the Instant Pot® Bible

Instant Pot®

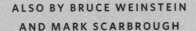

**ALSO BY BRUCE WEINSTEIN
AND MARK SCARBROUGH**

The Kitchen Shortcut Bible • The Ultimate Ice Cream Book •

The Ultimate Party Drink Book • The Ultimate Candy Book • The Ultimate Shrimp Book •

The Ultimate Brownie Book • The Ultimate Potato Book • Great Grilling • The Ultimate Muffin Book •

The Ultimate Chocolate Cookie Book • Cooking for Two • The Ultimate Frozen Dessert Book •

The Ultimate Peanut Butter Book • The Ultimate Cook Book • Pizza: Grill It! Bake It! Love It! •

Cooking Know-How • Ham: The Obsession with a Hindquarter • Real Food Has Curves •

Goat: Meat, Milk, Cheese • Lobsters Scream When You Boil Them •

The Complete Quick Cook • Grain Mains • The Great American SLOW COOKER Book •

Vegetarian Dinner Parties • The Great Big PRESSURE COOKER Book •

The Boozy Blender • A La Mode • The Turbo Blender Dessert Revolution •

All-Time Favorite Sheet Cakes and Slab Pies

the Instant Pot® Bible

MORE THAN 350 RECIPES AND STRATEGIES
THE ONLY BOOK YOU NEED
FOR EVERY MODEL OF INSTANT POT®

Bruce Weinstein and Mark Scarbrough
PHOTOGRAPHS BY ERIC MEDSKER

LITTLE, BROWN AND COMPANY
NEW YORK BOSTON LONDON

Little, Brown and Company
Hachette Book Group
1290 Avenue of the Americas, New York, NY 10104
littlebrown.com

First Edition: October 2018

Little, Brown and Company is a division of Hachette Book Group, Inc. The Little, Brown name and logo are trademarks of Hachette Book Group, Inc.

The publisher is not responsible for websites (or their content) that are not owned by the publisher.

The Hachette Speakers Bureau provides a wide range of authors for speaking events. To find out more, go to hachettespeakersbureau.com or call (866) 376-6591.

Photography © Eric Medsker
Interior design by Laura Palese
Cover design © Hachette Book Group

ISBN 978-0-316-52461-2
Library of Congress Control Number: 2018949181

10 9 8 7 6 5 4 3 2 1

LSC-C

Printed in the United States of America

Contents

Chapter 3: Chilis, Sloppy Joes, Pasta Sauces, and Ragùs   110

Chapter 4: Pasta Casseroles   152

Chapter 5: All Things Pulled   192

Chapter 6: All Things Curried   224

Chapter 7: All Things Steamed and Cooked with the Sous Vide Method   256

Chapter 8: Shorter Braises and Stews (Fewer than Twenty Minutes Under Pressure) 288

Chapter 9: Longer Braises and Stews (More than Twenty Minutes Under Pressure) 342

Introduction

WELCOME TO THE INSTANT POT REVOLUTION.

This extraordinary multipurpose countertop
cooker has changed the way millions of us cook, opening
up new opportunities in our kitchens and
saving us countless hours of time along the way.

The Instant Pot® Bible is the first cookbook written *for all models,* even the Instant Pot® Max, which features both a new, powerful MAX cooking function and the ability to cook sous vide. But you don't need a MAX for this book. You can have a Lux. A Duo. A Smart BT. An Ultra. A 3-quart Mini. Or an 8-quart of any sort. These recipes are fully forwards-and-backwards compatible no matter which Instant Pot you have. What's more, over a quarter of the recipes can use either the PRESSURE COOK or the SLOW COOK function, depending on what your timing needs are. Everybody uses their pot to cook fast. Some of us still like a slow cooker. Now we can choose. (And yes, this is the first Instant Pot book with sous vide recipes. Those are *only* for the Max machine. But the other 342 were crafted for every model, every make.)

That's a lot of good news, so permit us to be blunt: This cookbook is not an owner's manual. Because each model varies slightly from another, we won't tell you how to turn yours on, how to get the SAUTÉ function to the right heat, or how to open the pressure valve. Some models have preset buttons (MEAT/STEW, SOUP/BROTH, etc.); others don't. Some models require you to press START; others automatically switch the machine on after you've keyed in your cook time. You can find this sort of information in your owner's manual (or online, if yours has gone missing). We've accounted for the variables that matter once you start cooking, but we count on you to have a basic understanding of your model.

Then what is this book? The cover says it's a collection of 350 recipes. But it has many more. Countless, probably, given that we provide 25 flexible "road map" recipes: not standard recipes at all, but detailed layouts for chili and risotto, winter vegetable soup and rotisserie-style chicken. Each is a culinary outline that teaches you the basics and allows you to customize a dish with countless proteins, vegetables, herbs, and flavorful liquids. Consider these road maps to be gussied-up master recipes with the ratios set

and the variables laid out so you can prepare whatever you and yours prefer. (Desserts are a matter of greater precision, of course.)

In the more traditional recipes, we sometimes use the headnotes to explain how to make other, similar recipes in the pot. In the end, we hope you'll treat almost every recipe as a road map. Cook with a pen in hand so you can alter the recipe on the page. Or if you're scrolling on an e-reader, make notes in the recipe with the call-out function. And post your versions in the various Instant Pot Facebook or Instagram groups. We'd be more than flattered if you took our ideas and made them your own. Creativity is the best part of our job. We have a feeling it may be the same for you — at least, at times other than 5:45 p.m., when the kids are starving and you're about 20 minutes away from DEFCON 10.

But even with all those road maps and inventive recipes, there are a few dishes this book doesn't address. Most are utter basics. There's no plain rice recipe, for example. Nor ones for kefir or plain beans. These recipes are found in the booklet that accompanies each model. Some are even part of the owner's manual. And some, like those for yogurt, are too complicated to be written for all models, given the differences among the pots.

Instead, we offer a veritable bible of advice on mastering the art of using your machine. There are over 20 recipes for everything that can be pulled (chicken, pork, you name it). There are braises galore. There's a breakfast chapter, a sides chapter, and a dessert chapter. But most of this cookbook isn't laid out in a traditional manner. Instead, the main courses are divided into chapters like Pasta Casseroles, All Things Curried, Shorter Braises, and Longer Braises. If you look in one place and don't find a meat cut, a favorite vegetarian entrée, or a cooking technique you prefer, flip elsewhere or look in the index. For example, there are recipes for chicken thighs in the Soups, Pasta Casseroles, All Things Pulled, All Things Curried, All Things Steamed, Shorter Braises, Longer Braises, and even Rice and Grains chapters. As on any grand tour, your first stop probably isn't your last.

And there are lots of stops on the tour because this book is *big*. Try the Chicken Noodle Paprikash (page 172). Or the Eggnog Cheesecake (page 471). Or any one of the ten mouthwatering ragùs (starting on page 141). There's something in here for nearly every taste and occasion. And if you're curious about our favorite? Well, let's just say we made the Banana Bundt Bread (page 40) about half a dozen times *after* we got it right in testing because, well, banana bread is so great with a morning cup of coffee. Or at night in front of the TV while we binge-watched yet another Scandinavian crime series.

We live in rural New England and wrote this book during a long, hard winter. If the recipes in these pages helped us get through one of those, you'll be fine no matter where you are.

An Owner's Manual for this Cookbook

You need the manual for your Instant Pot, and you need one for this book. Ours is a little simpler. Keep the following seven points in mind:

1. Read the chapter openers.

We know: This is boiler-plate cookbook advice. But in those openers, we've included important information that you'll need again and again, especially under the FAQs header. Five minutes reading these will pay off since you'll understand how the recipes work.

2. Avoid the presets.

Many machines come with programmed, default features. Let's take timing as an example. When you press SAUTÉ and the heat level (say, LOW or LESS), or when you press the MEAT/STEW button (available in some but not all models), you get 10 minutes, maybe 15 on the timer. You can then manually adjust this

timing up or down. Some models will return to the timing you last selected the next time you press SAUTÉ or MEAT/STEW. Others return to the default. Just skip it all. We give you the timings (and more). Manually adjust the variables each time and you'll never go wrong.

3. Pay attention to the size of the pot in the main recipe.

We have written all the recipes with the **6-quart cooker** as the standard. However, more than three-quarters can also be made, *as stated*, in an **8-quart cooker**. In these recipes, there will be a note in the *Beyond* section on how to alter the recipe for a **3-quart cooker**. (Although a few times we note that the recipe unfortunately cannot be done in the smaller pot.) A few recipes were written for a **3- or 6-quart cooker.** Again, there will be notes in the *Beyond* section on how to up the ingredients so the recipe can work in an **8-quart cooker**. And some recipes can *only* be made as written in a **6-quart cooker**. The *Beyond* section will again explain the necessary alterations for both the **3- and 8-quart cookers.** Finally, a handful of recipes can be made in any size cooker.

4. Notice the two types of charts in the recipes.

One chart is for basic cooking techniques like browning a chicken breast or reducing a sauce — the same kinds of things you could also do on the stovetop. This chart is often the first and/or right before the last step of a recipe (see opposite page).

Read the chart left to right to figure out how to get the pot to the place it needs to be. The exact name for the heat level is different among the models — thus, "MEDIUM, NORMAL, or CUSTOM 300°F." That last "custom" marker is for the Max machine, which has a HIGH and a LOW for the SAUTÉ function, then adjustable temperatures in-between. The Ultra also has an adjustable sautéing temperature, plus a more traditional MEDIUM setting.

Pay careful attention to the heat level indicated for the SAUTÉ function. Although the vast majority of recipes in this book use MEDIUM, NORMAL, or CUSTOM 300°F, some use LOW or LESS; others, HIGH or MORE.

Notice, too, that when sautéing, we always round the time *up* to the nearest 5-minute mark. So a recipe may tell you to cook the onions for 2 minutes and the chart will say to set the time for 5 minutes, or the recipe will say to brown the roast for a total of 12 minutes and the chart will say 15 minutes. We built in a little extra time because we don't want the heating element to turn off on you — just in case your onion is juicier than ours, or your chuck roast takes a little longer to brown. As a result, you will often finish sautéing with a couple minutes on the timer to spare. Go right ahead and turn off the SAUTÉ function when you're ready to carry on with the recipe.

And one more thing: In all models, MAX or any other, the SAUTÉ function doesn't remain on for longer than 30 minutes. You may need to restart it to continue with a recipe that involves multiple browning and sautéing steps. Such recipes are super rare, but see the Bistro-Style Braised Short Ribs with Mushrooms on page 354 as an example. Here, we've given the timing as 35 minutes in the first chart, even though we well know that the setting is impossible, given the machines' limit. We wrote the recipe that way to avoid a second chart, to be honest. We trust you'll know how to turn it back on when the machine switches off. And let's face it: Most of us start sautéing before the machine actually beeps to tell us it's warmed up to the desired temperature. So the 30-minute cutoff in even the most complicated recipe may never worry those of us who lack saintly patience.

The other chart is for using the pot as a pressure cooker or a slow cooker (see page 14).

A Max machine *can* (but doesn't have to) cook at 15 psi — that is, pounds per square inch, the same pressure as almost all stovetop pressure cookers. The chart's top instructional row (under the headers) is for a Max machine *at its MAX setting.* This model also automatically opens or closes the valve, so you don't have to fiddle with it after you latch on the lid and set the cooking function. That's why there are dashes in the third box of that instructional row.

The second row, the one with the HIGH pressure setting, is the row you'll use if you have a Luxe, Duo, Smart, Ultra, or Mini. (You can also use it for a Max — see below.) All Instant Pot models except the Max cook at 12.6 psi (slightly higher than most other electric pressure cookers). For this row of the chart, you can either use the MANUAL or PRESSURE COOK setting or you can press (as here) the MEAT/STEW button (or other buttons like SOUP or GRAINS as the recipe indicates). We call out all the options in all the charts. But you must *always* override the presets to set the specific time noted in the chart.

We should also note that the Max machine *can* cook on the older HIGH setting. Max users can also use the chart's line for the HIGH setting, if they prefer a slightly longer cooking time and a slightly lower pressure setting.

Some charts are missing the last row, the SLOW COOK instructions. This is because these recipes cannot be completed using this function

The Chart for Basic Cooking Techniques

Press the button for	Set it for	Set the time for	If necessary, press
SAUTÉ	MEDIUM, NORMAL, or CUSTOM 300°F	5 minutes	START

Set the machine for	Set the level for	The valve must be	Set the time for	If necessary, press
PRESSURE COOK	MAX	—	3 minutes with the KEEP WARM setting off	START
MEAT/STEW, PRESSURE COOK, or MANUAL	HIGH	Closed	4 minutes with the KEEP WARM setting off	START
SLOW COOK	HIGH	Opened	3 hours with the KEEP WARM setting off (or on for 2 hours)	START

without major modifications to the ingredient list (in most cases: less liquid and oil, more spices and vegetables).

A few are even missing the first instructional row, the one with the Max instructions. It's not that these recipes can't be done in a Max machine. It's that they can't be done on the MAX pressure setting without, say, a cheesecake buckling into waves or more delicate ingredients dissolving into the sauce. These few recipes can only be done on HIGH, even in a Max machine.

5. Pay attention to the design and function changes in the Max machine.

For one thing, this pot's missing the old buttons for, say, MEAT/STEW or BEAN/CHILI. The Max machine is oriented toward cooking technique, not the type of dish cooked. While this change doesn't affect these recipes, don't get tripped up looking for the old functions, especially if you're used to another model or if you see those button indicators in the second instructional row of the chart.

The Max machine is not necessarily the first electric pressure cooker to cook at as high a pressure as a stovetop cooker. Some others hit that pressure mark and immediately fall off it. The Max is the first electric pressure cooker to *keep the pressure that high for the duration of the cooking.* Because of that and the Max model's design changes, you'll need to follow its

specific instructions and set the pot manually every time for all of these recipes.

One feature added to the Max is the SOUS VIDE function. We'll have much more to say about this feature in its chapter (page 256). For now, let's just say that this function is a game-changer for a home cook who wants to try out this cheffy technique.

One feature missing from the Max machine is the GRAIN button. On former models, this button was something of a wonder to us. It brought the water in the pot up to a certain temperature and held it there so the raw grains got a warm, 45-minute soak before the machine then flipped to pressure cooking for the stated time. Frankly, the GRAIN button resulted in the most perfect wheat berries and rye berries we've ever had. But we've found a way around the loss in the Max machine, as you'll see in the recipe for wheat berries on page 395.

The Max machine also offers a NUTRIBOOST feature that lets out steam in tiny bursts. Here's the deal: Every time the pressure valve opens, even for a second, the liquid in the pot goes from being super-heated but essentially placid to being almost apoplectic. When the valve closes again, the liquids calm back down until the next shock. Call it "intermittent fury," great for bone broth and more assertively flavored stocks, none of which will be clear (as they would be if the valve remained closed, followed by a natural release). These stocks would not be favored by a classically trained French chef who wants to be able to read his menu through them; but they are indeed bolder and more complex, better not only for sipping but even for cooking. We advocate using this feature only where we feel it's appropriate. For example, we don't feel the NUTRIBOOST function is right for broth-rich dishes like Beef Barley Soup (page 84). The grains become soft enough to dissolve and the soup, just too mucky.

6. Follow the release method for each recipe.

As you may know, cooking under pressure is as much about releasing said pressure as it is about building it. That pressure is made only one way: by steam. Liquids produce steam as they boil. That steam fills up the air space above the ingredients in the pot and eventually packs the space so tight that no more steam can be released from the liquids. The bubbling slows down and the pressure begins to build, ultimately bringing the liquids to a state in which they can't boil. (When a bubble pops, where would the gas go?) The result is that the boiling point of water in the pot rises from 212°F or 100°C to around 250°F or 112°C (the exact temperature depends on the model and the pressure it reaches). In addition, the *volume* of almost everything in the pot expands, wine to lamb shanks, carrots to cheesecakes.

Eventually, all that pressure has to go somewhere. There are two ways to get rid of it:

- the **quick-release method**

- the natural release method (worded in these recipes as "let the pressure **return to normal naturally**, about X minutes.")

For the **quick-release method**, the pressure valve on the lid must be opened to let go of the steam. Doing so requires different moves among different models. In some, you must turn the valve one way or another. For the Ultra, you must push a steam release

button next to the valve. For the Max, you must press the indicator on the touchpad without futzing with the valve. In all cases, steam will shoot out of the small hole in the valve.

Learning to release the pressure quickly is a key part of learning to cook in the pot. Don't ever release the steam under a cabinet overhang. Keep the geyser away from cabinet facings. And never consider the released steam an easy way to get a facial. Instead, put pets and small children out of the room until you get the hang of the method your machine requires. Don't be afraid; there are countless videos online to help you. We've even got two popular classes on *craftsy.com* that can get you more comfortable with the whole notion of pressure cooking.

By contrast, the **natural-release method** is easier. Basically, turn the cooker off (or let it lapse into stand-by mode) and wait. Over time, what's inside the pot will cool down enough that the steam in the pot's air space will condense. (Remember high-school physics?) At this point, the locking mechanism — a pin or cylinder in the lid called the "float valve" — will drop down (or, in fact, *release*). You can now unlatch the lid and open the pot. A natural release can take anywhere from 15 minutes to 1 hour, depending on the amount of liquid and the mass of the ingredients in the pot.

Do not vary the release from the one stated in the recipe, even if you skipped lunch earlier in the day and want that beef stew *right now*. The recipes were written to take into account the stated method. Although the machine is off and nothing appears to be happening, a natural release is not dead time. Those cubes of beef continue to cook as the pressure falls.

Why didn't we just write all the recipes with the **quick-release method?** Because of what happens inside the pot when you release the pressure in one fell swoop. As we've indicated, things in the pot are pretty calm when the pressure's on. You'll hear almost nothing. But the second that valve opens, it's as if the ingredients went from being a jalopy on a country road to a race car in the Indianapolis 500. In other words, the liquids jump to a furious boil. That sudden switch can help save delicate ingredients from getting overcooked, and it can offer faster soups and stews when it's warranted. But it can also turn braised vegetables to mush, cause potatoes or roots to cloud a sauce, and render more delicate cuts of meat a little too soft.

No, a quick release will not *ruin* a pork chop. But in testing the difference time and again, we found a quick release can make some cuts of meat a little too squishy for our taste. And they're not necessarily the ones we expected when we started writing about pressure cooking. Leaner cuts — like boneless skinless chicken breasts — are often able to withstand a quick release better than fattier ones like pork shoulder. (Our tests were conducted with cuts of meat in water in the pot. There are other factors that come into play in actual recipes — fat, starches, and even liquid-mass ratios — so we sometimes call for a quick release even with a fatty cut.)

Hey, we get it: The **natural-release method** makes pressure-cooker recipes look like bald-faced lies. "Twenty minutes under pressure yet the dish took an hour to make," someone inevitably says. We didn't want to fool you, so we always indicate about how long the natural release takes. Some writers shy away from these things. They want you to believe that a soup takes 10 minutes when in fact it takes 15 minutes to brown the meat and sweat the onions, another 10 minutes for the machine to come up to pressure, 10 minutes for it to cook under pressure, and 20 minutes for it to come back to normal pressure naturally. If you glance through a full recipe on any page of this book, you'll have a pretty good notion of the *real* timing.

7. Check out the *Beyond* for each recipe.
We started writing this book with an oath that we wouldn't call for any ingredient we couldn't find in our rural supermarket, a nicely stocked but not gigantic suburban Stop & Shop. That's why we substituted a mix of balsamic vinegar and Worcestershire sauce for Chinese black vinegar in a couple of recipes. True, the real-deal vinegar is available online with a click but otherwise only with a long drive for us. Yes, we can travel over an hour to some big gourmet supermarkets, even a decent Asian one and a great kosher one. But there was no Chinese black vinegar down the road. We should also admit up front that we made an exception for Sichuan peppercorns. There'll be more about them when we get to the two appropriate recipes.

Even though we (mostly) held to our oath, we often wanted to tell you how to nudge a recipe toward authenticity or how to make X, Y, and Z substitutions to our ingredient list that would make the dish, well, "cheffier" — and thus began the *Beyonds*. Over time, these grew to include serving suggestions and even garnishes. As we're indicated before, this section is also where you'll find any modifications needed to make a recipe work in a **3- or 8-quart pot.**

The Recipe Tags

We've tagged the recipes in this book to help you make better decisions about what to make for dinner. Not every recipe has every tag. Most have three or four. Here's what they mean:

FOR MAX MACHINES ONLY. Sous vide recipes are the only ones so marked.

SUPER FAST. These recipes are either 1) shockingly speedy, ready in just a few minutes, like the kid-friendly Buttery Noodles (page 155); or 2) absurdly quick given all that's going on in the pot — like a barbecue-sauce-based casserole with dried pasta that comes together in mere minutes (page 166).

SUPER EASY. In general, these recipes are what we call "dump and stir": Toss everything in the pot, stir things up, and cook under pressure (or slow cook at will). Most require no browning. If you buy prechopped onion and a jar of minced garlic, most require little to no work at a cutting board. In a few cases, we've marked a recipe as super easy even if it requires you to sweat some onions, boil down a sauce, or use frozen gnocchi to make a kicked-up casserole with a two-step pressure process.

FEWER THAN 10 INGREDIENTS. In other words, nine at most. Or to put it another way, about a third of the book's recipes. We don't play that funky game in which water, salt, and pepper don't count. They count. However, some of the road map recipes are tagged this way; when they claim you could use two or three items from a list, you can sometimes get away with using only one.

FAST/SLOW. These recipes can be made either under pressure or with the SLOW COOK function. Perhaps unbeknownst to you, there have been big changes in the heat levels for slow cooking among the Instant Pot models. One pot's low is *not* another's low. To keep things simple, all the SLOW COOK recipes have been written using the slow-cooker HIGH setting. Therefore, they cook more quickly. There are almost no 8-hour braises here. But you can use the KEEP WARM function to hold the dish until you're ready to eat it. By the way, some recipes tagged *Fast/slow* have the slow cooking instructions in the *Beyond* section attached to that recipe instead of in the chart in the recipe steps.

QUICK RELEASE. You must manually release the pressure at the end of cooking by opening the pressure valve, by pushing the button next to the valve (for the Ultra model), or by pressing the appropriate function on the touchpad (for the Max model).

MODIFIED QUICK RELEASE. Here, use the quick-release method to drop the pressure (and drop the temperature in the pot) but do not open the lid. Instead, leave it alone for a stated number of minutes with the valve open and the KEEP WARM setting off. This method is particularly useful for plumping grains and rice.

NATURAL RELEASE. After cooking, turn the pot off and let its pressure "**return to normal naturally**, about X minutes." Take special note: Some pots default to the KEEP WARM function. For a natural release, you must set the pot so it *does not*.

MODIFIED NATURAL RELEASE. In this case, turn the machine off and let its pressure come down naturally for a stated number of minutes — for example, "let the pressure **return to normal** for 10 minutes." After that, use the **quick-release method** to get rid of any residual pressure, either by opening the valve or pressing the quick-release function on the touchpad. This method is particularly useful for getting a little moisture back into a cut of lean meat.

QUICK RELEASE TWICE. NATURAL RELEASE TWICE. QUICK RELEASE, THEN NATURAL RELEASE. QUICK RELEASE, THEN MODIFIED NATURAL RELEASE. NATURAL RELEASE, THEN MODIFIED QUICK RELEASE. There are even more permutations. These are all the markers to indicate two-step recipes. Each one details what happens at the end of the first step, then what happens at the end of the second. These seem complicated now but don't worry: Each recipe tells you exactly what to do.

VEGETARIAN. There's no meat or seafood in the dish. There are, however, animal products like milk, honey, or eggs.

CAN BE VEGETARIAN. In this case, a simple swap will morph the recipe into a vegetarian one — for example, vegetable broth for chicken broth in an otherwise meatless recipe. Remember: Most Worcestershire sauce contains anchovies. Use vegetarian (or vegan) Worcestershire sauce, if it matters.

VEGAN. In this case, there are no animal products at all: no meat, honey, eggs, nada.

CAN BE VEGAN. Again, simple modifications can turn the recipe vegan: a swapped-out broth, or vegan Worcestershire sauce, or maybe oil for the butter.

GLUTEN-FREE. There's no wheat gluten in the recipe. However, your kitchen, cutting board, measuring spoons, and pot may have been contaminated. If you're cooking for someone who needs to eat gluten-free, you may need to take further precautions. For ingredients, we follow the Celiac Disease Foundation's requirements and rules. Some people have more drastic requirements or disagree with the organization. For reference, celiac.org is where we set the bar.

CAN BE GLUTEN-FREE. In this case, you need to substitute gluten-free versions of some ingredients without making any other alterations. We *do not* list the specific ingredients that need to be switched out. Those to watch out for include but are not limited to Worcestershire sauce, soy sauce, sausage meat (which can have wheat derivatives as filler or preservatives), some dried spice blends, and some condiments (particularly fat-free versions that may use wheat or a wheat derivative as a thickener.) Use certified gluten-free versions of these products (and more), even rolled and steel-cut oats. (Naturally gluten-free oats can be processed in facilities that also process wheat, the dust of which can get on the oats.) Watch out for hoisin sauce, a Chinese condiment. (We show how to make a gluten-free version in the *Beyond* section of the Vegetable Lo Mein recipe on page 184). And pay attention to baking powder. Although most made in the U. S. include cornstarch to preserve freshness (that is, to trap ambient humidity), baking powder from abroad may use wheat gluten. Finally, as to breadcrumbs, use Italian-seasoned gluten-free breadcrumbs or plain gluten-free panko breadcrumbs, both of which are increasingly available in stores and online.

FREEZES WELL. We tested these recipes with stacks of 1-quart, plastic, sealable containers on the counter. We put leftovers in the freezer. Those we enjoyed another day are so marked.

A Few Notes about Basic Ingredients

We give either the supermarket equivalent or the weight *as well as* the volume of common ingredients, particularly fresh produce that is prepped in a standard way. For example, a chopped onion is "1 medium yellow onion, chopped (1 cup)." However, we don't give the volume measure when that onion is sliced into thin half-moons, which are hard to measure accurately.

We assume you may well buy prechopped onion, bell pepper, celery, and carrots, as well as cubed and seeded butternut squash. We also assume you may have jars of minced garlic and ginger in the fridge. Feel free to use these ingredients. When using frozen chopped onion and bell pepper strips right out of the freezer, you'll have to cook them an extra minute or two.

Long-time cookbook readers will note that some ingredient volume equivalents seem a tad off. We say, for example, "1 medium garlic clove, peeled and minced (1 teaspoon)." A medium garlic clove minces up to more than 1 teaspoon. *However, we have given the volume amount for the convenience product.* This is because *jarred* minced garlic has (ahem) stewed in its own juices and is therefore more pungent than the freshly chopped stuff. Even prechopped onions and bell peppers have a more assertive flavor if they've sat around at the store.

On another note, the two of us *under-salt* food. It's not that we don't love salt. (One of us adds more to every tortilla chip.) It's just that we'd rather add crunchy sea salt or even kosher salt at the table.

In fact, we prefer *reduced-sodium* versions of common packaged ingredients in the Instant Pot. For our taste, a dish turns too salty if it includes standard cans of tomatoes, beans, and broth. We also tested every recipe that calls for soy sauce with the reduced-sodium version. But tastes vary. And this is not a health or diet book. So we have not specifically called for reduced-sodium ingredients unless we felt doing so was important to the dish's success.

Finally, we need to make a comment about butter. (Did you hear us sigh?) Unsalted butter is the holy grail of published recipes: always sought, never found. Every food writer makes a plea for it. We have, too. But the vast bulk of the butter sold in the United States is *salted*. Its sales are growing while the sales of unsalted butter plummet. As St. Paul learned on the road to Damascus, there's no use kicking against the cattle goads. So the butter in this book is salted, the American standard.

But we just blathered on about reduced-sodium ingredients. To compensate, we've even reduced the added salt in recipes to take salted butter into account. If you hold onto the righteousness of the culinary ideal and use unsalted butter, increase the salt in a recipe by at least half, if not double. But as for us and our house, we've gone with the flow.

All the Special Equipment You'll Need

Although there are now dozens, if not hundreds, of specialty cooking gadgets for the Instant Pot, not everyone wants to cough up so much money on gear. So beyond wooden spoons, rubber spatulas, measuring cups, and the like, we call for eight specialty items:

1. A 2-quart, high-sided, round soufflé dish.
That is, a round baking dish with 3½-inch (or 4-inch) sides that's also 7½ or 8 inches in diameter (outside edge to outside edge). It must be heat- and pressure-safe. Most are, but check with various manufacturers to be sure. Ours is made of thick porcelain. Not every piece of porcelain can withstand the cooker.

For the **3-quart cooker**, we often recommend halving the recipe and substituting a **1-quart high-sided soufflé dish,** which has 3- to 3½-inch sides and is 6 inches in diameter.

2. A 7-inch Bundt pan.

No matter the flutings and designs, the diameter is sacrosanct. Most fit snugly in a **3-quart cooker.** In this case, don't worry about the **Max Fill** line. The water level needed to make the steam is well below that mark, even if the Bundt pan sits above it.

Getting a 7-inch Bundt pan out of a **3-quart cooker** (or really any cooker) can be a pain. We stick the handle of a wooden spoon into the hole in the pan's center post, then use the spoon to leverage the pan up a bit before grasping its edge with oven mitts. Remember: That pan is super hot.

3. A 7-inch round springform pan.

This pan has a detachable side wall over a 7-inch bottom. Its sides should be 3 to 3½ inches tall. Because of the way the latch sticks out from the side of the pan, this gadget will not work in a **3-quart cooker**. You can substitute a 7-inch cheesecake pan (without a lip) in some cases but you may not be able to unmold the fare inside. We've heard there will soon be new Instant Pot springform pans without the latch, specifically designed for the Mini. These were not yet available as we finished writing this book.

4. A heat- and pressure-safe trivet.

We're talking about the one that comes with the machine. If you've misplaced your trivet, order another. If you don't have one and want to use whatever you've got, it must not have rubber feet and must be built to withstand the pressure's onslaught. Some pottery will not.

You can often turn a couple of small Pyrex custard upside down and use them as a base for a springform pan in a **6- or 8-quart cooker**. To do so, put them in the cooker *before* you add the water or other liquid for steaming. But the best advice is to use the trivet that comes with the pot. It has collapsible side handles, indispensable (as you'll see) in the sous vide recipes.

5. A heat- and pressure-safe collapsible steaming basket.

This is not the machine's trivet. This is an old-school, metal basket that opens out like daisy petals. Some new-fangled ones are made of silicone. These do not open out. Keep in mind the diameter of your pot. A giant silicone basket, made for a Dutch oven, won't work.

You'll need this gadget in rare instances to hold a lot of stuff so it doesn't sit in the water. The basket's feet should *not* be rubberized or plastic-coated. (Silicone is definitely okay.) The basket should have relatively tall legs. Always use the amount of water (or other steaming liquid) indicated in the recipe, even if it touches some of the food in the basket (thus the need for tall legs). The steam's the thing.

6. Heat- and pressure-safe 1-cup ramekins.

We used these in some desserts, particularly the puddings. We tested the recipes in Pyrex custard cups, the sort our grandmothers had. You can get fancier ones, but (again) they must be able to withstand the heat and pressure.

7. A fine-mesh sieve.

Small ingredients like wheat berries or rice grains can slip through the holes of a standard colander. A fine-mesh sieve can catch them. The best is a *chinois* (see page 48). We also always give you instructions on how to line a standard colander with cheesecloth or (sometimes) paper towels.

8. An aluminum foil sling.

Here's the one piece of equipment you must make. A sling is necessary because everything in the cooker is crazy hot, especially if you've quickly released the pressure and opened the lid right away. It's tough to reach in without touching the metal insert. Yes, the machine's trivet has collapsible handles. We still ended up with blisters on our knuckles. A sling gives you an easy way to raise and lower things into the pot (or even onto that trivet, provided its collapsible sides are up).

To make this sling, set *two* 2-feet-long pieces of aluminum foil on top of each other. Fold them together in half lengthwise (so that the thing is now a four-ply strip of foil). Put this sling on the counter as close to the cooker as possible, then set the baking dish or pan in the center of the sling. Fold its two ends over several times to create secure handles. Lift the whole contraption by these handles and put it in the cooker. Crimp the ends down so the lid will latch tightly but also so you can grab them later to lift the baking dish or pan out of the cooker.

And finally, while we never call for them, at the end of recipe-testing we discovered clamps with silicon-coated handles, designed for grabbing the edge of the Instant Pot's insert and lifting it out. We also discovered hand-length silicone gloves, perfect for grabbing the edge of the insert. If we'd had either of these while testing, our knuckles would have thanked us time and again.

A Dozen Up-Front FAQs

1. Why doesn't food squish flat when it cooks under pressure?

The pressure isn't coming straight down onto the food. The pressure comes from all directions at once. Think of a chicken breast. Think of a zillion arrows pointing at every spot on the breast, even every molecule. Then think of a zillion more arrows *inside* the breast, pushing out toward the surface. That's about how the pressure works. The chicken breast can't go flat. It's being pushed (quite literally) in every direction. That said, softer items — like cheesecake batters — can expand because the liquid inside is blowing up with the pressure. Batters billow, which is why they require extra care.

2. My pot has an elevation setting. Should I use it?

Sure. And you're talking about the Max pot. This elevation setting is specifically designed for the canning function. For all other models, don't worry about your specific elevation. A couple of years ago, we taped our pressure cooker classes for *craftsy.com* in the mile-high city of Denver, one class at a studio in a suburb with an elevation over 6,300 feet. We never canned anything but we also never had a single problem. Here's why: Although the pressure in the room was altered because of our higher elevation, the pressure in the pot was not. It's a sealed environment. It comes to HIGH (or LOW or MAX) internally. We even included quite a few baking recipes in those classes and did not make a single change to any cake, cheesecake, pie, or pudding.

3. What's with the weird verbiage in the road map recipes?

As we said, these recipes can be endlessly customized. The ingredient lists include culinary terms like "creamy liquid" or "flavor enhancer." These items are then immediately explained with a list of possible options and even ways to combine those options. We've set the ratios and left you to fill in the blanks, all while giving you plenty of options for those blanks. But in so doing, we had to use some terminology that smacks of chef school.

4. What's 0 minutes at pressure?

It's a way to make sure that delicate items like shrimp or orzo don't get overcooked. Every model lets you choose "0 minutes" as an option. The pot comes up to MAX or HIGH pressure and immediately stops cooking.

By the way, we should note a slightly alternate technique for some pasta dishes. We set the time for 1 minute, then release the pressure, not when the machine actually hits high pressure, but *the moment the lid's float valve jumps up and clicks closed* (that is, before the pot is actually all the way up to pressure). You'll also know the float valve (or pin) has closed because no more steam can escape from it (or from the pot at all). You'll hear it click and see it happen. For this rather odd technique, use the **quick-release method** to get rid of the pot's pressure right when the float valve closes, so delicate items don't stick, burn, or turn gummy.

5. You say to "turn the machine off" when it undergoes a natural release. Do I have to?

No. If the KEEP WARM setting has been turned off, the pot has turned off at the end of cooking (or actually, has moved to stand-by mode). That said, we're both a tad neurotic. OCD, really. One of us even unplugs the machine from the wall. (The writer, not the chef.) We turn the pot off just so nothing *can* happen. See? Neurotic.

6. What's with the lean ground beef, pork, and turkey?

Because of the way the lid fits tightly on the pot (even in the SLOW COOK mode with the valve open), there's almost no reduction among the liquids, even those trapped in interstitial fat. We find that standard ground meat results in dishes too oily for our taste. We prefer 90 percent (or more) lean ground beef, ground white meat turkey, and lean ground pork. Your taste may differ.

7. What's with scraping up *"every speck of browned stuff"* off the pot's bottom?

Many models of the Instant Pot have a safety feature that turns the pot off if things stick to the bottom of the insert and begin to burn. To avoid that, we've come up with ways to avoid the sticking problem altogether in pasta casseroles and some rice dishes. Even so, when proper browning happens, all sorts of natural sugars get stuck on the pot's bottom (aka the "browned stuff"). In a traditional stovetop braise, you would most likely deglaze a pot (starting the process of getting the browned bits unstuck from the bottom),

then the remainder of the stuff would eventually dissolve into the sauce over the next hour or so. In a pressure cooker, not enough time elapses. Some of the browned stuff hangs around and acts like glue on the pot's bottom. Ingredients fall down there or float by and get caught. They adhere and burn; the pot turns off.

In some recipes, you don't need to scrape up every speck. For instance, when you deglaze the pot with, say, wine or broth, we simply indicate that you should scrape it up without being assiduous. But for many pasta casseroles and grain dishes, you must get obsessive. In those, the direction *every speck of browned stuff* is in italics so you won't miss it. Listen, you want the caramelized stuff in the sauce anyway.

8. I tried to lock the lid onto my pot and it wouldn't do it. What gives?

Most likely, you've been cooking on the SAUTÉ function for a while. The pot is hot. There's steam inside the insert. Liquids may be boiling. The lid resists a firm lock because the pressure's already too high in the air space above the food. To remedy this problem, turn the SAUTÉ function off and wait a bit. Or if you've opened the pot after the first stage of a two-step cooking process, let the machine cool down a bit. Or — and this is the only case where such advice is *ever* applicable — use a skewer to press down the float valve (or the pin lock) so that it can't get in the way of locking the lid onto the pot. If none of these options work, you may need to contact Instant Pot for a repair.

9. My Max machine asks me how I want to release the pressure right up front. Should I do that?

You can but you don't need to. The machine will default to a natural release setting. Here's what we do: We let it default to the natural release function. When the machine beeps to indicate the timing is done, we press the quick-release function on the touchpad and let the pot rip. Of course, you can also set the pot to rip at the right moment when you start the pressure-cooking process. It's really a matter of taste. (And we're a bit fogeyish.) Just don't confuse the quick-release function with the one that has the Max machine make microbursts of pressure throughout the cooking, the NUTRIBOOST function.

10. The valve on my Max machine can't be manually closed. What do I do?

Nothing. The Max machine has been designed so that the valve opens or closes automatically, based on the function you request. This increased automation is why the requisite block in our charts for the valve's function has been left blank for the MAX setting on the Max machine. Remember, too, that you can also cook on HIGH in the Max machine and even use the SLOW COOK function. In all cases, setting the valve is irrelevant.

11. You call for a lot of dried spices. Seriously? I'm not running a spice store.

First off, many pressure cooker recipes yield better results with dried herbs, not fresh. The latter can end up squishy if they're not truly minced or if the braise is not well-stocked (in which case the herbs are more noticeable). What's more, the flavors of dried herbs and spices are often earthier and soften considerably under pressure, rendering them a great choice in many recipes since the pot tends to foreground sweet flavors in a dish.

In the end, you can't create wonderful food in the pot without layering the flavors. The pressure also kills a lot of the hot stuff in chiles. It can even mute some of the subtle notes in vegetables and herbs. To compensate, we need to up the spice game so the food isn't dull.

Here's an idea: Do you know other people in your neighborhood with multi-cookers? Run a spice ring. You take care of dried herbs, Henry takes care of dried spices, and Jane takes care of specialty blends. Now you don't have to run a spice store. You just have to have a few more house keys on your key ring.

12. Wait! What about when I...? Did you really mean to...? What if I can't eat...?

We can't predict every question, so look us up. We're around and happy to help. Bruce is on Facebook as Bruce Weinstein, on Twitter @bruceweinstein, and on Instagram as @bruceaweinstein. Mark is on all those platforms under Mark Scarbrough or @markscarbrough. Or go to our website: bruceandmark.com. Or listen to our podcast: Cooking with Bruce and Mark. We'd be honored to answer your questions wherever you find us.

In Conclusion...

Well, really, that's it. The rest we'll leave to the chapter openers and the recipes. You didn't buy an Instant Pot to read a book. You bought it to get busy. And to get a meal on the table. And then to get on with your morning, your day, your evening. You bought the pot to save time, right? So get cooking.

1
Breakfast

Although this is the first chapter of recipes, it's probably not the first place you'll turn. It shouldn't be the last either. True, weekday mornings are hectic. There are just a few recipes here to fit that schedule: the oatmeals, maybe the soft-boiled eggs. But when the weekend comes, consider your pot the best tool for getting a morning meal on the table.

Throughout, pay attention to the temperature of the eggs before they're cooked. The recipes for straight-on egg dishes — say, the ones for a frittata or for coddled eggs — were formulated for eggs right out of a 40°F refrigerator. But the recipes for the breakfast bread puddings and banana bread were tested with *room-temperature* eggs, so they quickly cohere into a custard or form a good crumb with the flour and leavening.

The quickest way to get eggs to room temperature is to fill a large bowl with warm (not hot) tap water, then submerge them in their shells in this water and let them sit for 5 to 10 minutes. Or you can go old-school and stumble into the kitchen to put them out on the counter for 25 to 30 minutes, then go take your shower. To us, doing so seems unthinkable moments just after an alarm (or a visiting baby) goes off.

And one more thing: We've been asked in countless cooking classes how to cook faster. Intriguingly, the question seems to come up most frequently when we're talking about breakfast or brunch. Time's precious in the morning, so we always give the same answer: We don't have a TV or a streaming device in the kitchen. And we can't see one from the kitchen. Keeping distractions to a minimum makes cooking faster and more efficient. And that's the whole reason you bought an Instant Pot, right?

FAQs

1. Can I use regular rolled oats instead of steel-cut oats?
No, both standard and instant rolled oats will foam too much. And since both are par-cooked, they'll turn to mush under pressure.

Listen, steel-cut oats are a pressure-cooker dream: a whole grain, the germ and bran intact, not compromised by all the processing rolled oats endure. And steel-cut oats are ready in a multi-cooker in about the same amount of time as regular oats require on the stove. Satisfying steel-cut oats are one of the biggest reasons to own an Instant Pot.

But with this warning: Steel-cut oats go rancid fairly quickly. If you open the can or bag and detect a funky odor like wet, dirty soaks filled with cilantro (ugh!), you'll know something's wrong. If you just bought that bag or can, take it back to the store for a refund. If you've had the oats on hand for a while, there's nothing to do but toss them out. We store ours in a tightly sealed container in the pantry for about 3 months or in the freezer for up to a year. Steel-cut oats can be used in the pot straight from the freezer.

2. What's with all the cream or milk added at the end? Can't I add it up front?

If online recipes are to be believed, many people do. These cooks must open the pot after cooking and stir like mad to get a smoother texture in the dish before they take a photo. They have to, because cream or milk breaks under pressure, unless it's put in a baking dish (to lift it off the hot bottom surface) or mixed into a batter of some sort. We add it at the end to avoid the gross gunk. All that said, evaporated milk does *not* break. We can add it directly to cereals before they undergo the pressure.

3. Must I use large eggs?

Yes. They're especially important for eggs cooked in their shells or (relatively) on their own — as in, say, hard-boiled eggs and coddled eggs. Only large eggs will come out right using the indicated timing. And for baking recipes, the calibration must be even more precise. We gave ground on the salted-butter issue (see page 19). We can't give ground here.

4. And while we're at it, how do you store coffee beans?

Now *that's* the eternal question. So let us ask you this: Ever walked into a coffee shop? Or noticed the coffee at the supermarket? Where are those beans? Out on the shelves (or maybe in the bulk bins). They're *not* stored in a refrigerator and *never* in a freezer. Cold temperatures can switch off certain flavor molecules that will never get turned on again, no matter how fancy your coffee maker is. And the ambient moisture in a humid refrigerator — or the condensation on the beans when they pop out of the freezer and onto the counter — can break down more flavor chemicals, rendering the coffee flat and dull. Keep coffee beans or even ground coffee in a cool, dark cabinet or pantry. A 12-ounce bag doesn't last two weeks in our house. Of course, we write books. Coffee comes with the territory. But we have a feeling yours won't last much longer if you enjoy a cup (or four) every morning.

Road Map: Basic Oatmeal

4 servings

Nothing could be easier than steel-cut oats from a multi-cooker. They're done in minutes, ready by the time you're onto your second cup of coffee (*second* one, because the natural release takes a little time). Don't be tempted to give it a quick release. The pot will sputter and spatter your cabinets. Worse yet, the oats won't be done because you'll have cut the cooking time short.

Unfortunately, oat milk will not work as the liquid in this recipe; it will break and turn stringy. But fat like butter or oil *is* necessary to help break up the foam the steel-cut oats inevitably produce. And we've left out the sweetener from this basic recipe; add whatever you like at the table.

2¾ cups liquid
Choose one or two from water, unsweetened apple cider, rice milk, cashew milk, soy milk, and/or almond milk — or a 50/50 combo of water and canned evaporated milk.

1 cup steel-cut oats

1 tablespoon fat
Choose butter, coconut oil, or vegetable, corn, canola, safflower, grape-seed, or any nut oil.

½ teaspoon table salt (optional)

1. Mix all the ingredients in a **3-, 6-, or 8-quart cooker**. Lock the lid onto the pot.

2.

Set the machine for	Set the level for	The valve must be	Set the time for	If necessary, press
PRESSURE COOK	MAX	—	3 minutes with the KEEP WARM setting off	START
PRESSURE COOK or MANUAL	HIGH	Closed	4 minutes with the KEEP WARM setting off	START

3. When the machine has finished cooking, turn it off and let its pressure **return to normal naturally**, about 15 minutes. Unlatch the lid and open the cooker. Stir well before serving.

Beyond

- You can (but don't need to) double this recipe if you have an **8-quart cooker.**

- Add your preferred sweetener to each bowlful: granulated white sugar, brown sugar, turbinado sugar, muscovado sugar, honey, maple syrup, agave syrup, date syrup, palm sugar, or coconut sugar.

- To add dried fruit — raisins, currants, blueberries, raspberries, chopped pitted dates or prunes, or chopped stemmed figs, nectarines, or peaches — stir it into the oatmeal after the pressure has been released. Set the lid askew for 2 to 3 minutes to warm and plump the dried fruit before serving.

- To use the SLOW COOK setting, increase the liquid to 4 cups and cook on HIGH with the pressure valve open for 4 hours, with the KEEP WARM setting off (or on for 2 hours).

3 tablespoons butter

1 cup steel-cut oats

2¾ cups water

¼ teaspoon table salt

Buttery Toasted Oatmeal

4 servings

Toasting raw oats in butter gives them a nutty flavor that is more complex than basic oatmeal. Again, there's no sweetener in the pot to keep the recipe basic. Add whatever you like to each serving.

Because steel-cut oats can sit on the shelf and are not sold quickly in this go-go world, they have varying amounts of remaining, residual moisture. If your oats are dried out, if they do not easily absorb liquid as they cook and end up soupy in the finished dish, set the lid askew over the pot for 5 minutes after opening. Once softened from the pressure, they will absorb liquid as they sit.

1.

Press the button for	Set it for	Set the time for	If necessary, press
SAUTÉ	MEDIUM, NORMAL, or CUSTOM 300°F	5 minutes	START

2. Melt the butter in a **3- or 6-quart cooker**. Add the oats and stir until they smell toasty, about 3 minutes. Turn off the SAUTÉ function; stir in the water and salt. Lock the lid onto the pot.

3.

Set the machine for	Set the level for	The valve must be	Set the time for	If necessary, press
PRESSURE COOK	MAX	—	3 minutes with the KEEP WARM setting off	START
PRESSURE COOK or MANUAL	HIGH	Closed	4 minutes with the KEEP WARM setting off	START

4. When the machine has finished cooking, turn it off and let its pressure **return to normal naturally** for 10 minutes. Then use the **quick-release method** to remove any residual pressure. Unlatch the lid and open the pot. Stir well before serving.

Beyond

- For an **8-quart cooker**, you must increase all the ingredients by 50 percent. Or you can double them in either a **6-quart** or **8-quart cooker**.

- For an even nuttier oatmeal, substitute a *toasted* or *roasted* nut oil of any sort (hazelnut, pecan, pistachio, walnut) for the butter.

- Letting the pot come back to normal pressure naturally for 10 minutes results in oatmeal that's still a tad chewy. If you want super creamy oatmeal, let it **return to natural pressure** for 20 minutes before releasing the remainder of the pressure with the **quick-release method**.

- To use the SLOW COOK mode, complete the recipe through step 2, then add the oats and increase the water to 4 cups. Cook on SLOW COOK on HIGH for 4 hours, with the KEEP WARM setting off (or on for 2 hours).

Cinnamon Apple Oatmeal

4 servings

Like a bakery breakfast bun in oatmeal form (huh?), this porridge is warm, comforting, and sweet. Adding the sugar up front gives the cereal a creamier finish. You can, of course, skip the sugar for a less-sweet breakfast. Or use an artificial sweetener (½ teaspoon liquid stevia works particularly well).

The dried apples should be chopped into small bits, the better to get one or two pieces per spoonful. To chop them without a hassle, spray your knife with nonstick spray, or simply wet the knife repeatedly as you chop the dried fruit. There's more liquid in this recipe than in the previous ones because the dried fruit also absorbs it under pressure.

2½ cups water

½ cup whole or low-fat evaporated milk (do not use fat-free)

1 cup steel-cut oats

½ cup chopped dried apples

2 tablespoons light or dark brown sugar (optional)

2 tablespoons butter

½ teaspoon ground cinnamon

½ teaspoon table salt (optional)

2 tablespoons half-and-half or heavy cream

1. Mix the water, milk, oats, apples, brown sugar (if using), butter, cinnamon, and salt (if using) in a **3-, 6-, or 8-quart cooker**. Lock the lid onto the pot.

2.

Set the machine for	Set the level for	The valve must be	Set the time for	If necessary, press
PRESSURE COOK	MAX	—	3 minutes with the KEEP WARM setting off	START
PRESSURE COOK or MANUAL	HIGH	Closed	4 minutes with the KEEP WARM setting off	START

3. When the machine has finished cooking, turn it off and let its pressure **return to normal naturally** for 15 minutes. Then use the **quick-release method** to get rid of any residual pressure in the pot. Unlatch the lid and open the cooker. Stir in the cream before serving.

Beyond

- You can double this recipe in a **6-quart cooker.** You can double or even triple it in an **8-quart cooker.**

- If you have leftovers, pack them into an 8-inch square pan or a small loaf pan lined with plastic wrap. Cover and refrigerate for up to 2 days. When ready, take the "cake" or "loaf" out of the pan and cut it into squares or slices. Fry these in butter in a nonstick skillet set over medium heat until brown and a little crunchy, turning several times. Serve with plenty of butter and maple syrup.

3 tablespoons butter

¼ cup packed dark brown sugar

2 very ripe bananas, peeled and
thinly sliced

2¾ cups water

1 cup steel-cut oats

2 teaspoons vanilla extract

½ teaspoon ground cinnamon

¼ teaspoon table salt

¼ cup half-and-half or heavy cream

Caramel Banana Oatmeal

4 servings

By creating a caramel-like sauce as the base for this hot breakfast
cereal, we turn it into a replica of Bananas Foster, the classic New
Orleans dessert (although — fun fact! — the recipe was first published in
The New York Times). The release here is just a straight-on natural one
because there's more sugar than in other oatmeal and porridge recipes
in this book. We need the sugar to make the caramel, of course. But hot
sugar syrup is particularly dangerous if it sputters from the vent.

1.

Press the button for	Set it for	Set the time for	If necessary, press
SAUTÉ	MEDIUM, NORMAL, or CUSTOM 300°F	5 minutes	START

2. Melt the butter in a **3- or 6-quart cooker.** Add the brown sugar and
stir until the sugar has dissolved and the mixture is bubbling. Stir in the
bananas to coat them in the sugar syrup. Turn off the SAUTÉ function.
Stir in the water, oats, vanilla, cinnamon, and salt. Lock the lid onto the
pot.

3.

Set the machine for	Set the level for	The valve must be	Set the time for	If necessary, press
PRESSURE COOK	MAX	—	3 minutes with the KEEP WARM setting off	START
PRESSURE COOK or MANUAL	HIGH	Closed	4 minutes with the KEEP WARM setting off	START

4. When the machine has finished cooking, turn it off and let its pressure
return to normal naturally, about 20 minutes. Unlatch the lid and open
the cooker. Stir in the cream before serving.

Beyond

- For an **8-quart cooker,** you must use
  ¼ cup (½ stick) butter and increase
  the remaining ingredients by 50
  percent.

- For brunch, add up to ½ teaspoon
  rum extract with the vanilla.

Tropical Oat Porridge

4 to 6 servings

We make this dairy-free porridge super creamy by overcooking the barley and the oats until they break down into a soft, warm cereal. Use only pearl barley, the sort without the hull or germ. It will almost disappear in the porridge.

3 cups water

½ cup pearl barley

½ cup steel-cut oats

½ cup unsweetened shredded coconut

¼ cup packed light brown sugar

1 tablespoon fresh lime juice

¼ teaspoon table salt

¼ cup coconut milk or coconut cream (do not use cream of coconut)

1. Mix the water, barley, oats, coconut, brown sugar, lime juice, and salt in a **3-, 6-, or 8-quart cooker**. Lock the lid onto the pot.

2.

Set the machine for	Set the level for	The valve must be	Set the time for	If necessary, press
PRESSURE COOK	MAX	—	12 minutes with the KEEP WARM setting off	START
PRESSURE COOK or MANUAL	HIGH	Closed	15 minutes with the KEEP WARM setting off	START

3. When the machine has finished cooking, turn it off and let its pressure **return to normal naturally**, about 20 minutes. Unlatch the lid and open the cooker. Stir in the coconut milk or coconut cream before serving.

Beyond

- You can double this recipe in an **8-quart cooker**.

- Garnish the servings with either chopped, peeled, and cored fresh pineapple or chopped dried pineapple with some toasted sliced almonds.

4½ cups (1 quart plus ½ cup) water

½ cup bulgur wheat, preferably medium or coarse grind

½ cup raw buckwheat groats

⅓ cup packed raisins or dried cranberries, chopped

¼ cup granulated white sugar

1 teaspoon vanilla extract

½ teaspoon ground cinnamon

¼ teaspoon table salt

½ cup heavy cream or half-and-half

Buckwheat and Bulgur Porridge

6 servings

In this oat-free hot cereal, bulgur offers both wheaty flavor and creamy texture, while buckwheat contributes a stickiness reminiscent of traditional oatmeal. Use only raw buckwheat groats, not toasted groats (often called "kasha"). Adding the cream at the end and bringing the porridge to a momentary bubble lets us avoid the irritatingly raw taste of heavy cream.

1. Mix the water, bulgur, buckwheat, raisins, sugar, vanilla, cinnamon, and salt in **3-, 6-, or 8-quart cooker**. Lock the lid onto the pot.

2.

Set the machine for	Set the level for	The valve must be	Set the time for	If necessary, press
PRESSURE COOK	MAX	—	12 minutes with the KEEP WARM setting off	START
PRESSURE COOK or MANUAL	HIGH	Closed	16 minutes with the KEEP WARM setting off	START

3. When the machine has finished cooking, turn it off and let the pressure **return to normal naturally**, about 15 minutes. Unlatch the lid and open the cooker.

4.

Press the button for	Set it for	Set the time for	If necessary, press
SAUTÉ	MEDIUM, NORMAL, or CUSTOM 300°F	5 minutes	START

5. Stir often as the porridge comes to a bubble. Stir in the cream or half-and-half and continue stirring over the heat for 1 minute. Turn off the SAUTÉ function and remove the *hot* insert from the machine to stop the cooking. Serve warm.

Beyond

- You can double this recipe in an **8-quart cooker**.
- Swap out the raisins for dried blueberries (which you needn't chop).
- For a bolder flavor, substitute turbinado or even date sugar for the granulated white sugar.

Cream of Rice Porridge

6 servings

By overcooking rice, we can get the grains to break down into something like boxed cream of rice cereal, but with a much better flavor (and less watery texture). Although you can use more expensive basmati, jasmine, or Texmati rice for this porridge, it works just as well with low-end, store-brand, long-grain white rice. Do not use par-cooked or instant rice.

6 cups (1½ quarts) water

1 cup raw long-grain white rice

3 tablespoons butter or a neutral-flavored oil like vegetable oil

½ teaspoon table salt

1. Mix all the ingredients in a **6- or 8-quart cooker**. Lock the lid onto the pot.

2.

Set the machine for	Set the level for	The valve must be	Set the time for	If necessary, press
PRESSURE COOK	MAX	—	35 minutes with the KEEP WARM setting off	START
PRESSURE COOK or MANUAL	HIGH	Closed	45 minutes with the KEEP WARM setting off	START

3. When the machine has finished cooking, turn it off and let its pressure **return to normal naturally**, about 35 minutes. Unlatch the lid and open the cooker. Stir well before serving.

Beyond

- You must halve the recipe for a **3-quart cooker**.

- The cereal is not sweet. Add your preferred sweetener to each serving to taste. See Road Map: Basic Oatmeal (page 27) for a fairly complete list.

- The hot cereal takes well to dried fruit such as raisins or dried blueberries. Stir these into individual servings with the sweetener.

- For a creamier cereal, use only 4½ cups water and add one 12-ounce can regular, low-fat, or fat-free evaporated milk.

1 cup water

1 to 12 large eggs, cold

Easy in-the-Shell Eggs

Makes up to 12 eggs

Here's the best way to make a variety of in-shell cooked eggs in the Instant Pot. But keep a few things in mind. First, the pressure is LOW, not HIGH (and certainly not MAX). Second, because of the way the pressure builds, the best results are to be had with *cold large eggs*, straight from the fridge. And finally, there's a range of timings given. You'll have perfect soft-boiled eggs in 3 minutes, the yolks not set and the whites barely set. (For a firmer set to those soft-boiled eggs, use the quick-release method but leave the lid on the pot after the pressure has escaped for 1 minute.) For soft-set eggs with a jammy yolk like you might find in a bowl of Ramen Broth (page 104), give them 6 minutes. And hard-boiled eggs take only 12 minutes.

By the way, the secret to a crunchy piece of toast is putting sliced bread straight from the *freezer* into the toaster for 1½ to 2 cycles.

1. Place a heat- and pressure-safe trivet inside a **6-quart cooker**. Or set a heat- and pressure-safe vegetable steamer in the pot. Pour in the water. Pile as many eggs as you like onto the trivet or steamer. Lock the lid onto the pot.

2.

Set the machine for	Set the level for	The valve must be	Set the time for	If necessary, press
PRESSURE COOK or MANUAL	LOW	Closed	3 minutes for soft-boiled eggs, 6 minutes for soft-set eggs, or 12 minutes for hard-boiled eggs with the KEEP WARM setting off	START

3. Use the **quick-release method** to bring the pot's pressure back to normal. Unlatch the lid and open the cooker. Transfer the eggs to a bowl or wire rack. Peel as soon as you can handle them.

Beyond

- For a **3-quart cooker**, you must use 1 cup water as stated, although you'll only be able to fit four or five eggs on the trivet.

- For an **8-quart cooker**, you must use 1½ cups water.

- Warm eggs peel more easily than cold. However, to save the eggs in their shells for a later use, transfer them from the pot to a bowl of cold water with an ice cube or two in it.

- An easy way to get the eggs out of the cooker without touching the hot metal inside is to use a large, balloon whisk. Gently press it down over one egg, capture the egg inside, and lift it out of the pot. (Or just use kitchen tongs with silicone tips.)

- The filling for our best deviled eggs is made by mixing 6 large hard-cooked yolks with 3 tablespoons mayonnaise, 2 tablespoons yellow mustard, 1 teaspoon dried dill, and ½ teaspoon table salt. Grind lots of ground black pepper over each filled egg half.

Coddled Eggs

1 to 6 servings

This recipe is the closest we can come to poached eggs in the cooker without simply using the SAUTÉ function to boil water and poach the eggs (at which point, seriously, there's no reason not to use a saucepan on the stove). The little bit of cream in each ramekin keeps the whites from turning tough.

Use only LOW pressure. The 2 minutes we suggest will result in soft-set eggs, the whites set but a little jiggly around the yolks. For a firmer set, give the eggs 3 minutes under LOW pressure, then continue on as directed.

1. Place a heat- and pressure-safe trivet in a **6-quart cooker**. Pour in the water. Butter or oil the inside of one to six heat- and pressure-safe 1-cup ramekins. Crack an egg into each, spoon 1 teaspoon cream on top, and season with salt and pepper to taste.

2. Place — or even stack — the ramekins on the trivet, making sure that no one ramekin completely covers another (that is, balancing a second layer as necessary on the rims of at least two ramekins in the row below). Lock the lid onto the pot.

3.

Set the machine for	Set the level for	The valve must be	Set the time for	If necessary, press
PRESSURE COOK or MANUAL	LOW	Closed	2 minutes with the KEEP WARM setting off	START

4. Use the **quick-release method** to bring the pot's pressure back to normal. Unlatch the lid and open the cooker. Transfer the *hot* ramekins to heat-safe serving plates and dig in.

1 cup water

Butter or vegetable, corn, canola, or olive oil for greasing the ramekins

1 to 6 large eggs

1 to 6 teaspoons heavy cream

Table salt and ground black pepper for garnishing

Beyond

- For a **3-quart cooker,** you must use 1 cup of water as directed although you'll only be able to fit four ramekins.

- For an **8-quart cooker,** you must use 1½ cups water, no matter how many eggs you make.

- Add finely minced herbs to each ramekin before you add the egg. Try chives, oregano leaves, or stemmed thyme leaves. For heat, add a pinch of red pepper flakes.

Fat for greasing the baking dish
Choose a solid fat like butter or coconut oil; or an oil like vegetable, corn, canola, safflower, olive, grape-seed, or a nut oil of any sort.

1½ cups water

9 large eggs

6 tablespoons creamy liquid
Choose whole milk, 2% milk, half-and-half, light cream, heavy cream, hemp milk, soy milk, coconut milk, cashew milk, or any nut milk.

½ teaspoon table salt

Up to 1 teaspoon ground black pepper

1½ cups filling
Choose one or several from chopped baby spinach; chopped, jarred roasted red pepper; cooked onions, shallots, or scallions (in butter or oil of any sort); cored, seeded, and finely chopped bell pepper; cooked sliced mushrooms; cooked diced and peeled potatoes; shredded semi-firm or hard cheese like Swiss, Cheddar, mozzarella, pecorino, or Parmigiano-Reggiano; sliced sun-dried tomatoes; and/or thawed, frozen broccoli or cauliflower florets.

Beyond

- For a **3-quart cooker**, you must use 6 large eggs, ¼ cup creamy liquid, ¼ teaspoon table salt, ¼ teaspoon ground black pepper, and ¾ cup filling. Put the egg mixture in a buttered or greased 1-quart, high-sided, round soufflé dish and add 1 cup water to the pot.

- Add fresh or dried herbs at will, up to 3 tablespoons fresh herbs or 1 tablespoon dried (or even a bottled dried herb blend). Add fresh herbs to the baking dish, then gently pour the egg mixture on top. Whisk dried herbs right into the egg mixture.

- For a spicy frittata, wait to pass Sriracha, Tabasco sauce, or another hot pepper sauce at the table. Bottled hot sauce can curdle the dairy if you add it before cooking.

Road Map: Instant Pot Frittata

4 to 6 servings

Okay, fair enough, this isn't a true frittata. It's more like an egg casserole—and a fine brunch entrée, no matter what you call it. Use this road map to create your own signature version. Go ahead, make notes right on this page so you remember what you did or what you want to do next time. But take note: Fat-free or 1% milk and rice milk are all too thin for a good result. And oat milk will break under pressure.

Step 5 offers directions for inverting the frittata onto a plate. You can skip the step and cut wedges right in the baking dish. They'll be uneven, maybe a little torn; but you also won't have to do a complicated kitchen dance with a hot dish early in the morning.

1. Pour the water into a **6- or 8-quart cooker**. Set a heat- and pressure-safe trivet in the pot. Butter or grease the inside of a 2-quart, high-sided, round soufflé dish. Make an aluminum foil sling (see page 20) and set the baking dish in the middle of it.

2. Whisk the eggs, creamy liquid, salt, and pepper in a large bowl until smooth and uniform, about 2 minutes. Stir in the filling mixture. Pour and scrape every drop of this mixture into the prepared baking dish. Cover it tightly with foil, then use the sling to pick it up and lower it onto the trivet. Fold down the sling's ends so they fit in the cooker. Lock the lid onto the pot.

3.

Set the machine for	Set the level for	The valve must be	Set the time for	If necessary, press
PRESSURE COOK or MANUAL	LOW	Closed	25 minutes with the KEEP WARM setting off	START

4. Use the **quick-release method** to bring the pot's pressure back to normal. Unlatch the lid and open the cooker. Use the sling to transfer the baking dish to a wire rack. Uncover the baking dish and cool the frittata for 5 minutes.

5. Run a flatware knife around the interior perimeter of the baking dish. Set a large plate or a serving platter over the top, then invert the *hot* baking dish and plate so that the frittata comes free. Cut into quarters or smaller wedges to serve.

No-Crust Ham and Spinach Quiche

4 servings

A traditional quiche is none too satisfying from the pot. The crust gets gummy and even bubbles up. We know: We've seen a zillion internet recipes, too. They've never worked for us.

But a crustless quiche does. We use a springform pan (rather than a 2-quart dish) so we can get even slices when unmolded. The spinach mixture gets packed into the pan, sitting at the seam to help seal it. That said, the pan's seam *must* be tight. Test your 7-inch round springform pan by filling it with water to see if it leaks.

1. Generously coat or butter the inside of a 7-inch round springform pan. Pour the water into a **6- or 8-quart cooker**. Set a heat- and pressure-safe trivet inside the pot. Make an aluminum foil sling (see page 20) and set the springform pan in the middle of it.

2. Mix the spinach, ham, oregano, pepper, and salt (if using) in a medium bowl and smooth it into an even layer in the pan. (Do not clean the bowl.) Sprinkle the cheese evenly over this mixture.

3. Whisk the eggs, milk, and flour in that same bowl until smooth, about 2 minutes. Gently pour this mixture over the ingredients in the pan (so as not to dislodge them). Cover the pan tightly with foil. Use the sling to pick it up and lower it onto the trivet in the pot. Fold the ends of the sling down to fit in the cooker. Lock the lid onto the pot.

4.

Set the machine for	Set the level for	The valve must be	Set the time for	If necessary, press
PRESSURE COOK or MANUAL	LOW	Closed	25 minutes with the KEEP WARM setting off	START

5. Use the **quick-release method** to bring the pot's pressure back to normal. Unlatch the lid and open the cooker. Use the sling to transfer the *hot* baking dish to a wire rack. Uncover and cool for 10 minutes. Run a flatware knife around the inside perimeter of the pan (or use a nonstick-safe knife for a nonstick pan). Unlatch the sides and remove the ring. Slice the quiche into quarters to serve.

Cooking spray or butter for greasing the baking dish

1½ cups water

One 10-ounce box frozen chopped spinach, thawed and squeezed dry by the handful

4 ounces smoked ham, any coatings removed, the meat diced

½ teaspoon dried oregano

½ teaspoon ground black pepper

¼ teaspoon table salt (optional)

3 ounces shredded Swiss or Monterey Jack cheese (¾ cup)

4 large eggs

½ cup whole milk

2 tablespoons all-purpose flour (for a gluten-free alternative, see the *Beyond* section)

Beyond

- Because of the way the latch is designed on the springform pan, this recipe cannot currently be made in a **3-quart cooker**.

- For a richer quiche, substitute half-and-half or even heavy cream for the milk.

- The flour is necessary to get the right set. However, if you need the recipe to be gluten-free, use a gluten-free baking mix, such as that sold by Bob's Red Mill, for a similar consistency. Make sure the ham doesn't have any wheat by-products injected into it or coated on it.

3 tablespoons butter

1 medium yellow onion, chopped (1 cup)

1 medium green bell pepper, stemmed, cored, and chopped (1 cup)

1 medium red bell pepper, stemmed, cored, and chopped (1 cup)

1 pound smoked deli ham (not thinly shaved), any coating removed, the meat diced

2 medium garlic cloves, peeled and minced (2 teaspoons)

1 teaspoon dried sage

1 teaspoon dried thyme

½ teaspoon celery seeds (optional)

¼ teaspoon table salt

¼ teaspoon ground black pepper

1 pound yellow potatoes, diced (no need to peel)

1½ cups chicken broth

Beyond

- For a **3-quart cooker**, you must use 1 cup broth and halve the remaining ingredients.

- For an **8-quart cooker**, you must increase all the ingredients by 50 percent.

- Substitute corned beef for the ham—or get fancy and substitute shredded, skinless boneless duck confit.

Breakfast Hash

4 to 6 servings

Not a side dish at all, this is a well-stocked breakfast entrée. Make sure the potatoes are *diced*—that is, in ½-inch cubes. They must be small and evenly sized to cook in the stated time. Skip processed sandwich meat and look for whole, roasted smoked ham at the deli counter. Have the butcher cut it into ½-inch slices to make the dicing easier for you.

1.

Press the button for	Set it for	Set the time for	If necessary, press
SAUTÉ	MEDIUM, NORMAL, or CUSTOM 300°F	5 minutes	START

2. Melt the butter in a **6-quart cooker**. Add the onion and both bell peppers. Cook, stirring occasionally, until softened, about 4 minutes. Add the ham, garlic, sage, thyme, celery seeds (if using), salt, and pepper. Cook, stirring often, until fragrant, about 1 minute.

3. Turn off the SAUTÉ function. Stir in the potatoes and broth, scraping up any browned bits on the pot's bottom. Lock the lid onto the cooker.

4.

Set the machine for	Set the level for	The valve must be	Set the time for	If necessary, press
PRESSURE COOK	MAX	—	10 minutes with the KEEP WARM setting off	START
PRESSURE COOK or MANUAL	HIGH	Closed	12 minutes with the KEEP WARM setting off	START

5. Use the **quick-release method** to bring the pot's pressure back to normal. Unlatch the lid and open the cooker. Stir well.

6.

Press the button for	Set it for	Set the time for	If necessary, press
SAUTÉ	HIGH or MORE	10 minutes	START

7. Bring the mixture to a simmer, stirring often. Continue without stirring until the liquid boils off and the hash touching the hot surface starts to brown, 3 to 4 minutes. Turn off the SAUTÉ function and remove the *hot* insert from the machine to stop the cooking. Some of the potatoes may have fused to the surface. Use a metal spatula to get them up. The point is to have some browned bits and some softer bits throughout the hash.

See photo in insert.

Pull-Apart Cinnamon Bread

6 servings

Monkey bread is a holiday tradition in the U.S., but here's a quicker, easier version that might put this breakfast specialty on the menu all year-round. It's made with canned biscuits and lots of butter, a real treat. Use only home-style (sometimes called "Southern-style") biscuits, not "flaky" biscuits. The biscuits need to cook up flat and dense, rather than light and layered.

1. Pour the water into a **6- or 8-quart cooker**. Place a heat- and pressure-safe trivet inside the pot. Generously butter the inside of a 7-inch round springform pan. Make an aluminum foil sling (see page 20) and set the prepared baking dish in the middle of it.

2. Mix the white sugar, brown sugar, cinnamon, and salt (if using) in a large, microwave-safe bowl. Cut the raw biscuits into quarters, then add them to this bowl and toss well to coat. Lightly pack the biscuits into the springform pan. (Much of the sugar mixture will stay behind in the bowl.)

3. Add the butter to the sugar mixture. Microwave on high in 15-seconds bursts, stirring after each, until the butter melts and the mixture bubbles. Pour and scrape this mixture over the biscuits in the pan. Use the sling to pick the pan up and lower it onto the trivet in the pot. Lay a piece of aluminum foil or parchment paper over the top of the pan without crimping or sealing it to the pan. Fold down the ends of the sling so they fit inside the machine. Lock the lid onto the cooker.

4.

Set the machine for	Set the level for	The valve must be	Set the time for	If necessary, press
PRESSURE COOK	MAX	—	15 minutes with the KEEP WARM setting off	START
MEAT/STEW, PRESSURE COOK, or MANUAL	HIGH	Closed	20 minutes with the KEEP WARM setting off	START

5. When the machine has finished cooking, turn it off and let its pressure **return to normal naturally** for 10 minutes. Then use the **quick-release method** to get rid of any residual pressure in the pot. Unlatch the lid and open the cooker. Use the sling to transfer the *hot* baking dish to a wire rack. Uncover and cool for 10 minutes, then run a flatware knife around the inside perimeter of the pan (or a nonstick-safe knife if the pan has a nonstick finish). Unlatch the sides and remove the ring. Serve by pulling apart the warm bread.

1½ cups water

⅓ cup granulated white sugar

⅓ cup packed light brown sugar

1½ teaspoons ground cinnamon

¼ teaspoon table salt (optional)

One 16.3-ounce can regular or buttermilk home-style biscuits (8 biscuits)

¼ cup (½ stick) butter, plus additional for greasing the pan

Beyond

- For a **3-quart cooker**, you must halve all the ingredients and make the pull-apart bread in a buttered 1-quart, high-sided, round soufflé dish. It won't unmold well, but you can pick it apart right in the baking dish.

- Sprinkle up to 3 tablespoons chopped raisins or dried cranberries among the biscuits before adding the melted butter mixture.

- Or sprinkle ¼ cup semi-sweet chocolate chips among the biscuit pieces as you layer them in the pan.

- For a bigger kick, add up to ¼ teaspoon grated nutmeg and/or ¼ teaspoon ground allspice with the cinnamon.

1½ cups water

Flour-and-fat baking spray

½ cup granulated white sugar

2 large eggs

3 tablespoons butter, at room temperature

2 very ripe medium bananas, peeled

½ cup regular, low-fat, or fat-free plain yogurt

2 tablespoons fresh lemon juice

1 teaspoon vanilla extract

1½ cups all-purpose flour

1½ teaspoons baking soda

¼ teaspoon table salt

½ cups walnuts

Beyond

- This recipe works in a **3-quart cooker** as written; a 7-inch Bundt pan will just fit. Make sure the paper towel doesn't catch on the rim of the lid. The amount of batter will rise up and almost touch the top of the cooker. It can get a little wet around the edges, but we didn't mind this in testing. For pitch-perfect aesthetics, when you fill the Bundt pan, leave a ½-inch space between the top of the batter and the top of the pan. (Discard that little bit of leftover batter.)

- Substitute any nut you like — pecans, almonds, skinned hazelnuts.

- Scrape the batter from the food processor into a bowl, then fold in up to ½ cup raisins, dried cranberries, or semi-sweet chocolate chips before getting the batter into the pan.

- A baking spray is easiest for getting the fat-and-flour mixture into every crevasse of a Bundt pan. But feel free to go old-school, using butter and all-purpose flour to coat the inside of the pan.

Bundt Banana Bread

8 servings

There's no worry about *this* banana bread drying out at the edges, given the pot's steamy environment. Here are the two secrets to success: First, make sure that pan is sprayed well, very nicely coated. If you think you've sprayed it enough, spray it a little more. The cake can stick like mad in the corners and indentations of the Bundt pan. And second, make sure the bananas are truly ripe, beyond the point you'd slice them onto cereal.

1. Pour the water into a **3-, 6-, or 8-quart cooker**. Set a heat- and pressure-safe trivet into the pot. Generously spray the inside of a 7-inch Bundt pan with baking spray, making sure the flour and fat mixture gets into all the crevices. Make an aluminum foil sling (see page 20) and set the pan in the middle of it.

2. Put the sugar, eggs, butter, and bananas in a food processor. Cover and process until smooth, stopping the machine once to scrape down the canister. Add the yogurt, lemon juice, and vanilla. Cover and process until smooth. Stop the machine and scrape down the inside.

3. Add the flour, baking soda, and salt. Cover and pulse until a uniform batter forms. Add the nuts and pulse to chop a bit and blend them in.

4. Pour, dollop, and scrape the batter into the prepared pan. Use a rubber spatula to smooth the top of the batter. Use the sling to pick up the pan and set it on the trivet in the pot. Fold down the ends of the sling so they fit into the pot without touching the batter. Lay a large paper towel over the top of the cake to cover it without touching the batter below. Lock the lid onto the cooker.

5.

Set the machine for	Set the level for	The valve must be	Set the time for	If necessary, press
PRESSURE COOK	MAX	—	18 minutes with the KEEP WARM setting off	START
PRESSURE COOK or MANUAL	HIGH	Closed	25 minutes with the KEEP WARM setting off	START

6. When the machine has finished cooking, turn it off and let the pressure **return to normal naturally**, about 25 minutes. Unlatch the lid and open the cooker. Remove the paper towel, then use the sling to lift the Bundt pan out of the cooker and onto a wire cooling rack. Cool for 5 minutes, then invert the pan onto a plate and shake gently to release the cake onto a cutting board. Slip the cake back onto the wire rack and continue cooling for at least 20 minutes before slicing into wedges.

See photo in insert.

Peanut Butter Bread Pudding

4 to 6 servings

Here's a bread pudding for breakfast, a treat that seems to cry out for crunchy bacon on the side. Use only natural-style peanut butter, without any added fat. If you use salt-free peanut butter, whisk in ½ teaspoon table salt with the peanut butter.

The best bread for this recipe (and for all subsequent bread puddings in this book) is packaged, sliced, "hearty" or "country-classic" white bread, rather than a loaf you might buy in the bakery, and certainly not sliced American "whipped" bread. The recipe calls for about half of a standard loaf.

And one more thing: Mound the bread cubes into the baking dish without pressing down. Otherwise, the liquids they've soaked up will come out and sear against the pan.

1. Pour the water into a **6- or 8-quart cooker**. Set a heat- and pressure-safe trivet in the pot.

2. Generously butter the inside of a 2-quart, high-sided, round soufflé dish. Make an aluminum foil sling (see page 20) and set the baking dish in the center of it.

3. Whisk the eggs, milk, half-and-half or cream, peanut butter, maple syrup, brown sugar, and vanilla in a large bowl until the peanut butter dissolves and the mixture is uniform, about 2 minutes. Add the bread cubes and toss well to soak up the egg mixture.

4. Pile the bread cubes into the prepared baking dish in a fairly even layer, pouring any additional liquid in the bowl over them. Cover the baking dish tightly with foil, then use the sling to pick up and lower the baking dish onto the trivet. Fold down the ends of the sling so they fit in the pot. Lock the lid onto the cooker.

5.

Set the machine for	Set the level for	The valve must be	Set the time for	If necessary, press
PRESSURE COOK	MAX	—	10 minutes with the KEEP WARM setting off	START
PRESSURE COOK or MANUAL	HIGH	Closed	12 minutes with the KEEP WARM setting off	START

6. Use the **quick-release method** to bring the pot's pressure back to normal. Unlatch the lid and open the cooker. Use the sling to transfer the *hot* baking dish to a wire rack. Uncover and cool for 5 minutes before serving by the big spoonful.

1½ cups water

Butter for greasing the baking dish

2 large eggs, at room temperature

¾ cup whole or low-fat milk

½ cup half-and-half or heavy cream

½ cup creamy natural-style peanut butter

¼ cup maple syrup

2 tablespoons light brown sugar

2 teaspoons vanilla extract

8 ounces white bread, preferably country-style bread, cut into 1-inch squares (do not remove the crusts)

Beyond

- For a **3-quart cooker**, you must halve all the ingredients and use a 1-quart, high-sided, round soufflé dish.

- Sprinkle up to 3 tablespoons chopped raisins among the bread cubes as you layer them into the baking dish.

- For PB&J bread pudding, omit the brown sugar and smear a light coating of your favorite fruit jam (not jelly or preserves) over the bread slices before you cut them into squares. Stir these gently in the liquid to keep the jam on the bread (as well as you can).

1½ cups water

Cooking spray or butter for greasing the baking dish

4 large eggs, at room temperature

2 cups whole milk

2 tablespoons light brown sugar

½ teaspoon vanilla extract

¼ teaspoon table salt

3 large cinnamon-raisin bagels, halved as if to toast them, then the halves cut into 1-inch pieces

Cinnamon-Raisin Bagel Bread Pudding

4 to 6 servings

Finally, here's a use for cinnamon-raisin bagels! (We have a long-running fight about their legitimacy. The Christian on our team thinks they aren't and the Jewish guy thinks they are. We live strange lives.) This bread pudding is chewy and dense. It's made with bagels, after all. They'll need to soak in the egg mixture for 10 minutes because they're so thick. Don't use thin ones, the sort you find in the freezer case. Instead, get fresh ones from the bakery department — or better yet, from a bagel shop.

1. Pour the water into a **6- or 8-quart cooker**. Set a heat- and pressure-safe trivet in the pot.

2. Generously coat or butter the inside of a 2-quart, high-sided, round soufflé dish. Make an aluminum foil sling (see page 20) and set the baking dish in the center of it.

3. Whisk the eggs, milk, brown sugar, vanilla, and salt in a large bowl until uniform, about 1 minute. Add the bagel pieces, toss well, and set aside for 10 minutes to soak up more of the egg mixture.

4. Stir the bagel mixture again, then pile the pieces into the prepared baking dish, pouring any additional liquid over them. (Do not press down to compact them but try to make as even a layer as possible.) Cover the baking dish tightly with foil, then use the sling to pick up and lower the baking dish onto the trivet. Fold down the ends of the sling so they fit in the pot. Lock the lid onto the cooker.

5.

Set the machine for	Set the level for	The valve must be	Set the time for	If necessary, press
PRESSURE COOK	MAX	—	10 minutes with the KEEP WARM setting off	START
PRESSURE COOK or MANUAL	HIGH	Closed	12 minutes with the KEEP WARM setting off	START

6. When the machine has finished cooking, turn it off and let its pressure **return to normal naturally** for 10 minutes. Then use the **quick-release method** to get rid of any residual pressure in the pot. Unlatch the lid and open the cooker. Use the sling to transfer the *hot* baking dish to a wire rack. Uncover and cool for 10 minutes before serving by the big spoonful.

Beyond

- For a **3-quart cooker**, you must use 1 cup of water, halve all the remaining ingredients, and use a 1-quart, high-sided, round soufflé dish.

- Use any flavored, sweet bagel — blueberry, chocolate chip — for this recipe.

- For a savory-sweet mix, fry up to 4 thin bacon slices until crunchy, then cool and chop into small bits to stir into the egg mixture with the bagel pieces.

Savory Sausage Bread Pudding

4 servings

This bread pudding has no added sugar, so it's a savory meal for a weekend morning. With cheese and sausage in the mix, there's plenty of fat — so feel free to use milk of any sort, even fat-free. (For a discussion about the right sort of bread, see the headnote for Peanut Butter Bread Pudding on page 41.)

1 tablespoon butter, plus more for greasing the baking dish

¾ pound smoked sausage links (such as kielbasa), diced

1½ cups water

3 large eggs, at room temperature

1½ cups whole, low-fat, or fat-free milk

8 ounces white bread, preferably country-style bread, cut into 1-inch squares (do not remove the crusts)

½ ounce Parmigiano-Reggiano, finely grated (¼ cup)

1 teaspoon dried thyme

½ teaspoon ground black pepper

1.

Press the button for	Set it for	Set the time for	If necessary, press
SAUTÉ	MEDIUM, NORMAL, or CUSTOM 300°F	5 minutes	START

2. Melt the butter in a **6- or 8-quart cooker**, then add the sausage. Cook, stirring often, until lightly browned, about 3 minutes. Turn off the SAUTÉ function. Scrape the contents of the *hot* insert into a large bowl. Set aside to cool for 15 minutes. Wipe out the insert and return it to the machine.

3. Pour the water into the cooker. Set a heat- and pressure-safe trivet in the pot. Generously butter the inside of a 2-quart, high-sided, round soufflé dish. Make an aluminum foil sling (see page 20) and set the baking dish in the center of it.

4. Whisk the eggs and milk in a second large bowl until uniform, about 2 minutes. Add the cooled sausage, the bread cubes, cheese, thyme, and pepper. Stir well until the bread is thoroughly coated in the egg mixture.

5. Pile the bread cubes into an even layer in the prepared baking dish, pouring any additional liquid over them (without pressing down on the bread). Cover the baking dish tightly with foil, then use the sling to pick up and lower the baking dish onto the trivet. Fold down the ends of the sling so they fit in the pot. Lock the lid onto the cooker.

6.

Set the machine for	Set the level for	The valve must be	Set the time for	If necessary, press
PRESSURE COOK	MAX	—	12 minutes with the KEEP WARM setting off	START
PRESSURE COOK or MANUAL	HIGH	Closed	16 minutes with the KEEP WARM setting off	START

7. When the machine has finished cooking, turn it off and let its pressure **return to normal naturally** for 10 minutes. Then use the **quick-release method** to get rid of any residual pressure in the pot. Unlatch the lid and open the cooker. Use the sling to transfer the *hot* baking dish to a wire rack. Uncover and cool for 10 minutes before serving by the big spoonful.

Beyond

- For a **3-quart cooker**, you must use 1 cup of water, halve all the remaining ingredients, and use a 1-quart, high-sided, round soufflé dish.

- There's no salt because of the butter, sausage, and cheese. Add some at will, probably at the table.

- Instead of the sausage links, substitute 12 ounces bulk breakfast sausage or mild or hot Italian sausage meat (that is, any casings removed).

- Drizzle maple syrup over the servings.

3 pounds tart apples, such as Granny Smith, peeled, cored, and chopped

1 cup unsweetened apple juice

Up to ¼ cup packed light brown sugar (optional)

1 tablespoon fresh lemon juice

½ teaspoon ground cinnamon

¼ teaspoon grated nutmeg

¼ teaspoon table salt

Spiced Applesauce

8 servings

Nothing beats *fresh*, warm applesauce, especially on a cold fall morning. It's so easy to make that you may never go back to the jarred stuff. But here's a warning: Pre-sliced apples won't work because they've softened and even dried out in storage. Their flavor may also have been compromised. Sorry about that. But if you're not going to open a jar, real applesauce is worth a little effort, no?

1. Stir all the ingredients in a **6-quart cooker** until the brown sugar dissolves. Lock the lid onto the pot.

2.

Set the machine for	Set the level for	The valve must be	Set the time for	If necessary, press
PRESSURE COOK	MAX	—	4 minutes with the KEEP WARM setting off	START
PRESSURE COOK or MANUAL	HIGH	Closed	6 minutes with the KEEP WARM setting off	START
SLOW COOK	HIGH	Opened	3 hours with the KEEP WARM setting off (or on for no more than 2 hours)	START

3. If you've used a pressure setting, when the machine has finished cooking, turn it off and let its pressure **return to normal naturally**, about 25 minutes.

4. Unlatch the lid and open the cooker. Use a potato masher to pulverize the apples into sauce right in the cooker. Serve warm or pack into two quart-sized containers, seal, and store in the fridge for up to 4 days, or in the freezer for up to 3 months.

Beyond

- For a **3-quart cooker**, you must use ¾ cup unsweetened apple juice and halve the other ingredients.

- For an **8-quart cooker**, you must increase all the ingredients by 50 percent.

- Add 1 cup fresh raspberries or fresh, pitted, sweet cherries to the mix.

- Serve with heaping spoonfuls of plain Greek yogurt.

Dried Fruit Compote

4 to 6 servings

You can use any dried fruit for this compote, although we suggest using larger pieces rather than raisins or dried cranberries, which become a bit too soft during cooking. Notice that the mixture is only cooked under LOW pressure. Doing so preserves the texture of the fruit (but won't save those raisins, if you use them).

1. Mix all the ingredients in a **3-, 6-, or 8-quart cooker** until the brown sugar dissolves. Lock the lid onto the pot.

2.

Set the machine for	Set the level for	The valve must be	Set the time for	If necessary, press
PRESSURE COOK or MANUAL	LOW	Closed	4 minutes with the KEEP WARM setting off	START
SLOW COOK	HIGH	Opened	2 hours with the KEEP WARM setting off (or on for no more than 2 hours)	START

3. If you've used the pressure setting, when the machine has finished cooking, turn it off and let its pressure **return to normal naturally**, about 15 minutes.

4. Unlatch the lid and open the cooker. Find and discard the cinnamon stick. Stir well before serving. If desired, store in a sealed container or covered bowl in the fridge for up to 3 days. (The compote will then taste better after it's been warmed in the microwave.)

1 pound mixed dried fruit, such as pitted prunes, apricots, quartered pear halves, and/or quartered nectarines or peaches

1 cup water

1 cup unsweetened apple juice

½ cup packed light brown sugar

1 tablespoon fresh lemon juice

¼ teaspoon table salt

One 4-inch cinnamon stick

Beyond

- Instead of using vanilla extract, halve a vanilla bean lengthwise and add it to the pot with the other ingredients.

- For a more sophisticated take, substitute red wine for the water.

- For more punch, substitute a star anise pod for the cinnamon stick.

- Serve the warm compote over plain Greek yogurt for breakfast, or over dollops of ricotta or scoops of vanilla ice cream for dessert.

2

Soups, Stocks, and Infusions

If you're an Instant Pot newbie, start here. A soup is the easiest way to introduce yourself to what the cooker can do: The large amount of liquid ensures there'll be plenty of steam; there are mostly no worries about delicate calibrations, so dinner is easy to accomplish; and you're relatively free to play around with ingredients.

Since this chapter also includes homemade stocks (even Ramen Broth!), we'd be remiss if we didn't talk a bit about stock and broth in general. We assume that you won't first make homemade stock for most of these recipes. You'll use the store-bought stuff, right? So here's another question: Have you ever tasted the stuff? We're amazed that so many people cook with this pantry staple yet have little understanding of what it tastes like.

If you want to take your cooking to the next level — and why not, since the Instant Pot makes it so easy? — invest 20 bucks and buy five or six brands of, say, chicken broth. Open them, put a little of each in separate cups, and barely warm them in the microwave before doing a side-by-side taste test. You'll discover one is too onion-y; another, too salty. One tastes like chicken; another, like a barnyard. One will be rich; another, watery. And since you're going all out, taste them side-by-side at room temperature, too. You'll soon know which suits your taste and which makes the best food for you and yours.

And since we're on this jag, let's add that you should do the same taste-testing with vegetable broths, which have an even wider range of acceptable (and unacceptable) flavors. You might be surprised that a less expensive brand tastes better. Price is not a guarantee of quality. It may be a function of a celebrity's face.

And one last note on the matter of patience: Even in the Instant Pot, soup takes time — not as much as it takes on the stove, but enough that dinner isn't a 5-minute job. It also shouldn't be a 5-minute stint at the table. Pour a glass of wine or iced tea. Settle in. Soup's on.

FAQs

1. Must I soak the dried beans?
For most of these recipes, yes. Soaked beans cook more quickly, whether under pressure or in the SLOW COOK mode. But more importantly, they cook more evenly and don't become as mushy since they're under pressure for less time.

That said, if soaked beans have not almost doubled in size from their dried state and if almost all of their wrinkles are not smoothed out, they may never get tender, no matter how long they endure the pot's pressure. Why? See the next answer.

2. What if the dried beans don't get tender in the time stated?
Here's some bad news: Dried beans do not move off store shelves quickly in our *I-want-it-now* world. The poor legumes hang out day after day, losing so much moisture through natural evaporation that they may not be tender in a recipe's stated time. You'll be able to tell if they're old by how they plump when they're soaked.

If, however, the dried beans did plump yet you find they're still too tough for your taste when you open the pot, do not add any vinegar or salt as the recipe may require at this stage. Instead, lock the lid back onto the pot and give them another 4 minutes at MAX or 5 minutes at HIGH, followed again by whichever method of pressure release the recipe requires.

3. Can you oversoak beans?

Yes, dried beans can get waterlogged, particularly dried beans that are relatively "fresh." Figure on 12 hours as the longest soak.

We may have just cramped your style. Most people want to do the soak overnight, even though they could just put the beans in water in the morning before they head off to the day. However, if you're an overnight fanatic, soak away, drain them in the morning, pour them into a large bowl, set a piece of plastic wrap right against their surface to protect them from moisture loss, and set them in the fridge for up to 12 hours.

4. Why do some beef stews call for beef *or* chicken broth?

Decent chicken broth is relatively easy to find; acceptable beef broth, next to impossible. In most cases, canned or packaged beef broth tastes like a bouillon cube soaked in murky water. Chicken broth usually has more oomph. (Beef trimmings, the sort to make stock, usually go to the dog-food industry, while chicken trimmings, not so much.) If you can find decent beef broth — or make your own (page 103) — you'll be well on your way to a better soup.

5. What's the difference between a stock and a broth?

It's an old-fashioned cookbook writers' trope that "stock" is the homemade stuff and "broth" is the store-bought variety. We've adhered to that difference in the ingredient lists in this book (if not always in the recipe titles).

There's nothing like homemade stock, not only on its own but as part of a recipe: an intense, deep, and satisfying base for a stew or braise. Make stock and squirrel it away in the freezer, especially since the prep is so easy in an Instant Pot. Even if you substitute 1 cup of homemade stock and use purchased broth for the remainder of the amount called for, the results will be dramatically better.

6. And what's a *chinois*?

A racist, culinary nightmare. Also, it's the term for a conical sieve with a very fine mesh, so called in French (*shee-NWAH*) because it's said to look like a Chinese guy's hat. (See?) The gadget's also called a "china cap" or a "bouillon strainer" (probably in a bid for a more PC kitchen). A good *chinois* runs about 20 bucks. It's the best tool for straining out fine, particulate matter from any soup or stock. A decent substitute is a standard colander lined with a double thickness of cheesecloth. But given that cheesecloth costs ten dollars a package, it's probably more economical to invest in the *chinois*.

Pesto Minestrone Soup

6 servings

This summer delight is a version of minestrone with the flavors of pesto: lots of basil and some nuts, even cheese stirred in at the end. We didn't sauté the onions and other vegetables first because we wanted a cleaner, brighter flavor. The soup's actually a bit sour, best on a warm evening (with a G&T — trust us). Calm it down with lots of crunchy bread to sop up every drop.

1. Mix the broth, beans, tomatoes, onion, carrots, celery, zucchini, basil, walnuts, garlic, salt, and red pepper flakes in a **6- or 8-quart cooker**. Stir in the pasta and lock the lid onto the pot.

2.

Set the machine for	Set the level for	The valve must be	Set the time for	If necessary, press
PRESSURE COOK	MAX	—	6 minutes with the KEEP WARM setting off	START
SOUP/BROTH, PRESSURE COOK, or MANUAL	HIGH	Closed	8 minutes with the KEEP WARM setting off	START
SLOW COOK	HIGH	Opened	3 hours with the KEEP WARM setting off (or on KEEP WARM for no more than 2 hours)	START

3. If you've used a pressure-cooking setting, use the **quick-release method** to bring the pot's pressure back to normal.

4. Unlatch the lid and open the pot. Stir in the cheese, set the lid askew over the pot, and set aside for about 5 minutes to blend the flavors.

See photo in insert.

1½ quarts (6 cups) vegetable broth

One 15-ounce can white beans, drained and rinsed (1¾ cups)

4 large round red tomatoes, chopped (4 cups)

1 medium yellow onion, chopped (1 cup)

2 medium carrots, chopped (1 cup)

2 medium celery ribs, chopped (⅔ cup)

1 medium zucchini (6 ounces), halved lengthwise and thinly sliced into half-moons

½ cup loosely packed fresh basil leaves, chopped

½ cup roughly chopped walnuts

Up to 3 medium garlic cloves, peeled and minced (1 tablespoon)

1 teaspoon table salt

Up to ½ teaspoon red pepper flakes

2 ounces regular, whole-wheat, or gluten-free elbow macaroni

2 ounces finely grated Parmigiano-Reggiano (1 cup)

Beyond

- You must halve the recipe for a **3-quart cooker**.
- Make the soup less sour by adding up to 1 tablespoon granulated white sugar with the vegetables.
- Substitute ¼ cup pine nuts for the walnuts.
- Substitute 6 ounces spiralized zucchini for the zucchini slices.
- Finish the bowls with a drizzle of fine, aromatic olive oil.

2 tablespoons liquid fat

Choose from olive oil, any vegetable or grain oil, or almond oil.

1 cup chopped or thinly sliced (and trimmed as necessary) allium aromatics

Choose one or two from onions (of any sort), scallions, shallots, and/or leeks (white and pale green parts only, well washed).

1 cup chopped (and seeded and/or trimmed as necessary) sturdier aromatics

Choose one or two from bell peppers of any color, celery, fennel, and/or radishes.

1½ quarts (6 cups) vegetable broth

2 pounds fresh tomatoes, stemmed and chopped

Use any variety, even cherry tomatoes — or a mix of tomatoes — so long as they smell fresh and sweet.

¼ cup packed chopped fresh herbs.

Choose one or even several from basil, dill, marjoram, oregano, parsley, rosemary, sage, savory, tarragon, and/or thyme.

6 cups chopped (and trimmed as necessary) quick-cooking summer vegetables

Choose a big selection from corn kernels, green beans, runner beans, snow peas, sugar snap peas, wax beans, yellow crookneck squash, and/or zucchini.

1 teaspoon table salt

Road Map: Summer Vegetable Soup

6 servings

When farmers' markets are bursting with tomatoes and summer vegetables, here's a way to make a soup that fits the season. This recipe's a two-stepper, even if it's summer and you'd rather be outside. During the first cooking under pressure, the tomatoes break down into the broth as the herbs infuse it. Then the vegetables get added for a second, super quick blitz under pressure so they don't turn mushy. During this second round of pressure, do not use the MAX setting (if it's available with your model). Bring the pot to HIGH pressure, then immediately release the pressure to keep the summery vegetables crisp and flavorful.

The real key to success is to chop everything to the same size: All the aromatics and tomatoes should be in ½-inch pieces; all the summer vegetables, about ¾-inch pieces.

Two particularly appealing herb combos are basil, tarragon, and thyme, and dill, parsley, and oregano.

1.

Press the button for	Set it for	Set the time for	If necessary, press
SAUTÉ	MEDIUM, NORMAL, or CUSTOM 300°F	10 minutes	START

2. Warm the oil in a **6- or 8-quart cooker** for a minute or two, then add both the allium and the sturdier aromatics. Cook, stirring often, until the allium aromatics begin to soften, 3 to 5 minutes. Stir in the broth, tomatoes, and fresh herbs. Turn off the SAUTÉ function and lock the lid onto the pot.

3.

Set the machine for	Set the level for	The valve must be	Set the time for	If necessary, press
PRESSURE COOK	MAX	—	10 minutes with the KEEP WARM setting off	START
SOUP/BROTH, PRESSURE COOK, or MANUAL	HIGH	Closed	14 minutes with the KEEP WARM setting off	START

4. When the machine has finished cooking, turn it off and let the pressure **return to normal naturally,** about 30 minutes. Unlatch the lid and open the pot. Stir in the quick-cooking summer vegetables. Lock the lid onto the pot.

5.

Set the machine for	Set the level for	The valve must be	Set the time for	If necessary, press
PRESSURE COOK or MANUAL	HIGH	Closed	0 minutes with the KEEP WARM setting off	START

6. Use the **quick-release method** to bring the pot's pressure back to normal. Unlatch the lid and open the pot. Stir in the salt before serving.

Beyond

- You must halve the recipe for a **3-quart cooker.**

- The best garnish on each serving is a highly flavorful olive oil.

- If you don't care about a vegan soup, use butter as the fat (and reduce the salt to ½ teaspoon).

- And grate lots of Parmigiano-Reggiano or pecorino over each bowlful.

- Or go all out and ladle the soup over big, crunchy croutons (see the *Beyond* section of the Beef Stew road map on page 345).

2 quarts (8 cups) vegetable broth

6 cups chopped (peeled and/or seeded as necessary) root vegetables

Choose one or several from butternut squash, carrots, celeriac, parsnips, potatoes of any variety, pumpkin, rutabaga, winter squash of any variety, and/or yellow beets.

1 cup chopped (and trimmed as necessary) allium aromatics

Choose one or a combo from onions (of any sort), shallots, and/or leeks (white and pale green parts only, well washed).

¼ cup soy sauce, preferably reduced-sodium

1 ounce small dried mushrooms, crumbled

Choose any sort from porcini, shiitake, chanterelle, morels, or even a purchased blend — but avoid large, dried mushrooms (like wood ear mushrooms), often found at Asian markets.

1½ tablespoons dried herbs

Choose dried basil, cilantro, oregano, rosemary, and/or thyme, or a purchased herb blend like an Italian blend or herbes de Provence.

Up to 3 medium garlic cloves, peeled and minced (1 tablespoon)

2 cups chopped stemmed greens

Choose one or several from kale, collard, escarole, mustard, and/or turnip greens.

Road Map: Winter Vegetable Soup

6 to 8 servings

This road map is designed to create a root vegetable soup with leafy greens in the mix. There are no tomatoes, of course. (Who's ever heard of a good tomato in December? And be quiet, if you live in Southern California.) Make sure you chop the root vegetables into 1-inch pieces. If you buy them prechopped from the produce section, you'll probably need to chop them more to get the right size. (Unless you have a vegetable concierge at your supermarket. Again, you Southern Californians need to be quiet.)

We listed some more common leafy greens. Use what you find, from dandelion greens to Chinese flowering broccoli. If you want to go all out, stop by an Asian supermarket some time to see the incredible range of leafy greens available. However, skip over chard, beet greens, and any baby greens for this soup. They turn too squishy.

1. Mix the broth, root vegetables, allium aromatics, soy sauce, dried mushrooms, herbs, and garlic in a **6- or 8-quart cooker**. Lock the lid onto the pot.

2.

Set the machine for	Set the level for	The valve must be	Set the time for	If necessary, press
PRESSURE COOK	MAX	—	10 minutes with the KEEP WARM setting off	START
SOUP/BROTH, PRESSURE COOK, or MANUAL	HIGH	Closed	12 minutes with the KEEP WARM setting off	START

3. Use the **quick-release method** to bring the pot's pressure back to normal. Unlatch the lid and open the pot.

4. Stir in the stemmed greens. Lock the lid back onto the pot.

5.

Set the machine for	Set the level for	The valve must be	Set the time for	If necessary, press
PRESSURE COOK or MANUAL	HIGH	Closed	0 minutes with the KEEP WARM setting off	START

6. Use the **quick-release method** to bring the the pressure back to normal. Unlatch the lid and open the pot. Stir well before serving.

Beyond

- You must halve the recipe for a **3-quart cooker.**
- For a simpler soup without the greens, simply omit steps 4, 5, and 6.
- Unfortunately, red beets turn the soup a lurid color. Maybe you don't mind. Our linens did.
- For heat, add up to 1½ teaspoons red pepper flakes with the dried herbs.
- The second cooking is designed to keep some chew in the greens. If you like softer greens, use a natural release in step 5.
- If you don't care about this soup being vegan, toss a 3-inch piece of Parmesan rind into the pot with the root vegetables — and set a poached egg in each serving.

2 tablespoons butter

2 thick-cut strips of bacon, chopped

1 medium yellow onion, chopped
(1 cup)

1 medium russet potato (about 6
ounces), peeled and cut into 1-inch
pieces

3 medium tart green apples, such as
Granny Smith, peeled, cored, and cut
into 1-inch pieces

½ teaspoon caraway seeds

½ teaspoon dried thyme

Up to ½ teaspoon table salt

½ teaspoon ground black pepper

1 quart (4 cups) vegetable broth

½ cup heavy cream

2 teaspoons cornstarch

Potato, Bacon, and Apple Chowder

6 servings

Yep, we put apples in chowder. They add an essential sweetness that pairs well with bacon in this easy soup, a welcome lunch or dinner in cooler weather. The potatoes are not cooked until they can be pureed, but rather just until tender.

Do not use flavored bacon here, or even pepper bacon. The soup needs a cleaner flavor profile to let the potatoes shine through.

1.

Press the button for	Set it for	Set the time for	If necessary, press
SAUTÉ	MEDIUM, NORMAL, or CUSTOM 300°F	10 minutes	START

2. Melt the butter in a **6- or 8-quart cooker**. Add the bacon pieces and cook, stirring often, until well browned, about 3 minutes. Add the onion and continue cooking, stirring more often, until the onion begins to soften, about 3 minutes.

3. Stir in the potatoes, apples, caraway seeds, thyme, salt, and pepper. Pour in the broth and scrape up *every speck of browned stuff* on the pot's bottom. Turn off the SAUTÉ function and lock the lid onto the pot.

4.

Set the machine for	Set the level for	The valve must be	Set the time for	If necessary, press
PRESSURE COOK	MAX	—	5 minutes with the KEEP WARM setting off	START
SOUP/BROTH, PRESSURE COOK, or MANUAL	HIGH	Closed	7 minutes with the KEEP WARM setting off	START
SLOW COOK	HIGH	Opened	3 hours with the KEEP WARM setting off (or on for no more than 2 hours)	START

5. If you've used a pressure-cooking setting, use the **quick-release method** to bring the pot's pressure back to normal.

6. Unlatch the lid and open the pot. Whisk the cream and cornstarch in a small bowl until smooth.

7.

Press the button for	Set it for	Set the time for	If necessary, press
SAUTÉ	MEDIUM, NORMAL, or CUSTOM 300°F	5 minutes	START

8. Bring the soup to a low simmer, stirring constantly. Add the cream slurry and continue cooking, stirring constantly, until thickened, about 1 minute. Turn off the SAUTÉ function and immediately remove the *hot* insert from the pot to stop any cooking. Serve warm.

Beyond

- You must halve the recipe for a **3-quart cooker.**
- Add up to 2 thinly sliced celery ribs (⅔ cup) with the onion.
- And/or add up to 2 medium garlic cloves, peeled and minced (2 teaspoons), with the onion.
- Stir up to 1 cup corn kernels (thawed if frozen) into the soup with the cream slurry.
- Use chicken broth for a much richer soup.

6 cups (1½ quarts) chicken or vegetable broth

3 pounds russet potatoes, peeled and chopped

1 small yellow onion, chopped (½ cup)

3 tablespoons butter, cut into three pieces

½ teaspoon table salt

½ teaspoon ground black pepper

½ cup regular or low-fat sour cream

4 ounces regular or low-fat cream cheese, cut into small bits

At least 2 tablespoons whole or low-fat milk, plus more as needed

Shredded American Cheddar cheese for garnishing

Finely chopped scallions, preferably just the green part, for garnishing

Loaded Baked Potato Soup

6 servings

For this baked-potato-in-a-bowl, you *must* use russets, the classic baking potatoes. Only these have the right amount of starch to make a soup that tastes like the classic steakhouse side. And you must chop those potatoes. Yes, it's a pain. Here's how to work efficiently: Peel them, then slice them into ½-inch-thick rounds. Cut these into ½-inch strips, gather them together, and cut these strips into ½-inch pieces.

Because potatoes endure long transport and often sit on the store's shelf a good while, there's no real way to judge how much internal moisture each holds. We give the amount of milk as a mere suggestion. In the end, you'll need to add enough to get the consistency you like — much looser than mashed potatoes, of course, but maybe not as loose as a more traditional soup.

1. Mix the broth, potatoes, onion, butter, salt, and pepper in a **6- or 8-quart cooker**. Lock the lid onto the pot.

2.

Set the machine for	Set the level for	The valve must be	Set the time for	If necessary, press
PRESSURE COOK	MAX	—	10 minutes with the KEEP WARM setting off	START
SOUP/BROTH, PRESSURE COOK, or MANUAL	HIGH	Closed	13 minutes with the KEEP WARM setting off	START

3. Use the **quick-release method** to bring the pot's pressure back to normal. Unlatch the lid and open the pot. Use a potato masher or the back of a wooden spoon to mash the potatoes into a coarse puree. (Do not use an immersion blender or even a regular blender to puree the soup as both will cool it down too quickly.) Without delay, whisk in the sour cream and cream cheese until smooth.

4. Add 2 tablespoons milk and whisk for a creamy consistency, adding more milk as needed to get your preferred texture. Serve in bowls, garnished with the Cheddar and scallions.

Beyond

- You must halve the recipe for a **3-quart cooker**.

- To take the soup over the top, also garnish the servings with crumbled, crisp-fried bacon.

- Or offer unexpected garnishes like pickled jalapeño rings, sliced avocado, and/or jarred pickled cocktail onions.

- If you're feeling luxurious, substitute half-and-half or heavy cream for the milk.

Kale-Is-the-New-Black Soup

6 servings

No doubt, kale's hip. Better, it's easy in this recipe, since you can use bagged, chopped kale. (Don't use baby kale, which will overcook.) You don't even need to wash bagged kale to get rid of any grit.

Of course, you can also use fresh whole leaves, particularly the more tender ones you can find at a farmers' market. Try red Russian, Toscano, scarlet, or red Ursa varieties.

The best way to wash kale leaves is to fill a clean kitchen sink with cool water, add stemmed leaves, and agitate the water a little. Let the leaves rest in the water for 5 minutes as the grit floats down, then skim them off the top of the water before pulling the stopper on the drain to wash away the grit.

For this recipe, brown the onions and cook the vegetables a little longer than you might usually, mostly to give these ingredients a deep, complex flavor to pair with the earthy, slightly bitter kale — which is itself cooked for a fairly long time to soften it considerably. A garnish of soy sauce brings everything into a more savory balance.

2 tablespoons olive oil

1 medium yellow onion, chopped (1 cup)

1 small fennel bulb, trimmed and chopped (1½ cups)

2 medium garlic cloves, peeled and minced (2 teaspoons)

6 cups packed chopped stemmed kale

1½ quarts (6 cups) vegetable broth

One 14-ounce can diced tomatoes (1¾ cups)

2 medium yellow potatoes (about 5 ounces each), such as Yukon Golds, diced (1½ cups)

2 tablespoons fresh rosemary leaves, chopped

2 tablespoons fresh sage leaves, chopped

Soy sauce for garnishing

1.

Press the button for	Set it for	Set the time for	If necessary, press
SAUTÉ	MEDIUM, NORMAL, or CUSTOM 300°F	15 minutes	START

2. Warm the oil in a **6- or 8-quart cooker** for a minute or two. Add the onion and fennel. Cook, stirring often, until the onion starts to get a little brown and even sweet, about 10 minutes. Stir in the garlic for a few seconds.

3. Add the kale. Stir well and continue cooking, stirring occasionally, until the greens wilt, about 3 minutes. Pour in the broth and scrape up the browned bits on the bottom of the pot. Turn off the SAUTÉ function and stir in the tomatoes, potatoes, rosemary, and sage. Lock the lid onto the pot.

4.

Set the machine for	Set the level for	The valve must be	Set the time for	If necessary, press
PRESSURE COOK	MAX	—	10 minutes with the KEEP WARM setting off	START
SOUP/BROTH, PRESSURE COOK, or MANUAL	HIGH	Closed	14 minutes with the KEEP WARM setting off	START

5. Use the **quick-release method** to bring the pot's pressure back to normal. Unlatch the lid and open the pot. Stir well, then ladle into bowls, garnishing each with a little soy sauce.

Beyond

- You must halve the recipe for a **3-quart cooker**.

- For heat, add up to 1 teaspoon red pepper flakes with the herbs.

- For a brighter flavor, add up to 2 teaspoons finely grated lemon zest with the herbs.

- If you don't need the soup to be vegan, use chicken broth for a bolder flavor and feel free to add up to ½ pound very thin slices of smoked kielbasa, bratwurst, or chorizo with the kale.

1 large fennel bulb (about 2 pounds), trimmed and chopped (4 cups)

1 quart (4 cups) vegetable broth

One 28-ounce can diced tomatoes (3½ cups)

1 medium yellow onion, chopped (1 cup)

½ cup golden raisins

3 tablespoons white wine vinegar

2 tablespoons light brown sugar

1 teaspoon dried dill

1 teaspoon caraway seeds

½ teaspoon celery seeds

½ teaspoon table salt

Not-Your-Jewish-Grandmother's Sweet-and-Sour Soup

6 servings

Back in the day (and on Delancey Street), a soup made with cabbage, tomatoes, and raisins was a standby, making an appearance at many a Shabbos dinner. We've updated the classic by substituting fennel for the cabbage. Cabbage can be, well, bland; but fennel gives the soup an aromatic hit, sort of like a big dose of celery with many herbaceous notes.

As you can imagine, the flavors are bright, even a little acidic, best on a summer evening when fennel is fresh at the farmers' market. (And best with a pale ale or a Hefeweizen.)

1. Mix all the ingredients in a **6- or 8-quart cooker**. Lock the lid onto the pot.

2.

Set the machine for	Set the level for	The valve must be	Set the time for	If necessary, press
PRESSURE COOK	MAX	—	15 minutes with the KEEP WARM setting off	START
SOUP/BROTH, PRESSURE COOK, or MANUAL	HIGH	Closed	20 minutes with the KEEP WARM setting off	START

3. Use the **quick-release method** to bring the pot's pressure back to normal. Unlatch the lid and open the pot. Set aside for 5 minutes to cool a bit, then stir well before serving.

Beyond

- You must halve the recipe for a 3-quart cooker.

- Garnish the servings with a drizzle of aromatic olive oil.

- And/or garnish with finely grated Parmigiano-Reggiano or pecorino.

- To make a more traditional cabbage soup, substitute 4 cups cored and chopped cabbage for the fennel.

- Soups like this one often included beef — particularly flanken (beef short ribs cut across the bones or "Korean-style"). To do that here, put up to 1 pound beef flanken and the broth in the pot and cook at MAX for 37 minutes or HIGH at 45 minutes, followed by a natural release. Open the pot, then continue with the recipe as written from step 1 (having already used the stated amount of broth).

The New Standard Cabbage Soup

6 servings

Here's our gussied-up version of the old-world cabbage soup that was transformed with fennel in the previous recipe. We've again modernized it, this time with apple, orange zest, and cinnamon, all to get more flavor in every bowl, a noble goal.

    Unfortunately, you can't use bagged shredded cabbage here. The strands are so thin, they'll turn into baby food under pressure. Halve a fresh cabbage, core it, then cut each half into ½-inch-thick slices, which you can then cut crosswise into ½-inch-thick strips.

1.

Press the button for	Set it for	Set the time for	If necessary, press
SAUTÉ	MEDIUM, NORMAL, or CUSTOM 300°F	10 minutes	START

2. Warm the oil in a **6- or 8-quart cooker** for a minute or two. Add the bacon and cook, stirring occasionally, until lightly browned, about 4 minutes. Add the onion and carrot; continue cooking, stirring more often, until the onion begins to soften, about 3 minutes.

3. Stir in the cabbage and cook, stirring all the while, until it begins to wilt, about 2 minutes. Pour in the broth and scrape up any browned bits on the bottom of the pot. Turn off the SAUTÉ function. Stir in the apple, vinegar, brown sugar, orange zest, nutmeg, black pepper, bay leaves, and cinnamon stick until the brown sugar dissolves. Lock the lid onto the pot.

4.

Set the machine for	Set the level for	The valve must be	Set the time for	If necessary, press
PRESSURE COOK	MAX	—	20 minutes with the KEEP WARM setting off	START
SOUP/BROTH, PRESSURE COOK, or MANUAL	HIGH	Closed	28 minutes with the KEEP WARM setting off	START
SLOW COOK	HIGH	Opened	4 hours with the KEEP WARM setting off (or on for no more than 3 hours)	START

5. If you've used a pressure-cooking setting, use the **quick-release method** to bring the pot's pressure back to normal.

6. Unlatch the lid and open the pot. Find and discard the bay leaves and cinnamon stick. Stir the soup well before serving hot.

1 tablespoon vegetable, corn, or canola oil

6 ounces thin-cut strips of pork, turkey, or beef bacon, chopped

1 medium red onion, chopped (1 cup)

1 medium carrot, chopped (½ cup)

1 medium green or red cabbage (about 1½ pounds), cored and thinly sliced into strips

1½ quarts (6 cups) chicken broth

1 medium tart green apple, such as Granny Smith, peeled, cored, and chopped

¼ cup apple cider vinegar

2 tablespoons dark brown sugar

1 tablespoon finely grated orange zest

½ teaspoon grated nutmeg

½ teaspoon ground black pepper

2 bay leaves

One 4-inch cinnamon stick

Beyond

- You must halve the recipe for a 3-quart cooker.

- For a richer soup, substitute up to 2 tablespoons butter for the oil.

- Dollop the servings with sour cream — or sour cream mixed with minced chives.

Tomato and Wheat Berry Soup

4 to 6 servings

4 cups water

1¾ pounds plum or Roma tomatoes, chopped (3½ cups)

1 medium yellow onion, chopped (1 cup)

½ cup dried wheat berries, preferably soft white wheat berries

½ cup sun-dried tomatoes packed in oil, chopped

2 tablespoons packed oregano leaves, minced

1 tablespoon packed rosemary leaves, minced

2 medium garlic cloves, peeled and minced (2 teaspoons)

Up to 1 teaspoon table salt

½ teaspoon fennel seeds

½ teaspoon ground black pepper

Whole grains are terrific in soups, although some people remain afraid of wheat berries in a pressure cooker — perhaps they once used a **quick-release method** at the end of cooking and splattered their kitchen cabinets with wheaty gunk. Those people also forgot the basic safety mechanism for cooking whole grains under pressure: Add a little fat. Here, the oil from the sun-dried tomatoes helps keep the wheat berries from foaming by breaking the surface tension in the liquid so bubbles cannot easily form. Ta da: a rich, summery-yet-whole-grain soup.

1. Mix all the ingredients in a **6- or 8-quart cooker**. Lock the lid onto the pot.

2.

Set the machine for	Set the level for	The valve must be	Set the time for	If necessary, press
PRESSURE COOK	MAX	—	35 minutes with the KEEP WARM setting off	START
HIGH PRESSURE or MANUAL	HIGH	Closed	45 minutes with the KEEP WARM setting off	START

3. When the machine has finished cooking, turn it off and let its pressure **return to normal naturally**, about 25 minutes. Unlatch the lid and open the pot. Stir well before serving.

Beyond

- You must halve the recipe for a **3-quart cooker.**

- For a richer (not vegan) soup, slice dried Spanish chorizo into ½-inch-thick rounds and stir them into the soup with the other ingredients.

- Or throw the small rind from a chunk of Parmigiano-Reggiano into the pot with the other ingredients. Or just grate lots of Parmigiano-Reggiano over each serving.

- For a gluten-free version, use certified gluten-free oat groats for the wheat berries. Increase the time under MAX to 43 minutes or HIGH pressure to 55 minutes.

Road Map: Creamy Vegetable Soup

4 to 6 servings

Here's culinary magic we can't conjure in a saucepan. By adding baking soda, we actually can change the pH of butter so that the milk solids don't burn while they're under pressure. We can then *poach* vegetables in butter, a trick we can never perform on the stovetop but only in a pressure cooker. The result is an intensely creamy soup without a smidgen of cream. Make several batches during a weekend cooking spree and get them into the freezer in individual servings. You'll have a fabulous dinner anytime you want to stream half a season of something.

1.

Press the button for	Set it for	Set the time for	If necessary, press
SAUTÉ	MEDIUM, NORMAL, or CUSTOM 300°F	5 minutes	START

2. Melt the butter in a **3- or 6-quart cooker**. Add the chopped vegetable and stir until fully coated in the butter. Turn off the SAUTÉ function. Add the salt, dried spice(s), and baking soda. Stir well, pour the water over everything, and lock the lid onto the pot.

3.

Set the machine for	Set the level for	The valve must be	Set the time for	If necessary, press
PRESSURE COOK	MAX	—	10 minutes with the KEEP WARM setting off	START
SOUP/BROTH, PRESSURE COOK, or MANUAL	HIGH	Closed	12 minutes with the KEEP WARM setting off	START

4. Use the **quick-release method** to bring the pot's pressure back to normal. Unlatch the lid and open the cooker. Pour in the liquid, then use an immersion blender right in the pot to puree the soup until smooth. Serve warm.

½ cup (1 stick) butter, cut into chunks

6 cups chopped vegetable

Choose from 1½-inch cauliflower florets (about 1½ pounds), 1½-inch broccoli florets and stems (about 1½ pounds), 1-inch peeled sweet potato cubes (about 1¾ pounds), 1-inch peeled celeriac cubes (about 1¾ pounds), 1-inch peeled turnip cubes (about 1¾ pounds), 1-inch peeled rutabaga cubes (about 1½ pounds), or 1-inch peeled and seeded winter or butternut squash cubes (about 1½ pounds).

½ teaspoon table salt

½ teaspoon dried spice or spice blend

Choose one from grated nutmeg, ground caraway, ground cardamom, ground cinnamon, ground cumin, sage, thyme, garam masala, curry powder, or other spice blends.

¼ teaspoon baking soda

¼ cup water

2½ cups liquid

Choose chicken, beef, or vegetable broth, or a combo of 2 cups broth and ½ cup dry white wine.

Beyond

- For an **8-quart cooker**, you must increase all the ingredients by 50 percent.

- For an even creamier texture, add up to ½ cup heavy cream before you puree the soup. Simmer for 1 minute with the SAUTÉ function on LOW or LESS if you don't like the taste of raw cream.

- If you don't have an immersion blender, pour the soup in batches into a blender, cover, remove the center knob, lay a clean kitchen towel over the opening, and blend until smooth, eventually getting all the batches into a large bowl and stirring them together.

- For a cleaner flavor, omit the dried herb or herb blend.

1 pound dried medium-sized beans

Choose one or two from Anazasi, appaloosa, azuki, bolita, calypso, cannellini, cranberry, great northern, lima, mortgage runner, pink, pinto, rattlesnake, red, red kidney, scarlet runner, Steuben yellow, Tolosana, and/or trout beans.

2 tablespoons fat

Choose from vegetable oil, corn oil, canola oil, safflower oil, olive oil, grape-seed oil, walnut oil, pecan oil, butter, coconut oil, rendered bacon fat, schmaltz, or lard.

3 cups chopped aromatic vegetables

Choose two to make up the total volume from onions (of any sort), shallots, leeks (white and pale green parts only, well washed), scallions, stemmed and cored bell peppers of any variety, celery, carrots, and/or trimmed fennel.

Up to 2 tablespoons dried herbs or spices

Choose two or three to make up the total volume from ground allspice, ground cinnamon, ground cumin, coriander seeds, dried basil, dried marjoram, dried oregano, dried rosemary, dried sage, dried savory, and/or dried thyme.

8 cups (2 quarts) broth

Use any sort.

2 tablespoons acid

Choose from lemon juice, lime juice, or vinegar of any sort.

½ teaspoon table salt

Road Map: Bean Soup

6 to 8 servings

There are a few things a pressure cooker seems to be made for. Steel-cut oatmeal? Sure thing. Beef short ribs? You bet. And bean soup. There's nothing like it: The tender beans release enough starch to enrich the broth, making pure comfort food.

Although this road map lets you concoct your own version, we find the best herb/spice combinations involve more dried, leafy herbs and less dried spices — for example, 1 tablespoon dried sage, 2 teaspoons dried thyme, and 1 teaspoon ground cinnamon; or 2 teaspoons dried oregano, 2 teaspoons dried rosemary, 1 teaspoon ground allspice, and 1 teaspoon coriander seeds. Really, the only way to tell which blend you like is to do exactly what we do when we're recipe-testing: Hold the bottles together under your nose and gently inhale.

1. Place the dried beans in a large bowl, fill it with cool tap water, and soak overnight, for at least 8 hours or up to 12 hours.

2.

Press the button for	Set it for	Set the time for	If necessary, press
SAUTÉ	MEDIUM, NORMAL, or CUSTOM 300°F	10 minutes	START

3. Warm the oil or melt the solid fat in a **6- or 8-quart cooker**. Add the aromatic vegetables and cook, stirring often, until they begin to soften, about 4 minutes. Add the dried herbs or spices; cook until aromatic, stirring all the while, just a few seconds.

4. Pour in the broth and scrape up any browned bits on the pot's bottom. Turn off the SAUTÉ function. Drain the beans in a colander set in the sink, then stir them into the pot. Lock the lid onto the cooker.

5.

Set the machine for	Set the level for	The valve must be	Set the time for	If necessary, press
PRESSURE COOK	MAX	—	15 minutes with the KEEP WARM setting off	START
SOUP/BROTH, PRESSURE COOK, or MANUAL	HIGH	Closed	20 minutes with the KEEP WARM setting off	START
SLOW COOK	HIGH	Opened	4 hours with the KEEP WARM setting off (or on for no more than 2 hours)	START

6. If you've used a pressure setting, when the machine has finished cooking, turn it off and let its pressure **return to normal naturally**, about 40 minutes. Unlatch the lid and open the cooker. Stir in the acid and salt before serving.

Beyond

- You must halve the recipe for a **3-quart cooker.**

- There are no black beans in this road map. They cook a bit differently. Use the method given here but use the **quick-release method** to return the machine's pressure to normal after cooking.

- If you'd like to skip the experiment with the herbs and spices, simply use a bottled spice blend.

- For more oomph, add up to 2 bay leaves with the herbs and spices. Or 1 star anise pod. And/or up to 1 teaspoon red pepper flakes.

- For a mealish bean soup, complete the recipe through adding the broth to the pot in step 4. At this point, add your choice of 1 lamb shank, trimmed; 1 veal shank; 1 beef shank; up to 12 ounces beef flanken; 1 fresh or smoked pork hock; or 2 turkey wings (smoked or not), cut into their individual segments. (Remember that smoked meats can be very salty.) Lock the lid onto the pot and put it under MAX pressure for 30 minutes or HIGH pressure for 40 minutes, followed by a quick release. Now add the soaked beans and carry on with the recipe as stated (leaving the meat in the pot). At the end of all the cooking, take the meat out of the pot, shred the meat off the bone, and stir the shredded meat back into the soup.

1 pound dried black beans

1½ tablespoons vegetable, corn, or canola oil

2 medium green bell peppers, stemmed, cored, and chopped (2 cups)

1 large yellow onion, chopped (1½ cups)

10 ounces smoked kielbasa, cut into 1-inch pieces

2 medium garlic cloves, peeled and minced (2 teaspoons)

2 teaspoons ground cumin

2 teaspoons dried oregano

2 teaspoons dried thyme

1 teaspoon ground allspice

½ teaspoon ground black pepper

1½ quarts (6 cups) chicken broth

2 tablespoons fresh lime juice

Black Bean and Kielbasa Soup

6 to 8 servings

Since black beans need special attention, we crafted this recipe to highlight their decidedly sweet flavor, pairing them with lots of vegetables, smoked sausage, and a blend of spices. The soup will be fairly thin when it's finished. If you want to thicken it, scoop out 1 cup cooked beans with some of the liquid and puree in a small blender or food processor until smooth, then stir it back into the pot.

1. Pour the beans into a large bowl, fill it with cool tap water, and set aside to soak at room temperature overnight, for at least 8 hours or up to 12 hours. Drain the beans in a large colander set in the sink.

2.

Press the button for	Set it for	Set the time for	If necessary, press
SAUTÉ	MEDIUM, NORMAL, or CUSTOM 300°F	10 minutes	START

3. Warm the oil in a **6- or 8-quart cooker** for a minute or two. Add the bell pepper and onion; cook, stirring often, until the onion begins to soften, about 4 minutes. Add the sausage and cook, stirring once in a while, just until lightly browned, about 3 minutes.

4. Stir in the garlic, cumin, oregano, thyme, allspice, and pepper until aromatic, just a few seconds. Pour in the broth and scrape up any browned bits on the pot's bottom. Turn off the SAUTÉ function, stir in the drained beans, and lock the lid onto the pot.

5.

Set the machine for	Set the level for	The valve must be	Set the time for	If necessary, press
PRESSURE COOK	MAX	—	15 minutes with the KEEP WARM setting off	START
SOUP/BROTH, PRESSURE COOK, or MANUAL	HIGH	Closed	20 minutes with the KEEP WARM setting off	START
SLOW COOK	HIGH	Opened	4 hours with the KEEP WARM setting off (or on for no more than 2 hours)	START

6. If you've used a pressure setting, when the machine has finished cooking, use the **quick-release method** to return its pressure to normal.

7. Unlatch the lid and open the pot. Stir in the lime juice and serve hot.

Beyond

- You must halve the recipe for a **3-quart cooker**.

- Substitute dried chorizo for the smoked sausage. Also add 1 tablespoon mild smoked paprika with the other spices.

- Garnish with sour cream or chopped, pitted, and peeled avocado, as well as minced red onion and cilantro leaves. Even top with shredded American Cheddar or Monterey Jack cheese.

Southern Black-Eyed Pea Soup

6 to 8 servings

Black-eyed peas don't need to be soaked before going under pressure. (When soaked, they turn too mealy.) Without that additional effort, we felt free to craft a slightly more complicated recipe. First, we make a rich base by cooking a ham hock for a good while, mostly to get all its flavor into the broth. Then we put the remaining ingredients in the pot for a second, quicker cooking.

By the way, you can complete the recipe through step 3 in advance. Pour the cooked broth and hock into a large bowl, cover, and refrigerate for up to 2 days. There's no need to return them to room temperature before proceeding with the remainder of the recipe.

1. Pour the broth into a **6- or 8-quart cooker**. Add the hock and lock the lid onto the pot.

2.

Set the machine for	Set the level for	The valve must be	Set the time for	If necessary, press
PRESSURE COOK	MAX	—	45 minutes with the KEEP WARM setting off	START
SOUP/BROTH, PRESSURE COOK, or MANUAL	HIGH	Closed	1 hour with the KEEP WARM setting off	START

3. Use the **quick-release method** to bring the pot's pressure back to normal. Unlatch the lid and open the pot. Stir in the black-eyed peas, onion, celery, bell pepper, rosemary, sage, thyme, pepper, and bay leaves. Lock the lid back onto the pot.

4.

Set the machine for	Set the level for	The valve must be	Set the time for	If necessary, press
PRESSURE COOK	MAX	—	18 minutes with the KEEP WARM setting off	START
SOUP/BROTH, PRESSURE COOK, or MANUAL	HIGH	Closed	25 minutes with the KEEP WARM setting off	START

5. Again use the **quick-release method** to bring the pot's pressure back to normal. Unlatch the lid and open the pot. Find and discard the bay leaves. Transfer the hock to a cutting board and set the lid askew over the pot. Cool the hock for a few minutes, then shred the meat from the bones. Stir the meat and the vinegar into the soup before serving.

---

7 cups (1 quart plus 3 cups) chicken broth

1 smoked ham hock (about ¾ pound)

1 pound dried black-eyed peas

1 medium yellow onion, chopped (1 cup)

4 medium celery ribs, thinly sliced (1⅓ cups)

1 medium green bell pepper, stemmed, cored, and chopped (1 cup)

1 teaspoon dried rosemary

1 teaspoon dried sage

1 teaspoon dried thyme

½ teaspoon ground black pepper

2 bay leaves

2 tablespoons apple cider vinegar

Beyond

- Because of the size of the hock, this recipe doesn't work well in a **3-quart cooker**.

- The hock provides plenty of salt to the dish. Pass more at the table, preferably kosher or coarse-grained salt.

- Hocks come with the skin attached. We like to chop it up after cooking and add it back to the soup with the meat. If doing so disgusts you (seriously?), discard the skin before chopping the meat.

- Add up to 2 chopped medium carrots (1 cup) with the other vegetables.

- Omit the rosemary and substitute a star anise pod for the bay leaves.

1 pound dried pinto beans

1½ quarts (6 cups) vegetable broth

1 large red onion, chopped (1½ cups)

2 large carrots, very thinly sliced (1½ cups)

1 small, thin-skinned orange, preferably a Valencia orange, chopped (the rind intact), any seeds removed

3 tablespoons packed fresh oregano leaves

2 tablespoons golden raisins

1 teaspoon ground cumin

1 teaspoon table salt

½ teaspoon ground cinnamon

½ teaspoon ground black pepper

Pinto Bean and (a Whole!) Orange Soup

6 to 8 servings

Indeed, this soup includes a *whole* orange. Chopped up, too. It's another trick you can't accomplish on the stovetop. The rind softens under pressure without turning bitter. In fact, it will almost melt and give the soup a spark of bright flavor. We'll admit that this recipe was a bit of a revelation when we were testing for this book: savory/sweet, mellow, and absurdly good with a drizzle of balsamic vinegar and lots of ground black pepper over each bowlful.

1. Pour the beans into a large bowl, fill it with cool tap water, and set aside to soak at room temperature overnight, for at least 8 hours or up to 12 hours.

2. Drain the beans in a large colander set in the sink; pour them into a **6- or 8-quart cooker**. Stir in the broth, onion, carrots, orange, oregano, raisins, cumin, salt, cinnamon, and black pepper. Lock the lid onto the pot.

3.

Set the machine for	Set the level for	The valve must be	Set the time for	If necessary, press
PRESSURE COOK	MAX	—	18 minutes with the KEEP WARM setting off	START
SOUP/BROTH, PRESSURE COOK, or MANUAL	HIGH	Closed	20 minutes with the KEEP WARM setting off	START

4. Use the **quick-release method** to bring the pot's pressure back to normal. Unlatch the lid and open the pot. Serve hot.

Beyond

- You must halve the recipe for a **3-quart cooker**.

- For a sweet-and-sour soup, open the pot after cooking and stir in 2 tablespoons apple cider vinegar and 2 tablespoons orange marmalade until it melts.

- Garnish the servings with sour cream and finely chopped chives, maybe even dusted with a little more ground cinnamon.

Pinto Bean and (Tons of!) Bacon Soup

6 to 8 servings

1 pound dried pinto beans

1 tablespoon butter

10 ounces thin slices of pork or turkey bacon, chopped

2 medium yellow bell peppers, stemmed, cored, and chopped (2 cups)

1 large yellow onion, chopped (1½ cups)

2 medium garlic cloves, peeled and minced (2 teaspoons)

2 teaspoons dried sage

1½ teaspoons dried thyme

½ teaspoon ground black pepper

1 cup dry white wine, such as Chardonnay

5 cups (1 quart plus 1 cup) chicken or vegetable broth

When it comes to bacon, why go halfway? Sure, you could cut back on the bacon here, to 6 ounces or so. But honestly, the flavor will be tamed by either the pressure or the slow cook. You might as well follow us up and over the top of this bacon mountain. That said, for a (slightly) healthier soup, spoon out all but 2 tablespoons rendered fat before adding the vegetables.

1. Pour the beans into a large bowl, fill it with cool tap water, and set aside at room temperature to soak overnight, for at least 8 hours or up to 12 hours.

2.

Press the button for	Set it for	Set the time for	If necessary, press
SAUTÉ	CUSTOM 300°F	15 minutes	START

3. Melt the butter in a **6- or 8-quart cooker**. Add the bacon and cook, stirring often, until browned but not crisp, about 5 minutes. Add the bell peppers, onion, and garlic. Continue cooking, stirring often, until the onion begins to soften, about 4 minutes. Stir in the sage, thyme, and pepper until aromatic, just a few seconds.

4. Pour in the wine and scrape up *every speck of browned stuff* on the pot's bottom. Turn off the SAUTÉ function and pour in the broth. Stir well and lock the lid onto the cooker.

5.

Set the machine for	Set the level for	The valve must be	Set the time for	If necessary, press
PRESSURE COOK	MAX	—	15 minutes with the KEEP WARM setting off	START
SOUP/BROTH, PRESSURE COOK, or MANUAL	HIGH	Closed	20 minutes with the KEEP WARM setting off	START
SLOW COOK	HIGH	Opened	4 hours with the KEEP WARM setting off (or on for no more than 2 hours)	START

6. If you've used a pressure setting, when the machine has finished cooking, turn it off and let the pressure **return to normal naturally**, about 35 minutes.

7. Unlatch the lid and open the pot. Stir the soup well before serving.

Beyond

- You must halve the recipe for a **3-quart cooker**.

- To omit the wine, substitute ⅔ cup unsweetened apple juice and increase the broth to 5½ cups.

- Add ½ teaspoon ground allspice with the sage and thyme.

- Add up to 2 teaspoons red pepper flakes with the herbs.

- For a more well-stocked stew, stir up to 3 cups baby arugula into the pot after cooking under pressure. Set aside with the lid askew over the pot for 5 minutes to wilt the greens.

1 pound dried lima beans

2 tablespoons olive oil

1 pound spicy pork or turkey Italian sausage links, cut into 1-inch pieces

2 medium yellow onions, chopped (2 cups)

1½ quarts (6 cups) chicken broth

4 fresh oregano sprigs

6 cups packed chopped stemmed kale leaves or 12 ounces bagged chopped kale leaves

1 tablespoon fresh lemon juice

Lima Bean, Kale, and Sausage Soup

6 to 8 servings

Lima beans' mild, slightly sweet, but still decidedly neutral taste makes them a flavor sponge, picking up the savoriness of whatever's around them. In this recipe, we've paired them with spicy Italian sausage to make a well-stocked soup reminiscent of a Sicilian braise.

1. Pour the beans into a large bowl, fill the bowl with cool tap water, and set aside overnight, for at least 8 hours or up to 12 hours.

2.

Press the button for	Set it for	Set the time for	If necessary, press
SAUTÉ	MEDIUM, NORMAL, or CUSTOM 300°F	10 minutes	START

3. Warm the oil in a **6- or 8-quart cooker** for a minute or two. Add the sausage pieces and brown *well,* stirring occasionally, about 6 minutes. Transfer the pieces to a nearby bowl.

4. Add the onion and cook, stirring often, until softened, about 3 minutes. Pour in the broth and scrape up *every speck of browned stuff* on the pot's bottom. Turn off the SAUTÉ function. Drain the beans in a colander set in the sink and add them to the pot along with all the sausage in the bowl and the oregano sprigs. Lock the lid onto the pot.

5.

Set the machine for	Set the level for	The valve must be	Set the time for	If necessary, press
PRESSURE COOK	MAX	—	12 minutes with the KEEP WARM setting off	START
SOUP/BROTH, PRESSURE COOK, or MANUAL	HIGH	Closed	15 minutes with the KEEP WARM setting off	START

6. Use the **quick-release method** to bring the machine's pressure back to normal. Unlatch the lid and open the pot. Find and discard the oregano sprigs, then stir in the kale. Lock the lid back onto the pot.

7.

Set the machine for	Set the level for	The valve must be	Set the time for	If necessary, press
PRESSURE COOK	MAX	—	4 minutes with the KEEP WARM setting off	START
SOUP/BROTH, PRESSURE COOK, or MANUAL	HIGH	Closed	5 minutes with the KEEP WARM setting off	START

8. When the machine has finished cooking, turn it off and let the pressure **return to normal naturally**, about 35 minutes. Unlatch the lid and open the pot. Stir in the lemon juice before serving.

Beyond

- Because kale is so bulky, this soup does not work well in a **3-quart cooker.**

- Add 1 teaspoon ground allspice or ¼ teaspoon ground cloves with the oregano sprigs.

- Add up to 1 tablespoon peeled and minced garlic just before you pour in the broth.

- For a more luxurious soup, omit the lemon juice and stir in up to ½ cup half-and-half or heavy cream in its place.

- Garnish the bowls with a grated hard cheese: pecorino, aged Asiago, a well-aged Gouda, even a hard goat cheese.

Lentil Soup with Carrots and Cinnamon

6 servings

Brown lentils break down under pressure, adding a creamy smoothness to this warming soup as well as an earthy savoriness, which is balanced by the honey. To make sure the soup doesn't get too sweet, we decided not to cook the onions as a first step, thereby leaving their sugars undeveloped and offering the broth a more aromatic finish.

During your prep, truly *chop* the carrots. Don't just slice them into rounds. Slice them lengthwise into ½-inch-thick strips, then slice these into ½-inch pieces.

And use only brown lentils — not red, pink, or green.

6 cups (1½ quarts) vegetable broth

1½ cups brown lentils

4 medium carrots, chopped (2 cups)

1 medium yellow onion, chopped (1 cup)

2 tablespoons honey or agave nectar

2 medium garlic cloves, peeled and minced (2 teaspoons)

½ teaspoon table salt

½ teaspoon ground black pepper

One 4-inch cinnamon stick

1. Stir all the ingredients in a **6- or 8-quart cooker**. Lock the lid onto the pot.

2.

Set the machine for	Set the level for	The valve must be	Set the time for	If necessary, press
PRESSURE COOK	MAX	—	15 minutes with the KEEP WARM setting off	START
SOUP/BROTH, PRESSURE COOK, or MANUAL	HIGH	Closed	20 minutes with the KEEP WARM setting off	START
SLOW COOK	HIGH	Opened	3 hours with the KEEP WARM setting off (or on for no more than 1 hour)	START

3. If you've used a pressure setting, when the machine has finished cooking, use the **quick-release method** to bring the pot's pressure back to normal.

4. Unlatch the lid and open the pot. Find and discard the cinnamon stick, then stir the soup well before serving.

Beyond

- You must halve the recipe for a **3-quart cooker**.

- For a sweeter soup, substitute 2 cups peeled and diced sweet potato or peeled, seeded, and diced butternut squash for the carrots.

- With cinnamon and lentils, this soup leans Middle Eastern in flavor. Add 1 teaspoon ground coriander and ½ teaspoon ground cardamom too — and/or drizzle pomegranate molasses over the bowls and serve with pita chips.

8 cups (2 quarts) chicken broth

¾ pound plain deli ham, chopped

2 cups dried green split peas

1 small yellow onion, chopped (½ cup)

1 teaspoon dried thyme

1 teaspoon finely grated lemon zest

½ teaspoon celery seeds

½ teaspoon ground black pepper

2 bay leaves

Absurdly Easy Split Pea Soup

6 servings

Of course, you could spend all day braising a ham hock or a ham bone to create split pea soup. But you bought an Instant Pot because you wanted dinner faster, right? This recipe takes the easy route and uses deli ham to make a wintry favorite in no time.

Most split-pea recipes for the pressure cooker have the peas go under pressure for a relatively long time, followed by a quick release. We opt for a shorter time under pressure, followed by a natural release, to avoid split-pea gunk spewing out of the valve. Also, when the pressure is released quickly, the soup jumps to an instant vigorous boil, causing the split peas to become more porridge-like. Frankly, we prefer soup, not paste.

1. Mix all the ingredients in a **6- or 8-quart cooker**. Lock the lid onto the pot.

2.

Set the machine for	Set the level for	The valve must be	Set the time for	If necessary, press
PRESSURE COOK	MAX	—	6 minutes with the KEEP WARM setting off	START
SOUP/BROTH, PRESSURE COOK, or MANUAL	HIGH	Closed	8 minutes with the KEEP WARM setting off	START

3. When the machine has finished cooking, turn it off and let its pressure **return to normal naturally**, about 15 minutes. Unlatch the lid and open the pot. Find and discard the bay leaves. Stir well before serving.

Beyond

- You must halve the recipe for a **3-quart cooker**.

- If the soup is too thin (yes, some people like wallpaper paste), set the machine to the SAUTÉ function at its MEDIUM, NORMAL, or CUSTOM 300°F (for the Max machine) setting after opening the pot. Simmer, stirring almost constantly, until the soup reaches your desired consistency, 5 to 10 minutes.

- If you can find roasted, on-the-bone ham at your supermarket's deli counter, buy a ¾-pound chunk and chop it up for the soup.

- Add up to 2 finely chopped medium carrots (1 cup) and 1 finely chopped peeled medium turnip (1 cup) with the other ingredients.

Yellow Split Pea Soup with Kimchi

6 servings

8 cups (2 quarts) vegetable broth

2 cups yellow split peas

1½ cups kimchi, chopped

1 medium leek, white and green part only, well washed and thinly sliced

3 medium garlic cloves, peeled and minced (1 tablespoon)

½ teaspoon ground dried turmeric

½ teaspoon ground black pepper

Kimchi is basically Korean sauerkraut: fermented cabbage packed with chiles. It adds a salty, savory base to this soup, which is thickened with yellow split peas (*not* chana dal, see page 229). If you can't find yellow split peas at your market (we, in fact, did), they're available via a quick online search. Sounds weird, right? Try it! The soup's a sweet-salty-spicy mash-up.

As to the kimchi, some brands are fiery; others, not so much. You can even find radish kimchi or chunkier, "country style" kimchi at larger supermarkets. And of course, you'll find an astounding array at Asian markets, particularly at H-Mart, the Korean grocery store chain that's come to most large U. S. cities.

1. Stir all the ingredients in a **6- or 8-quart cooker**. Lock the lid onto the pot.

2.

Set the machine for	Set the level for	The valve must be	Set the time for	If necessary, press
PRESSURE COOK	MAX	—	7 minutes with the KEEP WARM setting off	START
SOUP/BROTH, PRESSURE COOK, or MANUAL	HIGH	Closed	10 minutes with the KEEP WARM setting off	START

3. When the machine has finished cooking, turn it off and let the pressure **return to normal naturally**, about 20 minutes. Unlatch the lid and open the pot. Stir well before serving.

Beyond

- You must halve the recipe for a **3-quart cooker**.

- For a less assertive flavor in the soup, substitute drained sauerkraut for the kimchi.

- If you don't mind an army-green color, substitute green split peas for the yellow.

- This recipe's probably not a full meal. Consider serving it with skewers off the grill. Brush chicken breast or sirloin steak skewers with this marinade: ½ cup soy sauce, 2 tablespoons dark brown sugar, 1 tablespoon toasted sesame oil, and 2 teaspoons ground black pepper. Grill quickly over high heat, mopping with additional marinade as the meat cooks.

¼ cup (½ stick) butter

6 cups trimmed cauliflower florets

1 teaspoon table salt

½ teaspoon ground dried ginger

¼ teaspoon baking soda

3 cups vegetable broth

2 ounces white Cheddar cheese, shredded (½ cup)

¼ cup heavy cream

Cauliflower and White Cheddar Soup

4 to 6 servings

Using a modified version of the baking-soda-and-butter poaching technique, we used to make an absurdly creamy vegetable soup (see page 61). This recipe turns a mundane cauliflower soup into a cheese fest. White Cheddar works best, partly to keep the overall look of the soup pale, but also to offer a mellow flavor. At the end, you *must* remove the insert from the pot to wait for the flavors to meld. Otherwise, the cheese will break into an oily mess and any milk solids will stick to the still-hot bottom of the pot.

1.

Press the button for	Set it for	Set the time for	If necessary, press
SAUTÉ	MEDIUM, NORMAL, or CUSTOM 300°F	5 minutes	START

2. Melt the butter in a **3-, 6-, or 8-quart cooker**. Add the cauliflower and stir well until the florets are coated in butter. Stir in the salt, dried ginger, and baking soda. Turn off the SAUTÉ function, then pour in the broth and stir well. Lock the lid onto the pot.

3.

Set the machine for	Set the level for	The valve must be	Set the time for	If necessary, press
PRESSURE COOK	MAX	—	10 minutes with the KEEP WARM setting off	START
SOUP/BROTH, PRESSURE COOK, or MANUAL	HIGH	Closed	12 minutes with the KEEP WARM setting off	START

4. Use the **quick-release method** to bring the pot's pressure back to normal. Unlatch the lid and open the pot. Use an immersion blender to puree the soup right in the cooker. Or transfer about half the contents of the cooker to a large blender, cover but remove the center knob in the blender's lid, cover with a kitchen towel, and blend until smooth. Then transfer this puree to a large bowl and puree the rest of the soup before returning it all to the pot.

5.

Press the button for	Set it for	Set the time for	If necessary, press
SAUTÉ	LOW or LESS	5 minutes	START

6. Add the cheese and cream. Stir until quite steamy *but not yet boiling*, less than 1 minute. Turn off the SAUTÉ function, remove the *hot* insert from the machine, set the lid askew over it, and set aside for 5 minutes to blend the flavors.

Beyond

- For a more assertive taste, substitute an aged, semi-firm goat cheese for the white Cheddar.

- For a cheese beer soup, use only 2 cups broth and add 1 cup blond beer, lager, IPA, or pilsner.

- Make a broccoli Cheddar soup by substituting chopped broccoli florets and stems for the cauliflower. (The stems should be in pieces no more than 2 inches long.) Warning: the soup will be a rather garish green but still delicious.

- Garnish the bowls with caraway or fennel seeds.

Lemony Chicken Rice Soup

6 servings

Consider this our simplified version of *avgolemono,* a Greek (or probably Arabic) chicken soup made with rice and thickened with eggs. The broth is fairly sour, a good contrast to the sweet, white rice. In effect, we overcook that rice so that it thickens the soup.

Do not "cook" the soup after you whisk the egg mixture into it. Otherwise, the eggs will fail to emulsify into a thickener and simply scramble. Make sure they are *thoroughly* whisked with the lemon juice, then temper them by whisking in some of the hot soup before this combined mixture goes into the pot. All the while, don't let the whisk leave your hand.

And one more thing: There's no chicken in this recipe, other than the broth itself. Use the best broth you can find. Or use homemade stock (page 102).

1½ quarts (6 cups) chicken broth

⅔ cup raw long-grain white rice, such as white basmati

1 tablespoon finely minced fresh dill fronds

1 tablespoon finely minced fresh oregano leaves

1 tablespoon finely minced lemon zest

1 teaspoon table salt

4 large eggs, at room temperature

⅓ cup fresh lemon juice

1. Mix the broth, rice, dill, oregano, lemon zest, and salt in a **3-, 6-, or 8-quart cooker**. Lock the lid onto the pot.

2.

Set the machine for	Set the level for	The valve must be	Set the time for	If necessary, press
PRESSURE COOK	MAX	—	18 minutes with the KEEP WARM setting off	START
SOUP/BROTH, PRESSURE COOK, or MANUAL	HIGH	Closed	23 minutes with the KEEP WARM setting off	START

3. Use the **quick-release method** to bring the pot's pressure back to normal. Unlatch the lid and open the pot. Whisk the eggs and lemon juice in a large bowl until smooth. Whisk about 1 cup of the hot soup into the eggs mixture. Then whisk this combined mixture into the pot with the soup until smooth. Serve warm.

Beyond

- Garnish the servings with finely minced chives or the sliced green part of a scallion.

- Morph this into a Caribbean soup (sort of) by substituting lime zest for the lemon zest and ¼ cup fresh lime juice for the lemon juice. It'll also need a little heat: Add up to 2 teaspoons red pepper flakes with the herbs.

- If desired, top servings with cooked, peeled, and deveined shrimp or shelled crabmeat.

2 tablespoons olive oil

One 1-pound bone-in skinless chicken breast

Two 8-ounce bone-in skinless chicken thighs

½ teaspoon table salt, plus more if necessary

½ teaspoon ground black pepper

1½ quarts (6 cups) chicken broth

1 medium red onion, peeled and halved

4 medium carrots, peeled and cut in half widthwise

2 garlic cloves, peeled

3 fresh thyme sprigs

2 fresh sage sprigs

4 ounces wide egg or no-yolk noodles

1 tablespoon finely chopped fresh dill fronds

Chicken Noodle Soup

6 servings

Okay, all you chicken soup fanatics, forgive us. Our version is not pure yellow. We lobby for browning the chicken before cooking it in the broth with the vegetables and herbs (which we then discard since they've leached their flavor into the broth). The result is a cloudy stock, even brown. But the flavor is over the top: rich, decadent, and decidedly, well, chicken-y.

If you insist on old-school aesthetics, skip browning the chicken (omit the olive oil, too) and cook them in the broth with the vegetables and aromatics before carrying on as written. But honestly, why would anyone skimp on flavor for color?

1.

Press the button for	Set it for	Set the time for	If necessary, press
SAUTÉ	MEDIUM, NORMAL, or CUSTOM 300°F	15 minutes	START

2. Warm the oil in a **6- or 8-quart cooker** for a minute or two. Meanwhile, season the chicken pieces with ½ teaspoon salt and the pepper. Set the breast in the cooker and brown *well*, turning a couple of times, about 6 minutes. Transfer the breast to a nearby plate and add the thighs. Brown them, too, turning them a couple of times, about 5 minutes. Transfer them to that plate as well.

3. Pour in the broth, turn off the SAUTÉ function, and scrape up *every speck of browned stuff* on the pot's bottom. Return the chicken to the pot; add the onion, carrots, garlic, thyme, and sage. Lock the lid onto the cooker.

4.

Set the machine for	Set the level for	The valve must be	Set the time for	If necessary, press
PRESSURE COOK	MAX	—	15 minutes with the KEEP WARM setting off	START
SOUP/BROTH, PRESSURE COOK, or MANUAL	HIGH	Closed	18 minutes with the KEEP WARM setting off	START

5. Use the **quick-release method** to bring the pot's pressure back to normal. Unlatch the lid and open the pot. Transfer the chicken pieces to a large cutting board. Scoop out and discard all the vegetables and herbs. Stir the noodles and dill into the broth. Lock the lid onto the pot again.

6.

Set the machine for	Set the level for	The valve must be	Set the time for	If necessary, press
PRESSURE COOK	MAX	—	3 minutes with the KEEP WARM setting off	START
SOUP/BROTH, PRESSURE COOK, or MANUAL	HIGH	Closed	4 minutes with the KEEP WARM setting off	START

7. Meanwhile, remove and discard any bones and tough cartilage from the meat. Chop the meat into small, spoon-sized bits.

8. When the machine has finished cooking, use the **quick-release method** to bring its pressure again back to normal. Unlatch the lid and open the pot. Stir in the chicken meat and check for salt before serving.

Beyond

- For a **3-quart cooker,** you must omit the chicken breast and just use the two chicken thighs. Halve the remaining ingredients and cut the carrots into smaller pieces to fit in the pot.

- Substitute any herb sprigs you like: tarragon, rosemary, oregano, savory. And swap the dill out for just about any finely minced, leafy, green herb.

- For turkey noodle soup, substitute two 1-pound turkey thighs for the chicken breast and thighs; cook for 25 minutes at MAX or 30 minutes at HIGH, followed by a quick release.

- For more flavor, add up to 4 allspice berries with the herb sprigs during the first cooking (remove and discard the allspice as well).

- For a more peppery accent, skip sprinkling the chicken pieces with ground pepper and add up to 10 black peppercorns with the herbs during the first cooking (discard these peppercorns, too).

- For a discussion of the best kind of gluten-free noodles to use in a soup like this, see page 154.

See photo in insert.

Two 1-pound bone-in skinless chicken breasts

1 medium yellow onion, peeled and halved

Up to three 3-inch fresh ginger knobs, peeled and thinly sliced

1 medium head of garlic, any papery outer bits removed, sliced in half through the root end

1 tablespoon black peppercorns

1 teaspoon table salt

8 cups (2 quarts) water

1 pound zucchini, spiralized

Gingery Chicken Soup with Zucchini Noodles

6 servings

If you've got a winter cold, you *need* this soup, a mix of ginger and garlic without any pasta in the mix, just spiralized zucchini. The spiciness of the soup is determined by the amount of ginger.

In essence, the chicken is overcooked the first time under pressure to get its bony flavor into the broth and turn the meat luxuriously soft. The second cooking, however, is fast, just until the machine comes to full pressure. Don't overcook those vegetable noodles! They should provide a textural contrast to the chicken.

1. Place the chicken, onion, ginger, garlic, peppercorns, and salt in a **6- or 8-quart cooker**. Pour in the water and lock the lid onto the cooker.

2.

Set the machine for	Set the level for	The valve must be	Set the time for	If necessary, press
PRESSURE COOK	MAX	—	20 minutes with the KEEP WARM setting off	START
SOUP/BROTH, PRESSURE COOK, or MANUAL	HIGH	Closed	30 minutes with the KEEP WARM setting off	START

3. When the machine has finished cooking, turn it off and let its pressure **return to normal naturally**, about 35 minutes. Unlatch the lid and open the pot. Transfer the chicken breasts to a large cutting board. Fish out and discard all the other vegetables and aromatics in the pot.

4. Cool the chicken for a couple of minutes, then remove and discard any bones and tough cartilage. Chop the meat into small bits and stir these along with the zucchini noodles into the pot. Lock the lid back onto the cooker.

5.

Set the machine for	Set the level for	The valve must be	Set the time for	If necessary, press
PRESSURE COOK or MANUAL	HIGH	Closed	0 minutes with the KEEP WARM setting off	START

6. Use the **quick-release method** to bring the pot's pressure back to normal. Unlatch the lid and open the pot. Stir well before serving.

Beyond

- You must halve the recipe for a **3-quart cooker**.

- Spiralized zucchini is now available in almost all supermarkets.

- Substitute any other spiralized vegetable you might like: butternut squash, yellow summer squash, or whatever your market has in stock. If you use roots or winter squash, keep the timing as stated but don't open the pot for 5 minutes after you've released the pressure the second time to soften the "noodles" completely.

- Adding white wine will create a sweeter soup. Add no more than 1 cup with the water.

- For a more savory soup, omit the salt and garnish each bowlful with soy sauce.

Streamlined Pho

6 servings

This recipe puts a simplified version of this classic Vietnamese soup within reach of a weeknight dinner. (By the way, the name's pronounced something like "fun" without the "n.") Make the broth up to 4 days in advance and store it, covered, in the fridge — or store it in a sealed container in the freezer for up to 3 months. In either case, bring it to a simmer in the Instant Pot with the SAUTÉ function at HIGH or MORE before turning off that function, then add the remaining ingredients and continue with the recipe (that is, adding the beef, noodles, and fish sauce).

Straining the broth can be a challenge. Use a long-handled, spider strainer that you stick in the pot to pull out the ingredients. Or pour the entire contents of the *hot* insert through a fine-mesh sieve such as a *chinois* or through a colander lined with a double thickness of cheesecloth, into a big bowl. (You may have to work in batches.) Or do as any grandmother would do and fish things out one by one with a slotted spoon.

2 quarts (8 cups) water

3 pounds beef or pork soup bones

1 large yellow onion, peeled and halved

¼ cup chopped peeled fresh ginger

2 teaspoons table salt

1 teaspoon whole cloves

One 4-inch cinnamon stick

2 star anise pods

1½ pounds beef sirloin, sliced against the grain into stir-fry thin strips; or 1½ pounds beef cut up for stir-fry

2 tablespoons fish sauce

12 ounces dried rice stick noodles or rice noodles for pad Thai

1. Put the water, bones, onion, ginger, salt, cloves, cinnamon stick, and star anise pods in a **6- or 8-quart cooker**. Lock the lid onto the pot.

2.

Set the machine for	Set the level for	The valve must be	Set the time for	If necessary, press
PRESSURE COOK	MAX	—	30 minutes with the KEEP WARM setting off	START
SOUP/BROTH, PRESSURE COOK, or MANUAL	HIGH	Closed	40 minutes with the KEEP WARM setting off	START

3. When the machine has finished cooking, turn it off and let its pressure **return to normal naturally**, about 40 minutes. Unlatch the lid and open the pot. Strain out all the ingredients, leaving the aromatic broth behind. Stir in the beef and fish sauce. Add the rice noodles, breaking them as necessary so they fit. Lock the lid back onto the pot.

4.

Set the machine for	Set the level for	The valve must be	Set the time for	If necessary, press
PRESSURE COOK	MAX	—	3 minutes with the KEEP WARM setting off	START
MEAT/STEW, PRESSURE COOK, or MANUAL	HIGH	Closed	4 minutes with the KEEP WARM setting off	START

5. Use the **quick-release method** to bring the pot's pressure back to normal. Unlatch the lid and open the pot. Serve hot.

Beyond

- Because of the size of the bones, this soup is not easily made in a **3-quart cooker**.

- Make the broth in step 2 with the SLOW COOK setting. Cook with the pressure valve open on HIGH for 7 hours (the soup can then stay on the KEEP WARM setting for up to 4 hours).

- Garnish this streamlined pho with cilantro leaves, minced scallions, thinly sliced fresh serrano chiles, bean sprouts, basil leaves (particularly Thai basil leaves), and/or lime wedges.

5 cups (1 quart plus 1 cup) chicken broth

1 pound boneless skinless chicken breasts, diced

One 10-ounce can Rotel tomatoes with green chiles (1 cup plus 3 tablespoons)

One 4½-ounce can hot or mild diced green chiles (½ cup)

8 ounces white button mushrooms, thinly sliced

1 tablespoon standard chile powder

1 teaspoon ground cumin

1 teaspoon onion powder

1 teaspoon garlic powder

¼ teaspoon table salt

½ cup heavy cream

1½ tablespoons cornstarch

8 ounces shredded mild or sharp American Cheddar cheese (2 cups)

King Ranch Chicken Soup

6 servings

If you grew up in Texas, you already know about King Ranch chicken, a layered casserole with tomatoes, chiles, and chicken, something like a Texas version of lasagna with tortillas standing in for the noodles. You can't use tortillas in this soup (they'll fall to the bottom of the pot and scorch) but you can offer them alongside this admittedly whimsical concoction, made to taste like that Lone Star family favorite, now served in bowls, not on plates.

1. Mix the broth, chicken, tomatoes with chiles, green chiles, mushrooms, chile powder, cumin, onion powder, garlic powder, and salt in a **6- or 8-quart cooker**. Lock the lid onto the pot.

2.

Set the machine for	Set the level for	The valve must be	Set the time for	If necessary, press
PRESSURE COOK	MAX	—	10 minutes with the KEEP WARM setting off	START
SOUP/BROTH, PRESSURE COOK, or MANUAL	HIGH	Closed	13 minutes with the KEEP WARM setting off	START

3. Use the **quick-release method** to bring the pot's pressure back to normal. Unlatch the lid and open the pot.

4.

Press the button for	Set it for	Set the time for	If necessary, press
SAUTÉ	MEDIUM, NORMAL, or CUSTOM 300°F	5 minutes	START

5. Bring the soup to a bubble. Whisk the cream and cornstarch in a small bowl until smooth, then whisk this slurry into the soup. Continue cooking, whisking constantly, until thickened, about 1 minute. Turn off the SAUTÉ function and remove the *hot* insert from the pot to stop the cooking. Stir in the cheese, set the lid askew over the insert, and set aside for 5 minutes to melt the cheese. Stir well before serving.

Beyond

- You must halve the recipe for a **3-quart cooker**.

- Substitute any semi-firm cheese you wish, even a Tex-Mex blend of shredded cheeses (so long as there are no spices mixed into the cheese).

- Serve with lots of pickled jalapeño rings and peeled, pitted, and diced avocado.

- Crumble tortilla chips over each bowlful.

Buffalo Chicken Soup

6 servings

Who doesn't like buffalo chicken wings? Who hasn't always wanted them as soup? Okay, no one. Still, we took those flavors and morphed them into a satisfying meal, best on a winter evening. The pressure will take a lot of the sting out of the hot sauce: Pass more at the table for those (like us) who enjoy the burn.

1.

Press the button for	Set it for	Set the time for	If necessary, press
SAUTÉ	MEDIUM, NORMAL, or CUSTOM 300°F	10 minutes	START

2. Melt the butter in a **6- or 8-quart cooker**. Add the onion and celery. Cook, stirring often, until the onion begins to soften, about 4 minutes. Add the chicken and stir well until the pieces are coated in the butter. Turn off the SAUTÉ function.

3. Stir in the hot sauce, Worcestershire sauce, thyme, and garlic powder until everything is uniform and well coated. Pour in the broth and stir well. Lock the lid onto the pot.

4.

Set the machine for	Set the level for	The valve must be	Set the time for	If necessary, press
PRESSURE COOK	MAX	—	5 minutes with the KEEP WARM setting off	START
SOUP/BROTH, PRESSURE COOK, or MANUAL	HIGH	Closed	7 minutes with the KEEP WARM setting off	START

5. Use the **quick-release method** to bring the pot's pressure back to normal. Unlatch the lid and open the pot. Place the cream, cream cheese, and 2 cups of the broth from the pot in a food processor; cover and process until smooth and uniform. Whisk this mixture into the hot soup in the pot and serve at once, crumbling blue cheese over each bowl.

¼ cup (½ stick) butter, cut into chunks

1 medium yellow onion, chopped (1 cup)

4 medium celery stalks, thinly sliced (1 cup)

2 pounds boneless skinless chicken breasts, diced

⅓ cup hot red pepper sauce, preferably Texas Pete or Frank's RedHot

2 teaspoons Worcestershire sauce

1 teaspoon dried thyme

1 teaspoon garlic powder

1½ quarts (6 cups) chicken broth

½ cup heavy cream

4 ounces regular or low-fat cream cheese, cut into chunks

Crumbled blue cheese for garnishing

Beyond

- You must halve the recipe for a **3-quart cooker**.

- Because the cream cheese cannot be reheated (or it will break), the soup does not freeze well. That said, you could make the recipe through opening the pot in step 5, then cool and freeze the soup in a covered container for up to 4 months. Thaw and reheat on the stove, then remove it from the heat, prepare the cream cheese mixture as directed, and whisk it into the hot soup.

- For a sweeter finish, substitute a spicy barbecue sauce or Thai sweet chile sauce for the hot red pepper sauce.

1½ pounds boneless skinless chicken breasts cut for stir-fry (unseasoned, discard any flavor packets); or boneless skinless chicken breasts cut into ½ x ½-inch strips

1½ quarts (6 cups) chicken broth

1 large yellow onion, chopped (1½ cups)

1 cup frozen or fresh corn kernels (no need to thaw)

Up to 6 medium garlic cloves, peeled and minced (2 tablespoons)

Up to 2 medium fresh jalapeño chiles, stemmed, seeded, and chopped

2 tablespoons finely minced fresh oregano leaves

½ teaspoon table salt

4 medium Hass avocados, peeled, pitted, and diced

¼ cup fresh lime juice

Mexican-Style Chicken Soup

6 servings

The Yucatan was once the only place you could find versions of this tasty chicken-lime soup. It's since flashed across Mexico to become a favorite in every province. We leave the lime juice out of the mix until the very end to retain its tart bite (something the pressure would temper). There's a range for the amounts of garlic and jalapeño to use, so you can alter the soup to fit your tastes.

If you like it fiery, don't seed the chiles. Simply stem them and slice them into thin rings. If you dice the avocados as the soup cooks, stir the pieces with the lime juice in a medium bowl to keep them from turning brown.

1. Stir the chicken, broth, onion, corn, garlic, jalapeño, oregano, and salt in a **6- or 8-quart cooker**. Lock the lid onto the pot.

2.

Set the machine for	Set the level for	The valve must be	Set the time for	If necessary, press
PRESSURE COOK	MAX	—	5 minutes with the KEEP WARM setting off	START
SOUP/BROTH, PRESSURE COOK, or MANUAL	HIGH	Closed	7 minutes with the KEEP WARM setting off	START

3. Use the **quick-release method** to bring the pot's pressure back to normal. Unlatch the lid and open the cooker. Stir in the avocado and lime juice before serving.

Beyond

- You must halve the recipe for a **3-quart cooker**.

- Stir chopped, peeled, and deveined shrimp into the hot soup with the avocado and lime juice, then set the lid over the pot and set aside for 5 minutes to cook the shrimp.

- For a more Caribbean feel, use 1 quart (4 cups) chicken broth and 2 cups fish stock (see page 105). And really kick it up by substituting 1 fresh habanero chile, stemmed and chopped, for the jalapeños.

Turkey Rice Soup

4 to 6 servings

It doesn't get much simpler than using turkey cutlets for pressure-cooker soup. Since these cutlets lack any bones to put flavor into the broth, make sure you use a highly flavored chicken broth. Some larger supermarkets even sell turkey broth these days. Use that!

The cutlets should be chopped into pieces *no larger* than 1-inch square. You can even cut them into smaller bits, down to ½ inch each, the better to get more than one in each bite.

1. Stir the turkey, broth, onion, bell pepper, garlic, rice, thyme, zest, pepper, and salt in a **6- or 8-quart cooker**. Lock the lid onto the pot.

2.

Set the machine for	Set the level for	The valve must be	Set the time for	If necessary, press
PRESSURE COOK	MAX	—	12 minutes with the KEEP WARM setting off	START
SOUP/BROTH, PRESSURE COOK, or MANUAL	HIGH	Closed	15 minutes with the KEEP WARM setting off	START

3. Use the **quick-release method** to bring the pot's pressure back to normal. Unlatch the lid and open the pot. Stir in the lemon juice before serving.

1 pound turkey cutlets, cut into 1-inch pieces

1½ quarts (6 cups) chicken broth

1 medium red onion, chopped (1 cup)

1 small green bell pepper or medium Cubanelle pepper, stemmed, cored, and chopped (½ cup)

2 medium garlic cloves, peeled and minced (2 teaspoons)

¾ cup raw long-grain white rice, preferably white basmati

2 tablespoons fresh thyme leaves

2 teaspoons finely grated lemon zest

1 teaspoon ground black pepper

½ teaspoon table salt

1 tablespoon fresh lemon juice

Beyond

- You must halve the recipe for a **3-quart cooker**.

- For a heftier soup, add 1 medium carrot, chopped (⅓ cup) and/or 2 medium celery ribs, thinly sliced (½ cup) with the onion.

- Substitute minced oregano or parsley leaves for the thyme. Or substitute 1 tablespoon yellow curry powder for the thyme.

- Add up to ½ teaspoon red pepper flakes with the garlic.

1½ pounds turkey cutlets, cut into 1-inch pieces

6 cups (1½ quarts) chicken broth

6 ounces Brussels sprouts, trimmed and shaved (2 cups)

One 8-ounce jar peeled chestnuts, drained (if necessary), each chestnut halved

1 medium yellow onion, chopped (1 cup)

2 medium celery stalks, thinly sliced (½ cup)

½ cup fresh or frozen cranberries, chopped (no need to thaw)

1 tablespoon stemmed fresh thyme leaves

1 tablespoon minced fresh sage leaves

¼ teaspoon table salt

½ cup light, dry white wine, such as Pinot Grigio

1½ tablespoons cornstarch

2 cups seasoned bread cube stuffing mix

Beyond

- You must halve the recipe for a **3-quart cooker**.

- Skip the croutons and serve the soup over No-Drain Mashed Potatoes (page 424) for a hearty meal in a bowl.

- To make this soup more like an Italian bread soup, after you thicken the soup, remove the insert from the pot and stir in the seasoned bread cubes, then set the lid askew over the pot for 5 minutes to let the bread absorb some of the broth.

Thanksgiving in a Bowl

6 servings

Why wait until November to make a meal that tastes like the holiday? This soup's got all the fixings, right down to the purchased stuffing mix placed in the serving bowls to make a version of bread soup. The overall texture is more like a rich gravy that's been thinned out a bit. In other words, it's pretty substantial. To make prep easier, look for shredded Brussels sprouts in the produce section of most supermarkets.

1. Mix the turkey, broth, Brussels sprouts, chestnuts, onion, celery, cranberries, thyme, sage, and salt in a **6- or 8-quart cooker**. Lock the lid onto the pot.

2.

Set the machine for	Set the level for	The valve must be	Set the time for	If necessary, press
PRESSURE COOK	MAX	—	10 minutes with the KEEP WARM setting off	START
SOUP/BROTH, PRESSURE COOK, or MANUAL	HIGH	Closed	13 minutes with the KEEP WARM setting off	START

3. Use the **quick-release method** to bring the pot's pressure back to normal. Unlatch the lid and open the pot.

4.

Press the button for	Set it for	Set the time for	If necessary, press
SAUTÉ	MEDIUM, NORMAL, or CUSTOM 300°F	5 minutes	START

5. Bring the soup to a bubble. Whisk the wine and cornstarch in a small bowl until smooth. Whisk this slurry into the soup and cook, whisking constantly, until thickened, 1 to 2 minutes. Turn off the SAUTÉ function and remove the insert from the pot to stop the cooking. To serve, place ⅓ cup of the bread cube croutons in each of the serving bowls, then ladle the soup on top.

Turkey Meatball Soup with White Beans and Kale

6 servings

We used an Italian flavor profile for this well-stocked soup, which is almost a stew because it's so loaded. If you want a thinner, more traditional soup, increase the broth to 7 cups.

White bean and kale soups are often made with sausage. We used turkey because it has a milder, sweeter finish, then threw in a little salami for just a touch of porky goodness.

The meatballs are fairly simple with just a few flavorings from the breadcrumbs. They're also quite tender once they've gone under pressure. Even with those breadcrumbs in the mix, the soup needs hunks of crunchy bread for every bowlful.

1. Mix the ground turkey, breadcrumbs, and egg white in a large bowl until uniform. Use cleaned and dried hands to form the mixture into 16 balls, each made from about 2 tablespoons of the ground turkey mélange.

2.

Press the button for	Set it for	Set the time for	If necessary, press
SAUTÉ	MEDIUM, NORMAL, or CUSTOM 300°F	10 minutes	START

3. Warm the oil in a **6- or 8-quart cooker** for a minute or two. Add the onion, salami, and garlic; cook, stirring often, until the onion begins to soften, about 4 minutes. Stir in the kale; continue cooking, stirring more frequently, until the greens wilt, about 3 minutes.

4. Stir in the broth, turn off the SAUTÉ function, and scrape up the browned bits on the pot's bottom. Stir in the beans, oregano, and thyme. Add the meatballs and lock the lid onto the pot.

5.

Set the machine for	Set the level for	The valve must be	Set the time for	If necessary, press
PRESSURE COOK	MAX	—	15 minutes with the KEEP WARM setting off	START
SOUP/BROTH, PRESSURE COOK, or MANUAL	HIGH	Closed	19 minutes with the KEEP WARM setting off	START

6. Use the **quick-release method** to bring the pot's pressure back to normal. Unlatch the lid and open the pot. Stir gently (to preserve the meatballs) before serving.

1 pound lean ground turkey

½ cup Italian-seasoned dried breadcrumbs

1 large egg white

2 tablespoons olive oil

1 medium yellow onion, chopped (1 cup)

2 ounces hard salami, chopped

2 medium garlic cloves, peeled and minced (2 teaspoons)

4 cups chopped stemmed kale (about 8 ounces—do not use baby kale)

5 cups (1 quart plus 1 cup) chicken broth

One 15-ounce can white beans, preferably cannellini beans, drained and rinsed (1¾ cups)

1 teaspoon dried oregano

1 teaspoon dried thyme

Beyond

- You must halve the recipe for a **3-quart cooker**.

- If you want to go over the top, brown the meatballs with a little olive oil in the pot on its SAUTÉ function set for MEDIUM, NORMAL, or CUSTOM 300°F (for the Max machine). They're fairly fragile, so turn them gently with a thin spatula. Or brown them in olive oil in a skillet on the stove or on a lipped baking sheet in a 400°F oven for about 10 minutes.

- Substitute chopped pancetta for the salami.

- Top each bowl with lots of finely grated Parmigiano-Reggiano or even shredded semi-firm mozzarella.

1 tablespoon vegetable, corn, or canola oil

3 bone-in beef short ribs (about 1½ pounds)

1 cup frozen pearl onions (do not thaw)

2 medium celery ribs, thinly sliced (⅔ cup)

Up to 6 medium garlic cloves, peeled and minced (2 tablespoons)

1½ quarts (6 cups) beef or chicken broth

1 cup pearl barley

1 tablespoon stemmed fresh thyme leaves

½ teaspoon ground allspice

½ teaspoon table salt

½ teaspoon ground black pepper

1 tablespoon balsamic vinegar

Beef Barley Soup

6 servings

Rather than just dumping ingredients into the cooker for this classic soup, the best way to make it is to take advantage of the one of the machine's best features, its SAUTÉ function, to brown the beef short ribs and add a complex, savory flavor to the broth. Work to get the meat deeply colored, even along the sides. The pressure will then force both that flavor and the savory notes from the bones into the broth.

One warning: The browned bits on the bottom of the pot act like glue to the pearl barley, which can stick and burn. Make sure you scrape up every speck to prevent the pot from shutting off because of scorched grains.

1.

Press the button for	Set it for	Set the time for	If necessary, press
SAUTÉ	MEDIUM, NORMAL, or CUSTOM 300°F	15 minutes	START

2. Warm the oil in a **6- or 8-quart cooker** for a minute or two, then add the short ribs and brown *well* on all sides, turning several times, about 10 minutes. Transfer the short ribs to a bowl.

3. Add the pearl onions and celery to the pot. Cook, stirring often, until the onions begin to brown a bit, about 4 minutes. Stir in the garlic until fragrant, just a few seconds. Pour in the broth, turn off the SAUTÉ function, and scrape up *every single browned speck* on the pot's bottom.

4. Stir in the barley, thyme, allspice, salt, and pepper. Return the short ribs to the pot, as well as any liquid in their bowl. Lock the lid onto the cooker.

5.

Set the machine for	Set the level for	The valve must be	Set the time for	If necessary, press
PRESSURE COOK	MAX	—	35 minutes with the KEEP WARM setting off	START
SOUP/BROTH, PRESSURE COOK, or MANUAL	HIGH	Closed	45 minutes with the KEEP WARM setting off	START
SLOW COOK	HIGH	Opened	5 hours with the KEEP WARM setting off (or on for no more than 2 hours)	START

6. If you've used a pressure setting, when the machine has finished cooking, turn it off and let its pressure **return to normal naturally**, about 40 minutes.

7. Unlatch the lid and open the pot. Transfer the short ribs to a large cutting board; cool for 5 minutes.

8. Meanwhile, use a flatware tablespoon to skim any excess surface fat from the soup in the pot. Remove and discard the bones; chop the meat into small bits. Stir the meat as well as the balsamic vinegar into the soup, then serve warm.

Beyond

- For a **3-quart cooker**, you must use one large ¾-pound beef short rib and halve the remaining ingredients.

- For a heartier soup, add 1 medium carrot, thinly sliced, and/or 2 medium turnips, peeled and diced, with the pearl onions and celery.

- For a sweeter yet more complex soup, reduce the broth to 5 cups and use 1 cup light red wine, such as Pinot Noir, to deglaze the pot after all that browning.

- Garnish the bowls with minced chives or minced fresh dill fronds.

6 ounces thin bacon slices, chopped

1 large yellow onion, chopped (1½ cups)

1 medium green bell pepper, stemmed, cored, and chopped (1 cup)

3 medium garlic cloves, peeled and minced (1 tablespoon)

2 tablespoons pickle relish

1 tablespoon Dijon mustard

1 teaspoon dried thyme

1 teaspoon dried oregano

½ teaspoon ground black pepper

1½ quarts (6 cups) beef or chicken broth

1¼ pounds lean ground beef

½ cup half-and-half

2 tablespoons all-purpose flour

8 ounces mild American Cheddar cheese, shredded (2 cups)

Beyond

- You must halve the recipe for a **3-quart cooker**.

- Swap out the Cheddar cheese for Gouda, Gruyère, or even 4 ounces crumbled blue cheese (1 cup).

- Add up to 2 tablespoons hot red pepper sauce, such as Texas Pete, with the relish.

- If you miss the buns for your cheeseburger, cut two or three hamburger buns in half (into two rounds), then cut these into quarters. Toast them on a baking sheet in a 350°F oven until lightly browned, then serve them in the bowls as croutons.

Bacon Cheeseburger Soup

4 to 6 servings

This family-friendly soup takes all the flavors of a cheeseburger (even the pickle relish!) and turns them into a bowl of comfort. You don't have to settle for standard pickle relish. We've found dill relish and even more savory India relish at our local supermarket, either of which would work here. If you live in the South, you could even substitute chowchow, particularly a hot, vinegary version (rather than the sweeter ones that have lately gotten popular).

1.

Press the button for	Set it for	Set the time for	If necessary, press
SAUTÉ	MEDIUM, NORMAL, or CUSTOM 300°F	10 minutes	START

2. Add the bacon, onion, and bell pepper to a **6- or 8-quart cooker**. Cook, stirring occasionally, until the bacon begins to brown, about 5 minutes. Stir in the garlic, pickle relish, mustard, thyme, oregano, and pepper; cook until aromatic, just a few seconds.

3. Pour in the broth and scrape up any browned bits on the pot's bottom. Turn off the SAUTÉ function, then crumble in the ground beef, leaving it in pieces about the size of small marbles. Lock the lid onto the pot.

4.

Set the machine for	Set the level for	The valve must be	Set the time for	If necessary, press
PRESSURE COOK	MAX	——	5 minutes with the KEEP WARM setting off	START
SOUP/BROTH, PRESSURE COOK, or MANUAL	HIGH	Closed	7 minutes with the KEEP WARM setting off	START

5. Use the **quick-release method** to bring the pot's pressure back to normal. Unlatch the lid and open the cooker.

6.

Press the button for	Set it for	Set the time for	If necessary, press
SAUTÉ	MEDIUM, NORMAL, or CUSTOM 300°F	5 minutes	START

7. Bring the soup back to a simmer. Whisk the half-and-half and flour in a small bowl until smooth and uniform. Whisk this slurry into the soup and continue cooking, whisking almost constantly, until slightly thickened, 1 to 2 minutes. Turn off the SAUTÉ function and remove the *hot* insert from the pot. Stir in the cheese and set the lid askew over the insert for 5 minutes to melt the cheese. Stir again before serving.

German-Style Steak and Pickle Soup

6 servings

In essence, this soup mimics the flavors of German *rouladen* — that is, thin beef strips wrapped around dill pickles and served in a rich gravy. We deconstructed all that, then added apple cider so that the soup takes on a sweet-and-sour quality. The horseradish will mellow quite a bit, offering an aromatic, almost sweet flavor, creating the background for the other ingredients and enriching the broth to make the soup satisfying on a cold night.

1. Run your hand along the flank steak to determine the grain of the meat. Slice the meat into ¼-inch-thick strips against the grain, then cut these strips widthwise into 1-inch pieces. Put them and all the remaining ingredients in a **6- or 8-quart cooker**. Lock the lid onto the pot.

2.

Set the machine for	Set the level for	The valve must be	Set the time for	If necessary, press
PRESSURE COOK	MAX	—	18 minutes with the KEEP WARM setting off	START
SOUP/BROTH, PRESSURE COOK, or MANUAL	HIGH	Closed	22 minutes with the KEEP WARM setting off	START
SLOW COOK	HIGH	Opened	3 hours with the KEEP WARM setting off (or on for no more than 3 hours)	START

3. If you've used a pressure setting, when the machine has finished cooking, turn it off and let its pressure **return to normal naturally** for 10 minutes. Then use the **quick-release method** to get rid of any residual pressure in the pot.

4. Unlatch the lid and open the cooker. Stir the soup well before serving.

1½ pounds beef flank steak

5 cups (1 quart plus 1 cup) beef or chicken broth

1 cup unsweetened apple cider

3 large dill pickles, quartered lengthwise and sliced into ½-inch pieces

2 tablespoons jarred prepared white horseradish

1 teaspoon dried thyme

¼ teaspoon celery seeds

¼ teaspoon ground cloves

¼ teaspoon ground black pepper

Beyond

- You must halve the recipe for a 3-quart cooker.

- Serve over cooked white long-grain rice.

- Or skip the rice and toast slices of rye bread 4 to 6 inches from a heated broiler until a little crunchy, 1 to 2 minutes. Top each slice with a slice of Swiss cheese and broil until melted and gooey, about 1 minute. Ladle the soup into bowls and float one piece of cheese toast on each serving.

Beef Stir-Fry Soup

6 servings

This Asian-inspired soup is actually fairly light, despite the beef chuck. The flavors are brightened considerably by the allspice and five-spice powder, an aromatic contrast to the mildly bitter bok choy (which is merely warmed in the soup at the end).

When buying a large head of bok choy, look for stems that are white, not rust-colored, and leaves that are dark green without any noticeable wilt. The heads are notoriously gritty, especially in the white stems near the core. Separate the leaves and rinse well before slicing them into thin strips, the better to fit on a tablespoon when eating.

1 pound boneless beef chuck, cut into 1-inch pieces

1½ quarts (6 cups) beef or chicken broth

¼ cup soy sauce

1 medium red onion, chopped (1 cup)

2 medium carrots, thinly sliced (1 cup)

2 tablespoons minced peeled fresh ginger

1 teaspoon five-spice powder

1 large head of bok choy (about 1 pound), cored and thinly sliced

1. Mix the beef, broth, soy sauce, onion, carrots, ginger, and five-spice powder in a **6- or 8-quart cooker**. Lock the lid onto the pot.

2.

Set the machine for	Set the level for	The valve must be	Set the time for	If necessary, press
PRESSURE COOK	MAX	—	20 minutes with the KEEP WARM setting off	START
SOUP/BROTH, PRESSURE COOK, or MANUAL	HIGH	Closed	25 minutes with the KEEP WARM setting off	START
SLOW COOK	HIGH	Opened	4 hours with the KEEP WARM setting off (or on for no more than 3 hours)	START

3. If you've used a pressure setting, when the machine has finished cooking, turn it off and let its pressure **return to normal naturally**, about 30 minutes.

4. Unlatch the lid and open the pot. Stir in the bok choy. Set the lid askew over the top of the pot and set aside for 5 minutes to partially wilt the vegetable. Stir well before serving.

Beyond

- You must halve the recipe for a **3-quart cooker**.

- Add up to 1 cup drained and rinsed canned sliced water chestnuts or bamboo shoots with the bok choy.

- For a hotter soup, add 2 or 3 small dried red chiles, such as chiles de arbol, with the beef.

- Ladle the soup into bowls over cooked long-grain white rice.

- Five-spice powder is a traditional Chinese blend of spices, available in almost every spice rack. To make your own, toast 2 tablespoons Sichuan peppercorns (or black peppercorns for a less piquant taste), 2 tablespoons fennel seeds, 10 whole cloves, 5 star anise pods, and a 2-inch cinnamon stick broken into several pieces in a dry skillet over medium heat, stirring constantly until aromatic and lightly browned, about 4 minutes. Cool to room temperature, then transfer to a spice grinder and grind until powdery. Push through a fine-mesh sieve or strainer to get rid of any hard bits. Seal in a jar and keep in a cool, dark place for up to 6 months.

Beef and Roots Soup

6 servings

This is our version of the retro beef soup usually made with oatmeal as its thickener, an Old World bowl of comfort that's right for a meal after working around the house (or the farm, given how filling it is).

Unfortunately, rolled oats can stick and burn in a multi-cooker, so we've substituted brown rice and overcooked the grains so that they thicken the broth. Get *every speck of browned stuff* off the pot's bottom so no gluey bits can latch onto the rice grains and cause them to burn.

1.

Press the button for	Set it for	Set the time for	If necessary, press
SAUTÉ	MEDIUM, NORMAL, or CUSTOM 300°F	15 minutes	START

2. Melt the butter in a **6- or 8-quart cooker**. Add the onion and cook, stirring often, until softened, about 4 minutes. Add the beef and garlic; continue cooking, stirring once in a while, until all the pieces of beef have lost their raw, red color, about 4 minutes.

3. Pour in the broth and scrape up *every speck of browned stuff* on the pot's bottom. Turn off the SAUTÉ function. Stir in the rice, then lock the lid onto the pot.

4.

Set the machine for	Set the level for	The valve must be	Set the time for	If necessary, press
PRESSURE COOK	MAX	—	22 minutes with the KEEP WARM setting off	START
SOUP/BROTH, PRESSURE COOK, or MANUAL	HIGH	Closed	30 minutes with the KEEP WARM setting off	START

5. Use the **quick-release method** to bring the pot's pressure back to normal. Unlatch the lid and open the cooker. Stir in the rutabaga, carrots, oregano, thyme, and salt. Lock the lid back onto the pot.

6.

Set the machine for	Set the level for	The valve must be	Set the time for	If necessary, press
PRESSURE COOK	MAX	—	4 minutes with the KEEP WARM setting off	START
SOUP/BROTH, PRESSURE COOK, or MANUAL	HIGH	Closed	6 minutes with the KEEP WARM setting off	START

7. When the machine has finished cooking, turn it off and let its pressure **return to normal naturally**, about 30 minutes. Unlatch the lid and open the cooker. Stir well before serving. Garnish the bowls with lots of ground black pepper.

2 tablespoons butter

1 medium yellow onion, chopped (1 cup)

1½ pounds beef bottom round, cut into 1-inch pieces

2 medium garlic cloves, peeled and minced (2 teaspoons)

1½ quarts (6 cups) beef or chicken broth

⅓ cup raw long-grain brown rice

1 medium rutabaga (about 9 ounces), peeled and diced (2 cups)

2 medium carrots, thinly sliced (1 cup)

2 teaspoons dried oregano

2 teaspoons dried thyme

¼ teaspoon table salt

Ground black pepper for garnishing

Beyond

- You must halve the recipe for a **3-quart cooker**.

- Brighten the flavors by stirring up to 2 tablespoons red wine vinegar into the soup before serving.

- Substitute an equivalent weight amount of diced peeled turnips or diced peeled celeriac for the rutabaga. Or go for a mix of all these vegetables.

- Substitute dried marjoram for the oregano — or use 2 teaspoons of both.

- Skew the flavors sweeter by adding up to 2 tablespoons chopped raisins with the carrots and rutabaga.

- For an even heartier soup, stir in up to 1 cup heavy cream after it has finished cooking the second time. Set the lid over the pot and set aside for 5 minutes to take the edge off the cream's "raw" taste. (Don't add cream if you've also added vinegar.)

2 tablespoons butter

1 large beef shank (about 1½ pounds)

3 medium carrots, thinly sliced (1½ cups)

3 medium celery stalks, thinly sliced (1 cup)

1 medium yellow onion, chopped (1 cup)

1½ quarts (6 cups) beef or chicken broth

1 teaspoon dried thyme

1 teaspoon ground coriander

½ teaspoon ground cinnamon

¼ teaspoon table salt

½ cup raw long-grain brown rice

½ cup green lentils (that is, le Puy lentils)

Beyond

- For a **3-quart cooker**, you must halve all the ingredients. (You're going to have to track down a ¾-pound beef shank).

- For a sweeter soup, substitute 1 cup chopped, peeled, and seeded butternut squash for the carrots.

- For a brighter flavor, stir up to 2 tablespoons white balsamic vinegar into the soup after it has finished cooking.

Beef Shank, Rice, and Lentil Soup

6 servings

You may have to ask the butcher at your supermarket for a beef shank. It's probably in the back, left over after packaging the popular cuts. The shank will provide a big beefy hit to the soup—which is more like a lentil and rice soup with lots of beef flavor.

1.

Press the button for	Set it for	Set the time for	If necessary, press
SAUTÉ	MEDIUM, NORMAL, or CUSTOM 300°F	15 minutes	START

2. Melt the butter in a **6- or 8-quart cooker**. Add the beef shank and brown *well* on both sides, turning a couple of times, about 8 minutes. Transfer to a nearby bowl.

3. Add the carrots, celery, and onion to the pot. Cook, stirring often, until the onion begins to soften, about 4 minutes. Pour in the broth, turn off the SAUTÉ function, and scrape up the browned bits on the pot's bottom. Stir in the thyme, coriander, cinnamon, and salt. Return the shank and any juices in the bowl to the pot. Lock the lid onto the cooker.

4.

Set the machine for	Set the level for	The valve must be	Set the time for	If necessary, press
PRESSURE COOK	MAX	—	35 minutes with the KEEP WARM setting off	START
SOUP/BROTH, PRESSURE COOK, or MANUAL	HIGH	Closed	45 minutes with the KEEP WARM setting off	START

5. Use the **quick-release method** to bring the pot's pressure back to normal. Unlatch the lid and open the pot. Stir in the rice and lentils. Lock the lid back onto the pot.

6.

Set the machine for	Set the level for	The valve must be	Set the time for	If necessary, press
PRESSURE COOK	MAX	—	24 minutes with the KEEP WARM setting off	START
SOUP/BROTH, PRESSURE COOK, or MANUAL	HIGH	Closed	30 minutes with the KEEP WARM setting off	START

7. Again, use the **quick-release method** to bring the pot's pressure back to normal. Unlatch the lid and open the cooker. Transfer the shank to a cutting board. Remove the meat from the bone and discard the bone; chop the meat into spoon-sized bits. Stir these back into the soup before serving.

Ham and Potato Soup

6 servings

Using cooked deli ham, we can make a fairly fast soup. We're not talking about the shaved or sliced processed ham for sandwiches. Look for a big ham roast, preferably on the bone. Ask for several thick slices, each maybe ½ inch thick, that you can chop up. And truly *dice* the potatoes, into about ¼-inch cubes, so they'll cook quickly with the ham. The starch they give off will begin to thicken the broth as they cook, but the milk-and-flour slurry will finish the job and give the soup a creamy, rich texture.

1. Stir the broth, potatoes, ham, celery, onion, butter, sage, and pepper in a **6- or 8-quart cooker**. Lock the lid onto the pot.

2.

Set the machine for	Set the level for	The valve must be	Set the time for	If necessary, press
PRESSURE COOK	MAX	—	5 minutes with the KEEP WARM setting off	START
SOUP/BROTH, PRESSURE COOK, or MANUAL	HIGH	Closed	8 minutes with the KEEP WARM setting off	START

3. Use the **quick-release method** to bring the pot's pressure back to normal. Unlatch the lid and open the pot. Stir well.

4.

Press the button for	Set it for	Set the time for	If necessary, press
SAUTÉ	MEDIUM, NORMAL, or CUSTOM 300°F	5 minutes	START

5. Bring the soup to a simmer, stirring occasionally. Whisk the milk and flour in a medium bowl until smooth. Whisk this slurry into the bubbling soup. Continue cooking, whisking constantly, until thickened, 1 to 2 minutes. Turn off the SAUTÉ function and remove the *hot* insert from the pot to stop the cooking. Whisk a few more times to stop the bubbling, then serve hot.

2 quarts (8 cups) chicken broth

1½ pounds russet potatoes, peeled and diced

1½ pounds deli ham, any coating or fat removed, the meat diced

2 medium celery stalks, thinly sliced (⅔ cup)

1 small yellow onion, chopped (½ cup)

2 tablespoons butter, cut into small bits

1 teaspoon dried sage

½ teaspoon ground black pepper

1 cup whole or low-fat milk

¼ cup all-purpose flour

Beyond

- You must halve the recipe for a **3-quart cooker**.

- Morph this soup into a stew by decreasing the broth to 1 quart (4 cups). Keep the slurry thickener at the end at the stated amounts. The soup will have a chowder-like texture.

- Serve pretzel rolls smeared with mustard with this soup. Or for crunch, break up pretzels right over the bowls.

- Garnish the bowls with chopped fresh herbs: parsley, thyme, oregano, or savory.

1 to 2 tablespoons butter

2 pounds smoked kielbasa, cut into 1-inch sections

1 medium yellow onion, chopped (1 cup)

1 teaspoon dried sage

1 teaspoon dried thyme

½ teaspoon grated nutmeg

¼ teaspoon table salt

1 quart (4 cups) chicken broth

One 12-ounce bottle golden beer, preferably a pilsner

½ cup half-and-half

2 tablespoons all-purpose flour

6 ounces sharp American Cheddar cheese, shredded (1½ cups)

Sausage, Beer, and Cheddar Soup

6 servings

The success of this favorite soup depends on the quality of the kielbasa. If you want to go over the top, buy the sausage from a delicatessen or a specialty meat market — or check out Czerw's Kielbasy in Philadelphia (or through their online store) for some of the best we've ever tasted. We knew the place was right the first time we walked in and saw pictures of the Pope and JFK over the cash register.

1.

Press the button for	Set it for	Set the time for	If necessary, press
SAUTÉ	MEDIUM, NORMAL, or CUSTOM 300°F	10 minutes	START

2. Melt the butter in a **3- 6-, or 8-quart cooker**. Add the sausage pieces and cook, stirring occasionally, until lightly browned, about 4 minutes. Add the onion and continue cooking, stirring more often, until the onion begins to soften, about 3 minutes.

3. Stir in the sage, thyme, nutmeg, and salt until fragrant, just a few seconds. Pour in the broth and scrape up the browned bits on the pot's bottom. Turn off the SAUTÉ function and pour in the beer. Stir a few times to reduce the foam, then lock the lid onto the pot.

4.

Set the machine for	Set the level for	The valve must be	Set the time for	If necessary, press
PRESSURE COOK	MAX	—	5 minutes with the KEEP WARM setting off	START
SOUP/BROTH, PRESSURE COOK, or MANUAL	HIGH	Closed	7 minutes with the KEEP WARM setting off	START

5. Use the **quick-release method** to bring the pot's pressure back to normal. Unlatch the lid and open the cooker. Stir well.

6.

Press the button for	Set it for	Set the time for	If necessary, press
SAUTÉ	MEDIUM, NORMAL, or CUSTOM 300°F	5 minutes	START

7. Bring the soup to a simmer, stirring occasionally. Whisk the half-and-half and flour in a small bowl until smooth and uniform. Whisk this slurry into the simmering soup and continue cooking, whisking constantly, until slightly thickened, 1 to 2 minutes. Turn off the SAUTÉ function and stir in the cheese. Remove the *hot* insert from the pot, set the lid askew over the insert, and set aside for 5 minutes to melt the cheese and blend the flavors.

Beyond

- For a richer soup, use 2 medium onions, chopped (2 cups).
- For a thicker soup, reduce the broth to 3 cups.
- For a darker and sweeter soup, use beef broth and a dark beer, preferably a brown ale.
- For a "brothier" soup, skip the half-and-half slurry but also consider stirring in 4 ounces cooked and drained noodles before serving.

Italian-Style Sausage and White Bean Soup

6 servings

Despite its immigrant heritage, this soup has become an American standard. And no wonder: The flavors are mellow and satisfying enough to make a filling meal with little effort. But since the standard recipe is so prevalent, we couldn't resist gussying up our version with a bit with orange zest — and saffron (if you like). Even so, the success of the soup will turn on the quality of the sausage. If you buy large, house-made Italian sausages from a butcher shop or high-end supermarket, cut them into ½-inch-thick pieces.

1.

Press the button for	Set it for	Set the time for	If necessary, press
SAUTÉ	MEDIUM, NORMAL, or CUSTOM 300°F	10 minutes	START

2. Warm the oil in a **6- or 8-quart cooker** for a minute or two, then add the sausage pieces. Cook, stirring once in a while, until lightly browned, about 5 minutes. Add the carrots and onion; continue cooking, stirring more frequently, until the onion begins to soften, about 3 minutes.

3. Stir in the garlic, zest, oregano, saffron (if using), and salt until aromatic, just a few seconds. Pour in the broth and scrape up the most of the browned bits on the pot's bottom. Turn off the SAUTÉ function and stir in the tomatoes, white beans, and dried chiles (if using). Lock the lid onto the cooker.

4.

Set the machine for	Set the level for	The valve must be	Set the time for	If necessary, press
PRESSURE COOK	MAX	—	5 minutes with the KEEP WARM setting off	START
SOUP/BROTH, PRESSURE COOK, or MANUAL	HIGH	Closed	7 minutes with the KEEP WARM setting off	START
SLOW COOK	HIGH	Opened	4 hours with the KEEP WARM setting off (or on for no more than 2 hours)	START

5. If you've used a pressure setting, when the machine has finished cooking, use the **quick-release method** to bring the pot's pressure back to normal.

6. Unlatch the lid and open the cooker. If you've included the dried chiles, find and discard them. Stir well before serving.

2 tablespoons olive oil

1 pound sweet Italian sausage links, cut into 1-inch pieces

4 medium carrots, peeled and chopped (2 cups)

1 medium yellow onion, chopped (1 cup)

2 medium garlic cloves, peeled and minced (2 teaspoons)

2 teaspoons finely grated orange zest

2 teaspoons dried oregano

Up to ½ teaspoon saffron threads (optional)

½ teaspoon table salt

1½ quarts (6 cups) chicken broth

2 large round red tomatoes, stemmed and chopped (2 cups)

One 15-ounce can white beans, drained and rinsed (1¾ cups)

Up to 2 dried chiles de arbol (optional)

Beyond

- You must halve the recipe for a **3-quart cooker.**

- For a spicy soup, use hot Italian sausage links.

- Grate lots of Parmigiano-Reggiano over each serving, or dollop the servings with pesto.

- If desired, add up to 2 cups bagged chopped kale after the soup has cooked. Set the lid askew over the pot for 5 minutes to wilt the kale.

- For a Spanish-inspired soup, substitute fresh chorizo sausage for the Italian sausage. The chorizo will need to be cut into ½-inch-thick pieces. Also substitute one 14-ounce can of chickpeas, drained and rinsed, for the white beans; and one medium fennel bulb, trimmed and chopped, for the carrots.

1 pound boneless leg of lamb, any large pieces of fat removed, the meat cut into 1-inch pieces

2 medium garlic cloves, peeled and minced (2 teaspoons)

1 teaspoon dried oregano

1 teaspoon dried thyme

½ teaspoon ground dried turmeric

¼ teaspoon grated nutmeg

½ teaspoon table salt

2 tablespoons olive oil

1 medium red onion, chopped (1 cup)

2 quarts (8 cups) chicken broth

1 pound medium parsnips, peeled and cut into 1-inch pieces

1 pound small yellow potatoes such as Yukon Golds, none larger than a golf ball, each quartered

¼ cup loosely packed fresh cilantro leaves, finely chopped

Not-Your-Irish-Grandmother's Lamb and Potato Soup

6 servings

Here's the one and only lamb *soup* in this book. (There are plenty of lamb recipes in other chapters.) Frankly, we find lamb too strong for most soups that cook under pressure (or even in a slow cooker). The meat needs an oven reduction to mellow its flavors. However, by coating pieces of lamb in what's basically a barbecue rub, we gain some balance, getting bold flavors into the broth to match the meat.

Whenever you cut long, slender roots like parsnips and carrots, the dimensions stated for their size (here, 1-inch pieces) are always given for the fatter ends. As the root tapers, the slices should be cut a little longer for more even cooking.

1. Mix the lamb, garlic, oregano, thyme, turmeric, nutmeg, and salt in a large bowl until the meat is evenly and thoroughly coated. Set aside at room temperature for 10 minutes.

2.

Press the button for	Set it for	Set the time for	If necessary, press
SAUTÉ	MEDIUM, NORMAL, or CUSTOM 300°F	10 minutes	START

3. Warm the oil in a **6- or 8-quart cooker** for a minute or two. Add the onion and cook, stirring often, until it just begins to soften, about 4 minutes. Add the lamb and every speck of its rub. Cook, stirring frequently, until the lamb loses its raw, pink color, about 3 minutes. Pour in the broth, turn off the SAUTÉ function, and scrape up any browned bits on the pot's bottom. Lock the lid onto the pot.

4.

Set the machine for	Set the level for	The valve must be	Set the time for	If necessary, press
PRESSURE COOK	MAX	—	12 minutes with the KEEP WARM setting off	START
SOUP/BROTH, PRESSURE COOK, or MANUAL	HIGH	Closed	15 minutes with the KEEP WARM setting off	START

5. Use the **quick-release method** to bring the pot's pressure back to normal. Unlatch the lid and open the cooker. Stir in the parsnips and potatoes. Lock the lid back onto the pot.

6.

Set the machine for	Set the level for	The valve must be	Set the time for	If necessary, press
PRESSURE COOK	MAX	—	5 minutes with the KEEP WARM setting off	START
SOUP/BROTH, PRESSURE COOK, or MANUAL	HIGH	Closed	7 minutes with the KEEP WARM setting off	START

7. Again, use the **quick-release method** to bring the pot's pressure back to normal. Unlatch the lid and open the pot. Stir in the cilantro, then set the lid askew over the pot for 5 minutes to blend the flavors. Stir well before serving.

Beyond

- You must halve the recipe for a **3-quart cooker.**

- The soup could stand some heat. Add up to 3 dried chiles de arbol before the first cooking under pressure (remove these from the soup before serving). Or add up to 2 teaspoons red pepper flakes to the spice rub that goes on the lamb pieces.

- Don't like parsnips? Substitute 1 pound of carrots. Or even 1 pound of peeled and seeded butternut squash, cut into 1-inch cubes.

1½ quarts (6 cups) vegetable or chicken broth

4 ounces brown or white rice stick noodles, or rice noodles for pad Thai

3½ ounces shiitake mushroom caps, thinly sliced

2 tablespoons soy sauce, preferably reduced-sodium

1 tablespoon minced peeled fresh ginger

1 pound medium shrimp (about 30 per pound), peeled and deveined

8 ounces small bok choy, washed well for grit and roughly chopped

Shrimp and Rice Noodle Soup

4 servings

This simple soup is designed for a quick weekend lunch. It's straightforward, nothing heroic: a bowl of clean flavors with an umami richness from soy sauce.

1. Mix the broth, noodles, mushrooms, soy sauce, and ginger in a **6- or 8-quart cooker**. Lock the lid onto the pot.

2.

Set the machine for	Set the level for	The valve must be	Set the time for	If necessary, press
PRESSURE COOK	MAX	—	3 minutes with the KEEP WARM setting off	START
SOUP/BROTH, PRESSURE COOK, or MANUAL	HIGH	Closed	4 minutes with the KEEP WARM setting off	START

3. Use the **quick-release method** to bring the pot's pressure back to normal. Unlatch the lid and open the cooker.

4.

Press the button for	Set it for	Set the time for	If necessary, press
SAUTÉ	LOW or LESS	5 minutes	START

5. Bring the soup to a simmer. Stir the shrimp and bok choy into the soup. Cook, stirring occasionally, until the shrimp are pink and firm, about 2 minutes. Turn off the SAUTÉ function and serve warm.

Beyond

- The recipe doesn't work well in a **3-quart cooker** because the noodles have to be broken down into such small shards that they become rather irritating in the final dish.

- The noodles will most likely have to be broken into smaller pieces to fit in a **6-quart cooker** (depending on the brand of noodle you've got in hand). They may fit whole in an **8-quart cooker**.

- To go above and beyond, substitute white miso paste for the soy sauce.

- The bok choy will still be crunchy. If you like it softer, add it with the other ingredients to undergo the pressure cooking in step 2.

- If you can't find bok choy, substitute 8 ounces cored and chopped napa cabbage.

Spicy Shrimp and Rice Soup

6 servings

This spicy, coconut-milk soup is super thick, thanks to the rice, which absorbs much of the liquid as it cooks and creates something like a cross between a stew and a soup. If you have leftovers, thin out the soup with additional broth when reheating because the rice will continue to absorb more liquid in the refrigerator.

1. Mix the broth, tomatoes, coconut milk, onion, bell pepper, celery, rice, chiles, and oregano in a **6- or 8-quart cooker**. Lock the lid onto the pot.

2.

Set the machine for	Set the level for	The valve must be	Set the time for	If necessary, press
PRESSURE COOK	MAX	—	7 minutes with the KEEP WARM setting off	START
SOUP/BROTH, PRESSURE COOK, or MANUAL	HIGH	Closed	10 minutes with the KEEP WARM setting off	START

3. Use the **quick-release method** to return the pot's pressure to normal. Unlatch the lid and open the cooker.

4.

Press the button for	Set it for	Set the time for	If necessary, press
SAUTÉ	LOW or LESS	10 minutes	START

5. Stir the shrimp, parsley, and lemon juice into the soup. Continue cooking, stirring frequently, until the shrimp are pink and firm, about 2 minutes. Turn off the SAUTÉ function and serve warm.

1 quart (4 cups) chicken broth

One 28-ounce can crushed tomatoes (3½ cups)

1 cup regular or low-fat coconut milk

1 medium yellow onion, chopped (1 cup)

1 medium green bell pepper, stemmed, cored, and chopped (1 cup)

2 medium celery stalks, thinly sliced (⅔ cup)

½ cup raw long-grain white rice, preferably jasmine or basmati

Up to 2 small jalapeño chiles, stemmed, seeded, and finely chopped

2 tablespoons packed fresh oregano leaves, minced

1½ pounds medium shrimp (about 30 per pound), peeled and deveined

¼ cup loosely packed fresh parsley leaves, chopped

2 teaspoons fresh lemon juice

Beyond

- You must halve the recipe for a **3-quart cooker**.

- For much more flavor (and if you don't mind getting your fingers dirty at the table), devein the shrimp but leave them in their shells.

- For more heat, don't seed the chiles.

- For a sweeter soup, use 3 cups broth and 1 cup dry white wine, such as Chardonnay.

1 pound large shrimp (about 20 per pound)

1½ quarts (6 cups) chicken broth

2 medium carrots, thinly sliced (2 cups)

3 medium celery stalks, thinly sliced (1 cup)

1 medium yellow onion, chopped (1 cup)

2 small yellow potatoes (about 3 ounces each), such as Yukon Golds, chopped

½ cup fresh or frozen corn kernels (no need to thaw)

2 medium garlic cloves, peeled and minced (2 teaspoons)

2 tablespoons tomato paste

1 tablespoon stemmed fresh thyme leaves

¼ teaspoon table salt

½ pound pasteurized claw or "special" crabmeat, picked over for shell and cartilage

½ pound sea scallops, quartered

½ pound thin skinless white fish fillets, such as fluke, haddock, hake, or snapper, cut into 1-inch pieces

½ cup heavy cream

All-Out Fish Chowder

6 servings

This one's the real deal. You'll start by making shrimp broth with the shrimp shells. Then you'll add lots of vegetables and cook them under pressure before adding a vast array of fish — and some cream right at the end. The technique's complicated. The results are fresh and light — not pasty and thick — and best with a glass of white wine (rather than beer). By the way, there's no call for expensive lump (or even jumbo lump) crabmeat for this recipe. "Special" crabmeat is meat from the body, just not the large pieces.

1. Peel and devein the shrimp (discard the veins). Put the shells in a **6- or 8-quart cooker**. (Put the peeled shrimp on a plate, cover with plastic wrap, and set in the fridge.) Pour the broth into the cooker, stir well, and lock the lid onto the pot.

2.

Set the machine for	Set the level for	The valve must be	Set the time for	If necessary, press
PRESSURE COOK	MAX	—	3 minutes with the KEEP WARM setting off	START
SOUP/BROTH, PRESSURE COOK, or MANUAL	HIGH	Closed	5 minutes with the KEEP WARM setting off	START

3. Use the **quick-release method** to bring the pot's pressure back to normal. Unlatch the lid and open the cooker. Use a slotted spoon to fish out and discard all the shrimp shells, as well as any extraneous bits. Stir in the carrots, celery, onion, potatoes, corn, garlic, tomato paste, thyme, and salt until the tomato paste dissolves. Lock the lid back onto the pot.

4.

Set the machine for	Set the level for	The valve must be	Set the time for	If necessary, press
PRESSURE COOK	MAX	—	3 minutes with the KEEP WARM setting off	START
SOUP/BROTH, PRESSURE COOK, or MANUAL	HIGH	Closed	4 minutes with the KEEP WARM setting off	START

5. Again, use the **quick-release method** to bring the pot's pressure back to normal. Unlatch the lid and open the cooker.

6.

Press the button for	Set it for	Set the time for	If necessary, press
SAUTÉ	MEDIUM, NORMAL, or CUSTOM 300°F	5 minutes	START

7. Bring the soup to a simmer, stirring occasionally. Stir in the peeled shrimp, crabmeat, scallops, and fish. Continue cooking just until the shrimp are barely pink, 2 to 3 minutes. Turn off the SAUTÉ function, stir in the cream, and set the lid over the pot for 5 minutes to blend the flavors.

Beyond

- You must halve the recipe for a **3-quart cooker.**

- For a looser soup, use 2 quarts (8 cups) broth.

- If you want a thicker chowder, use 3 or 4 small yellow potatoes. In addition, whisk the cream with 1½ tablespoons cornstarch until smooth and stir this slurry into the soup after the shrimp are *fully* pink and firm. Continue cooking until thickened, all the while whisking gently (to keep the fish intact), about 1 more minute.

1½ quarts (6 cups) chicken broth

1 medium leek (about 4½ ounces), white and pale green parts only, halved lengthwise, washed well, and thinly sliced (⅓ cup)

1 very small butternut squash, diced, peeled, and seeded (2 cups)

Up to 2 fresh medium jalapeño chiles, stemmed and thinly sliced

2 medium garlic cloves, peeled and slivered

¼ cup loosely packed cilantro leaves, chopped

½ teaspoon ground allspice

½ teaspoon ground cinnamon

½ teaspoon table salt

2 pounds skinned sea bass, cut into 1-inch pieces

Fiery Jamaican-Style Fish Soup

4 to 6 servings

This recipe's a riff on a traditional Caribbean soup, sometimes made with chicken, sometimes (as here) with fish; sometimes pureed, sometimes (as here) left chunky. The only pain is dicing the butternut squash. If you buy it peeled, seeded, and chunked up from the supermarket, you'll still need to cut it down into ½-inch pieces at home.

You can make the recipe ahead, through the end of step 3. Cool the soup (without the fish), then store it in a sealed container in the fridge for up to 3 days, or in the freezer for up to 3 months. Bring the soup back to a simmer in a saucepan on the stove (or in the Instant Pot with the SAUTÉ function set at MEDIUM, NORMAL, or CUSTOM 300°F) before proceeding to cook the fish.

1. Mix the broth, leek, butternut squash, chiles, garlic, cilantro, allspice, cinnamon, and salt in a **6- or 8-quart cooker**. Lock the lid onto the pot.

2.

Set the machine for	Set the level for	The valve must be	Set the time for	If necessary, press
PRESSURE COOK	MAX	—	5 minutes with the KEEP WARM setting off	START
SOUP/BROTH, PRESSURE COOK, or MANUAL	HIGH	Closed	7 minutes with the KEEP WARM setting off	START

3. Use the **quick-release method** to bring the pot's pressure back to normal. Unlatch the lid and open the pot. Stir well.

4.

Press the button for	Set it for	Set the time for	If necessary, press
SAUTÉ	MEDIUM, NORMAL, or CUSTOM 300°F	10 minutes	START

5. Bring the soup to a simmer. Add the fish and cook, stirring occasionally but gently, until cooked through, 4 to 5 minutes. Turn off the SAUTÉ function and remove the *hot* insert from the pot to keep the fish from overcooking.

Beyond

- You must halve the recipe for a 3-quart cooker.

- For a more authentic Jamaican flavor, substitute peeled, seeded, and diced fresh pumpkin for the butternut squash.

- For greater intensity, use fish stock (see page 105) instead of chicken broth.

- For an even hotter soup, substitute one or even two stemmed, seeded, and chopped habanero chiles for the jalapeños.

- Garnish the bowls with toasted unsweetened coconut.

Vegetable Stock

Makes 10 cups

Here's our first recipe for homemade stock, the answer to all the insipid, watery vegetable broths on the market. Note that the Max machines instructions here call for both the pressure-cooking function to be set for SOUP/BROTH and for the NUTRIBOOST function to be turned on. Doing so will get the absolutely best flavor into the stock.

1. Put the onions, potato, carrots, celery, mushrooms, parsley, thyme, and peppercorns in a **6- or 8-quart cooker**. Pour in the soy sauce, then add as much of the water as possible without going over the **Max Fill** line. Stir well and lock the lid onto the pot.

2.

Set the machine for	Set the level for	The valve must be	Set the time for	If necessary, press
SOUP/BROTH and NUTRIBOOST	MAX	—	50 minutes with the KEEP WARM setting off	START
SOUP/BROTH, PRESSURE COOK, or MANUAL	HIGH	Closed	1 hour with the KEEP WARM setting off	START
SLOW COOK	HIGH	Opened	4½ hours with the KEEP WARM setting off (or on for no more than 4 hours)	START

3. If you've used a pressure setting, when the machine has finished cooking, turn it off and let its pressure **return to normal naturally**, about 40 minutes.

4. Unlatch the lid and open the cooker. Strain the contents of the insert through a fine-mesh sieve like a *chinois* (or through a colander lined with a double thickness of cheesecloth) and into a large bowl. Cool for 30 minutes, then store in covered containers in the fridge for up to 4 days, or in 1-cup covered containers in the freezer for up to 6 months.

2 large yellow onions, peeled and quartered

1 large yellow potato (about 9 ounces), washed and quartered

4 medium carrots, cut into quarters

4 medium celery stalks, including any leaves, cut into 2-inch pieces

½ pound cremini mushrooms, washed and halved

1 small bunch parsley, rinsed to remove grit

4 large thyme sprigs

1 teaspoon black peppercorns

¼ cup soy sauce, preferably reduced-sodium soy sauce

At most 2½ quarts (10 cups) water

Beyond

- You must halve the recipe for a **3-quart cooker**.

- This stock is a rich brown color, mostly because of the mushrooms and the soy sauce.

- If you're the type of person who freezes vegetable trimmings in the hopes of one day making stock, now's your chance. All the vegetables in the ingredient list come out to about 8 cups of chopped vegetables and/or trimmings. Feel free to substitute your stash.

- Add other vegetables at will. Use skinned, peeled, and chopped butternut squash instead of the carrots (the stock will be cloudier). Or substitute chopped trimmed fennel or even cubed peeled celeriac for the celery. Add 1 or 2 cubed peeled medium turnips for a slightly bitter flavor in the stock, or up to 1½ cups cubed peeled rutabaga for a sweeter flavor.

2½ pounds chicken wings, necks, and/or backs

2 medium carrots, cut into 2-inch pieces

2 medium parsnips, cut into 2-inch pieces

3 medium celery stalks including any leaves, cut into 2-inch pieces

1 large yellow onion, peeled and quartered

2 large garlic cloves, peeled

¼ cup loosely packed fresh dill fronds (optional)

2 teaspoons kosher salt

2 teaspoons black peppercorns

At most 2½ quarts (10 cups) water

Chicken Stock

Makes 10 cups

We have a friend who reads almost any recipe for a savory dish and says, "Well, it'll all be about the stock." Nothing could be truer. Making your own chicken stock on a weekend afternoon will be a sure-fire guarantee that your cooking is going to go over the top in the days (and months) ahead. Even if you reduce the purchased broth you use by 1 cup and sub in 1 cup of the homemade stuff, that recipe will come out better.

The dill here is optional, if traditional for so-called "Jewish penicillin." If you're making this stock to use in other recipes, leave it out. If you're making this stock because someone you know is ill and needs a healthy pick-me-up, or if you're going to use it to make a simple chicken noodle soup on your own with cooked spaghetti and chicken meat just stirred into it later, or even matzo ball soup at Passover, keep the dill in the mix.

1. Put the chicken, carrots, parsnips, celery, onion, garlic cloves, dill (if using), salt, and pepper in a **6- or 8-quart cooker**. Add as much of the water as possible without going over the **Max Fill** line. Lock the lid onto the pot.

2.

Set the machine for	Set the level for	The valve must be	Set the time for	If necessary, press
SOUP/BROTH and NUTRIBOOST	MAX	—	1 hour with the KEEP WARM setting off	START
SOUP/BROTH, PRESSURE COOK, or MANUAL	HIGH	Closed	1½ hours with the KEEP WARM setting off	START
SLOW COOK	HIGH	Opened	5 hours with the KEEP WARM setting off (or on for no more than 4 hours)	START

3. If you've used a pressure setting, when the machine has finished cooking, turn it off and let the pressure **return to normal naturally**, about 45 minutes.

4. Strain the contents of the insert through a fine-mesh sieve like a *chinois* (or through a colander lined with a double thickness of cheesecloth) and into a large bowl. Cool for 20 minutes, then store in covered containers in the fridge for up to 3 days, or in 1-cup covered containers in the freezer for up to 3 months.

Beyond

- You must halve the recipe for a **3-quart cooker**.

- For an old-world stock full of collagen and with an earthier, far-less-sweet flavor, add 1 or 2 well-cleaned chicken feet.

- For a more intense flavor, add several chicken hearts and/or gizzards (but no liver).

- And for an absurdly complex flavor (but not a yellow stock, rather a brown one), first roast the chicken pieces on a large, lipped baking sheet in a heated 450°F oven for 30 minutes before making the stock.

Beef Stock (aka Bone Broth)

Makes 10 cups

Those of us who've been making beef broth for years know its pleasures, no matter its name. But the surprise in our version may well be the vinegar. Beef is so naturally sweet that we feel that a little acid balances the flavor.

One warning: Don't use marrow bones. They'll cloud the results and lend a funky flavor. Of course, you can save back the bones from rib roasts and such for making stock, but make sure you've scraped off any seasonings or rubs.

And yes, this recipe takes more time than any other in this book. It's probably the definition of slow food. The point is to get all that collagen melted into the broth, enriching it considerably.

1. Position the rack in the center of the oven; heat the oven to 350°F. Lay the beef bones on a large lipped baking sheet and roast until lightly browned, about 30 minutes.

2. Transfer the bones and any juices to a **6- or 8-quart cooker**. (Add in any brown bits from the pan if you want a really rich — but not clear — stock.) Add the leek, carrots, garlic cloves, vinegar, thyme sprigs, peppercorns, salt, and bay leaves. Pour in as much as of the water as possible without going over the **Max Fill** line. Lock the lid onto the pot.

3.

Set the machine for	Set the level for	The valve must be	Set the time for	If necessary, press
SOUP/BROTH and NUTRIBOOST	MAX	—	2 hours with the KEEP WARM setting off	START
SOUP/BROTH, PRESSURE COOK, or MANUAL	HIGH	Closed	2½ hours with the KEEP WARM setting off	START
SLOW COOK	HIGH	Opened	6 hours with the KEEP WARM setting off (or on for no more than 4 hours)	START

4. If you've used a pressure setting, when the machine has finished cooking, turn it off and let its pressure **return to normal naturally**, about 1 hour.

5. Strain the contents of the insert through a fine-mesh sieve like a *chinois* (or through a colander lined with a double thickness of cheesecloth) and into a large bowl. Cool for 30 minutes, then skim the fat off the surface of the stock. Store in covered containers in the fridge for up to 3 days, or in 1-cup covered containers in the freezer for up to 3 months.

3 pounds beef bones with some meat attached, preferably beef neck bones, oxtails, short ribs with most of the meat removed, or a combination

1 large leek, trimmed of only the squiggly roots, the bulb end halved lengthwise, well washed, and the bulb and leaves thinly sliced

3 medium carrots, cut into 2-inch pieces

4 large garlic cloves, peeled

2 tablespoons apple cider vinegar

4 large fresh thyme sprigs

1 tablespoon black peppercorns

2 teaspoons kosher salt

2 bay leaves

At most 2½ quarts (10 cups) water

Beyond

- You must halve the recipe for a **3-quart cooker.**

- For a more aromatic broth, better for sipping than for recipes, add 1 star anise pod, 6 to 8 allspice berries, and/or one 4-inch cinnamon stick to the mix.

- For clearer stock, use a fat separator to skim the results. (Given the size of most home fat separators, you'll have to work in batches.)

1½ pounds chicken wings, necks, or backs

One 1-pound smoked ham hock

One 6-ounce chunk of salt pork or pancetta, cut into chunks

One 6-inch knob of fresh ginger, peeled and thinly sliced

6 medium scallions, trimmed and cut into 2-inch sections

¼ cup soy sauce, preferably reduced-sodium soy sauce

¼ cup mirin

At most 2½ quarts (10 cups) water

Ramen Broth

Makes 10 cups

Making the broth (well, really, the stock) for ramen can be a three-day affair by the time you cook all the individual parts — layering the flavors during a long, slow simmer in the oven, and then later on the stove, and then later back in the oven. But our Instant Pot recipe will let you make a knock-out ramen dinner for friends on the weekend. Or keep some in the freezer for when you're craving a bowl of comfort. See the *Beyond* section for ideas about turning the broth into dinner. If you prefer a clear ramen broth, set the Max machine just to PRESSURE COOK at MAX without the NUTRIBOOST feature.

1. Put the chicken, ham hock, salt pork, ginger, scallions, soy sauce, and mirin in a **6- or 8-quart cooker**. Pour in as much as of the water as possible without going over the **Max Fill** line. Lock the lid onto the pot.

2.

Set the machine for	Set the level for	The valve must be	Set the time for	If necessary, press
PRESSURE COOK, or SOUP/BROTH *and* NUTRIBOOST	MAX	—	2 hours with the KEEP WARM setting off	START
SOUP/BROTH, PRESSURE COOK, or MANUAL	HIGH	Closed	2½ hours with the KEEP WARM setting off	START
SLOW COOK	HIGH	Opened	6 hours with the KEEP WARM setting off (or on for no more than 4 hours)	START

3. If you've used a pressure setting, when the machine has finished cooking, turn it off and let its pressure **return to normal naturally**, about 50 minutes.

4. Strain the contents of the insert through a fine-mesh sieve like a *chinois* (or through a colander lined with a double thickness of cheesecloth) and into a large bowl. Cool for 30 minutes, then skim the fat from the surface of the stock. Store in covered containers in the fridge for up to 3 days, or in 2-cup covered containers in the freezer for up to 3 months.

Beyond

- This stock is not easily halved for a **3-quart cooker** because of the ham hock. It's almost impossible to find one small enough. That said, if you can find a very small, ½-pound hock, halve everything else and have at it!

- Serve the warm ramen broth over bowls of cooked and drained ramen, udon, or soba noodles, along with chopped greens (such as bok choy or kale), and bean sprouts.

- Take it over the top by adding more to the bowls: halved soft-cooked eggs (see page 34), slow-roasted pork belly, and/or small bits of nori (dried seaweed sheets).

Fish Stock

Makes 10 cups

If you want to get serious about making stock and wanted to know the one stock to make, we would say, "This one." Odd, no? But there are pretty decent versions of vegetable and chicken broth on the market. Fish broth is another matter. And there's no substitute for a fine fish stock in just about any fish soup, stew, or braise. Some people try to jury-rig a fish stock by adding bottled clam juice to canned chicken or vegetable broth. It's a pale imitation. If you really want to become a pro, make your own fish stock and mix it in about 50/50 proportions with purchased chicken or vegetable broth for any fish recipe in this book. Where do you get fish heads and such? Walk up to the fish counter of any large supermarket. Ask and you might receive.

3 pounds fish heads, tails, fins, skin, and bones, preferably with a little meat still adhering to them

4 medium carrots, cut into 2-inch pieces

4 medium celery stalks including any leaves, cut into 2-inch pieces

1 medium yellow onion, peeled and halved

1 tablespoon black peppercorns

1 teaspoon kosher salt

10 fresh parsley sprigs

2 bay leaves

At most 2½ quarts (10 cups) water

1. Put the fish parts, carrots, celery, onion, peppercorns, salt, and parsley sprigs in a **6- or 8-quart cooker**. Pour in as much water as possible without going over the **Max Fill** line. Lock the lid onto the pot.

2.

Set the machine for	Set the level for	The valve must be	Set the time for	If necessary, press
SOUP/BROTH and NUTRIBOOST	MAX	—	35 minutes with the KEEP WARM setting off	START
SOUP/BROTH, PRESSURE COOK, or MANUAL	HIGH	Closed	45 minutes with the KEEP WARM setting off	START
SLOW COOK	HIGH	Opened	4 hours with the KEEP WARM setting off (or on for no more than 2 hours)	START

3. If you've used a pressure setting, when the machine has finished cooking, turn it off and let its pressure **return to normal naturally**, about 40 minutes.

4. Unlatch the lid and open the cooker. Strain the contents of the insert through a fine-mesh sieve like a *chinois* (or through a colander lined with a double thickness of cheesecloth) and into a large bowl. Cool for 30 minutes, then skim any impurities off the surface of the stock. Store in covered containers in the fridge for up to 2 days, or in 1-cup covered containers in the freezer for up to 4 months.

Beyond

- You must halve the recipe for a **3-quart cooker**.

- To make shellfish stock (for étouffée, gumbo, and other Louisiana favorites), substitute 8 cups shrimp, lobster, and/or crab shells for the fish parts.

1 quart (4 cups) chicken broth

1 cup regular or low-fat coconut milk

½ cup chopped fresh turmeric (no need to peel)

2 medium garlic cloves, peeled and smashed

½ teaspoon table salt

Turmeric Broth

Makes 5 cups

This one's a hybrid, a broth mixed with a stock, or a stock made from a broth. It's really a sipping drink, maybe for sick-room care or on a day off when you need a little me-time. That said, you can also use the broth in any of the Asian- or Caribbean-inspired recipes in this book, provided they also have coconut milk in the mix.

Fresh turmeric has become so popular that it even shows up in our rural supermarket. Look for compact, plump pieces with tight skins, free of too many black spots, and certainly with no squishy bits. We suggest storing the broth in ½-cup increments in the freezer, so you can easily serve up a little dose when you need it.

1. Put all the ingredients in a **3-, 6-, or 8-quart cooker**. Lock the lid onto the pot.

2.

Set the machine for	Set the level for	The valve must be	Set the time for	If necessary, press
PRESSURE COOK	MAX	—	3 minutes with the KEEP WARM setting off	START
PRESSURE COOK or MANUAL	HIGH	Closed	5 minutes with the KEEP WARM setting off	START

3. Use the **quick-release method** to bring the pot's pressure back to normal. Unlatch the lid and open the cooker. Strain its contents through a fine-mesh sieve like a *chinois* (or through a colander lined with a double thickness of cheesecloth) and into a large bowl or a heat-safe pitcher. Serve warm — or store, covered, in the refrigerator for up to 1 week, or in the freezer for up to 6 months.

Beyond

• Add up to ¼ cup chopped, fresh ginger for a spicier broth.

Ginger Tea

Makes 2 quarts

2 quarts (8 cups) water

½ cup grated fresh ginger (no need to peel)

¼ cup honey

¼ cup fresh lemon juice

4 chamomile tea bags, any labels removed

One 4-inch cinnamon stick

If you've got a sore throat, here's your recipe. Or if you've got someone you care about who needs a little boost, here's the stuff. No doubt, it's spicy. It'll wake up those taste buds because the pressure cooker forces so much of the ginger into the tea to make a warm and healing drink.

1. Mix all the ingredients in a **6- or 8-quart cooker**. Lock the lid onto the pot.

2.

Set the machine for	Set the level for	The valve must be	Set the time for	If necessary, press
PRESSURE COOK	MAX	—	2 minutes with the KEEP WARM setting off	START
PRESSURE COOK or MANUAL	HIGH	Closed	4 minutes with the KEEP WARM setting off	START

3. Use the **quick-release method** to bring the pot's pressure back to normal. Unlatch the lid and open the cooker. Strain its contents through a fine-mesh sieve like a *chinois* (or through a colander lined with a double thickness of cheesecloth) and into a bowl or a heat-safe pitcher. Serve warm or cold. Store, covered, in the fridge for up to 1 week, or in the freezer for up to 6 months.

Beyond

- You must halve the recipe for a **3-quart cooker.**

- For more sweet-and-sour flavor, add up to 3 thin lemon slices with the other ingredients.

- For a less assertive flavor, substitute agave nectar for the honey.

5 cups (1 quart plus 1 cup) almond milk

5 black tea bags, any labels removed

10 green or white cardamom pods, crushed

10 whole cloves, crushed

1½ teaspoons fennel seeds

One 4-inch cinnamon stick

¼ teaspoon table salt

Almond Milk Chai

Makes 5 cups

Admittedly, this isn't standard chai made with whole milk. Unfortunately, milk can break under pressure without special safety precautions. So we've used almond milk and morphed the classic into a vegan drink. It's mildly sweet (thanks to that almond milk) and quite aromatic.

1. Mix all the ingredients in a **3-, 6-, or 8-quart cooker**. Lock the lid onto the pot.

2.

Set the machine for	Set the level for	The valve must be	Set the time for	If necessary, press
PRESSURE COOK	MAX	—	2 minutes with the KEEP WARM setting off	START
PRESSURE COOK or MANUAL	HIGH	Closed	3 minutes with the KEEP WARM setting off	START

3. Use the **quick-release method** to bring the pot's pressure back to normal. Unlatch the lid and open the cooker. Strain its contents through a fine-mesh sieve like a *chinois* (or through a colander lined with a double thickness of cheesecloth) and into a bowl or heat-safe pitcher. Serve hot or cold.

Beyond

- Sweeten the chai with a little brown sugar (if serving hot) or agave nectar (if serving cold).

- If you don't care about this being vegan, consider using honey as the sweetener.

Five Infused Waters

Makes about 1 quart each

The Instant Pot is the perfect tool to infuse fruit flavors into water, making a concentrate for cocktails, summer quenchers, or just a good swig after a hard day working in the yard. So here are five versions to set you up for summer. All offer powerful, assertive flavors. Serve over *lots* of ice, preferably crushed ice for more melt. Or dilute in a ratio of 3 parts plain seltzer to 1 part infused water for a pitcher of drinks.

    We made terrific Palomas as a celebration at the end of this book's photo shoot: For one tall drink, seed half a lime and cut it all into small bits, then muddle these with 2 teaspoons granulated white sugar in a cocktail shaker. Add 6 ounces Grapefruit Tarragon Water, 2½ ounces tequila, and ice cubes. Seal and shake well, then strain over fresh ice into a 16-ounce glass before topping with plain seltzer.

1. Place the ingredients for any infused water in a **3-, 6-, or 8-quart cooker**. Lock the lid onto the pot.

2.

Set the machine for	Set the level for	The valve must be	Set the time for	If necessary, press
PRESSURE COOK or MANUAL	HIGH	Closed	5 minutes with the KEEP WARM setting off	START

3. When the machine has finished cooking, turn it off and let its pressure **return to normal naturally**, 15 to 25 minutes (depending on the overall volume). Unlatch the lid and open the cooker. Strain its contents through a fine-mesh sieve like a *chinois* (or a colander lined with a double thickness of cheesecloth) and into a bowl. Store in a covered container in the fridge for up to 1 week, or in individual ½-cup containers in the freezer for up to 6 months.

Lime Blackberry Water

1 quart (4 cups) water

1 pint fresh blackberries

Juice of 1 medium lime

Grapefruit Tarragon Water

1 quart (4 cups) water

1 medium grapefruit, preferably a ruby red grapefruit, quartered

1 sprig fresh tarragon

Orange Mango Water

1 quart (4 cups) water

1 medium orange, preferably a blood orange, quartered

1 medium mango, peeled and chopped (include the pit and any fruit adhering to it)

Strawberry Lemon Water

1 quart (4 cups) water

1 quart strawberries, hulled

1 medium lemon, scrubbed to remove any waxy coating, then halved

Orange Cinnamon Water

1 quart (4 cups) water

2 medium juice oranges, quartered

One 2-inch cinnamon stick

Beyond

- Strain the infused water, then freeze undiluted in ice-cube trays to create fruit-laced cocktails this summer on the deck.

See photo in insert.

3

Chilis, Sloppy Joes, Pasta Sauces, and Ragùs

Our hunch is that these recipes represent some of the main reasons you bought a multi-cooker: hearty chilis and deep-flavored pasta sauces, all cooked under pressure in a fraction of the time they might take on the stove. Even so, about half of these recipes can also be made with the SLOW COOK function. You may not want to walk in the door and throw dinner together in seconds. You might want to put the ingredients in the pot earlier in the day and let them cook while you're off taking care of your life.

Please permit us to sound schoolmarmish and remind you that it's never a good idea to leave a slow cooker unattended. And the cooker should certainly not be left to its own devices if you've got a lively cat or a nosy dog, not to mention curious children.

Okay, back to the recipes. Many are full meals; some are not. The pasta sauces and ragùs, for example, will at least need cooked pasta to make them dinner, if not a side salad, too. In those recipes, the serving-size notation near the recipe title gives you a notion of how much pasta would work with the amount of sauce made, rather than a strictly defined number of portions. Some people chow down; others barely touch the stuff. We thought it best to explain how much cooked pasta a particular sauce will coat.

In some cases, the batch will be larger than you may want in a single sitting. Rather than halving the recipe (which usually proves impossible or even disastrous in a **6- or 8-quart cooker** with only half the liquid to make the necessary steam for pressure cooking), save the rest in the freezer for another day when you're too tired to pull out even the Instant Pot. Or just go on a weekend cooking spree, stocking quarts of tasty sauce in the freezer. You'll thank yourself some evening when you're too tired to cook.

FAQs

1. You want me to use dried chiles to make chili? Seriously?

Most of these recipes don't call for dried chiles. But two do, including one of the big ones in this chapter: the road map for Chile con Carne (page 116). We wanted to include a couple of honest-to-Texas chilis. So, yes, we call for dried chiles, which, mind you, show up even in our rural New England supermarket.

That said, they don't show up in abundance in our supermarket. So we always call for a variety of dried chiles in case the selection at yours is just as limited. Of course, you don't have to pick just one type if you can find more. New Mexico reds (familiar from Southwestern *ristras*) are sweet and moderately spicy; anchos are dried poblanos, a little citrusy and (as a rule) not as hot. Mulatos have an almost chocolate flavor; pasillas, a brighter bite, lemony at its base. Chipotles are smoked and dried jalapeños, usually fiery (one or two chipotles will suffice among other chiles in any of these recipes). And there are many more chile varieties in Latin American and Mexican American supermarkets. Experiment to create your own blend.

The rule for buying dried chiles is the same as the one for buying any dried fruit: They should be supple, not desiccated. They should show no bits of mold or wet decay. They should be intact or at least in large pieces, not chipped up, and certainly not powdery. And they should smell sweet, if also hot.

2. Why do these recipes call for so much chile powder?

Both the PRESSURE COOK and SLOW COOK functions destroy many of the flavor compounds found in chiles, even capsaicin, the stuff that brings on the burn. We need to use more chile powder than we might on the stovetop to preserve the characteristic flavor.

Buy chile powder in bulk, rather than in small jars. Look for large containers at most supermarkets or search online spice suppliers.

3. Why do you call for two kinds of chile powder?

Since we wanted a more complex flavor in some recipes and a more straightforward one in others, we used two types.

The first, *standard chile powder,* is the North American staple. It's actually a blend: ground dried chiles plus dried oregano, ground cumin, sometimes salt, and maybe a few other spices.

The second type, *pure chile powder,* is not a blend but (most often) one variety of chile that has been dried and ground, with no cumin and other spices. (Some bottlings are a blend of dried chiles, not one varietal.) We use a pure chile powder when we want a cleaner flavor profile, even when we go ahead and add, say, additional ground cumin to the mix.

We never specify *which* pure chile powder, leaving that decision to you and your supermarket's inventory. As a rule, pure ancho chile powder is sweeter and milder; chipotle chile powder is fiery and smoky. You can even find many more varieties of pure chile powder at gourmet supermarkets and from online spice shops.

And one more thing: When we call for *standard chile powder,* we often add more ground cumin. In our minds, there's never enough. Ground cumin may be even more essential to the flavor of American chili than ground dried chiles.

4. What are canned chipotles in adobo sauce?

They're smoked and dried jalapeños that have been put in a rich, vinegar-and-spice-laced sauce. It's a concoction originally from the Philippines but now popular in Latin American and Caribbean cooking. We have looked for — and found — small cans of chiles in adobo sauce at supermarkets across North America.

One warning: When the recipe calls for "1 canned chile in adobo sauce, stemmed and seeded," it doesn't mean that you should use one *entire can of* chiles in adobo sauce. (One of us is side-eying his sister.) Use only one or maybe two chiles *out of the can,* then cover the opened can and store it in the fridge for up to 3 months or in the freezer for perhaps a year, even longer.

5. What's the difference between a pasta sauce and a ragù?

Basically, a pasta sauce is thinner than a ragù. A pasta sauce has a fresher flavor, less "cooked." And a sauce is usually not as well stocked as a ragù. That said, a thousand Italian grandmothers are lining up right now to smack us for this sort of over-simplification. If you, too, think we're being sloppy, get in the queue.

6. What's the best way to serve the pasta sauces and ragùs?

The easiest way to make dinner out of any of the pasta sauces and many of the ragùs is to prepare and drain the pasta while the sauce is cooking. After the sauce has finished, stir the pasta right into the Instant Pot and toss with the sauce until well coated. Set aside for 2 minutes with the lid askew so the pasta can absorb more of the sauce. Throughout, we've also given more serving suggestions beyond simple pasta.

7. I want to use fresh pasta. What do I do?

To use fresh pasta (gluten-free or regular), the general rule is that *1 pound of dried pasta when cooked and drained is about the same as 1½ pounds of fresh pasta when cooked and drained*. Such thinking is not always accurate (based on the shape and thickness of the pasta), but it's close enough for weeknight purposes.

And there's another rule that dried pasta goes better with chunky, hearty sauces while fresh works best with sauces that include cream. We're not sure we buy it. Bolognese is a delight with fresh pasta. And a creamy tomato sauce works well with dried pasta as well as fresh.

8. Do I have to crush the canned tomatoes by hand? Haven't you heard of canned crushed tomatoes?

Yes, we have. And we sometimes call for them. But the pressure cooker is an unforgiving environment. We find that canned crushed tomatoes break down into tomato juice. For better texture, we advocate that you clean and dry your hands, then crush canned whole tomatoes one by one over (and into) the pot. You'll end up with a less watery, more textural sauce — and thank us later, despite the mess.

2 tablespoons fat

Choose one or a 50/50 combo from butter, rendered bacon fat, lard, schmaltz, duck fat, olive oil, vegetable oil, corn oil, canola oil, safflower oil, pecan oil, and/or walnut oil.

1 cup chopped allium aromatics

Choose one or combine any two from onions (of any sort), shallots, and/or well-cleaned, thinly sliced leeks (the white and pale green parts only).

1 cup chopped, seeded, and cored sweet pepper

Choose green, red, or yellow bell peppers, or even Cubanelle peppers.

Up to 2 medium garlic cloves, peeled and minced (2 teaspoons)

⅓ cup standard chile powder

Choose from mild, dark, smoked, roasted, or hot.

1 tablespoon ground cumin

1 tablespoon dried oregano

½ teaspoon table salt

One 28-ounce can diced tomatoes (3½ cups), preferably fire-roasted

1 cup clear liquid

Choose one or a 50/50 combo from broth of any sort, beer of any sort, and/or unsweetened apple cider.

One 15-ounce can beans, drained and rinsed (1⅔ cups)

Choose from red kidney, black, white, pink, navy, or even chickpeas.

1½ pounds lean ground meat

Choose one or a 50/50 combo from ground beef, pork, lamb, turkey, veal, and/or goat.

¼ cup tomato paste

Road Map: All-American Chili

6 servings

In this road map recipe, you choose the fat, the liquid, the beans, and even the type of ground meat to customize American chili to your taste. And don't stand on ceremony. Mix ground beef and pork, or ground veal and turkey. (And if you can find ground goat, good grief you live near a good supermarket!) In the end, the point is to make the chili you and yours would like for dinner. Have a blast. Make notes in the recipe margins. Create a signature recipe. It'll taste better because it's 100 percent yours. But one warning: Canned beans, after pressure cooking, do not stand up very well to freezing. Plan on eating it up!

1.

Press the button for	Set it for	Set the time for	If necessary, press
SAUTÉ	MEDIUM, NORMAL, or CUSTOM 300°F	10 minutes	START

2. Melt any solid fat or warm any liquid oil in a **6- or 8-quart cooker**. Add the allium aromatics, sweet pepper, and garlic. Cook, stirring often, until the vegetables soften, about 4 minutes.

3. Stir in the chile powder, cumin, oregano, and salt until aromatic, just a few seconds. Then stir in the tomatoes, liquid, and beans. Crumble in the ground meat and stir until well combined, not until the meat begins to brown. Turn off the SAUTÉ function and lock the lid onto the pot.

4.

Press the button for	Set it for	The valve must be	Set the time for	If necessary, press
PRESSURE COOK	MAX	—	6 minutes with the KEEP WARM setting off	START
BEAN/CHILI, PRESSURE COOK, or MANUAL	HIGH	Closed	8 minutes with the KEEP WARM setting off	START
SLOW COOK	HIGH	Opened	3 hours with the KEEP WARM setting off (or on for no more than 2 hours)	START

5. If you've used a pressure setting, when the machine has finished cooking, use the **quick-release method** to bring the pot's pressure back to normal.

6. When ready, unlatch the lid and open the cooker.

7.

Press the button for	Set it for	Set the time for	If necessary, press
SAUTÉ	MEDIUM, NORMAL, or CUSTOM 300°F	5 minutes	START

8. Bring the chili to a full bubble. Stir in the tomato paste until uniform throughout. Cook, stirring almost constantly, until slightly thickened, about 2 minutes. Turn off the SAUTÉ function, set the lid ajar over the pot, and let the chili rest for 10 minutes to blend the flavors.

Beyond

- You must halve the recipe for a **3-quart cooker.**

- For a bulkier chili, add ½ cup chopped celery and/or ½ cup chopped carrot with the allium aromatics and sweet pepper.

- There's not much heat (unless you used hot chile powder). For more spice, add one stemmed, seeded, and diced canned chipotle in adobo sauce with the allium aromatics and sweet pepper.

- For more umami flavor, omit the salt and add up to 2 tablespoons soy sauce.

- Serve topped with sour cream and shredded cheese, particularly Monterey Jack.

- Top with minced, seeded, and stemmed *fresh* jalapeños for their citrus-y bite.

- Use this chili to make a chili casserole: Layer it between corn tortillas and shredded cheese in a 9-inch square or even a 9 x 13-inch baking dish. Bake covered in a 350°F oven for 20 minutes, then uncovered until bubbling and gooey, about 10 more minutes.

12 dried red or black chiles, stemmed and seeded

Choose one or a combo from New Mexico reds, pasillas, mulatos, and/or anchos.

¼ cup loosely packed fresh oregano leaves

Up to 4 medium garlic cloves, peeled

2 teaspoons cumin seeds

½ teaspoon ground cinnamon

½ teaspoon table salt

2 tablespoons solid fat

Choose from butter, rendered bacon fat, lard, duck fat, or schmaltz.

2 medium yellow onions, chopped (2 cups)

3 medium bell peppers, cored, seeded, and chopped (3 cups)

Choose from green, red, orange, and/or yellow bell peppers.

3 pounds boneless, long-cooking red or white meat, diced

Choose from beef bottom round, beef sirloin, beef chuck, pork shoulder, or skinless chicken thighs.

1½ cups liquid

Choose from broth of any sort, or a 50/50 combo of broth and a dark beer, such as a stout or a porter.

Road Map: Chile con Carne

6 servings

Here's the real deal: no beans, no tomatoes, just "chiles with meat" (as its name in Spanish indicates). We've tested this recipe using just New Mexico reds (slightly sweeter and a little hot), a mix of New Mexico reds and anchos (a little more complex and certainly less sweet), a combination of mulatos and pasillas (a bit like a mole version of chili), and a mix of whatever chiles we had in the house and could pick up at the store (a little confusing, but darn tasty). We find that a two-chile mix is best. Crack the dried chiles open and remove all the seeds and as much of their spongy membranes as possible before soaking.

One important note: Whichever meat you choose must be diced to cook in the stated time, the pieces no more than ½ inch in size.

1. Bring a large saucepan of water to a boil over high heat. Turn off the heat, add the chiles, cover the pan, and soak the chiles for 20 minutes to soften. Or do this whole operation in the Instant Pot starting with the SAUTÉ function set to HIGH or MORE until the water boils.

2. Set a colander over a bowl in the sink. Drain the chiles into a colander, catching the soaking liquid below. Put the chiles in a large blender. Add the oregano, garlic, cumin seeds, cinnamon, and salt. Cover and blend, adding at least 1 tablespoon of the soaking liquid in dribs and drabs through the hole in the lid to create a coarse puree but stopping the machine at least once to scrape down the inside. Depending on the moisture content of the chiles, you may end up adding up to ¼ cup of the soaking liquid. Discard any remaining soaking liquid.

3.

Press the button for	Set it for	Set the time for	If necessary, press
SAUTÉ	MEDIUM, NORMAL, or CUSTOM 300°F	10 minutes	START

4. Melt the fat in a **6-quart cooker**. Add the onion and bell pepper. Cook, stirring often, until softened, about 5 minutes. Scrape every drop of the chile paste into the pot. Cook for 1 minute, stirring almost constantly to coat the vegetables.

5. Add the meat and stir to coat in the chile paste. Turn off the SAUTÉ function. Pour in the liquid and stir until uniform. Lock the lid onto the pot.

6.

Press the button for	Set it for	The valve must be	Set the time for	If necessary, press
PRESSURE COOK	MAX	—	10 minutes with the KEEP WARM setting off	START
BEAN/CHILI, PRESSURE COOK, or MANUAL	HIGH	Closed	13 minutes with the KEEP WARM setting off	START
SLOW COOK	HIGH	Opened	4 hours with the KEEP WARM setting off (or on for no more than 2 hours)	START

7. If you've used a pressure setting, when the machine has finished cooking, use the **quick-release method** to bring the pot's pressure back to normal.

8. When ready, unlatch the lid and open the cooker. Stir well before serving.

Beyond

- For a **3-quart cooker**, you must halve all the ingredients.

- For an **8-quart cooker**, you must keep the ingredients as they are but increase the liquid to 1½ cups—or simply double the recipe.

- Top the chili with sour cream, pickle relish, and pickled jalapeño rings.

- For a sweeter but more complex finish, use bourbon, brandy, or even whiskey—no more than 3 tablespoons, filling up the remainder of the liquid volume with broth.

- This is the chili for Frito pie: Lay Fritos on a plate, top with a big ladle of the chili, and then add lots of shredded cheese, even a Tex-Mex blend.

- This is also the chili for an enchilada casserole: Fill tortillas with shredded cheese, roll them up, and lay them in a 9 x 13-inch baking pan. Top with Chile con Carne, then add more shredded cheese on top. Cover and bake in a 350°F oven for 15 minutes, then uncover and continue baking until bubbling and hot, about another 10 minutes.

2 tablespoons olive, vegetable, corn, or canola oil

2 medium green bell peppers, stemmed, cored, and chopped (2 cups)

1 medium yellow onion, chopped (1 cup)

2 medium garlic cloves, peeled and minced (2 teaspoons)

2 pounds plum or Roma tomatoes, chopped (4 cups)

¼ cup standard chile powder

1 tablespoon dried oregano

2 teaspoons ground cumin

1 teaspoon ground coriander

1 teaspoon table salt

One 15-ounce can red kidney beans, drained and rinsed (1⅔ cups)

¾ cup chicken broth

2 pounds lean ground beef

¼ cup tomato paste

Beyond

- For a **3-quart cooker**, you must use ½ cup broth and halve the remaining ingredients.

- For an **8-quart cooker**, you must keep the ingredients as they are but increase the broth to 1¼ cups — or simply increase all the ingredients by 50 percent.

- Serve with dollops of sour cream or plain Greek yogurt.

- And/or serve with spoonfuls of pickle relish, or even purchased India relish (a more savory version of pickle relish), as well as bottled hot red pepper sauce.

- Use a 50/50 mix of lean ground beef and lean ground pork.

Firehouse Chili

6 servings

Here's a chili made with *fresh* tomatoes, not canned. We modeled it on the hearty, comfort-food chilis often made in firehouses across the United States. As such, it's a little more savory than some other offerings, if also admittedly a little more work.

1.

Press the button for	Set it for	Set the time for	If necessary, press
SAUTÉ	MEDIUM, NORMAL, or CUSTOM 300°F	10 minutes	START

2. Pour the oil into a **6-quart cooker** to warm for a minute or two. Then add the bell pepper, onion, and garlic. Cook, stirring often, until the onion softens, about 5 minutes. Stir in the tomatoes and continue cooking, stirring several times, until they begin to soften, about 2 minutes.

3. Stir in the chile powder, oregano, cumin, coriander, and salt until fragrant, just a few seconds. Add the beans and broth, then crumble in the ground beef and stir well. Turn off the SAUTÉ function and lock the lid onto the pot.

4.

Press the button for	Set it for	The valve must be	Set the time for	If necessary, press
PRESSURE COOK	MAX	—	6 minutes with the KEEP WARM setting off	START
BEAN/CHILI, PRESSURE COOK, or MANUAL	HIGH	Closed	8 minutes with the KEEP WARM setting off	START
SLOW COOK	HIGH	Opened	3 hours with the KEEP WARM setting off (or on for no more than 2 hours)	START

5. If you've used a pressure setting, when the machine has finished cooking, use the **quick-release method** to bring the pot's pressure back to normal.

6. Unlatch the lid and open the cooker.

7.

Press the button for	Set it for	Set the time for	If necessary, press
SAUTÉ	MEDIUM, NORMAL, or CUSTOM 300°F	5 minutes	START

8. Stir in the tomato paste. Bring to a full simmer, stirring all the while. Stir for 2 or 3 minutes at a full simmer until a little bit thickened and almost irresistible. Turn off the SAUTÉ function and remove the *hot* insert from the cooker to stop the cooking.

See photo in insert.

Turkey Chili Verde

Makes 6 servings

Good chili verde uses lots of tomatillos. They're a member of the gooseberry family, sort of like small, hard, green tomatoes. They have a tart but savory bite, not citrusy, more earthy-sour.

Fresh ones have a papery husk which must be removed. They can also be sticky at their skins. Give them a quick rinse before chopping.

1.

Press the button for	Set it for	Set the time for	If necessary, press
SAUTÉ	MEDIUM, NORMAL, or CUSTOM 300°F	15 minutes	START

2. Warm the oil in a **6- or 8-quart cooker** for a minute or two. Add the bell pepper, onion, jalapeño, and garlic. Cook, stirring often, until the onion begins to soften, about 5 minutes.

3. Crumble in the ground turkey. Cook, stirring once in a while and breaking up any large chunks, until the turkey begins to brown, about 4 minutes. Stir in the tomatillos, broth, cilantro, oregano, and salt. Turn off the SAUTÉ function and lock the lid onto the pot.

4.

Press the button for	Set it for	The valve must be	Set the time for	If necessary, press
PRESSURE COOK	MAX	—	5 minutes with the KEEP WARM setting off	START
BEAN/CHILI, PRESSURE COOK, or MANUAL	HIGH	Closed	8 minutes with the KEEP WARM setting off	START
SLOW COOK	HIGH	Opened	3 hours with the KEEP WARM setting off (or on for no more than 1 hour)	START

5. If you've used a pressure setting, use the **quick-release method** to bring the pot's pressure back to normal.

6. Unlatch the lid and open the cooker.

7.

Press the button for	Set it for	Set the time for	If necessary, press
SAUTÉ	MEDIUM, NORMAL, or CUSTOM 300°F	5 minutes	START

8. Bring the chili to a full simmer. Stir in the cornmeal. Cook, stirring constantly, until slightly thickened, about 4 minutes. Turn off the SAUTÉ function, set the lid loosely over the pot, and set aside to continue to thicken without any heat for 5 minutes.

2 tablespoons olive oil

2 medium green bell peppers, stemmed, seeded, and chopped (2 cups)

1 medium yellow onion, chopped (1 cup)

Up to 2 fresh medium jalapeño chiles, stemmed, seeded, and chopped (¼ cup)

2 medium garlic cloves, peeled and minced (2 teaspoons)

2 pounds ground turkey

1 pound fresh tomatillos, husked if necessary and chopped

1 cup chicken broth

½ cup loosely packed fresh cilantro leaves, chopped

2½ teaspoons dried oregano

1 teaspoon table salt

2 tablespoons yellow cornmeal

Beyond

- You must halve the recipe for a **3-quart cooker.**

- In a pinch, substitute *one and a half* 28-ounce cans of whole tomatillos, which you must drain and chop.

- Serve with lime wedges to squeeze over the bowls. And have warmed corn tortillas at the ready.

- It's hard to imagine turkey chili verde without sour cream.

- For a brunch, prepare the turkey chili verde as directed, then pour it into a 9 x 13-inch baking dish. Use a large spoon to make up to 8 wells in the chili, then crack a large egg into each. Cover with a light layer of shredded Monterey Jack. Bake in a 350°F oven for 8 to 15 minutes, depending on how you like them.

2 tablespoons vegetable, corn, or canola oil

1 medium yellow onion, chopped (1 cup)

1 pound lean ground beef

1 medium garlic clove, peeled and minced (1 teaspoon)

2 tablespoons standard chile powder

1½ tablespoons unsweetened cocoa powder

1 teaspoon ground allspice

1 teaspoon ground cinnamon

1 teaspoon ground cumin

½ teaspoon table salt

2 cups chicken broth

One 14-ounce can crushed tomatoes (about 1½ cups), preferably fire-roasted

1 tablespoon Worcestershire sauce

1 tablespoon red wine vinegar

8 ounces dried spaghetti

Cincinnati Chili

6 servings

Cincinnati chili is usually served *over* pasta. We decided to make it easier by cooking the pasta right in the pot *with* the chili. So shouldn't this recipe be in the chapter for pasta casseroles? Well, no — because the flavors are so decidedly "chili." The spaghetti picks them up as it cooks under pressure, turning the recipe into a one-pot wonder.

The cocoa powder may be a bit of a surprise. Trust us: Its slightly bitter notes enhance the dish's overall umami goodness. (You don't have to tell picky eaters about the cocoa powder.) Use regular dried spaghetti — not wide pappardelle or thick bucatini, and certainly not thin noodles, which will overcook and turn gummy.

1.

Press the button for	Set it for	Set the time for	If necessary, press
SAUTÉ	MEDIUM, NORMAL, or CUSTOM 300°F	10 minutes	START

2. Warm the oil in **6- or 8-quart cooker** for a minute or two. Add the onion and cook, stirring often, until softened, about 4 minutes. Crumble in the ground beef and cook, stirring often, until it loses its raw, red color, about 3 minutes.

3. Stir in the garlic, chile powder, cocoa powder, allspice, cinnamon, cumin, and salt until fragrant, less than 1 minute. Stir in the broth, crushed tomatoes, Worcestershire sauce, and vinegar.

4. Turn off the SAUTÉ function. Break the dried spaghetti in half and use a wooden spoon to push it into the liquid without its coming in contact with the bottom of the pot. Lock the lid onto the cooker.

5.

Press the button for	Set it for	The valve must be	Set the time for	If necessary, press
PRESSURE COOK	MAX	—	5 minutes with the KEEP WARM setting off	START
BEAN/CHILI, PRESSURE COOK, or MANUAL	HIGH	Closed	7 minutes with the KEEP WARM setting off	START

6. Use the **quick-release method** to bring the pot's pressure back to normal. Unlatch the lid and open the cooker. Stir well before serving.

Beyond

- For a **3-quart cooker**, you must halve the ingredients and break the uncooked spaghetti into thirds.

- For gluten-free pasta, we found the best success with spaghetti made from a mixture of rice and corn.

- Feel free to substitute lean ground pork for the ground beef.

- Top servings with shredded Monterey Jack or Cheddar, particularly a sharp Cheddar.

White Bean and Pumpkin Chili

8 servings

This tomato-free chili has become an American favorite in the past few years with versions served at lots of fast-casual restaurants. It's usually got quite a bit of sugar in the mix. For us, the canned pumpkin is sweet enough to do the trick. The number of servings is a little higher because the chili is so rich and filling. If you've got hearty eaters (or teenagers), it may only serve six.

1. Soak the beans in a big bowl of water for at least 8 hours or up to 12 hours. Drain in a colander set in the sink.

2.

Press the button for	Set it for	Set the time for	If necessary, press
SAUTÉ	MEDIUM, NORMAL, or CUSTOM 300°F	10 minutes	START

3. Warm the oil in a **6- or 8-quart cooker** for a minute or two, then add the onion. Cook, stirring often, until softened, about 3 minutes. Stir in the red pepper and garlic; cook for a few seconds.

4. Crumble in the ground beef. Cook, stirring often, until lightly browned, about 4 minutes. Stir in the chile powder, marjoram or oregano, cinnamon, ginger, and cloves. Cook a few seconds, then pour in the broth and pumpkin. Turn off the SAUTÉ function. Add the beans and stir well until uniform. Lock the lid onto the pot.

5.

Press the button for	Set it for	The valve must be	Set the time for	If necessary, press
PRESSURE COOK	MAX	—	18 minutes with the KEEP WARM setting off	START
BEAN/CHILI, PRESSURE COOK, or MANUAL	HIGH	Closed	25 minutes with the KEEP WARM setting off	START

6. Once the machine has finished cooking, turn it off and let the pressure **return to normal naturally**, about 20 minutes. Unlatch the lid and open the cooker. Stir well before serving.

2 cups dried great northern or cannellini beans

2 tablespoons olive oil

1 medium yellow onion, chopped (1 cup)

1 jarred roasted red pepper, chopped

2 medium garlic cloves, peeled and minced (2 teaspoons)

12 ounces lean ground beef

3 tablespoons standard chile powder

1½ tablespoons dried marjoram or oregano

1 teaspoon ground cinnamon

1 teaspoon ground dried ginger

½ teaspoon ground cloves

1 quart (4 cups) chicken broth

One 15-ounce can solid pack pumpkin (do not use pumpkin pie filling)

Beyond

- You must halve the recipe for a **3-quart cooker**.

- Feel free to substitute lean ground pork or lamb for the ground beef.

- You can substitute 2 teaspoons pumpkin pie spice blend for the cinnamon, ginger, and cloves. Make sure the blend includes no sugar or artificial sweetener.

- Stir in up to 1 cup half-and-half or heavy cream after cooking for a looser, creamier consistency.

- The chili's a little soupier than some others, mostly so there's enough liquid that the beans can cook properly. If it's too wet for your taste, use the SAUTÉ function at MEDIUM, NORMAL, or CUSTOM 300°F after cooking under pressure to boil it down for a couple minutes, stirring quite often.

8 dried chiles, preferably New Mexico
red, passila, ancho, and/or mulato
chiles, stemmed and seeded

½ small red onion, roughly chopped
(¼ cup)

1 canned chipotle in adobo sauce,
stemmed and seeded

2 medium garlic cloves, peeled

1½ tablespoons red wine vinegar

1½ tablespoons honey

1 tablespoon adobo sauce from the
can

1 tablespoon cumin seeds

1 tablespoon dried oregano

1 teaspoon table salt

2 tablespoons olive oil

2 pounds boneless beef brisket, diced

One 12-ounce bottle of beer
(1½ cups), preferably an amber
ale or a pilsner (gluten-free, if
necessary)

1 pound peeled butternut squash
cubes, about 1-inch pieces

Brisket and Butternut Squash Chili

Makes 4 servings

To be flat honest, this chili was our favorite. (It was also the favorite of
our neighbors who ate the results from testing the recipes in this book.)
Sort of like our road map for Chile con Carne (page 116), this one's a
more luxurious take on real-deal chili: savory fare made from dried
chiles, which become the basis for an aromatic paste — without a
tomato or a bean in sight. And using brisket ups the beef quotient
exponentially! To save yourself effort, ask your supermarket's butcher to
slice the meat into ½-inch strips — which you can then more easily dice
into ½-inch pieces. If you buy peeled, seeded, and cut-up butternut
squash in the produce section, you'll have to cut the chunks into smaller
bits.

Note that this recipe is a hybrid of sorts: The first part can be
cooked either under pressure or in the slow cooker, but the second
cooking is *only* done under pressure, thereby making this a potential
weekday dish. Make the chile paste the night before and store the
blender canister in the fridge. Slow-cook the chili during the day, then
add the butternut squash and finish the whole thing off under pressure
just before dinner.

1. Bring a large saucepan of water to a boil over high heat. Turn off the
heat, add the chiles, cover the pan, and soak for 20 minutes. Or do this
whole operation in the Instant Pot, starting with the SAUTÉ function set
to HIGH or MORE until the water boils.

2. Drain the chiles in a colander set in the sink and pile them into a
large blender. Add the onion, chipotle, garlic, vinegar, honey, adobo
sauce, cumin, oregano, and salt. Cover and blend into a coarse paste,
stopping the machine at least once to scrape down the inside.

3.

Press the button for	Set it for	Set the time for	If necessary, press
SAUTÉ	MEDIUM, NORMAL, or CUSTOM 300°F	5 minutes	START

4. Warm the oil in a **6-quart cooker** for a couple of minutes, then add every speck of the chile paste from the blender. Cook for 2 minutes, stirring often, to toast the paste. Add the brisket and stir well to get every little bit coated in the paste. Pour in the beer and stir well. Turn off the SAUTÉ function and lock the lid onto the pot.

5.

Press the button for	Set it for	The valve must be	Set the time for	If necessary, press
PRESSURE COOK	MAX	—	25 minutes with the KEEP WARM setting off	START
BEAN/CHILI, PRESSURE COOK, or MANUAL	HIGH	Closed	32 minutes with the KEEP WARM setting off	START
SLOW COOK	HIGH	Opened	4 hours with the KEEP WARM setting off (or on for no more than 3 hours)	START

6. If you've used a pressure setting, when the machine has finished cooking, use the **quick-release method** to bring the pot's pressure back to normal.

7. Unlatch the lid and open the cooker. Stir in the butternut squash cubes. Lock the lid back onto the pot.

8.

Press the button for	Set it for	The valve must be	Set the time for	If necessary, press
PRESSURE COOK	MAX	—	3 minutes with the KEEP WARM setting off	START
BEAN/CHILI, PRESSURE COOK, or MANUAL	HIGH	Closed	4 minutes with the KEEP WARM setting off	START

9. Use the **quick-release method** to bring the pot's pressure back to normal. Unlatch the lid and open the cooker. Stir well before serving.

Beyond

- For a **3-quart cooker**, you must use 1 cup beer and halve the remaining ingredients.

- For an **8-quart cooker**, you must add 1 cup beef broth with the beer.

- Our favorite dried chile combo was four New Mexico reds and four pasillas. A couple of dried chipotles would add a smoky flavor (and a lot more heat).

- We poured Alabama white barbecue sauce over our bowlfuls: Mix 2 cups regular or low-fat mayonnaise, 1 tablespoon ground black pepper, and 1 teaspoon granulated white sugar in a medium bowl. Whisk in ¼ cup distilled white vinegar, then continue adding more vinegar, maybe up to ¼ cup more, until the mixture is the consistency of a sauce, not a spread.

One 28-ounce can diced tomatoes
(3½ cups), preferably fire-roasted

One 12-ounce bottle Guinness stout
(1½ cups)

2 tablespoons pure chile powder

2 tablespoons mild smoked paprika

1 teaspoon ground cumin

1 teaspoon dried oregano

1 medium yellow onion, chopped
(1 cup)

2 pounds low-sodium raw corned
beef, rinsed and any spice packets
removed, the meat diced

Two 15-ounce cans pink beans
(3⅓ cups), drained and rinsed

Beyond

- You must halve the recipe for a
  3-quart cooker.

- To make a corned beef and cabbage
  chili, omit the beans and stir a
  1-pound bag of slaw mix into the
  stew in step 3 before the second
  round of cooking.

- The chili is a bit loose, a bit soupy.
  We preferred that texture with the
  corned beef. You can boil it down
  further by setting the machine to its
  SAUTÉ function at MEDIUM, NORMAL, or
  CUSTOM 300°F after step 5 and
  simmering it, uncovered, for a
  couple of minutes.

- To do without the alcohol, substitute
  1½ cups beef broth, ¼ cup
  unsweetened apple cider, and 2
  teaspoons apple cider vinegar for
  the beer.

- To cook this dish on the SLOW COOK
  mode, put all the ingredients in the
  pot up front, lock on the lid, keep the
  pressure valve open, and press the
  SLOW COOK function for 4 hours on
  HIGH with the KEEP WARM function set
  for up to 2 hours.

Corned Beef Chili with Guinness

Makes 6 servings

Purchased corned beef is terrific for chili! (The cut is just brisket, after
all.) It adds a briny savoriness, sort of like a New York deli version of
Midwestern comfort food, laced with stout and beans: a rib-sticker if
there ever was one. Stock up on corned beef after Saint Patrick's Day
when the packages are on sale. Put a couple in the freezer for a winter
night when you're ready for this hearty stew.

1. Mix the tomatoes, Guinness, chile powder, smoked paprika, cumin,
oregano, onion, and corned beef in a **6- or 8-quart cooker** until
uniform. Lock the lid onto the pot.

2.

Press the button for	Set it for	The valve must be	Set the time for	If necessary, press
PRESSURE COOK	MAX	—	22 minutes with the KEEP WARM setting off	START
BEAN/CHILI, PRESSURE COOK, or MANUAL	HIGH	Closed	30 minutes with the KEEP WARM setting off	START

3. Use the **quick-release method** to bring the pot's pressure back to
normal. Unlatch the lid and open the pot. Stir in the beans. Lock the lid
back onto the pot.

4.

Press the button for	Set it for	The valve must be	Set the time for	If necessary, press
PRESSURE COOK	MAX	—	3 minutes with the KEEP WARM setting off	START
BEAN/CHILI, PRESSURE COOK, or MANUAL	HIGH	Closed	4 minutes with the KEEP WARM setting off	START

5. Use the **quick-release method** to bring the pot's pressure back to
normal. Unlatch the lid, open the pot, and stir well before serving.

Bacon and Black Bean Chili

Makes 4 servings

Bacon? Chili? Together at last! Use thick-cut bacon strips so the chili has chunks of porky goodness in every spoonful. Or just use slab bacon. It's a pain to dice, but it will be even chewier in the mix. Also keep this in mind: Leaner bacon (of any sort) is a better choice. If the bacon's too fatty, it can leave an unappealing grease slick in the serving bowls.

1.

Press the button for	Set it for	Set the time for	If necessary, press
SAUTÉ	MEDIUM, NORMAL, or CUSTOM 300°F	15 minutes	START

2. Melt the butter in a **6- or 8-quart cooker**. Add the bacon and onion. Cook, stirring often, until the bacon begins to brown well, about 8 minutes. Stir in the beer. Scrape up *every speck of browned stuff* on the pot's bottom.

3. Turn off the SAUTÉ function. Stir in the tomatoes, black beans, chile powder, cumin, garlic, and canned chipotles. Lock the lid onto the pot.

4.

Press the button for	Set it for	The valve must be	Set the time for	If necessary, press
PRESSURE COOK	MAX	—	8 minutes with the KEEP WARM setting off	START
BEAN/CHILI, PRESSURE COOK, or MANUAL	HIGH	Closed	10 minutes with the KEEP WARM setting off	START
SLOW COOK	HIGH	Opened	4 hours with the KEEP WARM setting off (or on for no more than 2 hours)	START

5. If you've used a pressure setting, when the machine has finished cooking, use the **quick-release method** to bring the pot's pressure back to normal.

6. Unlatch the lid and open the cooker. Stir well before serving.

1 tablespoon butter

1 pound thick-cut or slab bacon (not pepper bacon or other flavored bacon), chopped

1 medium yellow onion, chopped (1 cup)

¾ cup amber beer or chicken broth

One 28-ounce can diced tomatoes (3½ cups)

One 15-ounce can black beans, drained and rinsed (1⅔ cups)

2½ tablespoons pure chile powder

2 teaspoons ground cumin

2 medium garlic cloves, peeled and minced (2 teaspoons)

Up to 2 canned chipotles in adobo sauce, stemmed, seeded, and chopped

Beyond

- You must halve the recipe for a **3-quart cooker**.

- This chili *needs* crunchy bread. Warm a baguette in the oven until the bread gets a crackly crust, so crackly it's almost a crouton.

- For a richer chili, whisk up to 1 cup plain Greek yogurt into the chili after cooking. Do not allow it to come back to a simmer or the yogurt will break.

- For more heat, search for super-hot ground Chimayo chile powder (usually found at East Indian markets).

- For a more sophisticated take, add ½ teaspoon ground cardamom, ½ teaspoon ground cinnamon, and/ or ¼ teaspoon grated nutmeg with the cumin.

1 pound boneless skinless chicken breasts, cut into ½-inch-wide strips

Two 15-ounce cans white beans, drained and rinsed (3⅓ cups)

1½ cups chicken broth

1 medium yellow onion, chopped (1 cup)

Two 4½-ounce cans mild or hot chopped green chiles (1 cup)

2 medium garlic cloves, peeled and minced (2 teaspoons)

2 teaspoons dried oregano

2 teaspoons ground cumin

¼ cup heavy cream

2 tablespoons yellow cornmeal

2 cups shredded Monterey Jack, Colby, or white Cheddar cheese

White Chili

Makes 4 servings

In the mood for a little decadence? Add cream to your chili! Here's a version of so-called "white" chili: sweet-and-sour (from canned green chiles), comforting, and hearty. It doesn't freeze well: The cream tends to break and the cornmeal settles to the bottom of the batch. Plan on eating it up when it's ready. By the way, there's no salt because the canned green chiles are notoriously sodium-rich. Pass salt at the table, if you wish.

1. Mix the chicken, beans, broth, onion, chiles, garlic, oregano, and cumin in a **6- or 8-quart cooker**. Lock the lid onto the pot.

2.

Press the button for	Set it for	The valve must be	Set the time for	If necessary, press
PRESSURE COOK	MAX	—	5 minutes with the KEEP WARM setting off	START
BEAN/CHILI, PRESSURE COOK, or MANUAL	HIGH	Closed	7 minutes with the KEEP WARM setting off	START

3. Use the **quick-release method** to bring the pot's pressure back to normal. Unlatch the lid and open the cooker.

4.

Press the button for	Set it for	Set the time for	If necessary, press
SAUTÉ	MEDIUM, NORMAL, or CUSTOM 300°F	5 minutes	START

5. Bring the chili to a simmer. Stir in the cream and cornmeal. Cook, stirring constantly, until the chili thickens somewhat, about 3 minutes. Turn off the SAUTÉ function and remove the *hot* insert from the machine. Sprinkle the cheese over the chili. Set the lid ajar over the insert for 5 minutes to melt the cheese.

Beyond

- You must halve the recipe for a **3-quart cooker**.

- We prefer the texture of the chicken strips. However, you can substitute 1 pound ground turkey (ground chicken gets depressingly squishy). Crumble the ground meat into marble-size bits in the pot.

- Add a heavy grind of black pepper (and even some red pepper flakes) over the melted cheese before serving.

Road Map: Bean Chili

Makes 6 servings

Nothing makes great bean chili like dried beans. But not every dried bean is created equal. Listen, the world's a mess. Hectic, too. Dried beans sit on the store's shelf for, um, forever. They can dry out so much that no matter how long you cook them, they never get tender.

Don't let any of that deter you from making your own brand of bean chili. Instead, look for plump beans (even in their dried state) in the package. They shouldn't be chipped up at the bottom of the bag. Once soaked, they should have definitely gotten fatter, doubled (or maybe even more) in size. For more information about dried beans, see page 47–48.

The herbs and spices you choose are what will make this your signature recipe. We have a preference for oregano, thyme, and cinnamon with a pinch of ground cloves. You might prefer all oregano, or a mix of sage and thyme with just a pinch of nutmeg.

If you open the pot and they're still too tough for your taste, lock the lid back in place and give them another 5 to 10 minutes at HIGH pressure, followed by the **quick-release method**.

1. Soak the dried beans in a big bowl of water for at least 8 hours or up to 12 hours, until nicely plumped. Drain in a colander set in the sink, then pour the beans into a **6- or 8-quart cooker**.

2. Stir in the broth, tomatoes, aromatics, root vegetables, quick-cooking vegetables, chile powder, fresh herbs and/or dried spices, enricher, and salt (if using). Lock the lid onto the pot.

3.

Press the button for	Set it for	The valve must be	Set the time for	If necessary, press
PRESSURE COOK	MAX	—	18 minutes with the KEEP WARM setting off	START
BEAN/CHILI, PRESSURE COOK, or MANUAL	HIGH	Closed	25 minutes with the KEEP WARM setting off	START

4. Once the machine has finished cooking, turn it off and let the pressure **return to normal naturally**, about 20 minutes. Unlock and open the lid. Stir well before serving.

2 cups medium-sized dried beans
Choose one or a combo from black, great northern, cannellini, pink, adzuki, and/or navy.

3 cups vegetable broth

One 14-ounce can crushed tomatoes (1¾ cups)

1½ cups chopped aromatics
Choose one or any combo from onions (of any sort), shallots, stemmed and seeded bell peppers of any sort, celery, trimmed fennel, and/or jarred roasted red peppers.

1½ cups diced root vegetables
Choose from carrots, parsnips, sweet potatoes, winter squash (such as butternut squash), yellow beets, turnips, or celeriac.

1 cup quick-cooking vegetables
Choose one or a 50/50 combo from diced zucchini, diced summer squash, trimmed and chopped green beans, chopped or small broccoli florets, chopped or small cauliflower florets, and/or corn kernels.

3 tablespoons pure chile powder
Choose from ancho, New Mexico red, New Mexico hatch, chipotle, or a pure chile blend.

2 tablespoons stemmed fresh green herbs or dried spices
Choose a blend from oregano, marjoram, sage, thyme, cumin, cinnamon, cloves, and/or nutmeg.

1 tablespoon flavor enricher
Choose from Dijon mustard, ketchup, sweet chile sauce, Worcestershire sauce, or chutney.

½ teaspoon table salt (optional)

Beyond

- You must halve the recipe for a **3-quart cooker**.
- Keep it vegan by garnishing the bowls with fresh, minced, seeded jalapeños, minced scallions, and even a vegan barbecue sauce.

1 quart (4 cups) vegetable broth

One 28-ounce can diced tomatoes (3½ cups), preferably petite diced

One 15-ounce can great northern or cannellini beans, drained and rinsed (1⅔ cups)

One 15-ounce can pink beans, drained and rinsed (1⅔ cups)

One 15-ounce can black beans, drained and rinsed (1⅔ cups)

One 12-ounce bottle beer (1½ cups), preferably a pale ale (and gluten-free, if necessary)

1 medium yellow onion, chopped (1 cup)

½ cup chana dal (that is, split and processed chickpeas)

½ cup buckwheat groats

½ cup green lentils (that is, le Puy lentils)

⅓ cup standard chile powder

1 tablespoon ground cumin

1 tablespoon dried oregano

½ teaspoon ground cloves

½ teaspoon ground dried mustard

½ teaspoon table salt

The Ultimate Vegan Chili

Makes 8 servings

You won't believe the texture of this chili! Even if you're a committed carnivore, you'll swear there's ground meat in the bowl, thanks to the mix of chana dal, buckwheat groats, and lentils. They provide an unbelievably savory foundation for a chili that's then stocked with beans. Admittedly, there are some funky ingredients in the list. Stock up because you're going to want to make this chili more than once. After all, there's nothing to it except stirring everything in the pot, then getting the pressure going. (For a discussion about why buckwheat is gluten-free, see page 407.)

1. Mix all the ingredients in a **6- or 8-quart cooker**. Lock the lid onto the pot.

2.

Press the button for	Set it for	The valve must be	Set the time for	If necessary, press
PRESSURE COOK	MAX	—	20 minutes with the KEEP WARM setting off	START
BEAN/CHILI, PRESSURE COOK, or MANUAL	HIGH	Closed	27 minutes with the KEEP WARM setting off	START
SLOW COOK	HIGH	Opened	4 hours with the KEEP WARM setting off (or on for no more than 2 hours)	START

3. If you've used a pressure setting, when the machine has finished cooking, use the **quick-release method** to bring the pot's pressure back to normal.

4. Unlock and open the lid. Stir well before serving.

Beyond

- You must halve the recipe for a **3-quart cooker**.

- If you don't want the alcohol, substitute 1½ cups unsweetened apple cider for the beer.

- There's no reason to stand on ceremony with the beans. You can use any combination — or just, for example, all pink beans. (Or whatever's on sale.) Use medium-sized beans, nothing big like lima beans or too small like navy beans.

Quinoa Chili

Makes 4 servings

Quinoa makes a thick, almost porridge-like chili — which is why the beans help give this version a little tooth, a better texture against the silkiness. Quinoa has a naturally occurring enzyme (a saponin) that protects the grains from, well, predators (aka us). Not only does the enzyme taste bitter, but it can foam in the pressure cooker and cause the pot to malfunction. Rinse the grains well in a fine-mesh sieve such as a *chinois* or in a colander lined with a double thickness of paper towels. We do this even if the package says they've already been rinsed.

1. Stir all the ingredients in a **6-quart cooker**. Lock the lid onto the pot.

2.

Press the button for	Set it for	The valve must be	Set the time for	If necessary, press
PRESSURE COOK	MAX	—	6 minutes with the KEEP WARM setting off	START
BEAN/CHILI, PRESSURE COOK, or MANUAL	HIGH	Closed	8 minutes with the KEEP WARM setting off	START
SLOW COOK	HIGH	Opened	3 hours with the KEEP WARM setting off (or on for no more than 1 hour)	START

3. If you've used a pressure setting, when the machine has finished cooking, use the **quick-release method** to bring the pot's pressure back to normal.

4. Unlock and remove the lid. Stir well before serving.

2 cups vegetable broth

1 cup red or white quinoa, well rinsed

One 15-ounce can red kidney beans, drained and rinsed (1¾ cups)

One 14-ounce can diced tomatoes (1¾ cups)

One 4½-ounce can mild or hot green chiles (½ cup)

2 jarred roasted red peppers, chopped

1 small zucchini (about 6 ounces), chopped

2 medium garlic cloves, peeled and minced (2 teaspoons)

1 tablespoon pure chile powder

2 teaspoons ground cumin

2 teaspoons dried oregano

Beyond

- For an **8-quart cooker**, you must increase all the ingredients by 50 percent.

- Because of the quinoa's need to dance in lots of liquid, we do not recommend making this chili in a **3-quart cooker**.

- Add up to ½ cup chopped onion and/or ½ cup chopped celery for a veggie-heavy chili.

- This chili would be a savory topping for chili dogs (whether you use vegan hot dogs or the more standard-issue ones).

2 tablespoons vegetable, corn, or canola oil

1 large yellow onion, chopped (1 cup)

1 medium red bell pepper, stemmed, cored, and chopped (1 cup)

2 celery ribs, thinly sliced (⅔ cup)

2 medium garlic cloves, peeled and minced (2 teaspoons)

1¾ pounds lean ground beef

1 cup beef or chicken broth

½ cup ketchup

1 tablespoon yellow mustard (don't you dare use Dijon)

1 tablespoon molasses

1 tablespoon standard chile powder

2 teaspoons apple cider vinegar

½ teaspoon table salt

6 to 8 regular hamburger buns

Beyond

- This chili may be gluten-free depending on the buns, of course—but more importantly, the ketchup. Some are made with vinegars crafted from wheat. Hunt's uses vinegar distilled from corn and is considered gluten-free.

- Sloppy joes are notoriously messy, maybe even a fork-and-knife affair. We tend to serve them to kids in hot dog buns.

- If you don't mind alcohol, substitute a pale ale or amber beer for the broth.

- Even though there's mustard in the mix, we still like to smear more on the buns before we add the sloppy joe mixture. Dill pickle slices are pretty tasty, too.

Classic Sloppy Joes

Makes 6 to 8 sandwiches

Hello, elementary school cafeteria! This recipe will give you the classic sloppy joe, an American favorite since the 1960s. Traditionally, the ground beef mixture is thickened with tomato paste. We felt it muddied the flavors and wanted a more characteristic, sweet/sour palette from the pot. So we advocate for using ketchup and boiling down the mixture after cooking. The flavors stay brighter. And you can control how sloppy you want your joes. We prefer a 20-napkin event.

1.

Press the button for	Set it for	Set the time for	If necessary, press
SAUTÉ	MEDIUM, NORMAL, or CUSTOM 300°F	10 minutes	START

2. Warm the oil in a **3-, 6-, or 8-quart cooker** for a minute or two, then add the onion, bell pepper, celery, and garlic. Cook, stirring often, until the onion begins to soften, about 4 minutes.

3. Crumble in the ground beef. Continue cooking, stirring fairly often and breaking up any clumps of ground beef, until the meat begins to brown, about 5 minutes. Turn off the SAUTÉ function. Stir in the broth, ketchup, mustard, molasses, chile powder, vinegar, and salt until uniform. Lock the lid onto the pot.

4.

Press the button for	Set it for	The valve must be	Set the time for	If necessary, press
PRESSURE COOK	MAX	—	4 minutes with the KEEP WARM setting off	START
BEAN/CHILI, PRESSURE COOK, or MANUAL	HIGH	Closed	5 minutes with the KEEP WARM setting off	START

5. Use the **quick-release method** to bring the pot's pressure back to normal. Unlatch the lid and open the cooker.

6.

Press the button for	Set it for	Set the time for	If necessary, press
SAUTÉ	LOW or LESS	10 minutes	START

7. Bring the mixture to a low simmer. Cook, stirring fairly often, until thickened and not as soupy, about 7 minutes. Turn off the SAUTÉ function, set the lid ajar over the pot, and set aside for 5 to 10 minutes to blend the flavors. Spoon the mixture into the hamburger buns.

Loaded Whole-Grain Sloppy Joes

Makes 6 to 8 sandwiches

Okay, these are not for the elementary school set. They're stocked with wheat berries and oats for a satisfying meal. There's no need to boil this mixture down since the oats will thicken it to hold together more easily than the filling for Classic Sloppy Joes (page 131). Plus, you can have old-school comfort food *and* eat healthy. Take your victories where you can.

1. Mix the water, wheat berries, and oil in a **6-quart cooker**. Lock the lid onto the pot.

2.

Press the button for	Set it for	The valve must be	Set the time for	If necessary, press
PRESSURE COOK	MAX	—	30 minutes with the KEEP WARM setting off	START
PRESSURE COOK or MANUAL	HIGH	Closed	40 minutes with the KEEP WARM setting off	START

3. Use the **quick-release method** to bring the pot's pressure back to normal. Unlatch the lid and open the cooker. Drain the wheat berries from the *hot* insert into a colander set in the sink. Rinse out the insert, return it to the cooker, and put the wheat berries back in the insert.

4. Stir in the tomatoes, chiles, onion, oats, molasses, mustard, Worcestershire sauce, vinegar, paprika, cloves, garlic powder, and salt. Crumble in the ground beef and stir until uniform, breaking up any large clumps. Lock the lid onto the pot.

5.

Press the button for	Set it for	The valve must be	Set the time for	If necessary, press
PRESSURE COOK	MAX	—	5 minutes with the KEEP WARM setting off	START
PRESSURE COOK or MANUAL	HIGH	Closed	7 minutes with the KEEP WARM setting off	START

6. Use the **quick-release method** to return the pot's pressure to normal. Unlatch the lid and open the cooker. Stir well before serving in hamburger buns.

3 cups water

½ cup dried wheat berries, preferably soft white wheat berries

1 tablespoon vegetable, corn, or canola oil

One 28-ounce can diced tomatoes (3½ cups)

One 4½-ounce can mild or hot chopped green chiles (½ cup)

1 small yellow onion, chopped (½ cup)

½ cup rolled oats (do not use quick-cooking or steel-cut)

¼ cup molasses

2 tablespoons Dijon mustard

2 tablespoons Worcestershire sauce

2 tablespoons red wine vinegar

2 tablespoons mild paprika

½ teaspoon ground cloves

½ teaspoon garlic powder

¼ teaspoon table salt

1½ pounds lean ground beef

6 to 8 hamburger buns

Beyond

- You must halve the recipe for a **3-quart cooker**.

- For an **8-quart cooker**, you must use the ingredients as stated but add ½ cup broth (or water) with the ground beef.

- Garlic powder gives the dish a more assertive garlic flavor than minced cloves. But if desired, substitute up to 2 teaspoons peeled and minced garlic.

1 tablespoon olive oil

1 medium yellow onion, chopped (1 cup)

1 medium red bell pepper, stemmed, cored, and chopped (1 cup)

3 cups vegetable broth

2 cups green lentils (that is, le Puy lentils)

One 14-ounce can crushed tomatoes (1¾ cups)

2 tablespoons soy sauce

1 tablespoon Dijon mustard

1 tablespoon dark brown sugar

1 teaspoon ground black pepper

6 hamburger buns

Vegan Sloppy Joes

Makes 6 sandwiches

Earthy lentils mixed with soy sauce and mustard make a pretty fine sloppy joe filling, provided you mash some of the cooked lentils into a puree to thicken the mixture. We've added some brown sugar because lentils are so savory. You could halve the amount of sugar, but don't omit it. Only use green lentils; the brown ones are too mushy for a successful sandwich filling.

1.

Press the button for	Set it for	Set the time for	If necessary, press
SAUTÉ	MEDIUM, NORMAL, or CUSTOM 300°F	5 minutes	START

2. Warm the oil in a **6- or 8-quart cooker** for a minute or two. Add the onion and bell pepper. Cook, stirring often, until the onion begins to soften, about 4 minutes. Turn off the SAUTÉ function. Stir in the broth, lentils, tomatoes, soy sauce, mustard, brown sugar, and pepper. Lock the lid onto the pot.

3.

Press the button for	Set it for	The valve must be	Set the time for	If necessary, press
PRESSURE COOK	MAX	—	18 minutes with the KEEP WARM setting off	START
BEAN/CHILI, PRESSURE COOK, or MANUAL	HIGH	Closed	24 minutes with the KEEP WARM setting off	START

4. When the pot is done cooking, turn it off and let its pressure **return to normal naturally**, about 25 minutes. Unlatch the lid and open the cooker. Use a potato masher or the back of a wooden spoon to mash some of the lentils into a puree, stirring them into the sauce to thicken it. Serve in hamburger buns.

Beyond

- You must halve the recipe for a **3-quart cooker**.

- For condiments in the buns, slice a red onion and a navel orange (peel and all) into very thin rounds (less than ¼ inch thick — and seeded for the orange). Coat these in olive oil and grill them until soft or even charred.

- Skip the buns and serve the lentil filling alongside scrambled eggs and grilled sausages for breakfast.

Buttery Marinara Sauce

Makes enough for 1½ pounds dried pasta

Here's a decadent marinara in the style of a recipe from the great and now-sadly-gone Italian cookbook author, Marcella Hazan. The whole thing's about as satisfying as any sauce we can imagine. We even thinned it out with extra broth and cream one day and ate it for lunch as tomato soup with crunchy toast. Pure heaven.

Two 28-ounce cans diced tomatoes (7 cups)

2 medium yellow onions, peeled and halved

Up to 4 medium garlic cloves, peeled and minced (4 teaspoons)

1 stick (8 tablespoons) butter, cut into chunks

1 teaspoon dried oregano

½ teaspoon ground black pepper

¼ teaspoon table salt

1. Stir all the ingredients in a **6-quart cooker**. Lock the lid onto the pot.

2.

Press the button for	Set it for	The valve must be	Set the time for	If necessary, press
PRESSURE COOK	MAX	—	4 minutes with the KEEP WARM setting off	START
PRESSURE COOK or MANUAL	HIGH	Closed	5 minutes with the KEEP WARM setting off	START

3. Use the **quick-release method** to return the pot's pressure to normal. Unlatch the lid and open the cooker. Fish out and discard the onion halves (or pieces, if they've come apart). Either use an immersion blender in the pot to puree the mixture into a sauce; or pour the mixture into a large blender, cover, and blend until smooth.

Beyond

- You must halve the recipe for a **3-quart cooker**.

- For an **8-quart cooker**, you must increase all the ingredients by 50 percent.

- To make this sauce even more savory, add up to 2 minced, tinned anchovy fillets and/or up to ½ teaspoon red pepper flakes with the other ingredients. (Omit the salt if adding anchovy fillets.)

Two 28-ounce cans whole tomatoes, drained

½ cup regular or low-fat evaporated milk

½ small yellow onion, chopped (½ cup)

¼ cup loosely packed fresh basil leaves, roughly chopped

1 tablespoon fresh rosemary leaves, chopped (optional)

½ teaspoon table salt

¼ cup heavy cream

2 tablespoons tomato paste

Creamy Tomato and Basil Pasta Sauce

Makes enough for 2 pounds dried pasta

This super rich pasta sauce is best in small doses with thick pasta like bucatini, rather than spaghetti. We've also made pasta casseroles with the sauce — and have even used it as the tomato sauce in a meat-free lasagna.

1. Wash and dry your hands. Crush the canned tomatoes one by one into a **6-quart cooker**. Add the evaporated milk, onion, basil, rosemary (if using), and salt. Stir well and lock the lid onto the pot.

2.

Press the button for	Set it for	The valve must be	Set the time for	If necessary, press
PRESSURE COOK	MAX	—	4 minutes with the KEEP WARM setting off	START
PRESSURE COOK or MANUAL	HIGH	Closed	5 minutes with the KEEP WARM setting off	START

3. Use the **quick-release method** to bring the pot's pressure back to normal. Unlatch the lid and open the cooker. Stir in the cream and tomato paste. Either use an immersion blender to puree the sauce right in the pot, or pour the contents of the pot into a large blender, cover, and blend until smooth, scraping down the canister's inside at least once.

Beyond

- For a **3-quart cooker**, you must use the full amount of evaporated milk but halve the remaining ingredients.

- For an **8-quart cooker**, you must add ½ cup vegetable or chicken broth with the evaporated milk.

- Add up to 1 teaspoon minced garlic with the basil.

- Grate nutmeg over the servings.

- Warm about ½ inch of olive oil in a large skillet set over medium-high heat until wavy. Fry whole basil leaves in the oil until blistered, about 1 minute, turning once. Use these to garnish the pasta.

- For a vodka sauce, substitute vodka for the evaporated milk.

See photo in insert.

Arrabbiata Sauce

Makes enough for 1 pound dried pasta

This version of the super-spicy sauce is fairly traditional in that it includes no onion — the better to let the heat blaze through. If you're worried, remember that pressure cookers eat up capsaicin, the burning chemical in chiles. Still, your first time you might want to use only one chile and cut down on the red pepper flakes (to, say, ½ teaspoon), just to make sure you like the fire as much as you think you do. However, red pepper flakes are not all created equal. Some are tame, almost dull; others, hellacious. Sample one of yours to know what you've got.

¼ cup olive oil

2 medium fresh Anaheim or jalapeño chiles, stemmed and thinly sliced

Up to 1 teaspoon red pepper flakes

6 medium garlic cloves, peeled and minced (2 tablespoons)

2 tinned anchovy fillets, minced

½ cup red (or sweet) vermouth

One 28-ounce can whole tomatoes (3½ cups)

1.

Press the button for	Set it for	Set the time for	If necessary, press
SAUTÉ	LOW or LESS	10 minutes	START

2. Warm the oil in a **3- or 6-quart cooker** for a minute or two. Add the chiles and red pepper flakes. Cook, stirring occasionally, until the oil turns orange and becomes spicy-fragrant, about 4 minutes. Add the garlic and anchovy. Cook, stirring almost constantly, until the anchovy bits almost dissolve, about 3 minutes. Pour in the vermouth and scrape up any browned bits on the bottom of the pot. Turn off the SAUTÉ function.

3. Clean and dry your hands. Pick up the whole tomatoes one by one from the can and crush them over the pot, letting the bits and pieces fall inside. When you've crushed all the tomatoes, pour in any remaining juice from the can. Lock the lid onto the pot.

4.

Press the button for	Set it for	The valve must be	Set the time for	If necessary, press
PRESSURE COOK	MAX	—	3 minutes with the KEEP WARM setting off	START
SOUP/BROTH, PRESSURE COOK, or MANUAL	HIGH	Closed	5 minutes with the KEEP WARM setting off	START

5. Use the **quick-release method** to bring the pot's pressure back to normal. Unlatch the lid and open the cooker. Stir well before serving.

Beyond

- For an **8-quart cooker**, you must add ¼ cup vegetable broth (or water) with the vermouth.

- Toss this pasta sauce with cooked and drained penne or ziti.

- Try a little balsamic vinegar as the condiment over the servings of pasta.

- Also, consider sprinkling each serving with finely chopped fresh parsley leaves.

3½ pounds cherry tomatoes, halved (use every drop of juice)

1 medium leek (about 4½ ounces), white and pale green part only, halved, washed well, and thinly sliced (⅓ cup)

¼ cup vegetable broth

¼ cup dry white wine or dry vermouth

3 tablespoons olive oil

2 tablespoons fresh rosemary leaves, minced

2 tablespoons fresh thyme leaves, minced

1 teaspoon granulated white sugar

1 teaspoon table salt

Cherry Tomato and Herb Pasta Sauce

Makes enough for 2 pounds dried pasta

Light, sweet, and herbaceous — what more can we say about this simple sauce made from cherry tomatoes? Use the freshest you can find — and none larger than a golf ball. Only true cherry tomatoes will work here, not grape or other tiny tomatoes. They're not juicy enough. If you find terrific ripe cherry tomatoes at a farmers' market, make a couple batches of the sauce for the freezer.

1. Mix all the ingredients in a **6- or 8-quart cooker**. Lock the lid onto the pot.

2.

Press the button for	Set it for	The valve must be	Set the time for	If necessary, press
PRESSURE COOK	MAX	—	4 minutes with the KEEP WARM setting off	START
PRESSURE COOK or MANUAL	HIGH	Closed	5 minutes with the KEEP WARM setting off	START

3. When the machine has finished cooking, turn it off and let the pot's pressure **return to normal naturally**, about 10 minutes. Unlatch the lid and open the cooker. Use a potato masher to crush the sauce into a loose puree, or use the back of a wooden spoon to press the sauce against the sides of the pot.

4.

Press the button for	Set it for	Set the time for	If necessary, press
SAUTÉ	MEDIUM, NORMAL, or CUSTOM 300°F	5 minutes	START

5. Bring the sauce to a simmer, stirring occasionally. Cook, stirring once in a while, until thickened somewhat, not pasty, just less soupy, about 3 minutes. Turn off the SAUTÉ function and stir well before serving.

Beyond

- For a **3-quart cooker**, you must use the full amount of broth and halve the remaining ingredients.

- For a more robust flavor, add up to 2 teaspoons minced garlic with the leek.

- If you don't have a leek on hand, substitute 2 chopped medium shallots.

- Stir chopped deli ham and broccoli florets into the hot sauce to make a heartier meal.

Eggplant and Caper Pasta Sauce

Makes enough for 1½ pounds dried pasta

This recipe makes a lot of sauce. And with pasta, it's more of a meal than a first course or a side dish, given how stocked the sauce is. We used jarred marinara because we wanted that smooth texture without having to create a marinara, puree it, and then carry on with the eggplant recipe. That said, you can always make your own Buttery Marinara Sauce (page 133) and use it here.

2 tablespoons butter

1 medium yellow onion, chopped (1 cup)

2 medium garlic cloves, peeled and minced (2 teaspoons)

One 1-pound eggplant, diced (3½ cups)

1 medium yellow or green bell pepper, stemmed, cored, and chopped (1 cup)

1 tablespoon drained and rinsed capers, chopped

One 24-ounce jar plain marinara sauce (3 cups)

½ cup vegetable broth

¼ cup loosely packed fresh parsley leaves

1.

Press the button for	Set it for	Set the time for	If necessary, press
SAUTÉ	MEDIUM, NORMAL, or CUSTOM 300°F	10 minutes	START

2. Melt the butter in a **3- or 6-quart pot**, then add the onion. Cook, stirring often, until softened, about 3 minutes. Add the garlic and cook for a few seconds, until fragrant.

3. Add the eggplant, bell pepper, and capers. Stir for 1 minute. Turn off the SAUTÉ function. Pour in the marinara sauce, broth, and parsley and stir until uniform. Lock the lid on the pot.

4.

Press the button for	Set it for	The valve must be	Set the time for	If necessary, press
PRESSURE COOK	MAX	—	6 minutes with the KEEP WARM setting off	START
PRESSURE COOK or MANUAL	HIGH	Closed	8 minutes with the KEEP WARM setting off	START
SLOW COOK	HIGH	Opened	2 hours with the KEEP WARM setting off (or on for no more than 1 hour)	START

5. If you've used a pressure setting, when the machine has finished cooking, use the **quick-release method** to bring the pot's pressure back to normal.

6. Unlatch the lid and open the cooker. Stir well before serving.

Beyond

- For an **8-quart cooker**, you must increase the broth to ¾ cup (use the remaining ingredients as stated).

- Top the sauced pasta with lots of finely grated Parmigiano-Reggiano or crumbled feta.

2 tablespoons butter

1 medium yellow onion, chopped (1 cup)

2 medium celery ribs, thinly sliced (½ cup)

1 medium carrot, thinly sliced (½ cup)

2 medium garlic cloves, peeled and minced (2 teaspoons)

1¼ pounds lean ground beef

½ cup canned regular or low-fat evaporated milk

One 28-ounce can whole tomatoes

2 tablespoons Italian seasoning blend, preferably salt-free

½ teaspoon grated nutmeg

¼ teaspoon table salt

¼ teaspoon ground black pepper

One 6-ounce can tomato paste

Classic Bolognese Sauce

Makes enough for 2 pounds dried pasta

Sometimes, nothing will do except the classic. Here's a sauce from the Instant Pot that preserves the traditional creamy/chunky texture so prized in a fine Bolognese, thanks mostly to the magic of evaporated milk (which won't break under pressure).

It's really more of a ragù, although not usually so labeled in American cooking — so this one's a main course (with pasta, of course, or maybe Polenta, page 443). While the recipe does require a bit of work, it doesn't force you into a half-day simmer on the stove, the way a more traditional recipe would. You'll still end up with a traditional meat sauce, the center of a great meal.

1.

Press the button for	Set it for	Set the time for	If necessary, press
SAUTÉ	MEDIUM, NORMAL, or CUSTOM 300°F	15 minutes	START

2. Melt the butter in a **6- or 8-quart cooker**. Add the onion, celery, carrot, and garlic. Cook, stirring often, until the onion begins to soften, about 5 minutes. Crumble in the ground beef and cook, breaking up any clumps, just until the meat loses all its pink, raw color, about 3 minutes.

3. Pour in the evaporated milk and scrape up any browned bits on the bottom of the pot. Cook, stirring quite a bit, until the milk comes to a full simmer, then continue cooking until the milk has reduced to about half its original volume, about 3 minutes.

4. Wash and dry your hands. Crush the whole tomatoes one by one into the pot, then pour any remaining juice from the can into the pot. Stir well, then turn off the SAUTÉ function. Stir in the seasoning blend, nutmeg, salt, and pepper. Lock the lid onto the pot.

5.

Press the button for	Set it for	The valve must be	Set the time for	If necessary, press
PRESSURE COOK	MAX	—	8 minutes with the KEEP WARM setting off	START
MEAT/STEW, PRESSURE COOK, or MANUAL	HIGH	Closed	10 minutes with the KEEP WARM setting off	START

6. Use the **quick-release method** to bring the pot's pressure back to normal. Unlatch the lid and open the cooker.

7.

Press the button for	Set it for	Set the time for	If necessary, press
SAUTÉ	MEDIUM, NORMAL, or CUSTOM 300°F	5 minutes	START

8. Stir in the tomato paste and bring the sauce to a full summer. Cook, stirring often, until somewhat thickened, about 3 minutes. Turn off the SAUTÉ function and set the lid ajar over the pot. Set aside for 10 minutes to blend the flavors.

Beyond

- You must halve the recipe for a **3-quart cooker**.

- Toss the sauce with wide noodles like pappardelle.

- Use a 50/50 combo of butter and olive oil for a silkier finish.

- Feel free to use ¾ pound lean ground beef and ½ pound lean ground pork.

- Make sure there's plenty of Parmigiano-Reggiano on hand to grate (or better, shave) over each serving.

- We tried various dairy substitutes, none with good results (some broke; some were too sweet). The best substitute was actually ½ cup chicken broth and 2 tablespoons rolled oats. The sauce is stickier but has a creamy feel, sort of like the original.

1 tablespoon olive oil

1 medium yellow onion, chopped (1 cup)

1 pound lean ground pork

1 pound sweet Italian sausage, any casings removed

½ cup chicken broth or dry white wine

One 28-ounce can diced tomatoes (3½ cups)

¼ cup loosely packed fresh basil leaves, finely chopped

2 tablespoons fresh oregano leaves, finely chopped

2 tablespoons fresh rosemary leaves, finely chopped

½ teaspoon table salt

Beyond

- For a **3-quart cooker**, you must use ⅓ cup wine or vermouth and halve the remaining ingredients.

- For an **8-quart cooker**, you must add ¼ cup chicken broth (or water) with the wine.

- For a richer finish, substitute butter for the olive oil. (Reduce or omit the salt if your butter is salted.)

- To go all out, grate aged Asiago or an aged goat cheese over the servings.

- To skip any dairy, garnish servings with a little syrupy balsamic vinegar — and maybe finely grated orange zest.

- Substitute 1 tablespoon fresh thyme leaves for the rosemary.

Pork and Basil Meat Sauce

Makes enough for 2 pounds dried pasta

This is a fairly traditional sauce, without the fuss of a Bolognese (see page 138–139). We pack extra flavor into the sauce by using sausage meat, already seasoned with fennel seeds and other aromatics. It can be a mess to take the casings off sausages, but you can often find bulk seasoned Italian sausage meat in the butcher case of larger supermarkets. The sausage meat may have been salted in advance. Check the label and if so, omit any salt here. (And some sausage meat, particularly when in casings, can have wheat fillers or thickeners. If this is a concern, check the label.)

The easiest way to chop all those herbs is to gather all three together on a cutting board (with or without the salt), then rock a chef's knife through them, repeatedly moving the blade on an axis around the herbs and gathering them together several times to start again.

1.

Press the button for	Set it for	Set the time for	If necessary, press
SAUTÉ	MEDIUM, NORMAL, or CUSTOM 300°F	10 minutes	START

2. Warm the oil in a **6-quart cooker** for a minute or two. Add the onion and cook, stirring often, until softened, about 4 minutes. Crumble in both the ground pork and the sausage meat. Cook, stirring often to break up any large clumps, until the meat is lightly browned, about 4 minutes.

3. Pour in the broth or wine and scrape up any browned bits on the pot's bottom. Turn off the SAUTÉ function. Stir in the tomatoes, basil, oregano, rosemary, and salt. Lock the lid onto the pot.

4.

Press the button for	Set it for	The valve must be	Set the time for	If necessary, press
PRESSURE COOK	MAX	—	8 minutes with the KEEP WARM setting off	START
MEAT/STEW, PRESSURE COOK, or MANUAL	HIGH	Closed	10 minutes with the KEEP WARM setting off	START

5. Use the **quick-release method** to bring the pot's pressure back to normal. Unlatch the lid and open the cooker. Stir well before serving.

Mushroom Ragù

Makes enough for 1 pound dried pasta

To put it bluntly, mushrooms grow in stuff you wouldn't want to eat. Don't believe the myth about not washing them. By all means, clean them with water before using them in this chunky but delicate pasta sauce. And there's no reason to use only cremini mushrooms. Consider stemmed, sliced shiitakes; sliced white button mushrooms, or even a range of more exotic mushrooms like porcini, hen of the wood, or oyster mushrooms. But skip portobello caps. The black gills turn the sauce a dark, unappetizing color.

2 tablespoons butter

2 medium shallots, chopped (½ cup)

1 medium carrot, chopped (½ cup)

1½ pounds small or medium cremini mushrooms

Up to 4 medium garlic cloves, peeled and minced (4 teaspoons)

One 28-ounce can diced tomatoes, preferably petite dice (3½ cups)

¼ cup vegetable broth

¼ cup loosely packed fresh basil leaves, finely chopped

1 teaspoon dried sage

¼ teaspoon red pepper flakes

¼ teaspoon grated nutmeg

¼ teaspoon table salt

1.

Press the button for	Set it for	Set the time for	If necessary, press
SAUTÉ	MEDIUM, NORMAL, or CUSTOM 300°F	10 minutes	START

2. Melt the butter in a **3-, 6-, or 8-quart cooker**, then add the shallots and carrot. Cook, stirring often, until the shallots begin to soften, about 3 minutes. Add the mushrooms and continue cooking, stirring occasionally, until they begin to soften, about 4 minutes.

3. Stir in the garlic and turn off the SAUTÉ function. Continue stirring in the residual heat for 1 minute to concentrate the liquid the mushrooms have begun to give off. Stir in the tomatoes, broth, basil, sage, red pepper flakes, nutmeg, and salt. Lock the lid onto the pot.

4.

Press the button for	Set it for	The valve must be	Set the time for	If necessary, press
PRESSURE COOK	MAX	—	8 minutes with the KEEP WARM setting off	START
PRESSURE COOK or MANUAL	HIGH	Closed	10 minutes with the KEEP WARM setting off	START

5. Use the **quick-release method** to bring the pot's pressure back to normal. Unlatch the lid and open the cooker.

6.

Press the button for	Set it for	Set the time for	If necessary, press
SAUTÉ	HIGH or MORE	10 minutes	START

7. Bring the sauce to a full simmer. Cook, stirring almost constantly, until thickened like a ragù, about 5 minutes. Turn off the SAUTÉ function and remove the *hot* insert from the machine to stop the cooking.

Beyond

- There are three other ways to thicken the ragù in the last step: 1) stir in ¼ cup tomato paste after pressure cooking and simmer for 1 minute, stirring often. Or 2) put about 1½ cups of the ragù in a blender, cover, blend until smooth, then stir this mixture back into the mushroom ragù without simmering it. Or 3) use an immersion blender right in the pot for 4 or 5 quick bursts to puree some of the mixture, then stir well before serving.

- For a richer ragù, increase the butter to ½ stick (¼ cup).

- Top the servings with finely grated Parmigiano-Reggiano, a smattering of finely grated lemon zest, and lots of freshly ground black pepper.

3 tablespoons butter

4 medium yellow onions, halved,
then thinly sliced into half-moons

1½ cups beef broth

¼ cup balsamic vinegar

2 tablespoons loosely packed fresh
rosemary leaves, minced

¼ teaspoon table salt

¼ teaspoon ground black pepper

2½ pounds lean ground beef

¼ cup tomato paste

Venetian-Style Sweet-and-Sour Ragù

Makes enough for 2 pounds dried pasta

The key to this classic sauce is to let the onions cook and cook (and cook some more) until they're super soft and sweet, all *without* letting them brown too much. Which means you'll need to stir quite a bit — particularly as they start to break down — as they lose much of their natural moisture while you're trying to concentrate their natural sugars. If you have an Ultra or a Max machine, you can drop the SAUTÉ level even lower (to, say, 228°F) and keep the onions even more mellow. After all that work, they'll pair perfectly with the balsamic vinegar. There's no need for an expensive bottle, just a tasty, sweet/sour vinegar you'd use to make a salad dressing.

1.

Press the button for	Set it for	Set the time for	If necessary, press
SAUTÉ	LOW or LESS	30 minutes	START

2. Melt the butter in a **6- or 8-quart cooker**, then add the onions. Cook, stirring once in a while at first, then more and more, until the onions are golden, very soft, and sweet, about 25 minutes.

3. Stir in the broth, vinegar, rosemary, salt, and pepper. Scrape up any browned bits on the bottom of the pot. Crumble in the ground beef. Turn off the SAUTÉ function but stir the beef over the residual heat for 1 minute. Lock the lid onto the pot.

4.

Press the button for	Set it for	The valve must be	Set the time for	If necessary, press
PRESSURE COOK	MAX	—	6 minutes with the KEEP WARM setting off	START
MEAT/STEW, PRESSURE COOK, or MANUAL	HIGH	Closed	8 minutes with the KEEP WARM setting off	START

5. Use the **quick-release method** to bring the pot's pressure back to normal. Unlatch the lid and open the cooker.

6.

Press the button for	Set it for	Set the time for	If necessary, press
SAUTÉ	MEDIUM, NORMAL, or CUSTOM 300°F	5 minutes	START

7. Stir in the tomato paste until uniform as the sauce comes back to a simmer. Cook, stirring often, until slightly thickened, about 2 minutes. Turn off the SAUTÉ function and remove the *hot* insert from the machine to stop the cooking.

Beyond

- You must halve the recipe for a 3-quart cooker.

- To make this sauce using the SLOW COOK setting, complete the recipe as written through step 3 without turning off the SAUTÉ function. Crumble in the ground beef, cook until lightly browned, then stir in the tomato paste until uniform. Turn off the SAUTÉ function. Lock the lid onto the pot but leave the valve open. Use the SLOW COOK function on HIGH to cook for 3 hours. The sauce can be kept on the KEEP WARM setting for up to 2 hours after cooking.

Picadillo-Style Ragù

Makes enough for 2 pounds dried pasta

Picadillo (*peek-ah-DEE-yoh*) is a traditional, sweet-and-savory ground beef "sauce," popular across the Caribbean and in Latin American. We morphed it into a ragù by making it a little wetter, the better to toss with cooked pasta (and the better to work in an Instant Pot without scorching). This is pretty fine deck food with a beer in the summer, considering you don't have to heat up the kitchen when the pot does its work. If it's really hot out, skip the pasta and scoop the sauce (via a slotted spoon) into lettuce cups.

2 tablespoons olive oil

1 large yellow onion, chopped
(1½ cups)

2 medium garlic cloves, peeled and minced (2 teaspoons)

1½ teaspoons cumin seeds

1 teaspoon coriander seeds

2 bay leaves

One 4-inch cinnamon stick

2 pounds lean ground beef

1 cup beef broth

½ cup raisins

½ cup sliced pitted green olives

1 tablespoon drained and rinsed capers, chopped

1 tablespoon fresh oregano leaves, finely chopped

One 6-ounce can tomato paste

½ cup loosely packed cilantro leaves, chopped

1.

Press the button for	Set it for	Set the time for	If necessary, press
SAUTÉ	MEDIUM, NORMAL, or CUSTOM 300°F	10 minutes	START

2. Warm the oil in a **3-, 6-, or 8-quart cooker** for a minute or two, then add the onion. Cook, stirring often, until softened, about 4 minutes. Stir in the garlic, cumin, coriander, bay leaves, and cinnamon stick. Cook for a few seconds until aromatic, stirring a few times.

3. Crumble in the ground beef. Cook, stirring several times to break up any large clumps, just until it loses its raw, pink color, about 4 minutes. Turn off the SAUTÉ function. Stir in the broth, raisins, olives, capers, and oregano, making sure you get any browned bits off the bottom of the pot. Lock the lid onto the pot.

4.

Press the button for	Set it for	The valve must be	Set the time for	If necessary, press
PRESSURE COOK	MAX	—	6 minutes with the KEEP WARM setting off	START
MEAT/STEW, PRESSURE COOK, or MANUAL	HIGH	Closed	8 minutes with the KEEP WARM setting off	START

5. Use the **quick-release method** to bring the pot's pressure back to normal. Unlatch the lid and open the cooker.

6.

Press the button for	Set it for	Set the time for	If necessary, press
SAUTÉ	MEDIUM, NORMAL, or CUSTOM 300°F	5 minutes	START

7. Stir in the tomato paste and cilantro as the mixture comes back to a boil. Cook, stirring often, until somewhat thickened if still a little soupy, about 3 minutes. Turn off the SAUTÉ function and remove the *hot* insert from the machine to stop the cooking. Find and discard the bay leaves and cinnamon stick and serve.

Beyond

- For a lighter ragù, substitute ground turkey for the beef and chicken broth for the beef broth.

- Although this dish can be tossed with pasta, we also like it over a bed of cooked long-grain white basmati rice.

- Garnish the servings with more sliced olives and even minced celery leaves.

- There's no salt in the mix because of the olives and capers. Pass some at the table.

- There's also no heat. Serve it with a hot red pepper sauce, such as Sriracha.

2 tablespoons olive oil

1 large yellow onion, chopped (1½ cups)

3 cups vegetable broth

One 14-ounce can diced tomatoes (1¾ cups)

1 cup brown lentils

½ cup green lentils (that is, le Puy lentils)

2 medium garlic cloves, peeled and minced (2 teaspoons)

1 tablespoon dried basil

1 teaspoon dried oregano

½ teaspoon ground allspice

½ teaspoon table salt

¼ teaspoon red pepper flakes

3 tablespoons tomato paste

Lentil Ragù

Makes enough for 1½ pounds dried pasta

Lentils make an exceptionally earthy ragù, a hearty meal that's best on a winter evening. There are two kinds of lentils here: brown and green. The brown will melt under pressure, thickening the sauce, while the green will stay firmer to give the ragù a more, well, ragù-ish texture. All lentils can have small stones hidden in their packages. Before using, spread the lentils on a big cutting board and pick through them to discard the stones and avoid expensive dental bills.

1.

Press the button for	Set it for	Set the time for	If necessary, press
SAUTÉ	MEDIUM, NORMAL, or CUSTOM 300°F	10 minutes	START

2. Warm the oil in a **3-, 6-, or 8-quart cooker** for a minute or two, then add the onion. Cook, stirring occasionally, until softened, about 5 minutes. Turn off the SAUTÉ function. Stir in the broth, tomatoes, brown lentils, green lentils, garlic, basil, oregano, allspice, salt, and red pepper flakes. Lock the lid onto the pot.

3.

Press the button for	Set it for	The valve must be	Set the time for	If necessary, press
PRESSURE COOK	MAX	—	10 minutes with the KEEP WARM setting off	START
CHILI/BEANS, PRESSURE COOK, or MANUAL	HIGH	Closed	12 minutes with the KEEP WARM setting off	START

4. When the pot has finished cooking, turn it off and let the pressure **return to normal naturally**, about 25 minutes. Unlatch the lid and open the cooker.

5.

Press the button for	Set it for	Set the time for	If necessary, press
SAUTÉ	MEDIUM, NORMAL, or CUSTOM 300°F	10 minutes	START

6. Bring the sauce to a simmer, stirring constantly. Stir in the tomato paste until uniform, then continue cooking, stirring almost the whole time, until thickened, about 2 minutes. Turn off the SAUTÉ function and remove the *hot* insert from the machine to stop the cooking.

Beyond

- To make this ragù with the SLOW COOK function, complete the recipe through step 2, stirring in the tomato paste before locking the lid on the pot. Leave the pressure valve open and use the SLOW COOK function to cook on HIGH for 3 hours with the KEEP WARM setting off (or on for up to 1 hour).

- If you're not interested in making a vegan ragù, substitute up to 3 tablespoons butter for the olive oil.

- Garnish the servings with pomegranate molasses and maybe with a light dusting of za'atar, the Middle Eastern spice blend.

Pork Ragù

Makes enough for 2 pounds dried pasta

This ragù uses pork shoulder, which can be notoriously fatty. We're all for those rich bits when the cut is roasted. However, whether you make this ragù under pressure or use the SLOW COOK function, look for the leanest piece of pork shoulder you can find to keep the sauce from being too oily.

We find that all our ragùs made with whole cuts of meat are better with dried pasta (rather than fresh). This ragù should go with substantial noodles, perhaps bucatini, pappardelle, or mafaldine.

1. Mix the pork, tomatoes, broth, onion, celery, oregano, rosemary, salt, and pepper in a **6- or 8-quart cooker**. Lock the lid onto the pot.

2.

Press the button for	Set it for	The valve must be	Set the time for	If necessary, press
PRESSURE COOK	MAX	—	35 minutes with the KEEP WARM setting off	START
MEAT/STEW, PRESSURE COOK, or MANUAL	HIGH	Closed	45 minutes with the KEEP WARM setting off	START
SLOW COOK	HIGH	Opened	4 hours with the KEEP WARM setting off (or on for no more than 2 hours)	START

3. If you've used a pressure setting, when the machine has finished cooking, turn it off and let its pressure **return to normal naturally**, about 25 minutes.

4. Unlatch the lid and open the cooker. Use a flatware tablespoon to skim any excess surface fat from the top of the sauce. Break up the pork pieces into smaller bits and shreds, stirring these into the sauce.

5.

Press the button for	Set it for	Set the time for	If necessary, press
SAUTÉ	MEDIUM, NORMAL, or CUSTOM 300°F	10 minutes	START

6. Bring the sauce to a simmer. Stir in the cream, then cook, stirring often, until somewhat thickened, about 4 minutes. Turn off the SAUTÉ function, remove the *hot* insert from the machine, and stir in the parsley just before serving.

2 pounds boneless pork shoulder, cut into 2-inch pieces and any large chunks of fat removed

2 pounds plum or Roma tomatoes, chopped (4 cups)

1 cup chicken broth

1 small yellow onion, chopped (½ cup)

2 medium celery stalks, thinly sliced (½ cup)

2 tablespoons fresh oregano leaves, finely chopped

2 tablespoons fresh rosemary leaves, finely chopped

½ teaspoon table salt

½ teaspoon ground black pepper

¼ cup heavy cream

¼ cup loosely packed parsley leaves, chopped

Beyond

- You must halve the recipe for a 3-quart cooker.

- If you don't want to add the cream, substitute 3 tablespoons tomato paste to thicken the sauce.

- For a much more savory stew, substitute goat milk for the cream. To serve, set a small mound of soft goat cheese in the bowls, top with hot, cooked, and drained bucatini or mafaldine, then ladle the sauce over the pasta.

2 tablespoons olive oil

2 pounds boneless beef chuck, trimmed of any large chunks of fat and cut in half

One 28-ounce can whole tomatoes (3½ cups)

½ cup frozen pearl onions (do not thaw)

¾ cup light dry red wine, such as Pinot Noir

1 tablespoon drained and rinsed capers, chopped

1 medium garlic clove, peeled and minced (1 teaspoon)

1 tablespoon dried rosemary

2 teaspoons dried oregano

1 bay leaf

½ teaspoon table salt

½ teaspoon ground black pepper

Italian Pot Roast Ragù

Makes enough for 2 pounds dried pasta

This recipe's a hybrid of sorts. Stew + Ragù = voilà!

You'll want to deeply brown the pieces of beef chuck. Seriously. Don't gray them. They should have dark spots across their surface, not just golden patches. Be patient and let all those natural sugars become more intensely flavored.

To balance all that browned goodness, we call for dried spices, rather than fresh, because the dried ones have a slightly earthier flavor, less bright and so more balanced in the ragù.

1.

Press the button for	Set it for	Set the time for	If necessary, press
SAUTÉ	MEDIUM, NORMAL, or CUSTOM 300°F	20 minutes	START

2. Warm the oil in a **6- or 8-quart cooker** for a minute or two. Add the beef in two batches and brown, turning a couple of times. Make sure the first piece is *well* browned before transferring it to a bowl and adding the second one. At the end, both pieces of beef should be in the bowl.

3. Wash and dry your hands. One by one, squeeze the whole tomatoes over the pot, then add any remaining juice from the can. Add the pearl onions and stir well to scrape up *all* the browned bits on the bottom of the pot. Cook for 2 minutes, stirring often, just until the onions begin to brown lightly. Turn off the SAUTÉ function.

4. Stir in the wine, capers, garlic, rosemary, oregano, bay leaf, salt, and pepper. Return the beef pieces and any juice in the bowl to the cooker. Lock the lid onto the pot.

5.

Press the button for	Set it for	The valve must be	Set the time for	If necessary, press
PRESSURE COOK	MAX	—	44 minutes with the KEEP WARM setting off	START
PRESSURE COOK or MANUAL	HIGH	Closed	55 minutes with the KEEP WARM setting off	START
SLOW COOK	HIGH	Opened	5 hours with the KEEP WARM setting off (or on for no more than 2 hours)	START

6. If you've used a pressure setting, when the machine has finished cooking, turn it off and let its pressure **return to normal naturally**, about 30 minutes.

7. Unlatch the lid and open the cooker. Use a flatware tablespoon to skim off any excess surface fat. Find and discard the bay leaf, then use two forks to shred the meat.

8.

Press the button for	Set it for	Set the time for	If necessary, press
SAUTÉ	HIGH or MORE	10 minutes	START

9. Bring the sauce to a full simmer. Cook, stirring occasionally, until reduced to a fairly wet ragù, about 5 minutes. Turn off the SAUTÉ function and set the lid askew over the pot for 5 minutes to blend the flavors.

Beyond

- You must halve the recipe for a **3-quart cooker**.

- Stir up to 2 tablespoons butter into the ragù just before serving.

- This ragù takes well to pasta shapes like rigatoni or fusilli. Or serve it as a stew over large spoonfuls of ricotta.

- Garnish with minced fresh parsley leaves.

See photo in insert.

One 28-ounce can diced tomatoes
(3½ cups)

½ cup red wine

4 medium shallots, peeled and thinly
sliced into rings

2 medium garlic cloves, peeled and
minced (2 teaspoons)

2 tablespoons fresh rosemary leaves,
finely chopped

1 teaspoon granulated white sugar

Up to 1 teaspoon table salt

½ teaspoon ground cinnamon

2 bay leaves

2 bone-in skinless turkey thighs
(about 1¼ pounds each)

2 tablespoons butter

Turkey Ragù

Makes enough for 1½ pounds dried pasta

Because we wanted to keep this ragù fairly thick, rather than soupy, we used turkey thighs, sometimes hard to track down but always available around the winter holidays when the butcher has been cutting the breasts off the turkeys for smaller holiday dinners. The easiest way to skin a turkey thigh is to grasp one corner of the skin with a paper towel and pull the skin diagonally across and off the meat. Also remove any large globs of fat underneath before adding the thighs to the cooker.

1. Stir the tomatoes, wine, shallots, garlic, rosemary, sugar, salt, cinnamon, and bay leaves in a **6- or 8-quart cooker**. Nestle the turkey thighs into this mixture. Lock the lid onto the pot.

2.

Press the button for	Set it for	The valve must be	Set the time for	If necessary, press
PRESSURE COOK	MAX	—	40 minutes with the KEEP WARM setting off	START
PRESSURE COOK or MANUAL	HIGH	Closed	50 minutes with the KEEP WARM setting off	START
SLOW COOK	HIGH	Opened	5 hours with the KEEP WARM setting off (or on for no more than 2 hours)	START

3. If you've used a pressure setting, when the machine has finished cooking, use the **quick-release method** to return the pot's pressure to normal.

4. Unlatch the lid and open the cooker. Use kitchen tongs to transfer the turkey thighs to a cutting board. Cool for a few minutes. Meanwhile, find, remove, and discard the bay leaves in the sauce.

5.

Press the button for	Set it for	Set the time for	If necessary, press
SAUTÉ	MEDIUM, NORMAL, or CUSTOM 300°F	5 minutes	START

6. Shred the meat off the bones. (Discard the bones and any cartilage.) Stir the meat into the sauce and add the butter. Cook at a full simmer, stirring frequently, until reduced to about the consistency of a fairly wet ragù, about 3 minutes. Turn off the SAUTÉ function and set the lid askew over the pot for 5 minutes to blend the flavors.

Beyond

- You must halve the recipe for a **3-quart cooker**.

- For a richer ragù, substitute evaporated milk for the red wine.

- For a dinner party–worthy dish, substitute 4 skinned duck leg quarters (½ to ¾ pounds each) for the turkey thighs. Make sure to garnish these servings with thyme leaves or finely chopped parsley leaves.

Creamy Beef Short Rib Ragù

Makes enough for 2 pounds dried pasta

Imagine old-school Swiss steak shredded up and served over pasta. Okay, that doesn't make any sense. But this ragù has a mid-century-modern, comfort-food feel, a rich mix of flavors in a creamy tomato sauce, as if Lunch Lady Doris had been a really good cook. By the way, the secret to that old-school flavor in mid-century recipes is the mix of thyme and allspice.

2 tablespoons olive oil

2 pounds boneless beef short ribs

½ teaspoon table salt

½ teaspoon ground black pepper

⅔ cup bold dry red wine, such as a Zinfandel

One 14-ounce can diced tomatoes (1¾ cups)

Up to 6 medium garlic cloves, peeled and minced (2 tablespoons)

½ cup regular or low-fat evaporated milk

1½ tablespoons fresh thyme leaves

½ teaspoon ground allspice

¼ cup heavy cream

1.

Press the button for	Set it for	Set the time for	If necessary, press
SAUTÉ	MEDIUM, NORMAL, or CUSTOM 300°F	20 minutes	START

2. Warm the oil in a **3-, 6-, or 8-quart cooker** for a minute or two. Season the short rib pieces with the salt and pepper. Brown them in three batches, turning them occasionally until they are *well* browned, then transfer to a nearby bowl and brown more. At the end, all the short ribs should be in the bowl.

3. Pour the wine into the cooker and scrape up *every speck of browned stuff* on the pot's bottom. Stir in the tomatoes and garlic. Cook, stirring often, until very aromatic, about 1 minute. Turn off the SAUTÉ function. Stir in the evaporated milk, thyme, and allspice. Return the short ribs and any liquid in the bowl to the cooker. Lock the lid onto the pot.

4.

Press the button for	Set it for	The valve must be	Set the time for	If necessary, press
PRESSURE COOK	MAX	—	40 minutes with the KEEP WARM setting off	START
MEAT/STEW or PRESSURE COOK	HIGH	Closed	50 minutes with the KEEP WARM setting off	START

5. When the cooker has finished, turn it off and let the pressure **come back to normal** for 10 minutes. Then use the **quick-release method** to get rid of any residual pressure. Unlatch the lid and open the cooker. Use a flatware tablespoon to skim off any excess surface fat. Shred the short ribs in the pot with two forks, then stir in the cream.

6.

Press the button for	Set it for	Set the time for	If necessary, press
SAUTÉ	MEDIUM, NORMAL, or CUSTOM 300°F	10 minutes	START

7. Bring the ragù to a simmer, then cook, stirring often, until reduced to a fairly thick pasta sauce, about 5 minutes. Turn off the SAUTÉ function and set the lid askew over the pot for 5 minutes to blend the flavors.

Beyond

- If you don't want to use wine, use an equivalent amount of beef broth plus 1 teaspoon dark brown sugar.

- Consider serving this ragù over Polenta (page 443).

- The ragù is so creamy it doesn't need cheese as a garnish. Instead, use chopped fresh parsley leaves and/or a smattering of dried cherries.

½ cup beef broth

⅓ cup reduced-sodium soy sauce

¼ cup packed dark brown sugar

3 medium garlic cloves, peeled and thinly sliced

2 teaspoons toasted sesame oil

1 teaspoon ground dried ginger

1 tablespoon ground black pepper

1 medium red onion, halved and sliced into thin half-moons

2½ pounds boneless beef chuck, cut into 3 pieces and any large bits of fat removed

2 tablespoons cornstarch

2 teaspoons water

Korean Beef Ragù

Makes enough for 2 pounds dried pasta

Here's a pure flight of fancy, a fusion of an Italian ragù with a Korean stew. It's a sweet, sticky, almost unreal concoction, best on a winter night with a glass of beer. Use only reduced-sodium soy sauce: Because the pot doesn't allow any evaporation and concentration of flavors, the regular stuff will end up making the ragù too salty.

1. Stir the broth, soy sauce, brown sugar, garlic, sesame oil, ginger, and black pepper in a **3-, 6-, or 8-quart cooker** until the brown sugar dissolves. Stir in the onion, then nestle the pieces of beef into the sauce. They won't all be submerged, but get them all coated. Lock the lid onto the pot.

2.

Press the button for	Set it for	The valve must be	Set the time for	If necessary, press
PRESSURE COOK	MAX	—	45 minutes with the KEEP WARM setting off	START
MEAT/STEW, PRESSURE COOK, or MANUAL	HIGH	Closed	55 minutes with the KEEP WARM setting off	START
SLOW COOK	HIGH	Opened	5 hours with the KEEP WARM setting off (or on for no more than 2 hours)	START

3. If you've used a pressure setting, when the machine has finished cooking, turn it off and let its pressure **return to normal naturally**, about 30 minutes.

4. Unlatch the lid and open the cooker. Use a flatware tablespoon to skim off any excess surface fat from the sauce. Shred the meat in the pot with two forks.

5.

Press the button for	Set it for	Set the time for	If necessary, press
SAUTÉ	MEDIUM, NORMAL, or CUSTOM 300°F	5 minutes	START

6. Bring the sauce to a full simmer, stirring often. Whisk the cornstarch and water in a small bowl or tea cup until smooth, then stir this slurry into the sauce. Continue cooking, stirring all the while, until the sauce is slightly thickened, about 1 minute. Immediately turn off the SAUTÉ function and remove the *hot* insert from the machine to stop the cooking. Set the lid askew over the insert for a couple of minutes to further thicken the sauce.

Beyond

- For an even more astounding set of flavors, add up to 2 tablespoons gochujang (a Korean chile paste) with the ingredients in step 1.

- Serve the ragù with cooked and drained egg noodles, rice noodles, or long-grain, white rice.

- No cheese, please! Garnish the servings with more toasted sesame oil.

Lamb Ragù

Makes enough for 2 pounds dried pasta

Our final ragù is a Greek-inspired concoction that's fairly rich. Since the tomato paste is so necessary to this dish, it's a good time to remember that one tomato paste is *not* like another. Some taste nothing but sweet; others, more like tomatoes. Spend ten bucks on several brands and do a taste test. You'll know exactly which one matches your taste.

3 tablespoons olive oil

1 large yellow onion, chopped (1½ cups)

2 medium carrots, chopped (1 cup)

4 medium garlic cloves, peeled and minced (4 teaspoons)

1½ pounds boneless leg of lamb, cut into 2-inch pieces

1 cup chicken broth

2 tablespoons fresh rosemary leaves, chopped

2 tablespoons fresh sage leaves, chopped

½ teaspoon table salt

½ teaspoon ground black pepper

One 6-ounce can tomato paste

1.

Press the button for	Set it for	Set the time for	If necessary, press
SAUTÉ	MEDIUM, NORMAL, or CUSTOM 300°F	10 minutes	START

2. Warm the oil in a **3-, 6-, or 8-quart cooker** for a minute or two. Add the onion and carrot. Cook, stirring often, until the onion begins to soften, about 5 minutes. Stir in the garlic and cook for a few seconds.

3. Add the lamb pieces; stir over the heat for 1 minute, just until the lamb is thoroughly mixed into the vegetables. Turn off the SAUTÉ function. Stir in the broth, rosemary, sage, salt, and pepper. Lock the lid onto the pot.

4.

Press the button for	Set it for	The valve must be	Set the time for	If necessary, press
PRESSURE COOK	MAX	—	23 minutes with the KEEP WARM setting off	START
MEAT/STEW, PRESSURE COOK, or MANUAL	HIGH	Closed	30 minutes with the KEEP WARM setting off	START

5. When the pot has finished cooking, turn it off and allow its pressure to **return to normal naturally**, about 30 minutes. Unlatch the lid and open the cooker. Use two forks to break up the meat into smaller pieces. Stir in the tomato paste until uniform.

6.

Press the button for	Set it for	Set the time for	If necessary, press
SAUTÉ	MEDIUM, NORMAL, or CUSTOM 300°F	10 minutes	START

7. Bring the sauce to a simmer, stirring constantly. Cook, stirring occasionally, until thickened, about 5 minutes. Turn off the SAUTÉ function and set the lid askew over the pot for 5 minutes to blend the flavors.

Beyond

- For more complex flavors, use ½ cup broth and ½ cup dry white wine.

- To give it a more Greek feel, omit the salt and add up to ¼ cup sliced pitted black olives. Also, substitute oregano for the sage.

- Try this with boneless goat leg meat sometime!

- Beyond pastas like farfalle or ziti, serve this ragù over cooked orzo or even Israeli couscous.

- Crumble feta over the servings. And drizzle them with a fine, aromatic olive oil.

4

Pasta Casseroles

Here comes serious comfort food: mac and cheese, tuna noodle casserole, chili mac, sausage gravy over noodles, cheeseburger casserole, and even some new favorites like dan dan noodles. True, not every recipe yields a casserole. Some are noodles in sauce—or as in the case of the first recipe, just in butter (heaven!). Most use standard dried pasta. A couple turn frozen gnocchi, a supermarket staple, into rich casseroles. And a few use rice noodles or Israeli couscous, a toasted pasta.

In no case will you make the noodles separately. Every recipe happens fully in the Instant Pot, starting with dried pasta (or frozen gnocchi, as the case might be). The creamy sauces are particularly astounding—although you *must* use canned evaporated milk, not regular milk (which can curdle under pressure without its being in a baking vessel of some sort or mixed into a batter). We'll let you know when low-fat evaporated milk can work. Fat-free never led to good results.

Dried pasta is a pantry must-have. The quality of the results will be directly related to the quality of the pasta. Cheaper isn't worse; more expensive, better. That said, it's sometimes worth it to spend a few extra quarters per pound for better dried pasta. Stock up when you see sales.

There are no *fast/slow* recipes in this chapter. The texture of pasta is too compromised over many hours in a slow cooker. We know there are plenty of internet recipes for the stuff. But we find slow-cooker pasta becomes unappealingly gummy without major modifications to the recipe. Because of those changes, we can't use the same ingredient list for both the fast and the slow settings. So we've opted out of the SLOW COOK function in this chapter. We hope you'll forgive us, given that there's so much comfort to go around.

FAQs

1. Why do you use jarred marinara sauce in some recipes?

Mostly, for convenience—but with this caveat: There's a *wide* variety of marinara sauce on the supermarket shelf. Read the labels carefully to find a brand that includes nothing more than what you'd put in that sauce, if you were making it from scratch. Don't use chunky bottled sauces or ones with cream or milk in the mix, but feel free to substitute jarred arrabbiata or fra diavolo sauce for the marinara in almost all cases.

Of course, you can use homemade Buttery Marinara Sauce (page 133) in every recipe that calls for marinara. And just to be shameless in self-promotion, we do have a knock-out, five-minute marinara sauce (made on the stovetop) in another of our books, *The Kitchen Shortcut Bible*.

2. What's "unseasoned rice vinegar"?

Technically, it's just "rice wine vinegar," although few manufacturers label it so. Rice vinegar comes in two forms: seasoned and so-called "unseasoned." The seasoned has added sugar and maybe a few aromatics. The unseasoned is a mild vinegar that is not sweet. It is *the only kind* called for in this book. As a maddening bit of labeling confusion, seasoned rice vinegar is sometimes, but not always, so labeled; and "unseasoned," the sort you want, is rarely labeled "unseasoned." Bottom line: Read the label and make sure there's no sugar or other sweetener in the bottle.

3. Can I substitute gluten-free noodles?

Yes, in almost all cases. We had better success with gluten-free noodles made from a combination of grains, rather than just one. We had the best success with dried pasta made with corn and rice. When it comes to the pasta casseroles that round out this chapter, multi-grain, gluten-free, no-boil lasagna noodles are available at large supermarkets or online suppliers.

4. Do I have to make adjustments for cooking gluten-free pasta?

Yes, especially if you use the multi-grain noodles we recommend. In all cases, increase the time under pressure by 1 minute (whether for the MAX or the HIGH setting). That said, tastes vary. Some people like chewier pasta. If you're in that lot, consider trying one of the recipes as written with gluten-free noodles and see if you prefer that texture to a softer feel.

5. What are egg noodles?

Some noodles — particularly fresh pasta — are always made with eggs. However, the egg pasta we're talking about are the familiar, wide, flat, *dried* noodles found in bags near the other pasta at the supermarket (and not in the refrigerator case). These are the noodles some of us grew up eating in tuna noodle casserole or even mac and cheese.

The extra-wide versions work best in the Instant Pot. We also tested the recipes with no-yolks noodles and found no difference in quality. And again, we found that the gluten-free egg noodles made from a mix of grains worked best. One note: There's no need to adjust the timing for gluten-free egg noodles.

6. What about rice noodles?

We call for two kinds: 1) rice stick noodles (also called "rice noodles for pad Thai" or even "stir-fry rice noodles" on some packages) and 2) rice vermicelli (sort of like a rice version of angel-hair pasta). Use the one specifically called for in the recipe, but feel free to substitute brown rice noodles *of the same variety* in any of these dishes with no other change in the recipe. But never substitute rice noodles for gluten-free noodles in any recipe in this chapter. The timing and the liquid ratios will be off.

Buttery Noodles

6 servings

Simple and satisfying, this pasta dish takes no time in an Instant Pot, a boon when you've got hungry kids in the house. One warning: You must stir constantly at the last step to make sure the delicate noodles do not stick.

Even without kids, make a pot when you're feeling under the weather. There's nothing like old-fashioned comfort food to perk you up. These noodles would also be welcome (and a little retro) alongside anything off the grill. You might want to fancy them up. See the suggestions in the *Beyond* section.

¼ cup (½ stick) butter

3 cups vegetable or chicken broth

12 ounces dried extra-wide egg or no-yolk noodles

¼ teaspoon table salt

1.

Press the button for	Set it for	Set the time for	If necessary, press
SAUTÉ	MEDIUM, NORMAL, or CUSTOM 300°F	5 minutes	START

2. Melt the butter in a **6- or 8-quart cooker**. Stir in the broth. Add the noodles and salt. Turn off the SAUTÉ function and lock the lid onto the pot.

Set the machine for	Set the level for	The valve must be	Set the time for	If necessary, press
PRESSURE COOK	MAX	—	3 minutes with the KEEP WARM setting off	START
PRESSURE COOK or MANUAL	HIGH	Closed	4 minutes with the KEEP WARM setting off	START

3. Use the **quick-release method** to bring the pot's pressure back to normal. Unlatch the lid and open the pot.

4.

Press the button for	Set it for	Set the time for	If necessary, press
SAUTÉ	MEDIUM, NORMAL, or CUSTOM 300°F	5 minutes	START

5. Stir constantly until any excess moisture evaporates and only buttered noodles remain, about 2 minutes. Turn off the SAUTÉ function, remove the *hot* insert from the machine to stop the cooking, stir well, and serve warm.

Beyond

- You must halve the recipe for a **3-quart cooker**.

- After cooking, season the noodles to taste with ground black pepper, poppy seeds, caraway seeds, and/or red pepper flakes.

- And/or stir up to ½ cup finely grated Parmigiano-Reggiano, pecorino, or an aged Asiago into the noodles.

One 16-ounce box dried pasta.
  Choose from cellentani, medium shells, large elbows, fusilli, or penne

3 cups water

1 cup regular or low-fat evaporated milk

2 tablespoons butter, cut into little bits

1 teaspoon onion powder

1 teaspoon ground dried mustard

¼ teaspoon table salt

1 cup heavy cream

12 ounces shredded cheese (3 cups)
  Choose one or a 50/50 combo from Swiss, American or English Cheddar, Monterey Jack, mozzarella, provolone, Gruyère, semi-firm Gouda, Havarti, fontina, Parmigiano-Reggiano, and/or Jarlsberg

Beyond

- You must halve the recipe for a **3-quart cooker**.

- Substitute a flavored cheese like pepper Jack or horseradish Cheddar. Or use a bagged, shredded cheese blend with spices (Italian, Mexican) for a bolder dish.

- There's no chance of a crunchy topping in the pot. Get one by spooning the finished casserole into a 9 x 13-inch baking dish; broil about 4 inches from the heating element until well browned and super crunchy, 3 to 4 minutes.

- Or toast fresh breadcrumbs in a skillet with a little olive oil or butter until lightly browned, stirring often, then sprinkle these over each serving. If desired, add dried herbs (parsley, thyme, and/or oregano) to those breadcrumbs before toasting.

- Or just crunch handfuls of thick, ruffle-cut potato chips over each serving.

Road Map: Mac and Cheese

6 servings

Here's the best way to create your own version of the ultimate American comfort food. Because the pasta cooks right in the evaporated milk, it becomes astoundingly luxurious, even better than a lot of oven versions. Note that you *cannot* use small pasta (like small elbows); they'll sink to the bottom of the pot and burn. And you can't use any thick-walled pasta like ziti or rigatoni because these won't cook in the time stated with the given liquid level. As a general rule, cooking dried pasta under pressure is mostly a matter of using a liquid level appropriate to the *thickness* of the pasta, rather than its length or shape.

1. Mix the pasta, water, evaporated milk, butter, onion powder, dried mustard, and salt in a **6- or 8-quart cooker**. Lock the lid onto the pot.

2.

Set the machine for	Set the level for	The valve must be	Set the time for	If necessary, press
PRESSURE COOK	MAX	—	4 minutes with the KEEP WARM setting off	START
PRESSURE COOK or MANUAL	HIGH	Closed	5 minutes with the KEEP WARM setting off	START

3. Use the **quick-release method** to bring the pot's pressure back to normal. Unlatch the lid and open the pot.

4.

Press the button for	Set it for	Set the time for	If necessary, press
SAUTÉ	MEDIUM, NORMAL, or CUSTOM 300°F	5 minutes	START

5. Stir in the cream and shredded cheese until uniform. Continue stirring constantly over the heat until the cheese melts and coats the pasta, 1 or 2 minutes. Turn off the SAUTÉ function, remove the *hot* insert from the machine, and set the lid ajar over the insert. Set aside for 5 minutes so the pasta can absorb most of the remaining liquid.

Creamy Tomato Mac and Cheese

6 servings

Consider this recipe a cross between mac and cheese and old-school tomato soup, a double dose of old-fashioned comfort. While testing recipes, we delivered a quart of this to a picky second-grader down our country road. He scarfed it up.

For us adults, the dish's sweet-tart bite calls out for something crunchy. If you're not in the mood to pair this with a baguette, stir thinly sliced carrots into the pot with the cheese to add texture.

1. Mix the pasta, broth, tomato puree, evaporated milk, thyme, nutmeg, salt, and pepper in a **6- or 8-quart cooker** until uniform. Lock the lid onto the pot.

2.

Set the machine for	Set the level for	The valve must be	Set the time for	If necessary, press
PRESSURE COOK	MAX	—	5 minutes with the KEEP WARM setting off	START
PRESSURE COOK or MANUAL	HIGH	Closed	7 minutes with the KEEP WARM setting off	START

3. Use the **quick-release method** to bring the pot's pressure back to normal. Unlatch the lid and open the pot. Add the cheese and cream; stir until the cheese melts. Set the lid ajar over the pot and set aside for 5 minutes to mellow the flavors.

One 16-ounce box dried ziti

3 cups vegetable or chicken broth

2 cups canned tomato puree

1 cup regular or low-fat evaporated milk

1 teaspoon dried thyme

½ teaspoon grated nutmeg

½ teaspoon table salt

½ teaspoon ground black pepper

8 ounces shredded white Cheddar or Swiss cheese (2 cups)

½ cup heavy cream

Beyond

- You must halve the recipe for a **3-quart cooker.**

- For a more aromatic dish, add dried herbs to the mix, up to 1 tablespoon total volume, choosing among thyme, oregano, parsley, basil, and/ or marjoram.

- For a more autumnal feel, substitute ground allspice for the nutmeg.

- For heat, add up to 1 teaspoon red pepper flakes with the nutmeg.

- For more richness, consider adding up to 2 tablespoons butter with the shredded cheese.

2 tablespoons butter

1 pound mild breakfast sausage meat (any casings removed)

1 teaspoon dried sage

12 ounces egg or no-yolk noodles

3 cups chicken broth

¾ cup heavy cream

Sausage Gravy and Noodles

6 servings

Nope, the title's not missing a comma between "sausage" and "gravy." This dish is Southern sausage gravy with noodles. We considered putting the recipe in the breakfast chapter. Then we ate half a pot for lunch one day. So voilà.

1.

Press the button for	Set it for	Set the time for	If necessary, press
SAUTÉ	MEDIUM, NORMAL, or CUSTOM 300°F	5 minutes	START

2. Melt the butter in a **6- or 8-quart cooker**. Crumble in the sausage meat; add the sage. Cook, stirring occasionally, until the meat loses its raw, pink color, about 3 minutes.

3. Mix in the noodles and broth. Stir well, although some of the noodles will stick up above the liquid. Turn off the SAUTÉ function and lock the lid onto the pot.

4.

Set the machine for	Set the level for	The valve must be	Set the time for	If necessary, press
PRESSURE COOK	MAX	—	3 minutes with the KEEP WARM setting off	START
PRESSURE COOK or MANUAL	HIGH	Closed	4 minutes with the KEEP WARM setting off	START

5. Use the **quick-release method** to bring the pot's pressure back to normal. Unlatch the lid and open the pot.

6.

Press the button for	Set it for	Set the time for	If necessary, press
SAUTÉ	MEDIUM, NORMAL, or CUSTOM 300°F	5 minutes	START

7. Stir in the cream and continue stirring over the heat until most of the liquid has been absorbed, about 1 minute. Turn off the SAUTÉ function, remove the *hot* insert from the pot, and set the lid ajar over the insert. Set aside for 5 minutes to allow the noodles to absorb most of the remaining liquid. Stir well before serving.

Beyond

- You must halve the recipe for a **3-quart cooker**.

- Stir up to ½ cup shredded mozzarella or finely grated Parmigiano-Reggiano into the noodles with the cream.

- For a sweeter finish, reduce the broth to 2 cups and add 1 cup dry white wine.

Creamy Mushroom Noodle Casserole

4 to 6 servings

Remember elementary school? Remember how bad the cafeteria food could be? Here's how it could have been better. We use more liquid here than in some other pasta casseroles, then thicken the sauce at the end to give it a classic cream-sauce texture. It's best warm right out of the pot. Plates, optional.

½ stick (¼ cup) butter

1 pound white button mushrooms, thinly sliced

Two 12-ounce cans regular or low-fat evaporated milk (3 cups)

3 cups vegetable or chicken broth

1 teaspoon dried sage

½ teaspoon dried thyme

¼ teaspoon table salt

¼ teaspoon ground black pepper

12 ounces wide egg or no-yolk noodles

¼ cup heavy cream

1 tablespoon cornstarch

1.

Press the button for	Set it for	Set the time for	If necessary, press
SAUTÉ	MEDIUM, NORMAL, or CUSTOM 300°F	10 minutes	START

2. Melt the butter in a **6- or 8-quart cooker**. Add the mushrooms and cook, stirring often, until they give off some liquid and start to soften, about 5 minutes.

3. Stir in the evaporated milk, broth, sage, thyme, salt, and pepper until uniform. Turn off the SAUTÉ function. Stir in the noodles. Not every noodle can be submerged; however, they should all be coated. Lock the lid onto the pot.

4.

Set the machine for	Set the level for	The valve must be	Set the time for	If necessary, press
PRESSURE COOK	MAX	—	3 minutes with the KEEP WARM setting off	START
PRESSURE COOK or MANUAL	HIGH	Closed	4 minutes with the KEEP WARM setting off	START

5. Use the **quick-release method** to bring the pot's pressure back to normal. Unlatch the lid and open the pot.

6.

Press the button for	Set it for	Set the time for	If necessary, press
SAUTÉ	MEDIUM, NORMAL, or CUSTOM 300°F	5 minutes	START

7. Whisk the cream and cornstarch into a small bowl until the cornstarch dissolves. Stir this slurry into the pot. Cook, stirring constantly, until the sauce thickens considerably, 1 or 2 minutes. Turn off the SAUTÉ function; remove the *hot* insert from the cooker to stop the cooking. Stir several more times, then serve warm.

Beyond

- You must halve the recipe for a **3-quart cooker**.

- For a fuller meal, stir up to 2 cups chopped skinless rotisserie chicken meat into the pot with the cream.

- Or stir in up to 1 cup chopped deli ham and up to 2 cups chopped broccoli florets.

2 tablespoons fat

Choose from olive oil, almond oil, vegetable oil, corn oil, canola oil, safflower oil, butter, rendered bacon fat, lard, or schmaltz.

1 medium yellow onion, chopped (1 cup)

1 or 2 medium sweet or mild peppers, stemmed, cored, and cut into strips (1 to 2 cups)

Choose from 1 red, yellow, orange, or green bell pepper; or 2 large Cubanelle peppers, or 2 large Anaheim chiles.

1 pound lean ground meat

Choose from beef, pork, veal, lamb, goat, or turkey—or a 50/50 combo.

Up to 2 medium garlic cloves, peeled and minced (1 teaspoon)

1½ tablespoons dried herb or seasoning blend

Choose from Cajun, French, Italian, Mediterranean, herbes de Provence, or other blends.

½ teaspoon table salt

One 28-ounce can diced tomatoes (3½ cups)

3 cups liquid

Choose from vegetable or chicken broth, or a 50/50 combo of broth of any sort with either dry white wine or pale amber beer.

1½ cups quick-cooking vegetables

Choose one or a combination of trimmed and chopped green beans, chopped broccoli florets, chopped cauliflower florets, thinly sliced carrots, thinly sliced celery, and/or thawed frozen artichoke heart quarters.

8 ounces dried pasta

Choose from ziti, penne, penne rigate, rigatoni, fusilli, tortiglioni, or radiatori.

One 6-ounce can tomato paste

4 ounces finely grated cheese (1 cup)

Choose from American, Cheddar, Swiss, Monterrey Jack, pepper Jack, Havarti, semi-firm Gouda, or Gruyère.

Road Map: Meat, Vegetable, and Pasta Casserole

4 servings

Here's another chance to make a signature recipe of your own in the Instant Pot! As we indicated in the book's introduction, we recommend using reduced-sodium or even salt-free ingredients (like the canned tomatoes and tomato paste here) because the pot tends to foreground salty flavors over earthy ones. (You can always add more salt at the table.)

The casserole isn't gooey until the cheese gets put on top at the end. If you have kids who like their casseroles to be extra-cheesy (or if you're a kid at heart), *stir* the cheese into the casserole before you set the lid askew over the pot.

1.

Press the button for	Set it for	Set the time for	If necessary, press
SAUTÉ	MEDIUM, NORMAL, or CUSTOM 300°F	10 minutes	START

2. Warm or melt the fat in a **6- or 8-quart cooker**. Add the onion and pepper. Cook, stirring often, until the onion softens, about 4 minutes. Crumble in the ground meat and cook, stirring often to break up any clumps, until it loses its raw, pink color, about 2 minutes.

3. Stir in the garlic, dried herb blend, and salt until aromatic, just a few seconds. Then stir in the tomatoes and liquid, scraping up *every speck of browned stuff* on the pot's bottom. Turn off the SAUTÉ function and stir in the quick-cooking vegetables and pasta. Stir well until the mixture is uniform. Lock the lid onto the pot.

4.

Set the machine for	Set the level for	The valve must be	Set the time for	If necessary, press
PRESSURE COOK	MAX	—	5 minutes with the KEEP WARM setting off	START
PRESSURE COOK or MANUAL	HIGH	Closed	7 minutes with the KEEP WARM setting off	START

5. Use the **quick-release method** to bring the pot's pressure back to normal. Unlatch the lid and open the pot.

6.

Press the button for	Set it for	Set the time for	If necessary, press
SAUTÉ	MEDIUM, NORMAL, or CUSTOM 300°F	5 minutes	START

7. Stir the tomato paste into the dish until dissolved. Continue stirring until thickened, about 2 minutes.

8. Sprinkle the cheese evenly over the top of the casserole. Remove the *hot* insert from the machine and set the lid ajar on top of the insert for 5 minutes to begin to melt the cheese. Serve by the big spoonful.

Beyond

- You must halve the recipe for a **3-quart cooker.**
- We don't recommend using ground chicken in this recipe, unless you use it in a 50/50 combo with ground beef or pork.
- Skip the cheese on top of the casserole and serve big spoonfuls of the casserole over mounds of regular or low-fat ricotta in the serving bowls.

2 tablespoons olive oil

1¼ pounds lean ground beef

One 24-ounce jar plain marinara sauce (3 cups)

3 cups chicken broth

12 ounces dried spaghetti

Easy Spaghetti and Meat Sauce

4 servings

If you keep dried spaghetti and jars of plain marinara sauce in the pantry, you can have a fast lunch or dinner any day of the week. The dried noodles must be broken in half so they can sit in the sauce.

Here's the general rule for sauced pastas under pressure: The noodles don't necessarily need to be submerged, but they should be stirred so they're well coated before you lock the lid onto the pot.

1.

Press the button for	Set it for	Set the time for	If necessary, press
SAUTÉ	MEDIUM, NORMAL, or CUSTOM 300°F	10 minutes	START

2. Warm the oil in a **6- or 8-quart cooker** for a minute or two. Crumble in the ground beef, stirring fairly often to break up any clumps, until well browned, about 4 minutes.

3. Stir in the marinara sauce and broth. Turn off the SAUTÉ function. Break the spaghetti noodles in half and stir them into the sauce in the pot. Lock the lid onto the pot.

4.

Set the machine for	Set the level for	The valve must be	Set the time for	If necessary, press
PRESSURE COOK	MAX	—	5 minutes with the KEEP WARM setting off	START
PRESSURE COOK or MANUAL	HIGH	Closed	6 minutes with the KEEP WARM setting off	START

5. Use the **quick-release method** to bring the pot's pressure back to normal. Unlatch the lid and open the pot. Stir well before serving.

Beyond

- For a **3-quart cooker**, cut all the ingredients in half. Also break the spaghetti into smaller bits so they'll fit.

- For more assertive flavors, feel free to substitute lean ground pork, mild Italian sausage meat (no casings), or even ground lamb for the ground beef. Or use a 50/50 combo of ground beef and ground pork.

Cheesy Chili Mac

6 servings

There may be no more quintessentially kid-friendly food in the U.S. than a combination of a tomato-based chili and mac and cheese. (For a variation on this theme, see Cincinnati Chili on page 120.) Make sure that you scrape every bit of browned stuff off the bottom of the pot when the broth goes in. Otherwise, the pasta can stick and burn.

1.

Press the button for	Set it for	Set the time for	If necessary, press
SAUTÉ	MEDIUM, NORMAL, or CUSTOM 300°F	10 minutes	START

2. Warm the oil in a **6- or 8-quart cooker** for a minute or two. Add the onion and cook, stirring often, until it begins to soften, about 2 minutes. Add the chiles and garlic. Continue cooking, stirring once in a while, until the liquid has mostly evaporated, about 2 minutes.

3. Crumble in the ground beef. Cook, stirring often to break up any clumps, until the meat loses its raw, pink color, about 2 minutes. Stir in the chile powder, cumin, and salt until fragrant, just a couple of seconds.

4. Stir in the broth and scrape up *every speck of browned stuff* on the bottom of the pot. Turn off the SAUTÉ function. Stir in the tomatoes, beans, and ziti until the pasta is coated. Lock the lid onto the pot.

5.

Set the machine for	Set the level for	The valve must be	Set the time for	If necessary, press
PRESSURE COOK	MAX	—	5 minutes with the KEEP WARM setting off	START
PRESSURE COOK or MANUAL	HIGH	Closed	7 minutes with the KEEP WARM setting off	START

6. Use the **quick-release method** to bring the pot's pressure back to normal. Unlatch the lid and open the pot. Stir in the cheese. Set the lid askew over the pot for 5 minutes to melt the cheese and mellow the flavors. Stir again before serving.

---

2 tablespoons olive oil

1 medium yellow onion, chopped (1 cup)

Two 4½-ounce cans mild or hot chopped green chiles (1 cup)

1 medium garlic clove, peeled and minced (1 teaspoon)

1½ pounds lean ground beef

¼ cup standard chile powder

2 teaspoons ground cumin

½ teaspoon table salt

2 cups beef or chicken broth

One 28-ounce can crushed tomatoes (3½ cups)

One 15-ounce can pink beans, drained and rinsed (1¾ cups)

8 ounces dried ziti

4 ounces shredded Cheddar (1 cup)

Beyond

- You must halve the recipe for a 3-quart cooker.

- For a silkier finish, substitute butter for the olive oil.

- For a hotter chili mac, use pure chipotle chile powder (or a mix of chipotle and standard chile powder). If using pure chipotle chile powder, increase the ground cumin to 1 tablespoon and add 2 teaspoons dried oregano.

- Or skip those substitutions: Use standard chile powder and switch to shredded pepper Jack instead of Cheddar.

2 tablespoons olive oil

2 pounds lean ground beef

1 teaspoon onion powder

1 teaspoon dried oregano

½ teaspoon garlic powder

¼ teaspoon table salt

¼ teaspoon ground black pepper

4 tablespoons ketchup

4 tablespoons pickle relish

2 tablespoons Dijon mustard

6 ounces dried large elbow macaroni or radiatore pasta (2 cups)

1½ cups chicken broth

8 ounces shredded Cheddar (2 cups)

Cheeseburger Casserole

6 servings

This one is actually a layered casserole with all the flavors of a cheeseburger (if you count the pasta as the bun). You can skip either the ketchup or mustard (why would you?), but the pickle relish adds essential moisture. Make the layers as even as possible, using the back of a flatware tablespoon to spread the various ingredients across the open surface of the casserole.

1.

Press the button for	Set it for	Set the time for	If necessary, press
SAUTÉ	MEDIUM, NORMAL, or CUSTOM 300°F	10 minutes	START

2. Warm the oil in a **6-quart cooker** for a couple of minutes. Crumble in the ground beef and cook, stirring often to break up any clumps, until well browned, about 5 minutes. Stir in the onion powder, oregano, garlic powder, salt, and pepper until aromatic, just a few seconds. Turn off the SAUTÉ function.

3. Use a large spoon to transfer two-thirds of the mixture from the pot to a nearby bowl. Now build the casserole. Spread out the remaining meat mixture in an even layer in the pot. Spread 2 tablespoons ketchup, 2 tablespoons relish, and 1 tablespoon mustard over the meat mixture. Top with 1 cup dried pasta. Add half of the remaining meat mixture in an even layer. Repeat with the rest of the ketchup, relish, and mustard, then the rest of the pasta. Spread the rest of the meat mixture in an even layer over the top, then pour the broth on and all around the casserole. Top with the cheese in an even layer. Lock the lid onto the pot.

4.

Set the machine for	Set the level for	The valve must be	Set the time for	If necessary, press
PRESSURE COOK	MAX	—	5 minutes with the KEEP WARM setting off	START
PRESSURE COOK or MANUAL	HIGH	Closed	7 minutes with the KEEP WARM setting off	START

5. Use the **quick-release method** to bring the pot's pressure back to normal. Unlatch the lid and open the pot. Remove the *hot* insert from the machine and set the lid ajar over the insert for 5 to 10 minutes to allow the casserole to set up.

Beyond

- You must halve the recipe for a 3-quart cooker.

- For an **8-quart cooker**, you must increase all the ingredients by 50 percent. You can then build all-around thicker layers in the pot, or simply add an extra layer.

- For a vegetarian casserole, use 1½ pounds textured soy protein (a ground beef substitute) and *2 cups* vegetable broth.

- For a barbecue cheeseburger casserole, use a shredded Tex-Mex cheese blend and barbecue sauce instead of the ketchup and mustard.

Easy Cheesy Meatballs and Ziti

4 servings

Consider this recipe a fast, Instant Pot version of spaghetti and meatballs. There's no need to soak the breadcrumbs in water or milk. Because of the way the pressure works, those breadcrumbs will soften to make the meatballs incredibly tender. The meatballs should also be fairly compact so they'll hold together. And make them small, no more than 2 inches in diameter, so they'll cook in the time stated.

1. Mix the ground beef, breadcrumbs, and cheese in a large bowl until uniform. Form into sixteen equal balls, about the size of large walnuts in their shells.

2. Mix the marinara sauce, broth, and wine in a **6-quart cooker**. Stir in the ziti; nestle the meatballs in one layer into the sauce. Lock the lid onto the pot.

3.

Set the machine for	Set the level for	The valve must be	Set the time for	If necessary, press
PRESSURE COOK	MAX	—	5 minutes with the KEEP WARM setting off	START
PRESSURE COOK or MANUAL	HIGH	Closed	7 minutes with the KEEP WARM setting off	START

4. Use the **quick-release method** to bring the pot's pressure back to normal. Unlatch the lid and open the pot. Stir gently before serving.

1 pound lean ground beef

¼ cup Italian-seasoned dried breadcrumbs

¼ cup finely grated Parmigiano-Reggiano

One 24-ounce jar plain marinara sauce (3 cups)

1 cup beef or chicken broth

½ cup dry white wine, such as Chardonnay

8 ounces dried ziti

Beyond

- You must halve the recipe for a **3-quart cooker**.

- For an **8-quart cooker**, you must increase all the ingredients by 50 percent.

- For a creamier dish, use ½ cup chicken broth and ½ cup evaporated milk.

- For a more refined dish, use the Cherry Tomato and Herb Pasta Sauce (page 136) in place of the bottled marinara sauce.

2 tablespoons vegetable, corn, or canola oil

1 large yellow onion, chopped (1½ cups)

1 medium green bell pepper, stemmed, cored, and sliced into thin strips

1¼ pounds lean ground beef

2 cups beef or chicken broth

1¼ cups barbecue sauce

8 ounces dried rigatoni

Barbecue Beef and Pasta Casserole

4 servings

What if you swapped out the marinara sauce for barbecue sauce in a pasta dish? Ta da! Customize this casserole by using whatever barbecue sauce you prefer. We tried it with both sweet and vinegary sauces. Both were good but we preferred the latter because the pressure cooker already highlights all sorts of sweet flavors (here: the onion and ground beef). The only sauces that didn't work were exceptionally chunky ones that didn't provide enough liquid for the requisite steam.

1.

Press the button for	Set it for	Set the time for	If necessary, press
SAUTÉ	MEDIUM, NORMAL, or CUSTOM 300°F	10 minutes	START

2. Warm the oil in a **6-quart cooker** for a minute or two. Add the onion and bell pepper; cook, stirring often, until the onion begins to soften, about 4 minutes. Crumble in the ground beef and cook, stirring frequently to break up any clumps, until lightly browned, about 4 minutes.

3. Pour in the broth and scrape up *every speck of browned stuff* on the pot's bottom. Turn off the SAUTÉ function. Stir in the barbecue sauce and pasta. Lock the lid onto the pot.

4.

Set the machine for	Set the level for	The valve must be	Set the time for	If necessary, press
PRESSURE COOK	MAX	—	5 minutes with the KEEP WARM setting off	START
PRESSURE COOK or MANUAL	HIGH	Closed	7 minutes with the KEEP WARM setting off	START

5. Use the **quick-release method** to bring the pot's pressure back to normal. Unlatch the lid and open the pot. Stir well before serving.

Beyond

- You must halve the recipe for a **3-quart cooker**.

- For an **8-quart cooker**, you must use 1¾ cups barbecue sauce and increase the remaining ingredients by 50 percent.

- Add cheese! Once you've opened the lid, stir up to 4 ounces (1 cup) shredded Cheddar into the casserole. Set the lid askew and set aside for 5 minutes, until the cheese has melted.

Mediterranean Ground Beef and Pasta Casserole

4 servings

Lemon, cinnamon, and dill — if you haven't tried this Greek mélange, you don't know how delicious it is: aromatic and sweet, almost irresistible. This sort of pasta casserole is traditionally made with orzo, the little rice-shaped pasta. Unfortunately, orzo is so small that the "grains" fall to the pot's bottom and burn. But this tasty one-pot meal comes out just as well with sturdier ziti. *Opa!*

- 2 tablespoons olive oil
- 1 small yellow onion, chopped (½ cup)
- 2 jarred anchovy fillets, minced (optional)
- 2 teaspoons finely grated lemon zest
- 2 medium garlic cloves, peeled and minced (2 teaspoons)
- ½ teaspoon ground black pepper
- 1 pound lean ground beef
- 1 cup dry white wine, such as Chardonnay
- 2 medium plum or Roma tomatoes, chopped (⅔ cup)
- ¼ cup fresh dill fronds, chopped
- ½ teaspoon ground cinnamon
- 8 ounces dried ziti
- 1½ cups beef or chicken broth

1.

Press the button for	Set it for	Set the time for	If necessary, press
SAUTÉ	MEDIUM, NORMAL, or CUSTOM 300°F	10 minutes	START

2. Warm the oil in a **6- or 8-quart cooker** for a minute or two. Add the onion and cook, stirring often, until it softens, about 2 minutes. If using, add the anchovies and stir for 1 minute until the bits begin to melt. Stir in the lemon zest, garlic, and pepper until fragrant, a few seconds.

3. Crumble in the ground beef and cook, stirring often to break up any clumps, until the meat loses its raw, pink color, about 3 minutes. Stir in the wine, tomatoes, dill, and cinnamon. Scrape up *every speck of browned stuff* on the pot's bottom. Turn off the SAUTÉ function. Stir in the pasta and broth until uniform. Lock the lid onto the pot.

4.

Set the machine for	Set the level for	The valve must be	Set the time for	If necessary, press
PRESSURE COOK	MAX	—	5 minutes with the KEEP WARM setting off	START
PRESSURE COOK or MANUAL	HIGH	Closed	7 minutes with the KEEP WARM setting off	START

5. Use the **quick-release method** to bring the pot's pressure back to normal. Unlatch the lid and open the pot. Stir well before serving.

Beyond

- You must halve the recipe for a **3-quart cooker.**
- If you omit the anchovy fillets, you should also add 1 teaspoon table salt with the ground black pepper.
- For a more herbaceous dish, add up to 1 tablespoon minced fresh oregano leaves with the dill.
- For a little heat, add up to ½ teaspoon red pepper flakes with the cinnamon.
- Feel free to substitute ground lamb for the ground beef.
- And be sure to crumble feta over the servings.

2 tablespoons vegetable, corn, or canola oil

1 small red onion, halved and sliced into thin half-moons

1 tablespoon minced peeled fresh ginger

1 pound ground beef

One 14-ounce can diced tomatoes (1¾ cups)

6 tablespoons almond butter

2 tablespoons honey

2 teaspoons mild paprika

1 teaspoon ground cinnamon

1 teaspoon ground cloves

1 teaspoon ground coriander

1 teaspoon ground cumin

1 teaspoon table salt

½ teaspoon cayenne

2¼ cups chicken broth

8 ounces dried bow-tie (or farfalle) pasta

Beef and Bow-Ties in Spicy Tomato-Almond Sauce

4 servings

This pasta casserole has the flavors of a Moroccan tagine: almonds, ginger, and a heavy dose of dried spices. It's aromatic, decidedly right for a cold evening. It's even got a long-simmered flavor thanks to the almond butter, which adds a complexity similar to that gained through the long process of reducing a sauce on the stove.

If you're fortunate enough to live near a large gourmet supermarket or a Middle Eastern market, substitute 1 tablespoon ras al hanout for the cinnamon, cloves, coriander, and cumin. *Ras el hanout* means something like "top shelf" and is a blend of Middle Eastern spices, each blend proprietary to its maker (although any you find would do here).

1.

Press the button for	Set it for	Set the time for	If necessary, press
SAUTÉ	MEDIUM, NORMAL, or CUSTOM 300°F	10 minutes	START

2. Warm the oil in a **6- or 8-quart cooker** for a minute or two. Add the onion and ginger; cook, stirring often, until the onion begins to soften, about 3 minutes. Crumble in the ground beef; continue cooking, stirring frequently to break up any clumps, until the meat loses its raw, pink color, about 3 minutes.

3. Stir in the tomatoes and almond butter until the almond butter dissolves in the sauce, all the while scraping up *every speck of browned stuff* on the pot's bottom. Stir in the honey, paprika, cinnamon, cloves, coriander, cumin, salt, and cayenne until uniform. Turn off the SAUTÉ function; stir in the broth and pasta. Lock the lid onto the pot.

4.

Set the machine for	Set the level for	The valve must be	Set the time for	If necessary, press
PRESSURE COOK	MAX	——	5 minutes with the KEEP WARM setting off	START
PRESSURE COOK or MANUAL	HIGH	Closed	7 minutes with the KEEP WARM setting off	START

5. Use the **quick-release method** to bring the pot's pressure back to normal. Unlatch the lid and open the pot. Stir well before serving.

Beyond

• You must halve the recipe for a 3-quart cooker.

• For a little heat, use canned diced tomatoes with chiles.

• For a (somewhat) more authentically Middle Eastern dish, substitute ground lamb for the ground beef and add 1 preserved lemon, seeded and chopped, with the diced tomatoes.

• Garnish with plain Greek yogurt.

• For a more savory dish, reduce the honey to 1 tablespoon and use 1¼ cups dry white wine and 1 cup broth.

Dan Dan Noodles

4 servings

Hot, spicy, and satisfying, this streamlined version of the classic Sichuan dish will take the chill off any evening. It's traditionally made with fresh noodles; but by cooking dried spaghetti right in the sauce, the flavors meld into some cross between a pasta casserole and a Chinese classic. Have lots of beer on hand!

1.

Press the button for	Set it for	Set the time for	If necessary, press
SAUTÉ	MEDIUM, NORMAL, or CUSTOM 300°F	10 minutes	START

2. Heat the oil in a **6- or 8-quart cooker** for a minute or two. Crumble in the pork and cook, stirring often and breaking up any clumps, until gray but not browned, about 4 minutes. Stir in the scallions, sambal oelek or hot sauce, garlic, and ginger. Cook until aromatic, just a few seconds.

3. Add the tahini, soy sauce, vinegar, honey, sherry (or its substitutes), and Worcestershire sauce. Stir well until the tahini is uniform in the mixture, then stir in the broth. Turn off the SAUTÉ function, add the spaghetti, and submerge the noodles in the sauce without their touching the bottom of the insert. Lock the lid onto the pot.

4.

Set the machine for	Set the level for	The valve must be	Set the time for	If necessary, press
PRESSURE COOK	MAX	—	4 minutes with the KEEP WARM setting off	START
PRESSURE COOK or MANUAL	HIGH	Closed	6 minutes with the KEEP WARM setting off	START

5. Use the **quick-release method** to bring the pot's pressure back to normal. Unlatch the lid and open the cooker. Stir well before serving.

2 tablespoons peanut oil (or vegetable, corn, or canola oil)

1 pound lean ground pork

6 medium scallions, trimmed and thinly sliced

Up to 2 tablespoons sambal oelek or a hot red pepper sauce such as Sriracha

3 medium garlic cloves, peeled and minced (1 tablespoon)

1 tablespoon minced peeled fresh ginger

¼ cup tahini

¼ cup soy sauce

3 tablespoons balsamic vinegar

2 tablespoons honey

2 tablespoons dry sherry, dry vermouth, or water

1 tablespoon Worcestershire sauce

2 cups chicken broth

8 ounces dried spaghetti, broken in half

Beyond

- You must halve the recipe for a 3-quart cooker.

- To make the flavor more authentic and less like sesame noodles, substitute sunflower seed butter for the tahini. Or skip the fancy stuff and use natural-style creamy peanut butter.

- To be more authentic, you can also substitute ¼ cup Chinese black vinegar for the balsamic vinegar and Worcestershire sauce.

- And substitute Shaoxing (a Chinese rice wine) for the sherry, vermouth, or water.

- Finally, use roasted Chinese chiles in oil, particularly Laoganma Spicy Chili Crisp Sauce, instead of the sambal oelek or hot sauce.

See photo in insert.

¼ cup sliced almonds

1 tablespoon butter

1 small yellow onion, chopped (½ cup)

1 pound unseasoned chicken breast cut for stir-fry, any flavoring packets discarded; or 1 pound boneless skinless chicken breast, cut into ½ x ½-inch strips

1¼ teaspoons dried sage

1 teaspoon dried thyme

½ teaspoon dried oregano

¼ teaspoon grated nutmeg

¼ teaspoon table salt

2½ cups chicken broth

8 ounces dried ziti

⅔ cup regular or low-fat evaporated milk

½ cup packed sun-dried tomatoes, sliced into very thin strips

½ cup heavy cream

1½ tablespoons all-purpose flour

1 ounce finely grated Parmigiano-Reggiano (½ cup)

Creamy Cheesy Chicken and Ziti Casserole

4 servings

This pasta casserole is just about the fanciest recipe in this chapter. The dish requires a thickened sauce, sliced sun-dried tomatoes, sliced almonds…a whole fandango of kitchen prep. It's not fast, but it sure is tasty, a great family meal.

1. Spread the sliced almonds in a medium dry skillet set over medium-low heat. Cook until lightly toasted, about 2 minutes, stirring often. Or toast the nuts in the pot — use the SAUTÉ function on LOW or LESS. Pour the almonds into a small bowl and set aside.

2.

Press the button for	Set it for	Set the time for	If necessary, press
SAUTÉ	MEDIUM, NORMAL, or CUSTOM 300°F	10 minutes	START

3. Melt the butter in a **6- or 8-quart cooker**. Add the onion and cook, stirring often, until softened, about 3 minutes. Add the chicken, sage, thyme, oregano, nutmeg, and salt. Stir over the heat just until the chicken loses its raw color, about 2 minutes.

4. Stir in the broth, ziti, evaporated milk, and sun-dried tomatoes until uniform. Turn off the SAUTÉ function. Lock the lid onto the pot.

5.

Set the machine for	Set the level for	The valve must be	Set the timer for	If necessary, press
PRESSURE COOK	MAX	—	5 minutes with the KEEP WARM setting off	START
PRESSURE COOK or MANUAL	HIGH	Closed	7 minutes with the KEEP WARM setting off	START

6. Use the **quick-release method** to bring the pot's pressure back to normal. Unlatch the lid and open the pot. Whisk the cream and flour in a small bowl until the flour dissolves.

7.

Press the button for	Set it for	Set the time for	If necessary, press
SAUTÉ	MEDIUM, NORMAL, or CUSTOM 300°F	5 minutes	START

8. Stir until the sauce comes to a simmer. Whisk the cream mixture one time to make sure the flour is thoroughly combined. Stir this slurry into the pot and continue cooking, stirring almost constantly, until thickened, about 2 minutes. Turn off the SAUTÉ function and remove the *hot* insert from the pot. Stir in the cheese and set the lid askew over the insert for a couple of minutes to blend the flavors. Sprinkle the toasted almonds over individual servings.

Beyond

- You must halve the recipe for a **3-quart cooker.**

- For a more authentic flavor, substitute pine nuts for the sliced almonds.

- For fewer ingredients, omit the sage, thyme, oregano, and nutmeg. Instead, use 2 teaspoons salt-free dried poultry seasoning blend.

4 tablespoons (½ stick) butter

1 medium yellow onion, chopped (1 cup)

1 pound unseasoned chicken breast cut for stir-fry, any flavoring packets discarded; or 1 pound boneless skinless chicken breast, cut into ½ x ½-inch strips

3 cups chicken broth

3 tablespoons mild paprika

½ teaspoon caraway seeds

¼ teaspoon grated nutmeg

¼ teaspoon table salt

¼ teaspoon ground black pepper

6 ounces wide egg or no-yolk noodles

½ cup regular or low-fat sour cream

Chicken Noodle Paprikash

4 servings

This dish is hardly an authentic Hungarian version of paprikash but an interpretation à la American roadside diners: a rich, buttery stew over noodles, here morphed further into a one-pot casserole.

Don't blanch at the amount of butter: It provides the bulk of the sauce's flavor. And do not heat the sour cream once it is added or it will break and turn the sauce into a watery mess. If you plan on making some and saving it back for another meal, omit the sour cream from that portion and reheat it later before adding the sour cream.

1.

Press the button for	Set it for	Set the time for	If necessary, press
SAUTÉ	MEDIUM, NORMAL, or CUSTOM 300°F	10 minutes	START

2. Melt the butter in a **6- or 8-quart cooker**. Add the onion and cook, stirring often, until softened, about 3 minutes. Stir in the chicken strips and cook until they lose their pink color, about 2 minutes.

3. Stir in the broth, paprika, caraway seeds, nutmeg, salt, and pepper until aromatic, about 1 minute. Turn off the SAUTÉ function. Stir in the noodles and lock the lid onto the pot.

4.

Set the machine for	Set the level for	The valve must be	Set the time for	If necessary, press
PRESSURE COOK	MAX	—	3 minutes with the KEEP WARM setting off	START
PRESSURE COOK or MANUAL	HIGH	Closed	4 minutes with the KEEP WARM setting off	START

5. Use the **quick-release method** to bring the pot's pressure back to normal. Unlatch the lid and open the pot. Stir in the sour cream until smooth just before serving.

Beyond

- You must halve the recipe for a **3-quart cooker**.

- For an added punch of flavor, add up to 2 teaspoons minced garlic with the chicken.

- Use a combination of mild and hot Hungarian paprika — or *all* hot Hungarian paprika (if you're brave).

Chicken Enchilada Casserole

4 servings

Given that this recipe is among the pasta casseroles, you already know it's not a true enchilada casserole. There are no corn tortillas. Instead, we created a good facsimile of the American favorite with purchased enchilada sauce and lots of chicken and vegetables, all turned into a pasta sauce for ziti. There's a wide range of heat quotients among prepared enchilada sauces. Make sure you get one that fits your needs.

1. Mix the enchilada sauce, chicken, broth, beans, bell pepper, corn, onion, smoked paprika, and cumin in a **6- or 8-quart cooker**. Stir in the ziti until coated. Lock the lid onto the pot.

2.

Set the machine for	Set the level for	The valve must be	Set the time for	If necessary, press
PRESSURE COOK	MAX	—	5 minutes with the KEEP WARM setting off	START
PRESSURE COOK or MANUAL	HIGH	Closed	7 minutes with the KEEP WARM setting off	START

3. Use the **quick-release method** to bring the pot's pressure back to normal. Unlatch the lid and open the pot.

4.

Press the button for	Set it for	Set the time for	If necessary, press
SAUTÉ	MEDIUM, NORMAL, or CUSTOM 300°F	5 minutes	START

5. Bring the sauce to a simmer, stirring constantly. Add the cornmeal and continue cooking, stirring constantly, until thickened about 1 minute. Turn off the SAUTÉ function and remove the *hot* insert from the pot. Set the lid askew over the insert for 5 minutes to blend the flavors and continue to thicken the sauce. Stir well before serving.

One 28-ounce can red enchilada sauce (3½ cups)

1 pound boneless skinless chicken breast, diced into ½-inch pieces

2 cups chicken broth

One 15-ounce can pink beans, drained and rinsed (1¾ cups)

1 large green bell pepper, stemmed, cored, and cut into thin strips

1 cup fresh or frozen corn kernels (if frozen, do not thaw)

1 small yellow onion, chopped (½ cup)

1 teaspoon mild smoked paprika

1 teaspoon ground cumin

8 ounces dried ziti

2 tablespoons yellow cornmeal

Beyond

- You must halve the recipe for a **3-quart cooker**.

- To add cheese, wait until the sauce has thickened with the cornmeal, then sprinkle up to 4 ounces (1 cup) shredded Monterey Jack or mozzarella evenly over the top of the casserole. As directed, set the pot's lid askew on top and set aside for 5 minutes to melt the cheese. But don't stir the stew at the end. Instead, dish up the cheese with the casserole below by the big spoonful.

- Garnish the servings with pickled jalapeño rings, chowchow, and/or sliced avocado.

2 cups chicken broth

1 cup regular or low-fat evaporated milk

4 ounces white button mushrooms, thinly sliced

2 medium celery stalks, thinly sliced (½ cup)

2 tablespoons butter

1 teaspoon onion powder

1 teaspoon ground dried mustard

¼ teaspoon table salt

12 ounces wide egg or no-yolk noodles

1 cup heavy cream

Two 6-ounce cans tuna, preferably yellow fin tuna packed in oil, drained

8 ounces grated Swiss cheese (2 cups)

Beyond

- You must halve the recipe for a 3-quart cooker.

- For a richer dish, look for canned or jarred *Italian* tuna packed in olive oil. Drain off the oil before stirring the chunks into the casserole.

- For a fresher flavor, add up to 1 tablespoon minced fresh herbs with the tuna: Tarragon, thyme, oregano, or parsley work best.

- For more kick, add up to ½ teaspoon garlic powder with the onion powder.

- Want a crunchy topping? Crush potato chips over the top of each serving. (Omit the salt from the recipe.)

- Substitute two 6-ounce cans salmon (drained), preferably wild Alaskan pink salmon, for the tuna for Salmon Noodle Casserole.

Tuna Noodle Casserole

6 servings

By cooking egg noodles in a mixture of broth and milk, we increase their silkiness, rendering this Instant Pot version of the classic casserole even more astounding.

We leave the tuna out until *after* cooking, so the dish doesn't turn too fishy. There won't be a crunchy top, but we have a suggestion for how to make one in the *Beyond* section.

1. Mix the broth, evaporated milk, mushrooms, celery, butter, onion powder, dried mustard, and salt in a **6- or 8-quart cooker**. Stir in the noodles until well coated. Lock the lid onto the pot.

2.

Set the machine for	Set the level for	The valve must be	Set the time for	If necessary, press
PRESSURE COOK	MAX	—	3 minutes with the KEEP WARM setting off	START
PRESSURE COOK or MANUAL	HIGH	Closed	4 minutes with the KEEP WARM setting off	START

3. Use the **quick-release method** to bring the pot's pressure back to normal. Unlatch the lid and open the pot. Stir in the cream.

4.

Press the button for	Set it for	Set the time for	If necessary, press
SAUTÉ	MEDIUM, NORMAL, or CUSTOM 300°F	5 minutes	START

5. Cook, stirring often, until the sauce is bubbling fairly well, about 1 minute. Turn off the SAUTÉ function and remove the *hot* insert from the pot. Gently stir in the tuna and cheese. Set the lid askew over the insert for a couple of minutes to melt the cheese.

Seafood Newburg Casserole

6 servings

Here's a multi-cooker version of a dish fashionable in the Mad Men '50s and '60s. We've turned it into a more hearty family dinner, suitable for a weeknight when you still want to pull out the stops.

The shrimp are fairly small in order to cook in the same time as the scallops. If you can only find medium shrimp (that is, about 30 per pound), peel and devein them, then chop them into pieces about as big as the scallop quarters.

1.

Press the button for	Set it for	Set the time for	If necessary, press
SAUTÉ	MEDIUM, NORMAL, or CUSTOM 300°F	5 minutes	START

2. Mix the broth, sherry, butter, tarragon, paprika, and salt in a **6- or 8-quart cooker**. Cook until the butter melts, stirring occasionally, about 3 minutes. Turn off the SAUTÉ function and stir in the noodles until coated. Lock the lid onto the pot.

3.

Set the machine for	Set the level for	The valve must be	Set the time for	If necessary, press
PRESSURE COOK	MAX	—	3 minutes with the KEEP WARM setting off	START
PRESSURE COOK or MANUAL	HIGH	Closed	4 minutes with the KEEP WARM setting off	START

4. Use the **quick-release method** to bring the pot's pressure back to normal. Unlatch the lid and open the pot.

5.

Press the button for	Set it for	Set the time for	If necessary, press
SAUTÉ	LOW or LESS	5 minutes	START

6. Whisk the cream and egg yolk in a small bowl. Whisk about 1 cup of the hot mixture from the pot into this cream mixture, then stir this combined mixture back into the pot along with the scallops and shrimp.

7. Cook, stirring constantly, just until the shrimp are firm, not more than 2 minutes. Immediately turn off the SAUTÉ function, remove the hot insert from the pot to stop the cooking, and continue stirring until any bubbling stops and the noodles are well coated.

2½ cups chicken broth

½ cup dry sherry

2 tablespoons butter

1 tablespoon fresh minced tarragon leaves

½ teaspoon mild paprika

¼ teaspoon table salt

12 ounces wide egg or no-yolk noodles

¾ cup heavy cream

1 large egg yolk

½ pound sea scallops, quartered

½ pound small shrimp (about 40 per pound), peeled, deveined, and cut in half lengthwise

Beyond

- You must halve the recipe for a **3-quart cooker.**

- Stir ½ pound pasteurized crab meat, picked over for shells and cartilage, into the casserole with the other seafood.

- If you don't want to use sherry, substitute an equivalent amount of bottled clam juice, available in almost all supermarkets (sometimes near the Italian food).

- For a little heat, add up to 1 teaspoon red pepper flakes with the tarragon.

- Garnish the servings with minced chives or the green bits of a scallion.

One 24-ounce jar plain marinara sauce (3 cups)

¼ cup red or sweet vermouth

1 pound boneless pork loin, cut into ½-inch cubes

One 14½-ounce bag frozen gnocchi (do not thaw)

1 cup frozen peas (do not thaw)

Gnocchi Casserole with Pork and Peas

4 servings

Frozen gnocchi are an incredibly easy pasta(-like) addition to this casserole, but there are two tricks to success. First, cut the pork into small cubes, each a little smaller than the gnocchi, so they'll cook efficiently and at the same time, none turning to mush.

Second, watch the pot during the second cooking. The moment the float valve comes up in the lid to lock the lid onto the pot, turn the machine off. In essence, the gnocchi don't cook under full pressure. They cook *just until* the lid locks into place. That second cooking should only be done at HIGH, not at MAX.

1. Mix the marinara sauce, vermouth, and pork in a **6- or 8-quart cooker**. Lock the lid onto the pot.

2.

Set the machine for	Set the level for	The valve must be	Set the time for	If necessary, press
PRESSURE COOK	MAX	——	7 minutes with the KEEP WARM setting off	START
PRESSURE COOK or MANUAL	HIGH	Closed	10 minutes with the KEEP WARM setting off	START

3. Use the **quick-release method** to bring the machine's pressure back to normal. Unlatch the lid and open the pot. Stir in the gnocchi and peas.

4.

Press the button for	Set it for	The valve must be	Set the time for	If necessary, press
PRESSURE COOK or MANUAL	HIGH	Closed	1 minute with the KEEP WARM setting off	START

5. *The moment* the float valve (or pin) pops up to lock the lid and the machine stops putting out steam, turn it off and let its pressure **return to normal naturally** for 1 minute. Then use the **quick-release method** to get rid of the residual pressure in the pot. Unlatch the lid and open the cooker. Stir well before serving.

Beyond

- You must halve the recipe for a **3-quart cooker**.

- To avoid the alcohol, substitute no-sugar-added cranberry juice for the vermouth.

- For added heat, stir up to 1 teaspoon red pepper flakes into the pot with the marinara sauce.

- Sprinkle up to 2 ounces (1 cup) finely grated Parmigiano-Reggiano over the top of the casserole in the pot.

- Substitute 1 pound boneless skinless chicken thighs, cut into ½-inch pieces, for the pork.

Breakfast Hash
(page 38)

Bundt Banana Bread (page 40)

Pesto Minestrone Soup (page 49)

Chicken Noodle Soup (page 74)

Infused Waters (page 109)

Fire House Chili (page 118)
with sour cream, pickle relish,
and pickled jalapeños

**Creamy Tomato
and Basil Pasta
Sauce (page 135)
with cavatappi**

**Italian Pot Roast
Ragù (page 146)
over ricotta**

**Dan Dan
Noodles
(page 169)**

**Vegetable Lo Mein with
Rice Vermicelli (page 184)**

Easy Lasagna Pie
(page 187)

All-American Pulled Pork (page 195)
on slider buns with cole slaw

**Pulled Brisket (page 206) over
No-Drain Mashed Potatoes (page 424)**

**Thanksgiving-Inspired Pulled Turkey
(page 221) over a corn muffin**

Three-Lentil
Dal Makhani
(page 233)

Better Butter Chicken (page 235) with cauliflower rice

Thai Seafood Curry
(page 253)

**Fried Chicken
(page 262)**

Cheesy Pesto Gnocchi Casserole

4 servings

Here's an easy dump-and-stir casserole, ready in minutes, the sort of miracle we all want from a multi-cooker. Look for a decent pesto, not an oily mess. The better stuff is sometimes found near the salad bar in supermarkets. See the *Beyond* for a homemade version.

As in the previous recipe, stop the cooking the moment the pressure valve or pin rises to lock onto the pot. In other words, don't step away from the cooker and don't even let it come all the way up to pressure. Such vigilance seems a small price to pay for a rich casserole, a quick meal on its own or a great thing to serve alongside steaks or chops off the grill.

1. Mix the gnocchi, ham, broth, evaporated milk, pimientos, and pesto in a **3- or 6-quart cooker**. Lock the lid onto the pot.

2.

Set the machine for	Set the level for	The valve must be	Set the time for	If necessary, press
PRESSURE COOK or MANUAL	HIGH	Closed	1 minute with the KEEP WARM setting off	START

3. *The moment* the float valve rises to lock the lid onto the pot and the machine stops putting out steam, turn it off and let its pressure **return to normal naturally** for 1 minute. Then use the **quick-release method** to get rid of the pot's residual pressure. Unlatch the lid and open the cooker. Stir the cheese and cream into the casserole. Set the lid askew over the pot for 5 minutes to melt the cheese.

One 14½-ounce bag frozen gnocchi (do not thaw)

1 cup diced smoked deli ham (about 5 ounces)

1 cup chicken broth

½ cup evaporated milk

One 4-ounce jar diced pimientos, drained (½ cup)

3 tablespoons purchased pesto

4 ounces shredded Swiss cheese (1 cup)

¼ cup heavy cream

Beyond

- For an **8-quart cooker**, you must increase all the ingredients by 50 percent.

- For a fast homemade pesto, put 2 cups loosely packed basil leaves, ⅓ cup olive oil, ⅓ cup finely grated Parmigiano-Reggiano, ¼ cup nuts (walnut, almonds, or pine nuts), 1 or 2 peeled medium garlic cloves, and ½ teaspoon salt in a food processor. Cover and process until smooth, adding dribs and drabs of water if you feel the sauce is too thick. Store extra pesto with a thin coating of olive oil over the top in a sealed container in the fridge for up to 4 days.

- Swap in another white cheese for the Swiss: mozzarella, Monterey Jack, provolone, pecorino, or white Cheddar (mild, not sharp).

One 24-ounce jar pizza sauce (3 cups)

1 pound sweet Italian pork or turkey sausage links, cut into 1-inch pieces

2 cups frozen bell pepper strips (do not thaw)

One 5-ounce package sliced pepperoni

½ cup chicken or vegetable broth

4 ounces mozzarella, diced

½ pound fresh pizza dough

¼ cup finely grated Parmigiano-Reggiano

Pizza Casserole

4 servings

Here's the best way to make a pizza in a multi-cooker. The dish is actually something like a pasta casserole, given that the pizza dough is rolled into balls, then floated like dumplings in a sauce that tastes just like the one on a sausage and pepperoni pizza.

As to the cooking technique, it's a bit unusual. First, the sauce and other pizza ingredients are put under pressure. Then the "dumplings" (made with pizza dough) are added and finished with the SLOW COOK function. Your model may not go as low as 25 minutes on that setting — in which case, you'll need to set it with the minimum amount of time possible and also set a more traditional timer for the proper time.

1. Mix the pizza sauce, sausage, bell pepper strips, pepperoni, and broth in a **6- or 8-quart cooker**. Lock the lid onto the pot.

2.

Set the machine for	Set the level for	The valve must be	Set the time for	If necessary, press
PRESSURE COOK	MAX	—	5 minutes with the KEEP WARM setting off	START
PRESSURE COOK or MANUAL	HIGH	Closed	6 minutes with the KEEP WARM setting off	START

3. Use the **quick-release method** to bring the pot's pressure back to normal. Unlatch the lid and open the cooker. Stir the mixture inside, then scatter the mozzarella cubes over the top.

4. Form the pizza dough into 8 balls, each about the size of a Ping-Pong ball. Nestle these about a quarter of the way into the sauce. Sprinkle the grated Parmigiano-Reggiano over the balls and the sauce.

5.

Set the machine for	Set the level for	The valve must be	Set the time for	If necessary, press
SLOW COOK	HIGH	Opened	25 minutes with the KEEP WARM setting off	START

6. Turn off the machine when done, open the pot, and serve without stirring.

Beyond

- You must halve the recipe for a **3-quart cooker**.

- For a more savory casserole, substitute plain marinara sauce for the pizza sauce.

- Add other pizza toppings you like with the pepperoni: 1 cup thinly sliced white or brown button mushrooms, ¼ cup sliced pitted black olives, ¼ cup chopped red onion, and/or 2 or 3 chopped anchovy fillets.

- Rather than sprinkling the Parmigiano-Reggiano over the casserole, knead it into the pizza dough before making the eight balls.

Israeli Couscous with Eggplant and Peppers

4 servings

Israeli couscous is something like pasta: little dried balls of semolina or wheat flour, also called "Jerusalem couscous," "pearl couscous," and "ptitim" (in Israel). The pasta has been toasted, so Israeli couscous has a bolder flavor, similar to barley. Israeli couscous stands up to big flavors in a casserole like this one — which is something like a thick Mediterranean stew, or maybe an Israeli couscous version of pasta puttanesca.

2 tablespoons olive oil

1 medium shallot, minced

1 tablespoon drained and rinsed capers, minced

3 medium garlic cloves, peeled and minced (1 tablespoon)

½ teaspoon red pepper flakes

One 1-pound eggplant, diced (no need to peel—4 cups)

2 medium green bell peppers, stemmed, cored, and chopped (2 cups)

2½ cups vegetable broth

One 14-ounce can diced tomatoes (1¾ cups)

1½ cups Israeli couscous

One 3- to 4-inch rosemary stalk

1.

Press the button for	Set it for	Set the time for	If necessary, press
SAUTÉ	MEDIUM, NORMAL, or CUSTOM 300°F	10 minutes	START

2. Warm the oil in a **6- or 8-quart cooker** for a minute or two. Add the shallot, capers, garlic, and red pepper flakes. Cook, stirring frequently, until the shallot softens, about 2 minutes. Stir in the eggplant and bell pepper. Continue cooking, stirring often, until the eggplant begins to soften, about 4 minutes.

3. Stir in the broth. Scrape up *every speck of browned stuff* on the pot's bottom. Turn off the SAUTÉ function. Stir in the tomatoes and couscous. Tuck the rosemary stalk into the mixture. Lock the lid onto the pot.

4.

Set the machine for	Set the level for	The valve must be	Set the time for	If necessary, press
PRESSURE COOK	MAX	—	7 minutes with the KEEP WARM setting off	START
PRESSURE COOK or MANUAL	HIGH	Closed	10 minutes with the KEEP WARM setting off	START

5. Use the **quick-release method** to bring the pot's pressure back to normal. Unlatch the lid and open the cooker. Find and discard the rosemary stalk. Stir well, then set the lid askew over the pot for 5 to 10 minutes so that the casserole continues to set up just before serving.

Beyond

- You must halve the recipe for a 3-quart cooker.

- Add 1 jarred anchovy fillet, minced, with the shallot and other ingredients. (The dish, of course, will no longer be vegan.)

- Add up to 3 fresh oregano sprigs with the rosemary stalk.

- Grate lots of Parmigiano-Reggiano over each serving. (Again, no longer vegan.)

2 tablespoons olive oil

1 large yellow onion, chopped
(1½ cups)

1 medium green bell pepper,
stemmed, cored, and chopped
(1 cup)

2 medium celery ribs, thinly sliced
(⅔ cup)

14 ounces smoked sausage,
preferably Cajun andouille, cut into
½-inch slices

2½ cups chicken broth

One 14-ounce can diced tomatoes
(1¾ cups)

1½ cups Israeli couscous

1 teaspoon dried thyme

1 teaspoon dried sage

½ teaspoon cayenne

½ teaspoon table salt

Cajun-Inspired Sausage and Israeli Couscous Casserole

4 servings

This one-pot supper is stocked with big flavors, the better to pair with those little, toasted pasta balls (aka Israeli couscous). If the dish is too soupy for your taste, boil it down in the pot for a couple minutes after pressure-cooking, using the SAUTÉ setting at MEDIUM, NORMAL, or CUSTOM 300°F.

However, don't make it too dry. The Israeli couscous will continue to absorb moisture as it sits. In fact, you'll need to thin out leftovers with a little extra broth when reheating.

1.

Press the button for	Set it for	Set the time for	If necessary, press
SAUTÉ	MEDIUM, NORMAL, or CUSTOM 300°F	5 minutes	START

2. Warm the oil in a **6- or 8-quart cooker** for a minute or two. Add the onion, bell pepper, and celery. Cook, stirring often, until the onion begins to soften, about 5 minutes. Add the sausage and cook, stirring fairly often, until all the sausage is warmed through and its oil has begun to loosen, about 3 minutes.

3. Stir in the broth and scrape up *every speck of browned stuff* on the pot's bottom. Turn off the SAUTÉ function. Stir in the tomatoes, couscous, thyme, sage, cayenne, and salt. Lock the lid onto the pot.

4.

Set the machine for	Set the level for	The valve must be	Set the time for	If necessary, press
PRESSURE COOK	MAX	—	7 minutes with the KEEP WARM setting off	START
PRESSURE COOK or MANUAL	HIGH	Closed	10 minutes with the KEEP WARM setting off	START

5. Use the **quick-release method** to bring the pot's pressure back to normal. Unlatch the lid and open the cooker. Set the lid askew over the cooker for 5 minutes to let the casserole set up. Stir well before serving.

Beyond

- You must halve the recipe for a **3-quart cooker.**

- Feel free to use smoked kielbasa or smoked bratwurst — although the dish won't have the characteristic Cajun flavor.

- The casserole may not be spicy enough for some tastes. Pass Tabasco sauce or other hot chile sauce at the table.

Thai-Inspired Chicken and Rice Noodles

4 servings

We've tried to recreate what's become something of an American classic: a sort of streamlined version of a rice noodle Thai stir-fry, less sweet than most versions, more true sweet-and-sour, even packed with savory flavors.

Quality fish sauce is the key. You can find it in the Asian aisle of almost every supermarket, even artisanal bottlings like Red Boat. Don't worry about its stinky aroma. It mellows beautifully as it cooks.

And one more thing: Sambal oelek is a hot, thick, red chile sauce, once from Southeast Asia but now found in almost every supermarket in North America. You can substitute any thick red chile sauce or paste, even a standard hot sauce like Texas Pete.

1.

Press the button for	Set it for	Set the time for	If necessary, press
SAUTÉ	MEDIUM, NORMAL, or CUSTOM 300°F	10 minutes	START

2. Warm the oil in a **6- or 8-quart cooker** for a minute or two. Add the bell peppers and shallots. Cook, stirring often, until the shallot softens, about 4 minutes. Add the chicken and garlic. Cook, stirring frequently, until the chicken loses its raw, pink color, about 3 minutes.

3. Stir in the broth, turn off the SAUTÉ function, and scrape up *every speck of browned stuff* on the pot's bottom. Stir in the lime juice, fish sauce, brown sugar, sambal oelek, and tomato paste until the brown sugar and tomato paste dissolve and the mixture is uniform in color. Stir in the rice noodles, basil, and peanuts. Lock the lid onto the pot.

4.

Set the machine for	Set the level for	The valve must be	Set the time for	If necessary, press
PRESSURE COOK	MAX	—	3 minutes with the KEEP WARM setting off	START
PRESSURE COOK or MANUAL	HIGH	Closed	4 minutes with the KEEP WARM setting off	START

5. Use the **quick-release method** to bring the pot's pressure back to normal. Unlatch the lid and open the cooker. Stir well and serve with lime wedges to squeeze over each portion.

1 tablespoon peanut oil (or vegetable, corn, or canola oil)

2½ cups frozen sliced bell pepper strips (do not thaw); or 2 medium red bell peppers, stemmed, cored, and sliced into thin strips

4 medium shallots, halved and thinly sliced lengthwise

2 pounds unseasoned chicken breast cut for stir-fry, any flavoring packets discarded; or 2 pounds boneless skinless chicken breast, cut into ½ x ½-inch strips

3 medium garlic cloves, peeled and minced (1 tablespoon)

1¼ cups chicken broth

¼ cup fresh lime juice

¼ cup fish sauce

¼ cup packed light brown sugar

2 tablespoons sambal oelek

1 tablespoon tomato paste

8 ounces dried rice stick noodles or rice noodles for pad Thai

½ cup loosely packed fresh basil leaves, roughly chopped

¼ cup chopped unsalted peanuts

Lime wedges for garnishing

Beyond

- You must halve the recipe for a 3-quart cooker.

- For a more authentic taste, substitute palm sugar or even coconut sugar for the brown sugar.

1¼ pounds lean ground turkey

¼ cup minced chives or the green parts of scallions

3 tablespoons yellow cornmeal

1 large egg white

1 teaspoon dried thyme

½ teaspoon table salt

½ teaspoon ground black pepper

2 medium shallots, chopped (about 1 cup)

3 cups chicken broth

2 tablespoons butter, cut into small bits

2 tablespoons finely chopped fresh sage leaves

¼ cup light, slightly sweet white wine, such as Pinot Grigio

7 ounces dried rice stick noodles or rice noodles for pad Thai

¼ cup heavy cream

Turkey Meatballs and Rice Noodles in Cream Sauce

4 servings

This straightforward meatball dish requires two different techniques under pressure. First, you'll partially cook the meatballs in the sauce; then you'll add the noodles and bring the pot not even to HIGH pressure, but *just until* the lid locks in place with the float valve or pin. Stopping the cooking at this moment ensures three things: 1) that the rice noodles don't stick, 2) that we don't have to make a soupy sauce to protect them, and 3) that the meatballs are done without being dry.

1. Stir the ground turkey, chives or scallions, cornmeal, egg white, thyme, salt, and pepper in a large bowl until uniform. Form into 16 moderately small, compact balls, each from about 2 rounded tablespoons of the mixture. Place these in a **6- or 8-quart cooker**.

2. Scatter the shallots over the meatballs. Pour in the broth, then add the butter, sage, and wine. Lock the lid onto the pot.

3.

Set the machine for	Set the level for	The valve must be	Set the time for	If necessary, press
PRESSURE COOK	MAX	—	2 minutes with the KEEP WARM setting off	START
PRESSURE COOK or MANUAL	HIGH	Closed	3 minutes with the KEEP WARM setting off	START

4. Use the **quick-release method** to bring the pot's pressure back to normal. Unlatch the lid and open the cooker. Use a slotted spoon to transfer the meatballs to a large bowl.

5. Break up the rice noodles to fit in the pot. Stir them into the liquid mixture. Set the meatballs back on top. Lock the lid back onto the pot.

6.

Set the machine for	Set the level for	The valve must be	Set the time for	If necessary, press
PRESSURE COOK or MANUAL	HIGH	Closed	1 minute with the KEEP WARM setting off	START

7. *The moment* the float valve (or pin) comes up to lock the lid in place and the machine stops putting out steam, turn it off and let its pressure **return to normal naturally** for 4 minutes. Then use the **quick-release method** to release any residual pressure in the pot. Unlatch the lid and open the pot again.

8.

Press the button for	Set it for	Set the time for	If necessary, press
SAUTÉ	MEDIUM, NORMAL, or CUSTOM 300°F	5 minutes	START

9. Stir in the cream. Bring the sauce to a low simmer, stirring gently, for less than 1 minute. Turn off the SAUTÉ function and remove the *hot* insert from the pot. Continue stirring gently until the bubbling stops and the sauce coats the noodles.

Beyond

- You must halve the recipe for a **3-quart cooker.**

- For a more sophisticated dish, add up to 2 tablespoons of any number of chopped, fresh, green, leafy herbs to the sauce with the cream — think rosemary, oregano, marjoram, or tarragon.

- For more kick, add up to 2 teaspoons minced garlic with the shallots.

- For a warm, comforting flavor, add up to ½ teaspoon grated nutmeg to the meatball mixture.

3 cups vegetable broth

6 tablespoons soy sauce

3 tablespoons unseasoned rice vinegar

2 tablespoons minced peeled fresh ginger

1 tablespoon hoisin sauce

2 medium garlic cloves, peeled and minced (2 teaspoons)

8 ounces dried rice vermicelli

1½ pounds bagged frozen vegetables for stir fry (do not thaw), any flavoring packets discarded

Vegetable Lo Mein with Rice Vermicelli

6 servings

It's hard to imagine an easier meal than this Instant Pot version of the take-out classic. Just mix the sauce in the cooker, then layer the noodles and frozen vegetables as directed in and onto the sauce. The machine doesn't really even come up to high pressure. When the float valve or pin rises to lock the lid onto the pot, turn it off and set it aside. Don't leave the pot unattended while it's coming to pressure. Pay attention to the cues in the instructions below.

1. Mix the broth, soy sauce, rice vinegar, ginger, hoisin sauce, and garlic in a **6- or 8-quart cooker**. Break the rice vermicelli to fit the pot and add them to the sauce. Pour the vegetables in an even layer over the top of everything. Lock the lid onto the pot.

2.

Press the button for	Set it for	The valve must be	Set the time for	If necessary, press
PRESSURE COOK or MANUAL	HIGH	Closed	1 minute with the KEEP WARM setting off	START

3. *The moment* the float valve (or pin) comes up to lock the lid in place and the machine stops putting out steam, turn it off and let its pressure **return to normal naturally** for 2 minutes. Then use the **quick-release method** to get rid of the residual pressure in the pot. Unlatch the lid and open the pot. Stir well before serving.

Beyond

- The dish will not work well in a **3-quart cooker** as not enough of the rice vermicelli will make it into the sauce.

- Hoisin sauce is a sweet, pasty condiment, often made from soy beans or sweet potatoes. There are versions of gluten-free hoisin sauce on the market but the quality varies. If you want to make your own, combine ¼ cup gluten-free soy sauce, 2 tablespoons creamy natural-style peanut butter, 2 tablespoons molasses, 1 tablespoon toasted sesame oil, 2 teaspoons unseasoned rice vinegar, 1 teaspoon minced garlic, 1 teaspoon Sriracha, ¼ teaspoon dried ground mustard, and ¼ teaspoon ground cloves in a small saucepan. Bring to a simmer over medium-low heat, stirring very often. Then reduce the heat and cook, stirring very often, almost constantly, until thickened, about 4 minutes. Store in a sealed, glass jar in the fridge for up to 2 weeks.

See photo in insert.

Vegetable Noodle Stroganoff

4 servings

Since this simple casserole contains so many vegetables, it's more like a full meal than some of the recipes in this chapter. (And check the suggestions among those in the *Beyond* section to add even more.)

    Because all those vegetables give off moisture as they cook, the sauce may be a little soupy when you open the pot. It's impossible to say exactly how much moisture any given vegetable will give off. That's why we boil down the sauce before adding the sour cream. But check the consistency when you open the pot. You may not need to do that extra step.

1.

Press the button for	Set it for	Set the time for	If necessary, press
SAUTÉ	MEDIUM, NORMAL, or CUSTOM 300°F	10 minutes	START

2. Melt the butter in a **6- or 8-quart cooker**. Add the onion and cook, stirring often, until softened, about 3 minutes. Add the mushrooms, zucchini, and garlic; cook, stirring often, until the mushrooms begin to soften, about 3 minutes.

3. Stir in the mustard, thyme, salt, and pepper until aromatic. Stir in the broth and scrape *every speck of brown stuff* on the bottom of the pot. Turn off the SAUTÉ function and stir in the noodles. All should be well coated but not all will be submerged. Lock the lid onto the pot.

4.

Set the machine for	Set the level for	The valve must be	Set the time for	If necessary, press
PRESSURE COOK	MAX	—	3 minutes with the KEEP WARM setting off	START
PRESSURE COOK or MANUAL	HIGH	Closed	4 minutes with the KEEP WARM setting off	START

5. Use the **quick-release method** to bring the pot's pressure back to normal. Unlatch the lid and open the pot.

6.

Press the button for	Set it for	Set the time for	If necessary, press
SAUTÉ	MEDIUM, NORMAL, or CUSTOM 300°F	5 minutes	START

7. Bring the sauce to a simmer, stirring all the while. Stir until most of the liquid has evaporated, about 1 minute. Turn off the SAUTÉ function. Remove the *hot* insert from the pot and stir in the sour cream until uniform just before serving.

2 tablespoons butter

1 small yellow onion, chopped (½ cup)

8 ounces cremini mushrooms, thinly sliced

1 medium zucchini, shredded and squeezed for moisture

1 medium garlic clove, peeled and minced (1 teaspoon)

1½ teaspoons Dijon mustard

1½ teaspoons dried thyme

¼ teaspoon table salt

¼ teaspoon ground black pepper

2 cups vegetable broth

6 ounces wide egg or no-yolk noodles

½ cup regular or low-fat sour cream

Beyond

- Unfortunately, this recipe does not work well in a **3-quart cooker** without major alterations.

- Feel free to substitute 1 chopped large shallot for the onion.

- For even more hearty vegetable goodness, add up to ½ cup shredded carrot or up to 1 cup chopped cauliflower florets with the zucchini.

- Garnish servings with fresh thyme leaves, finely grated lemon zest, and/or more ground black pepper.

1 tablespoon olive oil

1 pound lean ground beef

2 medium garlic cloves, peeled and minced (2 teaspoons)

2 teaspoons dried oregano

1 teaspoon fennel seeds

1 teaspoon dried thyme

½ teaspoon red pepper flakes

½ teaspoon table salt

One 28-ounce can diced tomatoes (3½ cups)

2 cups beef or chicken broth

8 ounces dried lasagna noodles, broken into 2- to 3-inch pieces to fit into the cooker

8 ounces shredded mozzarella (2 cups)

No-Layer Lasagna Casserole

2 to 4 servings

Before we get to the molded lasagnas and spaghetti pies, we thought we'd offer a lasagna-like casserole with broken-up lasagna noodles that's made right in the pot (that is, rather than layered in a springform pan and steamed under pressure). Serve it by the big spoonful, rather than in neat squares. Brown the ground beef deeply so that it offers a complex flavor in this otherwise super simple casserole.

1.

Press the button for	Set it for	Set the time for	If necessary, press
SAUTÉ	MEDIUM, NORMAL, or CUSTOM 300°F	10 minutes	START

2. Warm the oil in a **6- or 8-quart cooker** for a minute or two. Crumble in the ground beef and cook, stirring occasionally to break up the clumps, until lightly browned, about 6 minutes.

3. Stir in the garlic, oregano, fennel seeds, thyme, red pepper flakes, and salt until aromatic, a few seconds. Pour in the tomatoes and broth; scrape up *every speck of browned stuff* on the pot's bottom. Turn off the SAUTÉ function. Stir in the broken lasagna noodles and lock the lid onto the pot.

4.

Set the machine for	Set the level for	The valve must be	Set the time for	If necessary, press
PRESSURE COOK	MAX	—	5 minutes with the KEEP WARM setting off	START
PRESSURE COOK or MANUAL	HIGH	Closed	7 minutes with the KEEP WARM setting off	START

5. Use the **quick-release method** to return the machine's pressure to normal. Unlatch the lid and open the pot. Sprinkle the mozzarella over the casserole, then stir gently. Set the lid askew over the top of the pot for 5 minutes to melt the cheese and blend the flavors.

Beyond

• You must halve the recipe for a **3-quart cooker**.

• Feel free to use a 50/50 combo of ground pork and ground beef.

• For added complexity, use a 50/50 combo of red wine and broth.

• Rather than adding the mozzarella to the pot, serve the stew over large dollops of ricotta in the bowls. For more zest, mix a little finely grated lemon zest into the ricotta before using.

Easy Lasagna Pie

4 servings

Here's the simplest of our layered lasagnas, made with purchased marinara and no-boil noodles in a 7-inch round springform pan. Yes, the casserole takes time to build, cook, and set up, particularly because a natural release works best to let the noodles continue to cook without being bombarded by the pressure.

Of course, packaged lasagna noodles won't fit in this relatively small springform pan. They must be broken to fit. Don't worry about making solid layers of the noodle pieces. Since these are no-boil noodles, they will expand as they cook. And notice that this recipe is only to be cooked on HIGH (not on MAX, if your model offers that setting).

1. Generously coat the inside of a 7-inch round springform pan with olive oil. Set a heat- and pressure-safe trivet in a **6- or 8-quart cooker**. Add the water. Prepare an aluminum foil sling (see page 20).

2. Mix the ricotta, egg, and nutmeg in a medium bowl until uniform.

3. Spread a few tablespoons of the marinara sauce in the springform pan. Break one lasagna noodle to make a layer in the pan over the sauce, then dollop an even layer of ¼ cup of the ricotta mixture in tiny bits on top, followed by a sprinkled, even layer of ¼ cup mozzarella. Make three more layers, using ⅓ cup marinara sauce, a broken lasagna noodle, ¼ cup ricotta mixture, and ¼ cup mozzarella for each. After each layer, press the noodle bits down slightly to help spread out the ricotta below. Finish up with half the remaining marinara sauce, the last lasagna noodle, the remainder of the marinara sauce, and the Parmigiano-Reggiano in an even layer. Cover the springform pan tightly with aluminum foil. Use the sling to lower the pan onto the trivet in the pot; fold down the ends of the sling so they fit inside the pot. Lock the lid onto the cooker.

4.

Set the machine for	Set the level for	The valve must be	Set the time for	If necessary, press
PRESSURE COOK or MANUAL	HIGH	Closed	20 minutes with the KEEP WARM setting off	START

5. Once the machine has finished cooking at pressure, turn it off and let the pressure in the pot **return to normal naturally**, about 20 minutes. Unlatch the lid and open the pot. Use the sling to lift the springform pan out of the pot. Uncover the pan and set aside for 10 to 15 minutes so the lasagna sets up. Run a small knife around the interior edges to loosen the casserole from the pan, then unlatch the springform pan, remove the outer ring, and cut the lasagna into quarters to serve.

Olive oil or olive oil spray for the baking dish

2 cups water

1 cup regular ricotta

1 large egg

½ teaspoon grated nutmeg

1¾ cups purchased plain marinara sauce

5 no-boil dried lasagna noodles

4 ounces shredded mozzarella (1 cup)

¼ cup finely grated Parmigiano-Reggiano

See photo in insert.

Beyond

- Because of the size of the springform pan, none of these lasagnas will work in a **3-quart cooker**.

- Although the casserole doesn't come to the top of the springform pan (and so doesn't touch the foil), you can add a layer of parchment paper before the foil, if you're worried about it touching the acidic ingredients.

- Add basil or oregano leaves between some of the layers of the casserole.

- Add up to 1 teaspoon finely grated lemon zest to the ricotta mixture.

- Add up to 1 teaspoon red pepper flakes with the grated Parmigiano-Reggiano.

1 tablespoon olive oil, plus more for the pan

½ pound bulk sweet Italian sausage meat (or sausages, with any casings removed)

2 cups packed baby kale leaves

2 cups plain marinara sauce

2 cups water

6 dried no-boil lasagna noodles

12 ounces shredded mozzarella (3 cups)

Lasagna with Sausage and Kale

4 servings

This lasagna is a bit more like the classic standard (if made in an Instant Pot). However, we left out the ricotta and used only meat sauce and mozzarella, sort of like a pizza crossed with a lasagna, for more cheesy goodness in every bite. Don't stint on giving the lasagna time to set up; the no-boil noodles need to absorb more of the sauce as the casserole rests.

1.

Press the button for	Set it for	Set the time for	If necessary, press
SAUTÉ	MEDIUM, NORMAL, or CUSTOM 300°F	10 minutes	START

2. Warm the oil in a **6- or 8-quart cooker** for a minute or two. Crumble in the sausage and cook, stirring often to break up the clumps, until the meat loses its raw, red color, about 3 minutes. Add the kale and continue cooking, stirring once in a while, until the leaves have wilted, about 3 minutes.

3. Turn off the SAUTÉ function. Pour in the marinara sauce and mix well, then transfer every drop of contents of the *hot* insert to a large bowl. Clean the insert and return it to the pot.

4. Set a heat- and pressure-safe trivet inside the pot, then add the water. Generously oil the inside of a 7-inch round springform pan. Make an aluminum foil sling (see page 20).

5. Break up one lasagna noodle and use it cover the bottom of the prepared pan as well as you can. Top with even layers of a rounded ½ cup of the meat sauce and ½ cup of the mozzarella. Repeat five more times. Cover the springform pan tightly with foil. Use the sling to lower the pan onto the trivet in the pot. Fold down the ends of the sling and lock the lid onto the cooker.

6.

Set the machine for	Set the level for	The valve must be	Set the time for	If necessary, press
PRESSURE COOK or MANUAL	HIGH	Closed	20 minutes with the KEEP WARM setting off	START

7. Once the machine has stopped cooking, turn it off and let the pressure **return to normal naturally**, about 20 minutes. Unlatch the lid and open the pot. Use the sling to lift the springform pan out of the pot. Uncover and set aside for 15 minutes so the lasagna can set up. Run a small knife around the inside of the springform pan to loosen the casserole, then unlatch the pan, remove the outer ring, and cut the lasagna into quarters to serve.

Beyond

- For a more complex lasagna, use the Cherry Tomato and Herb Pasta Sauce (page 136).

- Feel free to substitute baby arugula for the baby kale.

- Go ahead and substitute fontina for the mozzarella.

Four-Cheese Spaghetti Pie

4 servings

Consider this a casserole version of an incredible four-cheese mac and cheese. Unfortunately, you must cook the spaghetti in advance. Make it a day or two earlier, storing it in a sealed plastic bag in the fridge until you're ready.

For this casserole (unlike the lasagnas that have come before), you can use the MAX setting, if available on your model, because the spaghetti has already been cooked (and isn't as delicate as the no-boil lasagna noodles). The spaghetti and cheese mixture makes quite a bit. Work to pack it into the pan as tightly as possible, pressing down against it with a rubber spatula to create an even layer of spaghetti pie.

1. Set a heat- and pressure-safe trivet inside a **6- or 8-quart cooker;** pour in the water. Generously butter the inside of a 7-inch round springform pan. Make an aluminum foil sling (see page 20).

2. Whisk the egg, oregano, nutmeg, and pepper in a large bowl until creamy. Add the cooked spaghetti and toss well to coat. Add the provolone, Swiss, and mozzarella; toss well until uniform. Pack this mixture tightly into the prepared pan. Top with the grated Parmigiano-Reggiano. Cover the pan tightly with foil. Use the sling to lower the pan onto the trivet in the pot. Fold down the ends of the sling and lock the lid onto the pot.

3.

Set the machine for	Set the level for	The valve must be	Set the time for	If necessary, press
PRESSURE COOK	MAX	—	12 minutes with the KEEP WARM setting off	START
PRESSURE COOK or MANUAL	HIGH	Closed	15 minutes with the KEEP WARM setting off	START

4. When the machine has finished cooking, turn it off and let its pressure **return to normal naturally**, about 20 minutes. Unlatch the lid and open the pot. Use the sling to transfer the pan to a wire cooling rack. Uncover the pan and set aside for 10 minutes for the pie to set up. Run a small knife around the interior of the pan to loosen the spaghetti pie from the sides, then unlatch the pan, remove the outer ring, and cut the spaghetti pie into quarters to serve.

Butter for greasing the pan

2 cups water

1 large egg

1 teaspoon dried oregano

¼ teaspoon grated nutmeg

½ teaspoon ground black pepper

8 ounces dried spaghetti, cooked, drained, rinsed, and cooled to room temperature

4 ounces shredded provolone (1 cup)

4 ounces shredded Swiss (1 cup)

4 ounces shredded mozzarella (1 cup)

2 tablespoons finely grated Parmigiano-Reggiano

Beyond

- As with the lasagnas, these spaghetti pies don't work in a 3-quart cooker because of the size of the springform pan.

- Go ahead and substitute shredded fontina for the provolone, or shredded Gruyère for the Swiss.

- For a little heat, add up to ½ teaspoon red pepper flakes with the oregano.

Butter for the pan

2 cups water

2 large eggs

1½ teaspoons dried dill

½ teaspoon grated nutmeg

½ teaspoon table salt

½ teaspoon ground black pepper

One 10-ounce box frozen chopped spinach, thawed and squeezed dry by the handful

1 cup whole or low-fat milk

½ cup whole-milk ricotta

¼ cup pine nuts

8 ounces dried spaghetti, cooked, drained, rinsed, and cooled to room temperature

Spinach and Ricotta Spaghetti Pie

4 servings

This casserole is a cross among a frittata, a creamy pasta dish, and a spaghetti pie. Consider it a rich treat for a cold evening. It needs a salad on the side: Dress mixed greens and sliced sugar snap peas with 1 part balsamic vinegar and 3 parts olive oil mixed with finely grated orange zest.

1. Set a heat- and pressure-safe trivet in a **6- or 8-quart cooker**, then pour in the water. Generously butter the inside of a 7-inch round springform pan. Prepare an aluminum foil sling (see page 20).

2. Whisk the eggs, dill, nutmeg, salt, and pepper in a large bowl until creamy. Stir in the spinach, milk, ricotta, and pine nuts until uniform. Add the spaghetti and toss until well coated. Pack this mixture tightly into the prepared pan, cover the pan tightly with aluminum foil, then use the sling to lower the pan onto the trivet in the pot. Fold down the ends of the sling and lock the lid onto the pot.

3.

Set the machine for	Set the level for	The valve must be	Set the time for	If necessary, press
PRESSURE COOK	MAX	—	15 minutes with the KEEP WARM setting off	START
PRESSURE COOK or MANUAL	HIGH	Closed	20 minutes with the KEEP WARM setting off	START

4. When the machine has finished cooking, turn it off and let the pressure **return to normal naturally**, about 20 minutes. Unlatch the lid and open the pot. Use the sling to transfer the springform pan to a wire cooling rack. Uncover the pan and set aside for 10 minutes for the casserole to set up. Run a small knife around the interior of the pan to loosen the spaghetti pie from the sides, then unlatch the pan, remove the outer ring, and cut the spaghetti pie into quarters to serve.

Beyond

- For a hint of sweetness, substitute golden raisins for the pine nuts.
- Try adding 1 teaspoon fennel seeds with the dill and nutmeg.
- Substitute soft goat cheese for the ricotta for a more intense flavor.
- Top the casserole with up to ½ cup finely grated Parmigiano-Reggiano before sealing with foil and cooking.

Spaghetti Carbonara Pie

4 servings

This one is something like a spaghetti quiche: a mix of eggs and bacon in a casserole with lots of noodles. We almost put the recipe in the breakfast chapter for a weekend brunch. (And maybe that's how you'll want to serve it.) In any event, cool the bacon before adding it, so it doesn't begin to cook the eggs.

1. Set a heat- and pressure-safe trivet in a **6- or 8-quart cooker**, then pour in the water. Generously butter the inside of a 7-inch round springform pan. Prepare an aluminum foil sling (see page 20).

2.

Press the button for	Set it for	Set the time for	If necessary, press
SAUTÉ	MEDIUM, NORMAL, or CUSTOM 300°F	10 minutes	START

3. Fry the bacon in the pot, stirring often, until crisp, about 6 minutes. Use a slotted spoon to transfer the bacon to a large bowl and cool for 10 minutes. Meanwhile, clean and dry the relatively hot insert before returning it to the machine.

4. Stir the eggs, cream, cheese, thyme, onion powder, and salt into the bowl with the bacon until uniform. Add the spaghetti and toss well until well coated. Pack this mixture into the prepared pan. Cover with aluminum foil. Then use the prepared sling to lower the pan onto the trivet in the cooker. Fold down the ends of the sling and lock the lid onto the pot.

5.

Set the machine for	Set the level for	The valve must be	Set the time for	If necessary, press
PRESSURE COOK	MAX	—	15 minutes with the KEEP WARM setting off	START
PRESSURE COOK or MANUAL	HIGH	Closed	20 minutes with the KEEP WARM setting off	START

6. When the machine has finished cooking, turn it off and let the pressure **return to normal naturally**, about 20 minutes. Unlatch the lid and open the pot. Use the sling to transfer the pan to a wire cooling rack. Uncover the pan and set aside for 10 minutes for the casserole to set up. Run a small knife around the interior of the pan to loosen the spaghetti pie from the sides, then unlatch the pan, remove the outer ring, and cut the pie into quarters to serve.

2 cups water

Butter for the pan

6 ounces bacon, chopped

2 large eggs, well whisked in a small bowl

1 cup heavy cream

2 ounces Parmigiano-Reggiano, finely grated (1 cup)

1 teaspoon dried thyme

½ teaspoon onion powder

¼ teaspoon table salt

8 ounces dried spaghetti, cooked, drained, rinsed, and cooled to room temperature

Beyond

- Feel free to substitute turkey bacon for the pork bacon.

- Try adding up to ½ ounce finely ground dried porcini mushrooms to the egg mixture. (Grind them in a spice grinder.)

- Sprinkle the top of the casserole with up to 1 teaspoon coarsely ground black pepper before covering with foil and cooking.

5

All Things
Pulled

Like a lot of people, we first got into pressure cooking because of the promise of pulled pork that didn't require manning a smoker all day. We even suspect that being able to make pulled pork in a fraction of the usual time is what has instigated the barbecue circuit's current obsession with burnt ends, the crunchy bits you can't get from a multi-cooker. Maybe the craze is coincidental, or maybe those pit masters are intimidated by a countertop cooker that locks moisture into the meat and produces some of the juiciest pork shoulder, chicken thighs, and even pulled vegetables we can imagine.

That said, recipes for all things pulled require some accommodations for what the pot can (and cannot) do. First, there must be enough liquid to create the necessary steam to bring on the pressure. As a result, some sauces are wet and need to be boiled down.

Must you do so? No, you can live well in a wetter pulled-pork world. You can even use kitchen tongs to pull some the meat from the pot and mop it with some of the thinner sauce left behind (although that sauce will have less pronounced flavors). Or you can just leave the shredded meat in the pot for a while. It will continue to absorb more sauce as it sits. But no doubt about it, boiling down the sauce for a few minutes at the end brings the dish closer to perfection — which may or may not be worth it on any given Saturday afternoon.

All these recipes except one end with a natural release. Such news may not be the best for busy people. A natural release can add 30 minutes, 40 minutes, even an hour to the total cooking time. But using a quick release just means we have to include 20, 30, maybe 40 minutes additional time under pressure anyway. More important, a quick release renders the meat too soft, even squishy, and makes for a wetter sauce. It doesn't allow the meat (or vegetables) to

slowly reabsorb some of the liquid. We decided that since we were saving ourselves 10 hours at the smoker, we could allow for this slower release method.

Most of these recipes require condiments of some sort: mustard, ketchup, mayonnaise, chutney. Also be prepared with various fixings: buns, lettuce, tomato, pico de gallo, salsa, even purchased coleslaw. Whatever's pulled is always a thing of beauty but it can look awfully lonely on the plate. It demands a party. Give it one.

FAQs

1. How do you pull the meat with two forks?
Although barbecue mavens insist on using meat forks, you can "get 'er done" with sturdy flatware forks. (Cheap, flimsy ones can bend.) Stab the meat with one fork, then press the tines of the other fork into the meat 1 to 3 inches away (depending on how thick the cut is). Pull that second fork away from the first, thereby beginning to shred the meat into its fibers. Once you've got the hunk of meat into smaller bits, you can begin to pull those apart with the two forks, usually right in the pot.

There's some debate about how "pulled" a pulled entree is. In our team, one of us likes them pulled until they're loose, meaty threads. The other (ahem, the Texan) leaves the meat in slightly larger hunks for (as he says) more "chew on the bun." Some people even like their pulled meat to be a knife-and-fork affair, leaving chunks of beef or pork that have to be further cut apart at the table. Then again, these people are probably serving the stuff in bowls and not on a bun.

2. Why do we sometimes remove that *hot* insert from the pot?

Some sauces have added sugar or are replete with natural sugars. The machine will continue to keep the stainless steel insert hot as it sits inside, especially on the bottom where the heating element lies. Think of the multi-cooker as an electric stovetop with burners that stay hot even after they're turned off. Removing the insert helps guarantee that any sugars will not burn against the insert's bottom.

The method for removing that *hot* insert is another matter entirely. For the first few times you do this, put kids and pets out of the kitchen. We suggest using silicone baking gloves to grab hold of its edges. If you don't have these, we find that a thick, clean, doubled-up kitchen towel in each hand works better than hot pads — which can either be too thin or don't bend enough to grasp the edge firmly. The insert can also tilt as it's lifted out. It can — even momentarily — come to rest against your forearm. A larger towel protects more of your skin. Trust us. We know.

3. What if the meat's not tender enough to pull?

Unfortunately, every cow or pig is not like every other cow or pig; no two cuts will ever get done at the exact same time. If we were manning a smoker or watching an oven, all we'd have to do is open the door and prod the meat to see if it's tender. But the Instant Pot has a locked-on lid. We can't check on how things are doing inside. Sometimes, that means waiting a long time for the pressure to come back to normal naturally, only to find that the brisket, pork loin, or chicken thighs are not tender enough to shred. If this happens, lock the lid back onto the cooker and bring the machine back to MAX for 5 minutes or HIGH for 6 minutes. Follow the same release pattern as the recipe indicates, open the pot, and try again.

Sorry about that. From our New England test kitchen, there's little we can do about the vagaries of modern meat. That said, the pressure does even matters out, more so than an oven would. We once roasted three seemingly identical briskets for a magazine article and found that one took 4 hours; the second, 4½ hours; and the last, 5½ hours. We never had such time swings in testing the cuts for this chapter. On a couple of occasions, a cut needed a few extra minutes under pressure. At that point, there's nothing to be done except to give the meat its due.

All-American Pulled Pork

8 servings

Here's our standard recipe for pulled pork. We use smoked paprika to give the meat that characteristic "smoker" flavor, rather than a bottled barbecue sauce that can end up too sweet. Even without burnt ends, the flavor will be intense and sweet.

Remove any big fatty blobs from the pork so that the sauce is not too greasy.

1. Pour the cider into a **6- or 8-quart cooker**. Mix the smoked paprika, brown sugar, chile powder, dried mustard, onion powder, garlic powder, salt, and pepper in a small bowl. Pat and rub this mixture all over the pork. Set the meat in the cooker and lock the lid onto the pot.

2.

Set the machine for	Set the level for	The valve must be	Set the time for	If necessary, press
PRESSURE COOK	MAX	—	1 hour with the KEEP WARM setting off	START
MEAT/STEW, PRESSURE COOK, or MANUAL	HIGH	Closed	1 hour 20 minutes with the KEEP WARM setting off	START
SLOW COOK	HIGH	Opened	5 hours with the KEEP WARM setting off (or on for no more than 4 hours)	START

3. If you've used a pressure setting, once the machine has finished cooking, turn it off and allow its pressure to **return to normal naturally,** about 30 minutes.

4. Unlatch the lid and open the pot. Use a meat fork and a large, slotted spoon or a large spatula to transfer the pork to a nearby cutting board (or transfer hunks of the pork, should the thing come apart). Use a flatware tablespoon to skim any excess surface fat from the sauce.

5.

Press the button for	Set it for	Set the time for	If necessary, press
SAUTÉ	MEDIUM, NORMAL, or CUSTOM 300°F	10 minutes	START

6. Bring the sauce to a boil, stirring a few times. Cook until the sauce has reduced to about half its volume, stirring occasionally, about 7 minutes. Meanwhile, shred the meat with two forks. When the sauce has reduced to the right consistency, turn off the SAUTÉ function and stir the shredded meat into the sauce in the pot. Set aside for 5 minutes with the lid on top but askew to blend the flavors and let the meat further absorb the sauce.

1½ cups unsweetened apple cider

2 tablespoons mild smoked paprika

2 tablespoons dark brown sugar

1 tablespoon standard chile powder

1 teaspoon ground dried mustard

1 teaspoon onion powder

1 teaspoon garlic powder

1 teaspoon table salt

½ teaspoon ground black pepper

3 pound boneless pork shoulder, cut in half and any large chunks of fat removed

See photo in insert.

Beyond

- For a **3-quart cooker,** you must use 1½ pounds pork, 1 cup unsweetened apple cider, and one-half of the dried spices for the rub.

- We prefer this pulled pork in slider buns, topped with lots of coleslaw.

- We also like it next to scrambled eggs for a weekend brunch.

- For a discussion of standard chile powder (vs. pure), see page 112.

- The best sauce for this pork is Alabama white sauce (see the *Beyond* at the Brisket and Butternut Squash Chili recipe on page 123).

1½ cups jarred pickle brine

1 teaspoon dried dill

1 teaspoon ground coriander

1 teaspoon ground dried mustard

1 teaspoon table salt

½ teaspoon red pepper flakes

3 pounds boneless pork shoulder, cut
in half and any large chunks of fat
removed

Pickled Pulled Pork

8 servings

If you're a fan of pulled pork that is more savory than sweet, don't throw out the pickle brine when you finish a jar of pickles. That brine is a ready-made marinade, even the base for a sauce, that adds a vinegary and herbaceous hit underneath the braised flavors. Use any sort of pickle brine you like: dill pickles, hot dills, super-vinegary pickles, you name it. And if you really do like sweet dishes, by all means use the brine from a jar of bread-and-butter pickles. Honestly, we've even made this recipe with a 50/50 combo of brines from a jar of sweet-and-sour pickles and a jar of pickled jalapeño rings.

By the way, if you're not ready to make this pulled pork the moment you finish a jar of pickles, seal the jar and freeze the brine in it for up to 4 months.

1. Pour the brine into a **6- or 8-quart cooker**. Mix the dill, coriander, dried mustard, salt, and pepper flakes in a small bowl. Spread this mixture evenly over the pork. Set the pork in the pot and lock on the lid.

2.

Set the machine for	Set the level for	The valve must be	Set the time for	If necessary, press
PRESSURE COOK	MAX	—	1 hour with the KEEP WARM setting off	START
MEAT/STEW, PRESSURE COOK, or MANUAL	HIGH	Closed	1 hour 20 minutes with the KEEP WARM setting off	START
SLOW COOK	HIGH	Opened	5 hours with the KEEP WARM setting off (or on for no more than 4 hours)	START

3. If you've used a pressure setting, once the machine has finished cooking, turn it off and let the pressure **return to normal naturally,** about 30 minutes.

4. Unlatch the lid and open the pot..Use a meat fork and a large slotted spoon to transfer the pork (or hunks of it) to a cutting board. Use a flatware tablespoon to skim any excess surface fat from the sauce.

5. Shred the meat with two forks; stir these shreds back into the pot. There will be too much liquid in the pot for decent pulled pork. But since this liquid is intensely flavorful and will continue to "marinate" the meat, keep the shredded meat in the liquid and use kitchen tongs to remove servings one at a time.

Beyond

- For a **3-quart cooker,** you must halve all the ingredients but leave the 1½-pound piece of pork shoulder whole.

- While buns are traditional, this pulled pork is also delicious on toasted rye bread with deli mustard.

- If you want a smoky flavor, add up to 1 tablespoon mild smoked paprika to the spice rub.

Cherry Chipotle Pulled Pork

8 servings

This pulled pork can be made with either a pork shoulder or a picnic ham (which is technically a portion of the larger pork shoulder). In either case, we call for a bone-in cut, mostly because the flavor of the bone (and its attendant cartilage) will bring more savory flavor to the sauce — which is sweet and smoky, thanks to the combination of the cherry jam and chiles in adobo sauce. True, those chiles are fiery. But the pressure cooker will tame most of the heat. However, use only one (or even half a chile), if you're concerned. Or if you love spicy food, use two chiles and don't seed them.

1½ cups beef or chicken broth

½ cup cherry jam (not jelly or preserves)

Up to 2 canned chipotle chiles in adobo sauce, stemmed, seeded (if desired), and chopped

3 tablespoons mild paprika

2 tablespoons Worcestershire sauce

1 teaspoon ground cumin

½ teaspoon ground cloves

½ teaspoon ground dried mustard

One 3½-pound bone-in pork shoulder or picnic ham, any skin and large chunks of fat removed

1. Whisk the broth, jam, chipotles, paprika, Worcestershire sauce, cumin, cloves, and dried mustard in a **6- or 8-quart cooker**. Add the pork and turn the piece in the sauce to coat all sides. Lock the lid onto the pot.

2.

Set the machine for	Set level for	The valve must be	Set the time for	If necessary, press
PRESSURE COOK	MAX	—	1 hour 10 minutes with the KEEP WARM setting off	START
MEAT/STEW, PRESSURE COOK, or MANUAL	HIGH	Closed	1 hour 30 minutes with the KEEP WARM setting off	START
SLOW COOK	HIGH	Opened	5½ hours with the KEEP WARM setting off (or on for no more than 4 hours)	START

3. If you've used a pressure setting, when the machine has finished cooking, turn it off and let the pressure **return to normal naturally,** about 30 minutes.

4. Unlatch the lid and open the pot. Use a meat fork and a large, slotted spoon to transfer the pork (or maybe pieces of it) to a nearby cutting board. Cut out and discard the bone. Then use a flatware tablespoon to skim the excess surface fat from the sauce in the pot.

5.

Press the button for	Set it for	Set the time for	If necessary, press
SAUTÉ	MEDIUM, NORMAL, or CUSTOM 300°F	15 minutes	START

6. Bring the sauce to a simmer, stirring occasionally. Cook until thickened like barbecue sauce, stirring more and more frequently to prevent scorching, 5 to 10 minutes. Meanwhile, shred the meat with two forks. Once the sauce has reduced to the right consistency, stir the meat back into it, turn off the SAUTÉ function, and serve warm.

Beyond

- Because of the size of the pork (even halved), all the recipes with bone-in cuts for pulled pork cannot easily be made in a **3-quart cooker**.

- If you boil down the sauce until it just coats the meat, this is the best pulled pork for quesadillas — served with lots of shredded American Cheddar.

- For a hotter version, add up to 1 tablespoon adobo sauce from the chipotle chile can with the broth, then pass extra hot red pepper sauce, like Tabasco or Texas Pete, at the table.

1½ cups water

4 ounces chopped dried pineapple (1 cup)

1 small red onion, chopped (½ cup)

One 4½-ounce can mild or hot green chiles (½ cup)

1 tablespoon molasses

Up to 1 teaspoon hot red pepper sauce, such as Tabasco sauce

1 teaspoon dried thyme

1 teaspoon ground dried ginger

1 teaspoon ground allspice

½ teaspoon ground dried turmeric

½ teaspoon celery salt

½ teaspoon grated nutmeg

½ teaspoon table salt

One 3½-pound bone-in pork shoulder or picnic ham, any skin and large blobs of fat removed

Caribbean-Style Pulled Pork

8 servings

No, it's not just the pineapple in the mix that gives this pulled pork an island feel. It's actually the combination of thyme, ginger, and allspice, with molasses as the sweetener. Those are the real secrets, although there's only a little molasses so the sauce isn't too sweet. We also don't care for the flavor of pineapple jam in this style of pulled pork, a common ingredient in recipes like this one. Instead, we opt for dried pineapple. The results highlight the natural sweetness of pork shoulder.

1. Stir the water, dried pineapple, onion, canned chiles, molasses, pepper sauce, thyme, ginger, allspice, turmeric, celery salt, nutmeg, and salt in a **6- or 8-quart cooker**. Add the pork and turn to coat on all sides. Lock the lid onto the pot.

2.

Set the machine for	Set level for	The valve must be	Set the time for	If necessary, press
PRESSURE COOK	MAX	—	1 hour 10 minutes with the KEEP WARM setting off	START
MEAT/STEW, PRESSURE COOK, or MANUAL	HIGH	Closed	1 hour 30 minutes with the KEEP WARM setting off	START
SLOW COOK	HIGH	Opened	5½ hours with the KEEP WARM setting off (or on for no more than 4 hours)	START

3. If you've used a pressure setting, when the machine has finished cooking, turn it off and let its pressure **return to normal naturally,** about 30 minutes.

4. Unlatch the lid and open the pot. Use a meat fork and a large, slotted spoon to transfer the pork (or pieces of it) to a nearby cutting board. Use a flatware tablespoon to skim any excess surface fat from the sauce.

5.

Press the button for	Set it for	Set the time for	If necessary, press
SAUTÉ	MEDIUM, NORMAL, or CUSTOM 300°F	15 minutes	START

6. Bring the sauce in the pot to a simmer, stirring occasionally. Simmer until reduced to about ½ cup, stirring more and more frequently as it cooks, 7 to 10 minutes. Meanwhile, shred the meat with two forks, discarding any additional blobs of fat. Stir the shredded meat into the sauce, turn off the SAUTÉ setting, and serve warm.

Beyond

- Again, it's almost impossible to find smaller, bone-in cuts that work in a **3-quart cooker.**

- For a simpler version, substitute 2 tablespoons bottled dry jerk seasoning blend for the hot red pepper sauce and spices. Check the bottling to see if it has any salt. If so, omit the salt in the recipe as well.

- Rather than serving this pulled pork in buns, try it in pita pockets garnished with purchased pico de gallo, sour cream, and fresh cilantro leaves.

Cuban-Style Pulled Pork

8 servings

This pulled pork is a whimsical, piggy riff on Ropa Vieja (for a more authentic version, see page 214). That dish is often made with the juice of sour oranges — which can be hard to find in North America. However, many brands of orange marmalade are made with sour oranges (read the labels), making the flavor combination easily within reach for anyone near a supermarket. Use only fresh lime juice. It has to be tart enough to stand up to the sugar in the marmalade. Some bottlings have dulled flavors.

1. Whisk the broth, marmalade, lime juice, garlic, chile, oregano, cumin, and salt in a **6- or 8-quart cooker**. Add the pork and turn to coat on all sides. Lock the lid onto the pot.

2.

Set the machine for	Set level for	The valve must be	Set the time for	If necessary, press
PRESSURE COOK	MAX	—	1 hour 10 minutes with the KEEP WARM setting off	START
MEAT/STEW, PRESSURE COOK, or MANUAL	HIGH	Closed	1 hour 30 minutes with the KEEP WARM setting off	START
SLOW COOK	HIGH	Opened	5½ hours with the KEEP WARM setting off (or on for no more than 4 hours)	START

3. If you've used a pressure setting, when the machine has finished cooking, turn it off and let its pressure **return to normal naturally,** about 30 minutes.

4. Unlatch the lid and open the pot. Use a meat fork and a large, slotted spoon to transfer the pork (or pieces of it) to a nearby cutting board. Remove and discard the bone. Use a flatware tablespoon to skim any excess surface fat from the sauce.

5.

Press the button for	Set it for	Set the time for	If necessary, press
SAUTÉ	MEDIUM, NORMAL, or CUSTOM 300°F	15 minutes	START

6. Bring the sauce in the pot to a simmer, stirring occasionally. Simmer until reduced to a fairly thick sauce, about like a bottled barbecue sauce, stirring more and more frequently as it cooks, 5 to 10 minutes (depending on how much moisture the pork has given off). Meanwhile, shred the meat with two forks, discarding any additional blobs of fat. When the sauce has reached the right consistency, stir the shredded meat into the sauce, turn off the SAUTÉ setting, and serve warm.

1 cup beef or chicken broth

1 cup orange marmalade, preferably made from sour oranges

¼ cup fresh lime juice

6 medium garlic cloves, peeled and thinly sliced

1 small or medium fresh jalapeño chile, stemmed and sliced into thin rings

2 tablespoons packed fresh oregano leaves

1 tablespoon ground cumin

1 teaspoon table salt

One 3½-pound bone-in pork shoulder or picnic ham, any skin and large blobs of fat removed

Beyond

- Again, it's almost impossible to find smaller, bone-in cuts that work in a **3-quart cooker**.

- Serve this pulled pork over Black Beans and Rice (see page 403).

- For a condiment, make a Cuban version of chimichurri: Pulse ⅔ cup olive oil, ½ cup packed fresh parsley leaves, 3 tablespoons fresh lime juice, 2 tablespoons red wine vinegar, 1 diced small red onion, up to 8 slivered and peeled medium garlic cloves, 2 teaspoons dried oregano, and 1 tablespoon table salt in a food processor until it forms a chunky sauce. Store in a covered container in the fridge for up to 2 weeks. To prevent browning, pour a slim coating of olive oil over the sauce before refrigerating. Scrape this hardened oil off the top before serving.

1 tablespoon finely minced lime zest

2 teaspoons ground dried ginger

2 teaspoons ground cumin

2 teaspoons ground black pepper

One 3-pound boneless pork shoulder, cut in half and any large bits of fat removed

2 large leeks (about 6 ounces each), white and pale green parts only, halved lengthwise, washed well, and thinly sliced (1 cup)

¾ cup beef or chicken broth

⅓ cup creamy natural-style peanut butter

⅓ cup soy sauce, preferably reduced-sodium soy sauce

⅓ cup packed light brown sugar

⅓ cup unseasoned rice vinegar

2 large garlic cloves, peeled

Pulled Pork in Peanut Sauce

8 servings

This pulled pork has a vaguely Southeast Asian feel, thanks mostly to the mix of peanut butter, vinegar, and soy sauce. It's actually more savory than you might think, even with the brown sugar. The peanut butter gives the sauce a natural thickness, so it doesn't need to be boiled down. And the shreds of pork will continue to absorb sauce as they sit in it, so any extra sauce will mostly be gone by the time you get to seconds.

1. Mix the zest, ginger, cumin, and pepper in a small bowl. Pat and rub this mixture all over the pork.

2. Stir the leeks, broth, peanut butter, soy sauce, brown sugar, and rice vinegar in a **6- or 8-quart cooker** until the peanut butter and brown sugar have dissolved. Add the coated pork. Drop the garlic cloves into the sauce. Lock the lid onto the pot.

3.

Set the machine for	Set level for	The valve must be	Set the time for	If necessary, press
PRESSURE COOK	MAX	——	1 hour with the KEEP WARM setting off	START
MEAT/STEW, PRESSURE COOK, or MANUAL	HIGH	Closed	1 hour 20 minutes with the KEEP WARM setting off	START
SLOW COOK	HIGH	Opened	5 hours with the KEEP WARM setting off (or on for no more than 4 hours)	START

4. If you've used a pressure setting, once the machine has finished cooking, turn it off and let its pressure **return to normal naturally,** about 30 minutes.

5. Unlatch the lid and open the pot. Use a slotted spoon to transfer the pork pieces to a nearby cutting board. Use a flatware tablespoon to skim any excess surface fat from the sauce in the pot.

6. Shred the meat with two forks and stir these shreds back into the sauce. Set the lid askew over the pot and set aside for 5 minutes to blend the flavors and let the meat continue to absorb the sauce.

Beyond

- For a **3-quart cooker,** you must halve all the ingredients but leave the 1½-pound piece of pork shoulder whole.

- Serve this pulled pork in flour tortillas (like soft tacos with an Asian flare) with sambal oelek, minced scallions, and/or chopped, unsalted peanuts as condiments.

Salsa Verde Pulled Pork

8 servings

This one's probably the easiest of all the pulled pork recipes, given that it uses jarred salsa verde. It's also both probably the spiciest, given that it includes the brine from a jar of pickled jalapeños and the chiles themselves. All that heat is a nice contrast to the fresh, tart taste of jarred salsa verde. The sauce isn't boiled down since the salsa verde and brine are fairly salty. Reducing it will only turn it more so. If the overall dish is too wet, use kitchen tongs to pull the meat out of the sauce for serving.

1. Mix the salsa verde, liquid from the jalapeño rings, and jalapeños in a **6- or 8-quart cooker**. Add the pork and turn to coat on all sides. Lock the lid onto the pot.

2.

Set the machine for	Set level for	The valve must be	Set the time for	If necessary, press
PRESSURE COOK	MAX	—	1 hour 10 minutes with the KEEP WARM setting off	START
MEAT/STEW, PRESSURE COOK, or MANUAL	HIGH	Closed	1 hour 30 minutes with the KEEP WARM setting off	START
SLOW COOK	HIGH	Opened	5½ hours with the KEEP WARM setting off (or on for no more than 4 hours)	START

3. If you've used a pressure setting, once the machine has finished cooking, turn it off and let its pressure **return to normal naturally**, about 30 minutes.

4. Unlatch the lid and open the pot. Use a meat fork and a slotted spoon to transfer the pork pieces to a nearby cutting board. Remove and discard the bone. Use a flatware tablespoon to skim any excess surface fat from the sauce in the pot. Shred the meat with two forks. Add these shreds to the pot along with the cilantro. Stir well before serving warm.

2 cups mild purchased salsa verde

¼ cup liquid from a jar of pickled jalapeño rings

2 tablespoons pickled jalapeño rings

One 3½ pound bone-in pork shoulder or picnic ham, any skin and large bits of fat removed

¼ cup packed fresh cilantro leaves, chopped

Beyond

- Because of the size of the bone in even a smaller pork shoulder, this recipe will not work in a **3-quart cooker**.

- Sprinkle shredded Monterey Jack over each serving.

- If you want pulled pork for an enchilada casserole, here's your best bet.

- To go all out, make your own salsa verde: Mix ½ pound husked and chopped tomatillos, ¾ cup water, ¼ cup chopped yellow onion, 1 chopped and stemmed small jalapeño chile, 1 tablespoon packed fresh oregano leaves, 1 tablespoon packed fresh cilantro leaves, 1 teaspoon minced garlic, and ½ teaspoon ground cumin in a **6- or 8-quart pot** set on the SAUTÉ function at MEDIUM, NORMAL, or CUSTOM 300°F — or in a medium saucepan set over medium heat. Bring to a simmer, then reduce the SAUTÉ level in the pot to LOW or LESS or reduce the heat on the stove to low. Simmer slowly, stirring often, until the tomatillos are soft, about 10 minutes. Cool for 10 minutes, then blend in a covered blender until smooth. Store any remaining sauce in a sealed container in the fridge for up to 1 week.

2 tablespoons vegetable, corn, or canola oil

One 3-pound boneless beef chuck roast, cut into two chunks and any large bits of fat removed

½ teaspoon table salt

½ teaspoon ground black pepper

1 cup water

1 cup ketchup

¼ cup apple cider vinegar

2 tablespoons Dijon mustard

2 tablespoons Worcestershire sauce

2 tablespoons mild paprika

2 teaspoons celery seeds

1 teaspoon garlic powder

1 teaspoon onion powder

All-American Pulled Beef

8 servings

Here's a standard version of pulled beef, best for sandwiches on hamburger buns — or maybe loaded into baked potatoes and topped with shredded American Cheddar cheese.

Brown the meat. Don't get impatient. You can even get some fairly well-done ends of the chuck, sort of like "burnt ends." These will remain chewy (if not crunchy) even after the meat has undergone its cooking and been pulled. Even more importantly, all that browning will step up the savory flavors of the dish, rendering this pulled beef far more than just a combo of meat and barbecue sauce.

1.

Press the button for	Set it for	Set the time for	If necessary, press
SAUTÉ	MEDIUM, NORMAL, or CUSTOM 300°F	20 minutes	START

2. Warm the oil in a **6- or 8-quart cooker** for a minute or two. Meanwhile, season the beef with the salt and pepper. Set one piece of chuck in the pot and brown well, turning once or twice, about 7 minutes. Transfer this piece of beef to a bowl and brown the second piece just as well before transferring it to the bowl.

3. Pour the water into the pot and scrape up the browned bits on the pot's bottom. Turn off the SAUTÉ function and stir in the ketchup, vinegar, mustard, Worcestershire sauce, paprika, celery seed, garlic powder, and onion powder. Return both pieces of meat and any juices in the bowl to the pot; turn the meat on all sides to coat it in the sauce. Lock the lid onto the pot.

4.

Set the machine for	Set level for	The valve must be	Set the time for	If necessary, press
PRESSURE COOK	MAX	—	1 hour with the KEEP WARM setting off	START
MEAT/STEW, PRESSURE COOK, or MANUAL	HIGH	Closed	1 hour 20 minutes with the KEEP WARM setting off	START
SLOW COOK	HIGH	Opened	5 hours with the KEEP WARM setting off (or on for no more than 3 hours)	START

5. If you've used a pressure setting, once the machine has finished cooking, turn it off and let its pressure **return to normal naturally,** about 30 minutes.

6. Unlatch the lid and open the pot. Use a meat fork and a large slotted spoon to transfer the pieces of meat to a nearby cutting board. Use a flatware tablespoon to skim any excess surface fat from the sauce in the pot.

7.

Press the button for	Set it for	Set the time for	If necessary, press
SAUTÉ	MEDIUM, NORMAL, or CUSTOM 300°F	15 minutes	START

8. Bring the sauce to a simmer, stirring often. Simmer until thickened, about like a loose wet barbecue sauce, stirring almost all the while, 5 to 10 minutes. Meanwhile, shred the beef into bits with two forks. Once the sauce has reached the desired consistency, stir the meat into it and cook for 1 minute, stirring often, until well coated. Turn off the SAUTÉ function and remove the *hot* insert from the pot. Set the lid askew over the insert and set aside for 5 minutes to blend the flavors and let the meat absorb more sauce.

Beyond

- For a **3-quart cooker,** you must halve all the ingredients. Keep the 1½-pound piece of meat intact.

- The best condiment for this version of pulled beef is coleslaw, right on the sandwich with the meat in the bun. To make a super easy coleslaw, stir a 1-pound bag of slaw mix with 1 cup bottled Ranch dressing.

1 tablespoon vegetable, corn, or canola oil

One 2½-pound boneless beef chuck roast, cut into two chunks and any large bits of fat removed

½ teaspoon table salt

½ teaspoon ground black pepper

½ cup amber beer, preferably a pilsner or a pale ale (a gluten-free beer, if necessary)

¾ cup beef broth

½ cup jarred prepared white horseradish

2 tablespoons Worcestershire sauce

1 teaspoon dried ground ginger

½ teaspoon ground dried turmeric

2 medium garlic cloves, peeled and minced (2 teaspoons)

2 bay leaves

Pulled Pot Roast

6 servings

We often make pot roast in the oven by slathering the beef chuck with jarred, prepared horseradish. The horseradish mellows into a sweet and savory mix that then flavors the sauce. We brought that recipe idea into pulled beef to create what feels to us like a pot roast turned into all-American sandwich filling.

1.

Press the button for	Set it for	Set the time for	If necessary, press
SAUTÉ	MEDIUM, NORMAL, or CUSTOM 300°F	20 minutes	START

2. Warm the oil in a **6- or 8-quart pot** for a minute or two. Meanwhile, season the beef with the salt and pepper. Add one piece to the pot and brown it *well*, turning once or twice, about 7 minutes. Transfer to a bowl and add the second piece of beef. Brown this one just as well on both sides before transferring it to the bowl.

3. Pour the beer into the pot. Scrape up the browned stuff on the pot's bottom, then turn off the SAUTÉ function. Stir in the broth, horseradish, Worcestershire sauce, ginger, turmeric, garlic, and bay leaves. Nestle the pieces of beef into this sauce, turning them to coat them on all sides. Lock the lid onto the pot.

4.

Set the machine for	Set level for	The valve must be	Set the time for	If necessary, press
PRESSURE COOK	MAX	—	55 minutes with the KEEP WARM setting off	START
MEAT/STEW, PRESSURE COOK, or MANUAL	HIGH	Closed	1 hour 10 minutes with the KEEP WARM setting off	START
SLOW COOK	HIGH	Opened	5 hours with the KEEP WARM setting off (or on for no more than 3 hours)	START

5. If you've used the pressure setting, once the machine has finished cooking, turn it off and let its pressure **return to normal naturally,** about 30 minutes.

6. Unlatch the lid and open the pot. Use a meat fork and a large, slotted spoon to transfer the pieces of meat to a nearby cutting board. Use a flatware tablespoon to skim any excess surface fat off the sauce. Also find and discard the garlic cloves and the bay leaves.

7.

Press the button for	Set it for	Set the time for	If necessary, press
SAUTÉ	MEDIUM, NORMAL, or CUSTOM 300°F	15 minutes	START

8. Bring the sauce to a simmer, stirring often. Simmer until thickened like a loose, wet barbecue sauce, stirring almost all the while, 5 to 10 minutes. Meanwhile, shred the meat with two forks.

9. When the sauce has reached the right consistency, stir the meat into it and cook, stirring often, until well coated and most of the liquid has been absorbed, about 1 minute. Turn off the SAUTÉ function and remove the *hot* insert from the pot. Set the lid askew over the insert and set aside for 5 minutes to blend the flavors and let the meat absorb more sauce.

Beyond

- For a **3-quart cooker,** you must use a 1½-pound piece of boneless beef chuck (keep it intact) and halve the remaining ingredients.

- For a sweeter sauce, add up to 2 tablespoons light brown sugar with the sauce ingredients.

- To use fresh horseradish, omit the prepared horseradish. Instead, grate 2 tablespoons peeled fresh horseradish into the sauce ingredients and add 1 tablespoon white wine vinegar.

- Serve this pulled beef on potato rolls with horseradish cream sauce. To make your own, whisk ½ cup regular or low-fat sour cream, ½ cup regular or low-fat mayonnaise, ¼ cup jarred prepared white horseradish, 1 teaspoon white balsamic vinegar, and ½ teaspoon ground black pepper in a medium bowl until smooth.

One 14-ounce can diced tomatoes
(1¾ cups)

½ cup bold red wine, such as
Zinfandel or Syrah

2 tablespoons balsamic vinegar

½ cup frozen pearl onions
(do not thaw)

8 baby carrots

8 pitted prunes

6 large pitted green olives, sliced

1 tablespoon fresh thyme leaves

2 medium garlic cloves, peeled and
minced (2 teaspoons)

½ teaspoon table salt

½ teaspoon ground black pepper

One 3-pound beef brisket, preferably
the flat cut, trimmed and cut in
half widthwise

Pulled Brisket

8 servings

This recipe is a not-quite-French-inspired braise turned into pulled beef. It's also not-quite-Jewish tzimmes turned into Midwestern American comfort food. And it's also like all of them combined. (Somehow.)

If not left whole, briskets come in two basic cuts. The flat cut (or "first cut") is less fatty than the "point cut." However, consider trimming even the flat cut of most of its exterior fat, just so it has about ¼ inch of so over the meat. The sauce will then have a brighter flavor.

The brisket needs a long time under pressure so that you can shred it, rather than just slice it. That said, it might not even be done with the timing stated. Brisket can be notoriously fussy, becoming tender at various times because of a range of factors well beyond just the size of the meat. If you find you can't shred the meat easily, put the hunk back in the sauce, bring it back to HIGH pressure, and cook for another 10 minutes, followed again by a natural release.

1. Mix the tomatoes, wine, and vinegar in a **6- or 8-quart cooker**. Stir in the pearl onions, carrots, prunes, olives, thyme, garlic, salt, and pepper. Nestle the meat into the sauce, then turn the cut over to coat both sides. Lock the lid onto the pot.

2.

Set the machine for	Set level for	The valve must be	Set the time for	If necessary, press
PRESSURE COOK	MAX	—	1 hour 10 minutes with the KEEP WARM setting off	START
MEAT/STEW, PRESSURE COOK, or MANUAL	HIGH	Closed	1 hour 30 minutes with the KEEP WARM setting off	START
SLOW COOK	HIGH	Opened	6 hours with the KEEP WARM setting off (or on no more than 4 hours)	START

3. If you've used the pressure setting, when the machine has finished cooking, turn it off and let its pressure **return to normal naturally,** about 30 minutes.

4. Unlatch the lid and open the cooker. Use a meat fork and a big slotted spoon to transfer the brisket (whole or in pieces) to a cutting board. Use a flatware tablespoon to skim excess surface fat from the sauce in the pot.

5.

Press the button for	Set it for	Set the time for	If necessary, press
SAUTÉ	MEDIUM, NORMAL, or CUSTOM 300°F	15 minutes	START

6. Bring the sauce to a simmer, stirring once in a while. Simmer, stirring a few times, until the sauce looks like a loose, wet barbecue sauce, 5 to 10 minutes. Meanwhile, shred the brisket using two forks — or perhaps a knife to cut thick slices that can then be shredded with a fork.

7. Once the sauce has reached the right consistency, stir the shredded brisket into it and cook, stirring often, until coated, about 1 minute. Turn off the SAUTÉ function and remove the *hot* insert from the pot. Set the lid askew over the insert and set aside for 5 minutes to blend the flavors and let the meat continue to absorb the sauce.

Beyond

- You must halve the recipe for a **3-quart cooker.**

- While you can serve this pulled brisket on potato rolls with pickle relish or pickled jalapeño rings, it's also great over No-Drain Mashed Potatoes (page 424).

- To omit the wine, substitute beef broth and add 2 teaspoons dark brown sugar.

- For a sweeter sauce, substitute ¼ cup raisins for the prunes.

- For a more complex flavor, substitute pomegranate molasses for the balsamic vinegar.

See photo in insert.

1 tablespoon butter

One 3-pound beef brisket, preferably the flat cut, trimmed and cut in half widthwise

1 large yellow onion, thinly sliced and separated into rings

1 cup very strong coffee

1 tablespoon molasses

½ cup beef broth

One 4-inch cinnamon stick

One 2-inch strip orange zest

1 teaspoon dried thyme

½ teaspoon ground allspice

½ teaspoon table salt

1 teaspoon ground black pepper

Pulled Brisket with Coffee

8 servings

Braising in coffee is a terrific thing: The acidic notes mellow into an undertone of dark, earthy flavors. Here, we include coffee in a highly spiced sauce, the better to pair with the bolder flavors of brisket.

Use strong coffee, perhaps double the strength you would drink. Even espresso would be welcome (if still more assertive). And use a vegetable peeler to remove a long strip of orange zest. We use a zest strip because one strip is easy to find and remove. Zillions of little threads of orange zest end up an irritation.

1.

Press the button for	Set it for	Set the time for	If necessary, press
SAUTÉ	MEDIUM, NORMAL, or CUSTOM 300°F	15 minutes	START

2. Melt the butter in a **6- or 8-quart cooker,** then add one piece of brisket and brown it *very* well on both sides, turning once or twice, about 5 minutes. Transfer to a bowl and brown the other piece of meat just as well on both sides before transferring it to the bowl.

3. Pour the coffee and molasses into the pot. As it comes to a simmer, scrape up any browned bits in the pot. Turn off the SAUTÉ function. Pour in the broth, then stir in the cinnamon stick, orange zest, thyme, allspice, salt, and black pepper. Set the pieces of meat back in the cooker, turning them in the sauce to coat on all sides. Lock the lid onto the pot.

4.

Set the machine for	Set level for	The valve must be	Set the time for	If necessary, press
PRESSURE COOK	MAX	—	1 hour 10 minutes with the KEEP WARM setting off	START
MEAT/STEW, PRESSURE COOK, or MANUAL	HIGH	Closed	1 hour 30 minutes with the KEEP WARM setting off	START
SLOW COOK	HIGH	Opened	6 hours with the KEEP WARM setting off (or on for no more than 4 hours)	START

5. If you've used the pressure setting, when the machine has finished cooking, turn it off and let its pressure **return to normal naturally,** about 30 minutes.

6. Unlatch the lid and open the cooker. Use a meat fork and a big slotted spoon to transfer the brisket (whole or in pieces) to a nearby cutting board. Use a flatware tablespoon to skim any excess surface fat from the sauce in the pot. Also fish out and discard the orange zest strip and cinnamon stick.

7.

Press the button for	Set it for	Set the time for	If necessary, press
SAUTÉ	MEDIUM, NORMAL, or CUSTOM 300°F	10 minutes	START

8. Bring the sauce to a simmer, stirring once in a while. Simmer, stirring occasionally, until it is a thin wet gravy, 5 to 6 minutes. Meanwhile, shred the brisket using two forks — or perhaps use a knife to cut thick slices that can then be shredded with a fork.

9. When the sauce has reached the desired consistency, stir the shredded brisket into it and cook, stirring often, until coated in the sauce, about 1 minute. Turn off the SAUTÉ function and remove the insert from the pot. Set the lid askew over the insert and set aside for 5 minutes to blend the flavors and let the meat continue to absorb the sauce.

Beyond

- For a **3-quart cooker,** use the full amount of butter and broth but halve the remaining ingredients.

- To make this a little easier, stop off at a coffee shop, buy a couple of shots of espresso, then use them with the rest of the volume of more standard drip coffee.

- For a sweeter flavor, substitute a dark beer, preferably a porter or a stout, for the beef broth.

- While this pulled beef is tasty in buns with mustard and even crisp-fried bacon strips, it's also good over cooked root vegetables mashed with butter, particularly mashed turnips and/or celeriac. Or boil cauliflower rice, add a little butter, and turn it into mashed cauliflower as a bed for the pulled beef.

2 small yellow onions, halved and thinly sliced into half-moons

2 large garlic cloves, peeled

1 cup plain cola (do not use a diet soda)

¼ cup Worcestershire sauce

2 tablespoons apple cider vinegar

2 tablespoons ketchup-like chili sauce, such as Heinz

1 tablespoon mild paprika

1 teaspoon ground dried mustard

1 teaspoon table salt

½ teaspoon ground cloves

One 3-pound boneless beef chuck roast, cut into two chunks and any large bits of fat removed

Cola Pulled Beef

6 servings

Although cola would seem to make this version of pulled beef super sweet, it's actually more of a sweet-and-sour mix, thanks to the vinegar and chili sauce. There's no browning here. We found that the more complex flavors gained from browning actually muddied the flavors of the sauce.

1. Mix the onion, garlic, cola, Worcestershire sauce, vinegar, chile sauce, paprika, ground mustard, salt, and cloves in a **6- or 8-quart cooker**. Set the pieces of beef into this sauce, then turn to coat on all sides. Lock the lid onto the pot.

2.

Set the machine for	Set level for	The valve must be	Set the time for	If necessary, press
PRESSURE COOK	MAX	—	1 hour with the KEEP WARM setting off	START
MEAT/STEW, PRESSURE COOK, or MANUAL	HIGH	Closed	1 hour 20 minutes with the KEEP WARM setting off	START
SLOW COOK	HIGH	Opened	5 hours with the KEEP WARM setting off (or on for no more than 3 hours)	START

3. If you've used the pressure setting, once the machine has finished cooking, turn it off and let its pressure **return to normal naturally,** about 30 minutes.

4. Unlatch the lid and open the pot. Use a meat fork and a large, slotted spoon to transfer the pieces of meat to a nearby cutting board. Use a flatware tablespoon to skim any excess surface fat off the sauce in the pot. Also find and discard the garlic cloves.

5.

Press the button for	Set it for	Set the time for	If necessary, press
SAUTÉ	MEDIUM, NORMAL, or CUSTOM 300°F	15 minutes	START

6. Bring the sauce to a simmer, stirring quite often. Simmer until thickened like a wet, loose barbecue sauce, stirring almost all the while, 5 to 10 minutes. Meanwhile, shred the beef with two forks. Once the sauce has reached the right consistency, stir the shredded meat into it and cook, stirring often, until well coated and most of the liquid has been absorbed, about 1 minute. Turn off the SAUTÉ function, remove the *hot* insert from the pot, set the lid askew over the insert, and set aside for 5 minutes to blend the flavors and let the meat absorb more sauce.

Beyond

- For a **3-quart cooker,** you must halve all the ingredients. Keep the 1½-pound piece of meat intact.

- Consider condiments like pickle relish, dill pickle slices, or chowchow.

- Or serve the pulled beef in hot dog buns with dill pickle sandwich slices running along one side of the bun.

- For a hotter version, reduce the Worcestershire sauce to 2 tablespoons and add up to 2 tablespoons liquid from a jar of pickled jalapeño rings with the other sauce ingredients.

Barbacoa

8 servings

Barbacoa is a Caribbean dish (although now found across the Americas) that is usually made of spiced shredded beef cooked over an open fire. Making barbacoa in an Instant Pot will never let you get crispy bits of shredded meat, but see the *Beyond* for an idea. This highly seasoned version makes the best taco meat in the book.

1. Stir the lime juice, paprika, cumin, oregano, onion powder, salt, and black pepper in a small bowl to make a paste. Rub this paste all over both sides of each piece of chuck.

2.

Press the button for	Set it for	Set the time for	If necessary, press
SAUTÉ	MEDIUM, NORMAL, or CUSTOM 300°F	10 minutes	START

3. Warm the oil in a **6- or 8-quart cooker**. Add one piece of the beef and brown *lightly* on both sides, turning once, about 3 minutes. Transfer to a bowl and brown the other piece of chuck in the same way before transferring it to the bowl.

4. Pour the broth into the pot, scrape up any browned bits on the pot's bottom, and turn off the SAUTÉ function. Stir in the tomato, garlic, chipotle, vinegar, and honey. Return the meat and any juices in the bowl to the pot; turn the pieces of beef in the sauce to coat them. Lock the lid onto the pot.

5.

Set the machine for	Set level for	The valve must be	Set the time for	If necessary, press
PRESSURE COOK	MAX	—	1 hour with the KEEP WARM setting off	START
MEAT/STEW, PRESSURE COOK, or MANUAL	HIGH	Closed	1 hour 20 minutes with the KEEP WARM setting off	START
SLOW COOK	HIGH	Opened	5 hours with the KEEP WARM setting off (or on for no more than 4 hours)	START

6. If you've used a pressure setting, when the machine has finished cooking, turn it off and let its pressure **return to normal naturally,** about 30 minutes.

7. Unlatch the lid and open the pot. Use a meat fork and a big slotted spoon to transfer the pieces of chuck to a cutting board. Use a flatware tablespoon to skim any excess surface fat from the sauce in the pot. Shred the meat with two forks, then stir it back into the sauce in the pot. Set the lid askew over the pot for 10 minutes to blend the flavors and allow the meat to continue to absorb the sauce.

1½ tablespoons fresh lime juice

1½ tablespoons mild paprika

1½ teaspoons ground cumin

1½ teaspoons dried oregano

1 teaspoon onion powder

1½ teaspoons table salt

½ teaspoon ground black pepper

One 3-pound boneless beef chuck roast, cut into two chunks and any large bits of fat removed

2 tablespoons olive oil

1¼ cups beef broth

1 large round red tomato, chopped (1 cup)

Up to 6 medium garlic cloves, peeled and minced (2 tablespoons)

Up to 1 canned chipotle chile in adobo sauce, stemmed, seeded (if desired), and chopped

5 tablespoons red wine vinegar

3 tablespoons honey

Beyond

- For a **3-quart cooker,** you must halve all the ingredients. Leave the 1½-pound piece of beef chuck in one piece.

- For a more traditional flavor (if not necessarily gluten-free), substitute a dark beer, preferably a brown ale, for the broth.

- If you miss the crisp bits, spread the sauced, shredded meat on a large lipped baking sheet, then pour and scrape any remaining sauce over the meat. Broil 4 to 6 inches from the heating element until a bit crunchy without burning, 1 to 3 minutes.

- Serve in tortillas topped with sliced avocado, pickled onions, pickled jalapeño rings, shredded cheese, and/or cilantro.

2 cups light but dry red wine, such as
Pinot Noir

2 pounds beef flank steak, cut into
3 pieces

3 fresh thyme sprigs

2 bay leaves

¼ cup olive oil

1 medium red onion, halved and
sliced into thin half-moons

2 medium red bell peppers,
stemmed, cored, and cut into thin
strips

2 medium garlic cloves, peeled and
minced (2 teaspoons)

2 teaspoons dried oregano

1 teaspoon ground cumin

1 cup canned crushed tomatoes with
lots of their juice

¼ cup beef or chicken broth

2 tablespoons red wine vinegar

Pulled Flank Steak with Red Peppers

6 servings

Without a doubt, this pulled dish is the fanciest in the book, more dinner party than weeknight supper. The flank steak is cut into pieces so that the shreds are smaller, more discreet — a better match to the vegetables which make a sweet-and-sour mix. It's great alongside mashed or scalloped potatoes or in homemade popovers. Consider garnishing the servings with lots of fresh herbs, particularly oregano and thyme.

One important note: The cooking is a two-step process, first the meat on its own, then the meat in the sauce. During the second cooking, only use the HIGH pressure setting, not MAX (if available on your machine).

1. Pour the wine into a **6- or 8-quart cooker**. Add the flank steak pieces and turn to coat. Tuck the thyme sprigs and bay leaves around the meat. Lock the lid onto the pot.

2.

Set the machine for	Set level for	The valve must be	Set the time for	If necessary, press
PRESSURE COOK	MAX	—	35 minutes with the KEEP WARM setting off	START
MEAT/STEW, PRESSURE COOK, or MANUAL	HIGH	Closed	45 minutes with the KEEP WARM setting off	START

3. When the machine has finished cooking, turn it off and let its pressure **return to normal naturally,** about 20 minutes. Unlatch and open the lid. Use a meat fork and a large, slotted spoon to transfer the pieces of flank steak to a cutting board. Shred the meat with two forks and set aside. Discard all the liquid and aromatics in the pot. Clean and dry the insert and return it to the cooker.

4.

Press the button for	Set it for	Set the time for	If necessary, press
SAUTÉ	MEDIUM, NORMAL, or CUSTOM 300°F	10 minutes	START

5. Warm the oil in the pot for a minute or two, then add the onion and bell pepper. Cook, stirring often, until the onion begins to soften, about 4 minutes. Add the garlic, oregano, and cumin; stir until aromatic, just a few seconds.

6. Turn off the SAUTÉ function and stir in the crushed tomatoes, broth, and vinegar. Stir the shredded meat and any juices on the cutting board into the pot. Continue stirring until uniform, then lock the lid onto the pot.

7.

Set the machine for	Set level for	The valve must be	Set the time for	If necessary, press
MEAT/STEW, PRESSURE COOK, or MANUAL	HIGH	Closed	0 minutes with the KEEP WARM setting off	START

8. When the machine has hit high pressure and finished cooking, turn it off and let the pressure **return to normal naturally,** about 5 minutes. Unlatch the lid and open the pot. Stir well before serving.

Beyond

- You must halve the recipe for a **3-quart cooker.**
- Consider this a pulled beef version of ragù, to be served with cooked fettuccini.
- Or keep the meat in the sauce, then use kitchen tongs to pick up some and drain it before putting it in an Italian hero with sliced provolone and sliced peperoncini.

1 cup drained jarred pickled onions

¾ cup pitted green olives, thinly sliced

¾ cup beef broth

¼ cup dry sherry or unsweetened apple juice

¼ cup raisins

2 tablespoons tomato paste

2 teaspoons dried oregano

2 teaspoons dried sage

½ teaspoon table salt

½ teaspoon ground black pepper

2 pounds beef flank steak

¼ cup chopped parsley leaves

Beyond

- For an **8-quart cooker,** you must increase the broth to 1½ cups and use the remaining ingredients as stated. The sauce will then need to be boiled down. Remove the meat from the pot and shred it on a cutting board as you cook the sauce on the SAUTÉ function at MEDIUM, NORMAL, or CUSTOM 300°F until reduced to a wet barbecue sauce, stirring occasionally. Stir the shredded meat and parsley into the sauce, then set aside as directed.

- For a **3-quart cooker,** you must use the full amount of broth (¾ cup) and halve the remaining ingredients. The sauce will also need to be reduced.

- Serve this pulled beef over Black Beans and Rice (page 403).

Ropa Vieja

6 servings

This legendary Cuban dish (the name of which means "old clothes" because the beef is shredded into "rags") is a boldly flavored concoction, often served atop rice and beans. There are undoubtedly as many versions of it as there are Cuban grandmothers. Ours has been streamlined a bit, the better to make it a weeknight standard. By using purchased pickled onions, raisins, and olives, we can get very close to the flavor of the long-simmered original.

1. Mix the pickled onions, olives, broth, sherry, raisins, tomato paste, oregano, sage, salt, and pepper in a **6-quart cooker**. Nestle the steak into this sauce, turning it to coat both sides. Lock the lid onto the pot.

2.

Set the machine for	Set level for	The valve must be	Set the time for	If necessary, press
PRESSURE COOK	MAX	—	40 minutes with the KEEP WARM setting off	START
MEAT/STEW, PRESSURE COOK, or MANUAL	HIGH	Closed	55 minutes with the KEEP WARM setting off	START
SLOW COOK	HIGH	Opened	4½ hours with the KEEP WARM setting off (or on for no more than 2 hours)	START

3. If you've used a pressure setting, when the machine finishes cooking, turn it off and let its pressure **return to normal naturally,** about 25 minutes.

4. Unlatch the lid and open the pot. Use two forks to shred the meat right in the pot. Stir in the parsley, then set the lid askew over the pot and set aside for 10 minutes to blend the flavors and allow the meat to continue to absorb the sauce.

All-American Pulled Lamb

8 servings

Years ago, we were researching a book all about ham and went on an expedition across Kentucky, looking for country ham producers. We got sidetracked at the Moonlite Bar-B-Q Inn in Owensboro and obsessed about their pulled mutton. Mutton may be too gamy for most people. With leg of lamb, we can turn out a pretty good imitation of this long-smoked barbecue.

1 tablespoon dark brown sugar

2 teaspoons mild smoked paprika

1½ teaspoons ground cumin

1 teaspoon ground dried mustard

1 teaspoon onion powder

1 teaspoon ground black pepper

½ teaspoon garlic powder

One 3-pound boneless leg of lamb, any netting removed, the meat opened up, cut in half, and any large chunks of fat removed

1 cup beef broth

¼ cup apple cider vinegar

2 tablespoons soy sauce

1. Mix the brown sugar, smoked paprika, cumin, dried mustard, onion powder, black pepper, and garlic powder in a large bowl. Pat the spice mixture over all sides of the lamb.

2. Stir the broth, vinegar, and soy sauce in a **6- or 8-quart cooker**. Set the meat into this sauce (do not turn over to coat). Lock the lid onto the pot.

3.

Set the machine for	Set level for	The valve must be	Set the time for	If necessary, press
PRESSURE COOK	MAX	——	1 hour 5 minutes with the KEEP WARM setting off	START
MEAT/STEW, PRESSURE COOK, or MANUAL	HIGH	Closed	1 hour 20 minutes with the KEEP WARM setting off	START
SLOW COOK	HIGH	Opened	4½ hours with the KEEP WARM setting off (or on for no more than 3 hours)	START

4. If using a pressure setting, when the machine has finished cooking, turn it off and let its pressure **return to normal naturally,** about 30 minutes.

5. Use a meat fork and a big, slotted spoon to transfer the meat (whole or in pieces) to a cutting board. Shred the meat with two forks. Then use a flatware tablespoon to skim any excess surface fat from the sauce.

6.

Press the button for	Set it for	Set the time for	If necessary, press
SAUTÉ	MEDIUM, NORMAL, or CUSTOM 300°F	10 minutes	START

7. Bring the sauce to a full simmer, stirring occasionally. Cook, stirring more and more frequently, until the sauce has reduced to half its volume, 5 to 8 minutes. Stir the shredded meat into the sauce and cook, stirring to make sure the meat is thoroughly coated, for 1 minute. Turn off the SAUTÉ function and remove the *hot* insert from the cooker. Set the lid askew over the insert and set aside for 5 to 10 minutes.

Beyond

- For a **3-quart cooker,** you must use ¾ cup broth and halve the remaining ingredients. Keep the 1½ pounds of boneless leg of lamb in one piece.

- This rub and braising technique will also work well for a 3-pound beef brisket, cut in half. In that case, let the meat go under pressure at MAX for 1 hour 20 minutes or at HIGH for 1 hour 45 minutes, either followed by a natural release.

- Serve with mayonnaise on toasted hamburger buns along with a slice of tomato and a paper-thin slice of red onion.

2 cups pomegranate juice

1 medium lemon, scrubbed to remove any waxy coating, then quartered, seeded, and finely chopped

4 medium garlic cloves, peeled and minced (4 teaspoons)

1 tablespoon dried oregano

2 teaspoons ground cinnamon

2 teaspoons dried dill

1 teaspoon table salt

One 3-pound bone-in lamb shoulder

1 large red onion, thinly sliced and broken into rings

2 tablespoons honey

Pulled Lamb Shoulder with Pomegranate and Cinnamon

8 servings

If you're a fan of bright flavors, this might be the pulled dish for you. The pomegranate juice retains much of its sour pop (aided, of course, by the chopped lemon). To really ramp things up, there's the incredible combination of cinnamon and dill: a savory and warming mix that works well with the relatively fatty cut of lamb.

1. Pour the pomegranate juice into a **6- or 8-quart cooker**. Mix the lemon, garlic, oregano, cinnamon, dill, and salt in a small bowl. Pat and rub this mixture evenly over the lamb shoulder. Set the meat in the cooker, scatter the onions all around and on the meat, and lock the lid onto the pot.

2.

Set the machine for	Set level for	The valve must be	Set the time for	If necessary, press
PRESSURE COOK	MAX	—	1 hour 10 minutes with the KEEP WARM setting off	START
MEAT/STEW, PRESSURE COOK, or MANUAL	HIGH	Closed	1½ hours with the KEEP WARM setting off	START
SLOW COOK	HIGH	Opened	5 hours with the KEEP WARM setting off (or on for more than 3 hours)	START

3. If you've used a pressure setting, when the machine finishes cooking, turn it off and let its pressure **return to normal naturally,** *about 30 minutes.*

4. Unlatch the lid and open the cooker. Use a meat fork and a large, slotted spoon to transfer the meat (whole or in pieces) to a cutting board. Shred the meat with two forks, discarding the bone as well as any additional bits of cartilage or fat. Then use a flatware tablespoon to skim any excess surface fat from the sauce in the pot.

5.

Press the button for	Set it for	Set the time for	If necessary, press
SAUTÉ	MEDIUM, NORMAL, or CUSTOM 300°F	15 minutes	START

6. Bring the sauce to a simmer, stirring occasionally. Stir in the honey and cook, stirring more and more frequently, until reduced to about half its volume, 5 to 10 minutes. Stir the meat into the sauce and cook, stirring to coat every thread of meat, for 1 minute. Turn off the SAUTÉ function and remove the insert from the cooker. Set the lid askew over the insert for 5 to 10 minutes to blend the flavors and allow the meat to continue to absorb the sauce.

Beyond

• This bone-in cut will not work well in a **3-quart cooker.**

• Serve with orzo pasta and top with minced fresh mint and parsley.

• Or serve in pita pockets with chopped lettuce and tahini sauce. To make enough sauce for 8 servings, whisk ⅓ cup tahini, ⅓ cup plain full-fat yogurt, and ¼ cup fresh lemon juice in a small bowl. Whisk in water by dribs and drabs until the mixture is the consistency of creamy salad dressing. Whisk in a pinch of salt and lots of ground black pepper.

All-American Pulled Chicken

6 servings

Root beer in pulled chicken? Stick with us. First off, what's more American than root beer? And second, it makes for a mix of herbal and sweet flavors that bring a subtle complexity to the sauce. Okay, so maybe the recipe isn't "all-American." Maybe we named it so in the hope it will become the standard, made with chicken breasts for a faster, less fatty, *and* more meaty pulled chicken.

1. Pour the root beer into a **6-quart cooker**. Add the chicken and stir well. Scatter the onions over the top, then dollop or sprinkle the barbecue sauce, Worcestershire sauce, black pepper, and garlic powder over everything. Lock the lid onto the pot.

2.

Set the machine for	Set level for	The valve must be	Set the time for	If necessary, press
PRESSURE COOK	MAX	—	18 minutes with the KEEP WARM setting off	START
MEAT/STEW, PRESSURE COOK, or MANUAL	HIGH	Closed	25 minutes with the KEEP WARM setting off	START
SLOW COOK	HIGH	Opened	2 hours with the KEEP WARM setting off (or on for no more than 1 hour)	START

3. If you've used a pressure setting, when the machine has finished cooking, turn it off and let its pressure **return to normal naturally,** about 20 minutes.

4. Unlatch the lid and open the pot. Use two forks to shred the chicken in the pot. Stir well, then set the lid askew over the top for 5 minutes to allow the meat to continue to absorb the sauce.

¾ cup root beer (do not use diet)

2½ pounds boneless skinless chicken breasts, preferably two or three giant breasts

2 small red onions, thinly sliced and broken into rings

6 tablespoons barbecue sauce of any sort, just not a chunky or creamy sauce

2 tablespoons Worcestershire sauce

1 teaspoon ground black pepper

½ teaspoon garlic powder

Beyond

- For a **3-quart cooker,** you must use ½ cup root beer and halve the remaining ingredients.

- For an **8-quart cooker,** you must increase *all* the ingredients by 50 percent.

- For a spicier pulled chicken, omit the Worcestershire sauce and use 2 tablespoons of a hot red pepper sauce like Tabasco sauce or even the brine from a jar of pickled jalapeño rings.

- Serve with vinegary condiments like pickle relish, dill relish, Dijon mustard, or spicy (not sweet) chowchow.

½ cup chicken broth

½ cup regular coconut milk

2 medium shallots, thinly sliced and separated into rings

4 medium garlic cloves, peeled and slivered

2 tablespoons thinly sliced thin lemongrass (peeled if necessary)

2 tablespoons hot red pepper sauce, preferably Sriracha

2 tablespoons light brown sugar

½ teaspoon ground dried turmeric

½ teaspoon table salt

2½ pounds boneless skinless chicken breasts, preferably two or three giant breasts

Thai-Inspired Pulled Chicken Breasts

6 servings

This recipe is a flight of fancy: an American pulled chicken combined with a Thai braise. Make sure you stir the solid fat into the coconut milk in the can to make the dish as rich as possible.

Lemongrass can be woody, even fibrous, especially the stuff that shows up in North American markets. Trim off any husk-like, desiccated outer rings and only use the tender inner parts of the white and pale green parts of the stalk.

1. Mix the broth, coconut milk, shallots, garlic, lemongrass, pepper sauce, brown sugar, turmeric, and salt in a **6-quart cooker** until the brown sugar dissolves. Set the chicken breasts into this sauce, turning the pieces to coat them on all sides. Lock the lid onto the pot.

2.

Set the machine for	Set level for	The valve must be	Set the time for	If necessary, press
PRESSURE COOK	MAX	—	18 minutes with the KEEP WARM setting off	START
MEAT/STEW, PRESSURE COOK, or MANUAL	HIGH	Closed	25 minutes with the KEEP WARM setting off	START
SLOW COOK	HIGH	Opened	2 hours with the KEEP WARM setting off	START

3. If you've used a pressure setting, when the machine has finished cooking, turn it off and let the pressure **return to normal naturally,** about 15 minutes.

4. Unlatch the lid and open the pot. Use two forks to shred the chicken right in the pot. Stir well, then set the lid askew over the pot and set aside for 5 to 10 minutes to blend the flavors and allow the meat to absorb some of the sauce.

Beyond

- For a **3-quart cooker,** you must use ½ cup broth and halve the remaining ingredients.

- For an **8-quart cooker,** you must increase *all* the ingredients by 50 percent.

- Serve over long-grain white rice and top the servings with fresh cilantro leaves, minced red onion, and fresh bean sprouts.

- For a hotter dish, add up to 2 small serrano chiles, stemmed and thinly sliced, with the other sauce ingredients.

- For a less aromatic but sweeter dish, substitute 2 tablespoons minced peeled fresh ginger for the lemongrass.

Tikka-Style Pulled Chicken Thighs

6 servings

Chicken tikka is a classic East Indian dish — but surely not ever a pulled dish! Oh, but yes. We've taken the classic flavors and revamped them to create a savory riff on an American classic: creamy, filling, with lots of warming spices. (Look elsewhere for Chicken Tikka Masala: page 242.) For the richest taste, use full-fat Greek yogurt, rather than fat-free.

1. Mix the tomatoes, broth, onion, ginger, smoked paprika, cinnamon, coriander, turmeric, and salt in a **6-quart cooker**. Add the chicken thighs and toss well to coat. Lock the lid onto the pot.

2.

Set the machine for	Set level for	The valve must be	Set the time for	If necessary, press
PRESSURE COOK	MAX	—	14 minutes with the KEEP WARM setting off	START
MEAT/STEW, PRESSURE COOK, or MANUAL	HIGH	Closed	20 minutes with the KEEP WARM setting off	START
SLOW COOK	HIGH	Opened	2 hours with the KEEP WARM setting off (or on for no more than 2 hours)	START

3. If you've used a pressure setting, when the machine has finished cooking, turn it off and let its pressure **return to normal naturally,** about 15 minutes.

4. Unlatch the lid and open the pot. Shred the meat with two forks in the pot. Add the yogurt and cilantro, then stir well until uniform.

One 14-ounce can diced tomatos (1¾ cups)

½ cup chicken broth

1 small red onion, chopped (½ cup)

2 tablespoons minced peeled fresh ginger

2 tablespoons mild smoked paprika

1 teaspoon ground cinnamon

1 teaspoon ground coriander

1 teaspoon ground dried turmeric

1 teaspoon table salt

2 pounds boneless skinless chicken thighs

¼ cup Greek yogurt

¼ cup lightly packed fresh cilantro leaves

Beyond

- For a **3-quart cooker,** you must use ⅓ cup broth and halve the remaining ingredients.

- For an **8-quart cooker,** you must increase *all* the ingredients by 50 percent.

- Serve over long-grain brown rice, a nutty contrast to the complex flavors.

- Or serve in pita pockets with a little minced red onion and a hearty dollop of chutney.

- For more heat, add up to 2 serrano chiles, stemmed and thinly sliced, with the onion.

¾ cup chicken broth

¼ cup balsamic vinegar

¼ cup strawberry jam (do not use sugar-free)

1 tablespoon Dijon mustard

1 tablespoon ground black pepper, preferably coarsely ground

1 teaspoon table salt

2½ pounds boneless skinless chicken thighs

1 large rosemary sprig

Balsamic–Black Pepper Pulled Chicken

6 servings

Since chicken thighs have a lot of meaty flavor, we felt free to use a lot of black pepper for a super-spicy bump. It's worth it to grind your own pepper for the freshest taste. The surprise here may well be the strawberry jam, a sweet contrast to the vinegar and pepper, a balance of flavors. Don't use jelly (too thin) or preserves (too thick).

1. Mix the broth, vinegar, jam, mustard, black pepper, and salt in a **6-quart cooker** until the jam dissolves. Add the chicken thighs and toss well to coat. Tuck the rosemary sprig into the mix and lock the lid onto the pot.

2.

Set the machine for	Set level for	The valve must be	Set the time for	If necessary, press
PRESSURE COOK	MAX	—	14 minutes with the KEEP WARM setting off	START
MEAT/STEW, PRESSURE COOK, or MANUAL	HIGH	Closed	20 minutes with the KEEP WARM setting off	START
SLOW COOK	HIGH	Opened	2 hours with the KEEP WARM setting off (or on for no more than 2 hours)	START

3. If you've used a pressure setting, when the machine has finished cooking, turn it off and let its pressure **return to normal naturally,** about 20 minutes.

4. Unlatch the lid and open the pot. Fish out and discard the rosemary sprig. Shred the meat with two forks in the pot, then stir well to coat with sauce. Set the lid askew over the pot for 5 to 10 minutes to allow the chicken to continue absorbing the sauce.

Beyond

- For a **3-quart cooker,** you must use ½ cup broth and halve the remaining ingredients.

- For an **8-quart cooker,** you must increase all the ingredients by 50 percent.

- Serve in radicchio cups with sour cream. Or serve over an undressed chopped salad of cucumber, celery, endive, and red onion.

Thanksgiving-Inspired Pulled Turkey

8 servings

The sun doesn't rise and set on pork, beef, and chicken when it comes to pulled dishes. You can even cook turkey tenderloins until they can be pulled into what can only be described as a one-pot version of a Thanksgiving meal, made with cranberry sauce, sage, and thyme. The shredded sweet potato adds lots of sweetness *and* thickens the sauce as the pieces melt into it.

Although turkey tenderloins work best because they shred into a "pulled" consistency, a chunk of boneless skinless turkey breast will do fine even if it's not so easy to shred. Cut it into three even pieces to match the approximate size and shape of turkey tenderloins.

1. Mix the broth, cranberry sauce, sage, thyme, and salt in a **6-quart cooker**. Stir in the shredded sweet potato, then set the turkey into this sauce, turning it to coat. Lock the lid onto the pot.

2.

Set the machine for	Set level for	The valve must be	Set the time for	If necessary, press
PRESSURE COOK	MAX	—	18 minutes with the KEEP WARM setting off	START
MEAT/STEW, PRESSURE COOK, or MANUAL	HIGH	Closed	25 minutes with the KEEP WARM setting off	START

3. When the machine has finished cooking, turn it off and let its pressure **return to normal naturally,** about 20 minutes. Unlatch the lid and open the pot. Shred the meat with two forks in the pot, then stir well until coated with sauce. Set the lid askew over the pot for 5 to 10 minutes to blend the flavors and allow the turkey to continue to absorb the sauce.

See photo in insert.

¾ cup chicken broth

½ cup whole berry cranberry sauce

2 tablespoons packed fresh sage leaves, finely chopped

2 teaspoons fresh thyme leaves

1 teaspoon table salt

1 small sweet potato (about 8 ounces), peeled and shredded through the large holes of a box grater

2½ pounds boneless skinless turkey tenderloins

Beyond

- For a **3-quart cooker,** you must use ½ cup broth and halve the remaining ingredients.

- For an **8-quart cooker,** you must increase *all* the ingredients by 50 percent.

- Unfortunately, this recipe doesn't work well on the slow cooker setting. The turkey dries out too quickly.

- For the full Thanksgiving treatment, buy corn muffins, split them in half, then toast them cut side down on a baking sheet in a 400°F oven until crisp at the edges. Serve the pulled turkey over them in bowls.

1 tablespoon lemon pepper
seasoning blend

2½ pounds boneless turkey
tenderloins, or boneless skinless
turkey breast cut into 3 pieces

⅔ cup chicken broth

¼ cup ginger jam

2 tablespoons fresh lemon juice

2 tablespoons red wine vinegar

2 tablespoons packed fresh oregano
leaves, minced

½ teaspoon red pepper flakes

Lemon and Ginger Pulled Turkey

6 servings

These are among the brightest flavors in this chapter: a sweet and tart
mix that's much more suited to a spring day than a winter one. In all
truth, this recipe is our pressure-cooker homage to the ever-popular
New York restaurant Rao's lemon chicken. It would even be great for
lunch on slices of toasted, whole-wheat bread, sort of like pulled turkey
salad. Check the label of your lemon pepper seasoning blend. If it
doesn't contain salt, add up to 1½ teaspoons salt with the sauce
ingredients.

1. Pat and massage the lemon pepper seasoning into the turkey
tenderloins or pieces. Mix the broth, jam, lemon juice, vinegar, oregano,
and red pepper flakes in a **6-quart cooker** until the jam dissolves into
the sauce. Set the turkey into this sauce (without turning the meat
over). Lock the lid onto the pot.

2.

Set the machine for	Set level for	The valve must be	Set the time for	If necessary, press
PRESSURE COOK	MAX	—	18 minutes with the KEEP WARM setting off	START
MEAT/STEW, PRESSURE COOK, or MANUAL	HIGH	Closed	25 minutes with the KEEP WARM setting off	START

3. When the machine has finished cooking, turn it off and let its
pressure **return to normal naturally,** about 20 minutes. Unlatch the lid
and open the pot. Shred the meat with two forks in the pot, then stir
well to coat with sauce. Set the lid askew over the pot for 5 to
10 minutes to blend the flavors and allow the meat to continue to
absorb the sauce.

Beyond

- For a **3-quart cooker,** you must use
  ½ cup broth and halve the remaining
  ingredients.

- For an **8-quart cooker,** you must
  increase *all* the ingredients by
  50 percent.

- Garnish with more fresh oregano
  leaves and finely grated lemon zest.

- Substitute lemon marmalade for the
  ginger jam for all-lemon pulled
  turkey.

All-American Pulled Vegetables

6 servings

By cooking lentils and then pureeing them, we can add a creamy texture that's often missing from pulled vegetables (and highly prized in the more meaty versions of pulled fare). We include lots of shredded (rather than chopped or diced) vegetables for a smooth, "pulled" finish.

    The sauce is quite smoky, thanks to a heavy hit of smoked paprika. However, there's just a touch of heat, since the pressure cooker will destroy much of it from the Rotel tomatoes. If you'd like a hotter dish, pass extra hot red pepper sauce at the table.

1. Mix the water and lentils in a **6-quart cooker**. Lock the lid onto the pot.

2.

Set the machine for	Set level for	The valve must be	Set the time for	If necessary, press
PRESSURE COOK	MAX	—	12 minutes with the KEEP WARM setting off	START
MEAT/STEW, PRESSURE COOK, or MANUAL	HIGH	Closed	15 minutes with the KEEP WARM setting off	START

3. Use the **quick-release method** to bring the pot's pressure back to normal. Unlatch the lid and open the pot. Drain the contents of the *hot* insert through a fine-mesh sieve such as a *chinois* or a colander lined with cheesecloth, either set in the sink. Cool a few minutes, then put the lentils in a food processor and process until smooth, stopping the machine and scraping down the inside at least once.

4. Do not clean the insert; set it back in the machine. Stir the sweet potato, red cabbage, green cabbage, carrots, Rotel tomatoes, onion, apple juice, Worcestershire sauce, mustard, brown sugar, smoked paprika, and chile powder into the pot. Lock the lid back on the cooker.

5.

Set the machine for	Set level for	The valve must be	Set the time for	If necessary, press
PRESSURE COOK	MAX	—	4 minutes with the KEEP WARM setting off	START
MEAT/STEW, PRESSURE COOK, or MANUAL	HIGH	Closed	5 minutes with the KEEP WARM setting off	START

6. Use the **quick-release method** to bring the pot's pressure back to normal. Unlatch the lid and open the pot. Scrape the lentil puree into the pot; stir well until uniform. Set the lid askew over the pot for 5 to 10 minutes to blend the flavors and allow the vegetables to continue to absorb the liquid.

2½ cups water

¾ cup green lentils (that is, le Puy lentils)

1 medium sweet potato (about 10 ounces), peeled and shredded through the large holes of a box grater

2 cups cored and shredded green cabbage (about half a large—or 3½-pound—green cabbage)

2 cups cored and shredded red cabbage (about half a large—or 3½-pound—red cabbage)

3 medium carrots, shredded through the large holes of a box grater (1½ cups)

One 10-ounce can Rotel tomatoes (1¼ cups)

1 small red onion, halved and thinly sliced into half-moons

¾ cup unsweetened apple juice

2 tablespoons Worcestershire sauce

2 tablespoons Dijon mustard

2 tablespoons dark brown sugar

2 tablespoons mild smoked paprika

1 tablespoon standard chile powder

Beyond

- For a **3-quart cooker,** you must use ½ cup apple juice and halve the remaining ingredients. For an **8-quart cooker,** you must increase the apple juice to 1 cup and use the stated amounts of the remaining ingredients.

- It's hard to predict exactly how much moisture all the vegetables will give off because various heads of cabbage will have varying water content. If you find the mix too soupy, don't boil it down. Instead, use a slotted spoon to serve up the pulled vegetables, letting some of the liquid drain back into the pot.

6

All Things Curried

Welcome to the biggest flavors in this book. Some of these recipes are not for the faint-hearted (or the third-grade set). From a road map for tagine-style suppers to an aromatic, irresistible chana dal, these dishes bring out the best of what the Instant Pot can do: preserve internal moisture in just about everything, mellow the flavors of dried spices, and save you time (and money) with tasty cuts and root vegetables.

Since curry is such a wide designation, you'll even find soups and noodle dishes here, recipes you might have expected in other chapters. For more about the specifics of curry and curry powder, see the FAQs below. But before the recipes, it's important to point out that most curry calls for cooked rice. So we should bend the discussion that way first.

Simply put, rice is not just rice. Even long-grain white rice is not just long-grain white rice. Some varietals have a delicate fragrance, a tantalizing blend of sweet and herbaceous flavors; others offer nothing more than a dull, flat, starchy ho-hum. It's tempting to say that you get what you pay for, but that's not always the case. Unfortunately, a taste test among brands is the only sure way to know. But for a shot at the best, look for plump grains, white or brown, either beautifully polished to a pearly luster or evenly brown across the batch.

Because of its intact germ and bran, brown rice can go bad relatively quickly; it will last maybe 4 months or a little longer if stored in a dark, cool pantry — or up to a year in a sealed container in the freezer. Raw, the rice should not smell musky or funky.

Rice grains come in various lengths. For our recipes, we've gone with the standard, North American three: short (almost never used in this book), medium (used a bit more often, if not much in this chapter), and long (the most common type throughout this chapter and the book as a whole). When it comes to long-grain rice, we prefer white or brown basmati or Texmati, simply because these are less floral than jasmine rice.

Medium-grain rice, most often found in North America as the varietal Arborio, has a stickier consistency. And short-grain rice, sometimes called "sushi rice," can be quite gummy. Either medium- or short-grain rice works well as a base for the soupy curries in this chapter, particularly those based on recipes from Thailand and Southeast Asia.

If you want to cook rice in the Instant Pot, be careful. The *Rice* function is calibrated differently among the models. Some will *not* automatically accommodate for brown rice; you must set the cook time manually. Read your pot's instruction manual. It (or the included recipe booklet) offers specific instructions on how to make plain rice in your model.

FAQs

1. What is curry powder?

Curry is the English version of a Tamil word that means "sauce." *Curry powder* is the blend of spices that flavor said sauce, which has either been rendered from the natural juices of meats and vegetables or created from ingredients like broth or coconut milk.

When most Americans think of curry powder, they think of a yellow, dried-spice blend. Where applicable, we call for it. Sometimes, in the *Beyond* section of a recipe, we even offer a specific blend you can concoct if you want to go all out. But with the advent of gourmet supermarkets and the growing food culture in North America, gone are the days when "yellow curry powder" meant just one thing. It and all other sorts of curry powders are now available in an almost overwhelming range of quality and flavor among proprietary blends. Some taste of nothing but acrid, low-grade turmeric; others offer an array of dried spices (and therefore a more complex flavor). In higher-end spice stores, you can even sample the offerings. If you search around at specialty spice stores or East Indian markets (even online), you'll be astounded at what's available.

2. Since curry powder is a spice blend, can I make my own?

Of course! Beyond any special blends we recommend in the recipes themselves, here's how to make a basic batch: Start with 1 tablespoon each of *at least* three, if not all four, of these spices: ground coriander, ground cumin, ground dried turmeric, and/or ground dried ginger. Add 1 teaspoon table salt and *up to* 1 teaspoon ground dried cayenne. Then add *at least* two but preferably three or four of the following: 1 teaspoon ground cinnamon, 1 teaspoon dried thyme, 1 teaspoon dried sage, ½ teaspoon grated nutmeg, ½ teaspoon ground fenugreek, ¼ teaspoon ground mace, and/or ¼ teaspoon ground cloves. You'll be the envy of your block.

3. Is there salt in commercial curry powder?

Sometimes, but not always. Check the label if you have health concerns or don't like a salty dish. If salt is among the ingredients, and particularly if it's near the top of the list, consider omitting any additional salt in the recipe and passing extra at the table.

4. Can I use other dried curry blends instead of the standard yellow powder?

By all means! There are red curry powders (usually quite fiery) as well as specialty, regional blends — not only from India, but also from Great Britain, South Africa, and the Caribbean. In truth, there are probably as many curry

powders used in Indian and Southeast Asian cooking as there are people in those regions standing at a stove right now. Don't get hung up on authenticity. Experiment, check out other bottlings, see what you like, and keep your experience in the kitchen fresh and exciting.

5. What is garam masala?

First off, it's a Hindi or Punjabi term that means "hot spice blend." The "hot" doesn't refer to its being spicy but to the way the spices are said to raise the body's internal temperature. In the same way, we might say "warming spices" for blends with, say, cinnamon and nutmeg: cozy flavors that are often associated with colder weather.

As with yellow curry powder, there's a wide range of quality and flavor among garam masalas on the market. You can also create your own. Over the years, we've come up with some blends that match various proteins. We're giving you house secrets here. Use them wisely. Each will make about 2 tablespoons of garam masala.

- For lamb and beef, mix together 2 teaspoons ground coriander, 1 teaspoon ground cinnamon, 1 teaspoon ground cumin, 1 teaspoon ground dried turmeric, ½ teaspoon ground cardamom, ¼ teaspoon ground cloves, and up to ¼ teaspoon ground dried cayenne.

- For pork, chicken, veal, or tofu, mix together 2 teaspoons ground coriander, 1 teaspoon ground cumin, 1 teaspoon mild paprika, 1 teaspoon fennel seeds, ½ teaspoon ground cinnamon, ¼ teaspoon ground allspice, and up to ¼ teaspoon ground dried cayenne.

- For fish and shellfish, mix together 2 teaspoons ground coriander, 1 teaspoon ground dried turmeric, 1 teaspoon mild paprika, ½ teaspoon ground fenugreek, ½ teaspoon ground dried ginger, ½ teaspoon ground dried mustard, ¼ teaspoon grated nutmeg, and up to ¼ teaspoon saffron threads.

6. What's a curry paste?

It's a wet blend of dried spices, fresh chiles, fresh aromatics, and oil or ghee. The basics are red, yellow, and green curry pastes, available in small jars, cans, or plastic tubs in the Asian or East Indian aisle of almost all supermarkets. Once opened, the packages can be covered and stored in the refrigerator for at least 4 months, maybe longer.

Red curry paste has a complex, bright flavor and is usually the hottest, although it can have plenty of sweet notes. Yellow curry paste is usually milder and more herbaceous than red (and sometimes milder than green). Green chile paste has sour notes and a fresh flavor, often from lemongrass. Some green chile pastes are absurdly hot since they're made from what seems like a metric ton of pulverized fresh green chiles.

But there are more blends than those three which you can use in these recipes. Massaman curry paste is heavy with warming spices (like cinnamon, cloves, and nutmeg) and is generally the mildest of the pastes. Penang curry paste is a fiery red mix, heavy with lemongrass and makrut lime leaves, guaranteed to knock your tongue for a loop. Sour vegetable curry paste is just what it sounds like: a sour, musty mélange missing coconut (which is in many of the others) but made with fermented shrimp paste (and therefore stinky, although it mellows over the heat).

No matter which of these you use, read the labels. If the first ingredient listed is chiles or cayenne, you've got a banging-hot version in hand. If you're worried, use half the stated amount of curry paste the first time you make a dish. But remember: You can't add more curry paste as a garnish. It'll be too pungent, too "raw." Instead, use a hot red pepper sauce like Sriracha for heat at the table.

7. What's ghee?

It's clarified butter — that is, butter with the milk solids removed. Whenever you melt butter, you've surely noticed those white blotchy bits at the bottom of the liquid fat. Take those out and essentially you've got ghee.

To make your own, put a cut-up stick of butter in a shallow bowl (a soup plate works best) and microwave on high in 10-second increments until melted, then cool for 15 to 20 minutes at room temperature to let the milk solids settle to the bottom. Skim the clear, oily fat off the top, leaving the solids (and inevitably some of the oil) behind. Store the clarified butter (the ghee) in a covered small glass jar in the fridge for a month or two. It will solidify again but you can scrape out what you need. Discard the solids and the small amount of oil with them — or save them for a few days in the fridge to add with the thickener to custards (particularly ice cream custards) for extra richness.

And one final note: Watch out if you buy ghee. Some brands are quite literally nothing more than butter-flavored shortening. Others are the real deal: clarified butter. Spring for the real deal.

8. What's chana dal?

Basically, these are split and processed chickpeas. (They are *not* yellow lentils, nor actually lentils of any sort.) The chickpeas (aka garbanzo beans) are of a specific variety that are then dried and cut into pieces about the size of corn kernels. They cook quickly with a grainy texture and an earthy flavor. You cannot substitute other sorts of lentils or "dal" (split pulses or legumes) for chana dal. Look for it in bags in the aisle near the whole grains.

1 tablespoon vegetable, corn, or canola oil

1 fresh serrano chile, stemmed, halved lengthwise, seeded, and chopped

1 teaspoon cumin seeds

1 teaspoon garam masala

1 teaspoon ground coriander

1 teaspoon ground dried turmeric

Up to ½ teaspoon ground dried cayenne

½ teaspoon granulated white sugar

½ teaspoon table salt

2 medium plum or Roma tomatoes, chopped (⅔ cup)

1¼ cups water

12 ounces baby spinach

1 pound extra-firm tofu, cut into 1-inch cubes

Vegan Saag Paneer

4 servings

Technically, this is "palak paneer" — that is, a *spinach* braise with a spicy sauce, although the dish is frequently called "saag paneer" on this side of the ocean, despite its lack of "saag," a mustard green.

The paneer is the real problem: It's a fresh cheese, common in India and Southeast Asia, but difficult to track down in the U.S. It has a fairly high melting point (for cheese anyway) and stays in chunks when it's folded into the sauce. We've crafted a vegan dish that's more accommodating to the limitations of our supermarkets by subbing extra-firm tofu for the cheese. Serve the stew over cooked white basmati rice.

1.

Press the button for	Set it for	Set the time for	If necessary, press
SAUTÉ	MEDIUM, NORMAL, or CUSTOM 300°F	10 minutes	START

2. Heat the oil in a **6- or 8-quart cooker** for a minute or two. Add the chile and cumin seeds. Cook, stirring all the while, just to toast the cumin seeds, about 1 minute. Stir in the garam masala, coriander, turmeric, cayenne, sugar, and salt until fragrant, just a few seconds.

3. Stir in the tomatoes and cook, stirring occasionally, until they begin to break down, about 2 minutes. Stir in the water and scrape up any browned bits on the pot's bottom. Turn off the SAUTÉ function, then stir in the spinach, pressing the leaves down into the liquid. Lock the lid onto the pot.

4.

Set the machine for	Set the level for	The valve must be	Set the time for	If necessary, press
PRESSURE COOK	MAX	—	6 minutes with the KEEP WARM setting off	START
PRESSURE COOK or MANUAL	HIGH	Closed	8 minutes with the KEEP WARM setting off	START

5. Use the **quick-release method** to bring the pot's pressure back to normal. Unlatch the lid and open the cooker. Gently stir in the tofu.

6.

Press the button for	Set it for	Set the time for	If necessary, press
SAUTÉ	MEDIUM, NORMAL, or CUSTOM 300°F	10 minutes	START

7. Cook, stirring occasionally but gently to keep the tofu intact, until the liquid has boiled down to a loose, wet sauce, about 5 minutes. Turn off the SAUTÉ function and set the lid askew over the pot for 5 minutes to blend the flavors. Stir gently again before serving.

Beyond

- You must halve the recipe for a **3-quart cooker.**

- Pure tofu is gluten-free. However, there are cross-contamination concerns with some brands. Buy certified gluten-free tofu if this is a concern.

- If you can find paneer, complete the recipe until you need to add the tofu. Omit the tofu, then continue on with step 6, boiling down the sauce as directed. After you turn off the SAUTÉ function, gently stir in 1 pound paneer, cut into 2-inch chunks. Set aside with the lid askew for 5 minutes to blend the flavors and warm the cheese.

Perfect Chana Dal

4 servings

Chana dal is something like a savory porridge, spicy and earthy. It is the single most important side dish you can make to go along with just about every East Indian–inspired curry in this chapter. It won't go with the dishes with noodles or any made from a wet curry paste; but it is exactly right with, say, Better Butter Chicken (page 235) or Savory-Sweet Beef and Tomato Curry (page 244). Serve it either alongside cooked rice in the bowls with the curry as the other third of the bowl or spoon it right on top of the curry. We even just top chana dal with a poached egg and call it a day.

2⅔ cups vegetable broth

1 cup chana dal (see page 227)

1 tablespoon vegetable, corn, or canola oil

1 teaspoon ground dried turmeric

1 teaspoon table salt

½ teaspoon ground cardamom

½ teaspoon ground cumin

½ teaspoon ground black pepper

1. Mix all the ingredients in a **3-, 6-, or 8-quart cooker.** Lock the lid onto the pot.

2.

Set the machine for	Set the level for	The valve must be	Set the time for	If necessary, press
PRESSURE COOK	MAX	—	7 minutes with the KEEP WARM setting off	START
PRESSURE COOK or MANUAL	HIGH	Closed	10 minutes with the KEEP WARM setting off	START

3. When the machine has finished cooking, turn it off and let its pressure **return to normal naturally,** about 25 minutes. Unlatch the lid and open the cooker. Stir well, then set the lid askew over the pot and set aside for 5 minutes so that the mixture continues to thicken. Serve warm.

Beyond

- This recipe can be (but doesn't have to be) doubled in an **6- or 8-quart cooker.**

- For an easy soup, add 3 cups vegetable (or chicken) broth after cooking and purée the soup right in the pot with an immersion blender.

- If you're not vegan, substitute butter or ghee for the oil. And stir up to ¼ cup heavy cream into the mixture *after* cooking. Set aside with the lid over the pot for 5 minutes to take the raw taste off the cream.

2 tablespoons butter

1 medium yellow onion, chopped (1 cup)

1 tablespoon minced peeled fresh ginger

1 tablespoon yellow curry powder

1 tablespoon light brown sugar

1 quart (4 cups) vegetable broth

2 pounds frozen butternut squash cubes (do not thaw)

Up to 2 tablespoons hot red pepper sauce, preferably Sriracha

¼ teaspoon table salt

1 cup regular or low-fat coconut milk

Spicy Curried Butternut Squash Soup

4 to 6 servings

This is a creamy (if cream-free) soup that uses frozen butternut squash cubes to make a tasty, light main course (or a starter course). The coconut milk adds an intense richness, a better foil to the heat.

We call for a lot of hot sauce in this recipe. If you're worried, make the soup the first time with only 1 tablespoon (or even less) of hot red pepper sauce. You can always add more before pureeing the soup.

If you have to puree the soup in batches in a blender, remove the center knob in the lid and cover the opening with a clean kitchen towel to prevent a pressure build-up and a subsequent explosion of soup all over your cabinets.

1.

Press the button for	Set it for	Set the time for	If necessary, press
SAUTÉ	MEDIUM, NORMAL, or CUSTOM 300°F	10 minutes	START

2. Melt the butter in a **6- or 8-quart cooker**. Add the onion and cook, stirring often, until softened, about 4 minutes. Add the ginger and stir until aromatic, just a few seconds. Stir in the curry powder and brown sugar until the brown sugar melts.

3. Pour in the broth and scrape up any browned bits on the pot's bottom. Turn off the SAUTÉ function, then stir in the butternut squash, hot sauce, and salt. Lock the lid onto the pot.

4.

Set the machine for	Set the level for	The valve must be	Set the time for	If necessary, press
PRESSURE COOK	MAX	—	7 minutes with the KEEP WARM setting off	START
SOUP/BROTH, PRESSURE COOK, or MANUAL	HIGH	Closed	10 minutes with the KEEP WARM setting off	START

5. Use the **quick-release method** to bring the pot's pressure back to normal. Unlatch the lid and open the pot. Add the coconut milk, then use an immersion blender to puree the soup in the pot. Or puree the soup in batches in a blender. Serve warm.

Beyond

- You must halve the recipe for a **3-quart cooker**.

- For a more substantial meal, set a mound of lump crab meat in the center of each bowl.

- Or hang cooked large cocktail shrimp off the rim of the bowl (or pile them on a plate nearby) to dip in the soup as you eat it.

- Or serve over cooked white rice and top with bean sprouts.

Empty-the-Root-Cellar Curry

6 servings

Okay, we don't have a root cellar. But here's a vegetarian curry — or even, vegan, if you use a vegan yogurt — that may be just the thing in the late fall when root vegetables are the only thing left fresh at the farmers' markets.

This curry has no added sweetener, letting the high-starch roots handle the job. You might be surprised how savory the dish is. Just make sure all the vegetables are chopped to the right size so they cook in the time stated. If you buy some of the roots prechopped (and why not?), you may need to cut the pieces down even smaller to match the requirements here.

1. Mix the parsnips, beets, potatoes, carrots, onion, broth, almonds, ginger, curry powder, and salt in a **6- or 8-quart cooker**. Stir well, then lock the lid onto the pot.

2.

Set the machine for	Set the level for	The valve must be	Set the time for	If necessary, press
PRESSURE COOK	MAX	—	7 minutes with the KEEP WARM setting off	START
PRESSURE COOK or MANUAL	HIGH	Closed	10 minutes with the KEEP WARM setting off	START

3. Use the **quick-release method** to bring the pot's pressure back to normal. Unlatch the lid and open the cooker. Stir well before serving in bowls with dollops of yogurt as a garnish.

---

1 pound medium parsnips (about 4), peeled and cut into 1-inch sections

1 pound yellow beets (about 3 large), peeled and cut into 1-inch cubes

1 pound large yellow potatoes, such as Yukon Golds (2 or 3 potatoes), cut into quarters

¾ pound medium carrots (about 5), peeled and cut into 1-inch sections

1 medium yellow onion, chopped (1 cup)

2 cups vegetable broth

½ cup whole roasted unsalted almonds

3 tablespoons minced peeled fresh ginger

2 tablespoons yellow curry powder

½ teaspoon table salt

Plain regular or low-fat yogurt for garnishing

Beyond

- You must halve the recipe for a **3-quart cooker**.

- Make your own curry blend: Instead of the store-bought curry powder, use 1½ teaspoons ground cinnamon, 1½ teaspoons ground cumin, 1½ teaspoon ground coriander, 1 teaspoon ground turmeric, and up to ½ teaspoon ground dried cayenne. Or use 2 tablespoons of a signature blend you can make, using the instructions on page 226.

- Dollop chutney as well as yogurt on each serving. Don't just think mango chutney. Try a cranberry one with these roots.

2 tablespoons vegetable, corn, or
canola oil

1 medium red onion, halved and
sliced into thin half-moons

1 fresh small serrano chile, stemmed,
halved, seeded, and thinly sliced

2 medium garlic cloves, peeled and
minced (2 teaspoons)

1 tablespoon minced peeled fresh
ginger

1 tablespoon garam masala

1 teaspoon ground cumin

1 teaspoon mild smoked paprika

½ teaspoon table salt

1½ cups vegetable broth

Two 15-ounce cans chickpeas,
drained and rinsed (3½ cups)

1 pound yellow potatoes, such as
Yukon Golds, cut into 1-inch cubes

½ cup regular or low-fat coconut milk

2 cups loosely packed baby spinach
leaves

1 tablespoon fresh lemon juice

Beyond

- You must halve the recipe for a
3-quart cooker.

- Make your own garam masala: Omit
the store-bought and use 1 teaspoon
ground coriander, ½ teaspoon
ground cardamom, ½ teaspoon
ground cinnamon, ¼ teaspoon
ground cloves, ¼ teaspoon ground
dried mustard, and a bay leaf.
Remove the bay leaf before serving.

- Heat about ½ inch of vegetable oil in
a small saucepan over medium-high
heat until the oil shimmers and
waggles. Add curry leaves and fry,
turning once, until crisp, about
1 minute. Lay these leaves over each
serving.

Smoky Chickpea and Potato Curry

4 servings

Chickpeas and potatoes are two of the most common ingredients in
East Indian cooking. We use them together in this simple, dairy-free
curry, substituting coconut milk for the more traditional yogurt. By
softening the vegetables and aromatics first, we can get natural sugars
into the stew without adding any other sweetener. The stew is so
delicious, it may well turn you into a vegan (or at least help you see that
eating vegan once in a while is a tasty thing).

1.

Press the button for	Set it for	Set the time for	If necessary, press
SAUTÉ	MEDIUM, NORMAL, or CUSTOM 300°F	10 minutes	START

2. Warm the oil in a **6- or 8-quart cooker** for a minute or two. Add the
onion and cook, stirring often, until softened, about 4 minutes. Add the
chile, garlic, and ginger. Continue cooking, stirring almost constantly,
for 1 minute.

3. Stir in the garam masala, cumin, smoked paprika, and salt until
fragrant, just a few seconds. Pour in the broth and scrape up any
browned bits on the pot's bottom. Turn off the SAUTÉ function. Stir in
the chickpeas, potatoes, and coconut milk until uniform. Lock the lid
onto the pot.

4.

Set the machine for	Set the level for	The valve must be	Set the time for	If necessary, press
PRESSURE COOK	MAX	—	5 minutes with the KEEP WARM setting off	START
PRESSURE COOK or MANUAL	HIGH	Closed	7 minutes with the KEEP WARM setting off	START

5. Use the **quick-release method** to bring the pot's pressure back to
normal. Unlatch the lid and open the pot. Stir in the baby spinach and
lemon juice. Set the lid askew over the pot; set aside for 5 minutes to
wilt the spinach and blend the flavors. Stir again before serving.

Three-Lentil Dal Makhani

6 servings

This one's a creamy lentil curry, often made with black lentils and kidney beans. Unfortunately, black lentils are tough to track down outside of specialty markets. Easier to find, red kidney beans do indeed break down and thicken the curry, giving it a characteristic texture. But dried kidney beans make the recipe overly complicated (soaking, pre-cooking separately, etc.). And canned kidney beans end up too squishy under pressure for this long. To solve all those problems, we use a mix of lentils to revamp this dish — even red lentils (sometimes called "pink lentils"), which dissolve under pressure and thicken the dish while giving it an earthy flavor. Although this is a vegetarian main course, feel free to serve it alongside almost anything from the grill. Pork loin would be welcome. Beef ribs, too.

1.

Press the button for	Set it for	Set the time for	If necessary, press
SAUTÉ	MEDIUM, NORMAL, or CUSTOM 300°F	5 minutes	START

2. Melt the butter in a **3-, 6-, or 8-quart cooker**. Add the garlic, ginger, garam masala, cumin, turmeric, salt, cayenne, cinnamon stick, cardamom pods, and bay leaves. Stir until fragrant, about 1 minute. Add the tomato and cook, stirring often, until it just begins to break down, 1 to 2 minutes.

3. Turn off the SAUTÉ function. Stir in the red lentils, brown lentils, and chana dal until coated in the spices. Stir in the water and lock the lid onto the pot.

4.

Set the machine for	Set the level for	The valve must be	Set the time for	If necessary, press
PRESSURE COOK	MAX	—	16 minutes with the KEEP WARM setting off	START
MEAT/STEW, PRESSURE COOK, or MANUAL	HIGH	Closed	20 minutes with the KEEP WARM setting off	START

5. Use the **quick-release method** to bring the pot's pressure back to normal. Unlatch the lid and open the cooker. Remove and discard the cinnamon stick, cardamom pods, and bay leaves. Stir in the cream until uniform, then set the lid askew over the pot for 5 minutes to blend the flavors. Stir again before serving.

See photo in insert.

2 tablespoons butter or ghee

6 medium garlic cloves, peeled and minced (2 tablespoons)

2 tablespoons minced peeled fresh ginger

1 tablespoon garam masala

1 teaspoon ground cumin

1 teaspoon ground dried turmeric

½ teaspoon table salt

Up to ½ teaspoon ground dried cayenne

One 4-inch cinnamon stick

4 green or white cardamom pods

2 bay leaves

1 large round red tomato, chopped (1 cup)

½ cup red lentils

½ cup brown lentils

½ cup chana dal

1 quart (4 cups) water

½ cup heavy cream

Beyond

- If you want to have the "full bean" experience (and a less thick curry), substitute dried black-eyed peas for the red lentils.

- Serve the curry with packaged na'an or other flatbreads.

3 pounds boneless skinless meat, cut into 1½- to 2-inch cubes

> **Choose** from chicken thighs, beef bottom round, beef arm roast, beef eye of round, leg of lamb, or fresh (not cured or smoked) ham.

2 tablespoons curry powder

> **Choose** from yellow, red, specialty blends, even tandoori or an Asian curry powder—or make your own (see page 226).

3 tablespoons oil

> **Choose** from vegetable, corn, canola, safflower, peanut, grape seed, avocado, coconut, or olive oil.

1½ cups chopped aromatics

> **Choose one or two** from onions (of any sort), shallots, scallions, fennel, celery, and/or leeks (white and pale green parts only, well washed).

2 tablespoons minced peeled fresh ginger

2 medium garlic cloves, peeled and minced (2 teaspoons)

½ cup dried fruit

> **Choose** from raisins (regular or golden), currants, chopped pitted prunes, chopped dried pineapple, chopped pitted dried nectarines, chopped pitted dried peaches, or chopped stemmed dried figs

½ cup unsalted shelled nuts

> **Choose** from pistachios, walnuts, pecans, or almonds.

1 cup liquid

> **Choose** a broth of any sort; or a 50/50 combo of broth and a dry white wine, such as Chardonnay.

½ teaspoon table salt

Beyond

- You must halve the recipe for a **3-quart cooker**.
- For an **8-quart cooker**, you must use 1¾ cups liquid and increase the remaining ingredients by 50 percent.

Road Map: Tagine-Style Curry

6 servings

A tagine is a North African curry, often a mix of meat, dried fruit, aromatics, and nuts, traditionally made in a shallow pot with a conical lid. Here's a streamlined recipe that allows you to create your own version in an Instant Pot. Leaner cuts of meat work better, so we don't recommend lamb, pork shoulder, or beef chuck, any of which produces an oily, thick sauce.

Serve the spiced stew over fluffed couscous, long-grain white rice, Israeli couscous, or plain mashed potatoes.

1. Toss the meat and curry powder in a large bowl until the pieces are evenly and thoroughly coated in the spices.

2.

Press the button for	Set it for	Set the time for	If necessary, press
SAUTÉ	MEDIUM, NORMAL, or CUSTOM 300°F	15 minutes	START

3. Warm the oil in a **6-quart cooker** for a minute or two, then add the aromatics. Cook, stirring often, until softened, 3 to 4 minutes. Add the ginger and garlic; cook, stirring often, until aromatic, less than 1 minute.

4. Add the meat, scraping every last speck of dried spices into the pot. Cook, stirring occasionally, until the meat loses its raw, pink color and browns lightly, about 5 minutes. Turn off the SAUTÉ function. Stir in the dried fruit and nuts, then the liquid and salt, just until everything is well combined. Lock the lid onto the pot.

5.

Set the machine for	Set the level for	The valve must be	Set the time for	If necessary, press
PRESSURE COOK	MAX	—	35 minutes with the KEEP WARM setting off	START
MEAT/STEW, PRESSURE COOK, or MANUAL	HIGH	Closed	45 minutes with the KEEP WARM setting off	START
SLOW COOK	HIGH	Opened	3 hours with the KEEP WARM setting off (or on for no more than 2 hours)	START

6. If you've used a pressure setting, when the machine has finished cooking, turn it off and let the pressure **return to normal naturally**, about 30 minutes.

7. Unlatch the lid and open the cooker. Stir well before serving.

Better Butter Chicken

6 servings

Here's our version of an internet craze: a buttery, tomato-laced, cream-rich sauce enrobing meaty pieces of chicken. Unfortunately, many recipes use cut-up bits of boneless, skinless chicken breast, which become tough shards; or chicken thighs, which leave the sauce greasy. We use bone-in skin-off chicken breasts to give the sauce a more savory, bony flavor, with some collagen melted into it to enrich every bite.

   To remove the skin from a chicken breast, grab the skin on the narrow, pointy end with a paper towel and pull the skin back and off the meat. Remove any large blobs of fat on the meat. Then cut each breast in half widthwise so there's about the same amount of meat in each portion.

1.

Press the button for	Set it for	Set the time for	If necessary, press
SAUTÉ	MEDIUM, NORMAL, or CUSTOM 300°F	5 minutes	START

2. Mix the tomatoes, broth or wine, onion, butter, curry powder, ginger, and salt in a **6-quart cooker**. Cook, stirring occasionally, until the butter melts, about 2 minutes. Turn off the SAUTÉ function, add the chicken, and toss well in the sauce to coat. Lock the lid onto the pot.

3.

Set the machine for	Set the level for	The valve must be	Set the time for	If necessary, press
PRESSURE COOK	MAX	—	12 minutes with the KEEP WARM setting off	START
MEAT/STEW, PRESSURE COOK, or MANUAL	HIGH	Closed	15 minutes with the KEEP WARM setting off	START

4. Use the **quick-release method** to bring the pot's pressure back to normal. Unlatch the lid and open the pot. Use kitchen tongs to transfer the chicken breasts to a serving platter or individual serving bowls.

5.

Press the button for	Set it for	Set the time for	If necessary, press
SAUTÉ	MEDIUM, NORMAL, or CUSTOM 300°F	5 minutes	START

6. Bring the sauce to a simmer, stirring quite frequently. Stir in the cream and cook the sauce at a low simmer, stirring quite often, until slightly thickened, about 2 minutes. Turn off the SAUTÉ function and spoon the sauce over the chicken breasts.

1½ cups canned crushed tomatoes

½ cup chicken broth or dry white wine

4 tablespoons (½ stick) butter, cut into bits

1 small yellow onion, chopped (½ cup)

2 tablespoons yellow curry powder

1 tablespoon minced peeled fresh ginger

¼ teaspoon table salt

Three 1-pound bone-in skinless chicken breasts, cut in half widthwise

½ cup heavy cream

See photo in insert.

Beyond

- You must halve the recipe for a **3-quart cooker**.

- For an **8-quart cooker**, you must increase all the ingredients by 50 percent.

- The curry's buttery enough to serve over mashed potatoes (page 424).

- Or serve it on top of split-open baked sweet potatoes.

- Or serve it over riced cauliflower. There's no need to cook the cauliflower. The warm sauce will do the job for you if you serve it immediately and set the bowls aside for a minute or two.

- Garnish servings with minced fresh cilantro and/or chives. And sprinkle unsalted shelled chopped pistachios over them, too.

2½ pounds large boneless skinless chicken thighs, halved

2 tablespoons red wine vinegar

1½ tablespoons vindaloo curry dried spice blend

2 teaspoons dark brown sugar

½ teaspoon ground cinnamon

2 tablespoons vegetable oil

2 medium yellow onions, halved and sliced into thin half-moons

1½ tablespoons minced fresh ginger

1 cup chicken broth

1¼ pounds yellow-flesh potatoes, cut into 1½-inch pieces

Plain Greek yogurt and mango chutney for garnishing

Chicken Vindaloo

4 servings

Vindaloo means "wine and potatoes," but it has come to mean "fiery hot" in North America. Actually, there's no wine in our version — a bit strange, we admit, but we wanted to skew the dish more savory, given that the pot highlights sweet flavors. Note that there's no need for rice. With the potatoes, this is a one-pot meal.

The recipe may seem to use a lot of vindaloo spice. You'll be amazed at how it mellows. If you're in doubt, or if you have children at the table, use at most 1 tablespoon and pass some bottled hot red chile sauce at the table to spice up some of the servings.

1. Mix the chicken, vinegar, spice blend, brown sugar, and cinnamon in a large bowl until evenly coated. Set aside at room temperature for up to 20 minutes. (Or cover and set in the fridge for up to 10 hours.)

2.

Press the button for	Set it for	Set the time for	If necessary, press
SAUTÉ	MEDIUM, NORMAL, or CUSTOM 300°F	10 minutes	START

3. Warm the oil in a **6-quart cooker** for a minute or two. Add the onions and cook, stirring often, until softened, about 5 minutes. Add the ginger and continue cooking, stirring often, until fragrant, about 1 minute.

4. Add the meat and every drop of its marinade and spices. Stir to mix among the onions. Turn off the SAUTÉ function, then pour in the broth and stir well. Lock the lid onto the pot.

5.

Set the machine for	Set the level for	The valve must be	Set the time for	If necessary, press
PRESSURE COOK	MAX	—	5 minutes with the KEEP WARM setting off	START
MEAT/STEW, PRESSURE COOK, or MANUAL	HIGH	Closed	8 minutes with the KEEP WARM setting off	START

6. Use the **quick-release method** to bring the pot's pressure back to normal. Unlatch the lid and open the cooker. Stir in the potatoes. Lock the lid back onto the pot.

7.

Set the machine for	Set the level for	The valve must be	Set the time for	If necessary, press
PRESSURE COOK	MAX	—	8 minutes with the KEEP WARM setting off	START
MEAT/STEW, PRESSURE COOK, or MANUAL	HIGH	Closed	10 minutes with the KEEP WARM setting off	START

8. Use the **quick-release method** to bring the pot's pressure back to normal. Unlatch the lid and uncover the cooker. Stir well, then serve with dollops of yogurt and a spoonful of chutney or two over each bowlful.

Beyond

- For a **3-quart cooker**, you must use ½ cup broth and halve the remaining ingredients.

- For an **8-quart cooker**, you must increase *all* the ingredients by 50 percent.

- If the curry is too soupy for your taste after the second cooking, bring the stew to a high simmer using the SAUTÉ function on its MEDIUM, NORMAL, or CUSTOM 300°F setting. Cook, stirring almost constantly, to reduce the sauce a bit, 2 to 3 minutes.

- Substitute butter or even ghee (clarified butter) for the vegetable oil.

- Omit the dried spice blend and make your own vindaloo powder: Increase the ground cinnamon to 1 teaspoon, and add the following spices to the bowl with the meat and vinegar: 1 teaspoon ground dried turmeric, 1 teaspoon hot paprika or ground dried red chiles, 1 teaspoon ground coriander, ½ teaspoon ground cumin, ½ teaspoon ground cloves, ½ teaspoon ground dried mustard, and ½ teaspoon table salt.

1 pound plain boneless skinless chicken breast cut for stir-fry; or boneless skinless chicken breasts cut into ½ x ½-inch strips

1 quart (4 cups) chicken broth

1½ cups regular or low-fat coconut milk

1 medium yellow bell pepper, stemmed, cored, and chopped (1 cup)

One 8-ounce can sliced bamboo shoots, drained (1 cup)

4 ounces shiitake mushroom caps, sliced

1 tablespoon minced peeled fresh ginger

1 tablespoon yellow curry powder

1 tablespoon granulated white sugar

1 tablespoon fresh lime juice

1 tablespoon hot red pepper sauce, such as Sriracha (optional)

Curried Chicken Soup

6 servings

There's no faster chicken soup in this book, particularly if you buy boneless skinless chicken breasts already prepped for stir-frying (that is, cut into long, thin strips). Make sure those strips are not marinated and discard any seasoning packets that come with them. And stir the coconut milk in the can with a fork before using to get the coconut solids mixed into the liquid.

1. Mix all the ingredients in a **6- or 8-quart cooker**. Lock the lid onto the pot.

2.

Set the machine for	Set the level for	The valve must be	Set the time for	If necessary, press
PRESSURE COOK	MAX	—	5 minutes with the KEEP WARM setting off	START
SOUP/BROTH, PRESSURE COOK, or MANUAL	HIGH	Closed	7 minutes with the KEEP WARM setting off	START
SLOW COOK	HIGH	Opened	3 hours with the KEEP WARM setting off (or on for 1 hour)	START

3. If using the pressure-cooking setting, when the machine has finished cooking, use the **quick-release method** to return its pressure to normal.

4. Unlatch the lid and open the pot. Stir well before serving.

Beyond

- You must halve the recipe for a **3-quart cooker.**

- For more flavor, add up to 1 tablespoon coriander seeds and/or 1 tablespoon yellow mustard seeds with the other ingredients.

- Put a handful of fresh bean sprouts in each bowl, ladle the soup on top, and garnish with fresh cilantro leaves as well as lime wedges to squeeze over each portion.

- For a bigger meal, serve the soup over cooked white or brown rice vermicelli.

Garlic Lovers' Chicken Curry

6 servings

If you're a fan of garlic, you know why you're here. But if you're a fan of sweeter curries, you've also come to the right place. There are so many onions (and then wine, plus raisins) that the curry's overall finish is a good balance between those sweet flavors and the heady aroma from all that garlic.

This curry cooks for a shorter amount of time but with a natural release. We changed the pressure-release method because of the amount of (natural) sugar in the recipe. There's now less chance of sputtering. Plus, the immediate, rapid boil of a quick release would turn the raisins to mush.

1. Mash the vinegar, garlic, ginger, coriander, cumin, cayenne, ground mustard, salt, and cloves in a small bowl into a paste. Set aside.

2.

Press the button for	Set it for	Set the time for	If necessary, press
SAUTÉ	MEDIUM, NORMAL, or CUSTOM 300°F	15 minutes	START

3. Melt the butter in a **6-quart cooker**. Add the onions and cook, stirring often, until softened, about 10 minutes. Stir in the garlic paste and the raisins; cook, stirring all the while, until fragrant, about 1 minute.

4. Add the chicken and stir well to coat in the spices and liquid. Pour in the broth and scrape up any browned bits on the pot's bottom. Turn off the SAUTÉ function and stir in the wine. Lock the lid onto the pot.

5.

Set the machine for	Set the level for	The valve must be	Set the time for	If necessary, press
PRESSURE COOK	MAX	—	7 minutes with the KEEP WARM setting off	START
MEAT/STEW, PRESSURE COOK, or MANUAL	HIGH	Closed	10 minutes with the KEEP WARM setting off	START

6. When the machine has finished cooking, turn it off and let its pressure **return to normal naturally,** about 20 minutes. Unlatch the lid and open the cooker. Stir well before serving.

1 tablespoon distilled white vinegar

6 medium garlic cloves, peeled and minced (2 tablespoons)

1 tablespoon minced peeled fresh ginger

½ teaspoon ground coriander

½ teaspoon ground cumin

½ teaspoon dried ground cayenne

½ teaspoon dried ground mustard

½ teaspoon table salt

¼ teaspoon ground cloves

4 tablespoons (½ stick) butter, cut into pieces

3 medium yellow onions, chopped (3 cups)

¼ cup golden raisins

2½ pounds large boneless skinless chicken thighs (6 to 8 thighs), cut in half and trimmed of any large hunks of fat

1 cup chicken broth

¼ cup sweet white wine, such as a Riesling, or unsweetened apple juice

Beyond

- For a **3-quart cooker,** you must use ¾ cup broth and halve the remaining ingredients.

- For an **8-quart cooker,** you must increase all the ingredients by 50 percent except use 1¼ cups broth.

- This curry needs cooked rice, particularly long-grain brown rice.

- Also serve this curry with lots of buttered, grilled bread (or maybe na'an).

¼ cup apple cider vinegar

2 teaspoons ground coriander

2 teaspoons ground cumin

1 teaspoon ground cardamom

1 teaspoon ground cinnamon

1 teaspoon table salt

1 teaspoon ground black pepper

½ teaspoon ground cloves

3 pounds bone-in skinless chicken thighs (about 8), any large chunks of fat removed

2 tablespoons vegetable, corn, or canola oil

2 teaspoons fennel seeds

1 medium yellow onion, chopped (1 cup)

1 tablespoon minced peeled fresh ginger

1 medium garlic clove, peeled and minced (1 teaspoon)

¾ cup chicken broth

½ cup sliced almonds

¼ cup canned tomato puree

1 tablespoon dark brown sugar

12 dried apricots, preferably California dried apricots, halved

Chicken Sali Boti

6 to 8 servings

Sali boti (or sometimes *salli boti*) is a curry from Parsi ethnic groups who practice Zoroastrianism and have settled mostly in the western parts of modern-day India. We prefer the *jardaloo* (apricot) version for the way the dried fruit adds a tart pop against the spices.

The dish is commonly made with lamb (or even mutton), although there are vegetarian renditions. We felt that chicken thighs worked better in the Instant Pot because lamb ended up a little too strongly flavored against the delicate spice blend. (Braising the meat in the oven would give the lamb a chance to mellow more than it does in the multi-cooker.)

No doubt about it: This one's got a lot of dried spices. It's also dramatic, even dinner-party worthy. You can't substitute a standard curry powder blend and get this very warming, aromatic mix. Stock up on spices and plan on making sali boti often.

1. Stir the vinegar, coriander, cumin, cardamom, cinnamon, salt, pepper, and cloves in a bowl to make a paste. Add the chicken thighs and toss well until they are thoroughly coated in the spice mixture. Set aside at room temperature for 15 minutes.

2.

Press the button for	Set it for	Set the time for	If necessary, press
SAUTÉ	MEDIUM, NORMAL, or CUSTOM 300°F	15 minutes	START

3. Warm the oil in a **6-quart cooker** for a minute or two. Add the fennel seeds and stir until toasted, about 1 minute. Add the onion, ginger, and garlic. Cook, stirring often, just until the onion turns fragrant, about 2 minutes.

4. Add the chicken thighs and every last bit of spices from the bowl. Stir well, then cook, turning and rearranging occasionally, until lightly browned, about 10 minutes.

5. Pour in the broth and scrape up the browned bits on the pot's bottom. Turn off the SAUTÉ function. Stir in the almonds, tomato puree, brown sugar, and apricots until the brown sugar dissolves. Lock the lid onto the pot.

6.

Set the machine for	Set the level for	The valve must be	Set the time for	If necessary, press
PRESSURE COOK	MAX	—	15 minutes with the KEEP WARM setting off	START
MEAT/STEW, PRESSURE COOK, or MANUAL	HIGH	Closed	18 minutes with the KEEP WARM setting off	START

7. When the machine has finished cooking, turn it off and let its pressure **return to normal naturally,** about 20 minutes. Unlatch the lid and open the pot. Stir well before serving.

Beyond

- For a **3-quart cooker**, you must use ½ cup broth and halve the remaining ingredients.

- For an **8-quart cooker**, you must use 1¼ cups broth and the stated amounts of the remaining ingredients. Or just double the recipe in an **8-quart cooker.**

- If you can't find bone-in chicken thighs without skin, remove the slippery skin from the meat by gripping one loose end with a paper towel and pulling the skin across and off the cut.

- Some versions of sali boti are made with potatoes — and this dish would indeed work well over mashed potatoes, particularly those with sour cream and butter in the mix.

- For a more authentic flavor, substitute grated jaggery for the brown sugar.

- For a sweeter dish, substitute 4 chopped dried pears for the dried apricots.

1 tablespoon butter or ghee

1 small yellow onion, chopped
(½ cup)

3 medium garlic cloves, peeled and
minced (1 tablespoon)

1 tablespoon minced peeled fresh
ginger

1 tablespoon garam masala

2 teaspoons granulated white sugar

1 teaspoon ground dried turmeric

1 teaspoon ground cumin

Up to 1 teaspoon ground dried
cayenne

½ teaspoon table salt

2½ pounds boneless skinless chicken
breasts, cut into 2-inch chunks

1 cup low-fat coconut milk

½ cup chicken broth

2 tablespoons tomato paste

¼ cup heavy cream

Chicken Tikka Masala

6 servings

Here's a take-out classic, morphed into a simple braise. Tikka masala is usually made with yogurt. But because yogurt can break under pressure, we use coconut milk for richness when cooking, then cream to finish the dish. That said, we had better success with low-fat coconut milk, which is not as heavy as full-fat.

1.

Press the button for	Set it for	Set the time for	If necessary, press
SAUTÉ	MEDIUM, NORMAL, or CUSTOM 300°F	10 minutes	START

2. Melt the butter in a **6- or 8-quart cooker**. Add the onion, garlic, and ginger. Cook, stirring often, until the onion softens, about 3 minutes. Stir in the garam masala, sugar, turmeric, cumin, cayenne, and salt until aromatic, just a few seconds.

3. Add the chicken and toss until the meat is well and evenly coated in the spices and aromatics. Pour in the coconut milk and broth. Add the tomato paste and stir until uniform. Turn off the SAUTÉ function and lock the lid onto the pot.

4.

Set the machine for	Set the level for	The valve must be	Set the time for	If necessary, press
PRESSURE COOK	MAX	—	5 minutes with the KEEP WARM setting off	START
MEAT/STEW, PRESSURE COOK, OR MANUAL	HIGH	Closed	7 minutes with the KEEP WARM setting off	START

5. Use the **quick-release method** to bring the pot's pressure back to normal. Unlatch the lid and open the cooker. Stir in the cream until uniform, then set the lid askew over the pot and set aside for 5 minutes to blend the flavors. Stir again before serving.

Beyond

- You must halve the recipe for a **3-quart cooker**.

- Garnish the servings with toasted unsweetened coconut.

- Try using homemade garam masala (see page 226 for a blend that works with chicken).

- Although the pairing is not traditional, the curry is good with peas: Add 1 cup fresh shelled or frozen peas (do not thaw) with the onion. If you use peas, omit the sugar.

Curried Chicken Couscous Casserole

4 to 6 servings

Hardly a standard couscous dish, this one's a one-pot supper — sort of like curried fried rice (that is, with couscous standing in for the rice). There may be a little liquid in the pot, even after it's been set aside for 10 minutes at the end. Scoop portions off the top and keep stirring the remainder after each serving. That extra liquid will continue to be absorbed into the couscous as the dish sits.

2 tablespoons butter or ghee

1 medium yellow onion, chopped (1 cup)

1½ pounds boneless skinless chicken breasts, cut into 1-inch chunks

2 teaspoons yellow curry powder

½ teaspoon ground cinnamon

½ teaspoon ground cumin

½ teaspoon table salt

¼ teaspoon ground cloves

1 quart (4 cups) chicken broth

½ cup raisins

¼ cup shelled unsalted pistachios

2⅔ cups quick-cooking (or instant) couscous

1.

Press the button for	Set it for	Set the time for	If necessary, press
SAUTÉ	MEDIUM, NORMAL, or CUSTOM 300°F	10 minutes	START

2. Melt the butter or ghee in a **6- or 8-quart cooker**. Add the onion and cook, stirring often, until softened, about 4 minutes. Add the chicken and cook, stirring frequently, just until it loses its raw, pink color, about 2 minutes.

3. Stir in the curry powder, cinnamon, cumin, salt, and cloves to coat the chicken. Pour in the broth and scrape up any browned bits on the pot's bottom. Turn off the SAUTÉ function, then stir in the raisins and pistachios. Lock the lid onto the pot.

4.

Set the machine for	Set level for	The valve must be	Set the time for	If necessary, press
PRESSURE COOK	MAX	—	5 minutes with the KEEP WARM setting off	START
PRESSURE COOK or MANUAL	HIGH	Closed	7 minutes with the KEEP WARM setting off	START

5. Use the **quick-release method** to bring the pot's pressure back to normal. Unlatch the lid and open the pot. Stir in the couscous until uniform. Remove the insert from the pot and set the lid askew over the insert for 10 minutes so that the couscous can absorb the liquid and get tender. Stir again before serving.

Beyond

- You must halve the recipe for a **3-quart cooker**.

- Try substituting chopped, pitted dates (preferably Medjool) for the raisins.

- Use a red curry powder blend for a hotter dish.

- Even with the yellow curry powder, pass extra hot sauce, particularly sambal oelek.

- Top the servings with chopped, stemmed chard or spinach that's been sautéed with a little butter or ghee (and perhaps a splash of broth to keep the thinner bits of the greens from sticking to the skillet's hot surface).

2 tablespoons vegetable, corn, or canola oil

2 large yellow onions, thinly sliced, the rings separated

2 tablespoons yellow curry powder

2 medium garlic cloves, peeled and minced (2 teaspoons)

2 large round red tomatoes, chopped (2 cups)

1 cup shredded unsweetened coconut

2½ pounds beef bottom round, trimmed and cut into 2-inch pieces

1 cup beef or chicken broth

3 tablespoons mango chutney

One 4-inch cinnamon stick

1 bay leaf

Savory-Sweet Beef and Tomato Curry

6 servings

Fresh tomatoes are a bit of an unusual ingredient in a curry. Unsweetened coconut is, too (although plenty of curries use coconut milk). But both the tomatoes and the coconut add a natural sweetness that blends nicely with beef, aromatic vegetables, and spices. Use only unsweetened coconut, sometimes called "desiccated coconut." You can find it at very large supermarkets, almost all health-food stores, and online.

1.

Press the button for	Set it for	Set the time for	If necessary, press
SAUTÉ	MEDIUM, NORMAL, or CUSTOM 300°F	10 minutes	START

2. Warm the oil in a **6- or 8-quart cooker** for a minute or two. Add the onions and cook, stirring often, just until they begin to soften, about 5 minutes. Stir in the curry powder and garlic until fragrant, just a few seconds.

3. Add the tomatoes and coconut. Cook, stirring occasionally, until the tomatoes begin to break down, about 4 minutes. Turn off the SAUTÉ function. Stir in the beef, broth, chutney, cinnamon stick, and bay leaf until the chutney melts. Lock the lid onto the pot.

4.

Set the machine for	Set level for	The valve must be	Set the time for	If necessary, press
PRESSURE COOK	MAX	—	30 minutes with the KEEP WARM setting off	START
MEAT/STEW, PRESSURE COOK, or MANUAL	HIGH	Closed	40 minutes with the KEEP WARM setting off	START

5. When the machine has finished cooking, turn it off and let its pressure **return to normal naturally,** about 30 minutes. Unlatch the lid and open the cooker. Remove and discard the cinnamon stick and bay leaf. Stir well before serving.

Beyond

- You must halve the recipe for a **3-quart cooker**.
- This curry is so heavily spiced, it would go well over Brown Rice and Lentils (page 404), Barley Pilaf (page 406), or Buckwheat Pilaf (page 407).

Choose-Your-Color Beef and Potato Curry

6 servings

The standard paste we would use in a recipe like this one is massaman curry paste — especially because of the potatoes, common in this style of dish. However, don't stand on ceremony. There are plenty of aromatics in the dish's mix, so any curry paste will work, a blend of flavors to match your taste. This one's not quite a road map recipe. But it can become a signature recipe when you find the curry paste you prefer. (Notice that the second cooking is only at HIGH pressure, even in a Max machine.)

1 tablespoon vegetable, corn, or canola oil

2 tablespoons wet red, yellow, green, massaman, Penang, or sour vegetable curry paste

3 pounds beef bottom round, cut into 2-inch pieces

One 4-inch cinnamon stick

6 green or white cardamom pods

10 whole cloves

1 cup regular or low-fat coconut milk

½ cup beef or chicken broth

2 tablespoons dark brown sugar

1½ pounds small white potatoes (do not use russets), each no larger than a Ping-Pong ball, halved

1.

Press the button for	Set it for	Set the time for	If necessary, press
SAUTÉ	MEDIUM, NORMAL, or CUSTOM 300°F	5 minutes	START

2. Warm the oil in a **6- or 8-quart cooker** for a minute or two. Add the curry paste and stir until toasty, about 1 minute. Add the beef, cinnamon stick, cardamom pods, and cloves. Stir until the beef is well coated in the curry paste.

3. Turn off the SAUTÉ function. Stir in the coconut milk and brown sugar until the brown sugar dissolves. Lock the lid onto the pot.

4.

Set the machine for	Set level for	The valve must be	Set the time for	If necessary, press
PRESSURE COOK	MAX	—	30 minutes with the KEEP WARM setting off	START
MEAT/STEW, PRESSURE COOK, OR MANUAL	HIGH	Closed	40 minutes with the KEEP WARM setting off	START

5. When the machine has finished cooking, turn it off and let its pressure **return to normal naturally,** about 25 minutes. Unlatch the lid and open the cooker. Stir in the potatoes. Lock the lid back onto the pot.

6.

Set the machine for	Set level for	The valve must be	Set the time for	If necessary, press
MEAT/STEW, PRESSURE COOK, or MANUAL	HIGH	Closed	5 minutes with the KEEP WARM setting off	START

7. Use the **quick-release method** to bring the pot's pressure back to normal. Unlatch the lid and open the cooker. Remove and discard the cinnamon stick, cardamom pods, and whole cloves. Stir again before serving.

Beyond

- You must halve the recipe for a **3-quart cooker.**

- To make a massaman curry paste, stem and seed 2 dried New Mexico red chiles, then pour boiling water over them in a large bowl. Soak for 10 minutes. Drain, reserving the soaking liquid. Place the chiles in a blender. Add 1 medium shallot, peeled and quartered; 4 large, peeled garlic cloves; 1 thinly sliced lemongrass stalk (white part only); one 1-inch ginger knob, peeled and cut into quarters; 1 teaspoon ground cinnamon; 1 teaspoon ground cardamom; 1 teaspoon table salt; ½ teaspoon ground cloves; ½ teaspoon grated nutmeg; and 6 fresh cilantro sprigs (including the stems). Cover and blend until smooth, adding a little soaking liquid to get a smooth paste. For a more authentic flavor, omit the salt and add 1 teaspoon shrimp paste. Store, covered, in a small container in the fridge for up to 1 week or freeze for up to 3 months.

2 teaspoons ground coriander

2 teaspoons ground dried ginger

1 teaspoon ground cinnamon

½ teaspoon ground cloves

½ teaspoon ground cumin

½ teaspoon ground dried turmeric

Up to ½ teaspoon ground dried cayenne

½ teaspoon table salt

2½ pounds beef bottom round, cut into 2-inch pieces

2 tablespoons vegetable, corn, or canola oil

1 medium yellow onion, chopped (1 cup)

2 cups beef or chicken broth

½ cup dry, light white wine, such as Pinot Grigio

½ cup dried wheat berries, preferably spring white wheat berries

½ cup small pitted green olives

1 tablespoon honey

Beyond

- You must halve the recipe for a **3-quart cooker.**

- For an **8-quart cooker,** you must increase the broth to 2½ cups but use the remaining ingredients as stated.

- Substitute dried Kamut berries for a more buttery flavor in the curry.

- Or substitute dried rye berries for an earthier yet more herbal flavor on top of the spices.

- To skip the wine, increase the broth to 1¾ cups and add ¼ cup unsweetened apple juice.

East-West Beef Curry with Wheat Berries

4 to 6 servings

We've fused the aromas of a curry — even created a unique spice blend — with a more Western flavor profile that includes wine and olives, sort of a Mediterranean undertow in the dish. We did all this because the curry is stocked with that hearty product of the American plains: wheat berries. It's a decidedly different take on the standard curry, sort of a global bowlful, best on a cold night.

1. Stir the coriander, ginger, cinnamon, cloves, cumin, turmeric, cayenne, and salt in a large bowl. Add the beef and toss until the pieces are evenly coated in the spices.

2.

Press the button for	Set it for	Set the time for	If necessary, press
SAUTÉ	MEDIUM, NORMAL, or CUSTOM 300°F	20 minutes	START

3. Warm the oil in a **6-quart cooker** for a minute or two. Add the onion and cook, stirring often, until softened, about 4 minutes. Add the meat and every last speck of dried spice from the bowl. Cook, stirring occasionally, until lightly browned, about 10 minutes.

4. Pour in the broth and scrape up *every speck of browned stuff* on the pot's bottom. Turn off the SAUTÉ function. Stir in the wine, wheat berries, olives, and honey until the honey dissolves. Lock the lid onto the pot.

5.

Set the machine for	Set level for	The valve must be	Set the time for	If necessary, press
PRESSURE COOK	MAX	—	35 minutes with the KEEP WARM setting off	START
MEAT/STEW, PRESSURE COOK, or MANUAL	HIGH	Closed	45 minutes with the KEEP WARM setting off	START

6. When the machine has finished cooking, turn it off and let its pressure **return to normal naturally,** about 35 minutes. Unlatch the lid and open the cooker. Stir well before serving.

Pork Shoulder Curry

4 servings

It seems almost sacrilegious to make curry with pork, yet we couldn't resist the hearty flavors of one made with pork shoulder. This one bends a little more Southeast Asian in its flavors with the rice vinegar and soy sauce, a sour curry with earthy notes from the turmeric.

1. Stir the turmeric, cinnamon, pepper, and cloves in a large bowl until uniform. Add the pork chunks and toss well until they are all coated evenly in the spice mixture.

2.

Press the button for	Set it for	Set the time for	If necessary, press
SAUTÉ	MEDIUM, NORMAL, or CUSTOM 300°F	10 minutes	START

3. Warm the oil in a **6-quart cooker** for a minute or two. Add the shallots, ginger, and garlic. Cook, stirring quite often, until the shallot starts to soften, 2 to 3 minutes. Add the meat and every last speck of spice in the bowl. Cook, stirring and rearranging once in a while, until all the meat has lost its raw, pink color, about 3 minutes.

4. Pour in the vinegar and soy sauce; scrape up any browned bits on the pot's bottom. Turn off the SAUTÉ function, pour in the broth, and stir well. Lock the lid onto the pot.

5.

Set the machine for	Set level for	The valve must be	Set the time for	If necessary, press
PRESSURE COOK	MAX	—	25 minutes with the KEEP WARM setting off	START
MEAT/STEW, PRESSURE COOK, or MANUAL	HIGH	Closed	35 minutes with the KEEP WARM setting off	START

6. When the machine has finished cooking, turn it off and let its pressure **return to normal naturally,** about 30 minutes. Unlatch the lid and open the cooker. Stir in the kale. Lock the lid back onto the pot.

7.

Set the machine for	Set level for	The valve must be	Set the time for	If necessary, press
MEAT/STEW, PRESSURE COOK, OR MANUAL	HIGH	Closed	5 minutes with the KEEP WARM setting off	START

8. Use the **quick-release method** to bring the pot's pressure back to normal. Unlatch the lid and open the cooker. Stir well before serving.

1 teaspoon ground dried turmeric

½ teaspoon ground cinnamon

½ teaspoon ground black pepper

¼ teaspoon ground cloves

2½ pounds boneless skinless pork shoulder, trimmed of any large hunks of fat, the meat cut into 2-inch pieces

2 tablespoons vegetable, corn, or canola oil

2 medium shallots, peeled and quartered

1 tablespoon minced peeled fresh ginger

3 medium garlic cloves, peeled and minced (1 tablespoon)

¼ cup unseasoned rice vinegar

2 tablespoons soy sauce

1 cup chicken broth

2 cups packed, stemmed, chopped kale

Beyond

- You must halve the recipe for a **3-quart cooker.**

- For an **8-quart cooker,** you must increase the broth to 1⅓ cups and use the remaining ingredients as stated.

- Skip long-grain white rice and serve over cornmeal grits.

- Take it over the top by using fresh turmeric: Omit the dried and add 1 tablespoon fresh minced peeled turmeric with the ginger.

- For a more traditional flavor, substitute boneless lamb shoulder, cut into 2-inch pieces, for the pork.

3 tablespoons butter

3 medium onions, roughly chopped (3 cups)

2 medium garlic cloves, peeled and minced (2 teaspoons)

2 teaspoons minced peeled fresh ginger

1½ pounds boneless center-cut pork loin chops, cut into 1½-inch cubes

1½ tablespoons yellow curry powder

1 tablespoon garam masala

2 cups chicken broth

1 pound medium carrots, peeled and cut into 2-inch pieces

1 tablespoon tomato paste

2 tablespoons soy sauce

1 tablespoon cornstarch or potato starch

The Pork Curry That Every Japanese Mom Makes

4 servings

If you watch as much Japanese TV as we do (you don't?), you know there's a certain pork curry that's a home staple, one of those childhood meals that becomes comfort food for adults. It seems as if every kid who has a bad day ends up eating this stuff! So here's our version, simplified for the Instant Pot and tweaked for the American supermarket.

Most Japanese pork curries use a boxed "curry roux," but we can build those flavors by starting with butter, then ending with tomato paste and soy sauce. Most Japanese versions also use quick-cooking shredded pork; but we feel that the center-cut pork chops give the dish a more American heartiness. Buy thicker, 1½-inch chops so that you can easily cut them into cubes.

1.

Press the button for	Set it for	Set the time for	If necessary, press
SAUTÉ	MEDIUM, NORMAL, or CUSTOM 300°F	10 minutes	START

2. Melt the butter in a **6- or 8-quart cooker**. Add the onion and cook, stirring often, until it begins to soften, about 5 minutes. Add the garlic and ginger; cook, stirring all the while, until fragrant, just a few seconds.

3. Add the meat and toss well until coated in the butter and aromatics. Stir in the curry powder and garam masala; keep stirring until the meat is evenly coated. Turn off the SAUTÉ function and pour in the broth. Stir in the carrots until uniform, then lock the lid onto the pot.

4.

Set the machine for	Set level for	The valve must be	Set the time for	If necessary, press
PRESSURE COOK	MAX	—	12 minutes with the KEEP WARM setting off	START
MEAT/STEW, PRESSURE COOK, or MANUAL	HIGH	Closed	15 minutes with the KEEP WARM setting off	START

5. Use the **quick-release method** to bring the pot's pressure back to normal. Unlatch the lid and open the cooker. Stir in the tomato paste until uniform.

6.

Press the button for	Set it for	Set the time for	If necessary, press
SAUTÉ	MEDIUM, NORMAL, or CUSTOM 300°F	5 minutes	START

7. As the sauce comes to a bubble in the pot, whisk the soy sauce and cornstarch or potato starch in a small bowl until smooth. Once the sauce is at a good simmer, stir this slurry into it and cook until thickened, no more than 1 minute. Turn off the SAUTÉ function and remove the *hot* insert from the pot. Set the lid askew on top of the insert and set aside for 5 minutes to blend the flavors.

Beyond

- You must halve the recipe for a **3-quart cooker.**
- Always serve this curry alongside white rice, preferably a medium-grain rice.
- Search for Japanese pickles, like daikon or carrots, to serve as a garnish.
- For a more authentic flavor, omit the yellow curry powder and garam masala and use 2½ tablespoons of an Asian curry powder, such as S & B Oriental Curry Powder, Asian Boy Curry Powder, or Golden Smell Curry Powder.

2 tablespoons peanut oil

3 medium red onions, halved and sliced into thin half-moons

2 tablespoons minced peeled fresh ginger

1 teaspoon coriander seeds

1 teaspoon fennel seeds

1 teaspoon whole cloves

One 2-inch cinnamon stick

½ teaspoon table salt

½ teaspoon ground black pepper

3 pounds boneless leg of lamb, trimmed of any big pieces of fat, the meat cut into 1½-inch pieces

¾ cup chicken broth

2 tablespoons red wine vinegar

1 tablespoon tomato paste

Lamb Curry 101

6 servings

Here's our basic lamb curry, an aromatic mix with lots of seeds and spices to bump up the flavors and pair them with the lamb. We use leg of lamb because it's less fatty than lamb shoulder. It also cooks a little more quickly than shoulder meat, without a tendency to break into squishy bits under pressure. By the way, the cloves are edible after cooking under pressure (but may be irritating to those not expecting them).

1.

Press the button for	Set it for	Set the time for	If necessary, press
SAUTÉ	MEDIUM, NORMAL, or CUSTOM 300°F	10 minutes	START

2. Warm the oil in a **6-quart cooker** for a minute or two. Add the onion and cook, stirring often, until softened, about 5 minutes. Stir in the ginger and cook until aromatic, just a few seconds. Add the coriander, fennel, cloves, cinnamon stick, salt, and pepper. Stir well for a few seconds until the spices are evenly distributed in the onions.

3. Add the meat and stir over the heat until the pieces are evenly coated in the onion and spice mixture. Turn off the SAUTÉ function, then stir in the broth, vinegar, and tomato paste until uniform. Lock the lid onto the pot.

4.

Set the machine for	Set level for	The valve must be	Set the time for	If necessary, press
PRESSURE COOK	MAX	—	35 minutes with the KEEP WARM setting off	START
MEAT/STEW, PRESSURE COOK, or MANUAL	HIGH	Closed	45 minutes with the KEEP WARM setting off	START
SLOW COOK	HIGH	Opened	4 hours with the KEEP WARM setting off (or on for no more than 3 hours)	START

5. If you've used a pressure setting, when the machine has finished cooking, turn it off and let its pressure **return to normal naturally,** about 30 minutes. Unlatch the lid and open the cooker. Stir well; discard the cinnamon stick and the whole cloves before serving.

Beyond

- For a **3-quart cooker**, you must use ½ cup broth and halve the remaining ingredients.

- For an **8-quart cooker**, you must increase *all* the ingredients by 50 percent.

- If you like, substitute butter or ghee for the oil.

- For a beef curry, use 3 pounds bottom round, cut into 1½-inch pieces.

- Serve over long-grain white rice that's been tossed with butter and a little soy sauce.

Pub-Style Korma

6 servings

The korma served in the United Kingdom is not an authentic korma; but it is a classic British comfort food, often made with nuts for richness as well as lots of coconut milk. We've adapted the traditional technique by creating a nut-and-spice mixture in a blender, then using this wet "sauce" in the Instant Pot as a vehicle for chunks of lamb.

1. Put the cashews, shallot, chile, garlic, ginger, garam masala, fennel seeds, coriander, cumin, turmeric, and salt in a large blender. Pour in the broth and coconut milk. Cover and blend until smooth, stopping the machine at least once to scrape down the inside.

2. Pour and scrape every drop of the spice mixture into a **6- or 8-quart cooker**. Add the lamb and stir until all the pieces are coated in the spice mixture. Lock the lid onto the pot.

3.

Set the machine for	Set level for	The valve must be	Set the time for	If necessary, press
PRESSURE COOK	MAX	—	35 minutes with the KEEP WARM setting off	START
MEAT/STEW, PRESSURE COOK, or MANUAL	HIGH	Closed	45 minutes with the KEEP WARM setting off	START
SLOW COOK	HIGH	Opened	4 hours with the KEEP WARM setting off (or on for no more than 3 hours)	START

4. If you've used a pressure setting, when the machine has finished cooking, turn it off and let its pressure **return to normal naturally,** about 30 minutes.

5. Unlatch the lid and open the cooker.

6.

Press the button for	Set it for	Set the time for	If necessary, press
SAUTÉ	MEDIUM, NORMAL, OR CUSTOM 300°F	5 minutes	START

7. Bring the sauce to a simmer, stirring frequently. Stir in the tomato paste until smooth. Continue cooking, stirring often, until thickened a bit, about like a wet gravy, 2 to 4 minutes. Turn off the SAUTÉ function, remove the *hot* insert from the machine, and set the lid askew over the insert for 5 minutes to blend the flavors. Stir well before serving.

6 tablespoons roasted unsalted cashews

1 large shallot, peeled and quartered

1 medium serrano chile, stemmed, halved lengthwise, and seeded (if desired)

5 medium garlic cloves, peeled

1½ tablespoons minced peeled fresh ginger

1 tablespoon garam masala

1½ teaspoons fennel seeds

1½ teaspoons ground coriander

1½ teaspoons ground cumin

1½ teaspoons ground dried turmeric

1 teaspoon table salt

1½ cups chicken broth

¾ cup regular coconut milk or coconut cream (do not use cream of coconut)

3 pounds boneless leg of lamb, trimmed of any large chunks of fat, the meat cut into 1½-inch pieces

3 tablespoons tomato paste

Beyond

- You must halve the recipe for a **3-quart cooker**.

- Although long-grain white rice is the traditional accompaniment, we prefer this curry over large cubes of toasted bread.

- Or even over French fries, the way it would be served in some pubs. (Try Tater Tots for an American version.)

2 tablespoons vegetable, corn, or canola oil

3 medium leeks (about 4½ ounces each), white and pale green parts only, halved lengthwise, well washed, and thinly sliced (1 cup)

1 tablespoon minced peeled fresh ginger

1½ teaspoons ground coriander

1½ teaspoons mild paprika

1½ teaspoons ground dried turmeric

1 teaspoon ground cinnamon

Up to ½ teaspoon ground dried cayenne

½ teaspoon table salt

3 pounds boneless leg of lamb, any large chunks of fat removed, the meat cut into 1½-inch pieces

1 cup chicken broth

½ cup buttermilk

2 tablespoons orange marmalade

Beyond

- You must halve the recipe for a **3-quart cooker.**

- Not all marmalades are created equally. Some are just jelly; others have large bits of orange in the mix. Some are "sweet marmalades," probably too sweet for the lamb. The best would be a marmalade made from sour oranges, a European specialty. Check the labels or look for brands like Bonne Maman or Dundee.

- Or substitute lemon or even lime marmalade for a more sour pop.

South African–Style Lamb Curry

6 servings

Curry is global fare. Here's a version from South Africa that uses buttermilk for a tangy richness. The buttermilk can break under pressure, so we stir it in at the end, then simmer it a little to mellow the flavors and thicken the sauce (with help from orange marmalade, which brings everything into balance).

1.

Press the button for	Set it for	Set the time for	If necessary, press
SAUTÉ	MEDIUM, NORMAL, or CUSTOM 300°F	5 minutes	START

2. Warm the oil in a **6- or 8-quart cooker** for a minute or two. Add the leeks and ginger; cook, stirring often, until softened, about 3 minutes. Stir in the coriander, paprika, turmeric, cinnamon, cayenne, and salt until fragrant, just a few seconds.

3. Add the lamb and toss until the meat is thoroughly coated in the spices and aromatics. Pour in the broth and stir well. Turn off the SAUTÉ function and lock the lid onto the pot.

4.

Set the machine for	Set level for	The valve must be	Set the time for	If necessary, press
PRESSURE COOK	MAX	—	35 minutes with the KEEP WARM setting off	START
MEAT/STEW, PRESSURE COOK, or MANUAL	HIGH	Closed	45 minutes with the KEEP WARM setting off	START
SLOW COOK	HIGH	Opened	4 hours with the KEEP WARM setting off (or on for no more than 3 hours)	START

5. If you've used a pressure setting, when the machine has finished cooking, turn it off and let its pressure **return to normal naturally,** about 30 minutes.

6. Unlatch the lid and open the cooker.

7.

Press the button for	Set it for	Set the time for	If necessary, press
SAUTÉ	MEDIUM, NORMAL, or CUSTOM 300°F	5 minutes	START

8. Stir in the buttermilk and marmalade as the sauce comes to a simmer. Continue cooking, stirring almost constantly, until a little thickened and reduced, about 2 minutes. Turn off the SAUTÉ function and set the lid askew over the pot for 5 minutes to blend the flavors. Stir again before serving.

Road Map: Thai Seafood Curry

4 to 6 servings

Thai curry is a spicy hodgepodge, made with coconut milk and lots of fresh vegetables, best served over *short-grain* white rice or white or brown rice noodles. One warning: the fish or shellfish will get done at varying times, a little difficult to note exactly in a road map recipe. If you see that the fish bits are done but the shrimp aren't quite pink yet, turn off the SAUTÉ function and set the lid askew over the pot for a couple of minutes so that the shrimp (in this case) cook in the residual heat. As a general rule, avoid oily fish (like salmon or trout) or thin, white-fleshed fish fillets (like sole, tilapia, or fluke).

1.

Press the button for	Set it for	Set the time for	If necessary, press
SAUTÉ	MEDIUM, NORMAL, or CUSTOM 300°F	10 minutes	START

2. Warm the oil in a **6- or 8-quart cooker** for a minute or two. Add the allium aromatics and cook, stirring often, until softened, 2 to 4 minutes. Add the ginger and cook until aromatic, just a few seconds.

3. Stir in the wet curry paste until everything is well coated, then add the tomatoes, coconut milk, lime juice, brown sugar, and fish sauce. Stir until the brown sugar has dissolved, then turn off the SAUTÉ function and lock the lid onto the pot.

4.

Set the machine for	Set level for	The valve must be	Set the time for	If necessary, press
PRESSURE COOK	MAX	—	5 minutes with the KEEP WARM setting off	START
MEAT/STEW, PRESSURE COOK, or MANUAL	HIGH	Closed	7 minutes with the KEEP WARM setting off	START

5. Use the **quick-release method** to bring the pot's pressure back to normal. Unlatch the lid and open the pot.

6.

Press the button for	Set it for	Set the time for	If necessary, press
SAUTÉ	MEDIUM, NORMAL, or CUSTOM 300°F	5 minutes	START

7. Bring the sauce to a full simmer. Stir in the fish or shellfish and the quick-cooking vegetables. Continue cooking, stirring gently, until the shellfish or fish is cooked through, 3 to 5 minutes. Turn off the SAUTÉ function, remove the *hot* insert from the machine, and serve warm.

See photo in insert.

2 tablespoons oil
   Choose from peanut oil, coconut oil, or any neutral-flavored oil you like: vegetable, corn, safflower, canola, avocado, or grape seed.

1½ cups chopped allium aromatics
   Choose from one or two onions (of any sort), scallions, leeks (white and pale green parts only, well washed), and/or shallots.

Up to ¼ cup minced peeled fresh ginger

Up to 2 tablespoons wet curry paste
   Choose from red, green, or yellow Thai curry paste, or even massaman or Penang curry paste.

One 14-ounce can diced tomatoes

1 cup regular or low-fat coconut milk

1½ tablespoons fresh lime juice

1½ tablespoons light brown sugar

1½ tablespoons fish sauce

1½ pounds fish or shellfish
   Choose from peeled and deveined medium shrimp (about 30 per pound), sea scallops, skinless swordfish fillets cut into 2-inch cubes, monkfish fillets cut into 2-inch pieces, skinless cod fillets cut into 2-inch pieces, skinless hake fillets cut into 2-inch pieces, or skinless halibut fillets cut into 1-inch pieces.

1 pound chopped quick-cooking vegetables
   Choose one or two from trimmed green or wax or other long beans, zucchini, yellow summer squash, stemmed and seeded bell peppers, cored napa cabbage, Chinese water spinach, cauliflower florets, broccoli florets, and/or sugar snap peas.

Beyond

- You must halve the recipe for a **3-quart cooker**.

- For a hotter chile, add 2 to 5 small, hot, red or green chiles (like Thai hots), stemmed and split.

2 tablespoons vegetable, corn, or canola oil

1 medium red onion, chopped (1 cup)

2 medium garlic cloves, peeled and minced (2 teaspoons)

2 tablespoons minced peeled fresh ginger

1 tablespoon yellow curry powder

2 teaspoons mild smoked paprika

½ teaspoon table salt

One 28-ounce can diced tomatoes with chiles (3½ cups)

1 pound frozen sliced okra (do not thaw)

½ cup water

1½ pounds skinless cod fillets, cut into 10 to 12 pieces

Curried Cod with Tomatoes and Okra

6 servings

Okra is such a common ingredient in curries that we felt we needed to include it in at least one recipe. Where we live in rural New England, we can only find fresh okra at an East Indian grocery store over an hour away. However, we can always find frozen okra at our Stop & Shop — and the frozen works better in the Instant Pot anyway (less slime, a better texture). We advocate for a much hotter curry here and get the burn by using canned diced tomatoes with chiles. But you can use regular diced tomatoes and pass bottled hot sauce at the table.

1.

Press the button for	Set it for	Set the time for	If necessary, press
SAUTÉ	MEDIUM, NORMAL, or CUSTOM 300°F	10 minutes	START

2. Warm the oil in a **6- or 8-quart cooker** for a minute or two. Add the onion and cook, stirring often, until softened, about 5 minutes. Add the garlic and ginger; cook until aromatic, stirring all the while, maybe half a minute. Stir in the curry powder, smoked paprika, and salt until fragrant, just a few seconds.

3. Pour in the tomatoes and scrape up any browned bits on the pot's bottom. Turn off the SAUTÉ function and stir in the okra and water. Lock the lid onto the pot.

4.

Set the machine for	Set level for	The valve must be	Set the time for	If necessary, press
PRESSURE COOK	MAX	—	4 minutes with the KEEP WARM setting off	START
PRESSURE COOK or MANUAL	HIGH	Closed	5 minutes with the KEEP WARM setting off	START

5. Use the **quick-release method** to bring the pot's pressure back to normal. Unlatch the lid and open the cooker. Nestle the cod pieces into the sauce. Set the lid askew over the pot.

6.

Press the button for	Set it for	Set the time for	If necessary, press
SAUTÉ	LOW or LESS	10 minutes	START

7. Simmer the cod in the sauce until cooked through, about 10 minutes. Turn off the SAUTÉ function and remove the *hot* insert from the pot to stop the cooking. Serve warm.

Beyond

- You must halve the recipe for a **3-quart cooker.**

- This curry needs rice in the bowls, preferably *brown* basmati for an earthier finish.

- For a sweeter finish to the curry, add 1 chopped medium carrot with the onion.

- Substitute swordfish fillets for the cod — or thinner, white-fleshed, skinless fillets like snapper, but cook thin fillets for only 2 to 3 minutes in the sauce.

Curried Shrimp with Rice Vermicelli

6 servings

Here's a simple, speedy curry made with rice noodles right in the pot. Remember: The world does not revolve around yellow curry powder. You could substitute other curry powders, even garam masala, a warming blend of dried spices without any heat (see page 226). Red curry powders can be quite hot, thanks to an abundance of cayenne. Check the labels to make sure you end up with one that suits your taste. Note that the dish can only be cooked on HIGH, even in a Max machine.

1. Mix the broth, soy sauce, rice vinegar, curry powder, and sambal oelek in a **6- or 8-quart cooker**. Break the vermicelli to fit in the pot and set them in the sauce. Lay the shrimp over the noodles and sauce, then pour the frozen mixed vegetables in an even layer on top. Lock the lid onto the pot.

2.

Set the machine for	Set the level for	The valve must be	Set the time for	If necessary, press
PRESSURE COOK or MANUAL	HIGH	Closed	0 minutes with the KEEP WARM setting off	START

3. *The moment* the float valve (or pin) pops up to lock the lid onto the pot and the machine stops putting out steam, turn off the machine and let the pressure **return to normal naturally** for 3 minutes, Then use the **quick-release method** to release any residual pressure in the pot. Unlatch the lid and open the pot. Stir well before serving.

3 cups chicken broth

6 tablespoons soy sauce

2 tablespoons unseasoned rice vinegar

1 tablespoon yellow curry powder

Up to 1 tablespoon sambal oelek

8 ounces dried rice vermicelli

¾ pound small shrimp (about 40 per pound), peeled and deveined

1 pound mixed frozen vegetables for stir-fry, any seasoning packets discarded (do not thaw)

Beyond

- This recipe does not work well in a **3-quart cooker** because the noodles have to be broken into too many, very small pieces.

- If you can't find small shrimp, use peeled and deveined medium shrimp (about 30 per pound) but cut each one lengthwise in half.

- If you don't want to use (or buy) sambal oelek, use Texas Pete hot sauce or Frank's RedHot.

7

All Things

Steamed and Cooked *with the* Sous Vide Method

Without a doubt, this chapter is the most "gourmet," the most cheffy. Technically, lots of dishes in a pressure cooker are steamed. But this chapter isn't about steaming a head of cauliflower (see page 428). Or making perfect whole grains (page 395). It's about using the pot's naturally steamy environment (and the attendant pressure) to make some pretty impressive meals: a giant crab cake in a Bundt pan, a family-friendly meatloaf, and some of the best-ever fried—yes, fried—chicken. This chapter is mostly not about "dinner in minutes." It's about upping your Instant Pot game, although a pot of steamed clams is awfully quick and tasty (see page 275).

This chapter also holds the recipes for the sous vide technique (French, *soo-veed*, "under"—or in—"a vacuum"). Basically, sous vide involves cooking food in an anaerobic environment at a low temperature to tenderize the interstitial cartilage without compromising any internal texture or losing any moisture.

Okay, wow, a lot—so let's break that down. An anaerobic environment is one without air—or more specifically, without oxygen (thus, the "vide" or vacuum in the terminology). We want to remove the air so that, ahem, bad bugs have nothing to live on as the meat or fish cooks below the temperature "kill point" for bacteria. So we seal the food in bags, as you'll see.

The low cooking temperature—way lower than what an oven can handle, even lower than the boiling point of water—is somewhere around 125°F (or 51°C). Maintaining that temperature in the pot, we then immerse the food in the warm water. And since the food is in a bag, it can't be waterlogged. We go to all this trouble so that the food is the most tender imaginable—and 1) we can get steaks that are rare edge to edge without a dried-out exterior, 2) we can actually eat super-tender but also rare short ribs that can be crunched up on the grill for just a minute or

two, 3) we can set eggs to a ridiculously jammy center, and 4) we can keep fish fillets moist and flavorful.

The Max machine allows you to turn the Instant Pot into a sous vide device without any other gadget. (Most sous vide cooking is done with an immersion circulator attached to a big pot of water.) The notion that the pot can make this jump to a cheffy level is pretty revolutionary in and of itself, even if cooking short ribs or a brisket by the sous vide method isn't right for a run-of-the-mill weeknight.

Because of the size and shape of the pot, the sous vide recipes don't make large quantities. There has to be enough room for the warm water's convection currents to circulate around the food. In the end, use these sous vide recipes as a way to introduce yourself to the technique. If you like what happens, try another recipe, then another, and soon you'll buy an immersion circulator, have a big pot of water with a dozen short ribs on the counter for a dinner party, and step off on the road to cheffy bliss.

Before you go, we need to address one or two safety concerns. Sous vide works because there is *no* air inside the bag that holds the food. Some online sous vide mavens are pretty lazy when it comes to this point. "Oh, just get the air out as good as you can," they say.

No, do it better. Get *all* the air out of the bag. Those so-called experts are trying to sell website clicks. They're not concerned about your safety.

We'll get to the specifics below in the FAQs, then the recipes themselves. And although sous vide is an Instant Pot game-changer, more than half of the recipes in this chapter can be used in any Instant Pot model. These recipes ask you to steam food as the first step in a culinary process that results in maximum rewards: not plain old broccoli florets or carrot spears but State Fair Turkey Legs (page 265) and some astonishing Brisket Skewers (page 266).

So head off to some of the most inventive dishes in the book. They'll help you use the pot to take your cooking to the next level.

FAQs

1. Okay, fine, but I still just want to open the pot and eat dinner. What's the deal?

In this chapter, head to the Down-Home Meatloaf (page 270), the Shrimp Boil (page 278), and the Crab Cake (page 276). Unlatch the lid and voilà! But after those and a few more, hie thee to other chapters. Some of this chapter's remaining recipes are more complicated. Without even mentioning the sous vide recipes, many of the steamed ones ask you to do something with the food once it's out of the pot: fry the chicken, crisp the steaks, grill the brisket skewers. Most of us got into pressure cooking because we wanted to get out of the kitchen quickly. Most of the recipes in this book are set up so we can. They're just not the bulk of this chapter.

2. Can I make the sous vide recipes in a machine other than the MAX?

No. Only the MAX has the capabilities to maintain the low temperature for safe and proper cooking. If you have another model of Instant Pot, you can, of course, make any of these sous vide recipes with a more traditional sous vide immersion circulator set up either on the side of the pot you have (preferably an **8-quart cooker**) or in a larger Dutch oven. But the trouble may not be worth it. Yes, some cooks have been using older models of the Instant Pot to make a sort of *ad hoc* sous vide machine. Such experiments are ill-advised. The recipes in this chapter are for smaller portions because of the narrowness of the Instant Pot's insert and the way convection currents have to move around the sealed bags.

3. Why do you give the thickness of the meat in the sous vide recipes?

Because in this specialized technique, the thickness is as important as the weight. In fact, the timings are *based* on the thickness. A 1-inch steak that is 4 inches long will cook via the sous vide method at the same rate as a 1-inch steak that's 8 or even 10 inches long. It's all about how the heat comes through the surface plane of the cut to permeate the core. Since sous vide is a professional chef's favorite trick, one would expect precision to be part of the game.

4. What's the water bath method for removing air in the bags?

First off, the best tool for removing air from the bags is a vacuum sealer. Unfortunately, it's an expensive gadget. More importantly, it pulls any liquids (along with the air) out of the bag. Some sealers have a so-called "moist setting." We find that even this function pulls most of the liquid out. (We tried and tried to make it work.) Sometimes, it's best to punt to the water bath method.

Put the food and any marinade in a zip-sealed plastic bag of the size we recommend. Fill a large bowl or pot with water. You can use water already in the Instant Pot insert for the sous vide process, so long as the machine has not yet been turned on and the water's still cool. With the bag open, grasp the two corners at the ends of the sealing strip and *slowly* lower the filled bag into the water. (Note the operative, italicized word in that sentence.) The surrounding water will push the air out of the bag as it's submerged. When the water level is right at the sealing strip, zip the bag closed and pull it out of the water.

5. If I'm putting something under sous vide for days, can I just leave the pot alone?

No. Please refer to the Max machine's instruction manual. You must open the lid occasionally and check the water level. It may have dropped. You may need to add more water. And you can't just add cold water or you'll throw the cooking time off and may induce food safety problems. You'll need to heat water on the stove to about the temperature of the water in the cooker (use an instant-read meat thermometer to be sure). Then add that warm water to the pot and lock the lid on top again.

2 tablespoons flavorful solid or liquid fat

Choose from room-temperature butter, room-temperature rendered bacon fat, room-temperature schmaltz, olive oil, avocado oil, walnut oil, pecan oil, hazelnut oil, or peanut oil.

2 tablespoons dried spices or a dried spice blend

Choose several to make the full amount from dried basil, chives, marjoram, parsley, rosemary, oregano, sage, savory, tarragon, or thyme — or choose a single spice blend such as Cajun, Italian, Greek, curry powder, herbes de Provence, za'atar, or another favorite.

1 teaspoon kosher salt

One 3½- to 4-pound whole chicken, any giblets or neck removed

2 cups chicken broth or water

Beyond

- Add up to 1 tablespoon liquid smoke to the water for a pseudo-smoked chicken.

- If you've used canned or boxed broth (and not liquid smoke), the liquid after cooking in the pot has become a terrific, rich, highly seasoned stock. Strain it and freeze it to use in place of or along with canned broth in another recipe.

- The chicken will no doubt taste better if it's browned before cooking. To do so, set the SAUTÉ function to LOW or LESS. Add 1 tablespoon vegetable, corn, canola, or olive oil to the pot, set the bird in it, and brown it on all sides, keeping it on one side until you can easily release it from the hot surface to turn it to another, 15 to 20 minutes in total. Transfer the browned chicken to a cutting board and cool for 10 minutes. Make the seasoning paste, rub it on the bird, continue with the recipe in step 2.

Road Map: Rotisserie-Style Chicken

4 to 6 servings

Why would you put a whole chicken in a multi-cooker when you can buy a rotisserie chicken at the grocery store? First, because you can catch sales on whole chickens and squirrel them away in the freezer to make this simple meal more economical. (But be forewarned: A frozen 4-pound bird will take 36 to 48 hours to thaw in the fridge.) Second (and more importantly), because the steam environment of the cooker makes a much juicier bird than those endlessly turning racks at the supermarket.

The easiest way to carve a chicken is with kitchen (or poultry) shears. A good pair costs about twenty dollars. Once the chicken has cooled for 10 minutes, pull the thigh and leg away from the body, then cut right in the center of the joints. For the breast, you can snip it off whole, about like using scissors to cut a ball out of fabric; then snip the meat into chunks right on the cutting board.

1. Use a fork to mash or mix the solid or liquid fat, dried herb(s), and salt in a small bowl until uniform. Rub this mixture all over the exterior of the chicken.

2. Pour the broth or water into a **6- or 8-quart cooker**. Set a heat- and pressure-safe trivet inside the pot. Set the bird breast side up on the trivet. Lock the lid onto the pot.

3.

Set the machine for	Set the level for	The valve must be	Set the time for	If necessary, press
PRESSURE COOK	MAX	—	30 minutes with the KEEP WARM setting off	START
STEAM, PRESSURE COOK or MANUAL	HIGH	Closed	36 minutes with the KEEP WARM setting off	START

4. When the machine has finished cooking, turn it off and let its pressure **return to normal naturally**, about 1 hour. Unlatch the lid and open the cooker. Cool the chicken in the pot for a few minutes, then use large kitchen tongs and a large metal spatula to transfer the bird to a nearby cutting board. Take care: The juices inside the bird will be hot. Put children and pets out of the room. Cool for another 5 to 10 minutes, then carve the bird as desired.

Road Map: Chicken Wings

4 to 6 servings

Here's how to turn chicken wings into a sure hit at your next gathering: Steam the wings in your Instant Pot to make them tender, then broil them to crisp the skin. Pair the spice blend in the pot with the coating mixture under the broiler: barbecue rub with barbecue sauce or curry powder with chutney. Think how the flavors will play out, especially after the wings have turned into tasty, crunchy bits on the baking sheet.

1. Place the chicken wing pieces, the dried spice blend, and the salt (if using) in a large bowl. Toss well until the chicken pieces are evenly and thoroughly coated in the spice blend.

2. Pour the liquid into a **6-quart cooker**. Set a heat- and pressure-safe collapsible steaming basket in the pot. Pile all the coated wings onto the basket. Lock the lid onto the cooker.

3.

Set the level for	The valve must be	Set the machine for	Set the time for	If necessary, press
MAX	—	PRESSURE COOK	4 minutes with the KEEP WARM setting off	START
HIGH	Closed	STEAM, PRESSURE COOK or MANUAL	5 minutes with the KEEP WARM setting off	START

4. When the machine has finished cooking, turn it off and let the pressure **return to normal naturally** for 10 minutes. Then use the **quick-release method** to get rid of any residual pressure in the pot. Unlatch the lid and open the cooker.

5. Use kitchen tongs or a big spoon to transfer the *hot* chicken wings to a large bowl. Add the coating mixture and toss well.

6. Position the rack 4 to 6 inches from the broiler heat source; heat the broiler for a few minutes. Spread the coated wings into a single layer on a large, lipped baking sheet. Broil until crisp and irresistible, turning once, about 5 minutes.

3¼ pounds chicken wings, cut into their three parts, any flappers removed and discarded; or 3 pounds chicken wingettes and/or drumettes

3 tablespoons dried spice blend

Choose from Cajun, Chinese, French, Italian, curry powder, herbes de Provence, five-spice powder (see page 88), or a favorite barbecue rub.

1 cup liquid

Choose from water, beer, white wine, broth, or unsweetened apple cider.

Up to 1 teaspoon table salt (optional)

1 cup coating mixture

Choose from barbecue sauce, chutney, French dressing, honey mustard, Ranch dressing, stir-fry sauce, Thai chili sauce, or a 50/50 combo of a hot red pepper sauce like Sriracha and ketchup.

Beyond

• For a **3-quart cooker**, you must use ¾ cup of the liquid but halve the amount of the remaining ingredients.

• For an **8-quart cooker**, you must use 1½ cups of the liquid but otherwise keep the stated amount of the other ingredients. Or you can increase everything by 50 percent in an **8-quart cooker**.

• For a dipping sauce, mix a hot red pepper sauce like Sriracha with lime zest, melted butter, and minced fresh mint or cilantro.

• Or mix apricot preserves with Dijon mustard and a little Worcestershire sauce.

1½ teaspoons mild paprika

1½ teaspoons kosher salt

1 teaspoon onion powder

½ teaspoon dried sage

½ teaspoon dried thyme

½ teaspoon ground black pepper

¼ teaspoon garlic powder

1½ cups water

Six 8- to 10-ounce bone-in skin-on chicken thighs

Peanut oil, vegetable oil, or solid vegetable shortening, for frying

Fried Chicken

6 servings

No, we're not frying in the pot. And we're not pressure-frying chicken. The pot's not built for such measures. Instead, we're using the pressure in the pot to tenderize the chicken and infuse the flavors into the meat, rendering out a little of the fat to make the thighs even crisper when they eventually hit the hot oil.

After cooking under pressure, we can't fry them in the pot with the SAUTÉ function on HIGH or MORE. First, we can only fit two at a time, slowing down the process. But more importantly, since we suggest pan-frying the chicken, rather than deep-frying it, the high-sided pot catches and keeps steam inside the insert, rendering the exposed skin above the oil too gummy.

1. Mix the paprika, salt, onion powder, sage, thyme, pepper, and garlic powder on a large plate until uniform. Pat the chicken thighs dry with paper towels and roll the chicken in this mixture to coat the pieces evenly and thoroughly.

2. Pour the water into a **6- or 8-quart cooker**. Set a heat- and pressure-safe trivet in the pot. Stack the thighs on the trivet. Lock the lid onto the cooker.

3.

Set the machine for	Set the level for	The valve must be	Set the time for	If necessary, press
PRESSURE COOK	MAX	—	10 minutes with the KEEP WARM setting off	START
STEAM, PRESSURE COOK, or MANUAL	HIGH	Closed	15 minutes with the KEEP WARM setting off	START

4. Use the **quick-release method** to bring the pot's pressure back to normal. Unlatch the lid and open the cooker. Line a large lipped baking sheet with paper towels. Use kitchen tongs to transfer the *hot* thighs to a large, lipped baking sheet. Set aside to dry for at least 20 minutes or up to 1 hour.

5. Set a 12-inch skillet over medium heat. Pour in enough oil to come about ½ inch up the sides — or melt enough shortening in the skillet to come to the same depth. Continue heating until the fat shimmers.

6. Slip three of the thighs skin side down into the oil. Fry until golden and crisp, about 10 minutes. Turn and continue frying until golden, crisp, and cooked through, about another 10 minutes. Transfer the thighs to a wire cooling rack and salt as desired. Add enough oil or shortening to get the depth back to ½ inch if necessary and wait a moment or two make sure the oil is again hot. Fry the remainder of the thighs in the same way. Serve warm.

See photo in insert.

Beyond

- You must halve the recipe for a 3-quart cooker.

- Pressure-cook the chicken ahead of time. Once the thighs have dried on the baking sheet for 20 minutes, transfer them to a bowl, cover it, and refrigerate for up to 1 day. Bring the thighs to room temperature before frying them.

- For crunchier skin, put about 1 cup all-purpose flour in a paper bag, add the cooked thighs, seal, and shake to coat them. Transfer them out one by one to the hot skillet, knocking off the excess flour before they get into the oil. Fry as directed.

- For a Korean-inspired dish, toss the cooked and fried thighs with up to ½ cup sweet Thai chili sauce before serving.

Chinese-Take-Out Lacquered Chicken Legs

4 to 6 servings

1 cup reduced-sodium soy sauce

¼ cup unseasoned rice vinegar

12 skin-on chicken legs

¼ cup granulated white sugar

Sticky, sweet, salty, and tender, these chicken legs make great deck snacks in the summer. They're equally good as part of a buffet on game day. But no matter the season, you'll need plenty of napkins. Use only reduced-sodium soy sauce so the basting liquid doesn't become too salty.

1. Pour the soy sauce and vinegar into a **6-quart cooker**. Set a heat- and pressure-safe collapsible steaming basket in the pot. Pile the chicken legs into the basket. Lock the lid onto the cooker.

2.

Set the machine for	Set the level for	The valve must be	Set the time for	If necessary, press
PRESSURE COOK	MAX	—	10 minutes with the KEEP WARM setting off	START
STEAM, PRESSURE COOK, or MANUAL	HIGH	Closed	12 minutes with the KEEP WARM setting off	START

3. Use the **quick-release method** to bring the pot's pressure back to normal. Unlatch the lid and open the cooker. Use kitchen tongs to transfer the chicken legs to a large, lipped baking sheet. Remove the steaming basket from the pot. Stir the sugar into the liquids in the pot.

4. Position the rack 4 inches from the broiler heat source; heat the broiler for a minute or two. Baste the legs with the sauce in the pot, then broil them until coated and crunchy, about 2 minutes, turning a couple of times and basting each time with more of the pot liquid. Serve warm.

Beyond

- You must halve the recipe for a **3-quart cooker**.

- For an **8-quart cooker**, you must increase all the ingredients by 50 percent — *or* simply increase the soy sauce and vinegar by 50 percent.

- For more flavor, put a 4-inch cinnamon stick, up to 6 green or white cardamom pods, and/or 1 star anise pod in the pot with the soy sauce and vinegar.

- Before serving, sprinkle sesame seeds all over the chicken legs.

2 tablespoons butter, softened to room temperature

1 teaspoon mild paprika

1 teaspoon kosher salt

½ teaspoon dried sage

½ teaspoon onion powder

½ teaspoon ground black pepper

¼ teaspoon garlic powder

One 4½- to 5-pound bone-in, skin-on turkey breast

2 cups chicken broth or water

Steam-Roasted Turkey Breast

6 to 8 servings

A turkey breast is our go-to make-ahead for weekend guests. We keep one in the fridge for sandwiches or for slices at breakfast for those who want a little more protein beyond granola. Some turkey breasts have a flat "bottom" so the breast meat sits nicely up top of the bones. Others have flapping bits of the ribs still attached (that can cause the meat to tip this way and that). Remove any extraneous bits with kitchen shears so the breast will sit flat in the cooker.

There's no way to crisp the skin in an Instant Pot. If you're making the turkey ahead, it may not matter, given that the bird will be cold. But see the *Beyond* for one way to get the job done.

1. Use a fork to mash the butter, paprika, salt, sage, onion powder, pepper, and garlic powder into a paste in a small bowl. Smear this mixture all over the skin of the turkey breast.

2. Pour the broth or water into a **6- or 8-quart cooker**. Set a heat- and pressure-safe trivet in the pot. Set the turkey breast skin side up on the trivet. Lock the lid onto the pot.

3.

Set the machine for	Set the level for	The valve must be	Set the time for	If necessary, press
PRESSURE COOK	MAX	——	18 minutes with the KEEP WARM setting off	START
STEAM, PRESSURE COOK or MANUAL	HIGH	Closed	25 minutes with the KEEP WARM setting off	START

4. When the machine has finished cooking, turn it off and let its pressure **return to normal naturally**, about 45 minutes. Unlatch the lid and open the cooker. Use large kitchen tongs and a large metal spatula to transfer the *hot* turkey breast to a nearby cutting board. Cool for 5 minutes, then carve into ¼- to ½-inch-wide slices.

Beyond

- Because of the size of the turkey breast, this recipe won't work in a **3-quart cooker**.

- For brown, crunchy skin, position the rack in the center of the oven and heat the oven to 450°F as the turkey cooks in the machine. When done, transfer the turkey breast skin side up to a small roasting or broiler pan. Roast until the skin has browned, about 10 minutes.

State Fair Turkey Legs

4 servings

Don't wait for the midway attractions! These turkey legs will fit the bill whenever the weather's warm and the day's gorgeous. In fact, if you want to make a barbecue or cookout more sophisticated, consider a tray of these legs for the under-twelve set. There will undoubtedly be an adult who's hankering to play Henry VIII.

1. Mix the chile powder, smoked paprika, onion powder, salt, and pepper in a small bowl until uniform. Smear ½ tablespoon oil on each turkey leg, then coat them evenly in the spice mixture.

2. Pour the water into a **6- or 8-quart cooker**. Set a heat- and pressure-safe trivet in the pot. Pile the legs onto the trivet. Lock the lid onto the pot.

3.

Set the machine for	Set the level for	The valve must be	Set the time for	If necessary, press
PRESSURE COOK	MAX	—	32 minutes with the KEEP WARM setting off	START
STEAM, PRESSURE COOK or MANUAL	HIGH	Closed	40 minutes with the KEEP WARM setting off	START

4. When the machine has finished cooking, turn it off and let its pressure **return to normal naturally** for 10 minutes. Then use the **quick-release method** to get rid of any residual pressure in the pot. Unlatch the lid and open the cooker. Use kitchen tongs to transfer the turkey legs to a large, lipped baking pan.

5. Position the rack 6 inches from the broiler heating element. Heat the broiler for 1 to 2 minutes. Meanwhile, whisk the honey, vinegar, and 1 to 2 teaspoons of the cooking water from the pot in a small bowl to make a sauce with the consistency of thick barbecue sauce.

6. Brush some of this honey mixture over the turkey legs, then broil to brown and crisp, about 2 minutes, turning a couple of times and basting with more of the mopping sauce. Cool for 5 minutes before serving.

1 tablespoon standard chile powder

1 teaspoon mild smoked paprika

1 teaspoon onion powder

1 teaspoon table salt

1 teaspoon ground black pepper

2 tablespoons vegetable, corn, or canola oil

Four ¾-pound skin-on turkey legs

2 cups water

¼ cup honey

1 tablespoon apple cider vinegar

Beyond

- Turkey legs are too long to fit well in a **3-quart cooker.**

- To make these turkey legs on the SLOW COOK setting, only add ½ cup water to the pot and do not use the trivet. Set the legs in the pot, latch on the lid, keep the pressure valve open (as necessary), and press the SLOW COOK function on HIGH. Cook for 4 hours with the KEEP WARM setting off or on for 2 hours. Broil as directed in steps 5 and 6.

2 pounds flat- or first-cut lean
brisket, cut into 1½-inch cubes

1 tablespoon mild smoked paprika

1 teaspoon onion powder

½ teaspoon garlic powder

½ teaspoon table salt

Twelve to sixteen 4-inch bamboo or
metal skewers

1 cup water

One 3½-ounce bottle liquid smoke

Beyond

- For a **3-quart cooker**, use 1 cup
  water but halve the remaining
  ingredients.

- For an **8-quart cooker**, you must use
  2 cups water and increase the
  remaining ingredients by 50
  percent — or simply increase the
  water to 2 cups (while keeping the
  stated amounts of the other
  ingredients).

- Serve the skewers with salsa verde,
  regular salsa, or even barbecue
  sauce for dipping.

- Make these skewers ahead of time.
  Cook them through step 4, then cool
  for a few minutes with the pot open.
  Use kitchen tongs to remove the
  trivet underneath them, then store
  the skewers (and meat) right in the
  steaming medium. Cool for
  20 minutes, then remove the insert
  from the machine, cover the insert
  with plastic wrap, and store it in the
  fridge for up to 24 hours. Grill the
  skewers an extra minute or so to
  warm them up.

Brisket Skewers

4 to 6 servings

Here's something we can *only* do in a multi-cooker: tenderize brisket
enough that it can be served as skewered cubes on kebabs. We use
liquid smoke to give the brisket a smokehouse flavor, then crisp the
skewers in a grill pan or on the grill until they're an unbelievable
combination of fatty brisket and tender beefiness.

   Use short skewers. You may need to break standard bamboo
skewers in half; watch out for splinters. But there's not much else to do.
Maybe provide a dip for the skewers? How about barbecue sauce,
ketchup, honey mustard, or even a creamy sour cream and horseradish
sauce? Oh, and beer. Not in the cooker. You'll need a cold beer in your
hand.

1. Toss the brisket cubes, smoked paprika, onion powder, garlic
powder, and salt in a large bowl until the meat is evenly and thoroughly
coated. Thread two cubes onto each of the skewers.

2. Pour the water and liquid smoke into a **6-quart cooker**. Set a
heat- and pressure-safe trivet in the pot. Pile the skewers onto the
trivet. Lock the lid onto the pot.

3.

Set the machine for	Set the level for	The valve must be	Set the time for	If necessary, press
PRESSURE COOK	MAX	—	42 minutes with the KEEP WARM setting off	START
STEAM, PRESSURE COOK or MANUAL	HIGH	Closed	50 minutes with the KEEP WARM setting off	START

4. When the machine has finished cooking, turn it off and let its
pressure **return to normal naturally**, about 20 minutes. Unlatch the lid
and open the pot.

5. Heat a large cast-iron grill pan over medium-high heat until smoking
or brush the grill grates and prepare the grill for high heat cooking
directly over the heat source. Grill the skewers (in batches in the grill
pan) until crisp and browned, about 2 minutes, turning occasionally.

See photo in insert.

SUPER EASY / FEWER THAN 10 INGREDIENTS / NATURAL RELEASE, THEN
MODIFIED NATURAL RELEASE / CAN BE GLUTEN-FREE / FREEZES WELL

ALL THINGS STEAMED AND COOKED
WITH THE SOUS VIDE METHOD **267**

Smoky Corned Beef

6 to 8 servings

In essence, this recipe uses purchased corned beef and the Instant Pot to make pastrami. It calls for a lot of corned beef. You may need to stack two 1½-pound packaged corned beefs on top of each other.

For a real treat, you then cook potatoes right in the smoky liquid in the pot. Of course, you needn't bother. You can skip steps 5 through 7 and simply slice the corned beef for sandwiches on rye bread topped with deli mustard and maybe purchased coleslaw.

1. Mix the dried mustard, coriander, and pepper in a small bowl. Dry the corned beef with paper towels, then pat this spice rub all over the meat.

2. Pour the water in a **6- or 8-quart cooker;** stir in the liquid smoke. Put a heat- and pressure-safe trivet in the pot, then set the coated corned beef on top. Lock the lid onto the pot.

3.

Set the machine for	Set the level for	The valve must be	Set the time for	If necessary, press
PRESSURE COOK	MAX	—	1 hour 10 minutes with the KEEP WARM setting off	START
MEAT/STEW, PRESSURE COOK, or MANUAL	HIGH	Closed	1 hour 30 minutes with the KEEP WARM setting off	START

4. When the machine has finished cooking, turn it off and let its pressure **return to normal naturally**, about 40 minutes. Unlatch the lid and open the pot. Transfer the corned beef to a nearby cutting board. Tent with foil to keep warm.

5. Remove the trivet from the pot. Stir the potatoes into the liquid inside. Lock the lid back onto the pot.

6.

Set the machine for	Set the level for	The valve must be	Set the time for	If necessary, press
PRESSURE COOK	MAX	—	7 minutes with the KEEP WARM setting off	START
STEAM, PRESSURE COOK, or MANUAL	HIGH	Closed	10 minutes with the KEEP WARM setting off	START

7. When the machine has finished cooking, turn it off and let its pressure **return to normal naturally** for 5 minutes. Then use the **quick-release method** to get rid of any residual pressure in the pot. Unlatch the lid and open the cooker. Drain the potatoes from the *hot* insert into a colander set in the sink. Slice the corned beef against the grain into ½-inch-thick strips and serve with the potatoes.

1 teaspoon ground dried mustard

1 teaspoon ground coriander

1 teaspoon ground black pepper

One 3- to 3½-pound corned beef, any spice packets removed and discarded, the meat well rinsed

2 cups water

Two 3.5-ounce bottles liquid smoke

2 pounds very small, red- or yellow-skinned potatoes, each about the size of a ping-pong balls, scrubbed of any surface dirt

Beyond

- For a **3-quart cooker,** halve all the ingredients. However, the 1½-pound corned beef may not fit. Slice it into two equal sections and stack these on each other on the rack.

- For the best Reuben sandwich, carve the warm pastrami against the grain into ½-inch-thick-slices. Set these on toasted rye bread with lots of sauerkraut and Russian dressing (see page 425). Notice what's missing? Cheese. Every single kosher deli cannot be wrong.

1 tablespoon mild smoked paprika

2 teaspoons dried oregano

2 teaspoons dried thyme

1 teaspoon ground dried mustard

1 teaspoon onion powder

½ teaspoon table salt

½ teaspoon ground black pepper

3½ pounds boneless beef short ribs

1½ cups water

2 tablespoons vegetable, corn, or canola oil

1 tablespoon granulated white sugar

1 tablespoon apple cider vinegar

Crisped and Mopped Beef Short Ribs

6 servings

Sure, the best thing about the Instant Pot is the ability to open the lid after cooking and look at dinner. But here, we use the pot to steam short ribs that have been coated in a fit-for-the-smoker rub. Those short ribs are put back into the pot later and made crisp over the heat. All in all, there's some effort required but a big dividend: crunchy short ribs that are meltingly tender, with a rich, sweet glaze.

1. Mix the smoked paprika, oregano, thyme, mustard, onion powder, salt, and pepper in a large bowl. Add the short ribs and toss well, until they are evenly and thoroughly coated. (There should be no dried spice mixture left in the bowl.)

2. Pour the water into a **6- or 8-quart cooker**. Set a heat- and pressure-safe collapsible steaming basket in the pot. Pile the coated short ribs into the basket, then lock the lid onto the pot.

3.

Set the machine for	Set level for	The valve must be	Set the time for	If necessary, press
PRESSURE COOK	MAX	—	35 minutes with the KEEP WARM setting off	START
STEAM, PRESSURE COOK, or MANUAL	HIGH	Closed	45 minutes with the KEEP WARM setting off	START

4. When the machine has finished cooking, turn it off and let its pressure **return to normal naturally**, about 20 minutes. Unlatch the lid and open the cooker. Use kitchen tongs to transfer the short ribs to a nearby bowl. Pour any liquid in the cooker into a second bowl, then clean and dry the machine's insert before returning it to the pot.

5.

Press the button for	Set it for	Set the time for	If necessary, press
SAUTÉ	MEDIUM, NORMAL, or CUSTOM 300°F	30 minutes	START

6. Warm the canola oil in the pot for a minute or two. Add about a third of short ribs and cook, turning occasionally, until crisped on all sides, about 6 minutes. Transfer these to a serving platter and brown the remaining two batches in the same way.

7. Once all the meat is on the platter, pour the reserved liquid into the pot and bring it to a full simmer. Stir in the sugar and vinegar. Continue cooking, stirring often, until this liquid has reduced to a thick glaze, about 6 minutes. Turn off the SAUTÉ function, then smear and spread this glaze over the short ribs before serving.

Beyond

- For a **3-quart cooker**, you must use 1 cup water but halve the remaining ingredients.

- Serve these with Baked Beans (page 444).

- Or serve them set over Creamy Black-Eyed Peas (page 438).

1½ pounds lean ground beef

One 8-ounce russet or baking potato, peeled and shredded through the large holes of a box grater

¼ cup plain panko breadcrumbs

1 large egg

2 tablespoons Worcestershire sauce

2 tablespoons ketchup

1 teaspoon dried oregano

1 teaspoon dried thyme

1 teaspoon onion powder

½ teaspoon garlic powder

1 teaspoon table salt

½ teaspoon ground black pepper

Olive oil spray

1½ cups water

Down-Home Meatloaf

6 servings

A Bundt pan makes a meatloaf in a snap in the Instant Pot. But you'll need one more piece of equipment: an instant-read meat thermometer. Taking the internal temperature of the loaf after cooking guarantees that the dish is safe to eat. Of course, some people like a crunchy top to an oven-roasted meatloaf. We've got a solution to that in the *Beyond* section. If you're looking for a braised meatloaf, see page 367.

1. Mix the ground meat, potato, breadcrumbs, egg, Worcestershire sauce, ketchup, oregano, thyme, onion powder, garlic powder, salt, and pepper in a large bowl until uniform.

2. Generously coat the inside of a 7-inch Bundt pan with olive oil spray. Pack the ground beef mixture into this pan, creating an even, smooth layer. Cover the pan with aluminum foil; poke a fairly large hole in the center of the foil where the hole exists in the center post of the Bundt pan.

3. Pour the water into a **3-, 6-, or 8-quart cooker**. Set a heat- and pressure-safe trivet inside the pot. Set the covered Bundt pan on the trivet. Lock the lid onto the cooker, taking care that the lid seals to the pot without any foil sticking out around the rim.

4.

Set the machine for	Set the level for	The valve must be	Set the time for	If necessary, press
PRESSURE COOK	MAX	——	22 minutes with the KEEP WARM setting off	START
STEAM, PRESSURE COOK or MANUAL	HIGH	Closed	30 minutes with the KEEP WARM setting off	START

5. When the machine has finished cooking, turn it off and let its pressure **return to normal naturally**, about 20 minutes. Unlatch the lid and open the cooker. Poke an instant-read meat thermometer through the foil and into the center of the loaf without touching metal in at least two places to make sure the meatloaf's temperature is 160°F.

If it is not, latch the lid onto the cooker with the pressure valve closed and cook for another 5 minutes at HIGH, followed by the **quick-release method**. Unlatch the lid, open the cooker, and take the meatloaf's internal temperature again.

6. Once done, use the handle of a wooden spoon leveraged into the center hole of the Bundt pan (also wear oven mitts) to transfer the *hot* Bundt pan to a wire rack. Cool for a few minutes, just until you can handle the pan. Using oven mitts, tip the Bundt pan a bit this way and that over a trash can to pour off any juices around the meatloaf. Set a platter over the pan, invert the whole thing (watch out for more hot juices!), and remove the pan. Cool for a few more minutes before slicing.

Beyond

- To glaze the meatloaf, whisk 2 tablespoons Worcestershire sauce; 2 tablespoons ketchup; and 1 tablespoon balsamic, sherry, or red wine vinegar in a small bowl until smooth. Invert the cooled meatloaf onto a large, lipped baking sheet, then smear this mixture over the top and sides of the meatloaf. Broil about 6 inches from a heated broiler element until bubbling and set, about 1 minute.

Olive oil spray

1½ teaspoons ground black pepper

1½ pounds lean ground pork

½ cup dehydrated potato flakes

1 large egg

2 tablespoons Dijon mustard

2 tablespoons Worcestershire sauce

2 teaspoons dried dill

1 teaspoon caraway seeds

½ teaspoon celery seeds

1½ cups water

Pork Meatloaf

4 to 6 servings

This meatloaf is a little smaller than the last one because it's missing all the shredded potato. We make up for it with dehydrated potato flakes (aka instant mashed potatoes). These catch and hold on to any released moisture, increasing in volume like little potato sponges, all to make sure the meatloaf is tender when cooked through. Beyond a fine entrée, this pork loaf is great when sliced into thin bits and served with toothpicks for a snack with cocktails. Slices also make a great sandwich on toasted multigrain bread with lots of deli mustard and sliced, ripe tomato.

1. Generously coat the inside of a 7-inch Bundt pan with olive oil spray. Sprinkle the pepper all over the interior pan, turning the pan this way and that to coat it evenly.

2. Mix the ground pork, potato flakes, egg, mustard, Worcestershire sauce, dill, caraway seeds, and celery seeds in a large bowl until uniform. Pack this mixture into the prepared pan, taking care not to knock the ground black pepper off the sides but getting the mixture into an even layer in the pan. Cover tightly with aluminum foil.

3. Pour the water into a **3-, 6-, or 8-quart cooker**. Set a heat- and pressure-safe trivet in the pot. Transfer the filled Bundt pan to the trivet. Lock the lid onto the cooker, taking care that the lid seals properly without any bit of foil sticking out of the rim.

4.

Set the machine for	Set the level for	The valve must be	Set the time for	If necessary, press
PRESSURE COOK	MAX	—	18 minutes with the KEEP WARM setting off	START
STEAM, PRESSURE COOK or MANUAL	HIGH	Closed	25 minutes with the KEEP WARM setting off	START

5. When the machine has finished cooking, turn it off and let its pressure **return to normal naturally**, about 20 minutes. Unlatch the lid and open the cooker. Poke an instant-read meat thermometer through the foil and into the center of the loaf without touching metal in at least two places to make sure the meatloaf's temperature is 160°F.

If it is not, cover the Bundt pan again, then latch the lid onto the cooker with the pressure valve closed and cook for another 5 minutes at HIGH, followed by the **quick-release method**. Unlatch the lid, open the cooker, and take the loaf's internal temperature again.

6. Transfer the Bundt pan to a wire cooling rack. Uncover and cool for a few minutes. Pick up the filled Bundt pan with oven mitts or hot pads and tip it just a bit over a trash can to pour off any hot juices around the interior perimeter of the pan. Set a serving platter over the pan, invert the whole thing, and remove the *hot* Bundt pan. Cool for a few more minutes before slicing and serving.

Beyond

- For a savory and sour kick, add ½ cup squeezed sauerkraut to the meat mixture before cooking.
- Or add ½ cup finely diced gherkin pickles.

1 pound lean ground beef

One 8-ounce can whole or sliced water chestnuts, drained and chopped (1 cup)

1 large egg white

2 tablespoons dry sherry, dry vermouth, or dry white wine

1 tablespoon minced peeled fresh ginger

¼ cup plus 1 tablespoon unseasoned rice vinegar

1 teaspoon five-spice powder (see page 88)

½ teaspoon ground black pepper

1 cup raw short-grain white rice

1 cup water

¼ cup soy sauce

¼ cup Worcestershire sauce

Chinese-Take-Out Porcupine Meatballs

2 to 4 servings

If you've never ordered these for takeout, now's the time to try them at home: tasty little meatballs covered in sticky rice. You can use medium-grain or even long-grain white rice to coat the balls, although chewy, short-grain sushi rice gives a decidedly chewy "coating" to the meatballs. The dipping sauce is fairly traditional, although you could skip it and use Chinese duck sauce or even just Sriracha thinned out with a little broth or sherry.

1. Mix the beef, chestnuts, egg white, sherry, ginger, 1 tablespoon vinegar, the five-spice powder, and pepper in a medium bowl until uniform. Form this mixture into 18 balls, each about the size of a golf ball, made from about 2 tablespoons of the mixture.

2. Pour the rice on a large plate, platter, or cutting board. Roll the balls in the rice, getting the grains to adhere evenly all over each ball.

3. Pour the water into a **6-quart cooker**. Set a heat- and pressure-safe collapsible steaming basket in the pot, opened out as much as you can. Pile the balls into the basket and lock the lid onto the pot.

4.

Set the machine for	Set the level for	The valve must be	Set the time for	If necessary, press
PRESSURE COOK	MAX	—	8 minutes with the KEEP WARM setting off	START
STEAM, PRESSURE COOK or MANUAL	HIGH	Closed	10 minutes with the KEEP WARM setting off	START

5. While the meatballs cook, whisk the soy sauce, Worcestershire sauce, and the remaining ¼ cup rice vinegar in a small serving bowl. Set aside.

6. When the machine has finished cooking, turn it off and let its pressure **return to normal naturally** for 10 minutes. Then use the **quick-release method** to get rid of any residual pressure in the pot. Unlatch the lid and open the cooker. Lift the *hot* steamer basket out of the cooker or gently transfer the balls one by one to a serving platter with kitchen tongs. Serve with the dipping sauce on the side.

Beyond

- You must halve the recipe for a **3-quart cooker**.

- For an **8-quart cooker**, you must use 1½ cups water but keep the remaining ingredients the same (there's no way to get a double recipe of 36 balls into a vegetable steamer).

- For more authentic flavor, substitute Shaoxing (a Chinese rice wine) for the sherry and ground white pepper for the black pepper.

- And use a 6-inch bamboo steaming basket, rather than a metal vegetable steamer.

Road Map: Steamed Clams

4 servings

There may be no better dinner to have while bingeing whatever's streaming tonight. Make a pot, remove the insert, carry it to the coffee table, set it on several hot pads, break out some bowls, grab a roll of paper towels for the drips, and have a crunchy baguette on hand to sop up the sauce.

The exterior of clam shells can be sandy, even if you don't feel the sand with your fingers. Scrub the shells well with a plastic brush or even a brand-new sponge that has a scouring side.

Sometimes, clams don't open after cooking — or sometimes they are a tad older and their shells' hinges are strong. If you find that over half aren't opened when you unlatch the pot's lid, put it back in place with the pressure valve open and bring the sauce to a simmer with the SAUTÉ function on MEDIUM, NORMAL, or CUSTOM 300°F. Cook for 1 to 2 minutes. They should all open. Discard any that do not. They could be locked closed with "sea muck" that you don't want in the sauce.

1. Mix the liquid, fat, acid, herbs, and garlic (if using) in a **6-quart cooker**. Stir in the clams. Lock the lid onto the pot.

2.

Set the machine for	Set the level for	The valve must be	Set the time for	If necessary, press
PRESSURE COOK	MAX	—	2 minutes with the KEEP WARM setting off	START
STEAM, PRESSURE COOK or MANUAL	HIGH	Closed	4 minutes with the KEEP WARM setting off	START

3. When the machine has finished cooking, turn it off and let its pressure **return to normal naturally**, about 15 minutes. Unlatch the lid and open the cooker. Spoon the clams into bowls. (Discard any that do not open.) Ladle lots of the sauce from the pot over them in the bowls.

1 cup liquid

> **Choose one or two** from wine of any sort, beer of any sort, broth of any sort, sherry, vermouth, and/or unsweetened apple juice.

2 tablespoons liquid or solid fat

> **Choose** from butter, rendered bacon fat, coconut oil, or lard — or olive, vegetable, corn, canola, safflower, or any nut oil.

2 tablespoons acid

> **Choose** from vinegar of any sort, lemon juice, or lime juice.

2 tablespoons minced fresh herb leaves

> **Choose one or preferably two** from basil, cilantro, marjoram, parsley, oregano, sage, savory, tarragon, and/or thyme.

Up to 3 medium garlic cloves, peeled and minced (1 tablespoon — optional)

3 pounds small littleneck, mahogany, or manila clams (8 to 9 per pound, about 24 to 36 clams in total), scrubbed

Beyond

- For a **3-quart cooker**, you must use ¾ cup liquid and halve the remaining ingredients.

- For an **8-quart cooker**, you must increase *all* the ingredients by 50 percent.

- For heat in the mix, add up to 1 medium fresh jalapeño, stemmed and sliced into thin rings; or up to 5 dried chiles de arbol or small dried Asian red chiles, the sort found in stir-fries.

2 tablespoons olive oil, plus additional for greasing the pan

2 medium celery stalks, thinly sliced (⅔ cup)

1 small yellow onion, chopped (½ cup)

1 small yellow bell pepper, stemmed, cored, and chopped (½ cup)

1½ cups water

1 teaspoon mild paprika

1 cup plain panko breadcrumbs

½ cup regular or low-fat mayonnaise

1 large egg

2 tablespoons Dijon mustard

1 tablespoon dried sage

1 teaspoon ground black pepper

½ teaspoon dried thyme

Several dashes hot red pepper sauce, such as Texas Pete or Tabasco Sauce (optional)

1 pound crabmeat, picked over for shells and cartilage

Crab Cake

6 servings

For us, this was the most surprising recipe after months of testing: a single Bundt pan crab cake, maybe a loaf cake, not fried crisp but steamed and light. No, it's not authentic, but it's a tasty meal with a salad on the side.

Don't use expensive giant or jumbo lump crabmeat. But also don't use the cheaper claw meat which can be quite fishy. Instead, use standard lump, back fin, or "special" crabmeat. The best crabmeat for this is found in pasteurized cans in the refrigerator case near the fish counter.

1.

Press the button for	Set it for	Set the time for	If necessary, press
SAUTÉ	MEDIUM, NORMAL, or CUSTOM 300°F	5 minutes	START

2. Warm the oil in a **3-, 6-, or 8-quart cooker** for a minute or two. Add the celery, onion, and pepper. Cook, stirring occasionally, until the onion softens, about 3 minutes. Scrape this mixture into a large bowl and set aside to cool to room temperature, about 20 minutes. Meanwhile, clean and dry the insert; return it to the pot.

3. Pour the water into the insert. Set a heat- and pressure-safe trivet in the pot. Generously oil the inside of a 7-inch Bundt pan. Sprinkle the paprika evenly around the interior of the pan, giving it a light coating.

4. Stir the breadcrumbs, mayonnaise, egg white, mustard, sage, pepper, thyme, and hot red pepper sauce (if using) into the onion mixture until uniform. Gently stir in the crabmeat, then pack this mixture into the prepared pan.

5. Cover the pan tightly with foil, then use a knife to poke a large hole in the center of the foil where the center hole of the Bundt pan is. Transfer the pan to the trivet in the cooker. Lock the lid onto the pot, making sure the lid seals tight without any foil sticking out around the rim.

6.

Set the machine for	Set the level for	The valve must be	Set the time for	If necessary, press
PRESSURE COOK	MAX	——	15 minutes with the KEEP WARM setting off	START
STEAM, PRESSURE COOK or MANUAL	HIGH	Closed	20 minutes with the KEEP WARM setting off	START

7. When the machine has finished cooking, turn it off and let its pressure **return to normal naturally**, about 20 minutes. Unlatch the lid and open the cooker. Transfer the *hot* Bundt pan to a wire cooling rack. Cool for 15 minutes, then set a plate over the pan, invert the whole thing, and remove the pan. Cool for another 5 minutes or so before slicing into wedges to serve.

Beyond

- The crab cake isn't crunchy. To make it crunchy, cool the unmolded cake to room temperature, about 1 hour. Slice it into thick wedges, then fry these in butter in a nonstick skillet set over medium heat, turning once, until browned on both sides, 3 to 4 minutes in all.

2 pounds shell-on small shrimp
(about 40 per pound), deveined

1½ pounds small red-skinned
potatoes, each slightly smaller than a
Ping-Pong ball, halved

2 tablespoons olive oil

Up to 2 tablespoons Old Bay
seasoning or other fish boil
seasoning

2 cups water

1 cup red chile sauce, such as Heinz
chili sauce

2 tablespoons fresh lemon juice

1 tablespoon prepared jarred white
horseradish

1 tablespoon minced fresh dill fronds

Several dashes hot red pepper sauce,
such as Tabasco Sauce

Shrimp Boil

4 servings

Well, okay, this isn't technically a shrimp boil as they'd prepare it along
the East Coast of the United States. But our rendition's close enough for
a great meal! By keeping the shells on the shrimp, the shrimp can
withstand a bit more of the pressure and the shells add more briny
flavor to the potatoes.

    To devein shrimp without peeling them, make a slit along the
convex curve — that is, the side of the shell opposite the legs. Use the tip
of a paring knife to nick up and remove the dark, squishy "vein" that runs
just under the meat. Or buy shell-on deveined shrimp, probably in the
freezer case at the supermarket. Yes, it's messy at the table to remove
the shells. The flavor is worth it!

1. Mix the shrimp, potatoes, olive oil, and seasoning blend in a large
bowl until the shrimp and potatoes are evenly and thoroughly coated.

2. Pour the water into a **6- or 8-quart cooker**. Set a heat- and
pressure-safe collapsible steaming basket in the pot. Open it out as
much you can. Pile the shrimp and potatoes into the basket. Lock the
lid onto the pot.

3.

Set the machine for	Set the level for	The valve must be	Set the time for	If necessary, press
PRESSURE COOK	MAX	—	7 minutes with the KEEP WARM setting off	START
STEAM, PRESSURE COOK or MANUAL	HIGH	Closed	10 minutes with the KEEP WARM setting off	START

4. Meanwhile, make the cocktail sauce. Whisk the chile sauce, lemon
juice, horseradish, dill, and hot red pepper sauce in a small serving
bowl. Set aside.

5. Use the **quick-release method** to bring the pot's pressure back to
normal. Unlatch the lid and open the pot. Lift the *hot* steamer out of the
pot and pour the shrimp and potatoes onto a serving plate. Serve with
the cocktail sauce on the side.

Beyond

- You must halve the recipe for a
  3-quart cooker.

- Skip the cocktail sauce and make a
  quick tartar sauce: Mix together 1 cup
  regular or low-fat mayonnaise,
  1½ tablespoons pickled relish,
  1 tablespoon finely minced green
  part of a scallion, 1 tablespoon fresh
  lemon juice, and ½ teaspoon table
  salt in a small bowl.

Perfect in-the-Shell Sous Vide Eggs

1 to 6 servings

Water as needed

1 to 6 large eggs, at room temperature

We already have a recipe for in-the-shell eggs (page 34). Why a second one? Because this one uses the sous vide function of the Max machine to produce absolutely perfect eggs every time. Although the recipe in the breakfast chapter is certainly faster, this one can keep the eggs at the right temperature for your taste for up to 1 hour. Any weekend when you have guests, set up the cooker and head back to the shower. By the time everyone's downstairs, the eggs will be waiting and perfect — and silkier, smoother than you can believe.

1. Set a heat-safe trivet inside a Max *Instant Pot*. Fill the insert two-thirds or to the **Max Fill** line with water.

2. Set the machine to its SOUS VIDE function. Set the timer for 2 hours. Set the temperature based on the following criteria:

- 145°F for soft-boiled eggs with barely set whites and loose, runny yolks
- 150°F for soft-boiled eggs with whites that hold their shape and yolks that are soft at their centers
- 155°F for soft-boiled eggs with definitely set whites and yolks with a jammy, caramel-like consistency, such as the eggs often placed in Ramen Broth (page 104)
- 160°F for hard-cooked eggs with firm whites and still-moist yolks
- 165°F for hard-cooked eggs with firm whites and drier yolks, better for chopping in egg salad

3. Lock the lid onto the pot. Press the START button.

4. When the machine reaches the appropriate temperature, uncover the pot and lower the eggs onto the trivet. (A slotted spoon works best.) Latch the lid back onto the pot (the valve will be open by default) and cook for 1 hour. The eggs will be ready at this point. However, they can be held at the set temperature for 1 additional hour.

Beyond

- For the best egg salad, mix 4 to 6 peeled and chopped hard-cooked eggs with 4 to 6 tablespoons regular or low-fat mayonnaise, up to ¼ cup finely minced celery, 1 tablespoon white wine vinegar, up to 2 teaspoons yellow mustard, 1 teaspoon granulated white sugar, 1 teaspoon table salt, and ½ teaspoon onion powder.

See photo in insert.

Water as needed

Two 10- to 12-ounce boneless beef strips steaks, each 1 inch thick

2 tablespoons olive oil

1 teaspoon kosher salt

½ teaspoon ground black pepper

12 fresh chives, cut in half widthwise

2 medium garlic cloves, peeled and thinly sliced

Sous Vide Strip Steaks with Chives and Garlic

2 servings

When you cook strip steaks with the sous vide technique, you end up with rare steaks all the way to the edge, a solid block of red (or pink) tender meat: incredibly juicy, perfect every time. Many so-called experts put the steaks in the water bath for 1½, maybe 2 hours — which may result in a faster dinner but not a better one. After two hours, the cartilage has not softened; the interstitial fat has not begun to melt. In our minds, such culinary silliness is only a souped-up version of bringing a steak to room temperature before grilling it. What's the point? If we're going to the trouble to put strip steaks through the sous vide process, we want them at maximum perfection. Thus, these go for 10 hours. After that, they are unbelievably tender and juicy, the best medium-rare steak you'll ever have.

1. Fill a MAX *Instant Pot* two-thirds or to the **Max Fill** line with water. Set the machine's heat-safe trivet in the pot's bottom. Latch the lid onto the pot.

2. Set the machine to its SOUS VIDE function. Set the timer for 10 hours. Set the temperature for 130°F. Press the START button.

3. As the water heats, rub the steaks with the oil; season them with salt and pepper. Set each steak in a small vacuum-sealer bag; add half the chives and half the garlic. Seal the bags on the regular setting of the vacuum sealer. If you don't have a vacuum-sealer, set each steak in a 1-quart zip-closed plastic bag, add the chives and garlic, and seal using the water method (see page 259).

4. When the water is at the right temperature, unlatch the pot's lid and open the cooker. Use kitchen tongs to lower each bag with its steak into the cooker; use the handles of the trivet to hold them down onto it. The bags must not touch; they must have enough room between them that convection currents can circulate between them, as well as between the bags and the insert's sides. Latch the lid onto the cooker again. Cook for 10 hours, paying careful attention to the water level in the pot (page 259).

5. When the steaks are ready, keep them in the water bath and set a cast-iron skillet over medium-high heat until smoking or brush the grill grates clean and prepare the grill for high-heat cooking (about 500°F). Unlatch the lid and open the cooker. Use kitchen tongs to get the bags out of the cooker. Open them and remove the steaks. Discard the chives and garlic, as well as the plastic bags.

6. Blot the steaks dry, then set them in the skillet or on the grate directly over the heat source. Cook for 1 to 2 minutes, turning once, for a good crust. Serve at once.

See photo in insert.

Beyond

- For the best steak sauce, whisk 6 tablespoons ketchup, 2 teaspoons soy sauce, 2 teaspoons Worcestershire sauce, ½ teaspoon onion powder, ¼ teaspoon red wine vinegar, ¼ teaspoon garlic powder, and several dashes of hot red pepper sauce, like Tabasco sauce.

Sous Vide Steak Teriyaki

2 servings

Once again, we ask the pertinent question for sous vide: What is the point of going to all the trouble if you're not going to do it long enough make a big difference? By letting a sirloin cook at a very low temperature in a soy and mirin mixture, the sweet flavors fuse against the outside of the steak, later producing a fantastic crust in a hot pan or on a hot grill. Soy and mirin, of course, are not a traditional teriyaki mixture. They're simpler. Mirin is a sweetened cooking rice wine. Look for it near the soy sauce in almost every supermarket.

Water as needed

One 1- to 1¼-pound, 1-inch-thick boneless beef sirloin

2 tablespoons soy sauce

2 tablespoons mirin

1. Fill a Max *Instant Pot* two-thirds or to the **Max Fill** line with water. Set the machine's heat-safe trivet in the pot's bottom. Latch the lid onto the pot.

2. Set the machine to its SOUS VIDE function. Set the timer for 10 hours. Set the temperature for 130°F. Press the START button.

3. Put the steak, soy sauce, and mirin in a 1-quart zip-closed freezer bag. Use the water method to remove the air from the bag (see page 259). Seal the bag shut.

4. When the water is at the right temperature, unlatch the pot's lid and open the cooker. Use kitchen tongs to lower the bag with the steak onto the trivet, using the trivet's handles to keep it in place without pressing down. Latch the lid onto the cooker again. Cook for 10 hours, paying careful attention to the water level in the pot (page 259).

5. When the steak is ready, keep it in the water bath and set a cast-iron skillet over medium-high heat until smoking or brush the grill grates clean and prepare the grill for high-heat cooking (about 500°F).

6. Unlatch the pot's lid and open the cooker. Use kitchen tongs to get the bag out of the cooker. Open it and remove the steak. Discard the bag and marinade.

7. Blot the meat dry and set it in the skillet or on the grate directly over the heat source. Cook for 2 minutes, turning once, for a good crust. Serve at once, slicing it into ¼-inch-thick strips against the grain (see page 87).

Beyond

- Garnish the steak with sesame seeds before slicing.

- Serve it with a simple sunomono salad: Slice an English (or seedless) cucumber into very thin rounds. Mix these with 1 teaspoon table salt and set aside for 10 minutes. Squeeze them dry by the handfuls over the sink. (Don't be scared of squishing them but also don't reduce them to pulp.) Place them in a serving bowl and dress them with 3 tablespoons unseasoned rice vinegar, 2 teaspoons granulated white sugar, and 1 teaspoon soy sauce. Toss well to before serving.

Water as needed

1 tablespoon dark brown sugar

1 teaspoon mild smoked paprika

½ teaspoon dried thyme

½ teaspoon onion powder

½ teaspoon kosher salt

¼ teaspoon garlic powder

Two 10- to 12-ounce, 1½-inch-thick
boneless beef short ribs

Sous Vide Southwestern Beef Short Ribs

2 servings

This recipe is the real deal, the whole reason you want to master the sous vide process. By cooking beef short ribs at such a low temperature for so long, the meat becomes impossibly tender yet still medium-rare. You'll end up with something like a cross between brisket and a strip steak — like a medium-rare, super-tender pot roast. It makes no sense. It's a miracle. It's sous vide.

1. Fill a MAX *Instant Pot* two-thirds or to the **Max Fill** line with water. Set the machine's heat-safe trivet in the pot's bottom. Latch the lid onto the pot.

2. Set the machine to its SOUS VIDE function. Set the timer for 48 hours. Set the temperature for 130°F. Press the START button.

3. Mix the brown sugar, paprika, thyme, onion powder, salt, and garlic powder on a plate until uniform. Roll the short ribs in this mixture to coat them on all sides. Put each of the short ribs in a small vacuum-sealer bag. Seal the bags on the regular setting of the vacuum sealer. If you don't have a vacuum-sealer, set each coated short rib in a 1-quart zip-closed plastic bag and seal using the water method (see page 259).

4. When the water is at the right temperature, unlatch the pot's lid and open the cooker. Use kitchen tongs to lower each bag with its rib onto the trivet; use the handles of the trivet to hold them down. The bags must not touch; they must have enough room between them that convection currents can circulate between them, as well as between the bags and the insert's sides. Latch the lid onto the cooker again. Cook for 48 hours, keeping watch on the water level in the pot (see page 259).

5. When the ribs are ready, keep them in the water bath and set a cast-iron skillet over medium-high heat until smoking, or brush a grill grate clean and prepare it for high-heat cooking (about 500°F).

6. Unlatch the lid and open the cooker. Use kitchen tongs to get the bags out of the cooker. Open them and remove the short ribs. Discard the bags.

7. Blot the short ribs dry and set them in the skillet or on the grate. Cook for 1 minute per larger side and ½ minute for short sides (the perimeter) to get a good crust. Serve at once.

Beyond

- You can double this recipe — but it will take double the time. Prepare two short ribs as directed, then drop them still in their bags into a big bowl of ice water. When cold, store the still-sealed bags in the refrigerator for 2 days while you make 2 more short ribs.

- Serve these as an appetizer at a dinner party. Slice the short ribs against the grain into ½-inch-thick strips, then either serve with toothpicks and cocktails, or set them in a pool of salsa, salsa verde, pico de gallo, or Butternut Squash Mash (page 432).

- Skip our barbecue rub and use any dried herb blend or rub you like, even a bottled, dry, barbecue rub.

Sous Vide Smokehouse Brisket

4 to 6 servings

We offer two ways to get a brisket done under sous vide. Either cook it for 72 hours at 140°F for an astonishingly rare but tender brisket that cuts like a steak but tastes like the work of a good smokehouse. Or cook it for 48 hours at 155°F for a more traditional texture, falling apart and very soft, the way a braised brisket can get (see page 352). Once cooked and cooled, the brisket can be sealed in plastic wrap and frozen for up to 2 months. Thaw in the fridge for 48 hours, then let it come to room temperature before crisping as suggested.

1. Fill a MAX *Instant Pot* to the **Max Fill** line with water. Set the machine's heat-safe trivet in the pot's bottom. Latch the lid onto the pot.

2. Set the machine to its SOUS VIDE function. Set the timer for either 48 hours at 155°F or 72 hours at 140°F. Press the START button.

3. Put the brisket in a 1-gallon-sized zip-closed plastic freezer bag. Add the liquid smoke and Worcestershire sauce. Seal the bag and rub the liquids all over the meat through the plastic. Open the bag and use the water method (see page 259). to remove all the air from the bag before sealing it tight.

4. When the water is at the right temperature, unlatch the pot's lid and open the cooker. Use kitchen tongs to lower the bag into the cooker; use the handles of the trivet to hold it down with pressing on it. Latch the lid onto the cooker again. Cook for 48 or 72 hours, paying careful attention to the water level in the cooker (see page 259).

5. When the brisket is ready, keep it in the water bath and set a cast-iron skillet over medium-high heat until smoking or brush a grill grate clean and heat the grill for high-heat cooking (about 500°F).

6. Unlatch the lid and open the cooker. Use kitchen tongs to get the bag out of the cooker. Open it and remove the brisket. Discard the bag and any liquid inside.

7. Blot the brisket dry and set it in the skillet or on the grate. Cook for 3 to 4 minutes, turning once for a good crust. Slice against the grain and serve at once.

Water as needed

One 1½-pound flat-cut or first-cut lean beef brisket with an even thickness

2 tablespoons liquid smoke

2 tablespoons Worcestershire sauce

Beyond

- Without grilling or searing it, carve the brisket against the grain into ¼-inch-thick slices for sandwiches. Make the best with toasted rye bread, plenty of deli mustard, iceberg lettuce leaves, and maybe sandwich-sliced dill pickles.

Water as needed

Two 8-ounce, 1-inch-thick boneless
skinless chicken breasts

½ cup purchased pesto (or homemade,
see page 177)

Sous Vide Pesto Chicken Breasts

2 servings

These chicken breasts are infused with the flavors of pesto. More importantly, after sous vide, they're ridiculously juicy. They're ready right out of the pot, but you can crisp them on the outside with a little olive oil in a hot grill pan. The meat will be white but tinged pink. It has been cooked to a temperature lower than the USDA recommends. However, because of the long time at that temperature, it is safe. If you have concerns, use only antibiotic-free, organic, local chicken. And skip this recipe for anyone who has a compromised immune system. For a fuller explanation of how sous vide cooking is safe, check out the sous vide section on the USDA website.

1. Fill a MAX *Instant Pot* two-thirds or to the **Max Fill** line with water. Set the machine's heat-safe trivet in the pot's bottom. Latch the lid onto the pot.

2. Set the machine to its SOUS VIDE function. Set the timer for 3 hours. Set the temperature for 150°F. Press the START button.

3. Put 1 chicken breast and half the pesto in each of two 1-quart zip-closed plastic freezer bags. Seal the bag and massage the pesto against the meat through the plastic. Open the bag and use the water method (see page 259) to remove all the air from the bag. Seal closed.

4. When the water is at the right temperature, unlatch the pot's lid and open the cooker. Use kitchen tongs to lower each bag with its chicken breast onto the trivet; use the trivet's handles to hold the bags down without pressing against them. The bags must not touch; they must have enough room between them that convection currents can circulate between them, as well as between the bags and the insert's sides. Latch the lid onto the cooker again. Cook for 3 hours.

5. When the cooking is finished, unlatch the lid and open the cooker. Use kitchen tongs to remove the bags from the water. Open them and remove the chicken breasts, keeping as much pesto on them as possible. Discard the bags. Slice the chicken breasts into ¼-inch-thick strips to serve.

Beyond

- Set these atop a composed salad made with chopped lettuce, cucumbers, celery, and tomatoes, dressing with olive oil, balsamic vinegar, and seasoned with salt, pepper, and dried oregano.

- Or make chicken salad: Cut the chicken slices into bite-sized bits, then mix them with mayonnaise, sour cream, sliced celery, sliced radishes, and minced onion—and maybe chopped walnuts, seedless green grapes, and/or chopped, marinated artichoke hearts.

Sous Vide Salmon Fillets

2 servings

Why would anyone go to the trouble of cooking fish with the sous vide method? Simply because the results are so sublime: soft, mellow salmon, about like confit. As in other recipes, you can't use a vacuum sealer to remove the air here. It would suck the olive oil right out of the bag.

1. Fill a MAX *Instant Pot* two-thirds or to the **Max Fill** line with water. Set the machine's heat- and pressure-safe trivet in the pot's bottom. Latch the lid onto the pot.

2. Set the machine to its SOUS VIDE function. Set the timer for 3 hours. Set the temperature for 130°F. Press the START button.

3. Put one salmon fillet, 2 tablespoons olive oil, and 2 dill fronds in each of two 1-quart zip-closed plastic freezer bags. Gently rub the oil into the fish through the plastic. Use the water method (see page 259) to get rid of any excess air in the bag. Seal closed.

4. When the water is at the right temperature, unlatch the pot's lid and open the cooker. Use kitchen tongs to lower each bag with its fillet onto the trivet; use the trivet's handles to hold the bags down without pressing them down. The bags must not touch; they must have enough room between them that convection currents can circulate between them, as well as between the bags and the insert's sides. Latch the lid onto the cooker again. Cook for 3 hours.

5. When the fish is ready, unlatch the lid and open the cooker. Use kitchen tongs to remove the bags from the water. Open the bags and remove the salmon fillets. Discard the bags, dill, and any liquid in the bags. Serve at once with a little more olive oil and some coarse salt sprinkled over each fillet.

Water as needed

Two 6- to 8-ounce skin-on salmon fillets

¼ cup olive oil, plus more for garnishing

4 fresh dill fronds

Kosher or crunchy sea salt for garnishing

Beyond

- For a light summer meal, serve these on a bed of Boston lettuce leaves. Top with thinly sliced red onion and some thinly sliced cucumber. Then mix mayonnaise with a little Sriracha or harissa and dollop it on top of each serving.

- Chill the salmon fillets and serve them cold with a horseradish sauce made by whisking together ¼ cup jarred prepared white horseradish, 2 tablespoons sour cream, 1 tablespoon mayonnaise, 2 teaspoons fresh lemon juice, ¼ teaspoon table salt, and several dashes hot red pepper sauce like Tabasco sauce.

Water as needed

Four 4- to 5-ounce raw frozen lobsters tails in their shells, thawed

¼ cup (½ stick) butter

4 large tarragon or thyme sprigs

Kosher or coarse sea salt and ground black pepper for garnishing

Sous Vide Buttery Lobster Tails

2 to 4 servings

Lobster tails can be notoriously rubbery, overcooked seconds after they're perfectly cooked. By using the sous vide method, we can poach them in butter with herbs and end up with pure luxury each time.

We should note that most of the lobster tails sold in the United States are from clawless, warm-water lobsters. Some of these are of inferior quality and can fall apart while cooking. The best lobster tails are those from Canada and the northern U.S., cold-water lobsters that have a sweeter, milder taste. Check the packaging, ask the fishmonger, and use the cold-water ones. You may also find *fresh* cold-water tails at markets along the East Coast, although these tails tend to be absurdly expensive.

The best lobster tails for this technique are small. Whether they make two servings or four servings with lots of sides is up to you. We can suggest Corn on the Cob (page 429) and Three-Bean Salad (page 445).

1. Fill a MAX *Instant Pot* two-thirds or to the **Max Fill** line with water. Set the machine's heat-safe trivet in the pot's bottom. Latch the lid onto the pot.

2. Set the machine to its SOUS VIDE function. Set the timer for 3 hours. Set the temperature for 130°F. Press the START button.

3. Remove the lobster tails from their shells with kitchen shears. Cut the pale white underside from the thicker end toward the fanned tail. Peel open the shell on either side, loosen the meat from the shell, and pull the meat out.

4. Put two tails in a small vacuum-sealer bag; add 2 tablespoons butter and 2 herb sprigs. Repeat with a second bag. Seal the bags on the regular setting of the vacuum sealer. If you don't have a vacuum-sealer, set two tails in a 1-quart zip-closed plastic bag; add half the butter and herb; prepare a second bag in the same way; and seal them both using the water method (see page 259).

5. When the water is at the right temperature, unlatch the pot's lid and open the cooker. Use kitchen tongs to lower each bag with its lobster tails onto the trivet; use the trivet's handles to hold the bags down without pressing on them. The bags must not touch; they must have enough room between them that convection currents can circulate between them, as well as between the bags and the insert's sides. Latch the lid onto the cooker again. Cook for 3 hours.

6. When the machine is finished cooking, ready, unlatch the lid and open the cooker. Use kitchen tongs to take the bags out of the cooker. Split them open and use kitchen tongs to pull out the tails. Discard the bags, herbs, and any liquid in them. Garnish the tails with salt and pepper to taste before serving.

Beyond

- The best lobster rolls start with hot dog buns. Slather the insides with mayonnaise, set a lobster tail in each (or maybe two in one bun!), and garnish with minced chives.

- Or brush the cut sides of the buns with melted butter and toast them cut side down on a griddle, in a grill pan, or on a grill until lightly browned, 1 to 2 minutes. Chop the poached tails into bite-sized pieces (none too small), then mix them with ½ cup regular or low-fat mayonnaise, 1 thinly sliced medium celery stalk, and 1 tablespoon fresh lemon juice. Pile this mixture into the warm hot dog buns and serve at once.

See photo in insert.

Shorter Braises and Stews

(Fewer than Twenty Minutes *Under Pressure*)

This chapter may well be where you found yourself as you first flipped through the book. There's a lot of comfort food here, no doubt. And the recipes are done quickly—although you'll notice from the title that the time signature only refers to the time under pressure, not any prepping you might do, nor any time the pot might have to come back to normal pressure naturally (rather than with a quick release). We're not trying to pull any funny stuff with that "Twenty Minutes" in the header. We're just trying to give you a heads-up about where to find some of the shorter braises and stews.

As you'd expect, there's a lot of chicken and ground beef in this chapter, even some pork chops. As you might *not* expect, there are fish and shellfish dishes. Cooking seafood in the pot requires careful timing, but we can also use this countertop appliance to build a flavorful sauce that the fish or shellfish then gets poached in.

There are just four road maps in this chapter: seared chicken breasts, ground beef stew, braised pork chops, and mussels. Many quick-cooking cuts require a little finesse to keep them from drying out and turning tough. We'll explain more in the headnotes, including why boneless skinless chicken breasts, while doable, are not doable except with pretty specific considerations. (Check out the pulled recipes that use boneless skinless chicken breasts, starting on page 291.) The same goes for boneless center-cut pork loin chops.

What you won't find are classic quick-cooking proteins like filet mignons, turkey scaloppini, or tilapia. Things that cook in a skillet or on the grill in a minute or two are simply not Instant Pot–worthy. For one thing, by the time the pot heats up and cooks under pressure, you could already be eating dinner with a more traditional preparation. And for another, the diminished fat and cartilage content of some of these items makes them a tough sell (or just tough) in the pot's über-hot environment.

And one important warning before you get to the recipes: Pay attention through to the differences among *bone-in*, *boneless*, *skin-on*, or *skinless*. These recipes have been developed and written to address specific problems associated with each.

Beyond those concerns, this chapter is probably the most diverse in the book. Some recipes include cooking tricks, some are unexpected concoctions, and some are just the sort of thing an average Wednesday night requires.

FAQs

1. What's the difference between a stew and a braise?

Definitions like these are endlessly debated among cookbook writers. By and large, a braise has less liquid than a stew. There's an old rule, advocated by the hoary dons, that the liquid in a braise must come no more than halfway up a piece of protein — and that by contrast, the liquid for a stew must swamp it. Maybe. In the end, many of these recipes fall on the line between a stew and a braise. Call them well-stocked stews. Or high-moisture braises. We've just tried to create the best flavor pairings we could, given the amount of liquid needed to make steam in the pot.

2. What happened to my favorite recipe for [insert entrée title here]?

It's probably elsewhere — like in the chapters on all things pulled, all things curried, and all things steamed, as well as among the pasta casseroles and pasta sauces. There are main-course casseroles in the grain chapter, too. (Try that chicken and rice sometime, page 412). In some ways, this chapter was designed to catch the things that didn't fall in those chapters: meatballs, mole, golumpkis, and much more.

Road Map: Perfect Seared Chicken Breasts

4 servings

Here's the problem: Despite the pot's high-moisture environment, boneless, skinless chicken breasts dry out and turn to shards in a multi-cooker. So here's our solution: Brown them first, then set them on a rack (or the machine's trivet) to keep them off the insert's superheated bottom when they undergo all that pressure. After cooking, a modified quick release lets them then sit in the steam a bit, so they can plump as they reabsorb some of their natural liquids.

Notice that these boneless skinless breasts are a bit larger than those sold in bulk bags at the supermarket. Notice, too, that you should brown the meat thoroughly. The chicken needs good color for the best flavor.

1.

Press the button for	Set it for	Set the time for	If necessary, press
SAUTÉ	MEDIUM, NORMAL, or CUSTOM 300°F	15 minutes	START

2. Melt the fat or warm the oil in a **6- or 8-quart cooker**. Season the chicken breasts with the dried herbs or seasoning blend and salt (if using). Set 2 breasts in the pot and brown *well*, turning once, about 6 minutes. Transfer these to a nearby plate and brown the other two breasts in the same way before getting them onto the plate.

3. Turn off the SAUTÉ function. Set a heat- and pressure-safe trivet in the pot. Pour in the liquid. Set all the chicken breasts on the trivet, overlapping thick ends over thin ends as necessary. Lock the lid onto the pot.

4.

Set the machine for	Set level for	The valve must be	Set the time for	If necessary, press
PRESSURE COOK	MAX	—	6 minutes with the KEEP WARM setting off	START
MEAT/STEW, PRESSURE COOK, or MANUAL	HIGH	Closed	8 minutes with the KEEP WARM setting off	START

5. Use the **quick-release method** to bring the pot's pressure back to normal — but *do not open the cooker*. Set it aside for 3 minutes with the valve open but the cooker off. Unlatch the lid and open the pot. Serve at once.

See photo in insert.

2 tablespoons solid or liquid fat

Choose from butter, lard, rendered bacon fat, schmaltz, or an oil of almost any sort: olive, avocado, vegetable, corn, canola, safflower, grape seed, walnut, almond, or pecan — or a 50/50 combo of a solid fat and a liquid fat.

Four 10- to 12-ounce boneless skinless chicken breasts

2 tablespoons dried herbs or a seasoning blend

Choose at least two or many to make up the total amount from any dried herb like thyme, oregano, or parsley; ground cinnamon, ground dried ginger, or ground dried turmeric; a curry powder of any sort, herbes de Provence, or any dried spice seasoning blend from Cajun to Italian, French to Greek.

½ teaspoon table salt (optional)

1½ cups liquid

Choose from water, broth of any sort, beer, wine of any sort, dry vermouth, dry sherry, unsweetened apple cider, unsweetened pear nectar, or a 50/50 combo of water or broth and wine.

Beyond

- You must halve the recipe for a **3-quart cooker**.

- After cooking, garnish the breasts with lots of ground black pepper.

- You'll get even better results if you brine the breasts: Buy chicken breasts that have *not* been injected with "a solution that may contain…." (read the package). Whisk 2 tablespoons kosher salt into 2 quarts (8 cups) cool water until dissolved, then submerge the breasts in the brine for at least 20 minutes but no more than 40 minutes. Discard the brine, pat the breasts dry, then proceed with the recipe.

- Or buy kosher boneless skinless chicken breasts. They're essentially prebrined!

2 cups chicken broth

1 small yellow onion, peeled and halved

1 medium carrot, cut into 2-inch pieces

¼ cup packed fresh parsley leaves

1 teaspoon table salt

1 teaspoon ground black pepper

Four 8- to 12-ounce boneless skinless chicken breasts

½ teaspoon mild paprika

½ teaspoon dried thyme

½ teaspoon garlic powder

½ teaspoon onion powder

Perfect Poached Chicken Breasts

4 servings

Here's another way to keep boneless skinless chicken breasts from becoming chicken splinters: Poach them in an aromatic broth, *then* coat them with a spice mixture while they're warm, so the spices adhere and the flavors have a chance to meld with the natural juices. As in the previous road map recipe, this one requires larger boneless skinless chicken breasts, not the small ones typically sold in bags of individually packaged breasts.

1. Stir the broth, onion, carrot, parsley, ½ teaspoon salt, and ½ teaspoon pepper in a **3, 6-, or 8-quart pot**. Set the chicken breasts in this sauce, then lock the lid onto the pot.

2.

Set the machine for	Set the level for	The valve must be	Set the time for	If necessary, press
PRESSURE COOK	MAX	—	7 minutes with the KEEP WARM setting off	START
MEAT/STEW, PRESSURE COOK, or MANUAL	HIGH	Closed	10 minutes with the KEEP WARM setting off	START

3. Meanwhile, mix the paprika, thyme, garlic powder, onion powder, the remaining ½ teaspoon salt, and the remaining ½ teaspoon ground black pepper in a small bowl until uniform.

4. Use the **quick-release method** to return the pot's pressure to normal. Unlatch the lid and open the cooker. Use kitchen tongs to transfer the chicken breasts to a cutting board; use a fork to pick off any extraneous bits like random parsley leaves. Sprinkle the paprika blend over the hot breasts on all sides and set aside for 5 to 10 minutes. Serve whole or slice at will — or store the chicken breasts, lightly covered on a plate, in the fridge for up to 3 days.

Beyond

- The broth in the pot is culinary gold. Strain it, then save it in the fridge or freezer to add to soups, stews, or braises.

- Like more garlic flavor? Add 2 large peeled garlic cloves to the pot with the onion.

- For the best chicken salad, chop two of the cooled chicken breasts and stir them in a bowl with ½ cup mayonnaise, ½ cup thinly sliced celery, ¼ cup sour cream, 1 tablespoon yellow mustard, and up to ¼ cup minced red onion.

Spicy Apricot Chicken Breasts

6 servings

A final way to keep boneless skinless chicken breasts moist and tender in the Instant Pot is to submerge them in a rich, thick, sugar-laced sauce that can protect them during the pressure siege.

Please note: Unlike the previous two recipes, these chicken breasts here are smaller, the sort usually individually packaged and sold in bags. Smaller, they can cook more quickly with this technique and thus preserve a better texture.

2 tablespoons butter

6 medium scallions, trimmed and thinly sliced

¾ cup chicken broth

⅓ cup apricot jam

2 tablespoons white wine vinegar

1 teaspoon ground dried mustard

Up to ½ teaspoon ground dried cayenne

¼ teaspoon table salt

Six 6- to 8-ounce boneless skinless chicken breasts

1.

Press the button for	Set it for	Set the time for	If necessary, press
SAUTÉ	MEDIUM, NORMAL, or CUSTOM 300°F	5 minutes	START

2. Melt the butter in a **6-quart cooker**. Add the scallions and cook, stirring often, until softened, about 2 minutes. Stir in the broth, jam, vinegar, mustard, cayenne, and salt until the jam melts. Turn off the SAUTÉ function; nestle the chicken breasts into the sauce. Lock the lid onto the pot.

3.

Set the machine for	Set the level for	The valve must be	Set the time for	If necessary, press
PRESSURE COOK	MAX	—	9 minutes with the KEEP WARM setting off	START
MEAT/STEW, PRESSURE COOK, or MANUAL	HIGH	Closed	12 minutes with the KEEP WARM setting off	START

4. Use the **quick-release method** to bring the pot's pressure back to normal. Unlatch the lid and open the pot. Serve the chicken breasts with the sauce ladled on them.

Beyond

- For a **3-quart cooker,** you must use ½ cup broth and halve the remaining ingredients.

- For an **8-quart cooker,** you must increase the broth to 1½ cups and the remaining ingredients by at least 50 percent. (You can also double the remaining ingredients.)

- Serve the breasts and their sauce over brown rice or brown or white rice stick noodles.

- Bulk up the meal by adding up to 2 thinly sliced medium celery ribs (⅔ cup) and/or 4 thinly sliced large radishes (⅔ cup) with the scallions.

- Enrich the sauce by removing the cooked chicken breasts and stirring up to 2 additional tablespoons butter into it before serving.

- The sauce may be too thin for your taste. Thicken it (or even turn it into a glaze) by using the SAUTÉ function set at MEDIUM, NORMAL, or CUSTOM 300°F, stirring quite often, for 3 to 6 minutes.

2 tablespoons olive oil

4 ounces lean ground pork

½ cup skinned hazelnuts, chopped

1 teaspoon ground cinnamon

1 teaspoon ground dried ginger

½ teaspoon table salt

2½ pounds boneless skinless chicken breasts, cut into ½-inch-thick strips

1 cup chicken broth

1 tablespoon honey

Up to ½ teaspoon red pepper flakes

Up to ¼ teaspoon saffron

1 tablespoon fresh lemon juice

Beyond

- You must halve the recipe for a **3-quart cooker**.

- For an **8-quart cooker**, you must increase all the ingredients by 50 percent.

- For a briny take, more reminiscent of authentic Portuguese cooking, add up to 2 minced jarred anchovy fillets with the hazelnuts. Or add one 6½-ounce can chopped clams, drained, with the honey and other spices.

- Increase the braise's flavor by toasting the hazelnuts in a dry skillet or in the Instant Pot with the SAUTÉ function on LOW or LESS until lightly browned in spots, stirring often, about 3 minutes. Cool the nuts, then chop them into smaller bits.

Portuguese-Inspired Chicken Braise with Hazelnuts

6 servings

This recipe's a sweet-and-savory mix, reminiscent of stews served in Portugal (although we've adapted the ingredients for the American supermarket). The dish includes a classic Portuguese combo, ground pork and hazelnuts, plus a little saffron for an earthy flavor. Look for skinned hazelnuts among the bulk nuts (or maybe near the dried fruit).

   Unfortunately, chicken already cut for stir-frying won't work in this recipe because the strips are too thin (and will overcook). Instead, you'll need to slice the breasts into long ½-inch-thick strips. To do so, set them on a cutting board so an axis line drawn from the narrowed end across the length of the breast lies parallel to you. Slice the meat on the diagonal to get the widest strips, particularly from the middle. If the breasts have their tenders attached, remove these and slice them separately.

1.

Press the button for	Set it for	Set the time for	If necessary, press
SAUTÉ	MEDIUM, NORMAL, or CUSTOM 300°F	10 minutes	START

2. Warm the oil in a **6-quart cooker** for a minute or two. Crumble in the ground pork and cook, stirring often to break up any clumps, until lightly browned, about 4 minutes. Add the hazelnuts, cinnamon, ginger, and salt, stirring until fragrant, for about 30 seconds.

3. Add the chicken and stir well until evenly coated. Stir in the broth, turn off the SAUTÉ function, and scrape up any browned bits on the pot's bottom. Stir in the honey, red pepper flakes, and saffron. Lock the lid onto the pot.

4.

Set the machine for	Set the level for	The valve must be	Set the time for	If necessary, press
PRESSURE COOK	MAX	—	3 minutes with the KEEP WARM setting off	START
MEAT/STEW, PRESSURE COOK, or MANUAL	HIGH	Closed	5 minutes with the KEEP WARM setting off	START

5. Use the **quick-release method** to bring the pot's pressure back to normal. Unlatch the lid and open the cooker. Stir in the lemon juice before serving.

Bone-in Chicken Breasts with Mushrooms

4 servings

Even *bone-in* chicken breasts need protection from the pressure, although they do have a natural defense: more fat and cartilage around the bones, especially when the skin is left on the meat. Although this recipe is not a road map, you can customize it by using various dried herb blends. Or mix together two or three dried herbs to make your own blend — like oregano, rosemary, and thyme; or thyme, sage, and allspice. If you use a bottled blend, consider using a salt-free one. Or if there's salt in the mix, omit it from the seasoning for the chicken.

2 tablespoons butter

Four 12-ounce bone-in skin-on chicken breasts, any rib bits or large hunks of fat removed

½ teaspoon table salt (optional)

½ teaspoon ground black pepper

1 large yellow onion, chopped (1½ cups)

8 ounces thinly sliced white button mushrooms

1 tablespoon dried spice blend, such as herbes de Provence, an Italian blend, a Cajun blend, or even Mrs. Dash

1 cup chicken broth

1.

Press the button for	Set it for	Set the time for	If necessary, press
SAUTÉ	MEDIUM, NORMAL, or CUSTOM 300°F	20 minutes	START

2. Melt the butter in a **6-quart cooker**. Season the chicken breasts with the salt (if using) and pepper, then add two of them skin side down to the pot. Brown *well* without turning, about 5 minutes. Transfer the breasts to a nearby bowl and brown the other two in the same way before transferring them to the bowl.

3. Add the onion and cook, stirring occasionally, until softened, about 4 minutes. Add the mushrooms and cook, stirring more often, until they give off their internal liquid and it reduces to a glaze, about 5 minutes.

4. Stir in the spice blend until aromatic, just a few seconds. Pour in the broth, turn off the SAUTÉ function, and scrape up any browned bits on the pot's bottom. Nestle the breasts skin side up in the sauce, overlapping them to fit. Lock the lid onto the cooker.

5.

Set the machine for	Set the level for	The valve must be	Set the time for	If necessary, press
PRESSURE COOK	MAX	—	10 minutes with the KEEP WARM setting off	START
MEAT/STEW, PRESSURE COOK, or MANUAL	HIGH	Closed	14 minutes with the KEEP WARM setting off	START

6. Use the **quick-release method** to bring the pot's pressure back to normal. Unlatch the lid and open the cooker. Use kitchen tongs to transfer the breasts to serving bowls. Spoon the sauce and vegetables over them.

Beyond

- For a **3-quart cooker**, you must use ⅔ cup broth and halve the remaining ingredients.

- For an **8-quart cooker**, you must increase all the ingredients by 50 percent.

- Go nuts and substitute more exotic, fresh mushrooms for the white button mushrooms: porcini, hen of the woods, or shiitake caps, for example. Remember that mushrooms grow in, um, "dirt" and should be washed. Don't use portobello caps or they'll turn the sauce a depressing brown-gray.

- The sauce may be too thin for your taste. (We actually liked this one fairly soupy when we were testing it.) Thicken the sauce after removing the chicken by boiling it on the SAUTÉ function at HIGH or MORE until about half its volume, stirring often, about 3 minutes.

- For a richer dish, add up to ½ cup heavy cream to the sauce before you boil it down.

2 tablespoons olive oil

Four 10- to 12-ounce bone-in skin-on chicken breasts

1 medium yellow onion, chopped (1 cup)

1 medium red bell pepper, stemmed, cored, and cut into thin strips

1 medium green bell pepper, stemmed, cored, and cut into thin strips

1 medium yellow bell pepper, stemmed, cored, and cut into thin strips

3 medium garlic cloves, peeled and minced (1 tablespoon)

1 tablespoon packed fresh rosemary leaves, minced

1 tablespoon packed fresh oregano leaves, minced

1 to 2 jarred anchovy fillets, finely chopped

¼ teaspoon table salt

2 tablespoons balsamic vinegar

1¼ cups chicken broth

Beyond

- You must halve the recipe for a **3-quart cooker**.

- As in other braises, the sauce may be a tad thin for your taste. Once the chicken breasts have been removed, reduce it by using the SAUTÉ function on MEDIUM, NORMAL, or CUSTOM 300°F, stirring often, 3 to 5 minutes.

- This dish needs garlic bread: Split a loaf of Italian bread or a French baguette in half lengthwise. Brush the cut sides with olive oil, then sprinkle them with minced garlic. Sprinkle finely grated Parmigiano-Reggiano over the cut sides, then broil cut side up 4 to 6 inches from the heat source until browned, 1 to 2 minutes.

Sicilian-Style Braised Bone-in Chicken Breasts

4 servings

This supper is packed with Mediterranean flavors. Make it easier by using 3¾ cups frozen multi-colored bell pepper strips (do not thaw) in place of the three fresh bell peppers. Make sure the chicken breasts are well browned. Otherwise, the skin will be squishy after braising. The anchovies add a bit of umami flavor to the sauce. No one will know they're there. They'll just remark on how savory the dish is.

1.

Press the button for	Set it for	Set the time for	If necessary, press
SAUTÉ	MEDIUM, NORMAL, or CUSTOM 300°F	15 minutes	START

2. Warm the oil for a minute or two in a **6- or 8-quart cooker**. Add two of the chicken breasts skin side down and brown *well* without turning, about 5 minutes. Transfer the breasts to a bowl and brown the other two in the same way before transferring them to the bowl.

3. Add the onion and all the bell pepper strips. Cook, stirring occasionally, until softened, about 4 minutes. Stir in the garlic, rosemary, oregano, anchovies (if using), and salt until aromatic, just a few seconds.

4. Pour in the vinegar and scrape up any browned bits on the pot's bottom. Turn off the SAUTÉ function. Pour in the broth and stir well. Nestle the chicken breasts skin side up in the sauce; drizzle any juice from their bowl over them. Lock the lid onto the pot.

5.

Set the machine for	Set the level for	The valve must be	Set the time for	If necessary, press
PRESSURE COOK	MAX	—	13 minutes with the KEEP WARM setting off	START
MEAT/STEW, PRESSURE COOK, or MANUAL	HIGH	Closed	16 minutes with the KEEP WARM setting off	START

6. Use the **quick-release method** to bring the pot's pressure back to normal. Unlatch the lid and open the pot. Transfer the chicken breasts to serving plates or a serving platter. Spoon some of the sauce over them before serving.

Chicken Bulgogi

4 servings

Bulgogi is a traditional Korean dish that starts as a braise (as here) but ends up as a skillet fry-up (see the *Beyond*). It's absurdly aromatic, although we've simplified it a bit for the American supermarket (again, see the *Beyond* to go over the top).

This dish is a sweet and spicy mix that should be served alongside cooked long-grain white rice and lots of kimchi.

1. Mix the onion, garlic, broth, cider, soy sauce, sesame oil, brown sugar, ginger, and chile paste in a **3- or 6-quart cooker** until the brown sugar dissolves. Stir the chicken into the sauce and lock the lid onto the pot.

2.

Set the machine for	Set the level for	The valve must be	Set the time for	If necessary, press
PRESSURE COOK	MAX	—	10 minutes with the KEEP WARM setting off	START
MEAT/STEW, PRESSURE COOK, or MANUAL	HIGH	Closed	12 minutes with the KEEP WARM setting off	START

3. Use the **quick-release method** to bring the pot's pressure back to normal. Unlatch the lid and open the pot. Spoon the chicken and sauce into bowls; top with the scallions and sesame seeds.

1 medium yellow onion, halved and sliced into thin half-moons

3 medium garlic cloves, peeled and minced (1 tablespoon)

¾ cup chicken broth

¼ cup unsweetened apple cider

3 tablespoons soy sauce

2 teaspoons toasted sesame oil

2 tablespoons light brown sugar

1 tablespoon minced peeled fresh ginger

1 tablespoon red chile paste, such as sambal oelek

1¾ pounds boneless skinless chicken thighs (6 to 8 thighs), any hunks of fat removed, the meat halved

Up to 4 medium scallions, trimmed and thinly sliced

2 teaspoons white sesame seeds

Beyond

- For an **8-quart cooker**, you must increase all the ingredients by 50 percent.
- Serve in lettuce wraps, particularly leaves of Boston lettuce.
- For a more traditional flavor, substitute *ssamjang*, a Korean chile paste, for the red chile paste.
- For a more traditional preparation, use kitchen tongs to remove the pieces of cooked chicken from the sauce. Use the SAUTÉ function on MEDIUM, NORMAL, or CUSTOM 300°F to boil the sauce almost to a glaze, stirring quite often, 6 to 8 minutes. Meanwhile, set a large, well-seasoned cast-iron skillet over medium-high heat until smoking. When the sauce is done, turn off the SAUTÉ function and remove the *hot* insert from the pot. Crisp the chicken pieces in the very hot skillet in batches, turning once, until charred in places, about 3 minutes per batch; then toss these with the glaze-sauce and serve with the scallions and sesame seeds as a garnish.

See photo in insert.

4 ounces thin strips of bacon, chopped

Four 10- to 12-ounce bone-in *skinless* chicken thighs

1 medium yellow onion, chopped (1 cup)

1 medium green bell pepper, stemmed, cored, and chopped (1 cup)

1 medium red bell pepper, stemmed, cored, and chopped (1 cup)

1 teaspoon Dijon mustard

½ teaspoon dried thyme

½ teaspoon caraway seeds

½ teaspoon celery seeds

½ teaspoon table salt

½ teaspoon ground black pepper

½ cup dry white wine, such as Chardonnay; or unsweetened apple cider

½ cup chicken broth

3 medium sweet potatoes (about 2 pounds), peeled and quartered lengthwise into wedges

Southern-Style Braised Bone-in Chicken Thighs

4 servings

Sweet potatoes, bacon, chicken — it doesn't get much more down-home than this recipe. Because of the long time the thighs cook, they must be skinless for this braise. (The skin would otherwise become too rubbery.) To remove the skin, grasp one "corner" at a thigh's smaller end with a paper towel, then pull the skin off the meat, holding onto the skin with the paper towel. (The skin can easily slip out of a bare hand.)

1.

Press the button for	Set it for	Set the time for	If necessary, press
SAUTÉ	MEDIUM, NORMAL, or CUSTOM 300°F	25 minutes	START

2. Cook the bacon in a **6-quart cooker** until crisp, stirring occasionally, about 4 minutes. Use a slotted spoon to transfer the bacon pieces to a nearby bowl. Add two of the thighs and brown *well* on both sides, turning a couple of times, about 6 minutes. Transfer these thighs to a bowl, add the other two, and brown them in the same way before transferring them to that bowl.

3. Add the onion and both bell peppers. Cook, stirring occasionally, until softened, about 4 minutes. Stir in the mustard, thyme, caraway seeds, celery seeds, salt, and pepper until aromatic, just a few seconds. Pour in the wine and scrape up any browned bits on the pot's bottom.

4. Turn off the SAUTÉ function. Pour in the broth and stir well. Return the chicken thighs and any juices in their bowl to the pot. Scatter the sweet potatoes pieces on top of everything. Lock the lid onto the cooker.

5.

Set the machine for	Set the level for	The valve must be	Set the time for	If necessary, press
PRESSURE COOK	MAX	—	13 minutes with the KEEP WARM setting off	START
MEAT/STEW, PRESSURE COOK, or MANUAL	HIGH	Closed	16 minutes with the KEEP WARM setting off	START
SLOW COOK	HIGH	Opened	4 hours with the KEEP WARM setting off (or on for no more than 2 hours)	START

6. If you've used a pressure setting, when the pot has finished cooking, use the **quick-release method** to bring its pressure back to normal.

7. Unlatch the lid and open the cooker. Use kitchen tongs to transfer the thighs and sweet potato pieces to serving plates or a serving platter. Use a flatware tablespoon to skim any excess surface fat from the sauce.

8.

Press the button for	Set it for	Set the time for	If necessary, press
SAUTÉ	HIGH or MORE	10 minutes	START

9. Bring the sauce to a boil and cook, stirring quite often, until reduced to about half its volume, 2 to 4 minutes. Turn off the SAUTÉ function. Spoon this sauce over the chicken and sweet potatoes before serving.

Beyond

- You must halve the recipe for a **3-quart cooker**.
- For an **8-quart cooker**, you must increase all the ingredients by 50 percent.
- Stir up to 1 cup drained and rinsed canned black-eyed peas, drained and rinsed canned hominy, and/or frozen sliced okra (do not thaw) into the sauce before you return the chicken to the cooker.
- Serve garnished with corn relish or chowchow.
- Although we suggest boiling down the sauce, you can skip that step—but the dish should then be served in bowls.
- For a cleaner flavor (without the smoky taste), substitute diced pancetta for the bacon.

2 tablespoons olive oil

Six 10- to 12-ounce bone-in skin-on chicken thighs

1 teaspoon table salt

½ teaspoon ground black pepper

1 large red onion, chopped (1½ cups)

2 tablespoons minced peeled fresh ginger

1 cup unsalted almonds, chopped

¼ cup loosely packed fresh cilantro leaves

1 tablespoon mild paprika

1 teaspoon ground coriander

1¼ cups chicken broth

Braised Chicken with Ginger and Almonds

6 servings

This braise is truly comforting, particularly for someone under the weather. The flavor profile is somewhat Middle Eastern — although the cilantro adds a grassy base to the sauce and the ginger gives it a peppery hit. Okay, it's hard to categorize the flavors, other than to say that they'd be welcome over No-Drain Mashed Potatoes (page 424), cooked and drained Israeli couscous, or medium-grain white or brown Arborio rice.

1.

Press the button for	Set it for	Set the time for	If necessary, press
SAUTÉ	MEDIUM, NORMAL, or CUSTOM 300°F	15 minutes	START

2. Warm the oil for 1 or 2 minutes in a **6- or 8-quart cooker**. Season the chicken pieces with the salt and pepper, then add about half of them skin side down to the pot and brown *well* without turning, about 4 minutes. Transfer these pieces to a nearby bowl and continue browning the remainder before transferring them to the bowl.

3. Add the onion and cook, stirring occasionally, until softened, about 4 minutes. Stir in the ginger and cook, stirring often, for 1 minute. Stir in the almonds, cilantro, paprika, and coriander until fragrant, just a few seconds.

4. Pour in the broth, turn off the SAUTÉ function, and scrape up any browned bits on the pot's bottom. Return the chicken pieces to the pot, overlapping them so that they mostly fit in the sauce. Pour any juices in their bowl over them, then lock the lid onto the cooker.

5.

Set the machine for	Set the level for	The valve must be	Set the time for	If necessary, press
PRESSURE COOK	MAX	—	13 minutes with the KEEP WARM setting off	START
MEAT/STEW, PRESSURE COOK, or MANUAL	HIGH	Closed	16 minutes with the KEEP WARM setting off	START
SLOW COOK	HIGH	Opened	4 hours with the KEEP WARM setting off (or on for no more than 2 hours)	START

5. If you've used a pressure setting, when the machine has finished cooking, use the **quick-release method** to bring the pot's pressure back to normal.

6. Unlatch the lid and open the cooker. Transfer the chicken to individual bowls or a large serving bowl. Use a flatware tablespoon to skim any excess surface fat from the sauce. Serve the chicken with lots of the sauce ladled around it.

Beyond

- You must halve the recipe for a **3-quart cooker.**

- Dollop the servings with plain Greek yogurt, garnish with a little minced red onion as desired, and offer pita bread alongside.

- For a more aromatic dish, substitute mild smoked paprika for the regular mild paprika.

- For an even more aromatic dish, toast whole almonds in a dry skillet set over low heat or in the pot with the SAUTÉ function on LOW or LESS until lightly browned and very aromatic, about 4 minutes. Cool before chopping the almonds into smaller bits.

4 tablespoons (½ stick) butter,
   2 tablespoons melted and cooled

1 small yellow onion, chopped
   (½ cup)

2 medium celery stalks, thinly sliced
   (⅔ cup)

1½ pounds ground chicken breast

1 teaspoon dried sage

1 teaspoon dried thyme

½ teaspoon ground black pepper

¼ teaspoon celery seeds (optional)

2 cups chicken broth

¾ cup frozen peas (do not thaw)

2 tablespoons Worcestershire sauce

1 tablespoon Dijon mustard

1 cup all-purpose flour

2 teaspoons baking powder

½ teaspoon table salt

½ cup regular buttermilk

½ teaspoon mild paprika

Chicken Stew with Buttermilk Dumplings

4 servings

Rather than using cut-up chicken (that would need to be browned, cooked, and taken off the bone), we simplified this recipe dramatically with ground chicken — which can dry out a bit under pressure. To compensate, we've upped the broth to make sure that the stew is moist, even a little soupy, although it will continue to reduce a bit as the dumplings cook at the end.

The second time the lid goes on the pot is for the SLOW COOK setting. If your cooker can only be set for 30 minutes at the lowest, or even 1 hour, you'll need to set a more run-of-the-mill timer for 20 minutes and stop the machine's cooking at that point.

1.

Press the button for	Set it for	Set the time for	If necessary, press
SAUTÉ	MEDIUM, NORMAL, or CUSTOM 300°F	10 minutes	START

2. Melt 2 tablespoons of the butter in a **6- or 8-quart cooker**. Add the onion and celery; cook, stirring occasionally, until the onion softens, about 3 minutes. Crumble in the ground chicken and continue cooking, stirring occasionally to break up any clumps, until the meat loses its raw, pink color, about 3 minutes.

3. Stir in the sage, thyme, black pepper, and celery seeds (if using) until aromatic, just a few seconds. Turn off the SAUTÉ function and stir in the broth, peas, Worcestershire sauce, and mustard until uniform. Lock the lid onto the pot.

4.

Set the machine for	Set the level for	The valve must be	Set the time for	If necessary, press
PRESSURE COOK	MAX	—	3 minutes with the KEEP WARM setting off	START
MEAT/STEW, PRESSURE COOK, or MANUAL	HIGH	Closed	5 minutes with the KEEP WARM setting off	START

5. As the stew cooks, whisk the flour, baking powder, and salt in a large bowl. Stir in the buttermilk and 2 tablespoons of melted and cooled butter until a wet dough forms.

6. When the stew has finished cooking, use the **quick-release method** to bring the pot's pressure back to normal. Unlatch the lid and open the cooker. Drop the dough in 6 even blobs across its surface. Sprinkle them with the paprika. Latch the lid onto the pot.

7.

Set the machine for	Set the level for	The valve must be	Set the time for	If necessary, press
SLOW COOK	HIGH	Opened	20 minutes with the KEEP WARM setting off	START

8. Turn off the SLOW COOK function, unlatch the lid, and open the pot. Set aside to cool for a few minutes, then serve by the big spoonful in bowls.

Beyond

- You must halve the recipe for a **3-quart cooker.**

- If you have an **8-quart pot** and want to make 6 servings, you *can* increase all the ingredients by 50 percent.

- For plain dumplings, swap out these for those with the beef stew on page 345.

- Omit the dumplings entirely and use pizza dough: Buy a ½ pound of fresh dough (not canned but fresh, usually in the refrigerator case — or right from a pizza shop). Divide the dough into 6 balls, drop them into the stew, sprinkle them with paprika, and cook the SLOW COOK function, covered and with the pressure valve open, until done, about 20 minutes.

- Or skip dumplings of any sort and simply serve the stew over Buttery Noodles (page 155).

2 tablespoons olive oil

Six 10- to 12-ounce bone-in skin-on chicken thighs

1 cup frozen pearl onions (do not thaw)

2 medium garlic cloves, peeled and minced (2 teaspoons)

½ teaspoon red pepper flakes

One 28-ounce can diced tomatoes (3½ cups)

⅔ cup pitted black olives

½ cup dry red wine, such as Cabernet Sauvignon; or chicken broth

2 teaspoons dried basil

2 teaspoons dried oregano

Chicken Cacciatore

6 servings

Cacciatore is a simple braise, a "hunter's stew" (or really, a "hunter's wife's stew," given how the name works out in its Italian dialect). We nixed any game meats (a traditional ingredient) and used *bone-in, skin-on* chicken thighs to enrich the sauce considerably. For the best success, look for oil- or brine-cured black olives on the salad bar at your supermarket, much better tasting than canned olives.

1.

Press the button for	Set it for	Set the time for	If necessary, press
SAUTÉ	MEDIUM, NORMAL, or CUSTOM 300°F	20 minutes	START

2. Warm the oil in a **6- or 8-quart cooker** for 1 to 2 minutes. Add three of the chicken thighs skin side down and brown *well* without turning, about 5 minutes. Transfer these to a nearby bowl and brown the remainder of the chicken thighs in the same way before transferring them to the bowl.

3. Add the pearl onions; cook, stirring occasionally, until lightly browned in spots, about 4 minutes. Stir in the garlic and red pepper flakes until aromatic, just a few seconds. Pour in the tomatoes and scrape up any browned bits on the pot's bottom.

4. Turn off the SAUTÉ function. Stir in the olives, wine or broth, basil, and oregano. Nestle the thighs skin side up in the pot, overlapping them to fit in the sauce. Pour any juices in their bowl over them and lock the lid onto the pot.

5.

Set the machine for	Set the level for	The valve must be	Set the time for	If necessary, press
PRESSURE COOK	MAX	—	13 minutes with the KEEP WARM setting off	START
MEAT/STEW, PRESSURE COOK, or MANUAL	HIGH	Closed	16 minutes with the KEEP WARM setting off	START

6. Use the **quick-release method** to bring the pot's pressure back to normal. Unlatch the lid and open the cooker. Use a large, slotted spoon to transfer the thighs to a large serving bowl or individual bowls; also scoop out and sprinkle the onions and olives over the chicken.

7.

Press the button for	Set it for	Set the time for	If necessary, press
SAUTÉ	MEDIUM, NORMAL, or CUSTOM 300°F	10 minutes	START

8. Bring the sauce to a full simmer; then cook, stirring often, until reduced to a wet pasta sauce rather than a soupy sauce, about 5 minutes. Turn off the SAUTÉ function and pour the sauce over the chicken.

Beyond

- You must halve the recipe for a **3-quart cooker.**

- Before browning the chicken, add up to 4 ounces diced pancetta to the pot and fry until crisp, stirring often, about 6 minutes. Use a slotted spoon to transfer these bits to a bowl before browning the chicken as directed.

- Add up to 1 cup chopped, trimmed fennel and/or ½ cup chopped carrots with the pearl onions.

- Serve the braise over Polenta (page 443).

16 dried chiles, preferably a blend of New Mexico red chiles and ancho chiles, stemmed and seeded

4 large garlic cloves, peeled

3 cups chicken broth

¼ cup sliced almonds

¼ cup raisins

½ teaspoon cumin seeds

½ teaspoon ground cloves

3 pounds chicken tenders

Chicken Mole Rojo

6 servings

Mole rojo ("red sauce" in Spanish, *MOH-lay ROH-hoh*), is a classic chile sauce — with as many variations as there are cooks in Oaxaca. Most pressure cooker versions call for the chicken to be shredded into the sauce after cooking because the meat inevitably gets overcooked and ends up none too appealing. Our version asks you to make a sauce first, puree it, and then quickly cook chicken tenders in it for much more flavor and a better texture in the meat. Call it "spicy bliss."

Note that the recipe only uses HIGH pressure (not MAX) on the first cooking — so that the chiles and raisins don't get too mushy before you add the chicken tenders. For more information about selecting, buying, and using dried chiles, see page 111.

1. Stir the chiles, garlic, broth, almonds, raisins, cumin, and cloves in a **6- or 8-quart cooker**. Lock the lid onto the pot.

2.

Set the machine for	Set the level for	The valve must be	Set the time for	If necessary, press
PRESSURE COOK or MANUAL	HIGH	Closed	4 minutes with the KEEP WARM setting off	START

3. Use the **quick-release method** to bring the pot's pressure back to normal. Unlatch the lid and open the cooker. Use an immersion blender to puree the ingredients in the pot. Or puree the contents of the pot in a covered blender with the lid's center knob removed and a clean kitchen towel placed over the opening. Pour the sauce back into the pot.

4. Add the chicken tenders and stir until they are evenly and thoroughly coated in the sauce. Lock the lid back onto the pot.

5.

Set the machine for	Set the level for	The valve must be	Set the time for	If necessary, press
PRESSURE COOK	MAX	—	4 minutes with the KEEP WARM setting off	START
MEAT/STEW, PRESSURE COOK, or MANUAL	HIGH	Closed	6 minutes with the KEEP WARM setting off	START

6. When the machine has finished cooking, turn it off and let its pressure **return to normal naturally**, about 15 minutes. Unlatch the lid and open the cooker. Use kitchen tongs to remove the tender from the sauce to serve.

Beyond

- You must halve the recipe for a **3-quart cooker**.

- Serve the meat in corn or flour tortillas filled with sliced avocado, sliced radishes, thinly sliced scallions, fresh cilantro leaves, regular or low-fat sour cream, shredded Jack cheese, and/or purchased pico de gallo.

- For a smoky flavor, substitute dried chipotles for up to two of the chiles.

- Substitute 3 pounds pork tenderloin, cut into 2-inch pieces, for the chicken.

- Or substitute 3 pounds turkey breast cutlets, each cut into 3 pieces.

- Or skip the tortillas and serve the chicken and the sauce over Black Beans and Rice (page 403).

Chicken Mole Verde

6 servings

As its name indicates, mole verde is a green sauce, made with *fresh* tomatillos and *fresh* chiles. We've calmed down the fire in this version, although you can bump it up by keeping the seeds in the jalapeño (or even adding another one for good measure). The flavors here are tart and bright, better as a summertime braise than winter comfort food.

1. Mix the broth, tomatillos, cilantro, pepitas, jalapeño, garlic, cumin, and salt in a **6-quart cooker**. Nestle the chicken pieces into the sauce, overlapping them as necessary. Lock the lid onto the cooker.

2.

Set the machine for	Set the level for	The valve must be	Set the time for	If necessary, press
PRESSURE COOK	MAX	—	13 minutes with the KEEP WARM setting off	START
MEAT/STEW, PRESSURE COOK, or MANUAL	HIGH	Closed	16 minutes with the KEEP WARM setting off	START
SLOW COOK	HIGH	Opened	4 hours with the KEEP WARM setting off (or on for no more than 2 hours)	START

3. If you've used a pressure setting, when the machine has finished cooking, turn it off and lets its pressure **return to normal naturally,** about 25 minutes.

4. Unlatch and open the lid. Use kitchen tongs to transfer the chicken pieces to a cutting board. Use an immersion blender right in the pot to puree the ingredients into a sauce. Or puree the contents of the pot in a covered blender with the center knob removed from the lid and a clean kitchen towel placed over the opening. Pour the sauce back into the pot.

5.

Press the button for	Set it for	Set the time for	If necessary, press
SAUTÉ	MEDIUM, NORMAL, or CUSTOM 300°F	15 minutes	START

6. Bring the sauce to a simmer; then cook, stirring quite often, until reduced to the consistency of marinara, 8 to 10 minutes. Return the chicken pieces to the pot, stir well, and cook for 1 minute. Turn off the SAUTÉ function, remove the *hot* insert from the pot, and set the lid askew over the insert for 5 minutes to blend the flavors.

1 cup chicken broth

8 ounces fresh tomatillos, husked and chopped

½ cup loosely packed fresh cilantro leaves, chopped

¼ cup pepitas (that is, green pumpkin seeds)

1 medium fresh jalapeño chile, stemmed, halved lengthwise, seeded (if desired), and thinly sliced

2 medium garlic cloves, peeled and minced (2 teaspoons)

1 teaspoon ground cumin

1 teaspoon table salt

Six 10- to 12-ounce skin-off, bone-in chicken thighs (see page 241 for instructions for removing the skin)

Beyond

- You must halve the recipe for a **3-quart cooker**.

- For an **8-quart cooker**, you must increase the broth to 1½ cups, but otherwise use the ingredient list as stated. The sauce will need another 3 to 4 minutes to boil down at the end.

- Once the chicken is returned to the reduced sauce and cooks for 1 minute, pour the contents of the insert into a 9 x 13-inch broiler-safe baking dish. Cover with 8 ounces shredded Cheddar, Monterey Jack, or a Tex-Mex blend (2 cups) and broil 4 to 6 inches from the heat source until the cheese melts, about 1 minute.

2 tablespoons vegetable, corn, or canola oil

Six 10- to 12-ounce bone-in skin-on chicken thighs

1 large yellow onion, chopped (1½ cups)

⅔ cup chicken broth

¼ cup apple cider vinegar

¼ cup soy sauce

2 tablespoons granulated white sugar

2 tablespoons sauce from a can of chipotle chiles in adobo sauce (optional)

6 medium garlic cloves, peeled and minced (2 tablespoons)

2 teaspoons mild paprika

2 teaspoons ground black pepper

2 bay leaves

Beyond

- You must halve the recipe for a 3-quart cooker.

- For a more traditional, thicker sauce, use kitchen tongs to transfer the cooked thighs to a cutting board. Strain the sauce through a fine-mesh sieve like a *chinois* (or a colander lined with a double thickness of cheesecloth), then discard the solids and return the sauce to the pot. Use the SAUTÉ function on MEDIUM, NORMAL, or CUSTOM 300°F to bring the sauce to a boil; then simmer, stirring quite often, until the sauce has reduced to two-thirds of its volume, about 5 minutes. Pour this sauce over the chicken before serving.

- Substitute six 10- to 12-ounce center-cut boneless pork loin chops for the chicken thighs. They'll brown much more quickly than the chicken skin.

- In true Filipino style, serve the meat and sauce over French fries, even frozen fries you've baked up.

Chicken Adobo

6 servings

Adobo is a traditional Filipino sauce, familiar to most North Americans from those cans of chipotles packed in adobo sauce (which get a lot of play in this book). Adobo sauce is a sweet and vinegary concoction. Rather than using the canned version, this recipe lets you create your own. Yes, for a little more body we suggest adding a little sauce from the can of chipotles in adobo to fill out our simplified sauce. (Maybe you've got some of the canned stuff saved back in the fridge after making another recipe in this book?) That canned sauce will add some extra spices we don't call for. But in truth, if you don't add it, the pot's sauce will be a little brighter in its flavors. If you want to make the sauce spicier, stem and chop one of the chipotles from that can and add it to the sauce with the other ingredients.

The pot's sauce will be a tad soupy. In recipe-testing, we liked this wetter sauce on long-grain, white rice.

1.

Press the button for	Set it for	Set the time for	If necessary, press
SAUTÉ	MEDIUM, NORMAL, or CUSTOM 300°F	20 minutes	START

2. Warm the oil in a **6- or 8-quart cooker** for a minute or two. Add half the chicken thighs skin side down and brown well without turning, about 5 minutes. Transfer the thighs to a nearby bowl and brown the remaining thighs in the same way before transferring to the bowl.

3. Add the onion and cook, stirring often, until softened, about 5 minutes. Pour in the broth and scrape up any browned bits on the pot's bottom. Turn off the SAUTÉ function and stir in the vinegar, soy sauce, sugar, adobo sauce (if using), garlic, paprika, pepper, and bay leaves.

4. Return the thighs skin side up to the pot, overlapping them to fit in the sauce. Add any juice from their bowl and lock the lid onto the cooker.

5.

Set the machine for	Set the level for	The valve must be	Set the time for	If necessary, press
PRESSURE COOK	MAX	—	13 minutes with the KEEP WARM setting off	START
MEAT/STEW, PRESSURE COOK, or MANUAL	HIGH	Closed	16 minutes with the KEEP WARM setting off	START

6. When the machine has finished cooking, turn it off and let its pressure **return to normal naturally**, about 20 minutes. Unlatch the lid and open the pot. Serve the chicken and sauce in bowls.

Turkey Burger Stew

6 servings

A ground turkey mixture is dropped into this stew in small bits (don't get OCD on their size, just small) so that they end up mimicking little bites of turkey burger in the tomato-laced stew. The croutons even stand in for the buns. You can buy boxed croutons or look for better ones in the bakery section of most supermarkets. Or make your own (page 345).

1. Mix the turkey, egg white, mustard, sage, salt, and pepper in a medium bowl until uniform. Set aside.

2.

Press the button for	Set it for	Set the time for	If necessary, press
SAUTÉ	MEDIUM, NORMAL, or CUSTOM 300°F	10 minutes	START

3. Melt the butter in a **6- or 8-quart cooker.** Add the onion and carrot. Cook, stirring often, until the onion softens, about 3 minutes. Add the mushrooms and cook, stirring more often, until they release their internal moisture and it thickens into a sauce, about 5 minutes. Stir in the garlic, thyme, and celery seeds until aromatic, just a few seconds.

4. Pour in the broth, scrape the browned bits off the pot's bottom, and turn off the SAUTÉ function. Stir in the tomatoes and tomato paste. Drop the ground turkey mixture in heaping teaspoonfuls into the stew. Stir very gently to keep from breaking them up, then lock the lid onto the pot.

5.

Set the machine for	Set the level for	The valve must be	Set the time for	If necessary, press
PRESSURE COOK	MAX	—	8 minutes with the KEEP WARM setting off	START
MEAT/STEW, PRESSURE COOK, or MANUAL	HIGH	Closed	10 minutes with the KEEP WARM setting off	START

6. Use the **quick-release method** to bring the pot's pressure back to normal. Unlatch the lid and open the pot. Stir gently. Serve in bowls with the croutons sprinkled on top.

1½ pounds lean ground turkey

1 large egg white

2 tablespoons Dijon mustard

2 teaspoons dried sage

½ teaspoon table salt

½ teaspoon ground black pepper

3 tablespoons butter

1 medium yellow onion, chopped (1 cup)

2 medium carrots, thinly sliced (1 cup)

8 ounces thinly sliced white button mushrooms

2 medium garlic cloves, peeled and minced (2 teaspoons)

1 teaspoon dried thyme

½ teaspoon celery seeds

1 quart (4 cups) chicken broth

One 14-ounce can diced tomatoes (1¾ cups)

1 tablespoon tomato paste

2 cups purchased plain croutons

Beyond

- You must halve the recipe for a **3-quart cooker.**

- To add greens (and more heft), stir 2 cups washed, stemmed, and chopped spinach leaves into the stew after opening it in step 5. Use the SAUTÉ function at MEDIUM, NORMAL, or CUSTOM 300°F to simmer the sauce until the spinach wilts, about 2 minutes.

- Sprinkle the servings with shredded Monterey Jack or pepper Jack cheese.

1 large jarred roasted red bell pepper

6 sun-dried tomatoes packed in oil

¼ cup dry but light red wine, such as Pinot Noir

1 tablespoon mild paprika

½ teaspoon ground cinnamon

½ teaspoon table salt

¼ teaspoon red pepper flakes

2 tablespoons butter

1 pound lean ground turkey

One 15-ounce can black-eyed peas, drained and rinsed (1½ cups)

One 14-ounce can diced tomatoes (1¾ cups)

½ cup chicken broth

2 tablespoons loosely packed fresh dill fronds, finely chopped

Beyond

- For an **8-quart cooker**, you must increase all the ingredients by 50 percent.

- To omit the wine, use chicken broth in its place but add 1 to 2 tablespoons unsweetened apple cider with the broth in step 4.

- Add greens for a bigger meal: After cooking, stir 1 cup chopped stemmed chard into a **3-quart cooker**, 2 cups chopped stemmed chard into a **6-quart cooker**, or 2½ cups chopped stemmed chard into an **8-quart cooker**. Set the lid over the pot and set aside for 5 minutes to wilt the greens.

Ground Turkey Stew with Black-Eyed Peas

4 servings

As a base for this simple stew, you'll first make a tasty condiment for the braising medium with jarred roasted red peppers, a concoction that's also a thickener as the stew cooks. Although final dish is a little saucy, we didn't feel the need to boil it down.

When you buy ground turkey, the package will say what you're getting: ground turkey breast, ground white meat turkey (usually with no skin and cartilage in the mix), or just ground turkey (which is about everything on the bird and so much fattier). We recommend only the first two in that list for a pressure or slow cooker since the rendered fat has no place to go except right in the sauce.

1. Put the roasted pepper, sun-dried tomatoes, wine, paprika, cinnamon, salt, and red pepper flakes in a food processor. Cover and pulse to create a coarse but thin sauce, stopping the machine at least once to scrape down the inside.

2.

Press the button for	Set it for	Set the time for	If necessary, press
SAUTÉ	MEDIUM, NORMAL, or CUSTOM 300°F	10 minutes	START

3. Melt the butter in a **3- or 6-quart cooker**. Crumble in the ground turkey and cook, stirring often to break up any clumps, until lightly browned, about 4 minutes. Scrape every bit of the red pepper paste into the cooker and cook, stirring all the while, for 1 minute.

4. Turn off the sauté function. Stir in the black-eyed peas, tomatoes, broth, and dill until uniform. Lock the lid onto the pot.

5.

Set the machine for	Set the level for	The valve must be	Set the time for	If necessary, press
PRESSURE COOK	MAX	—	3 minutes with the KEEP WARM setting off	START
MEAT/STEW, PRESSURE COOK, or MANUAL	HIGH	Closed	5 minutes with the KEEP WARM setting off	START

6. Use the **quick-release method** to bring the pot's pressure back to normal. Unlatch the lid and open the cooker. Stir well before serving.

Turkey Meatballs in a Lemony Sauce

4 to 6 servings

This braise is a Greek diner version of meatballs, served in a rich, lemony sauce thickened with eggs, maybe like a meatball version of avgolemono. (Check out our recipe for that soup on page 73.)

Whisk constantly and efficiently after the egg mixture goes into the pot. The sauce should never come back to a simmer or the eggs can scramble. Have your wits about you.

1. Mix the turkey, parsley, couscous, 1 egg, garlic, vinegar, onion powder, dill, oregano, salt, and pepper in a large bowl until uniform. Form this mixture into 16 balls using a scant ¼ cup of the mixture for each.

2. Pour the broth into a **6- or 8-quart cooker**. Put the meatballs in the pot in as even a layer (or two) as possible. Lock the lid onto the pot.

3.

Set the machine for	Set the level for	The valve must be	Set the time for	If necessary, press
PRESSURE COOK	MAX	—	2 minutes with the KEEP WARM setting off	START
MEAT/STEW, PRESSURE COOK, or MANUAL	HIGH	Closed	5 minutes with the KEEP WARM setting off	START

4. Use the **quick-release method** to bring the pot's pressure back to normal. Unlatch the lid and open the cooker. Use a slotted spoon to transfer the meatballs to a large bowl. (Be careful: they're fragile.)

5.

Press the button for	Set it for	Set the time for	If necessary, press
SAUTÉ	LOW or LESS	5 minutes	START

6. Bring the sauce in the cooker to a simmer. Meanwhile, whisk the lemon juice and cornstarch in a medium bowl until smooth. Whisk the remaining 3 eggs into this lemon juice mixture, then whisk about 1 cup of the sauce from the cooker into this mixture. Whisk this combined mixture into the sauce in the pot, whisking just until thickened, *not* returned to a boil. Immediately turn off the SAUTÉ function and remove the *hot* insert from the pot. Whisk a few more times, then return the meatballs to the sauce, tossing gently to coat them. Serve hot.

1½ pounds lean ground turkey

½ cup loosely packed fresh parsley leaves, finely chopped

½ cup instant couscous

4 large eggs

2 medium garlic cloves, peeled and minced (2 teaspoons)

3 tablespoons white wine vinegar

1 teaspoon onion powder

1 teaspoon dried dill

1 teaspoon dried oregano

1 teaspoon table salt

½ teaspoon ground black pepper

3 cups chicken broth

¼ cup fresh lemon juice

1½ tablespoons all-purpose flour

Beyond

- You must halve the recipe for a **3-quart cooker**.

- To pair this with a classic Greek diner salad, start with chopped iceberg lettuce, then add chopped cucumbers, sliced pitted black olives, and thinly sliced red onion. Add olive oil and red wine vinegar in a 4-to-1 oil to vinegar ratio; season the salad with dried oregano, table salt, and ground black pepper. Toss well and crumble feta over the top of each serving.

2 tablespoons olive oil

Two 1½- to 2-pound Cornish game hens, giblets and necks removed, each halved lengthwise

1 large leek (about 6 ounces), white and pale green parts only, halved lengthwise, well washed, and thinly sliced (½ cup)

1½ cups chicken broth

1 small lemon, scrubbed to remove any waxy coating, then halved and sliced into thin half-moons, any seeds removed

1 tablespoon honey

1 tablespoon stemmed fresh thyme leaves

1 teaspoon salt-free lemon pepper seasoning

1 teaspoon table salt

Beyond

- You must halve the recipe for a **3-quart cooker**.

- For a more classic sauce, remove the cooked game hens from the pot. Scoop out all the lemon pieces, too, reserving them as a garnish. Bring the remaining sauce in the pot to a simmer using the SAUTÉ function at MEDIUM, NORMAL, or CUSTOM 300°F. Cook, stirring often, until somewhat reduced, about 3 minutes. Turn off the SAUTÉ function and whisk in up to ¼ cup (½ stick) butter. Spoon this sauce over the birds, then top with some of the lemon bits.

- For a little heat, add up to ½ teaspoon red pepper flakes with the thyme.

Poached Game Hens in a Lemon-Thyme Sauce

4 servings

Although roasting game hens gives them a crisp skin, the birds can also be poached, particularly if the sauce is assertive enough to stand up to their slightly more aggressive flavor. Here, little bits of lemon will soften under pressure, a great match to the meat. Although we suggest removing the necks and giblets, you can certainly add the necks to the pot, even if you don't intend to eat them, mostly to give the sauce a more assertive "poultry" flavor. In fact, you can even chop up the hearts and gizzards, if available, and add them to the pot. (Leave out the liver.)

1.

Press the button for	Set it for	Set the time for	If necessary, press
SAUTÉ	MEDIUM, NORMAL, or CUSTOM 300°F	15 minutes	START

2. Warm the oil in a **6- or 8-quart cooker** for a minute or two. Add the two halves of one bird skin side down and brown *well* without turning, about 5 minutes. Transfer the halves to a bowl and brown the remaining halves in the same way before transferring them to that bowl.

3. Add the leek and cook, stirring often, until softened, about 3 minutes. Stir in the broth and scrape up any browned bits on the pot's bottom. Turn off the SAUTÉ function and mix in the lemon slices, honey, thyme, lemon pepper seasoning, and salt. Nestle the birds skin side up in the sauce, overlapping them to fit. Pour any juices from their bowl over them, then lock the lid onto the cooker.

4.

Set the machine for	Set the level for	The valve must be	Set the time for	If necessary, press
PRESSURE COOK	MAX	—	12 minutes with the KEEP WARM setting off	START
MEAT/STEW, PRESSURE COOK, or MANUAL	HIGH	Closed	15 minutes with the KEEP WARM setting off	START

5. Use the **quick-release method** to bring the pot's pressure back to normal. Unlatch the lid and open the pot. Serve the game hen halves in bowls with the pot's sauce over them.

Stuffed Peppers

4 servings

This old-school entrée is much easier in the cooker. But because of the way the pressure works, it's better to cook the filling for the peppers in advance. When we tested the peppers with a raw-meat filling, it was too "pudding-like," even mousse-y. And because the Italian seasoning blend and jarred marinara sauce may have added salt, we suggest adding the salt only if you like really salty food.

1.

Press the button for	Set it for	Set the time for	If necessary, press
SAUTÉ	MEDIUM, NORMAL, or CUSTOM 300°F	10 minutes	START

2. Warm the oil in a **6-quart cooker** for a minute or two. Crumble in the ground beef and cook, stirring occasionally, partly to break up any clumps, until browned, about 5 minutes. Stir in half of the cheese, the beans, rice, Italian seasoning blend, and salt (if using). Stir well, then turn off the SAUTÉ function and scrape this mixture from the *hot* insert into a large bowl. Return the insert to the cooker. (There's no need to clean it.)

3. Remove the "tops" of the peppers by cutting off the stem and about ½ inch of the pepper below it. Use a flatware spoon (preferably a serrated grapefruit spoon) to remove the core, seeds, and any white membranes from inside the peppers. Stuff them with the ground beef mixture.

4. Pour the marinara sauce and water into the cooker. Stand the peppers up in the sauce, leaning against each other and the sides of the cooker. Divide the remaining cheese among the tops of the stuffed peppers.

5.

Set the machine for	Set the level for	The valve must be	Set the time for	If necessary, press
PRESSURE COOK	MAX	—	10 minutes with the KEEP WARM setting off	START
MEAT/STEW, PRESSURE COOK, or MANUAL	HIGH	Closed	12 minutes with the KEEP WARM setting off	START

6. When the machine has finished cooking, turn it off and let its pressure **return to normal naturally** for 10 minutes. Then use the **quick-release method** to get rid of any residual pressure in the pot. Unlatch the lid and open the cooker. Use a large spoon and a metal spatula to transfer the peppers to serving bowls. Spoon lots of the sauce around them.

1 tablespoon olive oil

1 pound lean ground beef

4 ounces grated semi-firm mozzarella (1 cup)

½ cup canned and drained red kidney beans

¼ cup raw long-grain white rice

1 tablespoon dried Italian seasoning blend

½ teaspoon table salt (optional)

4 large bell peppers (green, yellow, orange, or red)

One 24-ounce jar classic marinara sauce (3 cups)

½ cup water

Beyond

- You must halve the recipe for a **3-quart cooker**.

- For an **8-quart cooker**, you must increase all the ingredients by 50 percent (in other words, make 6 stuffed peppers).

- Feel free to substitute lean ground turkey for the ground beef.

- To make a Tex-Mex version, substitute black beans for the kidney beans, 4 ounces purchased shredded Mexican blend of cheeses for the mozzarella, 1 tablespoon chile powder for the dried Italian seasoning blend, and 24 ounces plain bottled salsa for the marinara sauce.

1 tablespoon solid or liquid fat

Choose from vegetable, corn, canola, safflower, grape seed, olive, avocado, or any nut oil; or butter, coconut oil, lard, schmaltz, duck, goose, or rendered bacon fat.

1½ pounds lean ground beef

1 cup broth

Choose any sort.

2 tablespoons tomato paste

5 to 6 cups chopped quick-cooking vegetables

Choose at least two from cored and seeded bell peppers of any sort, broccoli florets, carrots, cauliflower florets, celery, corn kernels (if frozen, do not thaw), frozen edamame (do not thaw), frozen sliced okra (do not thaw), onions of any sort, peas (if frozen, do not thaw), trimmed green beans, and/or zucchini.

2 tablespoons vinegar

Choose from apple cider (with or without the mother), red wine, white wine, balsamic, or white balsamic (but not a flavored vinegar).

Up to 1½ tablespoons dried herbs and/or spices

Choose at least two from ground cinnamon, ground coriander, caraway seeds, celery seeds, fennel seeds, basil, oregano, parsley, rosemary, sage, savory, and/or thyme (remembering that dried spices are more powerful than dried herbs) — or a purchased spice blend such as herbes de Provence, a dried Italian blend, or other blends.

1 tablespoon soy sauce

1 teaspoon ground black pepper

Up to 1 teaspoon red pepper flakes (optional)

4 to 8 ounces shredded semi-firm cheese (1 to 2 cups)

Choose from American mild or sharp Cheddar, Monterey Jack, Swiss, or a purchased shredded cheese blend (without any added spices).

Road Map: Ground Beef Stew

6 servings

This cheesy ground-beef stew may well be one of the most classic expressions of American comfort food. Don't tell the kids, but we've snuck in lots of vegetables. We've used soy sauce, too, perhaps a bit of a surprise, a bid to bump up the umami flavors often lost under pressure.

This same stew will actually work with any ground meat — turkey, chicken, pork, veal, even buffalo. Just use a lean grind to keep the stew from becoming too fatty.

1.

Press the button for	Set it for	Set the time for	If necessary, press
SAUTÉ	MEDIUM, NORMAL, or CUSTOM 300°F	5 minutes	START

2. Warm the oil or melt the fat in a **6-quart cooker**. Crumble in the ground beef and cook, stirring often, partly to break up any clumps, until the meat loses its raw, pink color, 2 to 3 minutes. Pour in the broth and add the tomato paste. Stir until the paste has dissolved.

3. Turn off the SAUTÉ function. Add the quick-cooking vegetables, vinegar, dried herb and/or spice blend, soy sauce, black pepper, and red pepper flakes (if using). Stir until uniform, then lock the lid onto the pot.

4.

Set the machine for	Set the level for	The valve must be	Set the time for	If necessary, press
PRESSURE COOK	MAX	—	5 minutes with the KEEP WARM setting off	START
MEAT/STEW, PRESSURE COOK, or MANUAL	HIGH	Closed	7 minutes with the KEEP WARM setting off	START

5. Use the **quick-release method** to bring the pot's pressure back to normal. Unlatch the lid and open the cooker. Stir in the cheese, then set the lid askew over the pot for 5 minutes to melt the cheese and blend the flavors. Stir again before serving.

Beyond

- You must halve the recipe for a **3-quart cooker.**

- For an **8-quart cooker,** you must increase all the ingredients by 50 percent.

- If you'd rather not add the cheese, don't. Serve this simpler stew over long-grain white or brown rice or over cooked and drained wheat berries (see page 395) instead.

- Omit the semi-firm cheese and freeze 4 ounces cream cheese or fresh mozzarella for 30 minutes, then dice into small cubes and let it return to room temperature. Stir into the hot stew after cooking.

- Omit the stirred-in cheese and serve the stew over small mounds of ricotta.

- If you're looking for a ground beef and pasta casserole, see page 167.

2 tablespoons vegetable, corn, or canola oil

1 medium yellow onion, chopped (1 cup)

1½ pounds lean ground beef

2 medium carrots, thinly sliced (1 cup)

8 ounces fresh green beans, trimmed and cut into 1-inch pieces (1 cup)

2 medium garlic cloves, peeled and minced (2 teaspoons)

1 tablespoon Worcestershire sauce

1 tablespoon yellow mustard

1 tablespoon tomato paste

2 teaspoons dried thyme

1 teaspoon table salt

½ teaspoon ground black pepper

2 cups beef or chicken broth

1 cup plus 2 tablespoons all-purpose flour

1 teaspoon baking powder

1 teaspoon baking soda

1 teaspoon granulated white sugar

½ cup regular or low-fat milk

2 tablespoons butter, melted and cooled

Ground Beef and Vegetable Stew with Dumplings

4 to 6 servings

Tender dumplings can be a bit of a problem in the cooker, mostly because of the brilliant way it keeps moisture inside. But by stirring together a slightly wetter dough *and* making smaller dumplings (than perhaps normal), we can indeed steam dumplings over the stew as it simmers after cooking under pressure.

That said, the pot's interior environment is, well, humid. The dumplings will never become light and fluffy. They'll remain dense and slippery, if still a nice match to the stew underneath. If the timing of your machine cannot be set as low as 20 minutes on the SLOW COOK function, set it as low as it can, then set another timer for the dumplings.

1.

Press the button for	Set it for	Set the time for	If necessary, press
SAUTÉ	MEDIUM, NORMAL, or CUSTOM 300°F	10 minutes	START

2. Warm the oil in a **6- or 8-quart cooker** for a minute or two. Add the onion and cook, stirring occasionally, until softened, about 4 minutes. Crumble in the ground beef and cook, stirring often, partly to break up any clumps, until the meat loses its raw, pink color, about 2 minutes.

3. Stir in the carrots and green beans until uniform; then add the garlic, Worcestershire sauce, mustard, tomato paste, thyme, ½ teaspoon salt and the pepper. Stir until aromatic, just a few seconds. Pour in the broth and stir well to scrape up any browned bits on the pot's bottom. Turn off the SAUTÉ function and lock the lid onto the pot.

4.

Set the machine for	Set the level for	The valve must be	Set the time for	If necessary, press
PRESSURE COOK	MAX	—	5 minutes with the KEEP WARM setting off	START
MEAT/STEW, PRESSURE COOK, or MANUAL	HIGH	Closed	7 minutes with the KEEP WARM setting off	START

5. As the stew cooks, whisk the flour, baking powder, baking soda, sugar, and the remaining ½ teaspoon salt in a medium bowl until uniform. Stir in the milk and melted butter to form a wet dough, sort of like a thick batter.

6. When the machine has finished cooking, use the **quick-release method** to bring the pot's pressure back to normal. Unlatch the lid and open the cooker. Stir the stew, then drop the biscuit dough/batter by six or seven blobs over the top. Latch the lid back onto the pot.

7.

Set the machine for	Set the level for	The valve must be	Set the time for	If necessary, press
SLOW COOK	HIGH	Opened	20 minutes with the KEEP WARM setting off	START

8. Switch off the Slow Cook function. Unlatch the lid and open the pot. Cool for a few minutes, then serve by the big spoonful without stirring.

Beyond

- You must halve the recipe for a **3-quart cooker.**

- You *can* increase all the ingredients in an **8-quart cooker.**

- Add up to 2 tablespoons minced fresh parsley, oregano, or thyme to the dumpling dough/batter as you add the milk and butter.

- Or add up to 2 ounces (½ cup) shredded Cheddar, Jack, or Swiss cheese with the milk and butter.

- For a richer stew, omit the oil and cook the onion in 2 tablespoons butter.

- Swap out this dumpling dough for the one for buttermilk dumplings on page 302.

- Or skip making the dumplings altogether and use half of a 16.3-ounce can of home-style biscuits. Lay these biscuits on top of the stew in step 6.

One 28-ounce can diced tomatoes (3½ cups)

2 cups beef or chicken broth

1 medium green or red bell pepper, stemmed, cored, and chopped (1 cup)

1 small yellow onion, chopped (½ cup)

1 medium carrot, thinly sliced (½ cup)

2 teaspoons dried basil or oregano

1 teaspoon dried thyme

½ teaspoon table salt

¼ teaspoon grated nutmeg

1 pound lean ground beef

1 pound bulk sweet or mild Italian sausage (no casings)

1 large egg

½ cup Italian-seasoned dried breadcrumbs

¼ cup regular or low-fat milk

Beyond

- You must halve the recipe for a 3-quart cooker.

- The sauce is thin. If desired, transfer the meatballs to a serving platter, then stir ¼ cup tomato paste into the sauce and use the SAUTÉ function at MEDIUM, NORMAL, or CUSTOM 300°F to reduce and thicken the sauce, stirring often, 2 to 3 minutes.

- For more flavor, brown the meatballs before cooking them in the pot on a lipped baking sheet in a 350°F oven for 10 minutes, turning occasionally. (They are fragile—turn gently.)

- Grate lots of Parmigiano-Reggiano over the servings, and/or drizzle with balsamic vinegar.

Braised Italian Meatballs

6 servings

For these tasty meatballs poached in a light tomato sauce, we use Italian sausage and seasoned breadcrumbs so we don't have to empty a spice pantry to get the right flavors. You could even serve the meatballs on split Italian hero rolls with shredded mozzarella cheese and some of the sauce from the pot.

For more classic flair, skip the dried herbs and add 1 tablespoon each of minced fresh basil and oregano, as well as 2 teaspoons stemmed fresh thyme leaves.

1. Stir the tomatoes, broth, bell pepper, onion, carrot, basil or oregano, thyme, salt, and nutmeg in a **6- or 8-quart cooker**.

2. Mix the ground beef, sausage meat, egg, breadcrumbs, and milk in a large bowl until uniform. With clean, dry hands, form the mixture into 12 balls, using a scant ¼ cup of the mixture for each. Gently immerse these meatballs into the tomato mixture in the cooker. Lock the lid onto the pot.

3.

Set the machine for	Set the level for	The valve must be	Set the time for	If necessary, press
PRESSURE COOK	MAX	—	10 minutes with the KEEP WARM setting off	START
MEAT/STEW, PRESSURE COOK, or MANUAL	HIGH	Closed	12 minutes with the KEEP WARM setting off	START

4. When the machine has finished cooking, turn it off and let its pressure **return to normal naturally**, about 25 minutes. Unlatch the lid and open the pot. Serve the meatballs in bowls with lots of the sauce.

See photo in insert.

Meatballs with Red Cabbage, Tomato, and Dill

4 servings

If you're looking for something beyond the ordinary, try this meatball stew, made with a combination of cabbage, dill, and cinnamon. Some supermarkets sell red cabbage shredded into long, thin strips. If yours doesn't, split a medium head in half, remove the tough core, and set the cabbage head cut side down on a cutting board. Make ¼-inch-thick cuts across the head, then separate the shreds. Cut long shreds in half, if not thirds.

   As a technique note, the previous recipe had a natural release; this one, a quick release. There, we wanted a deeply "braised" flavor, letting the meatballs absorb some of the sauce as the pressure returned to normal. Here, we use a quick release to prevent the cabbage from getting too soft.

1. Mix the ground beef, egg, rice, oregano, garlic powder, onion powder, salt, and pepper in a large bowl until uniform. With clean and dry hands, form this mixture into 12 balls, using about 3 tablespoons of the mixture for each. Set them aside.

2.

Press the button for	Set it for	Set the time for	If necessary, press
SAUTÉ	MEDIUM, NORMAL, or CUSTOM 300°F	10 minutes	START

3. Warm the oil in a **6- or 8-quart cooker** for a minute or two. Add the onion and cook, stirring occasionally, until softened, about 4 minutes. Add the cabbage and cook, stirring more often, until it begins to wilt, about 3 minutes. Pour in the wine or cider and scrape up any browned bits on the pot's bottom.

4. Turn off the SAUTÉ function. Stir in the tomatoes, broth, dill, and cinnamon; scrape up any browned bits on the pot's bottom. Nestle the meatballs into this sauce. Lock the lid onto the pot.

5.

Set the machine for	Set the level for	The valve must be	Set the time for	If necessary, press
PRESSURE COOK	MAX	—	10 minutes with the KEEP WARM setting off	START
MEAT/STEW, PRESSURE COOK, or MANUAL	HIGH	Closed	12 minutes with the KEEP WARM setting off	START

6. Use the **quick-release method** to bring the pot's pressure back to normal. Unlatch the lid and open the cooker. Stir gently before serving.

1½ pounds lean ground beef

1 large egg

¼ cup raw long-grain white rice

½ teaspoon dried oregano

½ teaspoon garlic powder

½ teaspoon onion powder

½ teaspoon table salt

½ teaspoon ground black pepper

2 tablespoons olive oil

1 medium yellow onion, chopped (1 cup)

4 cups cored and shredded red cabbage (about half a medium head)

½ cup dry but fruit-forward red wine, such as Zinfandel; or unsweetened apple cider

One 14-ounce can diced tomatoes (1¾ cups)

½ cup beef or chicken broth

¼ cup loosely packed fresh dill fronds, minced

1 teaspoon ground cinnamon

Beyond

- You must halve the recipe for a **3-quart cooker**.

- For a brighter flavor, stir up to 2 tablespoons red wine vinegar or balsamic vinegar into the stew after cooking.

- Garnish the servings with sour cream.

- Serve with crunchy pretzels instead of bread. Or serve the meatballs and vegetables with a little sauce on pretzel rolls. (They'll be messy. Keep any white linens away from the table.)

2 tablespoons olive oil

1 small yellow onion, chopped
(½ cup)

1 medium carrot, chopped (½ cup)

1 medium celery rib, thinly sliced
(⅓ cup)

1 medium garlic clove, peeled and
minced (1 teaspoon)

1 teaspoon dried thyme

1½ pounds lean ground beef

1 cup fresh, shelled or frozen peas
(if frozen, do not thaw)

1¼ cup beef or chicken broth

1½ tablespoons tomato paste

1 tablespoon Worcestershire sauce

1½ pounds russet potatoes, peeled
and shredded through the large
holes of a box grater

1 teaspoon table salt

½ teaspoon onion powder

½ teaspoon ground black pepper

1 teaspoon mild paprika

Beyond

- You must halve the recipe for a
  3-quart cooker.

- For an **8-quart cooker,** you must
  increase all the ingredients by 50
  percent.

- Try seasoning the potatoes by
  omitting the onion powder and
  pepper and using up to 2 teaspoons
  of a dried spice blend. Or omit the
  onion powder and mix 1 medium
  scallion, trimmed and minced, with
  the potatoes.

- For a richer dish, dot up to
  2 tablespoons butter over the
  potatoes before the dish is cooked
  under pressure.

Mock Shepherd's Pie

4 to 6 servings

Why "mock"? Because we put seasoned, shredded potatoes over this
ground beef stew to mimic mashed potatoes. The potatoes won't be
fluffy and creamy, but they'll have a better texture (mashed potatoes
under pressure can get gummy). And the potatoes' starch will thicken
the stew below, turning this retro casserole into a one-pot meal.

1.

Press the button for	Set it for	Set the time for	If necessary, press
SAUTÉ	MEDIUM, NORMAL, or CUSTOM 300°F	10 minutes	START

2. Warm the oil in a **6-quart cooker** for a minute or two. Add the
onion, carrot, and celery. Cook, stirring occasionally, until the onion
softens, about 3 minutes. Stir in the garlic and thyme until aromatic,
just a few seconds.

3. Crumble in the ground beef and cook, stirring more often, partly to
break up any clumps, until the meat loses its raw, red color, about
3 minutes. Turn off the SAUTÉ function and stir in the peas, broth,
tomato paste, and Worcestershire sauce until the tomato paste
dissolves, scraping up any browned bits on the pot's bottom.

4. Toss the shredded potatoes, salt, onion powder, and pepper in a
large bowl until uniform. Scatter this mixture evenly over the top of the
ground beef mixture. Sprinkle the paprika evenly over the top. Lock the
lid onto the pot.

5.

Set the machine for	Set the level for	The valve must be	Set the time for	If necessary, press
PRESSURE COOK	MAX	—	7 minutes with the KEEP WARM setting off	START
MEAT/STEW, PRESSURE COOK, or MANUAL	HIGH	Closed	10 minutes with the KEEP WARM setting off	START

6. When the machine has finished cooking, turn it off and let its
pressure **return to normal naturally** for 10 minutes. Then use the
quick-release method to get rid of any remaining pressure in the pot.
Unlatch the lid and open the cooker. Serve by scooping up the potatoes
and stew by big spoonfuls and into bowls.

Pork Chops and Potatoes with Salsa Verde

4 servings

The surprising combination of butter and salsa verde (sometimes called "tomatillo salsa") gives this dish a range of sour and sweet flavors, a great way to make a simple braise more sophisticated. Salsa verde can be salty, so there's no added salt in the recipe.

1 cup jarred salsa verde

⅓ cup chicken broth

Four 1½-inch-thick, boneless, center-cut pork loin chops

Four 6-ounce yellow potatoes, preferably Yukon Gold, quartered

¼ cup (½ stick) butter, melted

½ teaspoon mild paprika

½ teaspoon ground black pepper

1. Mix the salsa verde and broth in a **6-quart cooker**. Nestle the pork chops into the mixture, overlapping them to fit. Make a layer with the potato wedges skin side down on top, then pour the melted butter over them. Sprinkle the potatoes with the paprika and pepper. Lock the lid onto the cooker.

2.

Set the machine for	Set the level for	The valve must be	Set the time for	If necessary, press
PRESSURE COOK	MAX	—	8 minutes with the KEEP WARM setting off	START
MEAT/STEW, PRESSURE COOK, or MANUAL	HIGH	Closed	10 minutes with the KEEP WARM setting off	START

3. When the machine has finished cooking, turn it off and let its pressure **return to normal naturally** for 5 minutes. Then use the **quick-release method** to get rid of any residual pressure in the pot. Unlatch the lid and open the cooker. Serve the potatoes and pork chops with the sauce ladled around them.

Beyond

- For a **3-quart cooker,** you must use ½ cup broth but halve the remaining ingredients.

- For an **8-quart cooker,** you must increase the broth to ¾ cup but use the stated amount of the remaining ingredients. Or you can increase all the ingredients by 50 percent in an **8-quart cooker.**

- Feel free to substitute four 8- to 10-ounce boneless skinless chicken thighs (the giant ones) for the pork chops.

2 tablespoons solid or liquid fat

Choose from butter, lard, schmaltz, duck fat, or goose fat; or vegetable, corn, canola, safflower, olive, avocado, or any nut oil — or choose a 50/50 combo of a solid and a liquid fat.

Four 10- to 12-ounce bone-in pork loin chops

½ teaspoon table salt

½ teaspoon ground black pepper

2 cups chopped quick-cooking vegetables

Choose at least two from carrots, celery, frozen artichoke heart quarters (do not thaw), leeks (white and pale green parts only, well washed), brown or white button mushrooms, onions (of any sort), shallots, shelled edamame (if frozen, do not thaw), shelled peas (if frozen, do not thaw), stemmed and cored bell pepper, trimmed scallions, trimmed fennel, yellow summer squash, and/or zucchini.

2 tablespoons minced fresh herbs

Choose one or two from marjoram, parsley, oregano, rosemary, sage, savory, and/or thyme.

Up to 1 teaspoon dried spices (optional)

Choose one or two from decorticated cardamom seeds, grated nutmeg, ground allspice, ground cardamom, ground coriander, ground cinnamon, ground fenugreek, and/or ground mace.

1½ cups liquid

Choose a broth of any sort, or a combination of broth and white wine, dry vermouth, or dry sherry — most likely in a ratio of 1 cup broth and ½ cup wine or perhaps in a ratio of 1¼ cups broth and ¼ cup wine for a more savory dish.

Road Map: Braised Pork Chops

4 servings

Although boneless center-cut pork loin chops need extra care in the pot to stay juicy, those with the bone attached have some natural protection, as well as more fat and cartilage. All of this guarantees a better meal. Pay careful attention here to the size of the chops: These are substantial cuts. (The thin ones cook in just a few minutes on the stovetop anyway.)

1.

Press the button for	Set it for	Set the time for	If necessary, press
SAUTÉ	MEDIUM, NORMAL, or CUSTOM 300°F	20 minutes	START

2. Melt the fat or warm the oil in a **6- or 8-quart cooker**. Season the pork chops with salt and pepper, then put two in the cooker. Brown well on both sides, turning a couple of times, about 6 minutes. Transfer the chops to a nearby bowl and brown the other two in the same way before transferring them to the bowl.

3. Add the chopped vegetable and cook, stirring often, until a little softened, about 3 minutes. Stir in the herbs and spices (if using) until aromatic, just a few seconds. Pour in the liquid and scrape up any browned bits on the pot's bottom.

4. Turn off the SAUTÉ function and nestle the pork chops into the sauce, overlapping them as necessary. Pour any juice from their bowl on top and lock the lid onto the cooker.

5.

Set the machine for	Set the level for	The valve must be	Set the time for	If necessary, press
PRESSURE COOK	MAX	—	9 minutes with the KEEP WARM setting off	START
MEAT/STEW, PRESSURE COOK, or MANUAL	HIGH	Closed	12 minutes with the KEEP WARM setting off	START

6. Use the **quick-release method** to return the pot's pressure to normal. Unlatch the lid and open the pot. Transfer the pork chops to serving plates or bowls; ladle the sauce on top.

Beyond

- You must halve the recipe for a **3-quart cooker**.

- For an **8-quart cooker**, you *can* increase the ingredients by 50 percent.

- To add a hint of sweetness, use some chopped, cored, and peeled apple as part of the quick-cooking mix. Or use peeled and seeded butternut or winter squash, diced into ¼-inch pieces.

- If the sauce is too thin for your taste, remove the cooked pork chops and use a slotted spoon to remove the vegetables, too. Bring the sauce to a simmer using the SAUTÉ function at MEDIUM, NORMAL, or CUSTOM 300°F. Cook for 1 minute, then stir in a slurry of 1 tablespoon cornstarch or potato starch whisked with 1 tablespoon water. Stir until thickened, then turn off the SAUTÉ function and remove the *hot* insert from the pot to stop the cooking.

2 teaspoons mild smoked paprika

1 teaspoon ground black pepper

½ teaspoon table salt

Four 1½-inch-thick, center-cut, boneless pork loin chops

2 tablespoons olive oil

4 ounces slab bacon, chopped

1 small red onion, chopped (½ cup)

2 medium garlic cloves, peeled and minced (2 teaspoons)

1 canned chipotle chile in adobo sauce, stemmed, seeded (if desired), and chopped

1 tablespoon adobo sauce from the can

1 teaspoon dried oregano

½ cup chicken broth

¾ cup porter, preferably a smoky porter

12 baby carrots or 2 medium carrots, cut into ½-inch sections

Smoky Pork Chops and Carrots

4 servings

To keep *boneless* center-cut pork chops juicy, they must be on the thick side: 1½ inches, in fact. We also increase the fats and sugars in the sauce so that it will coat and protect the meat. Consider these the guidelines for success with almost any boneless center-cut pork chop recipe in the pot.

If you can't find boneless center-cut pork chops this thick, buy a boneless center-cut pork loin and cut it into chops yourself. The slab bacon adds bits of chewy smokiness to the sauce. Feel free to substitute thick-sliced bacon, although the bits will be softer and not as luxurious.

1. Mix the smoked paprika, pepper, and salt in a small bowl. Pat the pork chops dry with paper towels, then pat and rub this spice mixture onto both sides of the meat. Set aside.

2.

Press the button for	Set it for	Set the time for	If necessary, press
SAUTÉ	MEDIUM, NORMAL, or CUSTOM 300°F	15 minutes	START

3. Warm the oil in a **6-quart cooker** for a minute or two. Set two pork chops in the cooker and brown lightly on both sides, turning a couple of times, about 4 minutes. Transfer them to a nearby bowl and brown the other two pork chops in the same way before transferring them to the bowl.

4. Add the slab bacon and onion. Cook, stirring often, until the bacon browns a bit and the onion softens, about 4 minutes. Stir in the garlic, chipotle, adobo sauce, and oregano until aromatic, about 30 seconds. Pour in the broth and scrape up any browned bits on the pot's bottom.

5. Turn off the SAUTÉ function. Stir in the porter, then nestle the pork chops into the sauce, overlapping them as necessary. Pour any juice from their bowl on top, scatter the carrots around the cooker, and lock the lid onto the pot.

6.

Set the machine for	Set the level for	The valve must be	Set the time for	If necessary, press
PRESSURE COOK	MAX	—	8 minutes with the KEEP WARM setting off	START
MEAT/STEW, PRESSURE COOK, or MANUAL	HIGH	Closed	10 minutes with the KEEP WARM setting off	START

7. When the machine has finished cooking, turn it off and let its pressure **return to normal naturally** for 5 minutes. Then use the **quick-release method** to get rid of any residual pressure in the pot. Unlatch the lid and open the cooker. Use kitchen tongs to transfer the chops to serving plates; spoon the carrots, onions, bacon, and sauce around them.

Beyond

- You must halve the recipe for a **3-quart cooker.**

- For an **8-quart cooker**, you must increase all the ingredients by 50 percent.

- Substitute additional broth for the porter but increase the smoked paprika to 1 tablespoon and add up to 2 teaspoons dark brown sugar with the garlic.

- For a built-in side, pile up to 1 to 2 cups shredded, cored green cabbage over the carrots and pork chops before locking the lid onto the cooker. (Do not pack ingredients above the **Max Fill** line.)

1 tablespoon olive oil

Four 1½-inch-thick, boneless, center-cut pork loin chops

½ teaspoon table salt

½ teaspoon ground black pepper

½ cup frozen pearl onions (do not thaw)

1 medium garlic clove, peeled and minced (1 teaspoon)

One 14-ounce can diced tomatoes with green chiles (1¼ cups)

¾ cup chicken broth

½ cup dried black-eyed peas

2 teaspoons mild paprika

1 teaspoon dried thyme

½ teaspoon grated nutmeg

3 cups frozen sliced okra (do not thaw)

1 tablespoon white wine vinegar

Pork Chops with Black-Eyed Peas and Okra

4 servings

This down-home braise is Southern comfort food, made a little spicy by the canned tomatoes with chiles. If desired, tame it by using regular canned diced tomatoes (preferably fire-roasted for more flavor). Or up the heat by also adding up to 1 teaspoon hot red pepper sauce, such as Tabasco sauce or Sriracha, with the dried spices.

1.

Press the button for	Set it for	Set the time for	If necessary, press
SAUTÉ	MEDIUM, NORMAL, or CUSTOM 300°F	10 minutes	START

2. Warm the oil in a **6-quart cooker** for a minute or two. Season the pork chops with the salt and pepper, then lightly brown two in the cooker, turning occasionally, about 3 minutes. Transfer them to a nearby bowl and brown the remaining two in the same way before transferring them to the bowl.

3. Add the pearl onions and cook, stirring occasionally, until lightly browned in a few places, about 3 minutes. Add the garlic and cook, stirring all the while, until aromatic, about 20 seconds. Stir in the tomatoes and broth; scrape up any browned bits on the pot's bottom.

4. Turn off the SAUTÉ function and stir in the black-eyed peas, paprika, thyme, and nutmeg until uniform. Lock the lid onto the cooker.

5.

Set the machine for	Set the level for	The valve must be	Set the time for	If necessary, press
PRESSURE COOK	MAX	—	10 minutes with the KEEP WARM setting off	START
MEAT/STEW, PRESSURE COOK, or MANUAL	HIGH	Closed	12 minutes with the KEEP WARM setting off	START

6. Use the **quick-release method** to bring the pot's pressure back to normal. Unlatch the lid and open the cooker. Nestle the pork chops into the hot sauce. Pour any juice from their bowl over them and scatter the okra on top. Lock the lid back onto the pot.

7.

Set the machine for	Set the level for	The valve must be	Set the time for	If necessary, press
PRESSURE COOK	MAX	—	10 minutes with the KEEP WARM setting off	START
MEAT/STEW, PRESSURE COOK, or MANUAL	HIGH	Closed	12 minutes with the KEEP WARM setting off	START

8. Once again, use the **quick-release method** to bring the pot's pressure back to normal. Unlatch the lid and open the cooker. Transfer the pork chops to serving plates or bowls. Stir the vinegar into the sauce with the okra, then ladle this mixture over the pork chops.

Beyond

- You must halve the recipe for a **3-quart cooker.**

- For an **8-quart cooker,** you must increase all the ingredients by 50 percent.

- Frozen okra works best because it won't be as slimy. Even if you buy fresh, it's best to cut it into 1-inch chunks and freeze it for this recipe.

1½ pounds lean ground pork

⅓ cup raw long-grain white rice, such as white basmati

1 large egg

½ teaspoon onion powder

½ teaspoon grated nutmeg

½ teaspoon table salt

½ teaspoon ground black pepper

1 large savoy cabbage

2 ounces thick-cut bacon, chopped

1 small yellow onion, chopped (½ cup)

1 medium carrot, chopped (½ cup)

1 medium celery stalk, thinly sliced (⅓ cup)

¼ cup raisins

2 cups chicken broth

¼ cup tomato paste

1 tablespoon red wine vinegar

1 teaspoon caraway seeds

Golumpkis

6 servings

A recipe for Polish stuffed cabbage rolls may seem an odd one in a chapter of *short* braises. But the pot does make the cooking go much faster than an hours-long simmer. Save this one for a winter night.

As an aside, if you've got our book *The Kitchen Shortcut Bible,* you already know that you can freeze the cabbage leaves and skip the step of blanching them for the rolls.

1. Mix the ground pork, rice, egg, onion powder, nutmeg, salt, and pepper in a large bowl until uniform. Set aside. Remove twelve leaves from the cabbage head. Reserve the remaining leaves for another purpose (and even freeze the core for a future batch of Vegetable Stock, page 101).

2.

Press the button for	Set it for	Set the time for	If necessary, press
SAUTÉ	HIGH or MORE	20 minutes	START

3. Fill a **6- or 8-quart cooker** about halfway with water and bring the water to a boil. Meanwhile, set up a large bowl of ice water on the counter. Submerge two or three cabbage leaves in the boiling water and blanch for 2 minutes, then transfer to the ice water. Continue cooking more cabbage leaves as directed, adding more ice to the water in the bowl to keep it cold.

4. Once all the leaves have been blanched, turn off the SAUTÉ function and drain the *hot* insert from the cooker. Return the insert to the machine.

5. Drain the cabbage leaves into a large colander set in the sink. Cut V-shaped notch out of the stem end of each leaf to remove any of the tough, pale white core.

6. Lay one cabbage leaf on your work surface with the V-shaped notch toward you. Set about ¼ cup of the ground pork filling in the middle of the leaf. Fold the two sides over the filling, then roll the leaf closed, starting at the V side. Set aside, seam side down, and make eleven more rolls.

7.

Press the button for	Set it for	Set the time for	If necessary, press
SAUTÉ	MEDIUM, NORMAL, or CUSTOM 300°F	5 minutes	START

8. Add the bacon to the cooker and sauté, stirring often, until lightly browned. Add the onion, carrot, celery, and raisins. Continue cooking, stirring often, until the onion softens, about 3 minutes. Use a slotted spoon to transfer about two-thirds of the mixture in the cooker to a nearby bowl. Turn off the SAUTÉ function.

9. Whisk the broth, tomato paste, vinegar, and caraway seeds in a medium bowl until the tomato paste dissolves. Pour ½ cup of this mixture into the cooker.

10. Layer about half the stuffed leaves seam side down in the cooker. Top with half of the reserved bacon mixture. Make a second layer of rolls seam side down and top with the remaining bacon mixture. Pour the remainder of the tomato paste mixture over the rolls.

11.

Set the machine for	Set the level for	The valve must be	Set the time for	If necessary, press
PRESSURE COOK	MAX	—	13 minutes with the KEEP WARM setting off	START
MEAT/STEW, PRESSURE COOK, or MANUAL	HIGH	Closed	18 minutes with the KEEP WARM setting off	START
SLOW COOK	HIGH	Opened	3 hours with the KEEP WARM setting off (or on for no more than 2 hours)	START

12. If you've used a pressure setting, turn the machine off when it has finished cooking and let its pressure **return to normal naturally,** about 30 minutes.

13. Unlatch the lid and open the cooker. Use a large spoon to transfer the stuffed rolls and the sauce to serving bowls.

Beyond

- You must halve the recipe for a **3-quart cooker.**

- Feel free to substitute ground turkey for the ground pork.

- For a fresher taste, add up to 1 chopped large tomato (1 cup) with the onions and other vegetables in the sauce, and/or add up to 1 tablespoon fresh lemon juice and/or 1 teaspoon finely minced lemon zest to the broth mixture.

- For a less sweet dish, omit the raisins as well as the salt from the filling. Add 1 tablespoon soy sauce to the tomato paste mixture.

2½ pounds smoked boneless ham, cut into 1-inch pieces, any coatings or rubs removed

1½ pounds small white "boiling" potatoes (do not use russets or baking potatoes), cut into 1-inch pieces

½ cup chicken broth

½ cup fresh orange juice

2 medium carrots, thinly sliced (1 cup)

1 to 2 medium fresh jalapeño chiles, stemmed, halved lengthwise, seeded (if desired), and thinly sliced

2 tablespoons orange marmalade

1 tablespoon apple cider vinegar

½ teaspoon ground cinnamon

½ teaspoon ground dried ginger

Up to ½ teaspoon ground cloves

Beyond

- You must halve the recipe for a 3-quart cooker.

- For an 8-quart cooker, you must increase all the ingredients by 50 percent.

- The ham is salty, so there's no added salt. For a saltier dish, add up to 1 tablespoon soy sauce with the vinegar.

- For a more aromatic stew, substitute ginger marmalade for the orange marmalade.

- For a less sweet stew, omit the orange marmalade and increase the broth to ¾ cup.

- If you don't want a spicy stew, omit the jalapeños, reduce the marmalade to 1 tablespoon, reduce the orange juice to ¼ cup, and increase the broth to ¾ cup.

Spicy Ham and Spud Stew

6 servings

Smoked ham is a great stewing meat for the Instant Pot: flavorful, porky, and luxurious. Here, it creates a dish that's like a glazed ham in stew form. Look for a whole, smoked ham in the deli case, or use the smoked ham slices (so-called "ham steaks") in the meat case of most supermarkets. Make sure there are no added flavorings to the meat. Slice off any rubs or marinade that may lay along its outer surface.

1. Stir all the ingredients in a **6-quart cooker** until the marmalade dissolves. Lock the lid onto the pot.

2.

Set the machine for	Set the level for	The valve must be	Set the time for	If necessary, press
PRESSURE COOK	MAX	—	6 minutes with the KEEP WARM setting off	START
MEAT/STEW, PRESSURE COOK, or MANUAL	HIGH	Closed	8 minutes with the KEEP WARM setting off	START
SLOW COOK	HIGH	Opened	3 hours with the KEEP WARM setting off (or on for no more than 2 hours)	START

3. If you've used a pressure setting, use the **quick-release method** to bring the pot's pressure back to normal.

4. Unlatch the lid and open the cooker. Stir well before serving.

Savory Ham and Sweet Potato Stew

6 servings

If sweet potato hash were turned into a tomato-based stew, you'd have this dish. Even consider it a weekend breakfast if you make biscuits to go alongside.

1.

Press the button for	Set it for	Set the time for	If necessary, press
SAUTÉ	MEDIUM, NORMAL, or CUSTOM 300°F	5 minutes	START

2. Warm the oil in a **6-quart cooker** for a minute or two. Add the onion and bell pepper; cook, stirring occasionally, until the onion softens, about 4 minutes. Turn off the SAUTÉ function.

3. Stir in everything else: the ham, sweet potatoes, tomatoes, broth, Worcestershire sauce, soy sauce, horseradish, cinnamon, celery seeds, cloves, and cayenne. Lock the lid onto the cooker.

4.

Set the machine for	Set the level for	The valve must be	Set the time for	If necessary, press
PRESSURE COOK	MAX	—	6 minutes with the KEEP WARM setting off	START
MEAT/STEW, PRESSURE COOK, or MANUAL	HIGH	Closed	8 minutes with the KEEP WARM setting off	START
SLOW COOK	HIGH	Opened	3 hours with the KEEP WARM setting off (or on for no more than 2 hours)	START

5. If you've used a pressure setting, use the **quick-release method** to bring the pot's pressure back to normal.

6. Unlatch the lid and open the cooker. Stir gently (to protect the sweet potatoes) before serving.

1 tablespoon vegetable, corn, or canola oil

1 medium yellow onion, chopped (1 cup)

2 medium green bell peppers, stemmed, cored, and chopped (2 cups)

2½ pounds boneless smoked ham, cut into 1-inch pieces, any coatings or rubs removed

2 large sweet potatoes (about 12 ounces each), peeled and cut into 1-inch pieces

1 cup canned diced tomatoes with plenty of their juice

½ cup chicken broth

1 tablespoon Worcestershire sauce

1 tablespoon soy sauce

1 tablespoon jarred white horseradish

½ teaspoon ground cinnamon

½ teaspoon celery seeds

¼ teaspoon ground cloves

Up to ¼ teaspoon ground dried cayenne

Beyond

- You must halve the recipe for a **3-quart cooker.**

- For an **8-quart cooker**, you must increase all the ingredients by 50 percent.

- For a sweeter stew, omit the soy sauce, increase the Worcestershire sauce to 2 tablespoons, and add 1 tablespoon light brown sugar with the ham and other ingredients in step 3.

One 28-ounce can diced tomatoes (3½ cups)

¼ cup packed dark brown sugar

2 to 3 tablespoons apple cider vinegar

2 tablespoons Worcestershire sauce

1 tablespoon mild smoked paprika

1 tablespoon ground dried mustard

2 teaspoons ground cumin

½ teaspoon ground cloves

½ teaspoon garlic powder

½ teaspoon onion powder

½ teaspoon ground black pepper

¼ teaspoon table salt

2½ pounds mild or hot Italian sausage links, cut into 1-inch pieces

2 tablespoons tomato paste

Barbecue Sausage Bites

6 to 8 servings

This easy sausage braise could become a standard on your Super Bowl buffet. It could also become an easy lunch or dinner any time you want a rich, sweet barbecue sauce to coat sausages. Yes, we're asking you to make your own barbecue sauce, rather than dumping in a bottle of the stuff. The flavors will be more balanced, more present, better all around.

1. Stir the tomatoes, brown sugar, vinegar, Worcestershire sauce, smoked paprika, dried mustard, cumin, cloves, garlic powder, onion powder, black pepper, and salt in a **6-quart cooker** until the brown sugar dissolves. Add the sausage and stir until evenly coated. Lock the lid onto the cooker.

2.

Set the machine for	Set the level for	The valve must be	Set the time for	If necessary, press
PRESSURE COOK	MAX	——	5 minutes with the KEEP WARM setting off	START
MEAT/STEW, PRESSURE COOK, or MANUAL	HIGH	Closed	7 minutes with the KEEP WARM setting off	START

3. Use the **quick-release method** to bring the pot's pressure back to normal. Unlatch the lid and open the cooker. Stir in the tomato paste.

4.

Press the button for	Set it for	Set the time for	If necessary, press
SAUTÉ	MEDIUM, NORMAL, or CUSTOM 300°F	5 minutes	START

5. Bring the dish to a simmer and cook, stirring often, until the sauce has thickened somewhat, about 3 minutes. Turn off the SAUTÉ function and serve as a stew in bowls or remove the insert and serve with toothpicks (for picking the sausage pieces out of the sauce).

Beyond

- You must halve the recipe for a **3-quart cooker**.

- For an **8-quart cooker**, you must increase all the ingredients by 50 percent.

- To make a larger meal, add a 1-pound bag of frozen mixed vegetables, thawed, with the tomato paste in step 3, and serve over cooked ziti.

Sausage, Greens, and Butternut Squash Stew

4 to 6 servings

Not much could be easier than this stew — especially if you buy bagged, chopped collard greens and already prepped butternut squash (which you'll probably need to cut into smaller pieces). The flavors skew a little more Italian than U.S. Southern, a surprising twist on a bowl of such comfort.

1.

Press the button for	Set it for	Set the time for	If necessary, press
SAUTÉ	MEDIUM, NORMAL, or CUSTOM 300°F	10 minutes	START

2. Warm the oil in a **6- or 8-quart cooker** for a minute or two. Add the sausage and brown well, turning occasionally, about 6 minutes. Add the collards and cook, stirring occasionally, until wilted, about 2 minutes.

3. Add the butternut squash, sage, fennel seeds, red pepper flakes, and nutmeg. Stir for 1 minute, then pour in the broth. Scrape up any browned bits on the pot's bottom and turn off the SAUTÉ function. Stir in the vinegar and lock the lid onto the pot.

4.

Set the machine for	Set the level for	The valve must be	Set the time for	If necessary, press
PRESSURE COOK	MAX	—	5 minutes with the KEEP WARM setting off	START
MEAT/STEW, PRESSURE COOK, or MANUAL	HIGH	Closed	7 minutes with the KEEP WARM setting off	START

5. Use the **quick-release method** to bring the pot's pressure back to normal. Unlatch the lid and open the cooker. Stir well, then sprinkle the cheese over the top. Set the lid askew over the cooker for 5 minutes to melt the cheese. Stir again before serving.

1 tablespoon olive oil

1½ pounds mild or sweet Italian sausage links, cut into 2-inch pieces

1½ pounds collard greens, washed, stemmed, and chopped (6 cups)

1 small butternut squash, peeled, seeded, and cut into 1-inch cubes (4 cups)

1 teaspoon dried sage

½ teaspoon fennel seeds

¼ teaspoon red pepper flakes

¼ teaspoon grated nutmeg

2½ cups chicken broth

1½ tablespoons white wine vinegar

2 ounces finely grated Parmigiano-Reggiano (½ cup)

Beyond

- Since collard greens are so bulky, this recipe does not work well in a **3-quart cooker**.

- Substitute Cajun andouille, smoked kielbasa, bratwurst, chicken and apple sausage, or even *fresh* chorizo for the Italian sausage.

- For a less assertive flavor, substitute stemmed and chopped kale or cored and chopped escarole for the collard greens. (Avoid chard and spinach, which can get too squishy.)

- For a sweeter dish, substitute 2 medium sweet potatoes, peeled and cut into 1-inch cubes, for the butternut squash.

1½ cups water

2 pounds Manila or small cherrystone clams, scrubbed for sand

2 tablespoons butter

2 tablespoons olive oil

1 medium yellow onion, chopped (1 cup)

1 small fennel bulb (about 6 ounces), trimmed and chopped (1 cup)

2 medium celery stalks, thinly sliced (⅔ cup)

1 medium carrot, chopped (½ cup)

1 small green bell pepper, stemmed, seeded, and chopped (½ cup)

3 medium garlic cloves, peeled and minced (1 tablespoon)

One 28-ounce can crushed tomatoes (3½ cups)

2 cups chicken broth

½ cup loosely packed fresh parsley leaves, finely chopped

2 tablespoons tomato paste

1 tablespoon Worcestershire sauce

1 teaspoon dried oregano

1 teaspoon dried thyme

½ teaspoon ground black pepper

½ pound thick-fleshed, skinless fish fillets, such as cod or halibut, cut into 1-inch pieces

½ pound medium shrimp (about 30 per pound), peeled and deveined

½ pound small sea scallops, halved

Red pepper flakes for garnishing (optional)

Cioppino-Style Seafood Stew

6 servings

Cioppino is a fast dish, but you may not know it was first made with ketchup — which we forgo in an pressure cooker in favor of crushed tomatoes and tomato paste for a better sauce in very little time. We can also cook the clams under pressure, thereby creating a flavorful clam broth for the stew ahead.

Beware: The water from the clams can be sandy. It must be strained. If you don't have a *chinois* (see page 48) or cheesecloth to line a colander, you can filter the liquid into a bowl through a coffee filter set in a small strainer. (Pour slowly so none of the liquid slops over the edge of the filter and into the bowl below.) Or just set the clam cooking liquid aside for 15 minutes to let the sand sink to the bottom of the bowl. Use only the top of the clam cooking liquid, avoiding the sand below and adding enough water to make 1½ cups total volume.

1. Pour the water into a **6- or 8-quart cooker**. Add the clams and lock the lid onto the pot.

2.

Set the machine for	Set the level for	The valve must be	Set the time for	If necessary, press
PRESSURE COOK	MAX	—	2 minutes with the KEEP WARM setting off	START
PRESSURE COOK or MANUAL	HIGH	Closed	3 minutes with the KEEP WARM setting off	START

3. Use the **quick-release method** to bring the pot's pressure back to normal. Unlatch the lid and open the cooker. Use a slotted spoon to transfer the clams to a large bowl. Discard any clams that do not open.

4. Strain the liquid in the *hot* insert through a fine-mesh sieve like a *chinois* (or a colander lined with a double layer of cheesecloth) into a bowl below. Rinse out the insert and return it to the machine.

5.

Press the button for	Set it for	Set the time for	If necessary, press
SAUTÉ	MEDIUM, NORMAL, or CUSTOM 300°F	10 minutes	START

6. Melt the butter in the oil, then add the onion, fennel, celery, carrot, bell pepper, and garlic. Cook, stirring often, until the onion softens and the vegetables are fragrant, about 6 minutes.

7. Stir in the tomatoes, broth, and the reserved, strained clam cooking water. Scrape up any browned bits on the pot's bottom and turn off the SAUTÉ function. Stir in the parsley, tomato paste, Worcestershire sauce, oregano, thyme, and pepper until the tomato paste dissolves. Lock the lid onto the pot.

8.

Set the machine for	Set the level for	The valve must be	Set the time for	If necessary, press
PRESSURE COOK	MAX	—	5 minutes with the KEEP WARM setting off	START
PRESSURE COOK or MANUAL	HIGH	Closed	7 minutes with the KEEP WARM setting off	START

9. Use the **quick-release method** to bring the pot's pressure back to normal. Unlatch the lid and open the cooker. Stir well.

10.

Press the button for	Set it for	Set the time for	If necessary, press
SAUTÉ	MEDIUM, NORMAL, or CUSTOM 300°F	5 minutes	START

11. Add the fish, shrimp, and scallops. Stir gently, then cook, stirring very carefully and only occasionally, until the shrimp are pink and firm, about 4 minutes. Turn off the SAUTÉ function and gently stir the reserved clams into the sauce. Set the lid askew over the pot and set aside for 5 minutes to warm the clams and blend the flavors. Serve in big bowls with red pepper flakes on the side, if desired, for sprinkling over each helping.

Beyond

- You must halve the recipe for a **3-quart cooker**.

- Because clams are salty and because we use Worcestershire sauce for its umami qualities, there's no added salt in this dish. Pass more at the table.

- For a fish-only version of this stew, ask the fishmonger for about ½ pound of fish tails, fins, heads, and bones. Cook these as you would the clams, then strain them out (and any particulate matter). Discard all that, keeping the cooking liquid to use in the stew. After the stew has been released from pressure the second time, omit the shellfish and add 1½ pounds thick-fleshed, skinned, white fish fillets and cook as directed in step 10.

5 cups vegetable broth

1 cup dry white wine, such as Chardonnay

1 small lemon, scrubbed to remove any waxy coating, then thinly sliced and seeded

4 or 5 fresh dill fronds

1 teaspoon black peppercorns

1 bay leaf

One 2-pound skin-on salmon fillet

½ cup regular or low-fat mayonnaise

½ cup regular or low-fat sour cream

2 tablespoons fresh lemon juice

2 tablespoons minced dill fronds

2 tablespoons jarred prepared white horseradish

1 tablespoon minced chives or scallion (green part only)

½ teaspoon ground black pepper

Beyond

- Because of the size of smaller salmon fillets, this recipe will not work well in a **3-quart cooker.**

- If you don't want to use wine, use 1½ quarts (6 cups) vegetable broth, but also add 1 teaspoon granulated white sugar to the sauce mixture.

- Serve portions of the salmon on Boston lettuce leaves with sliced radishes, chopped tomato, and/or sprouts, all topped with the horseradish sauce.

- Make an easy salmon salad for sandwiches by chopping the poached salmon and mixing it right into the horseradish sauce.

Poached Salmon with Horseradish Sauce

6 servings

Cold poached salmon may be summer's best meal: a make-ahead that's ready for lunch on the deck or patio whenever the time's right. Notice that the salmon poaches here at LOW pressure to preserve the meat and keep it from overcooking.

Look for a salmon fillet without a thick fat end and a thin, belly flap end. (Have the fishmonger cut an even piece from the middle of the fillet.) Also, make sure the pin bones have been removed. Run your fingers lightly over the fillet — careful! — to feel for them. Use cleaned tweezers to pull them out of the fish. Or ask that fishmonger to do the deed for you. If the salmon has been previously frozen, make sure the meat is not splitting and cracking but is intact and solid. Finally, fattier salmon (such as Atlantic) poaches better than leaner salmon (such as sockeye).

1. Mix the broth, wine, lemon, dill, peppercorns, and bay leaf in a **6- or 8-quart cooker**. Set the salmon skin side down in the broth mixture. Lock the lid onto the pot.

2.

Set the machine for	Set the level for	The valve must be	Set the time for	If necessary, press
PRESSURE COOK or MANUAL	LOW	Closed	4 minutes with the KEEP WARM setting off	START

3. Use the **quick-release method** to bring the pot's pressure back to normal. Unlatch the lid and open the cooker. Remove the *hot* insert from the cooker and set aside at room temperature for 10 minutes, then set the insert (with the salmon inside) on a towel on a shelf in the refrigerator and cool for 1 hour.

4. Meanwhile, whisk the mayonnaise, sour cream, lemon juice, dill, horseradish, chives, and pepper in a small bowl until smooth. Cover and refrigerate until you're ready to serve.

5. After an hour, transfer the salmon from the insert to a platter. Discard the liquid and solids in the insert. Slice the fish and serve at once — or cover and refrigerate for up to 2 days, offering the horseradish sauce on the side.

**Brisket Skewers
(page 266)**

Perfect in-the-Shell Sous Vide Eggs (page 279) with toast points

**Sous Vide Strip Steaks with Chives
and Garlic (page 280)**

Sous Vide Buttery
Lobster Tails
(page 286) turned
into lobster rolls

Perfect Seared Chicken Breasts (page 291) over Quinoa and Cauliflower Pilaf (page 408)

Sauté

Rice

Sous Vide

Cancel

Chicken Bulgogi
(page 297) with
lettuce wraps

Braised Italian Meatballs (page 318)

**Bistro-Style Braised Short Ribs
with Mushrooms (page 354)**

Kick-Butt Carnitas (page 376)

**Braised Stuffed
Turkey Breast
(page 380)**

**White Rice Pilaf (page 398) and
Wild Rice Pilaf (page 405)**

**Orange Beef
"Fried Rice"
Casserole
(page 413)**

Loaded Bundt Cornbread (page 431)

**Warm White Bean Salad (page 446)
with Italian canned tuna**

"Roasted" Garlic (page 450)

**Dulce de Leche (page 455)
over vanilla ice cream**

Classic Cheesecake
(page 466) with
Bing cherry sauce

**Chocolate Lava Cakes
(page 473) with
whipped cream**

Halibut Poached in Red Wine with Roasted Peppers

4 servings

We're not using pressure to cook these halibut fillets. We're using it to create a deeply flavored sauce. It may seem odd to cook fish in red wine, but it's actually a culinary practice that dates back to the Renaissance. The wine offers a bold flavor that's great with halibut, a fish with a more meat-like texture to stand up to all that surrounds it.

1. Mix the wine, red pepper, chickpeas, olives, garlic, oregano, cinnamon stick, and saffron (if using) in a **6- or 8-quart cooker**. Lock the lid onto the pot.

2.

Set the machine for	Set the level for	The valve must be	Set the time for	If necessary, press
PRESSURE COOK	MAX	—	5 minutes with the KEEP WARM setting off	START
PRESSURE COOK or MANUAL	HIGH	Closed	7 minutes with the KEEP WARM setting off	START

3. Use the **quick-release method** to bring the pot's pressure back to normal. Unlatch the lid and open the cooker. Remove and discard the cinnamon stick. Stir well.

4.

Press the button for	Set it for	Set the time for	If necessary, press
SAUTÉ	MEDIUM, NORMAL, or CUSTOM 300°F	10 minutes	START

5. Bring the sauce to a simmer, stirring occasionally. Slip the fillets into the sauce and set the cover askew over the pot. Cook until the fish is opaque throughout, 4 to 6 minutes. Turn off the SAUTÉ function and remove the *hot* insert from the pot to stop the cooking. Serve the fillets in bowls with lots of sauce around them.

1½ pounds full-bodied, fruit-forward red wine, such as Syrah

1 jarred roasted red pepper, chopped

½ cup drained canned chickpeas, rinsed

¼ cup pitted black olives

2 medium garlic cloves, peeled and minced (2 teaspoons)

2 teaspoons fresh oregano leaves, finely chopped

One 2-inch cinnamon stick

⅛ teaspoon saffron (optional)

Four 6- to 8-ounce skinless halibut fillets

Beyond

- You must halve the recipe for a **3-quart cooker**.

- For a richer sauce, transfer the cooked halibut fillets to serving bowls, then whisk up to 3 tablespoons butter into the sauce as it continues to simmer.

- For a more aromatic sauce, add up to 2 teaspoons finely minced orange zest to the red wine mixture before it cooks under pressure.

- Serve this stew over garlic bread croutons: Buy a loaf of ready-to-bake garlic bread. Cut the loaf into cubes and bake in a 375°F oven on a large, lipped baking sheet, stirring and turning occasionally, until crunchy, 10 to 12 minutes.

3 cups chicken broth or Fish Stock (see page 105)

1 cup beer, preferably an amber ale

½ cup (1 stick) butter, cut into chunks

⅓ cup tomato paste

Up to 6 medium garlic cloves, peeled and minced (2 tablespoons)

2 teaspoons dried thyme

1 teaspoon dried oregano

1 teaspoon fennel seeds

Up to 1 teaspoon red pepper flakes

½ teaspoon table salt

½ teaspoon celery seeds (optional)

3 pounds large shrimp (20 to 25 per pound), peeled and deveined

Crunchy bread, for serving

Spicy Buttery Shrimp

6 to 8 servings

Once again, we use the pressure cooker to build a sweet, buttery, and even tongue-spanking sauce, then gently poach the shrimp in it to keep them as tender as possible. The bread is not optional! You'll want it to sop up every drop.

1. Stir the broth, beer, butter, tomato paste, garlic, thyme, oregano, fennel seeds, red pepper flakes, salt, and celery seed (if using) in a **6- or 8-quart cooker**. Lock the lid onto the pot.

2.

Set the machine for	Set the level for	The valve must be	Set the time for	If necessary, press
PRESSURE COOK	MAX	——	5 minutes with the KEEP WARM setting off	START
MEAT/STEW, PRESSURE COOK, or MANUAL	HIGH	Closed	7 minutes with the KEEP WARM setting off	START

3. Use the **quick-release method** to bring the pot's pressure back to normal. Unlatch the lid and open the pot.

4.

Press the button for	Set it for	Set the time for	If necessary, press
SAUTÉ	MEDIUM, NORMAL, or CUSTOM 300°F	5 minutes	START

5. Stir the sauce as it comes to a simmer. Add the shrimp, stir well, and set the lid askew over the pot. Cook until the shrimp are pink and firm, about 2 minutes. Turn off the SAUTÉ function and remove the hot insert from the machine to stop the cooking. Pour the contents of the insert into a large serving bowl and serve with the crunchy bread to sop up the sauce.

Beyond

- You must halve the recipe for a **3-quart cooker**.

- For an **8-quart cooker**, you can (but don't have to) increase all the ingredients by 50 percent (for up to about 10 servings).

- For more flavor, use deveined medium shrimp still in their shells. You'll need to provide plenty of napkins for the peel-and-eat fest.

Shrimp Stew with White Beans and Spinach

4 servings

Surprisingly elegant, this Italian-inspired stew is a great supper for weekend guests. Don't use baby spinach but make sure you wash the larger spinach leaves to get rid of any sandy grit.

1.

Press the button for	Set it for	Set the time for	If necessary, press
SAUTÉ	MEDIUM, NORMAL, or CUSTOM 300°F	5 minutes	START

2. Warm the oil in a **6- or 8-quart cooker** for a minute or two. Add the onion and cook, stirring occasionally, until softened, about 4 minutes. Stir in the garlic, rosemary, and red pepper flakes (if using) until aromatic, just a few seconds.

3. Pour in the broth and scrape up any browned bits on the pot's bottom. Turn off the SAUTÉ function, add the beans, and stir well. Lock the lid onto the cooker.

4.

Set the machine for	Set the level for	The valve must be	Set the time for	If necessary, press
PRESSURE COOK	MAX	—	3 minutes with the KEEP WARM setting off	START
PRESSURE COOK or MANUAL	HIGH	Closed	4 minutes with the KEEP WARM setting off	START

5. Use the **quick-release method** to bring the pot's pressure back to normal. Unlatch the lid and open the cooker.

6.

Press the button for	Set it for	Set the time for	If necessary, press
SAUTÉ	MEDIUM, NORMAL, or CUSTOM 300°F	5 minutes	START

7. Bring the sauce to a simmer, stirring occasionally. Add the shrimp and spinach. Stir well, then set the lid askew over the pot and cook for 1 minute. Turn off the SAUTÉ function and stir in the lemon juice, salt, and pepper. Set the lid askew again over the pot and set aside for 3 minutes to blend the flavors and further cook the shrimp. Serve hot in bowls.

2 tablespoons olive oil

1 medium yellow onion, chopped (1 cup)

3 medium garlic cloves, peeled and minced (1 tablespoon)

1 tablespoon loosely packed fresh rosemary leaves, minced

Up to ½ teaspoon red pepper flakes (optional)

3 cups chicken broth

One 15-ounce can white beans, drained and rinsed (1¾ cups)

1 pound medium shrimp (about 30 per pound), peeled and deveined

4 cups packed, chopped, and stemmed spinach leaves

Up to 2 tablespoons fresh lemon juice

½ teaspoon table salt

½ teaspoon ground black pepper

Beyond

- You must halve the recipe for a **3-quart cooker.**

- Using even ½ cup of Fish Stock (page 105) — and thus only 2½ cups of chicken broth — will dramatically improve the flavor of the sauce.

- To give this dish a Spanish flair, substitute one 15-ounce can chickpeas, drained and rinsed, for the white beans. Add 1 teaspoon mild smoked paprika and ¼ teaspoon saffron with the rosemary.

2 tablespoons solid fat or liquid fat

Choose one or two from less assertive flavors like butter or schmaltz; or vegetable, corn, canola, safflower, olive, avocado, and/or grape seed oil.

4 ounces sausage or cured meat, chopped

Choose from sausage links of any sort (cut into ½-inch pieces), bacon (of any sort except flavored), pancetta, dried chorizo, or prosciutto.

½ cup chopped (and trimmed if necessary) allium aromatics

Choose from onion (of any sort), shallots, scallions, or leeks (white and pale green parts only, well washed).

Up to 1 tablespoon minced garlic or up to 1 tablespoon minced peeled fresh ginger (optional)

1 cup liquid

Choose either broth of any sort or a dry but light white wine such as Pinot Grigio — or a combo of both, either 50/50 or perhaps 75 broth/25 wine.

2 cups chopped (and stemmed and cored or trimmed as necessary) quick-cooking vegetables

Choose one or two from bell peppers, celery, fresh tomatoes of any sort, frozen artichoke heart quarters (do not thaw), shelled peas (if frozen, do not thaw), sugar snap peas, yellow summer squash, and/or zucchini.

2 tablespoons minced fresh herbs

Choose one or two from basil, cilantro, marjoram, parsley, oregano, rosemary, sage, savory, and/or thyme.

2 pounds mussels, scrubbed for exterior sand and debearded if necessary

Road Map: A Pot of Mussels

2 servings

There may be no better weeknight supper! By cooking mussels for just a minute or two under pressure, we make sure they flavor the broth but stay tender and juicy. Don't forget a bowl to hold all the shells.

1.

Press the button for	Set it for	Set the time for	If necessary, press
SAUTÉ	MEDIUM, NORMAL, or CUSTOM 300°F	10 minutes	START

2. Melt the fat or warm the oil in a **6- or 8-quart cooker.** Add the sausage or cured meat and cook, stirring often, until well browned, 4 to 6 minutes. Add the onion and cook, stirring occasionally, until the onion has softened, about 3 minutes. Stir in the garlic or ginger (if using) until aromatic, just a few seconds.

3. Pour in the liquid and scrape up any browned bits on the pot's bottom. Turn off the SAUTÉ function and stir in the quick-cooking vegetables and the herbs. Stir in the mussels, then lock the lid onto the pot.

4.

Set the machine for	Set the level for	The valve must be	Set the time for	If necessary, press
PRESSURE COOK	MAX	—	1 minute with the KEEP WARM setting off	START
PRESSURE COOK or MANUAL	HIGH	Closed	2 minutes with the KEEP WARM setting off	START

5. Use the **quick-release method** to bring the pot's pressure back to normal. Unlatch the lid and open the cooker. Discard any mussels that have not opened. Pour the contents of the *hot* insert into a large bowl to serve.

Beyond

- For a **3-quart cooker**, use ¾ cup liquid but halve the remaining ingredients.

- If when you open the cooker in step 5, more than a quarter of the mussels have not opened, they were larger than expected and have not cooked long enough. Lock the lid back onto the cooker and cook on HIGH only for 1 minute, followed by the **quick-release method**.

- You'll want bread for sopping up this mussel broth.

9

Longer Braises and Stews

(More than Twenty Minutes Under Pressure)

Back in the day, recipes like the ones in this chapter were the real reason our grandmothers bought their rather scary, stovetop pressure cookers: to make cheap cuts of meat in much less time than those cuts would take on the stovetop or in the oven.

Times have changed. First off, those cuts aren't cheap anymore. Have you priced a brisket? Or short ribs? The kids have caught on that chuck roast, pork butt, and lamb shoulder offer some pretty fine eating. Supply, demand: You know the story.

As a result, those cuts deserve more than a bag of baby carrots and a splash of that old standard, Kitchen Bouquet. They need to be gussied up to justify the cost. You probably want to make a celebration out of a 40-dollar piece of beef.

Start with one of the road maps in this chapter: beef stew, pot roast, brisket, or pork stew (which could be morphed into a lamb stew). These non-standard recipes will offer the best success for creating a satisfying meal, one customized to your taste. They'll also help you get the hang of the slightly larger set of complications that a once-inexpensive cut of meat requires.

Speaking of those flavors, we've felt free to bump them up in this chapter. Since many of these recipes require time and effort, we wanted to make them more sophisticated (or at least a little beyond the norm). Pork Belly Mapo Dofu (page 378)? It's absurdly delicious, since pork belly is so luxurious and the pot cooks it so quickly. In that recipe (and in others, too), we also offer ways to make the dish more legit, using some ingredients that might not be in your pantry. With one exception as you'll see, the recipes still retain our go-to rule: We only used ingredients we could find in our rural grocery store. But what lies in the *Beyond* section might require a little internet shopping.

So enjoy the time it takes to make what your grandmother would have considered a cheap cut of meat. Just as she did, you, too, can make it in a fraction of the time.

FAQs

1. What does it mean when it says to "slice the meat against the grain"?

Meat — or to be accurate *and* gross, muscle tissue — is fibrous. To do its job, it has to bend, flex, and twist. For poultry and most pork, the matter of its grain is moot. The meat has been butchered in such a way that the fibers already run against the cuts, so slicing a pork loin, for example, into individual rounds is no problem. But beef (along with veal and buffalo) is not typically butchered to make slicing and carving an easy task. (At least not in the U.S. Other countries butcher red meat more in keeping with its grain.).

To get long slices that don't fall apart or turn to stringy bits, slice cuts like sirloin or brisket "against the grain." Once cooked, run your fingers across the meat's surface. Notice which way the fibers run. Now carve 90 degrees from the direction of those fibers, cutting across them (that is, "against" them).

2. What's with all the frozen pearl onions?

Have you ever tried to peel fresh ones? Maddening! They're worse than garlic: zillions of bits of papery hull. Frozen pearl onions are already peeled. Ta-da! But more importantly, they hold up better under pressure, especially if they're still frozen when they hit the pot. As they brown, their exteriors contract with moisture loss, the interiors are still a little chilled, and the onions remain (basically) intact once the pressure hits. Sure, a few come apart. But they offer a great way to get texture and tooth into a long-braised dish. And one more thing: they're easy to have on hand, a few bags in the freezer ready to go.

2 tablespoons fat

Choose from butter, lard, schmaltz, rendered bacon fat, goose fat, duck fat, olive oil, vegetable oil, corn oil, canola oil, safflower oil, peanut oil, grape seed oil, avocado oil, sesame oil, or any nut oil—or a 50/50 combo of a solid fat and a liquid fat.

6 ounces cured and/or smoked meat, chopped

Choose from bacon (of any sort but not flavored), pancetta, prosciutto, or chorizo.

2½ pounds beef stew meat, cubed

Choose from bottom round, top round, boneless chuck, boneless arm roast, or "stew meat."

1 cup chopped (and trimmed if necessary) allium aromatics

Choose from onions (of any sort), shallots, or leeks (white and pale green part only, well washed).

2 cups sliced mushrooms (optional)

Choose any variety (but no shiitake mushroom stems).

½ cup *dried* fruit (optional)

Choose from raisins, currants, pitted and chopped prunes, chopped apricots, or stemmed and chopped figs.

1 tablespoon stemmed, minced fresh herbs

Choose one or a combination from basil, chives, marjoram, parsley, oregano, rosemary, sage, savory, tarragon, and/or thyme.

1½ teaspoons dried spices

Choose one or two from caraway seeds, fennel seeds, ground allspice, ground cinnamon, ground coriander, ground cumin, mild regular and/or smoked paprika.

Up to 3 medium garlic cloves, peeled and minced (1 tablespoon)

1 tablespoon flavor enhancer

Choose from vinegar or any sort, Dijon mustard, fresh lemon juice, Worcestershire sauce, hoisin sauce (page 184), soy sauce, pesto, pomegranate molasses, tomato paste, barbecue sauce, chowchow, or vinegary pickle relish

Road Map: Beef Stew

6 to 8 servings

We hope this recipe becomes the basis of one of your weeknight standards. There's quite a bit of variety here, including the choice between mushrooms and dried fruit. Mushrooms, of course, will give the stew an earthier edge. (If you really want to develop umami in the stew, use mushrooms *and* soy sauce—and even consider omitting the fresh herbs.) Dried fruit will yield a sweeter stew, probably a little more in line with what a lot of Americans consider comfort food. You can even use both mushrooms and dried fruit for a very complex mix of flavors.

As to the herb choices, particularly good combinations are thyme, cinnamon, and allspice; parsley, tarragon, and regular paprika; and oregano, thyme, fennel seeds, and smoked paprika.

1.

Press the button for	Set it for	Set the time for	If necessary, press
SAUTÉ	MEDIUM, NORMAL, or CUSTOM 300°F	25 minutes	START

2. Melt the fat or warm the oil in a **6- or 8-quart cooker**. Add the smoked and/or cured meat. Cook, stirring occasionally, until well browned or even crisp, 3 to 5 minutes. Use a slotted spoon to transfer the meat to a nearby bowl.

3. Add the stew meat and cook, stirring occasionally and rearranging the pieces, until *well* browned, about 10 minutes. Add the allium aromatic(s) and continue cooking, stirring more often, until it begins to soften, 2 to 3 minutes. If desired, stir in the mushrooms and/or dried fruit until well combined.

4. Stir in the fresh herbs, dried spices, and garlic until aromatic, just a few seconds, then stir in the flavor enhancer. Turn off the SAUTÉ function, pour in the liquid, and scrape up the browned bits on the pot's bottom. Lock the lid onto the pot.

5.

Set the machine for	Set the level for	The valve must be	Set the time for	If necessary, press
PRESSURE COOK	MAX	—	40 minutes with the KEEP WARM setting off	START
MEAT/STEW, PRESSURE COOK, or MANUAL	HIGH	Closed	50 minutes with the KEEP WARM setting off	START
SLOW COOK	HIGH	Opened	4 hours with the KEEP WARM setting off (or on for no more than 3 hours)	START

6. If you've used a pressure setting, when the machine finishes cooking, turn it off and let its pressure **return to normal naturally,** about 30 minutes.

7. Unlatch the lid and open the cooker. Stir in the potatoes and carrots. Lock the lid onto the pot.

8.

Set the machine for	Set the level for	The valve must be	Set the time for	If necessary, press
PRESSURE COOK	MAX	—	5 minutes with the KEEP WARM setting off	START
MEAT/STEW, PRESSURE COOK, or MANUAL	HIGH	Closed	7 minutes with the KEEP WARM setting off	START

9. Use the **quick-release method** to bring the pot's pressure back to normal. Unlatch the lid and open the cooker. Stir well. Because there's no way to figure out the amount of salt in your particular version, garnish servings with salt as desired.

1½ cups liquid

Choose from beef or chicken broth, beer, or a 50/50 combo of broth with either red wine, white wine, dry sherry, or dry vermouth.

1 pound yellow potatoes, such as Yukon Golds, cut into 1-inch pieces

1 pound medium carrots, cut into 1-inch pieces

Table, kosher, or coarse sea salt for garnishing (optional)

Beyond

- You must halve the recipe for a **3-quart cooker.**

- For a simpler stew, omit the potatoes and carrots (that is, skip steps 7, 8, and 9). We then recommend thickening the stew. First, increase the meat's cooking time to 45 minutes for MAX or 57 minutes on HIGH in step 5. (The time for slow-cooking the stew will not change.) Then whisk 2 tablespoons water and 1½ tablespoons cornstarch in a small bowl until smooth. Once you've opened the pot, use the SAUTÉ setting on MEDIUM, NORMAL, or CUSTOM 300°F to bring the sauce to a simmer. Stir in the cornstarch slurry and cook, stirring often until thickened, 1 to 2 minutes. Immediately turn off the SAUTÉ function and remove the *hot* insert from the pot to stop the cooking.

- If the stew is too wet for your taste *with* the potatoes and carrots, we don't advise using a slurry to thicken it. Instead, boil it down with the SAUTÉ setting on HIGH or MORE, stirring quite often, 1 to 3 minutes.

- Our favorite way to serve beef stew, even with potatoes in the mix, is over big, crunchy croutons: Buy a baguette, cut it into 1-inch-thick slices, and toast these on a lipped baking sheet in a 375°F oven, turning occasionally, until brown and crisp.

2 tablespoons fat

Choose from either a solid fat like butter, rendered bacon fat, lard, schmaltz, goose fat, or duck fat; or a tasty liquid fat like olive oil, sesame oil, walnut oil, pecan oil, or pumpkin seed oil — or a 50/50 combo of solid and liquid fat.

One 3½-pound boneless chuck roast

½ teaspoon table salt (optional)

½ teaspoon ground black pepper

1½ cups chopped (and trimmed if necessary) allium aromatics

Choose from onions (of any sort), shallots, or leeks (white and pale green parts only, well washed).

2 medium garlic cloves, peeled and minced (2 teaspoons)

2 large sprigs of fresh herbs

Choose from basil, marjoram, oregano, parsley, rosemary, sage, tarragon, or thyme.

Up to 1½ teaspoons dried spice

Choose one or two from ground allspice, ground coriander, ground cumin, mild paprika, mild smoked paprika, fennel seeds, caraway seeds, and/or mustard seeds.

1½ cups liquid

Choose from broth of any sort; or a 50/50 combo of broth and wine of any sort, beer, dry sherry, or dry vermouth; or a two-thirds/one-third combo of broth and gin, whiskey, and/or bourbon.

2 tablespoons flavor enhancer

Choose from tomato paste, barbecue sauce, Dijon mustard, chutney, jarred prepared horseradish, pesto, tapenade, red chili sauce (such as Heinz), sweet Thai chile sauce, tamarind paste, or hoisin sauce (see page 184).

1½ pounds peeled (and seeded, necessary) roots or tubers, chopped into 2-inch pieces

Choose one or a selection from yellow potatoes, red-skinned potatoes, sweet potatoes, parsnips, carrots, turnips, rutabaga, celeriac, and/or yellow beets.

2 tablespoons water

1½ tablespoons cornstarch

Road Map: Pot Roast

6 to 8 servings

Well over three-quarters of the U.S. would call a braised chuck roast a "pot roast." For the rest of you, see Road Map: Braised Brisket on page 352.

The road map given here for a chuck roast will let you customize the preparation to suit your taste and let you experiment with the dish for years to come. But think about whether you want to salt the meat before you do so. The flavor enhancer you use may be loaded with salt.

There are various types of chuck roast on the market: some thick, almost "rolls" of meat; others flatter and wider. Any will work. However, flatter cuts may come apart after being under pressure for so long. For better aesthetics, consider tying the meat. Wrap butchers' twine around its perimeter and tie securely but not tightly, holding the meat in place without scrunching it up. Snip this twine off the roast before carving.

If you don't mind a soupier sauce, ignore steps 9 and 10. In all honesty, we often decide whether we want to thicken the sauce once we open the pot and remove the meat in step 8.

1.

Press the button for	Set it for	Set the time for	If necessary, press
SAUTÉ	MEDIUM, NORMAL, or CUSTOM 300°F	20 minutes	START

2. Melt the fat or warm the oil in a **6- or 8-quart cooker**. Season the roast with the salt (if using) and pepper. Set it in the cooker and brown *well* on both sides, turning once or twice, 8 to 10 minutes. Transfer the roast to a nearby cutting board.

3. Add the allium aromatics and cook, stirring often, until softened, 2 to 5 minutes. Stir in the garlic until aromatic, just a few seconds; then add the fresh herb sprigs and the dried spice(s).

4. Stir well, turn off the SAUTÉ function, pour in the broth, and scrape up the browned bits on the pot's bottom. Stir in the flavor enhancer until smooth and nestle the chuck roast into the sauce. Pour any juices on the cutting board into the pot and lock the lid onto the cooker.

5.

Set the machine for	Set level for	The valve must be	Set the time for	If necessary, press
PRESSURE COOK	MAX	—	40 minutes with the KEEP WARM setting off	START
MEAT/STEW, PRESSURE COOK, or MANUAL	HIGH	Closed	55 minutes with the KEEP WARM setting off	START

6. Use the **quick-release method** to bring the pot's pressure back to normal. Unlatch the lid and open the cooker. Scatter the roots or tubers around the meat. Lock the lid back onto the pot.

7.

Set the machine for	Set level for	The valve must be	Set the time for	If necessary, press
PRESSURE COOK	MAX	—	20 minutes with the KEEP WARM setting off	START
MEAT/STEW, PRESSURE COOK, or MANUAL	HIGH	Closed	28 minutes with the KEEP WARM setting off	START

8. When the machine has finished cooking, turn it off and let its pressure **return to normal naturally**, about 30 minutes. Unlatch the lid and open the cooker. Use a wide spatula and a large cooking spoon (for balance) to transfer the meat to a nearby cutting board (the cut may fall into large chunks, especially if it wasn't tied). Use a flatware tablespoon to skim any excess surface fat from the sauce in the pot.

9.

Press the button for	Set it for	Set the time for	If necessary, press
SAUTÉ	MEDIUM, NORMAL, or CUSTOM 300°F	15 minutes	START

10. As the sauce and vegetables come to a simmer, whisk the water and cornstarch in a small bowl until smooth. Once the sauce is bubbling, stir this slurry into the pot. Continue cooking, stirring constantly, until thickened, 1 to 2 minutes. Turn off the SAUTÉ function and remove the *hot* insert from the pot to stop the cooking. Slice the meat into chunks and serve in bowls with lots of the sauce and vegetables.

Beyond

- You must halve the recipe for a **3-quart cooker.**

- To use the SLOW COOK setting, complete the recipe through step 4. Scatter the roots and/or tubers on top of and around the beef. With the pressure valve open, lock the lid onto the pot and cook on HIGH for 6 hours (then leave on the KEEP WARM setting for up to 2 hours). When done, complete the second half of step 8, as well as steps 9 and 10 as written.

1 tablespoon butter

1 tablespoon olive oil

One 3- to 3½-pound boneless beef chuck roast

2 medium yellow onions, halved and sliced into thin half-moons

2 medium garlic cloves, peeled and minced (2 teaspoons)

1 tablespoon stemmed fresh thyme leaves

1 teaspoon fennel seeds

¼ teaspoon grated nutmeg

¼ teaspoon red pepper flakes

1 large round red tomato, chopped (1 cup)

¼ cup chopped pitted black olives

¼ cup raisins

1¼ cups beef or chicken broth

2 tablespoons tomato paste

Braised Chuck Roast with Raisins and Olives

6 servings

If you're not in the mood to figure out your own road map for a pot roast, try this recipe with its sweet-and-savory sauce, a nice match to the naturally sweet flavors in the beef. There's no salt in the sauce; the olives add plenty. If you miss the salt (or want a more savory dish), drizzle the servings with soy sauce.

1.

Press the button for	Set it for	Set the time for	If necessary, press
SAUTÉ	MEDIUM, NORMAL, or CUSTOM 300°F	20 minutes	START

2. Melt the butter in the oil in a **6- or 8-quart cooker**. Add the chuck roast and brown *well* on all sides, even around the perimeter, turning occasionally but not too much, about 10 minutes. Use a wide metal spatula and a big cooking spoon (for balance) to transfer the chuck roast to a nearby cutting board.

3. Add the onions and cook, stirring often, until they begin to soften, about 4 minutes. Stir in the garlic, thyme, fennel seeds, nutmeg, and red pepper flakes until fragrant, just a few seconds. Add the tomato, olives, and raisins.

4. Stir well, turn off the SAUTÉ function, pour in the broth, and scrape up any browned bits on the pot's bottom. Whisk the tomato paste into the sauce. Return the beef and any juices on the cutting board to the pot. Lock the lid onto the cooker.

5.

Set the machine for	Set the level for	The valve must be	Set the time for	If necessary, press
PRESSURE COOK	MAX	—	1 hour with the KEEP WARM setting off	START
MEAT/STEW, PRESSURE COOK, or MANUAL	HIGH	Closed	1 hour 20 minutes with the KEEP WARM setting off	START
SLOW COOK	HIGH	Opened	5 hours with the KEEP WARM setting off (or on for no more than 3 hours)	START

6. If you've used a pressure setting, when the machine has finished cooking, turn it off and let its pressure **return to normal naturally,** about 30 minutes.

7. Unlatch the lid and open the cooker. Use that same large spatula and a big spoon to transfer the roast to a cutting board (the meat may fall into chunks). Cool for a couple of minutes. Meanwhile, use a flatware tablespoon to skim the excess surface fat off the sauce in the pot. Chunk the meat into pieces or slice it into ½-inch-thick rounds, then serve in bowls with lots of the sauce.

Beyond

- You must halve the recipe for a **3-quart cooker.**

- Look for better quality olives at the prepared foods bar at your supermarket.

- Serve this braise in split-open baked potatoes — or even on top of cooked wheat berries (see page 359).

- Although the thyme/fennel/nutmeg combo is particularly pleasing with the olives, try tarragon/caraway seeds/ground allspice in equal measures to the original set of spices.

2 tablespoons vegetable, corn, or canola oil

One 3- to 3½-pound boneless beef chuck roast

½ teaspoon ground black pepper

6 medium scallions, trimmed and thinly sliced

3 medium garlic cloves, peeled and minced (1 tablespoon)

Up to 2 small fresh jalapeño chiles, stemmed, halved lengthwise, seeded, and thinly sliced

1 tablespoon packed fresh oregano leaves

½ teaspoon ground allspice

¼ teaspoon grated nutmeg

1 bay leaf

1 cup plain cola (do not use diet)

¾ cup beef or chicken broth

¼ cup dark rum, such as Myers's

1 tablespoon soy sauce

Cuba Libre–Braised Chuck Roast

6 servings

Cuba Libre is that classic cruise-ship cocktail: a rum and Coke. However, in pressure cooking, standard gold or white rum doesn't have enough oomph to stand up to the pressure and the complicated sauce. Use only dark rum, a sweet and sticky concoction that turns pot roast into something special.

1.

Press the button for	Set it for	Set the time for	If necessary, press
SAUTÉ	MEDIUM, NORMAL, or CUSTOM 300°F	15 minutes	START

2. Warm the oil in a **6- or 8-quart cooker** for a minute or two. Season the roast with the pepper, set it in the cooker, then brown *well* on all sides, even the perimeter, turning occasionally, about 10 minutes. Transfer the roast to a nearby cutting board.

3. Add the scallions, garlic, jalapeño(s), oregano, allspice, nutmeg, and bay leaf. Stir well until aromatic, just a few seconds. Pour in the cola and scrape up any browned bits on the pot's bottom. Turn off the SAUTÉ function.

4. Stir in the broth, rum, and soy sauce. Return the beef and any juices on the cutting board to the cooker. Lock the lid onto the pot.

5.

Set the machine for	Set the level for	The valve must be	Set the time for	If necessary, press
PRESSURE COOK	MAX	—	1 hour with the KEEP WARM setting off	START
MEAT/STEW, PRESSURE COOK, or MANUAL	HIGH	Closed	1 hour 20 minutes with the KEEP WARM setting off	START
SLOW COOK	HIGH	Opened	5 hours with the KEEP WARM setting off (or on for no more than 3 hours)	START

6. If you've used a pressure setting, when the machine has finished cooking, turn it off and let its pressure **return to normal naturally**, about 30 minutes.

7. Unlatch the lid and open the cooker. Use a large metal spatula and a big cooking spoon to transfer the roast to a clean cutting board. Cool for 5 to 10 minutes. Meanwhile, fish out and discard the bay leaf. Use a flatware tablespoon to skim any excess surface fat from the sauce. Chunk the meat into pieces or slice it into ½-inch-thick rounds, then serve in bowls with lots of the sauce.

Beyond

- You must halve the recipe for a **3-quart cooker**.

- Add up to 4 ounces chopped bacon. Crisp it in the oil, then use a slotted spoon to transfer the bacon to a nearby bowl before browning the beef.

- Rather than potatoes, serve this over Black Beans and Rice (page 403).

2 tablespoons solid or liquid fat

Choose form butter, lard, schmaltz, rendered bacon fat, goose fat, duck fat, olive oil, avocado oil, sesame oil, vegetable oil, corn oil, canola oil, safflower oil, peanut oil, grape seed oil, or any nut oil — or a 50/50 combo of solid and liquid fat.

One 3-pound beef brisket, preferably the flat (or first) cut, any surface fat trimmed to ¼ inch thick

½ teaspoon table salt (optional)

½ teaspoon ground black pepper

2 cups chopped (and trimmed if necessary) allium aromatics

Choose one or two from onions (of any sort), scallions, shallots, leeks (white and pale green parts only, well washed), and/or frozen pearl onions (do not thaw).

4 medium garlic cloves, peeled

1 tablespoon dried herbs and/or spices

Choose at least two from basil, chervil, fennel seeds, marjoram, oregano, rosemary, sage, savory, thyme, ground allspice, ground cinnamon, ground coriander, ground cumin, mild paprika, and/or mild smoked paprika; or choose an dried herb blend, such as herbes de Provence, an Italian blend, a Cajun blend, or others (keeping in mind that dried spices are usually more potent than dried herbs).

½ cup liquid enhancer

Choose from red wine, white wine, dry vermouth, dry sherry, brandy, bourbon, unsweetened apple cider, or beer (particularly a dark beer or a porter).

¾ cup broth

Choose any sort.

Up to ¼ cup flavor booster

Choose one from a range of condiments: mustard of any sort, ketchup, chutney of any sort, barbecue sauce of any sort, soy sauce, orange marmalade, hoisin sauce (page 184), or oyster sauce.

Road Map: Braised Brisket

6 to 8 servings

Here's a way to make what at least parts of New England and New York call "pot roast" — that is, braised brisket.

This recipe calls for a flat-cut (or first-cut) brisket: a leaner piece without a cap of fatty meat at one end. Choose a brisket with a fairly even thickness. A 3-pound brisket might not fit in a **6-quart cooker**, depending on its overall shape. It's fine to cut one in half widthwise and stack the pieces on each other (you'll probably have to brown them in two steps). And it's fine to mush a single piece of brisket against the sides of the pot *a bit* (but not a lot) because the meat will shrink as it cooks.

As you make up your own version of this recipe, keep the flavors fairly simple. Work with a purchased spice blend if you're unsure how to blend spices. Over the long cooking, the meat will become quite soft, almost velvety. It won't be much good for slicing for sandwiches, but the leftovers will make a fine, tasty, chopped beef sandwich the next day.

1.

Press the button for	Set it for	Set the time for	If necessary, press
SAUTÉ	MEDIUM, NORMAL, or CUSTOM 300°F	20 minutes	START

2. Melt the fat on its own or in some oil, or warm the oil for a minute or two in a **6- or 8-quart cooker**. Season the brisket with the salt (if using) and pepper, then set it in the pot and brown *well* on both sides, turning only once or twice, about 10 minutes. Transfer the brisket to a nearby cutting board.

3. Add the allium aromatics and cook, stirring often, until they begin to soften, 2 to 4 minutes. Add the garlic cloves and the dried spices, stir well, then pour in the liquid enhancer. Scrape up any browned bits on the pot's bottom as it comes to a simmer.

4. Turn off the SAUTÉ function, then stir in the liquid and some of the flavor enhancer. Taste the sauce for salt and add more flavor enhancer, if desired. Return the brisket and any juices on the cutting board to the pot, nestling the meat into the sauce. Lock the lid onto the pot.

5.

Set the machine for	Set the level for	The valve must be	Set the time for	If necessary, press
PRESSURE COOK	MAX	—	1 hour with the KEEP WARM setting off	START
MEAT/STEW, PRESSURE COOK, or MANUAL	HIGH	Closed	1 hour 20 minutes with the KEEP WARM setting off	START

6. When the machine has finished cooking, turn it off and let its pressure **return to normal naturally,** about 30 minutes.

7. Unlatch the lid and open the cooker. Transfer the brisket to a clean cutting board. Cool for 5 to 10 minutes. Meanwhile, use a flatware tablespoon to skim any excess surface fat from the sauce in the pot. Slice the brisket into ½-inch-wide strips against the grain. Serve lapped with the sauce from the pot.

Beyond

- You must halve the recipe for a **3-quart cooker.**

- For a traditional Jewish brisket, substitute 1 cup canned diced tomatoes for the liquid enhancer *and* the flavor booster. Increase the broth to 1 cup. If desired, add up to ¼ cup raisins with the garlic and dried spices.

- For a thicker sauce, use an immersion blender after you've removed the brisket to puree the allium aromatics and thicken sauce.

- Or after transferring the brisket to a cutting board, boil down the sauce using the SAUTÉ function at its HIGH or MORE setting, stirring often, until reduced to about half its volume, 4 to 6 minutes.

- Or transfer the brisket to a cutting board, then bring the sauce to a simmer using the SAUTÉ function at its MEDIUM, NORMAL, or CUSTOM 300°F setting. Whisk 2 tablespoons water and 1 tablespoon cornstarch in a small bowl until smooth, then scrape every drop of this slurry into the sauce. Cook, stirring all the while, until thickened, 1 to 2 minutes. Immediately turn off the SAUTÉ function and remove the insert from the pot to stop the cooking.

2 thin strips of bacon, chopped

2½ tablespoons butter,
1½ tablespoons of it at room
temperature

3½ pounds boneless beef short ribs

1 small red onion, chopped (½ cup)

1 pound thinly sliced brown cremini
mushrooms

1 cup dry red wine, such as Cabernet
Sauvignon

½ cup beef or chicken broth

2 teaspoons dried thyme

1 teaspoon dried sage

½ teaspoon table salt

½ teaspoon ground black pepper

2 bay leaves

1½ tablespoons all-purpose flour

Bistro-Style Braised Short Ribs with Mushrooms

6 servings

Although cooking beef short ribs in the Instant Pot cuts down on the time they need to braise, we haven't shaved any time off any of the other steps in this fairly traditional recipe, even using a classic *beurre manié* (French, *burh mahn-YAY*, a butter and flour mixture) to thicken the sauce into silky richness. The meat will be so tender that you'll barely need knives at the table, so the short ribs are best served in bowls.

1.

Press the button for	Set it for	Set the time for	If necessary, press
SAUTÉ	MEDIUM, NORMAL, or CUSTOM 300°F	35 minutes	START

2. Melt 1 tablespoon butter in a **6- or 8-quart cooker**. Add the bacon and fry until crisp, stirring occasionally, about 4 minutes. Use a slotted spoon to transfer the bacon to a nearby large bowl.

3. Add half the short ribs and brown them *well* on all sides, turning occasionally, about 10 minutes. Transfer these to that bowl and add the remaining short ribs, browning them in just the same way. Transfer these to the bowl, too.

4. Add the onion and cook, stirring often, until softened, about 3 minutes. Add the mushrooms and continue cooking, stirring occasionally, until they give off their internal moisture and that liquid evaporates to a glaze in the pot, about 5 minutes.

5. Pour in the wine and scrape up the browned bits on the pot's bottom. Turn off the SAUTÉ function and stir in the broth, thyme, sage, salt, pepper, and bay leaves. Return the short ribs, bacon, and any juices in that bowl to the pot. Stir well, then lock the lid onto the cooker.

6.

Set the machine for	Set level for	The valve must be	Set the time for	If necessary, press
PRESSURE COOK	MAX	—	1 hour 10 minutes with the KEEP WARM setting off	START
MEAT/STEW, PRESSURE COOK, or MANUAL	HIGH	Closed	1 hour 30 minutes with the KEEP WARM setting off	START
SLOW COOK	HIGH	Opened	4 hours with the KEEP WARM setting off (or on for no more than 3 hours)	START

7. If you've used a pressure setting, when the machine has finished cooking, turn it off and let its pressure **return to normal naturally**, about 30 minutes.

8. Unlatch the lid and open the cooker. Find and discard the bay leaves. Use kitchen tongs and a slotted spoon to transfer the short ribs, bacon, and any vegetables to a serving platter. Tent with aluminum foil to keep warm. Use a flatware tablespoon to skim any excess surface fat from the sauce in the pot.

9.

Press the button for	Set it for	Set the time for	If necessary, press
SAUTÉ	MEDIUM, NORMAL, or CUSTOM 300°F	5 minutes	START

10. As the sauce comes to a simmer, use a fork to make a smooth paste out of the flour and the remaining, room-temperature 1½ tablespoons butter in a small bowl. As the sauce simmers, whisk this flour mixture into the pot in dribs and drabs, just a little at a time, whisking until it's all been added and the sauce has thickened, 1 to 2 minutes. Turn off the SAUTÉ function and pour the sauce in the *hot* insert over the meat and vegetables on the platter.

Beyond

- You must halve the recipe for a **3-quart cooker.**
- For a sweet finish in the sauce, add up to 2 medium carrots, chopped (1 cup), with the onion.
- Or add up to 2 teaspoons minced garlic with the dried herbs.
- Serve this stew alongside (or even over) crunchy roasted potatoes.

See photo in insert.

1½ pounds boneless beef chuck roast, tied around its perimeter with butchers' twine

1½ pounds bone-in beef short ribs

1 medium yellow onion, peeled and halved

1 medium head of garlic, any loose papery bits removed, then halved

6 large thyme sprigs

1 tablespoon black peppercorns

1 teaspoon table salt, plus more as necessary

1 bay leaf

Water, as needed

2 medium leeks, white and pale green parts only, halved lengthwise and well washed

4 medium carrots, peeled and halved widthwise

4 medium parsnips, peeled and halved widthwise

4 medium yellow potatoes, quartered

Streamlined Pot au Feu

4 to 6 servings

Pot au feu (French, *paw-toh-FUH*, "pot on the fire") may well be the definition of homesickness for many a French national living abroad. It's also the definition of an all-day dish — or was until now. In essence, it's boiled meat, rather plain (although we add interest with vegetables like parsnips). It's quite brothy, like a rich soup with meat and vegetables. Our process takes two steps: first, to build the broth, then to cook the meat in that broth with other vegetables until everything's meltingly tender, just about ready for a spoon.

1. Put the chuck roast, short ribs, onion, garlic, thyme, peppercorns, 1 teaspoon salt, and the bay leaf in a **6- or 8-quart cooker**, arranging the meat in fairly compact layers. Add enough water to just cover everything without going above the **Max Fill** line. Lock the lid onto the pot.

2.

Set the machine for	Set level for	The valve must be	Set the time for	If necessary, press
PRESSURE COOK	MAX	—	40 minutes with the KEEP WARM setting off	START
MEAT/STEW, PRESSURE COOK, or MANUAL	HIGH	Closed	55 minutes with the KEEP WARM setting off	START

3. When the machine has finished cooking, turn it off and let its pressure **return to normal naturally**, about 45 minutes. Unlatch the lid and open the cooker. Use kitchen tongs and a large, metal spatula to transfer the meat to a nearby cutting board.

4. Strain the liquid in the cooker through a fine-mesh sieve like a *chinois* (or a colander lined with a double thickness of cheesecloth) into a large bowl below. Discard all the solids; pour the strained broth into the cooker. Return the meat and any juices as well.

5. Add the leeks, carrots, parsnips, and potatoes, submerging them as much as possible in the liquid. (If for any reason the broth, meat, and vegetables come above the **Max Fill** line, ladle out enough broth so that the liquid level falls below that marker.) Lock the lid back onto the cooker.

6.

Set the machine for	Set level for	The valve must be	Set the time for	If necessary, press
PRESSURE COOK	MAX	—	7 minutes with the KEEP WARM setting off	START
MEAT/STEW, PRESSURE COOK, or MANUAL	HIGH	Closed	10 minutes with the KEEP WARM setting off	START

7. Use the **quick-release method** to return the pot's pressure to normal. Unlatch the lid and open the cooker. Dish the meat, vegetables, and broth into large serving bowls. Season with more salt, as needed.

Beyond

- You must halve the recipe for a **3-quart cooker**.

- Garnish the meat in each serving with a little Dijon mustard and serve with a crunchy baguette on the side.

- For an old-world version, omit the potatoes and use 4 medium turnips, peeled and quartered.

- Some traditional cooks add a little wine to sweeten the broth. Add up to ½ cup light red wine, such as Pinot Noir, with the vegetables in step 5.

2 tablespoons butter

1 large yellow onion, chopped
(1½ cups)

2 medium carrots, chopped (1 cup)

2½ pounds beef sirloin tips, cut into
1-inch pieces

2 tablespoons packed sage leaves,
finely chopped

1 tablespoon packed stemmed thyme
leaves

½ teaspoon table salt

½ teaspoon ground black pepper

2½ cups beef or chicken broth

1 cup dried black-eyed peas

Sirloin Tips Braised with Black-Eyed Peas

6 servings

Sirloin tips are economical and flavorful, with little bits of cartilage and fat held in the meat. Those inner bits melt under pressure, offering you quick one-pot comfort food.

Don't cut up a sirloin steak for this recipe. It'll overcook and dry out. And quickly glance over the dried black-eyed peas, just to make sure there are no little hulls, stones, or extraneous bits among them.

1.

Press the button for	Set it for	Set the time for	If necessary, press
SAUTÉ	LOW or LESS	20 minutes	START

2. Warm the butter in a **6- or 8-quart cooker** for a minute or two. Add the onion and carrot. Cook, stirring often, until the onion is exceptionally soft, even a little browned, about 15 minutes. Add the sirloin tips and continue cooking, stirring occasionally, until they lose their pink, raw color, about 3 minutes.

3. Stir in the sage, thyme, salt, and pepper until aromatic, just a few seconds. Pour in the broth and scrape up any browned bits on the pot's bottom. Turn off the SAUTÉ function and stir in the black-eyed peas. Lock the lid onto the cooker.

4.

Set the machine for	Set level for	The valve must be	Set the time for	If necessary, press
PRESSURE COOK	MAX	—	20 minutes with the KEEP WARM setting off	START
MEAT/STEW, PRESSURE COOK, or MANUAL	HIGH	Closed	30 minutes with the KEEP WARM setting off	START

5. Use the **quick-release method** to bring the pot's pressure back to normal. Unlatch the lid and open the cooker. Stir well before serving.

Beyond

- You must halve the recipe for a **3-quart cooker.**

- Try these flavor variations: Add 1 large round red tomato, chopped, with the black-eyed peas.

- And/or add up to 1 tablespoon minced garlic with the fresh herbs.

- And/or add up to 2 teaspoons finely minced orange zest.

- And/or add up to ½ teaspoon red pepper flakes.

Tea-Braised Eye of Round Roast

6 to 8 servings

A smoky tea is an amazing braising medium, especially under pressure. It becomes irresistibly sweet, turning the broth for this down-home, Chinese braise into a spiced sensation. You needn't add the Sichuan peppercorns, although they're readily available these days at large supermarkets (and from hundreds of online suppliers). We'll confess that their use here breaks our oath about using ingredients only from our rural supermarket. Thus, those peppercorns are optional. (For more information, see the headnote to Pork Belly Mapo Dofu on page 378.)

1. Bring the water to a boil in a medium saucepan set over high heat. Remove the pan from the heat and stir in the loose tea or add the tea bags. Cover and set aside until very dark, about 10 minutes. Strain the tea into a medium bowl or remove and discard the bags.

2.

Press the button for	Set it for	Set the time for	If necessary, press
SAUTÉ	MEDIUM, NORMAL, or CUSTOM 300°F	15 minutes	START

3. Warm the oil in a **6- or 8-quart cooker** for a minute or two. Add the beef and brown it *well* on all sides, turning occasionally, about 10 minutes. Transfer the meat to a nearby cutting board. Pour the tea into the pot and stir to get up all the browned bits on the pot's bottom.

4. Turn off the SAUTÉ function; stir in the ginger, Sichuan peppercorns (if using), and salt. Return the roast to the pot. Add the leeks and chile, making sure these are mostly in the broth. Lock the lid onto the pot.

5.

Set the machine for	Set level for	The valve must be	Set the time for	If necessary, press
PRESSURE COOK	MAX	—	55 minutes with the KEEP WARM setting off	START
MEAT/STEW, PRESSURE COOK, or MANUAL	HIGH	Closed	1 hour 15 minutes with the KEEP WARM setting off	START
SLOW COOK	HIGH	Opened	5 hours with the KEEP WARM setting off (or on for no more than 4 hours)	START

6. If you've used a pressure setting, when the machine has finished cooking, turn it off and let its pressure **return to normal naturally,** about 30 minutes.

7. Unlatch the lid and open the pot. Transfer the roast to a cutting board and cool for 5 minutes. Carve into ½-inch-thick slices and serve in bowls with lots of the broth from the pot.

2 cups water

¼ cup loose Lapsang Souchong tea or 6 Lapsang Souchong tea bags, any labels removed

2 tablespoons vegetable, corn, or canola oil

One 3-pound beef eye of round roast

1 teaspoon ground dried ginger

1 teaspoon Sichuan peppercorns (optional)

½ teaspoon table salt

1 medium leek, white and pale green part only, halved lengthwise, washed well, and thinly sliced (⅓ cup)

1 small fresh serrano chile, stemmed, halved lengthwise, seeded (if desired), and thinly sliced

Beyond

- You must halve the recipe for a **3-quart cooker.**

- Make the tea in the Instant Pot: Set the SAUTÉ function on HIGH or MORE and bring the water to a simmer. Add the tea or tea bags and turn off the SAUTÉ function. Cover and steep as directed, then either strain the liquid into another bowl to remove the loose tea or remove and discard the tea bags and pour the liquid into a nearby bowl.

- Stir a little hot red chile sauce like sambal oelek into individual servings.

- Use other sorts of smoky tea, particularly Pu'er (sometimes spelled "pu-erh"), a tea that's been allowed to ferment until rich and whiskey-like.

- Don't throw out any extra broth after serving dinner. Store it in the fridge. The next day, heat it up and mix it with cooked and drained rice noodles, a little sliced scallion, and plenty of fresh bean sprouts.

2 tablespoons peanut or toasted sesame oil

One 2- to 2½-pound beef flank steak, cut in half widthwise

10 medium scallions, trimmed and cut into 2-inch pieces

8 ounces shiitake mushrooms, the stems discarded and the caps thinly sliced

2 medium garlic cloves, peeled and minced (2 teaspoons)

2 tablespoons minced peeled fresh ginger

1½ cups beef or chicken broth

2 tablespoons soy sauce

2 tablespoons dark brown sugar

3 medium carrots, cut into 1-inch chunks

Teriyaki-Style Braised Flank Steak

6 servings

This recipe's a braise-y cross between teriyaki and negimaki, those rolls of beef around scallions in a sweet sauce that are served as appetizers in North American Japanese restaurants. We deconstructed all those flavors into a rich broth for the flank steak. It will be too large for the pot, so cut it in half and overlap these pieces without setting one directly on top of the other.

1.

Press the button for	Set it for	Set the time for	If necessary, press
SAUTÉ	MEDIUM, NORMAL, or CUSTOM 300°F	25 minutes	START

2. Warm 1 tablespoon oil in a **6- or 8-cooker** for 1 to 2 minutes. Add one piece of flank steak and brown it on both sides, turning occasionally, about 8 minutes. Transfer the steak to a nearby cutting board, add the remaining 1 tablespoon oil, and brown the second piece of flank steak in the same way before getting it to the cutting board.

3. Add the scallions, mushrooms, garlic, and ginger to the pot. Cook, stirring often, until the mushrooms begin to soften, about 2 minutes. Pour in the broth and scrape up any browned bits on the pot's bottom.

4. Turn off the SAUTÉ function, then stir in the soy sauce and brown sugar until dissolved. Return the meat and any juices to the pot. Put the carrots on top and lock the lid onto the cooker.

5.

Set the machine for	Set the level for	The valve must be	Set the time for	If necessary, press
PRESSURE COOK	MAX	——	50 minutes with the KEEP WARM setting off	START
MEAT/STEW, PRESSURE COOK, or MANUAL	HIGH	Closed	1 hour 5 minutes with the KEEP WARM setting off	START
SLOW COOK	HIGH	Opened	5 hours with the KEEP WARM setting off (or on for no more than 3 hours)	START

6. If you've used a pressure setting, when the machine has finished cooking, turn it off and let its pressure **return to normal naturally,** about 35 minutes.

7. Unlatch the lid and open the pot. Transfer the meat to a clean cutting board. Slice the meat against the grain into ½-inch-thick slices and serve in bowls with the sauce and carrots.

Beyond

- For a **3-quart cooker,** you must use 1 cup broth and halve the remaining ingredients.

- To thicken the sauce, transfer the carrots to the cutting board with the meat. Use the SAUTÉ function at MEDIUM, NORMAL, or CUSTOM 300°F to bring the sauce to a simmer. Whisk 2 tablespoons water and 1 tablespoon cornstarch in a small bowl until smooth, then whisk this mixture into the sauce. Cook, whisking constantly, until thickened, 1 to 2 minutes. Turn off the SAUTÉ function and remove the *hot* insert from the pot to stop the cooking. Spoon the sauce over the slices.

- Serve the slices and broth over cooked and drained rice noodles of any sort, or even vermicelli.

3½ to 4-pound beef bottom round roast

1 medium yellow onion, peeled and halved

2 medium carrots, halved widthwise

2 medium celery stalks, halved widthwise

One 6-inch rosemary sprig

6 large fresh sage leaves

2 teaspoons kosher salt

1 teaspoon ground black pepper

2 bay leaves

1 cup plus 1 tablespoon white wine vinegar

Water as needed

1 cup fresh breadcrumbs

4 cups loosely packed fresh parsley leaves and stems (about 2 medium bunches)

Up to 4 jarred anchovy fillets

Up to 3 medium garlic cloves, peeled and minced (1 tablespoon)

2 teaspoons drained and rinsed capers

Up to ½ cup olive oil

Streamlined Bollito Misto

8 servings

Bollito misto, like Pot au Feu (page 356), is a boiled meat dish, although this one is Italian rather than French. We've streamlined it by using only beef bottom round (rather than a big range of meat cuts, so ours is not really a bollito *misto*, more like a bollito *uno*).

Don't eat the vegetables after cooking. In culinary terms, they're "spent" — that is, they've added all their flavor to the savory broth that's served with the meat. But the broth and the meat will be pure bliss, savory and satisfying.

1. Set the beef in a **6- or 8-quart cooker**. Put the onion, carrots, celery, rosemary, sage, salt, pepper, and bay leaves around the beef. Drizzle 1 tablespoon vinegar over everything, then add enough water to a depth of about three-quarters of the way up the meat. (The liquid level must not go above the **Max Fill** line. Set the meat in the pot so that it's as flat as possible.) Lock the lid onto the pot.

2.

Set the machine for	Set the level for	The valve must be	Set the time for	If necessary, press
PRESSURE COOK	MAX	—	1 hour with the KEEP WARM setting off	START
MEAT/STEW, PRESSURE COOK, or MANUAL	HIGH	Closed	1 hour 30 minutes with the KEEP WARM setting off	START
SLOW COOK	HIGH	Opened	5½ hours with the KEEP WARM setting off (or on for no more than 4 hours)	START

3. Meanwhile, mix the breadcrumbs and the remaining 1 cup vinegar in a large bowl and set aside for 20 minutes.

4. If you've used a pressure setting, when the machine has finished cooking, turn it off and let its pressure **return to normal naturally**, about 40 minutes.

5. Unlatch the lid and open the cooker. Use a large, metal spatula and a big cooking spoon (mostly for balance) to transfer the beef to a nearby cutting board. Use a slotted spoon to find and discard everything else in the pot. Tent the meat with aluminum foil while you make the parsley sauce.

6. Squeeze the breadcrumbs dry by handfuls over the sink, then add them to a food processor. Add the parsley, anchovies, capers, and ¼ cup olive oil. Cover and pulse to create a coarse sauce, stopping the machine to scrape down the inside occasionally and adding more olive oil through the feed tube to get a saucy consistency (but no more than ¼ cup additional olive oil).

7. Carve the beef into ½-inch-thick slices and serve with lots of the parsley sauce on top. The leftover sauce can stay in a covered container in the fridge for up to 3 days, so long as you smooth it out in a container and pour a thin layer of olive oil on top of it to prevent oxidation (aka browning).

Beyond

- You must halve the recipe for a **3-quart cooker.**

- Make a full meal by offering traditional antipasto ingredients on the side: jarred roasted red peppers, marinated artichoke hearts, olives, even small mozzarella balls.

- Or serve this dish with Better Syracuse Potatoes (page 425).

1 tablespoon butter

1 tablespoon vegetable, corn, or canola oil

2½ pounds beef bottom round roast

½ teaspoon table salt

½ teaspoon ground black pepper

1 large yellow onion, chopped (1½ cups)

2 medium carrots, chopped (1 cup)

2 medium garlic cloves, peeled and minced (2 teaspoons)

½ cup dry but fruit-forward red wine, such as Zinfandel

½ cup beef broth

½ cup red wine vinegar

1 teaspoon granulated sugar

½ teaspoon caraway seeds

½ teaspoon ground allspice

4 bay leaves

1 tablespoon tomato paste

Sauerbraten-Style Pot Roast

4 to 6 servings

Taking advantage of the way pressure can (sort of) marinate meat *as* it cooks, here's a way to prepare a tasty replica of more traditional sauerbraten just about any weekend evening. Beef bottom round gives the dish some richness (top round would be too dry) without becoming too oily (as, say, chuck would). Use good-quality, very flavorful red wine, the sort you're apt to finish the evening you make this meal.

1.

Press the button for	Set it for	Set the time for	If necessary, press
SAUTÉ	MEDIUM, NORMAL, or CUSTOM 300°F	20 minutes	START

2. Melt the butter in the oil in a **6- or 8-quart cooker**. Season the beef with the salt and pepper, get it in the pot, and brown it *well*, turning a couple of times, about 10 minutes. Transfer the beef to a nearby cutting board.

3. Add the onion and carrot; cook, stirring often, until the onion just begins to soften, about 2 minutes. Add the garlic and stir until aromatic, just a few seconds. Pour in the wine and scrape up any browned bits on the pot's bottom.

4. Turn off the SAUTÉ function. Stir in the broth, vinegar, sugar, caraway seeds, allspice, and bay leaves. Return the meat and any juices to the pot, nestling the meat into the sauce. Lock the lid onto the pot.

5.

Set the machine for	Set the level for	The valve must be	Set the time for	If necessary, press
PRESSURE COOK	MAX	—	55 minutes with the KEEP WARM setting off	START
MEAT/STEW, PRESSURE COOK, or MANUAL	HIGH	Closed	1 hour 15 minutes with the KEEP WARM setting off	START
SLOW COOK	HIGH	Opened	5 hours with the KEEP WARM setting off (or on for no more than 4 hours)	START

6. If you've used a pressure setting, when the machine has finished cooking, turn it off and let its pressure **return to normal naturally**, about 40 minutes.

7. Unlatch the lid and open the cooker. Using a large, metal spatula and a big cooking spoon (mostly for balance), transfer the meat to a clean cutting board. Find and discard the bay leaves.

8.

Press the button for	Set it for	Set the time for	If necessary, press
SAUTÉ	MEDIUM, NORMAL, or CUSTOM 300°F	5 minutes	START

9. When the sauce comes to a simmer, stir in the tomato paste and cook, stirring often, until the sauce has thickened slightly, 2 to 3 minutes. Turn off the SAUTÉ function, then remove the *hot* insert from the machine to stop the cooking. Slice the meat against the grain into ½-inch-thick slices. Serve in bowls with lots of the sauce.

Beyond

- You must halve the recipe for a **3-quart cooker.**
- This version is not very sweet. Increase the sugar to 1 tablespoon, if desired.
- Serve the meat and sauce over Buttery Noodles (page 155).

2 tablespoons olive oil

6 bone-in ½- to ¾-inch-thick beef shanks, each about ¾ pound

4 ounces frozen pearl onions (1 cup—no need to thaw)

6 ounces thinly sliced brown cremini mushrooms

1 cup dark beer, preferably brown ale

¾ cup beef or chicken broth

2 tablespoons Worcestershire sauce

1 tablespoon Dijon mustard

1 teaspoon caraway seeds

1 teaspoon dried thyme

Beer-Braised Beef Shanks

6 servings

Beef shanks are the fantastic cut of beef: like osso buco but more savory, less soft, a hearty meal for chilly weather. The shanks are big—they won't all be submerged in the cooking liquids. Overlap them as necessary.

And one note: We also tested this recipe with grass-fed-and-finished beef shanks. They needed an extra 5 minutes under pressure at either pressure level (but no additional time on the SLOW COOK function).

1.

Press the button for	Set it for	Set the time for	If necessary, press
SAUTÉ	MEDIUM, NORMAL, or CUSTOM 300°F	30 minutes	START

2. Warm the oil in a **6- or 8-quart cooker** for a minute or two. Add two or three of the shanks and brown well, turning a few times, about 10 minutes. Transfer these to a nearby bowl and soldier on, browning the remaining shanks without crowding them before getting them into the bowl.

3. Add the pearl onions and mushrooms to the pot. Cook, stirring often, until the mushrooms begin to soften, about 3 minutes. Pour in the beer and scrape up the browned bits on the pot's bottom.

4. Turn off the SAUTÉ function. Stir in the broth, Worcestershire sauce, mustard, caraway seeds, and thyme. Return the shanks and any juices to the pot, nestling them into the sauce as well as you can. Lock the lid onto the pot.

5.

Set the machine for	Set the level for	The valve must be	Set the time for	If necessary, press
PRESSURE COOK	MAX	—	40 minutes with the KEEP WARM setting off	START
MEAT/STEW, PRESSURE COOK, or MANUAL	HIGH	Closed	50 minutes with the KEEP WARM setting off	START
SLOW COOK	HIGH	Opened	5 hours with the KEEP WARM setting off (or on for no more than 4 hours)	START

6. If you've used a pressure setting, when the machine has finished cooking, turn it off and let its pressure **return to normal naturally,** about 30 minutes.

7. Unlatch the lid and open the pot. Serve the shanks in bowls with lots of the sauce around them.

Beyond

- You must halve the recipe for a **3-quart cooker.**

- Have toast on hand so that you can cut it on the diagonal and use the tip to dig the marrow out of the bones before spreading it on the toast.

- Serve the shanks, vegetables, and broth over cooked and drained orzo.

Italian-Style Braised Meatloaf

4 to 6 servings

Braising a meatloaf gives it a smooth, luxurious texture. The breadcrumbs do not have to be soaked because they take on so much liquid and soften so well under pressure. If the breadcrumbs you buy have salt in the mix, reduce the Worcestershire sauce to 1½ teaspoons. (And for a more traditional — if made in a Bundt pan — meatloaf, see page 270.)

The only way to get this behemoth of a loaf out of the pot after cooking is with a wide, flexible, metal spatula. If you're worried, cut the loaf in half in the pot, then transfer the two halves to a cutting board.

1. Mix the tomatoes, onion, bell pepper, garlic, broth, vinegar, basil, oregano, nutmeg, red pepper flakes, and salt in a **6-quart cooker**.

2. Stir the ground beef, breadcrumbs, egg, Worcestershire sauce, garlic powder, and pepper in a large bowl until uniform. (The egg must be thoroughly mixed in.) Using clean, dry hands, form this mixture into a 7-inch meatloaf, about like a football cut in half from point to point, then the ends rounded to form a more compact loaf. Set this loaf into the sauce in the cooker; spoon some of the sauce over the loaf. Lock the lid onto the pot.

3.

Set the machine for	Set the level for	The valve must be	Set the time for	If necessary, press
PRESSURE COOK	MAX	—	18 minutes with the KEEP WARM setting off	START
MEAT/STEW, PRESSURE COOK, or MANUAL	HIGH	Closed	25 minutes with the KEEP WARM setting off	START

4. When the machine has finished cooking, turn it off and let its pressure **return to normal naturally**, about 25 minutes. Unlatch the lid and open the cooker. Transfer the meatloaf to a cutting board. Cool for a few minutes, then slice and serve with the sauce from the pot.

One 14-ounce can diced tomatoes (1¾ cups)

1 small yellow onion, chopped (½ cup)

1 small green bell pepper, stemmed, cored, and chopped (½ cup)

1 medium garlic clove, peeled and minced (1 teaspoon)

½ cup beef or chicken broth

1 tablespoon balsamic vinegar

2 teaspoons dried basil

2 teaspoons dried oregano

½ teaspoon grated nutmeg

½ teaspoon red pepper flakes

½ teaspoon table salt

2 pounds lean ground beef

½ cup Italian-seasoned dried breadcrumbs

1 large egg

1 tablespoon Worcestershire sauce

½ teaspoon garlic powder

½ teaspoon ground black pepper

Beyond

- For a **3-quart cooker**, you must use ½ cup broth (as stated in the recipe) but halve the remaining ingredients.

- For an **8-quart cooker**, you must increase *all* the ingredients by 50 percent.

- If the sauce is too wet for your taste, bring it to a simmer with the SAUTÉ setting on MEDIUM, NORMAL, or CUSTOM 300°F. Whisk in 2 tablespoons tomato paste, then continue cooking, whisking occasionally, until thickened, 2 to 4 minutes.

2 tablespoons fat

Choose from either a solid fat like butter, lard, or rendered bacon fat, or a tasty liquid fat like olive oil, sesame oil, walnut oil, pecan oil, or pumpkin seed oil — or a 50/50 combo of solid and liquid fat.

4 pounds bone-in shoulder chops, cut into 1-inch pieces; or bone-in pork stew meat

½ teaspoon table salt

½ teaspoon ground black pepper

2 medium garlic cloves, peeled and minced (2 teaspoons)

1 tablespoon dried spices

Choose a selection from whole cloves, coriander seeds, cumin seeds, fennel seeds, mild smoked paprika, mild paprika, dried oregano, dried thyme, and/or dried sage — or a bottled blend such as an Italian or Cajun blend, even herbes de Provence (but probably not any sort of curry powder).

One 2-inch cinnamon stick (optional)

2 cups liquid

Choose broth of any sort or a 50/50 combo of broth and beer or white wine.

¼ cup flavor enhancer

Choose from soy sauce, mustard of any type, chutney, marmalade, pesto, tapenade, barbecue sauce, or chowchow.

2 tablespoons acid

Choose from vinegar of any sort except white distilled vinegar, lemon juice, lime juice, orange juice, or grapefruit juice.

Road Map: Pork Stew

6 to 8 servings

This road map recipe results in a simple stew, without onions, other allium aromatics, or even root vegetables. The point is to make truly porcine fare, letting the flavors of the meat shine. It works best with 1-inch-thick pork *shoulder* chops, which have a mix of fat, meat, and bone that makes for a satisfying stew.

1.

Press the button for	Set it for	Set the time for	If necessary, press
SAUTÉ	MEDIUM, NORMAL, or CUSTOM 300°F	20 minutes	START

2. Warm the oil or melt the fat in a **6- or 8-quart cooker**. Season the pork with the salt and pepper; then add about half the meat to the cooker and brown *well*, turning and rearranging occasionally, about 7 minutes. Use kitchen tongs or a slotted spoon to transfer the pork pieces to a nearby bowl and brown the remainder of the pork in the same way before transferring to the bowl.

3. Add the garlic, spices, and cinnamon stick (if using) to the pot. Stir until aromatic, just a few seconds. Pour in the liquid and scrape up any browned bits on the pot's bottom. Turn off the SAUTÉ function, then stir in the flavor enhancer and the acid. Return the pork and any juices to the pot, stir well, and lock the lid onto the cooker.

4.

Set the machine for	Set the level for	The valve must be	Set the time for	If necessary, press
PRESSURE COOK	MAX	—	24 minutes with the KEEP WARM setting off	START
MEAT/STEW, PRESSURE COOK, or MANUAL	HIGH	Closed	30 minutes with the KEEP WARM setting off	START
SLOW COOK	HIGH	Opened	4 hours with the KEEP WARM setting off (or on for no more than 2 hours)	START

5. If you've used a pressure setting, when the machine has finished cooking, turn it off and let its pressure **return to normal naturally,** about 20 minutes.

6. Unlatch the lid and open the pot. Use a slotted spoon to transfer the pieces of pork to a large bowl. Discard the cinnamon stick, if you've used it. Use a flatware tablespoon to skim any excess surface fat from the sauce. Stir the pork back into the sauce and serve in bowls.

Beyond

- You must halve the recipe for a **3-quart cooker.**

- The sauce is wet, like a stew. Boil it down, if desired. Remove the pork from the pot as directed. Turn the SAUTÉ function on HIGH or MORE. Cook, stirring almost constantly, as the sauce boils, reducing it to about half its original volume, about 5 minutes. Turn off the SAUTÉ function and stir well before serving.

- Serve this dish over cooked medium-grain white rice, cooked and drained orzo, Butternut Squash Mash (page 432), White Bean Purée (page 451), or Polenta (page 443).

- Use this same road map to make an easy lamb stew by substituting 4 pounds bone-in lamb shoulder chops, cut into 1-inch pieces, for the pork.

One 14-ounce can diced tomatoes with chiles (1¾ cups)

½ cup natural-style smooth or crunchy peanut butter

¾ cup chicken broth

1 tablespoon packed fresh oregano leaves, minced

½ teaspoon grated nutmeg

Up to ½ teaspoon ground dried cayenne

½ teaspoon table salt

2 tablespoons peanut oil

One 3-pound boneless skinless pork shoulder, cut in half

1 large red onion, halved and sliced into very thin half-moons

2 medium garlic cloves, peeled and minced (2 teaspoons)

1 tablespoon minced peeled fresh ginger

⅓ cup light but dry white wine, such as Sauvignon Blanc

2 bay leaves

2 tablespoons fresh lime juice

Pork Shoulder and Peanut Butter Stew

6 servings

This stew has a West African flavor profile — although it's made with pork shoulder, which is not exactly traditional in the area. The pork gives the stew a rich flavor that is a great match to both the heat from the chiles and the smooth, creamy texture the peanut butter gives to the sauce. Similar stews are made with ground peanuts, but peanut butter gives the stew a "reduced" flavor, as if it's simmered for hours (provided, however, that you use a natural-style variety, without extra fat or sugar).

1. Whisk the tomatoes, peanut butter, broth, oregano, nutmeg, and salt in a large bowl until the peanut butter dissolves. Set aside.

2.

Press the button for	Set it for	Set the time for	If necessary, press
SAUTÉ	MEDIUM, NORMAL, or CUSTOM 300°F	15 minutes	START

3. Warm the oil in a **6-quart cooker** for a minute or two. Add half the pork shoulder and brown *lightly* on all sides, turning occasionally, about 4 minutes. Transfer to a bowl and brown the other half in the same way before transferring it to a bowl.

4. Add the onion and cook, stirring often, until softened, about 4 minutes. Stir in the garlic and ginger until aromatic, just a few seconds. Pour in the wine, add the bay leaves, and scrape up any browned bits on the pot's bottom.

5. Turn off the SAUTÉ function. Pour in the tomato mixture. Return the pork and any juices to the pot, then lock the lid onto the cooker.

6.

Set the machine for	Set the level for	The valve must be	Set the time for	If necessary, press
PRESSURE COOK	MAX	—	40 minutes with the KEEP WARM setting off	START
MEAT/STEW, PRESSURE COOK, or MANUAL	HIGH	Closed	50 minutes with the KEEP WARM setting off	START
SLOW COOK	HIGH	Opened	5 hours with the KEEP WARM setting off (or on for no more than 3 hours)	START

7. If you've used a pressure setting, when the machine has finished cooking, turn it off and let its pressure **return to normal naturally,** about 30 minutes.

8. Unlatch the lid and open the pot. Transfer the pork to a cutting board; find and discard the bay leaves. Use a flatware tablespoon to skim any excess surface fat from the sauce in the pot. Stir the lime juice into the sauce. Carve the pork into ½-inch-thick slices (or just small chunks) and serve with the sauce ladled on top.

Beyond

- You must halve the recipe for a **3-quart cooker.**

- For an **8-quart cooker,** you must increase all the ingredients by 50 percent.

- For more vegetables in the stew, add up to 2 chopped medium carrots; six 5-ounce yellow potatoes, halved; 8 ounces frozen sliced okra (do not thaw); and/or 1 large, stemmed, cored, and roughly chopped red bell pepper with the tomato mixture.

- Serve with flatbread: lavash, lefse, even large flour tortillas.

1 tablespoon vegetable, corn, or canola oil; or peanut oil

6 ounces slab bacon, diced

1 large leek (about 6 ounces), white and pale green parts only, halved lengthwise, well washed, and thinly sliced (½ cup)

2 tablespoons minced peeled fresh ginger

2½ pounds boneless pork loin, cut into 2-inch cubes

Two 8-ounce cans whole water chestnuts, drained (about 1 cup)

1¼ cup beef or chicken broth

½ cup reduced-sodium soy sauce

One 4-inch cinnamon stick

1 star anise pod

2 tablespoons water

1 tablespoon cornstarch

Chinese Take-Out Pork Loin and Bacon Stew

4 to 6 servings

This easy version of a classic American-Chinese stew is given a decidedly comfort-food twist with the addition of slab bacon. Use only reduced-sodium soy sauce to avoid an overly salty dish. The water chestnuts will keep a lot of their crunch, even under pressure.

1.

Press the button for	Set it for	Set the time for	If necessary, press
SAUTÉ	MEDIUM, NORMAL, or CUSTOM 300°F	10 minutes	START

2. Warm the oil in a **6- or 8-quart cooker** for a minute or two. Add the slab bacon and cook, stirring occasionally, until well browned, about 4 minutes. Add the leek and ginger; continue cooking, stirring more often, until the leek has softened, about 2 minutes.

3. Add the pork and toss well to combine. Turn off the SAUTÉ function; stir in the water chestnuts, broth, soy sauce, cinnamon stick, and star anise pod. Lock the lid onto the cooker.

4.

Set the machine for	Set the level for	The valve must be	Set the time for	If necessary, press
PRESSURE COOK	MAX	—	16 minutes with the KEEP WARM setting off	START
MEAT/STEW, PRESSURE COOK, or MANUAL	HIGH	Closed	20 minutes with the KEEP WARM setting off	START
SLOW COOK	HIGH	Opened	3 hours with the KEEP WARM setting off (or on for no more than 2 hours)	START

5. If you've used a pressure setting, when the machine has finished cooking, turn it off and let its pressure **return to normal naturally,** about 20 minutes.

6. Unlatch the lid and open the cooker. Find and discard the cinnamon stick and star anise pod.

7.

Press the button for	Set it for	Set the time for	If necessary, press
SAUTÉ	MEDIUM, NORMAL, or CUSTOM 300°F	5 minutes	START

8. Bring the sauce to a low simmer. Meanwhile, whisk the water and cornstarch in a small bowl until smooth. Whisk this slurry into the simmer stew, then cook, stirring all the while, until thickened, 1 to 2 minutes. Turn off the SAUTÉ function and remove the *hot* insert from the machine to stop the cooking. Set the lid askew over the insert for 5 minutes to blend the flavors. Stir again before serving

Beyond

- You must halve the recipe for a **3-quart cooker.**

- You *can* increase all the ingredients by 50 percent in an **8-quart cooker.**

- Serve the stew over long-grain white rice and/or wilted spinach — or better yet, steamed and crisp-tender Chinese water spinach.

- Drizzle the servings with toasted sesame oil — and maybe Sriracha.

2 tablespoons olive oil

6 bone-in country-style pork ribs
(2 to 2½ pounds total weight)

1 medium red onion, chopped (1 cup)

1 cup unsweetened apple cider

½ cup chopped dried apples

½ cup chicken broth

1 tablespoon Dijon mustard

2 teaspoons dark brown sugar

1 teaspoon dried sage

1 teaspoon dried thyme

½ teaspoon table salt

Cider-Braised Country-Style Pork Ribs

6 servings

It's hard to make a successful pork chop braise in a pressure cooker without using thick bone-in pork chops (for a road map to do just that, see page 321). As an easier alternative, look for bone-in country-style pork ribs. They'll help create a fine pork braise with little fuss. One note: This dish, while lip-smackingly fatty and rich, is not a full meal. It needs Brown Rice and Lentils (page 404) or maybe Buckwheat Pilaf (page 407) on the side.

1.

Press the button for	Set it for	Set the time for	If necessary, press
SAUTÉ	MEDIUM, NORMAL, or CUSTOM 300°F	20 minutes	START

2. Warm the oil in a **6- or 8-quart cooker** for a minute or two. Add half the country-style ribs and brown *well* on all sides, turning occasionally, about 8 minutes. Transfer the meat to a nearby bowl and brown the remaining country-style ribs in the same way before getting them into that bowl.

3. Add the onion and cook, stirring often, until softened, about 3 minutes. Pour in the cider, turn off the SAUTÉ function, and scrape up any browned bits on the pot's bottom. Stir in the dried apples, broth, mustard, brown sugar, sage, thyme, and salt. Nestle the ribs into the sauce; add any juice from their bowl. Lock the lid onto the pot.

4.

Set the machine for	Set the level for	The valve must be	Set the time for	If necessary, press
PRESSURE COOK	MAX	—	28 minutes with the KEEP WARM setting off	START
MEAT/STEW, PRESSURE COOK, or MANUAL	HIGH	Closed	35 minutes with the KEEP WARM setting off	START
SLOW COOK	HIGH	Opened	4 hours with the KEEP WARM setting off (or on for no more than 2 hours)	START

5. If you've used a pressure setting, when the machine has finished cooking, turn it off and let its pressure **return to normal naturally**, about 25 minutes.

6. Unlatch the lid and open the pot. Use kitchen tongs to transfer the country-style ribs to a serving platter. Use a flatware tablespoon to skim any excess surface fat from the sauce.

7.

Press the button for	Set it for	Set the time for	If necessary, press
SAUTÉ	HIGH or MORE	10 minutes	START

8. Bring the sauce in the pot to a boil. Cook, stirring often, until reduced to half its original volume, about 5 minutes. Turn off the SAUTÉ function. Serve the country-style ribs with lots of the sauce drizzled over them — and more on the side for dipping.

Beyond

- Because of the length of the country-style ribs, this recipe will not work well in a **3-quart cooker**.

- For a more savory dish, reduce the apple cider to ½ cup and increase the chicken broth to 1 cup.

- For a sweeter, more aromatic dish, add up to 2 chopped, medium carrots and up to 1 tablespoon minced ginger with the onion.

- Feel free to swap out the sage for parsley or dill.

1½ cups chicken broth

½ cup lime marmalade

¼ cup packed fresh basil leaves, chopped

6 medium garlic cloves, peeled and minced (2 tablespoons)

2 teaspoons ground cumin

1 teaspoon table salt

One 3-pound boneless skinless pork butt, any large hunks of fat removed, the meat cut into 2-inch pieces

At least 2 tablespoons vegetable, corn, or canola oil; lard; or rendered bacon fat

Kick-Butt Carnitas

6 servings

There are a million different sauces and glazes for carnitas, a Mexican staple. After a trip eating our way through Texas last year, we became enamored of the mix of lime and basil, a sort of *nouveau* Southwestern tweak on the classic. The lime marmalade will not only provide the essentially sour pop but offer some sugar which will be crucial in the next step: frying the pieces of cooked pork to render them irresistibly crunchy.

1. Whisk the broth, marmalade, basil, garlic, cumin, and salt in a **6- or 8-quart cooker** until the marmalade dissolves. Add the pork pieces and stir until uniform. Lock the lid onto the pot.

2.

Set the machine for	Set the level for	The valve must be	Set the time for	If necessary, press
PRESSURE COOK	MAX	——	30 minutes with the KEEP WARM setting off	START
MEAT/STEW, PRESSURE COOK, or MANUAL	HIGH	Closed	40 minutes with the KEEP WARM setting off	START

3. When the machine has finished cooking, turn it off and let its pressure **return to normal naturally**, about 20 minutes. Unlatch the lid and open the cooker. Use kitchen tongs to transfer the pieces of pork to a large cutting board. Use a flatware tablespoon to skim any excess surface fat from the sauce in the pot.

4.

Press the button for	Set it for	Set the time for	If necessary, press
SAUTÉ	HIGH or MORE	10 minutes	START

5. Bring the sauce to a boil and cook, stirring very often, until reduced to the consistency of a barbecue sauce, 6 to 7 minutes. Turn off the SAUTÉ function and pour the sauce into a small, heat-safe serving bowl.

6. Heat the oil or melt the fat in a large skillet set over medium heat. Add about a third of the pork pieces (maybe more — but no crowding!) and cook, turning occasionally, until brown and crisp, about 5 minutes. Transfer to a serving platter and continue browning more of the pork. When done, ladle the thickened sauce over the pieces to serve.

Beyond

- You must halve the recipe for a **3-quart cooker**.

- You can fry the pork right in the Instant Pot, using the SAUTÉ function ON HIGH OR MORE. Because the surface area of the pot is smaller than that of a skillet, you'll need to work with a greater number of batches.

- For a more savory dish, reduce the lime marmalade to ⅓ cup and add 1 tablespoon soy sauce.

- For a sweeter dish, substitute orange marmalade for the lime.

- Serve with lots of corn or flour tortillas, sour cream, and purchased pico de gallo.

See photo in insert.

Pork Belly Braised in Ginger Beer

6 servings

Pork belly is fatty luxuriance — and best either smoked or finished with a sweet flavor profile (as here, with ginger beer). To compensate for the sweetness of that liquid, we bumped up the aromatics with orange zest, star anise, and cinnamon.

     Pork belly is often sold without the skin these days — but not always. If you can only find one with the skin still on, buy a 2¼-pound piece. You must then slice off the skin or have the butcher do it for you.

1.

Press the button for	Set it for	Set the time for	If necessary, press
SAUTÉ	HIGH or MORE	25 minutes	START

2. Warm the oil in a **6- or 8-quart cooker** for a minute or two. Add half the pork belly pieces and brown *well* on all sides, turning occasionally, about 10 minutes. Transfer these to a nearby bowl and brown the remaining pieces the same way before transferring them into that bowl.

3. Pour the ginger beer into the cooker and scrape up any browned bits on the pot's bottom. Turn off the SAUTÉ function, then stir in the soy sauce, orange juice, scallions, orange zest, garlic, ginger, cinnamon, and star anise pods. Return the pork belly pieces and any juices to the cooker. Lock the lid onto the pot.

4.

Set the machine for	Set the level for	The valve must be	Set the time for	If necessary, press
PRESSURE COOK	MAX	—	25 minutes with the KEEP WARM setting off	START
MEAT/STEW, PRESSURE COOK, or MANUAL	HIGH	Closed	35 minutes with the KEEP WARM setting off	START

5. Use the **quick-release method** to bring the pot's pressure back to normal. Unlatch the lid and open the cooker. Transfer the pork belly to a serving platter or serving bowls. Find and discard the star anise pods. Use a flatware tablespoon to skim the excess surface fat from the sauce. Chunk up the meat, then spoon the sauce and scallions over it in bowls.

1 tablespoon vegetable, corn, or canola oil

2 pounds skinless pork belly, cut into 6 pieces

One 12-ounce bottle non-alcoholic ginger beer

⅓ cup soy sauce, preferably reduced-sodium

⅓ cup fresh orange juice

4 medium scallions, trimmed and cut into 1-inch pieces

2 tablespoons finely minced orange zest

1 medium garlic clove, peeled and minced (1 teaspoon)

2 tablespoons minced peeled fresh ginger

½ teaspoon ground cinnamon

2 star anise pods

Beyond

- You must halve the recipe for a **3-quart cooker.**

- For a thicker sauce, skim it of fat, then reduce it using the SAUTÉ function at MEDIUM, NORMAL, or CUSTOM 300°F, stirring quite often, until thickened, 7 to 8 minutes.

- Serve the broth, pork belly, and scallions over cooked and drained udon noodles.

- For a heartier dish, open the pot in step 5 after cooking, then lay 4 cups packed, stemmed, and chopped kale on top of the pork and sauce. Lock the lid back onto the pot and cook at MAX for 2 minutes or at HIGH for 3 minutes, followed by a quick release. You won't be able to skim the sauce because of the greens (which will have been coated in pork fat!).

1 tablespoon toasted sesame oil

1 pound skinless pork belly, cut into ½-inch pieces

4 medium scallions, trimmed and thinly sliced

1 tablespoon minced peeled fresh ginger

1 teaspoon Sichuan peppercorns

2 tablespoons chili paste, such as sambal oelek

1 teaspoon granulated white sugar

1 cup chicken broth

1 tablespoon soy sauce

1 tablespoon balsamic vinegar

1 tablespoon Worcestershire sauce

1 pound extra-firm silken tofu, such as Mori-Nu brand, drained and cut into ½-inch cubes

1 tablespoon cornstarch

1 tablespoon water

Pork Belly Mapo Dofu

4 to 6 servings

Mapo dofu (literally, "old pock-marked grandmother's tofu") is a traditional Sichuan braise that's notorious in North America for being absurdly hot. More authentic versions are balanced and aromatic. The dish is usually made with a little ground pork or maybe ground beef. We couldn't resist swapping out those for pork belly since the Instant Pot cooks it so quickly.

Our version has some tweaks to fit most modern American supermarkets with one exception: Sichuan peppercorns, the one ingredient for which we broke our local-supermarket-only rule. These are not peppercorns at all but rather the dried hulls from seeds of a citrus plant. They are highly prized for their spicy *and* numbing quality, an absolutely essential flavor for this dish. Look for Sichuan peppercorns at Asian markets and from an almost endless array of online sellers. For a more authentic version of the sauce, see the *Beyond* attached to this recipe.

1.

Press the button for	Set it for	Set the time for	If necessary, press
SAUTÉ	MEDIUM, NORMAL, or CUSTOM 300°F	10 minutes	START

2. Warm the oil in a **3- or 6-quart cooker** for a minute or two. Add the pork belly and cook, stirring often, until the pieces are lightly browned at the edges, about 4 minutes. Stir in the scallions, ginger, and peppercorns until aromatic, about 1 minute.

3. Add the chili paste and sugar; cook until bubbling and sizzling with the meat, about 1 minute. Stir in the broth and scrape up any browned bits on the pot's bottom. Turn off the SAUTÉ function and stir in the soy sauce, balsamic vinegar, and Worcestershire sauce. Lock the lid onto the pot.

4.

Set the machine for	Set the level for	The valve must be	Set the time for	If necessary, press
PRESSURE COOK	MAX	—	10 minutes with the KEEP WARM setting off	START
MEAT/STEW, PRESSURE COOK or MANUAL	HIGH	Closed	12 minutes with the KEEP WARM setting off	START

5. When the machine has finished cooking, turn it off and let its pressure **return to normal naturally**, about 20 minutes. Unlatch the lid and open the cooker.

6.

Press the button for	Set it for	Set the time for	If necessary, press
SAUTÉ	MEDIUM, NORMAL, or CUSTOM 300°F	5 minutes	START

7. Stir the dish as it comes to a simmer. Add the tofu and cook, stirring gently once or twice, for 1 minute. Meanwhile, whisk the cornstarch and water in a small bowl or teacup until smooth, then gently stir this slurry into the simmering sauce. Cook, stirring gently a few times, until thickened, less than 1 minute. Turn off the SAUTÉ function and remove the *hot* insert from the machine. Set the lid askew over the insert and set aside for 5 minutes to blend the flavors.

Beyond

- For an **8-quart cooker**, you must increase all the ingredients by 50 percent.

- For a more authentic flavor, make these three substitutions: 1) dobanjiang paste (a fermented bean and chili paste from Asian markets) for the chili paste; 2) 2 tablespoons Chinese black vinegar for the balsamic vinegar *and* Worcestershire sauce; and 3) drizzle (or bathe) the servings with red chile oil.

- Although it's almost always served over long-grain white rice, we prefer our *nouveau* version over medium-grain white rice, such as Arborio or Valencia.

2 tablespoons butter

1 medium shallot, minced

1 medium garlic clove, peeled and minced (1 teaspoon)

4 ounces bulk sweet Italian sausage meat (or links with the casings removed)

¼ cup raisins, chopped

1 cup fresh breadcrumbs

1 teaspoon finely grated lemon zest (optional)

½ teaspoon fennel seeds

One 2½-pound boneless skinless turkey breast, butterflied flat and opened up

½ teaspoon table salt

½ teaspoon ground black pepper

1½ cups chicken broth

2 fresh oregano sprigs

1½ tablespoons water

1 tablespoon cornstarch

Braised Stuffed Turkey Breast

4 to 6 servings

This recipe's a fair amount of work, but you'll end up with a dish worthy of a holiday table. The turkey breast is butterflied, then stuffed with meat and breadcrumbs before being rolled, tied, and braised.

The easiest way to butterfly a boneless skinless turkey breast is to have the butcher do it for you. Just ask! To DIY it: Set the breast on a cutting board so that the smoother side that had the skin is facing down. Holding the blade of a large chef's knife parallel to the cutting board, cut into the thinner side of the meat as if you were cutting into the pages of an open book from the side, working the knife through the meat until about 1 inch remains at the fatter side. Open the breast up like said book, that 1-inch section now like a book's spine.

1.

Press the button for	Set it for	Set the time for	If necessary, press
SAUTÉ	MEDIUM, NORMAL, or CUSTOM 300°F	10 minutes	START

2. Melt 1 tablespoon butter in a **6- or 8-quart cooker**. Add the shallot and garlic; cook, stirring often, until softened, 2 minutes. Crumble in the sausage meat. Cook, stirring to break it up, until well browned, about 4 minutes.

3. Turn off the SAUTÉ function and scrape the contents of the pot's insert into a large bowl. Cool for 5 minutes; then stir in the raisins, breadcrumbs, lemon zest (if using), and fennel seeds. Cool for 10 minutes.

4. Lay the turkey breast split side up on a large cutting board. Spread the breadcrumb mixture in an even layer over the meat. Roll the meat up from the long edge to form a compact spiraled "log," then tie this log in three places with butchers' twine to keep it closed. Season the outside of the log with the salt and pepper.

5.

Press the button for	Set it for	Set the time for	If necessary, press
SAUTÉ	MEDIUM, NORMAL, or CUSTOM 300°F	10 minutes	START

6. Melt the remaining 1 tablespoon butter in the cooker. Add the stuffed turkey breast (bending it to fit if need be) and brown *lightly* on all sides, turning occasionally, about 5 minutes. Turn off the SAUTÉ function, then pour in the broth. Tuck the oregano sprigs around the meat and lock the lid onto the cooker.

7.

Set the machine for	Set the level for	The valve must be	Set the time for	If necessary, press
PRESSURE COOK	MAX	—	25 minutes with the KEEP WARM setting off	START
MEAT/STEW, PRESSURE COOK, or MANUAL	HIGH	Closed	35 minutes with the KEEP WARM setting off	START

8. When the machine has finished cooking, turn it off and let its pressure **return to normal naturally**, about 25 minutes. Unlatch the lid and open the cooker. Find and discard the oregano sprigs. Use a large, metal spatula and a spoon (for balance) to transfer the turkey roll to a nearby cutting board.

9.

Press the button for	Set it for	Set the time for	If necessary, press
SAUTÉ	MEDIUM, NORMAL, or CUSTOM 300°F	5 minutes	START

10. As the sauce comes to a simmer, whisk the water and cornstarch in a small bowl until smooth. Whisk this slurry into the sauce and continue cooking, whisking constantly, until thickened somewhat, 1 to 2 minutes. Immediately turn off the SAUTÉ function and remove the insert from the pot to stop the cooking. Slice the stuffed turkey breast into 1-inch-thick slices and serve with the sauce ladled on top.

See photo in insert.

Beyond

- Because of the size of this roll, the recipe will not work well in a **3-quart cooker.**
- Serve with Perfect Sweet Potatoes (page 427) and Spicy Collard Greens (page 437).
- Try swapping out the sweet Italian sausage meat for raw chorizo sausage meat, and the fennel seeds for cumin seeds.

1 cup bold red wine, such as Cabernet Franc

¾ cup chicken broth

2 tablespoon hoisin sauce (see page 184)

2 tablespoons honey

2 tablespoons soy sauce

4 medium scallions, trimmed and thinly sliced

2 medium garlic cloves, peeled and minced (2 teaspoons)

1 tablespoon minced peeled fresh ginger

½ teaspoon five-spice powder (see page 88)

2 tablespoons peanut oil

4 turkey legs, each about ¾ pound

Turkey Legs Braised in Red Wine with Asian Spices

4 servings

Turkey legs are often better braised than roasted, although we also turn them into state-fair–worthy drumsticks on page 265. Braised, more of the meat at the tendons gets tender and the tasty bits around them get softer. Here, we braise them in red wine with a few aromatics for a new twist on an old favorite.

Unfortunately, only certain turkey legs can fit in an Instant Pot. They can be no longer than 7 inches end to end. Sad to say, the only way to be sure is to take a tape measure to the store. People will think you're nuts but you won't be caught without a dinner plan that evening.

1. Whisk the wine, broth, hoisin sauce, honey, and soy sauce in a medium bowl until smooth. Stir in the scallions, garlic, ginger, and five-spice powder. Set aside.

2.

Press the button for	Set it for	Set the time for	If necessary, press
SAUTÉ	MEDIUM, NORMAL, or CUSTOM 300°F	15 minutes	START

3. Warm the oil in a **6- or 8-quart cooker**. Add two turkey legs and brown *well*, turning occasionally, about 6 minutes. Transfer to a nearby bowl and brown the other two turkey legs in the same way before getting them into that bowl.

4. Pour in the wine mixture and scrape up any browned bits on the pot's bottom. Turn off the SAUTÉ function. Put the turkey legs back in the pot, stacking and arranging them so that they are each in some of the sauce. Lock the lid onto the pot.

5.

Set the machine for	Set the level for	The valve must be	Set the time for	If necessary, press
PRESSURE COOK	MAX	—	21 minutes with the KEEP WARM setting off	START
MEAT/STEW, PRESSURE COOK, or MANUAL	HIGH	Closed	30 minutes with the KEEP WARM setting off	START
SLOW COOK	HIGH	Opened	4 hours with the KEEP WARM setting off (or on for no more than 2 hours)	START

6. If you've used a pressure setting, when the machine has finished cooking, turn it off and let its pressure **return to normal naturally,** about 20 minutes.

7. Unlatch the lid and open the cooker. Transfer the turkey legs to a serving platter; tent with aluminum foil to keep warm.

8.

Press the button for	Set it for	Set the time for	If necessary, press
SAUTÉ	MEDIUM, NORMAL, or CUSTOM 300°F	5 minutes	START

9. Bring the sauce in the cooker to a boil, stirring occasionally. Cook, stirring more frequently especially as it boils down, until reduced to a third of its original volume, about 6 minutes. Turn off the SAUTÉ function. Spoon and pour this sauce over the turkey legs before serving.

Beyond

- Because of their size, turkey legs will not fit in a **3-quart cooker.**

- If you want crisp skin on the legs, put them on a large, lipped baking sheet after cooking and broil 4 to 6 inches from a heated broiler element, turning occasionally, until crisp and dark brown, about 6 minutes.

5 tablespoons butter, at room temperature

Two 1½-pound skin-on, bone-in turkey thighs

1 large yellow onion, chopped (1½ cups)

3 medium celery stalks, thinly sliced (1 cup)

1 teaspoon dried sage

½ teaspoon dried thyme

½ teaspoon table salt

½ teaspoon ground black pepper

1½ cups chicken broth

⅔ cup jarred peeled whole chestnuts (about 6 ounces)

⅓ cup dried cranberries

3 tablespoons all-purpose flour

Braised Turkey Thighs with Cranberries and Chestnuts

4 servings

Turkey thighs are terrific for cooking under pressure (or slow cooking) — with one problem: their skin. You *must* brown it well. Leave the skin against the hot surface in the pot until the natural sugars caramelize and the whole thing can be popped off the bottom without tearing. You'll probably be able to fit both thighs in an **8-quart cooker**; you may have to work in batches in a **6-quart cooker**. Afterwards, carve turkey thighs by slicing the meat off the bones in long strips. (The bones offer tremendous gnawing possibilities.)

1.

Press the button for	Set it for	Set the time for	If necessary, press
SAUTÉ	MEDIUM, NORMAL, or CUSTOM 300°F	20 minutes	START

2. Melt 2 tablespoons butter in a **6- or 8-quart cooker**. Season the turkey thighs with the salt and pepper, then add them skin side down to the pot, working in batches if necessary to avoid crowding. Brown *well* without turning, until the skin easily releases from the pot's surface, 4 to 5 minutes. Turn and continue browning until golden, about 3 minutes. Transfer them to a nearby bowl.

3. Add the onion and celery; cook, stirring often, until the onion begins to soften, about 4 minutes. Stir in the sage, thyme, salt, and pepper until fragrant, just a few seconds. Pour in the broth and scrape up the browned bits on the pot's bottom.

4. Turn off the SAUTÉ function, then stir in the chestnuts and dried cranberries. Nestle the thighs skin side up into the sauce and add any juices from their bowl. Lock the lid onto the pot.

5.

Set the machine for	Set the level for	The valve must be	Set the time for	If necessary, press
PRESSURE COOK	MAX	—	25 minutes with the KEEP WARM setting off	START
MEAT/STEW, PRESSURE COOK, or MANUAL	HIGH	Closed	32 minutes with the KEEP WARM setting off	START
SLOW COOK	HIGH	Opened	4 hours with the KEEP WARM setting off (or on for no more than 2 hours)	START

6. Meanwhile, use a fork to mash the flour into the remaining 3 tablespoons butter to make a paste in a small bowl.

7. If you've used a pressure setting, when the machine is finished cooking, use the **quick-release method** to bring its pressure back to normal.

8. Unlatch the lid and open the pot. Transfer the turkey thighs to a serving platter. Use a slotted spoon to get the vegetables and dried fruit onto the platter with the thighs.

9.

Press the button for	Set it for	Set the time for	If necessary, press
SAUTÉ	MEDIUM, NORMAL, or CUSTOM 300°F	5 minutes	START

10. Bring the sauce to a simmer, whisking often. Whisk in the butter paste in small dribs and drabs, letting each get incorporated into the sauce before adding the next. Once all the paste has been added, continue whisking over the heat until the sauce has thickened, about 1 minute. Turn off the SAUTÉ function and remove the *hot* insert from the pot to stop the cooking. Ladle the sauce over the turkey thighs when serving.

Beyond

• You must halve the recipe for a **3-quart cooker.**

• Many dried cranberries have been sweetened. For a more savory dish, search out those without the additives, at health-food stores or online.

2 tablespoons butter

Two 1½-pound skin-on, bone-in turkey thighs

¼ teaspoon table salt

¼ teaspoon ground black pepper

½ cup frozen pearl onions (do not thaw)

1 pound white button mushrooms, thinly sliced

¼ cup brandy

⅔ cup chicken broth

2 teaspoons dried tarragon or thyme

1 teaspoon Dijon mustard

¼ cup heavy cream

Braised Turkey Thighs with Mushrooms and Cream

4 servings

These turkey thighs are cooked for less time than those in the previous recipe. Here, we want them to have a more "roasted" texture to go with the cream sauce, rather than the falling-off-the-bone dark-meat texture that went better with the last braise's sauce.

1.

Press the button for	Set it for	Set the time for	If necessary, press
SAUTÉ	MEDIUM, NORMAL, or CUSTOM 300°F	25 minutes	START

2. Melt the butter in a **6-quart cooker**. Season the turkey thighs with the salt and pepper, then add them skin side down to the cooker, working in batches if necessary. Brown *well* without turning, until the skin easily releases from the pot's surface, 4 to 5 minutes. Turn and continue browning until golden, about 3 minutes. Transfer them to a nearby bowl.

3. Add the pearl onions and cook, stirring occasionally, until lightly browned in places, about 4 minutes. Add the mushrooms and continue cooking until they give off their internal liquid and it reduces to a glaze, about 5 minutes.

4. Pour in the brandy and scrape up any browned bits on the pot's bottom. Turn off the SAUTÉ function and stir in broth, tarragon, and mustard. Nestle the thighs into the sauce and pour any of their juice in the bowl over them. Lock the lid onto the pot.

5.

Set the machine for	Set the level for	The valve must be	Set the time for	If necessary, press
PRESSURE COOK	MAX	—	16 minutes with the KEEP WARM setting off	START
MEAT/STEW, PRESSURE COOK, or MANUAL	HIGH	Closed	20 minutes with the KEEP WARM setting off	START

6. When the machine is finished cooking, turn it off and let its pressure **return to normal naturally**, about 15 minutes. Unlatch the lid and open the cooker. Transfer the thighs to a cutting board.

7.

Press the button for	Set it for	Set the time for	If necessary, press
SAUTÉ	MEDIUM, NORMAL, or CUSTOM 300°F	5 minutes	START

8. Bring the sauce to a simmer, stirring occasionally. Stir in the cream and continue cooking for 2 minutes, to reduce the sauce a little and thoroughly incorporate the flavors of the cream. Turn off the SAUTÉ function and remove the insert from the pot to stop the cooking. Ladle the sauce over the turkey thighs when serving.

Beyond

- For a **3-quart cooker**, you must use ½ cup broth and halve the remaining ingredients.

- For an **8-quart cooker**, you must increase *all* the ingredients by 50 percent.

- Go ahead and use more exotic mushrooms, like porcini, hen of the wood, or shiitake caps. But avoid cremini mushrooms or portobello caps. Both will turn the sauce a dark brown.

- Rather than mashed potatoes, try this dish over Yellow Rice Pilaf (page 400).

2 tablespoons olive oil

One 3- to 4-pound boneless leg of lamb

1 teaspoon table salt

½ teaspoon ground black pepper

1 cup dry, light red wine, such as Pinot Noir

½ cup chicken broth

1 medium yellow onion, peeled and halved

4 whole cloves

3 medium Roma or plum tomatoes, chopped (⅔ cup)

2 large carrots, cut into 2-inch sections

6 large garlic cloves, peeled

2 teaspoon dried thyme

Spoon Lamb

6 to 8 servings

This is the fastest way to make *gigot à sept heures* (French, ʒee-GOH-ah-set-uhr, "seven-hour leg of lamb"). The meat becomes so tender, it won't need a knife.

Some boneless legs of lamb are sold in nets. They're hunks of leg meat that have been bagged together. If you can only find a boneless leg of lamb in such a condition, have the butcher remove it from its net and tie it into a compact, cylindrical roast.

Or if the supermarket sells only butterflied, boneless leg of lamb (mostly for the grill), roll it into a compact log and tie it in several places with butchers' twine.

1.

Press the button for	Set it for	Set the time for	If necessary, press
SAUTÉ	MEDIUM, NORMAL, or CUSTOM 300°F	15 minutes	START

2. Warm the oil in a **6- or 8-quart cooker** for a minute or two. Season the lamb with the salt and pepper, then set it in the pot and brown well on all sides, even the ends, turning occasionally, about 12 minutes. Transfer the leg of lamb to a nearby bowl.

3. Pour in the wine and broth, then scrape up any browned bits on the pot's bottom. Turn off the SAUTÉ function. Stud the onion pieces with the whole cloves; add these to the pot along with the tomatoes, carrots, garlic, and thyme. Return the lamb to the cooker and lock the lid onto the pot.

4.

Set the machine for	Set the level for	The valve must be	Set the time for	If necessary, press
PRESSURE COOK	MAX	—	1 hour 10 minutes with the KEEP WARM setting off	START
MEAT/STEW, PRESSURE COOK, or MANUAL	HIGH	Closed	1 hour 30 minutes with the KEEP WARM Setting off	START
SLOW COOK	HIGH	Opened	5 hours with the KEEP WARM setting off (or on for no more than 2 hours)	START

5. If you've used a pressure setting, when the machine has finished cooking, turn it off and let its pressure **return to normal naturally,** about 25 minutes.

6. Unlatch and open the lid. Transfer the leg of lamb to a clean cutting board.

7. Fish out and discard the onions, carrots, and the cloves that have slipped off the onions. Use an immersion blender right in the cooker to blend the remaining ingredients in the pot into a sauce — or pour the contents of the insert into a blender, cover, remove the center knob, cover the hole with a clean kitchen towel, and blend until smooth. To serve, carve the meat into 1-inch slices and/or chunks, then serve them with the sauce ladled on top.

Beyond

- You must halve the recipe for a **3-quart cooker.**

- For an aromatic kick, substitute gin for the red wine. Also add 4 juniper berries and 4 allspice berries when you add the onions.

2 tablespoons olive oil

2½ pounds boneless leg of lamb, any chunks of fat removed and the meat cut into 1½-inch pieces

1 large yellow onion, chopped (1½ cups)

2 medium garlic cloves, peeled and minced (2 teaspoons)

1 cup dry white wine, such as Chardonnay

½ cup chicken broth

1 medium butternut squash, peeled, seeded, and cubed (4 cups)

½ cup golden raisins

1 tablespoon apple cider vinegar

½ teaspoon table salt

½ teaspoon ground black pepper

1 large rosemary sprig

2 large thyme sprigs

2 bay leaves

Beyond

- You must halve the recipe for a **3-quart cooker**.

- To omit the wine, use ½ cup unsweetened apple cider and increase the broth to 1 cup.

- For heat, add up to 4 dried small red chiles, preferably chiles de arbol. Remove these before serving.

- Brighten the flavors with a little lemon juice just before serving.

- For a more savory stew, omit the salt, reduce the raisins to 3 tablespoons, and add 2 tablespoons soy sauce.

Lamb and Butternut Squash Stew

6 servings

Although this is a *fast/slow* stew, the overall texture will differ depending on which function you've used — which is often the case with fairly fatty cuts of meat. Under pressure, the lamb and the butternut squash will retain some of their natural chew; with the SLOW COOK mode, the meat and vegetables will become very tender, almost velvety. No matter which method you use, the easiest way to make this stew is to buy chopped, peeled, and seeded butternut squash. If you do, cut each piece into 1½-inch pieces.

1.

Press the button for	Set it for	Set the time for	If necessary, press
SAUTÉ	MEDIUM, NORMAL, or CUSTOM 300°F	25 minutes	START

2. Warm the oil in a **6- or 8-quart cooker**. Add half the lamb pieces and brown well, turning occasionally, about 8 minutes. Transfer the lamb to a nearby bowl and brown the remaining lamb pieces in the same way before getting them into that bowl.

3. Add the onion and cook, stirring often, until softened, about 4 minutes. Stir in the garlic until aromatic, just a few seconds. Pour in the wine and scrape up any browned bits on the pot's bottom.

4. Turn off the SAUTÉ function and stir in the broth, butternut squash, raisins, vinegar, salt, pepper, rosemary, thyme, and bay leaves. Return the lamb pieces and any juices in their bowl to the cooker. Stir well, then lock the lid onto the pot.

5.

Set the machine for	Set the level for	The valve must be	Set the time for	If necessary, press
PRESSURE COOK	MAX	—	21 minutes with the KEEP WARM setting off	START
MEAT/STEW, PRESSURE COOK, or MANUAL	HIGH	Closed	30 minutes with the KEEP WARM setting off	START
SLOW COOK	HIGH	Opened	3½ hours with the KEEP WARM setting off (or on for no more than 3 hours)	START

6. If you've used a pressure setting, when the machine has finished cooking, use the quick-release method to **return the pressure to normal naturally**, about 25 minutes.

7. Unlatch the lid and open the cooker. Find and discard the herb sprigs and the bay leaves. Stir well before serving.

Buttery Lamb Stew with Wheat Berries and Pecans

6 servings

This big bowl of stew with whole grains is best on a day when you're in from a fall garden cleanup or a winter run on the slopes — or shoveling the driveway. Lamb shoulder chops require a long time to get tender, so there's a built-in time lag that can be used to cook the wheat berries, too. In this recipe (unlike all others in this book), we soak the wheat berries to ensure they're done at the same time as the lamb.

½ cup dried wheat berries, preferably soft white wheat berries

¼ cup (½ stick) butter

2½ pounds boneless lamb shoulder, any chunks of fat removed, the meat cut into 2-inch pieces

1 large yellow onion, chopped (1½ cups)

2½ cups chicken broth

½ cup chopped pecans

2 teaspoons dried sage

½ teaspoon red pepper flakes

½ teaspoon table salt

1. Soak the wheat berries in a big bowl of water for at least 8 hours or up to 12 hours. Drain in a fine-mesh sieve or a small-holed colander set in the sink.

2.

Press the button for	Set it for	Set the time for	If necessary, press
SAUTÉ	MEDIUM, NORMAL, or CUSTOM 300°F	25 minutes	START

3. Melt 2 tablespoons butter in a **6- or 8-quart cooker**. Add about half the lamb pieces and brown well, turning and rearranging occasionally, about 8 minutes. Transfer these to a nearby bowl, add the remaining 2 tablespoons butter, and brown the remainder of the lamb in the same way before transferring the pieces to the bowl.

4. Add the onion and cook, stirring occasionally, until softened, about 4 minutes. Pour in the broth and scrape up any browned bits on the pot's bottom. Turn off the SAUTÉ function, then stir in the soaked wheat berries, as well as the pecans, sage, red pepper flakes, and salt. Return the lamb pieces and any of the juices in their bowl to the cooker. Stir well and lock the lid onto the pot.

5.

Set the machine for	Set the level for	The valve must be	Set the time for	If necessary, press
PRESSURE COOK	MAX	—	30 minutes with the KEEP WARM setting off	START
MEAT/STEW, PRESSURE COOK, or MANUAL	HIGH	Closed	40 minutes with the KEEP WARM setting off	START

6. When the machine is finished cooking, turn it off and let its pressure **return to normal naturally**, about 25 minutes. Unlatch the lid and open the cooker. Stir well before serving.

Beyond

- You must halve the recipe for a **3-quart cooker**.

- To enrich the sauce, add up to ½ cup heavy cream after cooking. Set the SAUTÉ function on MEDIUM, NORMAL, or CUSTOM 300°F and bring to a simmer for 1 minute, stirring often, to cook out the cream's raw taste and blend the flavors.

10

Rice and Grains

(Mains and Sides)

This chapter has a split personality. A little over half of its recipes are for grain side dishes: a range of pilafs (rice to quinoa) as well as a road map for risotto and even a hearty combination of beans and lentils that goes alongside anything from the grill. The remainder of the recipes are grain-based main courses, from a good ole chicken-and-rice casserole to aromatic biryani and even paella.

But don't miss the first recipe for perfect wheat berries. We're whole grain fanatics. We almost always keep cooked wheat berries in the fridge to toss into soups, add to salads, or bulk up smoothies. We'd like to convince you to do the same.

And now for an inevitable warning: Grains, whole or not, can be funky. Yes, a multi-cooker prepares them quickly and efficiently. But grains don't move off a grocery store's shelf quickly. They can go rancid. If you open the package and the grains have an acrid smell, take them back for a refund.

Even so, there's also the question of the grains' internal moisture content. Individual grains contain varying amounts — which means they get tender at different times.

Because of these variables, consider the timings here as educated guesses, more so than those in any other chapter of this book. Yes, we tested the recipes several times. Often, we wrote timings that were an average of the results: 7 minutes for one batch, 9 for another, 8 for a third — so 8 minutes appears in this book.

If you open the pot and find the grains are still a tad too "al dente," lock the lid back on, open the pressure valve, and set the machine aside for a few minutes. If the grains are too hard to soften this way, check to make sure there's still enough liquid in the pot (you'll need about ¾ cup in a **3-quart,** 1¼ cups in a 6-quart, or 1¾ cups in an **8-quart**), lock the lid back on, and bring it to HIGH pressure (not MAX) for 1 or 2 minutes, followed by the **quick-release method**. At this point, the valve may sputter. Have a clean kitchen towel on hand to lay over it.

Frankly, such culinary futzing seems a small price to pay for a pilaf in minutes or a comforting rice casserole in a few more.

FAQs

1. How do I store all these grains?
Whole grains aren't really whole. For the most part, they include three parts of the grain: the germ, the bran, and the endosperm. In almost all cases (except for corn), the hulls are missing because they are indigestible. Refined grains like white rice or pearl barley, by contrast, are missing the germ and bran. Refined grains withstand longer storage (up to 8 months in some cases) in a sealed container in a cool, dry pantry because they are missing all the natural oils in the germ and bran, the very things that get smelly. We keep all whole grains (like wheat berries and brown rice) in labeled, sealed, plastic containers in a dark pantry for a couple of months, or in the freezer for up to 1 year.

2. Why do grain dishes sometimes turn out soupy?
There's only one way to make the pot work: boiling liquid ➜ steam ➜ pressure. You must increase the liquid in the pot more than you might in a stovetop saucepan to make sure 1) you get the pressure needed, and 2) you have enough liquid that the grains (or lentils or beans) can dance in the water as they cook without ending up burned on the pot's bottom. All this means you may have to boil a dish down after cooking to keep it from being too soupy. Of course, you can skip the whole process and serve the grains with a slotted spoon or even in bowls.

3. What's with all the white *basmati* rice?
We feel it's the best variety for a pressure cooker. Standard, low-rent, packaged, long-grain rice (that is, the store brand) can turn hideously gummy as the kernels break down. Basmati and its kin like Texmati hold up better. True, basmati is more expensive; but we find the payoff worth it.

Perfect Wheat Berries

Makes about 3 cups cooked grains

1 quart (4 cups) water

1 cup raw, soft, white (or spring) wheat berries

1 tablespoon vegetable, corn, canola or olive oil; or butter

In this recipe, we don't provide a chart of cooking times because of the way different models of the Instant Pot work. But no matter which you own, the recipe is a time-saver because the raw grains cook more quickly under pressure. They also don't need to be soaked overnight, the way they would if we were cooking them on the stovetop.

Toss cooked and drained wheat berries in any green salad, use them in tuna or chicken salad to bulk it up, add them to chickpeas to make a thicker hummus in a food processor, toss them into chilis or stews for the last 5 minutes of cooking, use them instead of cooked rice for a new take on fried "rice" in a wok, add a few to a smoothie to make it richer, or enjoy them as a better cold breakfast cereal with milk, blackberries, and a little sugar.

1. Stir the water, wheat berries, and fat in a **3-, 6-, or 8-quart cooker**. Lock the lid onto the pot with the pressure valve closed.

2. For **Lux, Duo, Smart,** or **Ultra** models, press the MULTIGRAIN button for HIGH pressure. Set the time for 30 minutes and press START if necessary. The machine will automatically soak the grains in a 45-minute warm-water bath, then cook them at HIGH pressure for 30 minutes. When the machine has finished cooking, turn it off and let its pressure **return to normal naturally,** about 30 minutes.

For a **Max** machine, turn on the SAUTÉ function to HIGH and heat the contents until it is quite steamy but not boiling. Switch the SAUTÉ function off, latch the lid onto the pot, and set aside for 45 minutes. Then set the machine to cook at MAX for 25 minutes. Press START. When the machine has finished cooking, turn it off and let its pressure **return to normal naturally,** about 25 minutes.

3. Unlatch the lid and open the cooker. Drain the wheat berries from the *hot* insert into a fine-mesh sieve such as a *chinois* or through a colander lined with a double thickness of paper towels. Cool for 5 minutes, then refresh the grains with cool tap water to stop any residual cooking. Shake the sieve or colander a few times to get rid of excess moisture. Use the cooked wheat berries at once or store them in a sealed container in the fridge for up to 3 days or in the freezer for up to 2 months.

Beyond

- For a more buttery flavor, substitute Kamut berries, an organic strain of khorasan wheat.

- For raw hard red (or winter) wheat berries, rye berries, hull-less barley, or raw oat groats (*not* steel-cut or rolled oats of any sort but the whole groats), use the first technique for cooking at HIGH in older models for 40 minutes, followed by a **natural release;** or use the second technique for warming the water, then cooking at MAX for 35 minutes, followed by a **natural release.**

2 tablespoons solid or liquid fat

Choose from butter, lard, schmaltz, coconut oil, goose fat, or duck fat; or olive, vegetable, corn, canola, safflower, grape seed, avocado, or any nut oil — or a 50/50 combo of a solid fat and a liquid fat.

1 cup chopped (and trimmed if necessary) allium aromatics.

Choose from onions (of any sort), shallots, leeks (white and pale green parts only, well washed), or scallions.

1½ cups raw medium-grain white rice, preferably white Arborio rice

½ cup flavor-enhancing liquid

Choose from white wine (of any sort), dry vermouth, dry sherry, strongly brewed tea, a pale-colored beer such as an IPA or a Pilsner, unsweetened apple juice, or mushroom broth.

2 tablespoons minced fresh herb leaves

Choose one or several from basil, chives, marjoram, oregano, parsley, rosemary, sage, savory, tarragon, and/or thyme.

Up to 3 medium garlic cloves, peeled and minced (1 tablespoon)

Up to ¼ teaspoon saffron threads (optional)

1 quart (4 cups) broth

Use any sort — chicken, beef, vegetable, turkey, or fish — or (better) use a homemade stock, even in as little as a 25/75 ratio with store-bought broth.

Road Map: Risotto

4 to 6 servings

This road map leads you to a simple risotto. You can but don't need to add vegetables. If you make plain risotto to serve with a steak off the grill, you'll get about six servings out of the pot. But this road map can also create a full dinner. If you make a risotto stocked with vegetables, plan on four servings for a main course.

Use only white medium-grain rice. Arborio is the standard, although you can use bomba, Valencia, and even more generic varieties. This technique won't work with brown Arborio, nor with short- or long-grain rice of any sort.

The risotto may be a tad soupy when you open the pot, depending on the moisture content of the uncooked rice grains and the natural moisture packed into the vegetables. Solve this soupiness in two ways. After you add the cheese in step 5, set the pot aside with the lid askew for several minutes, even up to 10. The rice will continue to absorb moisture. Or *before* you add any cheese, use the SAUTÉ function on LOW or LESS to gently simmer the risotto, stirring almost constantly, until most of the liquid has been absorbed, maybe 2 or 3 minutes.

1.

Press the button for	Set it for	Set the time for	If necessary, press
SAUTÉ	MEDIUM, NORMAL, or CUSTOM 300°F	10 minutes	START

2. Melt the fat or heat the oil in a **3-, 6-, or 8-quart cooker** for a minute or two. Add the allium aromatics and cook, stirring often, until softened, 3 to 5 minutes. Stir in the rice and cook until it is coated in the fat and the tips of the grains have begun to turn translucent, about 1 minute.

3. Stir in the flavor-enhancing liquid and scrape up any browned bits on the pot's bottom. Stir in the herbs, garlic (if using), and saffron (if using) until aromatic, just a few seconds. Turn off the SAUTÉ function, pour in the broth, scrape up any browned bits on the pot's bottom, and stir in the quick-cooking vegetables (if using). Lock the lid onto the cooker.

4.

Set the machine for	Set the level for	The valve must be	Set the time for	If necessary, press
PRESSURE COOK	MAX	—	7 minutes with the KEEP WARM setting off	START
PRESSURE COOK or MANUAL	HIGH	Closed	9 minutes with the KEEP WARM setting off	START

5. Use the **quick-release method** to bring the pot's pressure back to normal. Unlatch the lid and open the cooker. Add the cheese and stir well. Set the lid askew over the pot for about 2 minutes to melt the cheese. Stir again and season with salt and pepper as desired.

Up to 2 cups prepped quick-cooking vegetables (optional)

Choose one or two from cored and chopped endive; diced carrots; frozen butternut squash cubes (do not thaw); frozen edamame (do not thaw); frozen mixed vegetables of any sort without any spice or flavorings added (do not thaw); jarred peeled chestnuts; diced peeled carrots or parsnips; diced, seeded, and peeled fresh butternut squash or other winter squash; shelled peas (fresh or frozen); washed and stemmed chard, kale, or other leafy greens; thinly sliced shiitake mushroom caps; thinly sliced white or brown button mushrooms; and/or thinly sliced fresh porcini mushrooms.

½ to 1 cup grated semi-firm or firm cheese

Choose from Asiago, Cheddar, Colby, Havarti, Gorgonzola, Gouda, Jack, mozzarella, Parmigiano-Reggiano, pepper Jack, pecorino, or Swiss — or even a smoked cheese like Jack or Gouda.

Table salt and ground black pepper for garnishing

Beyond

- You must halve the recipe for a **3-quart cooker**.

- For a variation in flavor and texture, substitute up to ½ cup of a soft cheese like chèvre or ricotta (or even ½ cup crème fraîche) for the semi-firm or firm cheese. Stir well to melt.

- For heat, add up to 1 teaspoon red pepper flakes with the fresh herbs.

3 tablespoons olive oil

Up to 3 medium garlic cloves, peeled and minced (1 tablespoon)

Up to ¼ teaspoon saffron threads (optional)

2 cups raw long-grain white rice, such as white basmati or Texmati

1 quart (4 cups) vegetable broth

6 tablespoons packed raisins, chopped

6 tablespoons sliced almonds

1 teaspoon table salt

½ teaspoon ground allspice

½ teaspoon ground black pepper

White Rice Pilaf

6 *servings*

This straightforward rice side goes with almost anything roasted or grilled — like a platter of olive oil–slathered and lemon zest–sprinkled, grilled endive, fennel slices, quartered cauliflower heads, and/or zucchini spears. There's plenty of broth to cook the rice so the grains stay tender and have enough room to move in the pot without sticking to the bottom. Most of that liquid should get absorbed when you set the pot aside in the last step, steaming the rice to perfection.

1.

Press the button for	Set it for	Set the time for	If necessary, press
SAUTÉ	MEDIUM, NORMAL, or CUSTOM 300°F	10 minutes	START

2. Heat the oil in a **3-, 6-, or 8-quart cooker** for a minute or two. Add the garlic and saffron (if using) and cook, stirring often, until aromatic, about 20 seconds. Stir in the rice and get the grains coated in the oil and spices.

3. Turn off the SAUTÉ function. Stir in the broth, raisins, almonds, salt, allspice, and pepper. Lock the lid onto the pot.

4.

Set the machine for	Set the level for	The valve must be	Set the time for	If necessary, press
PRESSURE COOK	MAX	—	7 minutes with the KEEP WARM setting off	START
PRESSURE COOK or MANUAL	HIGH	Closed	9 minutes with the KEEP WARM setting off	START

5. Use the **quick-release method** to bring the pot's pressure back to normal — but *do not open the cooker*. Set aside with the lid latched and the valve open for 10 minutes. Unlatch the lid and open the pot. Stir well before serving.

Beyond

- If the pilaf is too soupy, set the SAUTÉ function on LOW or LESS function and cook, uncovered, for a few minutes, stirring quite often to make sure the rice doesn't stick.

- Feel free to swap out the almonds for pine nuts, chopped walnuts, or chopped pecans.

- For a less sweet pilaf, substitute 2 thinly sliced, medium celery ribs (⅔ cup) for the raisins.

See photo in insert.

Brown Rice Pilaf

6 servings

Brown rice pilaf is not often a successful dish. The grains get hard on the outside before they're tender on the inside, then half of them start to break apart and become like a porridge before the rest are done. But the high-steam environment inside a multi-cooker makes all the grains plump and chewy. It also puts this healthy side within reach almost any weekday. In fact, with a poached egg on top of each serving, this pilaf can easily become a main course.

1.

Press the button for	Set it for	Set the time for	If necessary, press
SAUTÉ	MEDIUM, NORMAL, or CUSTOM 300°F	5 minutes	START

2. Melt the butter in a **3-, 6-, or 8-quart cooker**. Add the onion and cook, stirring occasionally, until softened, about 3 minutes. Add the pecans, thyme, sage, salt, and pepper. Stir until aromatic, just a few seconds. Add the rice and cook, stirring often, until coated in the herbs and fat.

3. Pour in the broth and scrape up *every speck of browned stuff* on the pot's bottom. Turn off the SAUTÉ function and stir in the cranberries. Lock the lid onto the cooker.

4.

Set the machine for	Set the level for	The valve must be	Set the time for	If necessary, press
PRESSURE COOK	MAX	—	22 minutes with the KEEP WARM setting off	START
PRESSURE COOK or MANUAL	HIGH	Closed	28 minutes with the KEEP WARM setting off	START

5. Use the **quick-release method** to bring the pot's pressure back to normal — but *do not open the pot*. Set it aside with the lid latched but the pressure valve open for 10 minutes. Unlatch the lid and open the cooker. Stir well before serving.

2 tablespoons butter

1 medium red onion, chopped (1 cup)

1 cup chopped pecans

1 teaspoon dried thyme

1 teaspoon dried sage

¼ teaspoon table salt

¼ teaspoon ground black pepper

2 cups raw brown long-grain rice, such as brown basmati or Texmati

1 quart (4 cups) vegetable broth

¼ cup packed dried cranberries, chopped

Beyond

- You can use this recipe as a road map for a brown rice pilaf. Swap out the butter for just about any fat. The same goes for the pecans and dried cranberries, substituting other nuts or dried fruits (chopped as necessary) to create your own signature version.

1 tablespoon very warm water

½ teaspoon saffron threads

3 tablespoons olive oil

1 large yellow onion, chopped
(1½ cups)

Up to 1 teaspoon ground dried
turmeric

½ teaspoon ground dried ginger

½ teaspoon table salt

¼ teaspoon red pepper flakes

1½ cups raw long-grain white rice,
preferably jasmine

3 cups vegetable broth

Beyond

- Try adding any number of other
things to the pot before you lock the
lid on. Consider ½ cup packed baby
kale leaves; ½ cup shelled peas
(thawed if frozen); ¼ cup drained
and chopped jarred pimientos; or
¼ cup sliced, pitted green olives.

- For a little crunch, add up to ⅓ cups
shelled, unsalted pistachios with the
spices. Or finely chop those pistachios
and sprinkle them over each serving.

- For a richer (if not vegetarian)
version, substitute chicken broth for
the vegetable broth.

Yellow Rice Pilaf

6 servings

Wow, people love those packages of yellow rice (sometimes called
"Spanish rice") at the supermarket! But let's face it: The rice doesn't
taste like much more than salt. Here's a recipe for a true "yellow" rice
pilaf, also once called "Spanish rice" in the U.S., almost always made
with saffron and turmeric. This pilaf is the best bed for skewers or
kebabs.

1. Pour the water over the saffron threads in a small bowl or a teacup.
Set aside as you continue with the recipe.

2.

Press the button for	Set it for	Set the time for	If necessary, press
SAUTÉ	MEDIUM, NORMAL, or CUSTOM 300°F	10 minutes	START

3. Heat the oil in a **3-, 6-, or 8-quart cooker** for a minute or two. Add
the onion and cook, stirring often, until softened, about 5 minutes. Stir
in the turmeric, ginger, salt, and red pepper flakes until fragrant, just a
few seconds.

4. Add the rice and cook, stirring all the while, until the grains are
evenly coated in the oil and spices. Turn off the SAUTÉ function, pour in
the broth, and scrape up *every speck of browned stuff* on the pot's
bottom. Stir in the saffron and its soaking water. Lock the lid onto the
cooker.

5.

Set the machine for	Set the level for	The valve must be	Set the time for	If necessary, press
PRESSURE COOK	MAX	—	10 minutes with the KEEP WARM setting off	START
PRESSURE COOK or MANUAL	HIGH	Closed	12 minutes with the KEEP WARM setting off	START

6. Use the **quick-release method** to bring the pot's pressure back to
normal — but *do not open the cooker.* Set it aside with the lid still latched
and the pressure valve open for 10 minutes. Unlatch the lid and open
the pot. Stir well before serving.

Herbed Green Rice

6 servings

No, we don't mean rice that ends up green because it has been soaked in the juice squeezed from chlorophyll-rich young bamboo. We mean a highly herbed rice side dish, a great idea with a spring meal. The fresh herbs can get squishy after so long under pressure. Make sure they are truly minced so they almost melt into the mix.

1.

Press the button for	Set it for	Set the time for	If necessary, press
SAUTÉ	MEDIUM, NORMAL, or CUSTOM 300°F	5 minutes	START

2. Melt the butter in a **3-, 6-, or 8-quart cooker**. Add the leek and cook, stirring constantly, until softened, about 2 minutes. Stir in the chiles and garlic until fragrant, about 1 minute. Pour in the rice and stir until the grains are evenly and thoroughly coated in the butter and aromatics.

3. Turn off the SAUTÉ function and stir in the broth, parsley, cilantro, oregano, and salt. Lock the lid onto the pot.

4.

Set the machine for	Set the level for	The valve must be	Set the time for	If necessary, press
PRESSURE COOK	MAX	—	10 minutes with the KEEP WARM setting off	START
PRESSURE COOK or MANUAL	HIGH	Closed	12 minutes with the KEEP WARM setting off	START

5. Use the **quick-release method** to bring the pot's pressure back to normal — but *do not open the cooker*. Set it aside with the lid still latched and the pressure valve open for 10 minutes. Unlatch the lid, open the cooker, and stir well before serving.

2 tablespoons butter

1 large leek (about 6 ounces), white and pale green parts only, halved lengthwise, well washed, and thinly sliced (½ cup)

One 4½-ounce can chopped mild or hot green chiles (½ cup)

2 medium garlic cloves, peeled and minced (2 teaspoons)

1½ cups raw long-grain white rice, preferably jasmine

3 cups vegetable broth

1 cup loosely packed fresh parsley leaves, minced

⅓ cup loosely packed fresh cilantro leaves, minced

2 tablespoons loosely packed fresh oregano leaves, minced

½ teaspoon table salt

Beyond

- Swap out the green herbs we suggest for others you might like. The parsley is integral to the dish, but try rounding it out with sage and savory or oregano and thyme or just tarragon. In total (with the parsley), you're looking for a little less than 1½ cups of loosely packed fresh herbs before mincing.

1 cup small dried red beans, such as small red Colorado beans

2 tablespoons vegetable, corn, or canola oil

1 medium yellow onion, chopped (1 cup)

1 medium bell pepper, stemmed, cored, and chopped (1 cup)

3 medium celery ribs, thinly sliced (1 cup)

3 medium garlic cloves, peeled and minced (1 tablespoon)

1½ cups raw long-grain white rice, preferably basmati

1 teaspoon dried thyme

1 teaspoon dried sage

½ teaspoon celery seeds

Up to ½ teaspoon ground dried cayenne

½ teaspoon table salt

2 bay leaves

3¾ cups vegetable or chicken broth

Red Beans and Rice

4 to 6 servings

This recipe yields a Louisiana version of the classic grain/legume side dish. (See the next recipe for our take on the Cuban version.) There are many variations for this dish among Cajun cooks — some with myriad spices and additions; others, little more than the grain and the legume together. Ours is about midway between the fussy and the simple. Consider it a go-to starchy side to put underneath any spicy stew or braise.

1. Soak the beans in a large bowl of water for 8 hours or up to 12 hours. Drain them in a colander set in the sink.

2.

Press the button for	Set it for	Set the time for	If necessary, press
SAUTÉ	MEDIUM, NORMAL, or CUSTOM 300°F	10 minutes	START

3. Warm the oil in a **6- or 8-quart cooker** for a minute or two. Add the onion, bell pepper, and celery. Cook, stirring occasionally, until the onion softens, about 4 minutes. Add the garlic and cook, stirring more frequently, for 1 minute. Add the rice, thyme, sage, celery seeds, cayenne, salt, and bay leaves. Stir until the grains are evenly and thoroughly coated in the fat and mixed into the vegetables.

4. Pour in the broth and scrape up *every speck of browned stuff* on the pot's bottom. Turn off the SAUTÉ function. Stir in the beans and lock the lid onto the pot.

5.

Set the machine for	Set the level for	The valve must be	Set the time for	If necessary, press
PRESSURE COOK	MAX	—	10 minutes with the KEEP WARM setting off	START
PRESSURE COOK or MANUAL	HIGH	Closed	12 minutes with the KEEP WARM setting off	START

6. Use the **quick-release method** to bring the pot's pressure back to normal — but *do not open the cooker.* Set it aside with the lid latched and the pressure valve open for 10 minutes. Unlatch the lid and open the cooker. Find and discard the bay leaves. Stir well before serving.

Beyond

- You must halve the recipe for a **3-quart cooker.**

- For a meatier (and by some accounts, more classic) version, cook up to ½ cup loose sausage meat, preferably Louisiana andouille, in the oil. Transfer the meat to a bowl, then continue on with the recipe. Add the meat back with the drained beans.

Black Beans and Rice

4 to 6 servings

Here's a Cuban version of the classic grain/legume side dish (see the previous recipe for our simplified take on the Louisiana version). This one goes great under our Picadillo-Style Ragù (page 143). It is also the gold standard for taco night and alongside a grilled Southwest-style rubbed pork loin.

1. Soak the beans in a large bowl of water for 8 hours or up to 12 hours. Drain them in a colander set in the sink.

2. Pour the beans into a **6- or 8-quart cooker**. Add the remaining ingredients and stir well. Lock the lid onto the cooker.

3.

Set the machine for	Set the level for	The valve must be	Set the time for	If necessary, press
PRESSURE COOK	MAX	—	10 minutes with the KEEP WARM setting off	START
PRESSURE COOK or MANUAL	HIGH	Closed	12 minutes with the KFFP WARM setting off	START

4. Use the **quick-release method** to bring the pot's pressure back to normal—but *do not open the cooker.* Set it aside with the lid latched and the pressure valve open for 10 minutes. Unlatch the lid and open the cooker. Stir well before serving.

1 cup dried black beans

3¾ cups vegetable or chicken broth

1½ cups raw long-grain white rice, preferably basmati

Up to ½ cup loosely packed cilantro leaves, minced

One 4½-ounce can chopped mild or hot green chiles (½ cup)

1½ teaspoons dried oregano

½ teaspoon ground cumin

½ teaspoon table salt

½ teaspoon ground black pepper

Beyond

- You must halve the recipe for a **3-quart cooker.**

- For heat, add up to 1 medium fresh jalapeño, stemmed, halved lengthwise, seeded (if desired), and thinly sliced to the mix.

- For more zip, add up to 2 teaspoons finely minced orange zest; up to a 4-ounce jar of chopped pimientos, drained and rinsed; and/or up to 1 teaspoon mild smoked paprika.

¼ cup olive oil

6 medium garlic cloves, peeled and minced (2 tablespoons)

½ teaspoon red pepper flakes

½ cup vermouth, either dry (white) or sweet (red)

2 cups raw long-grain brown rice

½ cup green lentils (that is, le Puy lentils)

1 teaspoon table salt

1 quart (4 cups) vegetable or chicken broth

Brown Rice and Lentils

6 servings

This easy side dish is highly spiced because the oil steeps with the aromatics before you assemble the dish. Although it's great alongside a roast of just about any sort, it also makes the base for a great breakfast. Serve it up on plates, then top each serving with a fried egg (or two) and hot sauce, like Sriracha.

1. Before turning on the heat, pour the oil into a **3-, 6-, or 8-quart cooker**. Add the garlic and red pepper flakes.

2.

Press the button for	Set it for	Set the time for	If necessary, press
SAUTÉ	LOW or LESS	5 minutes	START

3. Heat the oil slowly until the garlic is golden at the edges, stirring often, 3 to 4 minutes. Stir in the vermouth and scrape up any browned bits on the pot's bottom.

4. Pour in the rice, lentils, and salt. Stir until the rice grains are evenly and thoroughly coated in the fat and aromatics. Turn off the SAUTÉ function and stir in the broth. Lock the lid onto the pot.

5.

Set the machine for	Set the level for	The valve must be	Set the time for	If necessary, press
PRESSURE COOK	MAX	—	23 minutes with the KEEP WARM setting off	START
PRESSURE COOK or MANUAL	HIGH	Closed	30 minutes with the KEEP WARM setting off	START

6. When the machine has finished cooking, turn it off and let its pressure **return to normal naturally**, about 20 minutes. Unlatch the lid and open the cooker. Stir well before serving.

Beyond

- For a real treat, use super aromatic Wehani rice.

- For more punch, mince 1 tinned anchovy fillet; add it with the garlic and red pepper flakes—but omit the salt.

- To avoid using alcohol, substitute ¼ cup unsweetened apple juice and an additional ¼ cup vegetable broth for the red vermouth—or use all broth.

- If you've used a **6- or 8-quart cooker**, try stirring up to 2 cups packed baby arugula or baby kale and 1 tablespoon balsamic vinegar into the finished dish. Set the lid askew over the pot for 2 or 3 minutes to wilt the greens.

Wild Rice Pilaf

6 servings

Wild rice is not rice. It's a grass grain, once found almost exclusively in the upper Midwest and the southern portions of Ontario. Today, there are many varietals on the market: some brown, some black, many grown in California. This recipe was designed for *black* wild rice, the sort that splits when cooked to reveal a creamy, white core.

There's something of a reversal in this technique: The wild rice is cooked under pressure, then the other ingredients are added to the pot. We found that keeping the apple and scallions out from under the pressure gave them a better texture to match the wild rice.

1 cup raw black wild rice

3 tablespoons butter

½ cup chopped walnuts

1 firm, sour, green apple, such as Granny Smith, cored and diced (no need to peel)

2 medium scallions, trimmed and thinly sliced

1 medium celery stalk, thinly sliced (⅓ cup)

1 tablespoon packed fresh sage leaves, minced

½ teaspoon table salt

1. Pour the wild rice in a **3-, 6-, or 8-quart cooker**, add 1 tablespoon of the butter, and fill the cooker with water until the wild rice is submerged by 2 inches. Lock the lid onto the pot.

2.

Set the machine for	Set the level for	The valve must be	Set the time for	If necessary, press
PRESSURE COOK	MAX	—	28 minutes with the KEEP WARM setting off	START
PRESSURE COOK or MANUAL	HIGH	Closed	40 minutes with the KEEP WARM setting off	START

3. Use the **quick-release method** to bring the pot's pressure back to normal. Unlatch the lid and open the pot. Drain the wild rice from the hot insert into a fine-mesh sieve such as a *chinois* or through a colander lined with a single layer of cheesecloth. Rinse out the insert and return it to the machine.

4.

Press the button for	Set it for	Set the time for	If necessary, press
SAUTÉ	MEDIUM, NORMAL, or CUSTOM 300°F	10 minutes	START

5. Melt the remaining 2 tablespoons butter in the pot, then add the walnuts, apple, scallions, and celery. Cook, stirring occasionally, until the scallions soften, about 3 minutes. Stir in the cooked and drained wild rice, then add the sage and salt. Cook, stirring all the while, to blend the flavors, about 1 minute. Turn off the SAUTÉ function and remove the *hot* insert from the pot to stop the cooking. Serve warm.

See photo in insert.

Beyond

- For a sweeter finish, substitute 1 firm ripe pear, cored and chopped, for the apple.

- Feel free to substitute pecans or even skinned hazelnuts for the walnuts.

2 tablespoons vegetable, corn, or canola oil; or butter

2 medium shallots, peeled and chopped (½ cup)

2 medium garlic cloves, peeled and minced (2 teaspoons)

1½ cups raw pearl barley

2½ cups vegetable or chicken broth

1 medium carrot, shredded through the large holes of a box grater (⅓ cup)

2 tablespoons packed fresh dill fronds, minced

Up to 1 tablespoon fresh lemon juice

1 teaspoon finely grated lemon zest

½ teaspoon table salt

½ teaspoon ground black pepper

Barley Pilaf

6 servings

Pearl barley has a mild, sweet flavor that pairs well with lemon and dill. This one's a filling side dish, a welcome addition to a holiday table alongside roast beef or turkey.

1.

Press the button for	Set it for	Set the time for	If necessary, press
SAUTÉ	MEDIUM, NORMAL, or CUSTOM 300°F	10 minutes	START

2. Heat the oil for a minute or two (or melt the butter) in a **6- or 8-quart cooker**. Add the shallots and cook, stirring occasionally, until softened, about 3 minutes. Add the garlic and cook until fragrant, just a few seconds. Stir in the barley until it is evenly and thoroughly coated in the fat.

3. Pour in the broth, turn off the SAUTÉ function, and scrape up *every speck of browned stuff* on the pot's bottom. Stir in the carrot, dill, lemon juice, lemon zest, salt, and pepper. Lock the lid onto the pot.

4.

Set the machine for	Set the level for	The valve must be	Set the time for	If necessary, press
PRESSURE COOK	MAX	—	18 minutes with the KEEP WARM setting off	START
PRESSURE COOK or MANUAL	HIGH	Closed	25 minutes with the KEEP WARM setting off	START

5. When the machine has finished cooking, turn it off and let its pressure **return to normal naturally**, about 20 minutes. Unlatch the lid and open the cooker. Stir well before serving.

Beyond

- You must halve the recipe for a **3-quart cooker**.

- Garnish servings with crumbled feta or soft goat cheese. Or even crumbled blue cheese.

- This pilaf is also good as a bed for sausages off the grill, particularly smoked bratwurst or kielbasa.

Buckwheat Pilaf

6 servings

Buckwheat may not sound gluten-free ("wheat," after all); but it is *not* a cereal grain. It's the seed from a grass cultivar not even distantly related to wheat. It cooks up sticky and thick, with a subtle texture of oats but with a more herbaceous flavor. Do not use kasha — that is, *toasted* buckwheat groats. The flavor will be far too strong, even bitter. Plain buckwheat groats go rancid quickly at room temperature. Store them in a sealed container in the freezer for up to 6 months.

1.

Press the button for	Set it for	Set the time for	If necessary, press
SAUTÉ	MEDIUM, NORMAL, or CUSTOM 300°F	10 minutes	START

2. Warm the oil for a minute or two (or melt the butter) in a **6- or 8-quart cooker**. Add the onion and celery; cook, stirring occasionally, until the onion has softened, about 3 minutes. Add the pecans, cranberries, sage, and thyme; stir well until fragrant, about 30 seconds.

3. Pour in the broth, turn off the SAUTÉ function, and scrape up *every speck of browned stuff* on the pot's bottom. Stir in the buckwheat and salt. Lock the lid onto the cooker.

4.

Set the machine for	Set the level for	The valve must be	Set the time for	If necessary, press
PRESSURE COOK	MAX	—	3 minutes with the KEEP WARM setting off	START
PRESSURE COOK or MANUAL	HIGH	Closed	5 minutes with the KEEP WARM setting off	START

5. Use the **quick-release method** to bring the pot's pressure back to normal — but *do not open the pot*. Set it aside with the lid latched and the pressure valve open for 7 minutes. Unlatch the lid and open the cooker. Stir well before serving.

1 tablespoon vegetable, corn, or canola oil; or butter

1 small yellow onion, chopped (½ cup)

2 medium celery ribs, thinly sliced (⅔ cup)

½ cup chopped pecans

½ cup dried cranberries

2 tablespoons packed fresh sage leaves, minced

1 tablespoon stemmed fresh thyme leaves

1 quart (4 cups) vegetable or chicken broth

2 cups raw buckwheat groats

½ teaspoon table salt

Beyond

- You must halve the recipe for a 3-quart cooker.

- Because of varying amounts of moisture in uncooked groats, the pilaf may be a little soupy. If so, use the SAUTÉ function on MEDIUM, NORMAL, or CUSTOM 300°F to boil away the excess liquid, stirring almost constantly, 2 to 3 minutes. Be careful: The groats can quickly fuse to the pot's bottom. Turn off the SAUTÉ function and immediately remove the *hot* insert from the pot to stop the cooking, continuing to stir the mixture a few times to keep the buckwheat from sticking.

2 tablespoons butter

1 medium yellow onion, chopped (1 cup)

2 medium garlic cloves, peeled and minced (2 teaspoons)

½ teaspoon cumin seeds

½ teaspoon ground dried ginger

1 cup raw red or white quinoa, thoroughly rinsed in a fine-mesh sieve or a colander lined with cheesecloth

2 cups vegetable broth

1 pound cauliflower florets, roughly chopped (3 cups)

One 14-ounce can diced tomatoes (1¾ cups)

¼ teaspoon table salt

Quinoa and Cauliflower Pilaf

4 to 6 servings

There has been a debate recently about whether quinoa has a protein similar enough to gluten to knock it out of the diets of those with celiac disease or gluten sensitivities. Extensive tests published in *The American Journal of Gastroenterology* discovered that those with gluten intolerances can actually improve their overall digestive health by including quinoa among their choices. So make this tasty pilaf side dish for weekend or holiday gatherings when you know someone at the table can't enjoy the bread or the stuffing in the turkey. Or just make it for yourself: a tasty, earthy side dish to glitz up the simplest meal.

1.

Press the button for	Set it for	Set the time for	If necessary, press
SAUTÉ	MEDIUM, NORMAL, or CUSTOM 300°F	10 minutes	START

2. Melt the butter in a **6- or 8-quart cooker**. Add the onion and cook, stirring occasionally, until softened, about 4 minutes. Add the garlic, cumin seeds, and ground ginger; stir until aromatic, just a few seconds. Pour in the quinoa and stir until the grains are evenly distributed through the other ingredients.

3. Pour in the broth, turn off the SAUTÉ function, and scrape up *every speck of browned stuff* on the pot's bottom. Stir in the cauliflower, tomatoes, and salt. Lock the lid onto the cooker.

4.

Set the machine for	Set the level for	The valve must be	Set the time for	If necessary, press
PRESSURE COOK	MAX	—	4 minutes with the KEEP WARM setting off	START
PRESSURE COOK or MANUAL	HIGH	Closed	5 minutes with the KEEP WARM setting off	START

5. Use the **quick-release method** to bring the pot's pressure back to normal. Unlatch the lid and open the cooker.

6.

Press the button for	Set it for	Set the time for	If necessary, press
SAUTÉ	MEDIUM, NORMAL, or CUSTOM 300°F	5 minutes	START

7. Cook, stirring often, until the liquid has boiled down to a sauce, about 3 minutes. Turn off the SAUTÉ function and remove the *hot* insert from the machine to stop the cooking. Set the lid askew over the top of the insert and set aside for 5 minutes so the grains continue to absorb the liquid and the flavors meld.

Beyond

- You must halve the recipe for a **3-quart cooker.**

- If you skip steps 6 and 7, the dish will be soupier, better for small bowls than served right alongside the main course on a plate.

- Turn this into a quinoa and tomato soup by increasing the broth to 6 cups in a **6- or 8-quart cooker.**

See photo in insert.

2 tablespoons vegetable, corn, or canola oil; or butter

1 medium yellow onion, chopped (1 cup)

1¼ cups raw red or white quinoa, rinsed in a fine-mesh sieve or a colander lined with cheesecloth

¼ cup raw buckwheat groats (do not use kasha—aka toasted buckwheat groats)

¼ cup dry white wine, such as Chardonnay

3½ cups vegetable or chicken broth

One 14-ounce can diced tomatoes (1¾ cups)

1 teaspoon dried thyme

¼ teaspoon grated nutmeg

¼ teaspoon table salt

1 ounce finely grated Parmigiano-Reggiano (½ cup—optional)

Quinoa and Buckwheat Risotto

6 servings

In this tweaked take on risotto, there's no rice. Instead, the buckwheat lends the dish the creamy texture of the Italian classic. It's faux risotto, a bit healthier than the original and a great match for Bollito Misto (page 362) or Perfect Seared Chicken Breasts (page 291).

1.

Press the button for	Set it for	Set the time for	If necessary, press
SAUTÉ	MEDIUM, NORMAL, or CUSTOM 300°F	10 minutes	START

2. Warm the oil for a minute or two (or melt the butter) in a **6- or 8-quart cooker**. Add the onion and cook, stirring occasionally, until softened, about 3 minutes. Stir in the quinoa and buckwheat groats until coated in the fat.

3. Pour in the wine and scrape up *every speck of browned stuff* on the pot's bottom. Turn off the SAUTÉ function. Stir in the broth, tomatoes, thyme, nutmeg, and salt. Lock the lid onto the cooker.

4.

Set the machine for	Set the level for	The valve must be	Set the time for	If necessary, press
PRESSURE COOK	MAX	—	6 minutes with the KEEP WARM setting off	START
PRESSURE COOK or MANUAL	HIGH	Closed	8 minutes with the KEEP WARM setting off	START

5. Use the **quick-release method** to bring the pot's pressure back to normal. Unlatch the lid and open the cooker. Stir in the cheese (if using). Set the lid askew over the pot for 5 minutes to blend the flavors. Stir again before serving.

Beyond

• You must halve the recipe for a **3-quart cooker**.

• To bulk up this side dish, add up to 2 cups chopped carrots, peeled sweet potatoes, or chopped seeded peeled winter or butternut squash.

• Or stir in up to 2 cups packed baby kale with the cheese in step 5.

Beef, Barley, and Mushroom Casserole

6 servings

Here's the first of our grain main courses: a favorite soup turned into a savory, sloppy joe–style casserole. Sloppy joe fillings can be sweet, but this preparation is quite savory and even "dry" — in keeping with its casserole consistency, rather than the filling for a messy sandwich (which you can find on page 131). This main course can be even more savory if you use grass-fed beef. Because of the way a pressure cooker works, the barley picks up lots of the beefy flavor. And because we opted for ground beef, rather than a cubed cut of meat, the casserole is relatively easy to prepare.

2 tablespoons butter

1 medium yellow onion, chopped (1 cup)

8 ounces thinly sliced cremini mushrooms

2 medium garlic cloves, peeled and minced (2 teaspoons)

¾ pound lean ground beef

1 cup pearl barley

1 large round red tomato, chopped (1 cup)

1 tablespoon packed fresh sage leaves, chopped

Up to ½ teaspoon grated nutmeg

½ teaspoon table salt

½ teaspoon ground black pepper

1⅔ cups beef or chicken broth

1.

Press the button for	Set it for	Set the time for	If necessary, press
SAUTÉ	MEDIUM, NORMAL, or CUSTOM 300°F	15 minutes	START

2. Melt the butter in a **3-, 6-, or 8-quart cooker**. Add the onion and cook, stirring occasionally, until softened, about 3 minutes. Add the mushrooms and continue cooking, stirring more frequently, until they give off their internal moisture and it evaporates to a glaze, about 5 minutes. Stir in the garlic until aromatic, just a few seconds.

3. Crumble in the ground beef and cook, stirring occasionally to break up any clumps, until the meat loses its raw, pink color, about 2 minutes. Stir in the barley, tomato, sage, nutmeg, salt, and pepper until the barley is evenly distributed throughout the mixture.

4. Pour in the broth, turn off the SAUTÉ function, and scrape up any browned bits on the pot's bottom. Lock the lid onto the cooker.

5.

Set the machine for	Set the level for	The valve must be	Set the time for	If necessary, press
PRESSURE COOK	MAX	—	18 minutes with the KEEP WARM setting off	START
PRESSURE COOK or MANUAL	HIGH	Closed	25 minutes with the KEEP WARM setting off	START

6. When the machine has finished cooking, turn it off and let its pressure **return to normal naturally**, about 25 minutes. Unlatch the lid and open the pot. Stir well, then set the lid askew over the pot and set aside for 5 minutes to blend the flavors.

Beyond

- Substitute ground turkey or even ground pork for the beef — or use a 50/50 combo of different kinds of ground meat. (However, ground chicken is not successful in this casserole.)

- Make this vegetarian by using ¾ pound unseasoned soy (or other plant-based) protein crumbles rather than ground beef, and 1⅔ cups vegetable broth rather than beef or chicken.

1 tablespoon butter

¾ pound smoked pork sausage links, such as kielbasa, cut into 1-inch pieces

1 medium yellow onion, chopped (1 cup)

1½ pounds boneless skinless chicken thighs, any large bits of fat removed, the meat cut into 1-inch pieces

1 cup raw long-grain white rice, preferably basmati

1 cup shelled peas (if frozen, no need to thaw)

1½ teaspoons mild paprika

½ teaspoon dried sage

½ teaspoon dried thyme

¼ teaspoon table salt

2 cups chicken broth

Beyond

- You must halve the recipe for a **3-quart cooker**.

- For an **8-quart cooker**, you must increase all the ingredients by 50 percent.

- If you want to omit the sausage and return to a more standard rendition, use 2 pounds of boneless, skinless chicken thighs.

- For a bit more heft, add 1 stemmed, cored, and chopped medium bell pepper (of any color) with the onion.

- Also try adding up to ½ pound thinly sliced white or brown button mushrooms with the onions. Cook, stirring occasionally, until the mushrooms give off their liquid and it reduces to a glaze, about 6 minutes.

- For more kick, substitute mild or hot smoked paprika for the regular paprika.

Chicken and Rice Casserole

4 to 6 servings

This is really a chicken, *sausage*, and rice casserole. The addition of a little porky goodness turns the family favorite into something special even on a Wednesday night. It's like a cross between arroz con pollo and the well-known American stand-by.

1.

Press the button for	Set it for	Set the time for	If necessary, press
SAUTÉ	MEDIUM, NORMAL, or CUSTOM 300°F	15 minutes	START

2. Warm the butter in a **6-quart cooker** for a minute or two. Add the sausage and cook, stirring occasionally, until it begins to brown at the edges, about 4 minutes. Add the onion and cook, stirring occasionally, until softened, about 3 minutes. Add the chicken and stir just until it loses its raw, pink color, about 2 minutes.

3. Stir in the rice, peas, paprika, sage, thyme, and salt until uniform. Stir in the broth, turn off the SAUTÉ function, and scrape *every speck of browned stuff* off the pot's bottom. Lock the lid onto the cooker.

4.

Set the machine for	Set the level for	The valve must be	Set the time for	If necessary, press
PRESSURE COOK	MAX	——	10 minutes with the KEEP WARM setting off	START
PRESSURE COOK or MANUAL	HIGH	Closed	12 minutes with the KEEP WARM setting off	START

5. Use the **quick-release function** to bring the pot's pressure back to normal—but *do not open the cooker*. Set it aside with the lid latched and the pressure valve open for 10 minutes. Unlatch the lid, open the pot, and stir well before serving.

Orange Beef "Fried Rice" Casserole

4 servings

We can't make fried rice well in a multi-cooker. But we can make main-course rice casseroles that use the flavors of classic Chinese take-out dishes, morphing them into a cross between more traditional fried rice and an American casserole. The beef needs longer to cook, so brown rice is a better alternative here (rather than having to cook the dish in two steps, beef for a while, then rice added later).

1.

Press the button for	Set it for	Set the time for	If necessary, press
SAUTÉ	MEDIUM, NORMAL, or CUSTOM 300°F	10 minutes	START

2. Warm the oil in a **3- or 6-quart cooker** for a minute or two. Add the scallions, ginger, and zest. Cook, stirring often, just until the scallions begin to soften, about 1 minute. Add the beef and cook, stirring occasionally, until it loses its raw, red color, about 2 minutes. Add the rice and stir well until the grains are uniformly distributed throughout.

3. Pour in the broth, turn off the SAUTÉ function, and scrape up *every speck of browned stuff* on the pot's bottom. Stir in the soy sauce, orange juice, hoisin sauce, and vinegar until uniform. Lock the lid onto the cooker.

4.

Set the machine for	Set the level for	The valve must be	Set the time for	If necessary, press
PRESSURE COOK	MAX	—	17 minutes with the KEEP WARM setting off	START
PRESSURE COOK or MANUAL	HIGH	Closed	20 minutes with the KEEP WARM setting off	START

5. Use the **quick-release method** to bring the pot's pressure back to normal—but *do not open the cooker.* Set it aside with the lid latched and the pressure valve open for 10 minutes. Unlatch the lid, open the pot, and stir well before serving.

See photo in insert.

2 tablespoons vegetable, corn, or canola oil

6 medium scallions, trimmed and thinly sliced

2 tablespoons minced peeled fresh ginger

2 tablespoons finely minced orange zest

1 pound beef flank steak, cut in half lengthwise, then cut against the grain into ¼-inch-thick strips

1 cup raw long-grain brown rice

1¼ cups beef broth

¼ cup soy sauce

¼ cup fresh orange juice

2 tablespoons hoisin sauce (see page 184)

1 tablespoon apple cider vinegar

Beyond

- For an **8-quart cooker**, you must increase all the ingredients by 50 percent.

- For a more vegetable-heavy dish, add up to ½ cup frozen edamame (do not thaw) with the rice and/or up to 1 cup frozen broccoli florets (do not thaw) with the broth.

- Go ahead and substitute an equivalent amount of boneless skinless chicken thighs, cut into ¼-inch-thick strips, for the beef.

- Garnish with minced chives or the green parts of a scallion.

2 tablespoons vegetable, corn, or canola oil

1 medium yellow onion, chopped (1 cup)

¼ cup minced peeled fresh ginger

1 pound lean ground pork

2 medium garlic cloves, peeled and minced (2 teaspoons)

2 cups chicken broth

1¼ cups raw long-grain white rice, preferably basmati

¼ cup soy sauce

¼ cup unseasoned rice vinegar

½ teaspoon five-spice powder (see page 88)

Ground Pork and Ginger "Fried Rice" Casserole

4 servings

This recipe has a traditional flavor profile for fried rice — except it uses *a lot* of ginger. Feel free to cut down on the copious amount, although we feel all that ginger gives the dish an irresistible, aromatic flair. Because we used ground pork, definitely a quick-cooker, we chose white rice instead of longer-cooking brown rice.

1.

Press the button for	Set it for	Set the time for	If necessary, press
SAUTÉ	MEDIUM, NORMAL, or CUSTOM 300°F	10 minutes	START

2. Warm the oil in a **3- or 6-quart cooker** for a minute or two. Add the onion and ginger. Cook, stirring often, until the onion begins to soften, about 4 minutes. Crumble in the ground pork and cook, stirring occasionally to break up any clumps, until it loses its raw, pink color, about 4 minutes. Stir in the garlic until aromatic, just a few seconds.

3. Pour in the broth, turn off the SAUTÉ function, and scrape up *every speck of browned stuff* on the pot's bottom. Add the rice, soy sauce, vinegar, and five-spice powder. Stir well until the grains are evenly distributed, then lock the lid onto the pot.

4.

Set the machine for	Set the level for	The valve must be	Set the time for	If necessary, press
PRESSURE COOK	MAX	—	7 minutes with the KEEP WARM setting off	START
PRESSURE COOK or MANUAL	HIGH	Closed	9 minutes with the KEEP WARM setting off	START

5. Use the **quick-release method** to bring the pot's pressure back to normal — but *do not open the cooker*. Set it aside with the lid latched and the pressure valve open for 10 minutes. Unlatch the lid, open the pot, and stir well before serving.

Beyond

- For an **8-quart cooker**, you must increase all the ingredients by 50 percent.

- For a fresher flavor, substitute 6 medium scallions, trimmed and thinly sliced, for the onion.

- For heat, add up to 1 tablespoon red chile paste, such as sambal oelek or Sriracha, with the broth.

Chicken Biryani Casserole

4 to 6 servings

Although biryani is usually a layered rice dish, we've turned it into a one-pot casserole. The spice mixture for biryani can be complex, so we simplified it to just garam masala and fresh ginger, mostly in the interest of getting dinner on the table quickly. (To make your own garam masala, see page 226.) Because of the way the rice continues to absorb moisture in the dish, this one's not very successful as leftovers the next day.

1. Mix the water and saffron in a small bowl or teacup. Set aside.

2. Whisk the yogurt, garlic, ginger, garam masala, lemon juice, turmeric, cayenne, and salt in a large bowl until uniform. Add the chicken and toss well to coat evenly and thoroughly. Set aside.

3.

Press the button for	Set it for	Set the time for	If necessary, press
SAUTÉ	MEDIUM, NORMAL, or CUSTOM 300°F	15 minutes	START

4. Melt 2 tablespoons butter in a **6- or 8-quart cooker**. Add the onion and cook, stirring often, until golden, even lightly browned, about 10 minutes. Use a slotted spoon to transfer half the onions to a nearby bowl.

5. Add the remaining 2 tablespoons butter, then the chicken and every bit of its marinade as well as the bay leaves. Cook, stirring almost constantly, for 2 minutes. Pour in the broth, turn off the SAUTÉ function, and scrape up *every speck of browned stuff* on the pot's bottom. Sprinkle the rice over the top of the dish; stir gently just so the grains are submerged (they need not be thoroughly and evenly incorporated). Lock the lid onto the cooker.

6.

Set the machine for	Set the level for	The valve must be	Set the time for	If necessary, press
PRESSURE COOK	MAX	—	7 minutes with the KEEP WARM setting off	START
PRESSURE COOK or MANUAL	HIGH	Closed	9 minutes with the KEEP WARM setting off	START

7. Use the **quick-release method** to bring the pot's pressure back to normal — but *do not open the cooker*. Set it aside with the lid latched and the pressure valve open for 10 minutes.

8. Stir the water and saffron threads into the reserved onions and spread this mixture over the top of the casserole in the cooker without stirring it. Set the lid askew over the pot for 5 minutes to heat the onions and blend the flavors. Serve big spoonfuls, discarding the bay leaves as you find them.

1 tablespoon warm tap water

Up to 1 teaspoon saffron threads

¾ cup plain regular or low-fat yogurt (do not use fat-free or Greek yogurt)

3 medium garlic cloves, peeled and minced (1 tablespoon)

1 tablespoon minced peeled fresh ginger

1 tablespoon garam masala

1 tablespoon fresh lemon juice

½ teaspoon ground dried turmeric

Up to ½ teaspoon ground dried cayenne

½ teaspoon table salt

2½ pounds boneless skinless chicken thighs, any large bits of fat removed, the meat quartered

¼ cup (½ stick) butter or ghee (see page 227)

2 large yellow onions, halved and cut into thin half-moons

2 bay leaves

3 cups chicken broth

1½ cups raw long-grain white basmati rice

Beyond

- You must halve the recipe for a 3-quart cooker.

- Garnish individual servings with lots of minced fresh cilantro and mint leaves.

- Go ahead and add up to 1 cup shelled green peas (thawed if frozen) with the rice before the second cooking.

2 tablespoons vegetable, corn, or canola oil

2 medium yellow onions, halved and sliced into thin half-moons

2 teaspoons coriander seeds

1 teaspoon cumin seeds

1 teaspoon table salt

½ teaspoon ground dried turmeric

½ teaspoon ground black pepper

8 green or white cardamom pods, lightly crushed

8 whole cloves

One 4-inch cinnamon stick

1 bay leaf

1½ cups raw long-grain brown rice

2 pounds boneless leg of lamb, any large bits of fat removed, the meat cut into 1-inch pieces

2½ cups beef or chicken broth

Lamb Biryani Casserole

6 servings

This recipe uses long-grain *brown* rice to make a biryani-style casserole, with sweet flavors to match the earthy whole grain and lots of spices for big pops of flavor. Those spices are whole and will soften under pressure. You might not find many spice bits because of the way the pressure acts on them. But warn anyone who won't appreciate a sudden mouthful to pick out any whole spices found on their plate.

1.

Press the button for	Set it for	Set the time for	If necessary, press
SAUTÉ	MEDIUM, NORMAL, or CUSTOM 300°F	15 minutes	START

2. Warm the oil in a **6- or 8-quart cooker** for a minute or two. Add the onion and cook, stirring occasionally, until golden yellow, about 8 minutes. Stir in the coriander seeds, cumin seeds, salt, turmeric, pepper, cardamom pods, cloves, cinnamon stick, and bay leaf until aromatic, about 20 seconds. Stir in the rice until the grains are evenly distributed throughout the mix.

3. Stir in the lamb until it's evenly coated in the spices and rice. Pour in the broth, turn off the SAUTÉ function, and scrape up *every speck of browned stuff* on the pot's bottom. Stir well and lock the lid onto the cooker.

4.

Set the machine for	Set the level for	The valve must be	Set the time for	If necessary, press
PRESSURE COOK	MAX	—	17 minutes with the KEEP WARM setting off	START
PRESSURE COOK or MANUAL	HIGH	Closed	20 minutes with the KEEP WARM setting off	START

5. When the machine has finished cooking, turn it off and let its pressure **return to normal naturally**, about 25 minutes. Unlatch the lid and open the cooker. Find and discard the cinnamon stick and bay leaf. Stir well before serving.

Beyond

- You must halve the recipe for a **3-quart cooker**.

- Garnish the servings with chutney of any sort, as well as toasted sliced almonds.

- Or drizzle the servings with crème fraîche and top them with chopped fresh parsley, cilantro, and/or mint leaves.

- Serve with Perfect Chana Dal (page 229).

Spicy Vegetable Biryani Casserole

4 servings

Flavorful and comforting, this casserole can get very hot if you use the full amount of jalapeño (even though the pressure cooker tames the capsaicin in the chile). Even with the heat, for us this casserole is the most comforting of any in the book. It goes best with beer, like a pale ale or an IPA.

1.

Press the button for	Set it for	Set the time for	If necessary, press
SAUTÉ	MEDIUM, NORMAL, or CUSTOM 300°F	10 minutes	START

2. Warm the oil in a **6- or 8-quart cooker** for a minute or two. Add the coriander seeds, cumin seeds, cardamom pods, cloves, and bay leaves. Stir until very aromatic, about 1 minute. Add the onion and jalapeño. Cook, stirring often, until the onion begins to soften, about 3 minutes. Stir in the garlic, ginger, garam masala, and smoked paprika until aromatic, just a few seconds.

3. Stir in the rice, bell pepper, okra, cauliflower, and peas until the rice grains are evenly distributed throughout the mixture. Pour in the broth, turn off the SAUTÉ function, and scrape up *every speck of browned stuff* on the pot's bottom. Lock the lid onto the cooker.

4.

Set the machine for	Set the level for	The valve must be	Set the time for	If necessary, press
PRESSURE COOK	MAX	—	7 minutes with the KEEP WARM setting off	START
PRESSURE COOK or MANUAL	HIGH	Closed	9 minutes with the KEEP WARM setting off	START

5. Use the **quick-release method** to bring the pot's pressure back to normal — but *do not open the cooker*. Set it aside with the lid latched and the pressure valve open for 10 minutes. Unlatch the lid and open the cooker. Find and discard the bay leaves. Stir well and serve big spoonfuls.

2 tablespoons vegetable, corn, or canola oil

1 teaspoon coriander seeds

1 teaspoon cumin seeds

4 green or white cardamom pods, lightly crushed

8 whole cloves

2 bay leaves

1 large red onion, chopped (1½ cups)

Up to 2 medium fresh jalapeño chiles, stemmed, halved lengthwise, seeded (if desired), and thinly sliced

1 medium garlic clove, peeled and minced (1 teaspoon)

1 teaspoon minced peeled fresh ginger

1 teaspoon garam masala (see page 226)

1 teaspoon mild smoked paprika

1½ cups raw long-grain white rice, preferably basmati

1 large red bell pepper, stemmed, cored, and chopped (1½ cups)

1 cup frozen sliced okra (do not thaw)

1 cup chopped fresh cauliflower florets (do not use frozen)

½ cup frozen peas (do not thaw)

3 cups vegetable broth

Beyond

- You must halve the recipe for a **3-quart cooker**.

- Garnish the servings with roasted cashews and chopped fresh cilantro leaves.

- And/or top them with vegan yogurt (or plain Greek yogurt, if you don't mind the dairy).

½ pound mussels (about 20), their shells scrubbed, the mussels debearded (if necessary)

6 small mahogany or littleneck clams, their shells scrubbed

6 very large shrimp (about 10 per pound—deveined but shell-on)

1½ cups water

2 tablespoons olive oil

1 medium yellow onion, chopped (1 cup)

1 medium green bell pepper, stemmed, cored, and chopped (1 cup)

¾ pound mild or hot Italian sausage links, cut into 1-inch pieces

1 pound boneless skinless chicken thighs, any large hunks of fat removed, the meat cut into 1-inch pieces

2 teaspoons mild smoked paprika

2 teaspoons dried oregano

½ teaspoon fennel seeds

¼ teaspoon saffron threads

¼ teaspoon table salt

One 14-ounce can diced tomatoes (1¾ cups)

1¾ cups chicken broth

1¼ cups raw medium-grain white rice, such as Arborio, bomba, or Valencia rice

Yes, Paella

6 servings

It's hard to believe that paella can come from an Instant Pot. True, you won't get a crunchy bottom, the way paella turns out in a giant pan over an open fire. Even so, this recipe's a fine imitation, fit for weekend company.

Steaming the shellfish first makes a great stock. If you've got cheesecloth, triple-line a colander and drain the shellfish into this contraption in step 3, catching the stock in a bowl below. It should now be free of sand. Then in step 6, use ½ cup of this shellfish stock as a replacement for ½ cup of the chicken broth (and, therefore, also use 1¼ cups chicken broth) for a way tastier paella. Save any extra shellfish stock in a small, sealed container in the freezer for up to 1 year to add to other seafood soups or stews.

1. Put the mussels, clams, and shrimp in a **6- or 8-quart cooker**. Add the water and lock the lid onto the pot.

2.

Set the machine for	Set the level for	The valve must be	Set the time for	If necessary, press
PRESSURE COOK	MAX	—	2 minutes with the KEEP WARM setting off	START
PRESSURE COOK or MANUAL	HIGH	Closed	4 minutes with the KEEP WARM setting off	START

3. When the machine has finished cooking, turn it off and let its pressure **return to normal naturally**, about 10 minutes. Unlatch the lid and open the cooker. Drain the contents of the *hot* insert into a colander set in the sink. Wipe out the insert and return it to the machine.

4.

Press the button for	Set it for	Set the time for	If necessary, press
SAUTÉ	MEDIUM, NORMAL, or CUSTOM 300°F	10 minutes	START

5. Warm the oil in the cooker for a minute or two, then add the onion and bell pepper. Cook, stirring occasionally, until the onion softens, about 4 minutes. Add the sausage and chicken; cook, stirring more often, just until the chicken loses its raw, pink color, about 2 minutes. Stir in the smoked paprika, oregano, fennel seeds, saffron, and salt until aromatic, just a few seconds.

6. Pour in the tomatoes, turn off the SAUTÉ function, and scrape up *every speck of browned stuff* on the pot's bottom. Stir in the broth and rice until the rice is evenly mixed throughout. Lock the lid onto the pot.

7.

Set the machine for	Set the level for	The valve must be	Set the time for	If necessary, press
PRESSURE COOK	MAX	—	9 minutes with the KEEP WARM setting off	START
PRESSURE COOK or MANUAL	HIGH	Closed	12 minutes with the KEEP WARM setting off	START

8. Use the **quick-release method** to bring the pot's pressure back to normal. Unlatch the lid and open the cooker. Stir the rice mixture in the cooker, then pile the seafood on top. Cover the cooker without engaging the pressure valve. Set aside for 10 minutes to continue steaming the rice and warm the seafood. Turn off the KEEP WARM setting and open the pot. Serve in bowls by the big spoonful.

Beyond

- You must halve the recipe for a **3-quart cooker**.

- For an **8-quart cooker**, you *can* (but don't have to) increase all the ingredients by 50 percent.

- For an even heartier meal, cube up to ½ pound skinless *thin* white-fleshed fish fillets (such as tilapia, flounder, or fluke) into 1-inch pieces, then gently stir into the rice in step 8 before piling the shellfish on top and steaming the dish for 10 minutes.

- Add up to 1 cup shelled green peas (thawed if frozen) with the broth and rice.

- For heat, add up to 2 teaspoons red pepper flakes with the saffron and other spices.

11

More Sides

Maybe this chapter's title should be Faster Sides. Or Better Sides? As you'll see, we solved the perennial problems of mushy carrots and overcooked green beans by altering standard pressure-cooker methods with a bit of culinary school know-how.

What's more, there's no point in trying to cook some greens like Swiss chard in an Instant Pot, unless it's part of a well-stocked soup. Chard is done in minutes on the stovetop. Meanwhile, the multi-cooker is still coming up to pressure. We love leafy greens but add them late in the cooking process of most dishes to retain as much of their vibrancy and flavor as possible.

Or maybe the chapter should have been More Sides That Could Become Main Courses. Many of these side dishes can be vegetarian or vegan entrées on their own. And many more can become a main course with a small tweak: Add a poached egg on top of the Warm White Bean Salad (page 446), pile the Buttery Cheesy Mushrooms (page 442) into baked potatoes, or serve the Loaded Cornbread (page 431) alongside a chopped salad.

These days, side dishes are often afterthoughts. They're assembled, rather than cooked — or just boxed up from a supermarket's buffet. We see a lot of people shopping the salad bar with a package of raw chicken breasts in their carts.

Fair enough, because life moves fast. But that's why you've got an Instant Pot. Consider having a second, smaller cooker just to make sides to go along with the main course; most of these recipes work well in a **3-quart cooker**. Those Creamy Black-Eyed Peas (page 438) would be welcome with Fried Chicken (page 262) or Brisket Skewers (page 266). And Baked Beans (page 444) are great all summer long — especially ones made right, the real way, with dried beans and lots of aromatic spices. What could be better?

FAQS

1. What's a potato masher?

Your grandmother knew. It's a hand-held old-school gadget, either a wire zigzag on a metal handle or a flat circle (or oval) with slats across its surface. You work it the way you might suspect: by pressing down into cooked potatoes so that they "mash" through or against the metal. You have to work it through the spuds (or other ingredients) many times. The more you do, the creamier the mash.

When it comes to mashed potatoes, we prefer a potato masher to an electric mixer. We've never been a fan of those ultra-creamy, French-bistro potatoes, the kind with just enough potato in the batch to hold the cream and butter in suspension. We prefer hearty, American-style mashed potatoes, even a little chunky, with the skins still on the spuds.

2. My raw potatoes are turning green. What do I do?

Cut out those green bits! In fact, cut them out deeply, maybe a quarter of the potato. The potato has been exposed to light for too long. (It did grow underground, after all.) It's started to produce chlorophyll (which isn't bad for you) and so has also started to produce solanine (which is bad and can cause an upset stomach). Make sure you pick spuds at the store without green bits. Once these start, they're not going away. We rarely buy potatoes in bags. We pick them out one by one.

By the way, did you know the fridge is no good for potatoes? The cooler temperatures cause the potato's natural starches to begin to convert into sugars — making the tuber sweeter, less earthy, and less flavorful. It's best to store potatoes in a cool, dark place, a spot somewhere around 50°F. That's hard to find at home. Maybe a basement closet? Failing that, buy them and use them promptly. The store often has a cool room where it can store spuds properly until they're ready to move to the produce shelf — and then to your home.

3. How do I store all these leafy greens?

Many of these side dishes use greens in some way. For cabbage heads, do not wash them when you get them home. Instead, wrap them tightly in plastic wrap and store them in the coolest part of the fridge for up to a week. For most other leafy greens, again do not wash them. Wrap slightly damp paper towels around the bunch, then seal it in plastic wrap and store it in the coolest part of the fridge for up to 4 days.

Kale is the exception. You still don't wash the leaves, but you should chop them into smaller bits if desired and store them in a sealed but perforated plastic bag in the coolest part of the refrigerator for just a day or two.

Baked Potatoes

4 to 6 servings

All the best toppings for baked potatoes? Got those? Then go ahead and make this classic side dish as fancy as you want it. We even keep an already-baked potato or two in the fridge at all times so we can cut one into wedges and dip them in ketchup for an afternoon snack.

   Make sure the potatoes are equal in size so they cook at the same rate. They are also super-heated when they come out of the pot. Keep them away from kids until they've cooled a bit.

1. Pour the water into a **6- or 8-quart cooker**. Set a heat- and pressure-safe trivet in the pot. Prick the potatoes in several places with a fork. Set them on the trivet either stacked flat or stood up like soldiers. Lock the lid onto the pot.

2.

Set the machine for	Set the level for	The valve must be	Set the time for	If necessary, press
PRESSURE COOK	MAX	—	10 minutes with the KEEP WARM setting off	START
PRESSURE COOK or MANUAL	HIGH	Closed	12 minutes with the KEEP WARM setting off	START

3. When the machine has finished cooking, turn it off and let the pressure **return to normal naturally** for 10 minutes. Then use the **quick-release method** to get rid of any residual pressure in the pot. Unlatch the lid and open the cooker. Use large kitchen tongs to transfer the potatoes to a serving platter or serving plates. Cool for several minutes before serving.

1 ½ cups water

4 to 6 medium russet or baking potatoes (8 ounces each)

Beyond

- You must halve the recipe for a **3-quart cooker.**

- If you like a crisp skin on a baked potato, position the rack in the center of the oven and heat it to 425°F as the pot cooks. When the potatoes are done, transfer them to a baking sheet and roast until the skin dries out and becomes crunchy, 10 to 15 minutes.

2½ pounds yellow potatoes, such as Yukon Gold, cut into halves or quarters, so each piece is about the size of a small apricot

1¼ cups vegetable or chicken broth

3 tablespoons butter

½ teaspoon table salt

⅓ cup heavy cream, half-and-half, or whole milk

¼ cup regular or low-fat sour cream

1 tablespoon Dijon mustard

Ground black pepper for garnishing

No-Drain Mashed Potatoes

4 to 6 servings

By cooking cut-up potatoes in broth, we can create a rich version of mashed potatoes without ever draining the insert. The leached starch is invaluable for thickening the broth (a bit) and making the mashed potatoes creamy. If you don't have a potato masher, dump the contents of the insert into a large bowl and use an electric mixer at medium-low speed to make the mashed potatoes. (If possible, use only the paddle attachment.) However, they will be a little looser than those mashed directly in the pot.

1. Stir the potatoes, broth, butter, and salt in a **6- or 8-quart cooker**. Lock the lid onto the pot.

2.

Set the machine for	Set the level for	The valve must be	Set the time for	If necessary, press
PRESSURE COOK	MAX	——	7 minutes with the KEEP WARM setting off	START
PRESSURE COOK or MANUAL	HIGH	Closed	10 minutes with the KEEP WARM setting off	START

3. When the machine has finished cooking, turn it off and let its pressure **return to normal naturally**, about 20 minutes. Unlatch the lid and open the cooker. Add the cream, sour cream, and mustard. Use a potato masher right in the pot to mash the potatoes to your liking, chunky or smooth. Grind black pepper over individual servings, if desired.

Beyond

- You must halve the recipe for a **3-quart cooker**.

- We like a coarser texture in mashed potatoes. If you like ultra-smooth mashed potatoes, peel the potatoes before cooking.

- For *hot* mashed potatoes, turn the SAUTÉ function on LOW or LESS after opening the pot, then add the ingredients in step 3 and mash over this low heat. Turn off the SAUTÉ function when the potatoes are right and remove the insert from the machine.

- Feel free to omit the cream, mustard, and sour cream. Add 4 tablespoons (½ stick) additional butter to the pot after you open it.

Better Syracuse Potatoes

6 servings

Syracuse potatoes are sometimes called "salt potatoes" because they're cooked in brine under pressure. They're delicious — but we've improved the recipe with the addition of vinegar, which complements the natural sweetness of the spuds and makes them absurdly addictive.

This dish is only cooked on HIGH, even in the Max machine. The higher MAX pressure would split the potatoes.

Also, this recipe will not work if you use larger potatoes and halve them, or if you peel the potatoes or poke them in any way. The skin protects the delicate, creamy white richness underneath.

6 cups water

1 cup kosher salt

1 cup distilled white vinegar

3 pounds small red-skinned potatoes, each 1 to 1½ inches in diameter

1. Mix the water, salt, and vinegar in a **6- or 8-quart cooker** until the salt dissolves. Add the potatoes and stir well. Lock the lid onto the cooker.

2.

Set the machine for	Set the level for	The valve must be	Set the time for	If necessary, press
PRESSURE COOK or MANUAL	HIGH	Closed	2 minutes with the KEEP WARM setting off	START

3. When the machine has finished cooking, turn it off and let its pressure **return to normal naturally** for 15 minutes. Then use the **quick-release method** to get rid of any residual pressure in the pot. Unlatch the lid and open the cooker. Drain the potatoes in a large colander set in the sink. Serve warm.

Beyond

- You must halve the recipe for a 3-quart cooker.

- Pour the cooked potatoes on a baking sheet and cool them to room temperature. The salt will form a crust on each spud. Serve on toothpicks with cold cocktails.

- Or pile the hot potatoes in a bowl and pour a little melted butter over them, add lots of ground black pepper, and toss well.

- Or serve potatoes tossed with a quick Russian dressing: Whisk 1 cup regular or low-fat mayonnaise, ¼ cup bottled red chili sauce such as Heinz Chili Sauce, and 2 tablespoons pickle relish in a medium bowl. Add some or all of this to the potatoes and toss well. (Save any remaining dressing in a covered bowl in the fridge for up to 3 days.)

3 pounds russet or baking potatoes, peeled and cut into 1-inch pieces

2 cups water

¼ cup apple cider vinegar

3 large eggs

1 cup regular or low-fat mayonnaise

3 medium celery ribs, thinly sliced (1 cup)

Up to 1 small red onion, chopped (½ cup)

Up to ¼ cup loosely packed fresh dill fronds, chopped

2 tablespoons white balsamic vinegar

1 tablespoon Dijon mustard

1 tablespoon Worcestershire sauce

Up to 1½ teaspoons table salt

½ teaspoon ground black pepper

Up to ½ teaspoon garlic powder

Potato Salad

8 servings

Here's a great idea: Cook potatoes and eggs together in the Instant Pot, then add them to a creamy, spicy dressing for an (almost) instant salad. Waxy red-skinned potatoes proved too dry here; yellow potatoes broke down too much. Russets or other baking potatoes, although not traditional in stovetop recipes, have the right amount of starch to hold together yet become creamy and delicate in the salad.

1. Put the potatoes into a **6- or 8-quart cooker**. Pour in the water and apple cider vinegar. Set the eggs on top of the potatoes. Lock the lid onto the cooker.

2.

Set the machine for	Set the level for	The valve must be	Set the time for	If necessary, press
PRESSURE COOK or MANUAL	LOW	Closed	10 minutes with the KEEP WARM setting off	START

3. As the potatoes and eggs cook, whisk the mayonnaise, celery, onion, dill, vinegar, mustard, Worcestershire sauce, salt, pepper, and garlic powder in a large bowl. Set aside.

4. When the machine has finished cooking, use the **quick-release method** to bring the pot's pressure back to normal. Unlatch the lid and open the cooker. Transfer the eggs to a cutting board. Drain the potatoes in a colander set in the sink. Add them hot to the dressing and toss well. Peel the still-warm hard-cooked eggs, chop them, add them to the potato mixture, and stir gently. Serve warm or cover and refrigerate for up to 1 day.

Beyond

- You must halve the recipe for a **3-quart cooker**. (Use 1 or 2 eggs.)

- Feel free to omit the Dijon and add 1 tablespoon prepared jarred white horseradish to the dressing.

- Add crunch with 1 cup sliced radishes, diced cucumber, or thinly sliced carrots.

- The dressing is not sweet; add up to 1 tablespoon granulated white sugar, if desired.

Perfect Sweet Potatoes

Makes 1 to 6 sweet potatoes

1½ cups water

1 to 6 small sweet potatoes (6 ounces each and 5 to 6 inches long)

Pressure cooking sweet potatoes makes them smoother, silkier, and creamier than oven-roasting them. Oddly enough, they're also less sweet and more savory, since the sugars are not condensed and concentrated as in the oven. This makes them a better side to beef and chicken stews that already have a sweet edge. Make sure the sweet potatoes are the same size for even cooking.

1. Pour the water into a **6- or 8-quart cooker**. Set a heat- and pressure-safe trivet inside the pot. Pile the potatoes onto the trivet. Lock the lid onto the pot.

2.

Set the machine for	Set the level for	The valve must be	Set the time for	If necessary, press
PRESSURE COOK	MAX	—	15 minutes with the KEEP WARM setting off	START
PRESSURE COOK or MANUAL	HIGH	Closed	20 minutes with the KEEP WARM setting off	START

3. When the machine has finished cooking, turn it off and let its pressure **return to normal naturally**, about 20 minutes. Unlatch the lid and open the cooker. Use large kitchen tongs to transfer the sweet potatoes to a serving platter or serving plates. Cool for a few minutes before serving.

Beyond

- Because of the sweet potatoes' size and shape, this recipe will not work well in a **3-quart cooker**.

- For sweet potato mash, cool the sweet potatoes for 5 minutes. Peel them and put them in a large bowl. Add up to 6 tablespoons butter, cut into small pieces, as well as 1 teaspoon table salt. Use a potato masher to mash them right in the bowl until creamy.

- Go beyond butter, salt, and pepper. Split cooked sweet potatoes open and top them with vanilla yogurt, cranberry sauce, or Heinz Chili Sauce.

- Seal a few cooled, cooked sweet potatoes in plastic wrap and store them in the fridge for up to 4 days to add them by quarters to smoothies.

1½ cups water

1 teaspoon table salt

**1 medium cauliflower, 1 to
1½ pounds, any green leaves
removed**

Steamed Cauliflower

4 to 6 servings

This recipe yields a rather unadorned, steamed *head* of cauliflower. What you do with it is up to you, but see the *Beyond* for several ideas.

Did you know that green leaves on a head of cauliflower are edible and provide a big punch of flavor to stocks of almost any sort? Save them in a zip-sealed plastic bag in the freezer for up to 6 months until you're ready to make stock (see the recipes starting on page 101).

1. Stir the water and salt in a **3-, 6-, or 8-quart cooker** until the salt dissolves. Set a heat- and pressure-safe trivet in the pot. Set the cauliflower stem side up on the trivet. Lock the lid onto the pot.

2.

Set the machine for	Set the level for	The valve must be	Set the time for	If necessary, press
PRESSURE COOK	MAX	—	4 minutes with the KEEP WARM setting off	START
PRESSURE COOK or MANUAL	HIGH	Closed	6 minutes with the KEEP WARM setting off	START

3. Use the **quick-release method** to bring the pot's pressure back to normal. Unlatch the lid and open the pot. Use two large forks (even large flatware forks) to stab the cauliflower on either side, then lift it out of the cooker and onto a serving platter. Serve warm.

Beyond

- Cool the cauliflower for 5 minutes, then use two forks to break it into florets. Toss these with melted butter. Or with yogurt and yellow curry powder. Or with the same dressing used to make potato salad (page 426).

- Cool the cauliflower for 20 to 30 minutes, then slice it into ½-inch-thick "steaks." Oil these and rub them with your favorite spice blend. Grill over high heat until lightly browned, 1 to 2 minutes per side.

- Or set the warm cauliflower in a serving bowl and pour a cheese sauce on top. Melt 2 tablespoons butter in a medium saucepan over medium heat. (Or in the cleaned and dried insert with the SAUTÉ function on MEDIUM, NORMAL, or CUSTOM 300°F.) Whisk in 2 tablespoons all-purpose flour until smooth, then whisk in 1 cup whole or low-fat milk in small bits until smooth. Once all the milk has been added, cook until slightly thickened, whisking constantly, about 1 minute. Whisk in 4 ounces (1 cup) shredded American Cheddar, Swiss, or Monterey Jack until smooth. Remove from the heat, cool a minute or two, and pour over the cauliflower.

Corn on the Cob

2 to 8 servings

1½ cups water

2 to 8 medium corn ears, shucked

Steaming corn in the Instant Pot ensures that the kernels are tender and plump. Better yet, you don't have to be ready to serve the corn the moment it's done if you use the KEEP WARM setting.

The best way to shuck corn is to grab the individual green leaves and any silks around them, then pull these down and back toward the stem. Work your way around the ear, leaf section by leaf section. At the end, lightly moisten a paper towel and rub it along the ear to remove any errant silks.

1. Pour the water into a **6- or 8-quart cooker**. Set a heat- and pressure-safe trivet in the pot. Pile and stack the ears of corn on the trivet. Lock the lid onto the pot.

2.

Set the machine for	Set the level for	The valve must be	Set the time for	If necessary, press
PRESSURE COOK	MAX	—	0 minutes with the KEEP WARM setting on for up to 30 minutes	START
PRESSURE COOK or MANUAL	HIGH	Closed	1 minute with the KEEP WARM setting on for up to 30 minutes	START

3. Use the **quick-release method** to bring the pot's pressure back to normal. If desired, set aside with the pressure valve open and the KEEP WARM setting on for up to 30 minutes. Unlatch the lid and open the cooker. Use kitchen tongs to transfer the corn ears to a serving platter or serving plates.

Beyond

- For a **3-quart cooker**, you must break each ear in half to make them fit. At most, three halved ears will fit well in the pot. Use 1 cup water.

- Serve steamed corn with a compound butter: Soften ½ cup (1 stick) butter at room temperature, about 30 minutes. Add up to 2 tablespoons minced fresh herbs or 2 teaspoons dried herbs or 1 teaspoon garlic or onion powder. Also add up to ½ teaspoon table salt. Mash the ingredients together to serve with the warm corn.

- Or forgo tradition and serve the corn with finely grated Parmigiano-Reggiano, finely grated lemon zest, and ground black pepper.

2 pounds frozen corn kernels, thawed

⅔ cup whole milk

4 ounces regular cream cheese

2 tablespoons butter, melted and cooled to room temperature, plus more for greasing the baking dish

2 teaspoons granulated white sugar

½ teaspoon dried thyme

Up to 1 teaspoon red pepper flakes (optional)

½ teaspoon table salt

½ teaspoon ground black pepper

1½ cups water

Cream-Style Corn

6 to 8 servings

We loved cream-style corn when we were kids. Of course, growing up in the convenience-crazed seventies, we only knew about the canned stuff. We've always wanted to make a "cornier" version, less pasty and porridge-like. We've tried dozens of recipes in the pot. Most break (ick), a few curdle (ick, again), many are too oily (still ick), and the rest are just plain forgettable. So here's our take: a creamy, somewhat soupy side dish that should be served up in small bowls near the main plate.

1. Pour about one quarter of the corn kernels into a blender. Add the milk, cream cheese, butter, sugar, thyme, red pepper flakes (if using), salt, and pepper. Cover and blend until fairly smooth.

2. Generously butter the inside of a 2-quart, high-sided, round baking dish. Make an aluminum foil sling (see page 20) and set this dish in the center of the sling. Pour the remaining three-quarters (or so) of the corn kernels into this dish. Add the purée from the blender and stir gently but well. Cover the baking dish with aluminum foil.

3. Pour the water into a **6- or 8-quart cooker**. Set a heat- and pressure-safe trivet in the cooker. Use the sling to pick up and transfer the baking dish to the trivet. Fold down the ends of the sling so they fit in the pot. Lock the lid onto the cooker.

4.

Set the machine for	Set the level for	The valve must be	Set the time for	If necessary, press
PRESSURE COOK	MAX	—	15 minutes with the KEEP WARM setting off	START
PRESSURE COOK or MANUAL	HIGH	Closed	20 minutes with the KEEP WARM setting off	START

5. Use the **quick-release method** to bring the pot's pressure back to normal. Unlatch the lid and open the cooker. Use the sling to transfer the *hot* baking dish to a wire cooling rack. Uncover, cool for a couple of minutes, and serve hot.

Beyond

• For a **3-quart cooker**, you must use 1 cup water, halve the remaining ingredients, and use a 1-quart, high-sided, round soufflé fish.

Loaded Bundt Cornbread

8 servings

This easy cornbread is a great addition to your Thanksgiving table — or to any summer barbecue. It's packed with cheese, corn, even chiles — almost a meal. Our recipe is not very sweet. You can even halve the sugar. We find that less sugar means more of the other great flavors.

1. Whisk the cornmeal, flour, baking powder, sugar, and salt in a medium bowl until uniform. Set aside.

2. Pour the water into a **6- or 8-quart cooker**. Set a heat- and pressure-safe trivet in the pot. Generously butter the inside of a 7-inch Bundt pan. Make an aluminum foil sling (see page 20) and set the pan in the middle of the sling.

3. Whisk the eggs and buttermilk in a large bowl until smooth and creamy. Stir in the corn, mozzarella, butter, and chiles. Pour in the cornmeal mixture and stir until the flour and cornmeal are moistened and uniform throughout the batter. Pour and scrape into the prepared pan.

4. Use the sling to pick up and transfer the pan to the trivet in the cooker. Lay a large paper towel on top of the Bundt pan. Fold down the ends of the sling so they fit in the cooker without touching the paper towel. Lock the lid onto the cooker.

5.

Set the machine for	Set the level for	The valve must be	Set the time for	If necessary, press
PRESSURE COOK	MAX	—	20 minutes with the KEEP WARM setting off	START
PRESSURE COOK or MANUAL	HIGH	Closed	25 minutes with the KEEP WARM setting off	START

6. When the machine has finished cooking, turn it off and let its pressure **return to normal naturally**, about 20 minutes. Unlatch the lid and open the cooker. Use the sling to transfer the Bundt pan to a wire cooling rack. Remove the paper towel and cool for 5 to 10 minutes. To unmold, set a cutting board over the pan and turn both the (still warm) pan and cutting board upside-down. Jiggle the pan to loosen the cake, then remove the pan. If desired, reinvert the cake so it sits right side up. Continue cooling for at least 10 minutes before slicing into wedges.

See photo in insert.

Ingredients

1 cup yellow cornmeal

¾ cup all-purpose flour

2 teaspoons baking powder

2 teaspoons granulated white sugar

½ teaspoon table salt

1½ cups water

2 large eggs, at room temperature

¾ cup regular buttermilk

1 cup frozen corn kernels, thawed

2 ounces semi-firm mozzarella, shredded (½ cup)

4 tablespoons (½ stick) butter, melted and cooled to room temperature, plus more for greasing the pan

¼ cup canned hot or mild chopped green chiles (about half a 4.5-ounce can)

Beyond

- For a **3-quart cooker**, use the ingredients as stated but do not set a paper towel on top of the Bundt pan in the cooker. If you want a perfect edge, fill the pan only to within ½ inch of the rim. (Discard the remaining batter.)

- For more pizzazz, cook up to 1 chopped medium yellow onion (1 cup) and up to 1 stemmed, cored, and chopped medium green bell pepper (1 cup) in some butter in a skillet set over medium heat (or in the pot on the SAUTÉ function at MEDIUM, NORMAL, or CUSTOM 300°F) until quite soft, stirring often, about 5 minutes. Cool to room temperature, then add to the batter with the cheese and chiles.

1½ cups water

2 pounds butternut squash, peeled, halved, seeded, and cut into 4-inch pieces

¼ cup (½ stick) butter

2 tablespoons heavy cream, half-and-half, or whole milk

1 tablespoon packed fresh sage leaves, minced

½ teaspoon table salt

½ teaspoon ground black pepper

Butternut Squash Mash

6 servings

The next time you have a savory braise for dinner, ladle the meat, vegetables, and sauce right on top of this creamy puree in bowls. You'll need a vegetable steamer insert for this recipe, not the more standard trivet we often use. Without a steamer, the butternut squash pieces will fall through the trivet and end up waterlogged. You can use purchased, cut-up butternut squash; but for proper cooking, the pieces must be 4 inches long and 1 to 2 inches thick, slightly larger than some prepped butternut squash in the produce section.

1. Pour the water into a **3-, 6-, or 8-quart cooker**. Set a heat- and pressure-safe vegetable steamer inside the pot. Pile the butternut squash pieces into the steamer. Lock the lid onto the cooker.

2.

Set the machine for	Set the level for	The valve must be	Set the time for	If necessary, press
PRESSURE COOK	MAX	—	5 minutes with the KEEP WARM setting off	START
PRESSURE COOK or MANUAL	HIGH	Closed	8 minutes with the KEEP WARM setting off	START

3. Use the **quick-release method** to bring the pot's pressure back to normal. Unlatch the lid and open the steamer. Pick up the *hot* vegetable steamer and take it out of the pot. Drain the liquid in the pot. Return all the butternut squash pieces to the pot.

4.

Press the button for	Set it for	Set the time for	If necessary, press
SAUTÉ	LOW or LESS	5 minutes	START

5. Use a potato masher to begin mashing the squash. Add the butter, cream, sage, salt, and pepper. Continue to mash the ingredients together until as smooth as you like, about 1 minute. Turn off the SAUTÉ function and remove the *hot* insert from the pot to stop the cooking. Serve warm.

Beyond

- For more warming flavors, omit the sage and add up to 1 teaspoon ground cinnamon, ½ teaspoon ground allspice, and/or ½ teaspoon grated nutmeg to the mash in its place.

Maple Glazed Carrots

6 to 8 servings

This easy side dish is great for the winter holidays or at a barbecue in the summer. Maple syrup gives the carrots a more complex flavor than brown sugar would. Do not use pancake syrup. Go for the real thing.

2 pounds medium carrots, peeled and cut into 1-inch pieces

2 cups water

3 tablespoons butter

2 tablespoons maple syrup

½ teaspoon table salt

1. Put the carrots and water in a **3-, 6-, or 8-quart cooker**. Lock the lid onto the pot.

2.

Set the machine for	Set the level for	The valve must be	Set the time for	If necessary, press
PRESSURE COOK	MAX	—	2 minutes with the KEEP WARM setting off	START
PRESSURE COOK or MANUAL	HIGH	Closed	3 minutes with the KEEP WARM setting off	START

3. Use the **quick-release method** to bring the pot's pressure back to normal. Unlatch the lid and open the cooker. Drain the carrots in the *hot* insert into a colander set in the sink.

4.

Press the button for	Set it for	Set the time for	If necessary, press
SAUTÉ	MEDIUM, NORMAL, or CUSTOM 300°F	5 minutes	START

5. Melt the butter in the cooker. Stir in the syrup and salt until bubbling. Add the carrots and continue cooking, stirring constantly, until the carrots are glazed, 2 to 3 minutes. Turn off the SAUTÉ function and remove the *hot* insert from the cooker to stop the cooking. Pour the carrots and any remaining glaze into a serving bowl and cool for a couple of minutes before serving.

Beyond

- Try adding spices to the butter glaze: ½ teaspoon ground allspice, ½ teaspoon ground cardamom, ½ teaspoon ground cinnamon, ¼ teaspoon ground cloves, or ¼ teaspoon grated nutmeg.

- Add heat to the butter glaze with several dashes of hot red pepper sauce.

1 cup pomegranate juice

½ cup plus 1 tablespoon water

¼ cup packed light brown sugar

1 canned chipotle chile in adobo
sauce, stemmed, seeded
(if desired), and minced

1 tablespoon adobo sauce from the
can of chipotle chiles

¼ teaspoon table salt

2 pounds cored and shredded red
cabbage (8 cups)

3 large thyme sprigs

2 teaspoons cornstarch

Spicy and Tangy Red Cabbage

6 to 8 servings

Cooked red cabbage should be a standard along with sausages or
wieners from a grill pan, a griddle, or the grill. Our version makes the
usual a little more elegant with the zing of canned chipotles in adobo
sauce *and* the pop of pomegranate juice — a bright, almost citrusy flavor
with the cabbage. If you use bagged shredded cabbage, make sure the
pieces are not tiny threads but slightly larger bits for a better texture.

1. Stir the juice, ½ cup water, brown sugar, chipotle chile, adobo sauce,
and salt in a **6- or 8-quart cooker** until the brown sugar dissolves. Add
the cabbage and thyme sprigs. Toss well until evenly and thoroughly
coated. Lock the lid onto the pot.

2.

Set the machine for	Set the level for	The valve must be	Set the time for	If necessary, press
PRESSURE COOK	MAX	—	10 minutes with the KEEP WARM setting off	START
PRESSURE COOK or MANUAL	HIGH	Closed	12 minutes with the KEEP WARM setting off	START

3. Use the **quick-release method** to bring the pot's pressure back to
normal. Unlatch the lid and open the cooker.

4.

Press the button for	Set it for	Set the time for	If necessary, press
SAUTÉ	MEDIUM, NORMAL, or CUSTOM 300°F	5 minutes	START

5. Whisk the remaining 1 tablespoon water and the cornstarch in a
small bowl until smooth. Stir this slurry into the bubbling cabbage
mixture. Continue cooking, stirring almost constantly, until the liquid in
the pot thickens to a sauce, 1 to 2 minutes. Turn off the SAUTÉ function
and remove the *hot* insert from the cooker to stop the cooking. Pour the
cabbage and any sauce into a large serving bowl and cool for a couple
of minutes before serving.

Beyond

- You must halve the recipe for a
  3-quart cooker.

- For a more vinegary sauce, stir up to
  2 tablespoons red wine vinegar into
  the pomegranate juice mixture
  before adding the cabbage.

- Or use up to 3 tablespoons pickle
  brine from a jar of dill or kosher
  pickles.

- Or for a much hotter dish, add up to
  3 tablespoons of the brine from a jar
  of pickled jalapeño rings.

Spiced Green Cabbage with Yogurt

6 to 8 servings

This East Indian–inspired side is loaded with all sorts of seeds which will soften and almost melt into the sauce. The flavorful mélange is great with curries and on top of baked potatoes for an easy vegetarian meal.

1.

Press the button for	Set it for	Set the time for	If necessary, press
SAUTÉ	MEDIUM, NORMAL, or CUSTOM 300°F	10 minutes	START

2. Melt the butter in a **6-quart cooker**. Add the mustard seeds, coriander seeds, cumin seeds, turmeric, and red pepper flakes. Cook, stirring constantly, until aromatic, less than 1 minute. Add the onion and cook, stirring occasionally, until softened, about 4 minutes.

3. Turn off the SAUTÉ function. Add the cabbage and stir well until evenly and thoroughly coated in the fat and spices. Pour in the broth and stir well. Lock the lid onto the cooker.

4.

Set the machine for	Set the level for	The valve must be	Set the time for	If necessary, press
PRESSURE COOK	MAX	—	8 minutes with the KEEP WARM setting off	START
PRESSURE COOK or MANUAL	HIGH	Closed	10 minutes with the KEEP WARM setting off	START

5. Use the **quick-release method** to bring the pot's pressure back to normal. Unlatch the lid and open the cooker. Add the yogurt and stir well until uniform. Pour into a large serving bowl and serve hot.

2 tablespoons butter

2 teaspoons brown mustard seeds

1½ teaspoons coriander seeds

1½ teaspoons cumin seeds

½ teaspoon ground dried turmeric

Up to ½ teaspoon red pepper flakes

1 large yellow onion, halved and sliced into thin half-moons

One 2-pound green cabbage, cored and shredded (8 cups)

1 cup chicken or vegetable broth

¾ cup plain full-fat, low-fat, or fat-free Greek yogurt

Beyond

- For a **3-quart cooker**, you must use ½ cup broth and halve the remaining ingredients.

- For an **8-quart cooker**, you must increase all the ingredients by 50 percent.

- Top the serving dish or individual servings with toasted, unsweetened coconut.

1½ cups water

2 pounds frozen cut leaf spinach, thawed and squeezed dry by the handful

1 cup whole milk

¾ cup heavy cream

2 ounces semi-firm mozzarella, shredded (½ cup)

2 tablespoons butter, melted and cooled to room temperature, plus more for greasing the baking dish

2 tablespoons regular cream cheese, cut into tiny bits

½ teaspoon onion powder

¼ teaspoon garlic powder

Up to ¼ teaspoon grated nutmeg

¼ teaspoon table salt

¼ teaspoon ground black pepper

Creamed Spinach

6 to 8 servings

This steakhouse side is faster and easier than ever, so long as you use only frozen cut-leaf spinach (not chopped spinach). Cut-leaf spinach won't turn into a squishy mess in the pot. Our version is not soupy or pasty. Rather, it's spinach in a creamy sauce. It's also made in a 2-quart baking dish and should be served by the big spoonful. It needs a New York strip or a rib-eye. Fire up the barbecue.

1. Pour the water into a **6- or 8-quart cooker**. Set a heat- and pressure-safe trivet in the pot. Generously butter the inside of a 2-quart, high-sided, round baking dish. Make an aluminum foil sling (see page 20) and set the baking dish at the center of the sling.

2. Mix the spinach, milk, cream, mozzarella, melted butter, cream cheese, onion powder, garlic powder, nutmeg, salt, and pepper in a large bowl until uniform. Pile this mixture into the prepared baking dish and cover tightly with aluminum foil. Use the sling to pick up and transfer the baking dish to the trivet. Lock the lid onto the pot.

3.

Set the machine for	Set the level for	The valve must be	Set the time for	If necessary, press
PRESSURE COOK	MAX	—	15 minutes with the KEEP WARM setting on for up to 30 minutes	START
PRESSURE COOK or MANUAL	HIGH	Closed	20 minutes with the KEEP WARM setting on for up to 30 minutes	START

4. Use the **quick-release method** to bring the pot's pressure back to normal. Unlatch the lid and open the cooker. Use the sling to transfer the *hot* baking dish to a wire cooling rack. Uncover and cool for 5 minutes before serving.

Beyond

- For a **3-quart cooker**, you must use 1 cup water, halve the remaining ingredients, and use a 1-quart, high-sided, round soufflé dish.

- To add heat, increase the ground black pepper to up to 1 or even 2 teaspoons.

- For more flavor, add up to 4 medium scallions, thinly sliced, with the other ingredients.

Spicy Collard Greens

6 servings

Long before kale became the "it" green, Southerners knew about collard greens. They're a bit chewier, never spongy, with a pleasant, herbal flavor that's a little grassy and just a tad bitter — a good contrast to roasted meat. This version makes a spectacular addition to wraps with thinly sliced ham or turkey and cheese. If you use the collards this way, pull the greens out of any sauce with kitchen tongs so the wrap isn't too soupy.

1.

Press the button for	Set it for	Set the time for	If necessary, press
SAUTÉ	MEDIUM, NORMAL, or CUSTOM 300°F	10 minutes	START

2. Warm the oil in a **6-quart cooker** for a minute or two. Add the garlic and red pepper flakes; cook, stirring often, until fragrant, about 20 seconds. Add the tomato and cook, stirring occasionally, until it breaks down a bit, about 3 minutes. Stir in the broth and scrape up any browned bits on the pot's bottom.

3. Turn off the SAUTÉ function. Stir in the wine and salt. Add the collards and toss well until evenly and thoroughly coated in the sauce and spices. Lock the lid onto the pot.

4.

Set the machine for	Set the level for	The valve must be	Set the time for	If necessary, press
PRESSURE COOK	MAX	—	4 minutes with the KEEP WARM setting off	START
PRESSURE COOK or MANUAL	HIGH	Closed	5 minutes with the KEEP WARM setting off	START

5. Use the **quick-release method** to bring the pot's pressure back to normal. Unlatch the lid and open the cooker. Stir well before serving.

2 tablespoons olive oil

3 medium garlic cloves, peeled and minced (1 tablespoon)

Up to 1 teaspoon red pepper flakes

1 large round red tomato, chopped (1 cup)

½ cup vegetable broth

½ cup dry white wine, such as Chardonnay

½ teaspoon table salt

1½ pounds collard greens, stemmed and chopped (8 packed cups)

Beyond

- For a **3-quart cooker,** you must use ⅔ cup broth and halve the remaining ingredients.

- For an **8-quart cooker,** you must increase the broth to 1 cup and use the remaining ingredients as stated.

- To omit the wine, add the same amount of additional broth plus 1 tablespoon unsweetened apple juice or cider.

- For a hotter, more sophisticated dish, omit the red pepper flakes and add up to 2 tablespoons purchased harissa with the garlic.

- For a curried take, omit the red pepper flakes and add up to 1 tablespoon wet red curry paste with the garlic.

¼ cup (½ stick) butter, cut into chunks

1 medium yellow onion, chopped (1 cup)

1 medium red bell pepper, stemmed, cored, and chopped (1 cup)

2 medium garlic cloves, peeled and minced (2 teaspoons)

1 teaspoon dried thyme

1 teaspoon dried sage

1 teaspoon mild paprika

½ teaspoon table salt

¼ teaspoon celery seeds

¼ teaspoon grated nutmeg

3 cups vegetable or chicken broth

2 cups dried black-eyed peas

½ cup heavy cream

Creamy Black-Eyed Peas

6 servings

Black-eyed peas have long been a harbinger for good luck on New Year's Day in some parts of the United States. But don't make this recipe a seasonal one. Consider it a fine "starch side" all year long: more than just black-eyed peas and vegetables but a creamy, rich side dish, best with roasted or grilled proteins. There is an extra step here that uses a puree of some of the peas and cream to make a thickener for the sauce.

1.

Press the button for	Set it for	Set the time for	If necessary, press
SAUTÉ	MEDIUM, NORMAL, or CUSTOM 300°F	5 minutes	START

2. Melt the butter in a **6- or 8-quart cooker**. Add the onion and bell pepper; cook, stirring occasionally, until the onion softens, about 3 minutes. Stir in the garlic, thyme, sage, paprika, salt, celery seeds, and nutmeg until fragrant, just a few seconds.

3. Pour in the broth and scrape up any browned bits on the pot's bottom. Turn off the SAUTÉ function and stir in the black-eyed peas. Lock the lid onto the cooker.

4.

Set the machine for	Set the level for	The valve must be	Set the time for	If necessary, press
PRESSURE COOK	MAX	—	19 minutes with the KEEP WARM setting off	START
PRESSURE COOK or MANUAL	HIGH	Closed	23 minutes with the KEEP WARM setting off	START

5. Use the **quick-release method** to bring the pot's pressure back to normal. Unlatch the lid and open the cooker. Stir well, then transfer 2 cups of the pea and liquid mixture in the pot to a blender. Add the cream, cover, remove the center knob in the blender's lid, place a clean kitchen towel over the opening, and blend until a smooth puree. Pour this mixture into the remaining black-eyed peas and stir well before serving.

Beyond

- You must halve the recipe for a **3-quart cooker**.

- Rather than thickening the dish in step 5, omit the cream (and pureeing the beans). Instead, stir up to 3 cups packed baby kale into the pot, then set the lid askew over it and set it aside for 5 minutes to blend the flavors and wilt the greens.

- Or add the cream but skip the thickening step; instead, stir up to ¼ cup instant couscous into the pot after cooking. Again, set the lid over the pot and set it aside for 5 minutes to soften the couscous (which will absorb much of the cooking liquid).

Spaghetti Squash with Herbs and Butter

6 servings

It's fast and easy to steam a spaghetti squash in an Instant Pot. The flesh, once cooked, separates into tiny threads, like little bits of spaghetti (or more like bright yellow short spiralized butternut squash noodles). We've fancied up this simple preparation a bit with fresh herbs and lots of butter. The easiest way to remove the seeds from the squash halves before steaming is with a serrated grapefruit spoon.

1. Pour the water into a **6- or 8-quart cooker**. Put the spaghetti squash halves skin side down in the pot—not both flat, of course, but maybe one flat and one angled up against it. Lock the lid onto the cooker.

2.

Set the machine for	Set the level for	The valve must be	Set the time for	If necessary, press
PRESSURE COOK	MAX	—	8 minutes with the KEEP WARM setting off	START
PRESSURE COOK or MANUAL	HIGH	Closed	10 minutes with the KEEP WARM setting off	START

3. Use the **quick-release method** to bring the pot's pressure back to normal. Unlatch the lid and open the cooker. Use large kitchen tongs and a metal spatula to transfer the *hot* squash halves to a nearby cutting board. Cool for 10 minutes. Discard the water in the insert. Use a fork to scrape the flesh into threads and into a large bowl.

4.

Press the button for	Set it for	Set the time for	If necessary, press
SAUTÉ	MEDIUM, NORMAL, or CUSTOM 300°F	5 minutes	START

5. Melt the butter in the cooker. Add the oregano, thyme, salt, and pepper. Stir well, then add the squash threads. Cook, stirring almost constantly, until the squash has absorbed the butter and the herbs are evenly distributed, 1 to 2 minutes. Turn off the SAUTÉ function, pour the contents of the *hot* insert into a serving bowl, and cool for a minute or two before serving.

1½ cups water

One 3- to 3½-pound spaghetti squash, halved lengthwise, the seeds scraped out

¼ cup (½ stick) butter, cut into pieces

1 tablespoon packed fresh oregano leaves, finely chopped

1 tablespoon stemmed fresh thyme leaves

½ teaspoon table salt

½ teaspoon ground black pepper

Beyond

- For a **3-quart cooker**, look for a small, 1¼- to 1½-pound spaghetti squash. Use 1 cup water and halve the remaining ingredients.

- Use the cooked squash "threads" as a substitute for pasta: Don't put them back in the pot with the butter and herbs. Rather, use them as a bed for Buttery Marinara Sauce (page 133) or Cherry Tomato and Herb Pasta Sauce (page 136).

- Use any fresh herbs you like: basil, marjoram, parsley, rosemary, or savory, among others, in any proportions—whether all 2 tablespoons of one or a mix between two (or even three).

- For a more sophisticated flavor, substitute 3 tablespoons walnut or pecan oil for the butter.

2 tablespoons olive oil

1½ pounds cherry tomatoes, halved

2 medium garlic cloves, peeled and minced (2 teaspoons)

½ teaspoon table salt

1½ pounds fresh green beans, trimmed

¼ cup loosely packed fresh basil leaves, finely chopped

2 tablespoons pine nuts

Warm Green Beans and Smashed Tomatoes

6 servings

Here's a side dish that's great alongside sandwiches in the winter when large round tomatoes aren't at their best. Believe it or not, there's enough liquid in the cherry tomatoes as they break down to create the necessary steam without any added broth — but *only if you use cherry tomatoes*. Grape, pear, and almost all other small tomatoes are not juicy enough for this technique. Because the green beans cook quickly (and are easily overcooked), only use LOW pressure for this dish.

1.

Press the button for	Set it for	Set the time for	If necessary, press
SAUTÉ	MEDIUM, NORMAL, or CUSTOM 300°F	5 minutes	START

2. Warm the oil in a **6-quart cooker** for a minute or two. Add the tomatoes, garlic, and salt. Cook, stirring often, until the tomatoes begin to break down and give off their liquid, 2 to 3 minutes. Stir in the green beans and turn off the SAUTÉ function. Lock the lid onto the pot.

3.

Set the machine for	Set the level for	The valve must be	Set the time for	If necessary, press
PRESSURE COOK or MANUAL	LOW	Closed	1 minute with the KEEP WARM setting off	START

4. Use the **quick-release method** to bring the pot's pressure back to normal. Unlatch the lid and open the cooker. Stir in the basil and pine nuts, then set aside with the lid askew over the pot to blend the flavors for 5 minutes.

Beyond

- For a **3-quart cooker**, you must use 1 pound of cherry tomatoes, halved, and halve the remaining ingredients.

- For an **8-quart cooker**, you must use 2 pounds of cherry tomatoes, halved, and the remaining ingredients as stated.

- Swap in another finely chopped nut for the pine nuts: pecans, walnuts, even skinned hazelnuts.

Eggplant, Zucchini, and Tomatoes

6 servings

This side dish is like a mock ratatouille, made faster with canned tomatoes (and the pot's pressure, of course). There's enough liquid in the tomatoes and vegetables to make the requisite steam for a **6-quart cooker**. See the *Beyond* instructions to add more liquid for an **8-quart cooker**.

1. Stir all the ingredients in a **6-quart cooker**. Lock the lid onto the pot.

2.

Set the machine for	Set the level for	The valve must be	Set the time for	If necessary, press
PRESSURE COOK	MAX	—	5 minutes with the KEEP WARM setting off	START
PRESSURE COOK or MANUAL	HIGH	Closed	7 minutes with the KEEP WARM setting off	START

3. Use the **quick-release method** to bring the pot's pressure back to normal. Unlatch the lid and open the cooker. Stir well; fish out and discard the bay leaf. Set the lid askew over the pot and set aside for 5 minutes to blend the flavors before serving in small bowls.

One 28-ounce can diced tomatoes with or without chiles (3½ cups)

2 medium zucchini (about 1 pound), diced

1 medium eggplant (about 1 pound), stemmed and diced (no need to peel)

1 small yellow onion, chopped (½ cup)

Up to 4 medium garlic cloves, peeled and minced (4 teaspoons)

2 tablespoons olive oil

1 tablespoon fresh lemon juice

1 teaspoon dried oregano

1 teaspoon dried thyme

½ teaspoon table salt

½ teaspoon ground black pepper

1 bay leaf

Beyond

- You must halve the recipe for a **3-quart cooker**.

- For an **8-quart cooker**, you must add ½ cup broth or water and use the remaining ingredients as stated.

- If the mixture is too soupy for your taste, use the SAUTÉ function at LOW or LESS after cooking to boil the mixture down for a minute or two, stirring almost constantly.

1¼ cups boiling water

1 ounce dried porcini mushrooms

2 tablespoons butter

1 medium shallot, peeled and chopped (¼ cup)

1½ pounds thinly sliced white button or cremini mushrooms

¼ cup dry vermouth, dry white wine, or vegetable broth

2 teaspoons stemmed fresh thyme leaves

½ teaspoon table salt

½ teaspoon ground black pepper

1 ounce Parmigiano-Reggiano, finely grated (½ cup)

¼ cup loosely packed fresh parsley leaves, finely chopped

Buttery Cheesy Mushrooms

6 servings

This simple side belongs next to chicken or fish off the grill. Or use it as a condiment right on top of steaks or chops. Or spoon the mushrooms over baked potatoes.

Unfortunately, mushrooms lose a little of their flavor pop in a multi-cooker. We solve that by including dried mushrooms. Although we call for porcini (because they're common in our supermarket), substitute any sort of dried mushroom you like, even a less expensive blend of dried mushrooms. Do not substitute large Chinese dried mushrooms.

1. Pour the boiling water over the dried mushrooms in a small bowl. Set aside at room temperature for 10 minutes.

2.

Press the button for	Set it for	Set the time for	If necessary, press
SAUTÉ	MEDIUM, NORMAL, or CUSTOM 300°F *al*	10 minutes	START

3. Melt the butter in a **3-, 6-, or 8-quart cooker**. Add the shallot and cook, stirring occasionally, until softened, about 2 minutes. Add the mushrooms and cook, stirring occasionally, until they give off their internal moisture and it evaporates to a glaze, about 4 minutes.

4. Turn off the SAUTÉ function and pour in the vermouth. Scrape up any browned bits on the pot's bottom. Stir in the thyme, salt, and pepper; pour in the soaked mushrooms and their soaking liquid. Stir well, then lock the lid onto the cooker.

5.

Set the machine for	Set the level for	The valve must be	Set the time for	If necessary, press
PRESSURE COOK	MAX	—	6 minutes with the KEEP WARM setting off	START
PRESSURE COOK or MANUAL	HIGH	Closed	8 minutes with the KEEP WARM setting off	START

6. Use the **quick-release method** to bring the pot's pressure back to normal. Unlatch the lid and open the cooker. Stir well.

7.

Press the button for	Set it for	Set the time for	If necessary, press
SAUTÉ	HIGH or MORE	10 minutes	START

8. Bring the mushroom mixture to a full simmer, stirring occasionally. Continue cooking until the liquid in the pot has reduced to a glaze, stirring more and more frequently as it does, 5 to 6 minutes. Turn off the SAUTÉ function; stir in the cheese and parsley. Set the lid askew over the pot to meld the flavors for a couple of minutes before serving.

Beyond

- For a sweeter dish (better alongside smoked foods), substitute red (or sweet) vermouth for the dry vermouth.

- For a creamier dish, almost a sauce, add up to ½ cup heavy cream to the mix before you reduce it down in step 8. In this case, don't get rid of all the moisture in the pot but keep the final dish a little "loose."

Polenta

4 to 6 servings

This is a quick and easy way to make the classic Italian side dish in an Instant Pot. Serve this polenta as a bed for any ragù or thick pasta sauce in this book. *Don't use* cornmeal or instant polenta; rather use coarse-ground yellow polenta, sometimes called "polenta corn grits."

1 quart (4 cups) water

¼ cup (½ stick) butter

½ teaspoon table salt

1 cup regular polenta

1 ounce finely grated Parmigiano-Reggiano (½ cup)

1.

Press the button for	Set it for	Set the time for	If necessary, press
SAUTÉ	MEDIUM, NORMAL, or CUSTOM 300°F	10 minutes	START

2. Put the water, butter, and salt in a **3- or 6-quart cooker**. Cook, stirring occasionally, until the butter melts and the mixture starts to bubble, 3 to 4 minutes. Stir in the polenta and cook, stirring quite often, for 2 minutes. Turn off the SAUTÉ function and lock the lid onto the cooker.

3.

Set the machine for	Set the level for	The valve must be	Set the time for	If necessary, press
PRESSURE COOK	MAX	—	6 minutes with the KEEP WARM setting off	START
PRESSURE COOK or MANUAL	HIGH	Closed	8 minutes with the KEEP WARM setting off	START

4. When the machine has finished cooking, turn it off and let its pressure **return to normal naturally**, about 20 minutes. Unlatch the lid and open the cooker. Stir in the cheese, then set the lid askew for a couple of minutes to melt the cheese and blend the flavors. Stir well before serving warm.

Beyond

- For an **8-quart cooker**, you must increase all the ingredients by 50 percent — or even double them.

- For a richer polenta, warm up to ½ cup heavy cream or half-and-half in a small saucepan on the stove over medium-low heat until bubbles fizz around its perimeter. Stir this into the polenta along with the cheese. Set aside, partially covered, for 5 minutes.

- Substitute other cheeses for the Parmigiano-Reggiano: a similar amount of finely shredded pecorino of any sort or a hard, aged goat cheese. Or substitute 2 ounces (½ cup) shredded semi-firm cheese like Swiss, Gruyère, or Emmentaler.

- For Southern-style comfort, omit the cheese. Pour the cooked polenta into a buttered 9-inch square baking dish and cool to room temperature, then cover and refrigerate for up to 2 days. Turn out the solidified polenta cake onto a cutting board, cut into squares, and fry them in butter in a nonstick skillet set over medium heat until brown and crunchy, turning a couple of times. Serve this "fried mush" with fried, scrambled, or poached eggs.

1 pound dried pinto beans

8 ounces slab bacon, diced

1 medium yellow onion, chopped (1 cup)

2½ cups chicken or vegetable broth

½ cup canned crushed tomatoes

¼ cup molasses, preferably unsulfured

¼ cup packed light brown sugar

2 tablespoons apple cider vinegar

2 teaspoons ground dried mustard

½ teaspoon ground cloves (optional)

½ teaspoon table salt

½ teaspoon ground black pepper

Beyond

• You must halve the recipe for a **3-quart cooker**.

• The beans will continue to set up as the mixture cools. If it's too soupy for your taste, stir 2 to 3 tablespoons tomato paste into the hot mixture and set aside for 5 minutes with the lid askew over the pot before serving.

• For less sweet but hotter baked beans, reduce the brown sugar to 2 tablespoons and add up to 2 tablespoons hot red pepper sauce, such as Sriracha or sambal oelek with the molasses. Also, omit the salt and add up to 2 teaspoons soy sauce.

Baked Beans

8 servings

Baked beans are a summer treat. But who wants to heat up the kitchen in the middle of July? The pot's the answer! Better yet, plug it in on the deck or patio, never bringing any of that steam into the house. The ground cloves are optional but they do give the dish the ketchup-y quality some people like in baked beans.

1. Soak the beans in a large bowl of water for at least 8 hours or up to 12 hours. Drain in a colander set in the sink.

2.

Press the button for	Set it for	Set the time for	If necessary, press
SAUTÉ	MEDIUM, NORMAL, or CUSTOM 300°F	10 minutes	START

3. Add the bacon to a **6- or 8-quart cooker**. Cook, stirring often, until the pieces begin to get brown and crisp, about 4 minutes. Add the onion and cook, stirring occasionally, until the onion softens, about 3 minutes. Pour in the broth and scrape up *every speck of browned stuff* on the pot's bottom.

4. Turn off the SAUTÉ function. Stir in the drained beans, the tomatoes, molasses, brown sugar, vinegar, mustard, cloves (if using), salt, and pepper. Lock the lid onto the pot.

5.

Set the machine for	Set the level for	The valve must be	Set the time for	If necessary, press
PRESSURE COOK	MAX	—	10 minutes with the KEEP WARM setting off	START
PRESSURE COOK or MANUAL	HIGH	Closed	12 minutes with the KEEP WARM setting off	START

6. When the machine has finished cooking, turn it off and let its pressure **return to normal naturally**, about 30 minutes. Unlatch the lid and open the cooker. Stir well before serving.

Not-Your-Mother's Three-Bean Salad

6 servings

Why don't you just open a few cans of beans and make a salad? Because of the texture of those beans! If you've got the time, dried beans (and here, chickpeas) will produce a more luxurious salad, better alongside burgers and hot dogs. And with fresh green beans, too, the salad will seem like summer on the plate.

    The dish is best while the beans are fresh from the pot, added warm to the dressing. That said, you can cover the salad and set it in the fridge for up to 2 days, although the scallions and beans will leach moisture as they sit in the dressing, rendering the whole dish quite a bit soupier.

1. Soak the beans and chickpeas in a big bowl of water for at least 8 hours or up to 12 hours. Drain in a colander set in the sink.

2. Pour the beans into a **6- or 8-quart cooker**. Add enough water so that they're submerged by 2 inches. Add 1 tablespoon olive oil and lock the lid onto the pot.

3.

Set the machine for	Set the level for	The valve must be	Set the time for	If necessary, press
PRESSURE COOK	MAX	—	10 minutes with the KEEP WARM setting off	START
PRESSURE COOK or MANUAL	HIGH	Closed	12 minutes with the KEEP WARM setting off	START

4. Use the **quick-release method** to bring the pot's pressure back to normal. Unlatch the lid and open the cooker. Stir in the green beans. Set the lid askew over the pot and set aside for 2 minutes, then drain the contents of the *hot* insert into a large colander set in the sink. Rinse with cool tap water to stop the cooking. Drain well, shaking the colander to get rid of excess moisture.

5. Whisk the remaining ¼ cup oil and the vinegar in a large serving bowl until uniform. Stir in the scallions, garlic, salt, oregano, cumin, smoked paprika, and pepper. Add the contents of the colander and toss well.

1 cup dried red kidney beans

1 cup dried chickpeas

Water as needed

¼ cup plus 1 tablespoon olive oil

8 ounces fresh green beans or wax beans, trimmed and cut into ½-inch pieces

3 tablespoons red wine vinegar

4 medium scallions, trimmed and thinly sliced

1 medium garlic clove, peeled and minced (1 teaspoon)

1 teaspoon table salt

½ teaspoon dried oregano

½ teaspoon ground cumin

½ teaspoon mild smoked paprika

½ teaspoon ground black pepper

Beyond

- You must halve the recipe for a **3-quart cooker**.

- Substitute dried great northern, cannellini, Roman, or pinto beans for either the kidney beans or the chickpeas.

- We offer up our favorite dressing for this salad. But you can skip it and use up to ½ cup bottled Italian dressing instead.

1½ cups dried cannellini or great northern beans

Water as needed

¼ cup plus 1 tablespoon olive oil

2 tablespoons white wine vinegar

1 small red onion, chopped (½ cup)

¼ cup loosely packed fresh parsley leaves, finely chopped

2 medium garlic cloves, peeled and minced (2 teaspoons)

2 teaspoons drained and rinsed capers, finely chopped

2 teaspoons fresh rosemary leaves, finely chopped

½ teaspoon table salt

¼ teaspoon red pepper flakes

Warm White Bean Salad

6 servings

This side has Italian flavors, so consider it a go-to accompaniment for shrimp or scallops in just about any way you can prepare them. Or make a Tuscan T-bone by rubbing the meat with olive oil, a little minced garlic, crunchy sea salt, and ground black pepper, then grilling to rare or medium-rare. Serve this warm salad spooned on top of the steak.

1. Soak the beans in a big bowl of water for at least 8 hours or up to 12 hours. Drain in a colander set in the sink.

2. Pour the beans into a **6- or 8-quart cooker**. Add enough water so they're submerged by 2 inches. Add 1 tablespoon olive oil and lock the lid onto the cooker.

3.

Set the machine for	Set the level for	The valve must be	Set the time for	If necessary, press
PRESSURE COOK	MAX	—	10 minutes with the KEEP WARM setting off	START
PRESSURE COOK or MANUAL	HIGH	Closed	12 minutes with the KEEP WARM setting off	START

4. As the beans cook, whisk the remaining ¼ cup olive oil and the vinegar in a large, heat-safe serving bowl until smooth. Stir in the onion, parsley, garlic, capers, rosemary, salt, and red pepper flakes.

5. When the machine has finished cooking, use the **quick-release method** to bring the pot's pressure back to normal. Unlatch the lid and open the cooker. Drain the contents of the *hot* insert into a colander set in the sink. Shake the colander to make sure the beans dry well. Dump them into the bowl with the dressing and toss well. Serve warm.

Beyond

- You must halve the recipe for a **3-quart cooker**.

- This salad is a good base for canned, Italian-style tuna, particularly the tuna packed in olive oil. Crumble it on top or toss it into the salad after you've mixed the beans into the dressing.

See photo in insert.

Lima Beans and Greens

6 servings

Here's a hearty side that could become a light main course or lunch, particularly on a chilly day. Or top each serving with a poached egg for an easy dinner. It's a bit soupy, so plan on serving it in bowls.

    Escarole is a traditional Italian green, a compact if floppy head with moderately thick leaves and a sweet but pleasingly bitter flavor that mellows when cooked. The inner leaves can be quite sandy. Rinse them well and pat them dry with paper towels. If you can't find escarole, substitute stemmed collard greens or large stemmed kale leaves.

1. Soak the lima beans in a large bowl of water for at least 8 hours or up to 12 hours. Drain in a colander set in the sink.

2.

Press the button for	Set it for	Set the time for	If necessary, press
SAUTÉ	MEDIUM, NORMAL, or CUSTOM 300°F	10 minutes	START

3. Warm the oil in a **6- or 8-quart cooker** for a minute or two. Add the onion and cook, stirring occasionally, until softened, about 3 minutes. Stir in the garlic, oregano, and red pepper flakes until fragrant, just a few seconds. Stir in the tomatoes and scrape up any browned bits on the pot's bottom.

4. Turn off the SAUTÉ function and stir in the broth, wine, vinegar, and salt. Add the escarole and drained lima beans. Stir well and lock the lid onto the cooker.

5.

Set the machine for	Set the level for	The valve must be	Set the time for	If necessary, press
PRESSURE COOK	MAX	—	7 minutes with the KEEP WARM setting off	START
PRESSURE COOK or MANUAL	HIGH	Closed	9 minutes with the KEEP WARM setting off	START

6. When the machine has finished cooking, turn it off and let its pressure **return to normal naturally**, about 20 minutes. Unlatch the lid and open the cooker. Stir well before serving.

2 cups dried lima beans

2 tablespoons olive oil

1 medium yellow onion, chopped (1 cup)

2 medium garlic cloves, peeled and minced (2 teaspoons)

2 teaspoons minced fresh oregano leaves

Up to ½ teaspoon red pepper flakes

One 14-ounce can crushed tomatoes (1¾ cups)

1 cup vegetable broth

½ cup fairly fruit-forward white wine, such as Pinot Grigio; or unsweetened apple cider

2 tablespoons apple cider vinegar

½ teaspoon table salt

1 small head of escarole (about 8 ounces), cored and chopped (about 4 cups)

Beyond

- You must halve the recipe for a 3-quart cooker.

- For more heft, stir up to 1 cup finely grated Parmigiano-Reggiano (2 ounces) into the pot after cooking. Set the lid askew over the top and set aside for 5 minutes to melt the cheese.

- If you don't care about the dish being vegan, fry bacon strips and crumble them over each serving.

2 tablespoons butter or olive oil

1 cup frozen pearl onions
(do not thaw)

2 medium garlic cloves, peeled and
minced (2 teaspoons)

2 cups vegetable broth

2 tablespoons tomato paste

1 tablespoon stemmed fresh thyme
leaves

1 tablespoon packed fresh sage
leaves, minced

½ teaspoon table salt

½ teaspoon ground black pepper

2 bay leaves

Two 15-ounce cans great northern or
cannellini beans, drained and rinsed
(3½ cups)

1 pound celeriac, peeled and chopped
(2½ cups)

1 pound medium parsnips, peeled
and cut into 1-inch sections

White Beans and Roots

8 servings

If you don't want to fool with soaking dried beans, try this simple side (or a satisfying vegan main course) that uses canned beans for an earthy, slightly braise-y mix.

Celeriac is the root of a specific varietal of celery. It should be firm (not soft and mushy in places) and have an herbaceous, celery-like aroma. It can be hard to peel because it's gnarled and "hairy" with little root filaments. We find that a vegetable peeler works best to get most of the peel off, then a paring knife gets into the crevices. Make sure the cubes are no larger than 1 inch so the celery root cooks in the time stated.

1.

Press the button for	Set it for	Set the time for	If necessary, press
SAUTÉ	MEDIUM, NORMAL, or CUSTOM 300°F	10 minutes	START

2. Melt the butter in a **6- or 8-quart cooker**. Add the pearl onions and cook, stirring occasionally, until lightly browned in places, about 4 minutes. Stir in the garlic until aromatic, just a few seconds. Turn off the SAUTÉ function, add the broth, and scrape up any browned bits on the pot's bottom.

4. Stir in the tomato paste, thyme, sage, salt, pepper, and bay leaves until the tomato paste dissolves. Add the beans, celeriac, and parsnips. Stir well and lock the lid onto the cooker.

5.

Set the machine for	Set the level for	The valve must be	Set the time for	If necessary, press
PRESSURE COOK	MAX	—	5 minutes with the KEEP WARM setting off	START
PRESSURE COOK or MANUAL	HIGH	Closed	8 minutes with the KEEP WARM setting off	START

6. Use the **quick-release method** to bring the pot's pressure back to normal. Unlatch the lid and open the cooker. Stir well before serving.

Beyond

- You must halve the recipe for a **3-quart cooker**.

- For a main course (that's obviously not vegan), serve the mixture over a big spoonful of whole-milk ricotta.

Red Beans, Spinach, and Sweet Potatoes

6 to 8 servings

Larger spinach leaves can turn squishy under pressure unless they are few in number and surrounded by lots of liquid. In this hearty side dish, we use baby spinach for a milder flavor — *and* for a better texture since those small leaves never undergo pressure but are simply warmed in the sauce.

1.

Press the button for	Set it for	Set the time for	If necessary, press
SAUTÉ	MEDIUM, NORMAL, or CUSTOM 300°F	5 minutes	START

2. Warm the oil in a **6- or 8-quart cooker** for a minute or two. Add the onion and cook, stirring occasionally, until softened, about 3 minutes. Add the garlic, ginger, coriander, red pepper flakes, and salt. Cook, stirring often, until aromatic, about 20 seconds.

3. Turn off the SAUTÉ function, add the broth, and scrape up any browned bits on the pot's bottom. Stir in the tomatoes, sweet potatoes, and beans. Lock the lid onto the cooker.

4.

Set the machine for	Set the level for	The valve must be	Set the time for	If necessary, press
PRESSURE COOK	MAX	—	6 minutes with the KEEP WARM setting off	START
PRESSURE COOK or MANUAL	HIGH	Closed	8 minutes with the KEEP WARM setting off	START

5. Use the **quick-release method** to bring the pot's pressure back to normal. Unlatch the lid and open the cooker. Add the spinach and stir well. Set the lid askew over the pot and set aside for 5 minutes to wilt the spinach and blend the flavors. Stir well before serving.

2 tablespoons vegetable, corn, or canola oil

1 medium yellow onion, chopped (1 cup)

3 medium garlic cloves, peeled and minced (1 tablespoon)

1 tablespoon minced peeled fresh ginger

1 teaspoon ground coriander

Up to ½ teaspoon red pepper flakes

½ teaspoon table salt

1 cup vegetable broth

One 14-ounce can diced tomatoes (1¾ cups)

1½ pounds sweet potatoes, peeled and cut into 1-inch cubes

One 15-ounce can kidney beans, drained and rinsed (1½ cups)

2 cups packed baby spinach leaves

Beyond

- You must halve the recipe for a **3-quart cooker.**

- To turn this side into a full meal, add up to ¾ cup thinly sliced smoked sausage links, such as smoked kielbasa or bratwurst, with the onions.

1 cup water

2 to 4 garlic heads

About 1 to 2 tablespoons olive oil

"Roasted" Garlic

Makes 2 to 4 garlic heads

No, you can't roast garlic in the pot. But you can make a pretty good approximation in a few minutes (versus an hour). True, the garlic will not "reduce"—that is, internal moisture will not condense in the cloves, making them exceptionally sweet. And they will not brown. But they *will* have a more intense, garlicky punch—terrific to mix with butter and spread on bread, to drop into olive oil for a few days to flavor it, to add to stews and braises for a flavor kick, or to mix into mashed potatoes for a garlicky side dish.

1. Pour the water into a **3- or 6-quart cooker**. Set a heat- and pressure-safe trivet in the pot.

2. Cut the top quarter off each garlic head (that is, the end toward the tip, away from the wider, flat root end), partly exposing the garlic cloves below. (Not every single clove need be exposed.)

3. Rub about ½ tablespoon olive oil into the cut part of the garlic head, getting the olive oil down among the cloves, particularly inside the papery skins. Set the garlic heads cut side up on the trivet in the pot. Lock the lid onto the cooker.

4.

Set the machine for	Set the level for	The valve must be	Set the time for	If necessary, press
PRESSURE COOK	MAX	——	5 minutes with the KEEP WARM setting off	START
PRESSURE COOK or MANUAL	HIGH	Closed	7 minutes with the KEEP WARM setting off	START

5. When the machine has finished cooking, turn it off and let its pressure **return to normal naturally**, about 20 minutes. Unlatch the lid and open the cooker. Use kitchen tongs to gently pick up and transfer the garlic heads to a large plate. Cool for several minutes, then either squeeze the warm cloves out of their paper hulls; or cool to room temperature, about 1 hour, then seal the heads individually in plastic wrap and refrigerate for up to 1 week.

Beyond

- For an **8-quart cooker**, you must use 1½ cups water.

- To brown the garlic, drizzle the cooked heads with a little more olive oil, then set them cut side up on a lipped baking sheet. Broil 4 to 6 inches from the heating element until lightly browned, 1 to 3 minutes.

See photo in insert.

White Bean Puree

6 to 8 servings

Is this a dip for celery ribs, baby carrots, or cucumber spears before dinner? Is it a spread for wraps? Is it a substitute for mashed potatoes under a rich beef or chicken stew? Is it a sauce that goes on top of a steak or chop off the grill? Yes! Depending on how much olive oil you add, you can control the final consistency: dip, puree, or sauce.

1 cup dried great northern or cannellini beans

Water as needed

At least ⅓ cup olive oil

1 jarred roasted yellow pepper

½ cup sliced almonds

1 large garlic clove, peeled and minced

1 tablespoon white wine vinegar

1 teaspoon fennel seeds

½ teaspoon table salt

½ teaspoon ground black pepper

1. Soak the beans in a big bowl of water for at least 8 hours or up to 12 hours. Drain in a colander set in the sink.

2. Pour the beans into a **3-, 6-, or 8-quart cooker**. Add enough water so they're submerged by 2 inches. Add 1 tablespoon olive oil and lock the lid onto the pot.

3.

Set the machine for	Set the level for	The valve must be	Set the time for	If necessary, press
PRESSURE COOK	MAX	—	10 minutes with the KEEP WARM setting off	START
PRESSURE COOK or MANUAL	HIGH	Closed	12 minutes with the KEEP WARM setting off	START

4. Use the **quick-release method** to bring the pot's pressure back to normal. Unlatch the lid and open the cooker. Drain the contents of the *hot* insert into a colander set in the sink. Shake the colander to remove excess water, then pour the warm beans into a large food processor.

5. Add 2 tablespoons olive oil, the roasted pepper, almonds, garlic, vinegar, fennel seeds, salt, and pepper. Cover and process until smooth, adding more olive oil through the feed tube in 1-tablespoon increments until the puree is smooth and creamy. Serve warm.

Beyond

- If you're not going to serve the puree right away, scrape it into a medium bowl and refrigerate, covered, for up to 3 days. Warm it up in the microwave on high in 15-second bursts, stirring after each and thinning with additional broth or water as needed.

12

Desserts

We'll confess that when we first got into pressure cooking, we were more surprised about a chapter like this one than almost anything else. It just didn't seem right: steam + pressure = cake. Seriously?

Well, it *doesn't* make sense for some desserts. No, you'll never get the same crumb in a pressure-cooker cake that you can get in one from the oven. And no, you'll never get the chewy density of a New York–style cheesecake out of an Instant Pot without some added chemical craziness that we don't care for.

You wouldn't ask a food processor to make a roast beef. You shouldn't ask an Instant Pot to make a three-layer birthday cake. But if you work within the parameters of what the machine can do, you can make wonderful desserts — and some of the best cheesecakes we know, even if they're not the NY deli standard.

In fact, the pot seems made for puddings. And for steamed cakes, those British classics that are due for a renaissance. It's also the only way we make Dulce de Leche these days (page 455).

More than any other chapter, these recipes are set in stone. Baking is chemistry and works because of certain, long-established ratios. There are no road maps in this chapter because the formulas are sacrosanct. Experiment only if you know what you're doing before you do it.

With this chapter, we come to the end of the book and bid you a sweet, happy farewell. Yes, cook more often. You bought a pot to do so. But slow down. Make dinner, even if it's a faster meal. The world needs time, in shorter supply than ice in the Arctic. In our lives, there are three ways to find that lost time: walks down New England country roads with our collies, hours spent binge-watching Scandinavian shows, and having dinner with friends and family. That last is hands down the best. We hope we've shared it with you.

FAQs

1. What's the best way to make a graham cracker crust in a springform pan?

By using your clean dry fingers. Once you get the crumbs and the butter mixed together, dump them into the pan, just not right in its center. Spread them out as you pour them in. Get your fingers into the pan to press and shape the mixture evenly across the bottom, then up the sides. Make a fairly compact and flat bottom, then begin to work that bottom toward the pan's seam and up the edges, starting at the center and eventually pushing the crumb mixture up the sides (and working around and around the pan as you do so, of course). Once the crust is in place, check to make sure that it's not too thick at the seam (where the side meets the bottom). Push this excess back toward the center of the bottom crust or up the sides of the pan.

2. Why are the eggs at room temperature here?

Because just like you, egg proteins curl up when they're cold. By bringing them to room temperature, they stretch out. When they're elongated, they can create a better structure in the batter, catching the air and holding it in the mix (along with the gluten in the flour). Lighter, more tender baked goods — even those made in a steamy pot — are better every time with room-temperature eggs. For advice on getting eggs to room temperature, see page 25.

3. Why does my cheesecake smell like curry?

There's a running debate among Instant Pot users about how much the sealing ring in the pot's lid translates the odors of former dishes into the one currently under pressure. For almost every recipe in this book, we barely noticed a difference: a curry followed by a beef stew, a chicken casserole followed by a pasta one. But one day we tested the Dulce de Leche (page 455) right after the Brisket Skewers (page 266) and ended up with a smoky, meatish dessert sauce. Put simply: *No, thanks.* So our best advice is to buy a couple of extra rings, especially for more delicate desserts like cheesecake and Butterscotch Pudding (page 458). There are even color-coded rings available, if you're a supertaster. Just remember which ring is for which sort of dish.

Dulce de Leche

Makes 1 cup

Normally, dulce de leche is an exercise in patience: stirring, stirring, stirring in a saucepan. But the Instant Pot makes it an (almost) everyday treat: a creamy, sweet sauce that can be made in about an hour, start to finish. The results are thick and honey-like, with the distinct taste of caramelized sugar.

1. Pour 1½ cups water into a **6- or 8-quart cooker**. Set a heat- and pressure-safe trivet in the pot. Whisk the remaining 3 tablespoons warm water and the baking soda in a 2-quart, high-sided, round soufflé dish. Whisk in the condensed milk until smooth. Set this bowl on the trivet and lock the lid onto the cooker.

2.

Set the machine for	Set the level for	The valve must be	Set the time for	If necessary, press
PRESSURE COOK	MAX	—	30 minutes with the KEEP WARM setting off	START
PRESSURE COOK or MANUAL	HIGH	Closed	40 minutes with the KEEP WARM setting off	START

3. When the machine has finished cooking, turn it off and let its pressure **return to normal naturally**, about 15 minutes. Unlatch the lid and open the cooker. Whisk the dulce de leche until smooth or use an immersion blender right in the insert to make the sauce super smooth. Pour the sauce into a small bowl and set it in the fridge for an hour or two. Cover and refrigerate for up to 5 days, microwaving small portions to loosen them up before serving.

1½ cups water plus 3 tablespoons warm water

½ teaspoon baking soda

One 14-ounce can full-fat sweetened condensed milk

Beyond

- Unfortunately, dulce de leche cannot be made in a soufflé dish smaller than the one required here — and therefore cannot be made in a **3-quart cooker.** Even halved, the mixture roils too much to be contained in a 1-quart baking dish. The recipe also *cannot* be doubled in the standard 2-quart baking dish we call for.

- Serve dulce de leche over vanilla, butter pecan, chocolate, or any nut ice cream. It's particularly delicious over cashew milk ice cream.

- Drizzle warm dulce de leche over blackberries — and top with whipped cream.

- Or spread it on toast as a change from Nutella.

- Or dip salty pretzel logs into the sauce as a great dessert.

See photo in insert.

4 large eggs

2 cups whole milk

3 tablespoons granulated white sugar

½ teaspoon vanilla extract

¼ teaspoon table salt

1½ cups water

Silky Vanilla Custard

4 servings

Custards from a multi-cooker come out a little firmer than those from the stovetop, similar in texture to silken tofu (and definitely not dry, given the pot's moist environment). They also don't need to set up in the refrigerator but are ready to eat warm from the cooker.

Make sure the eggs are whisked fully into the custard base with no bits of the whites floating loose. The easiest way to get the egg mixture into the custard cups is to use a ladle, rather than trying to pour from the rim of a bowl (unless your mixing bowl has a pouring spout).

1. Whisk the eggs, milk, sugar, vanilla, and salt in a large bowl until very smooth. Divide this mixture evenly among four heat- and pressure-safe 1-cup ramekins. Cover each ramekin with a small piece of aluminum foil.

2. Pour the water into a **6- or 8-quart cooker**. Set a heat- and pressure-safe trivet in the cooker. Stack the ramekins in the cooker (probably 3 on the rack and then one balanced in the middle on the edges of the three below). Lock the lid onto the cooker.

3.

Set the machine for	Set the level for	The valve must be	Set the time for	If necessary, press
PRESSURE COOK	MAX	—	3 minutes with the KEEP WARM setting off	START
PRESSURE COOK or MANUAL	HIGH	Closed	5 minutes with the KEEP WARM setting off	START

4. When the machine has finished cooking, turn it off and let its pressure **return to normal naturally**, about 15 minutes. Unlatch the lid and open the cooker. Transfer the *hot* covered ramekins to a wire rack, uncover, and cool for 15 minutes. Serve warm, or cover again and refrigerate for at least 2 hours or up to 4 days.

Beyond

- Because of the size of the ramekins, this recipe cannot be halved for a **3-quart cooker**.

- You can (but don't have to) increase all the ingredients by 50 percent and make six 1-cup ramekins of pudding in an **8-quart cooker**. Or you can cut the recipe by half (or even cut it to a quarter of its original and make just one custard) using 2 ramekins (or just 1) in a **6- or 8-quart cooker**. However, you *must* keep the water the same (1½ cups).

- Sprinkle up to ½ teaspoon ground cinnamon and/or ½ teaspoon grated nutmeg onto each ramekin of custard base before baking.

- Try adding up to ½ teaspoon rum, almond, or lemon extract with the vanilla extract.

Chocolate Pudding

4 servings

Our chocolate pudding is made with melted chocolate, not cocoa powder. That chocolate gives the pudding a thick, super rich texture, like a cross between pudding and frosting. A little goes a long way, although whipped cream would be welcome to (ahem) lighten the dessert.

1. Place both types of chocolate in a large, heat-safe bowl. Set aside.

2. Pour the milk and cream into a medium, microwave-safe bowl. Heat on high until steaming, 1 to 2 minutes. Pour the hot milk mixture over the chocolate and steep for 1 minute. Stir until creamy and melted. Cool for 5 minutes, whisking occasionally.

3. Whisk in the egg yolks, vanilla, and salt until smooth. Divide this mixture between four heat- and pressure-safe 1-cup ramekins. Cover each tightly with aluminum foil. Pour the water into a **6- or 8-quart cooker**. Set a heat- and pressure-safe trivet in the pot, then stack the ramekins on the trivet, probably three on the bottom and one on top in the center on their edges. Lock the lid onto the cooker.

4.

Set the machine for	Set the level for	The valve must be	Set the time for	If necessary, press
PRESSURE COOK	MAX	—	10 minutes with the KEEP WARM setting off	START
PRESSURE COOK or MANUAL	HIGH	Closed	12 minutes with the KEEP WARM setting off	START

5. When the machine has finished cooking, turn it off and let its pressure **return to normal naturally**, about 20 minutes. Unlatch the lid and open the pot. Transfer the *hot* covered ramekins to a wire rack, uncover, and cool for 15 minutes. Serve warm or cover again and refrigerate for at least 2 hours until chilled or up to 4 days.

6 ounces semi-sweet chocolate, chopped; or 6 ounces semi-sweet morsels (about 1 cup)

½ ounce unsweetened chocolate, chopped (half of a 1-ounce square of standard baking chocolate, or about 1½ tablespoons chopped unsweetened chocolate)

1 cup whole milk

½ cup heavy cream

4 large egg yolks

Up to 2 teaspoons vanilla extract

¼ teaspoon salt

1½ cups water

Beyond

- Because of the size of the ramekins, this recipe cannot be halved for a **3-quart cooker**.

- The best whipped cream is made with chilled utensils: Set the bowl and the beaters of a mixer (or a whisk, if you're old-school) in the refrigerator for at least 3 hours or up to 24 hours before making whipped cream. Our preferred ratio is 1 tablespoon confectioners' sugar and ¼ teaspoon vanilla extract for every ⅔ cup heavy cream. Pour the cream into the chilled bowl and beat at high speed with a stand mixer with the whip attachment or a hand-held electric mixer (or even with a whisk by hand) until somewhat thickened. Add the sugar and vanilla and continue beating on high until soft, light peaks can be formed off the ends of the turned-off whisk attachment or beaters (or the hand-held whisk).

3 tablespoons butter

½ cup packed dark brown sugar

1½ cups whole milk

½ cup heavy cream

6 large egg yolks

¼ teaspoon vanilla extract

⅛ teaspoon salt

1½ cups water

Butterscotch Pudding

4 servings

This pudding is like butterscotch *pot de crème*, made by turning butter and brown sugar into caramel, then creating a custard base to steam-cook in the ramekins. The results are wonderfully smooth. Don't be surprised if it really serves just two (since each of you will eat two).

1.

Press the button for	Set it for	Set the time for	If necessary, press
SAUTÉ	MEDIUM, NORMAL, or CUSTOM 300°F	10 minutes	START

2. Melt the butter in a **6- or 8-quart cooker**. Stir in the brown sugar until smooth and cook until constantly bubbling, about 3 minutes. Stir in the milk and cream until the sugar mixture melts again and becomes smooth. Turn off the SAUTÉ function and pour the mixture from the *hot* insert into a nearby large bowl. Cool for 15 minutes. Meanwhile, clean and dry the insert; return it to the machine.

3. Whisk the egg yolks, vanilla, and salt into the milk mixture until smooth. Divide this mixture evenly among four heat- and pressure-safe 1-cup ramekins. Cover each with aluminum foil.

4. Pour the water into the cooker and set a heat- and pressure-safe trivet in the machine. Stack the ramekins on the trivet, balancing a second layer on the edge of more than one ramekin below. Lock the lid onto the pot.

5.

Set the machine for	Set the level for	The valve must be	Set the time for	If necessary, press
PRESSURE COOK	MAX	—	7 minutes with the KEEP WARM setting off	START
PRESSURE COOK or MANUAL	HIGH	Closed	10 minutes with the KEEP WARM setting off	START

6. When the machine has finished cooking, turn it off and let its pressure **return to normal naturally**, about 20 minutes. Unlatch the lid and open the cooker. Transfer the *hot* covered ramekins to a wire rack, uncover, and cool for 15 minutes. Serve warm or cover again and refrigerate for at least 2 hours or up to 4 days.

Beyond

- Because of the size of the ramekins, this recipe cannot be halved for a **3-quart cooker**.

- In an **8-quart cooker**, you can (but don't have to) increase all the ingredients by 50 percent (if desired) and make six 1-cup ramekins of pudding. Use 1½ cups water, as directed, in the cooker.

- If you've used oven-safe ramekins, you can put a meringue on these puddings (as long as they're still hot). To do so, beat 3 large egg whites and ⅛ teaspoon table salt in a medium bowl with an electric mixer (with a whisk attachment, if available) at medium speed until foamy, about 1 minute. Beat in 6 tablespoons granulated white sugar in a slow, steady stream until the sugar dissolves and you can form soft peaks off the end of a rubber spatula dipped into the mixture. Divide this mixture among the tops of the puddings, sealing it to the edges. Use the spatula to make peaks and valleys in the beaten egg-white mixture. Set the *hot* ramekins on a large lipped baking sheet and bake in a 375°F oven until lightly browned, 8 to 10 minutes. Cool for at least 15 minutes before serving.

Tapioca Pudding

4 to 6 servings

We followed the advice of eight bazillion internet recipes and tried (and tried and tried) to make tapioca pudding right in the pot's insert. It burned every time, no matter what size tapioca pearls we used. The only sure path to success was to use a soufflé dish in the pot, then whisk an egg and an egg yolk into the pudding after cooking to make the whole thing rich and creamy.

For this recipe, you must use instant tapioca, the stuff your grandmother used to thicken pie fillings. It's found in the baking aisle near the baking soda. You cannot use larger tapioca pearls, familiar from bubble teas. And for safety's sake, use only organic eggs (because they're not cooked but only heated in the rice mixture). If you are cooking for someone with immune system problems, search out in-the-shell pasteurized eggs.

3 cups whole, low-fat, or fat-free milk

½ cup granulated white sugar

½ cup instant tapioca

1 teaspoon vanilla extract

¼ teaspoon table salt

1½ cups water

1 large egg, at room temperature

1 large egg yolk, at room temperature

1. Whisk the milk, sugar, tapioca, vanilla, and salt in a 2-quart, high-sided, round, heat- and pressure-safe soufflé dish until the sugar dissolves. Do not cover.

2. Pour the water into a **6- or 8-quart cooker**. Set a heat- and pressure-safe trivet in the pot. Set the baking dish on the trivet and lock the lid onto the pot.

3.

Set the machine for	Set the level for	The valve must be	Set the time for	If necessary, press
PRESSURE COOK	MAX	—	5 minutes with the KEEP WARM setting off	START
PRESSURE COOK or MANUAL	HIGH	Closed	7 minutes with the KEEP WARM setting off	START

4. When the machine has finished cooking, turn it off and let its pressure **return to normal naturally**, about 20 minutes. Unlatch the lid and open the cooker. Whisk the hot mixture in the baking dish until smooth, scraping up any clumped tapioca on the bottom.

5. Whisk the egg and egg yolk in a medium bowl until smooth. Whisk the hot tapioca custard in small portions into the eggs, then more and more of it, until all of the milk mixture is incorporated and smooth. Set in the refrigerator to chill for 2 hours, then serve or cover and store in the fridge for up to 4 days.

Beyond

- For a **3-quart cooker**, you must use 1 cup of water in the cooker, halve all the remaining ingredients, and use a 1-quart, high-sided, round soufflé dish.

- Stir dried fruit into the pudding after you've incorporated all the eggs. Try ½ cup dried blueberries, cranberries, currants, or raisins.

- Or stir up to 2 thinly sliced, peeled bananas into the pudding after the eggs have been incorporated.

1 tablespoon butter

¾ cup raw white Arborio rice

One 12-ounce can whole or low-fat evaporated milk (1½ cups)

½ cup water

½ cup granulated white sugar

Up to 2 teaspoons vanilla extract

¼ teaspoon table salt

1 large egg, at room temperature

1 large egg yolk, at room temperature

⅓ cup heavy cream

Rice Pudding

4 to 6 servings

Our rice pudding recipe is basically a sweetened modification of our risotto recipe — and the whole thing gets enriched with eggs and cream. As in the previous recipe for Tapioca Pudding, only use organic or even in-the-shell pasteurized eggs for safety's sake.

1.

Press the button for	Set it for	Set the time for	If necessary, press
SAUTÉ	MEDIUM, NORMAL, or CUSTOM 300°F	5 minutes	START

2. Melt the butter in a **6-quart cooker**. Add the rice and cook, stirring constantly, until the tips of the grains turn translucent, about 1 minute. Stir in the evaporated milk, water, sugar, vanilla, and salt until the sugar dissolves. Turn off the SAUTÉ function and lock the lid onto the pot.

3.

Set the machine for	Set the level for	The valve must be	Set the time for	If necessary, press
PRESSURE COOK	MAX	—	7 minutes with the KEEP WARM setting off	START
PRESSURE COOK or MANUAL	HIGH	Closed	10 minutes with the KEEP WARM setting off	START

4. When the machine has finished cooking, turn it off and let its pressure **return to normal naturally**, about 15 minutes. Unlatch the lid and open the cooker. Stir the rice mixture a couple of times.

5. Whisk the egg, egg yolk, and cream in a large bowl until smooth. Whisk about 1 cup of the rice mixture into this egg mixture until smooth, then whisk this combined mixture back into the remaining rice mixture in the pot. Set aside for 5 minutes, then serve warm or spoon into a large, clean bowl and refrigerate until chilled, about 1 hour. Covered, the pudding can stay in the fridge for up to 2 days.

Beyond

- For a **3-quart cooker**, you must halve all the ingredients.

- For an **8-quart cooker**, you must increase all the ingredients by 50 percent.

- Stir in up to ½ cup dried fruit after the combined egg-and-pudding mixture has cooled for 5 minutes. Choose raisins, currants, or cranberries — or choose among any chopped dried fruit like pineapple, nectarines, pitted dates, or stemmed figs.

- Once cooled, stir in up to ½ cup mini chocolate chips. Or go Italian and stir in up to ⅓ cup finely chopped glacé (or candied) cherries, candied orange rind, or candied citron (any of that chopped fruitcake fruit).

Sweet Coconut Rice with Mango

6 servings

Here's a quick rendition of a dessert served in Thai restaurants across North America. You'll need sweet glutinous rice, not sushi or other short-grain varietals of white rice. You should be able to find it in an Asian market or you can order it online — although we did luck out and find it at our rural supermarket on two occasions. It's sometimes called "sweet rice." But beware: Some manufacturers label other short-grain white rices as "sweet." Just be sure it has the word "glutinous" on the label. (By the way, there is no wheat gluten in glutinous rice.)

One 14-ounce can full-fat coconut milk or coconut cream (but not cream of coconut)

½ cup granulated white sugar

½ teaspoon vanilla extract

½ teaspoon table salt

3½ cups water

1½ cups raw, sweet, glutinous white rice

3 medium ripe mangos, peeled, pitted, and cut into bite-size chunks

1.

Press the button for	Set it for	Set the time for	If necessary, press
SAUTÉ	MEDIUM, NORMAL, or CUSTOM 300°F	10 minutes	START

2. Mix the coconut milk, sugar, vanilla, and salt in a **6- or 8-quart cooker**. Cook, stirring often, until bubbling, about 4 minutes. Turn off the SAUTÉ function, remove the *hot* insert from the machine, and scrape every drop of the coconut mixture into a heat-safe, large bowl. Set aside.

3. Clean the insert and return it to the machine. Pour 1½ cups water into the pot, then set a heat- and pressure-safe trivet in the pot. Mix the rice and the remaining 2 cups water in a 2-quart, high-sided, round soufflé dish. Set this dish on the trivet and lock the lid onto the pot.

4.

Set the machine for	Set the level for	The valve must be	Set the time for	If necessary, press
PRESSURE COOK	MAX	—	12 minutes with the KEEP WARM setting off	START
PRESSURE COOK or MANUAL	HIGH	Closed	15 minutes with the KEEP WARM setting off	START

5. Use the **quick-release method** to bring the pot's pressure back to normal — *but do not open the pot*. Set aside for 10 minutes, then unlatch the lid and open the cooker. Remove the *hot* bowl from the trivet.

6. Stir all but ⅓ cup of the coconut milk mixture into the cooked rice. Serve the rice warm in bowls with mango pieces all over the top and drizzle the portions with as much of the remaining coconut milk mixture as desired.

Beyond

- For a **3-quart cooker**, you must use 1 cup of water in the cooker, halve the remaining ingredients, and use a 1-quart, high-sided, round soufflé dish.

- This dessert is much easier with presliced mangos, often available in the refrigerator case in the supermarket's produce section. They are often sold in spears, which you can chop into smaller pieces.

- Split a vanilla bean in half lengthwise and add it with the sugar to the coconut milk mixture. Remove the vanilla bean halves before serving.

½ plus ⅓ cup granulated white sugar

1½ cups plus 3 tablespoons water

3 large eggs

1¼ cups heavy cream

¾ cup whole milk

2 teaspoons vanilla extract

⅛ teaspoon table salt

Burnt Sugar Flan

4 servings

These little custard cups steam with a burnt sugar sauce in the bottom of each. The sugar syrup is first poured into the cups, it hardens, then turns wet again as the custards cook and cool. How dark you cook that sugar syrup is a matter of culinary debate. If you like a sweet, mild flavor, cook it only until it is barely amber. Go darker for a more robust flavor. But remember: It will continue to cook (and darken) for a bit after the pot has been removed from the heat.

Why not just cook the syrup with the SAUTÉ function on HIGH in the pot? Because it's hard to judge exactly how dark the syrup has gotten inside the pot and because it's very difficult to pour from the insert.

1. Melt the ½ cup sugar and the 3 tablespoons water in a small saucepan set over medium heat until amber or even a little darker, stirring occasionally until the sugar melts then undisturbed to your desired color, 4 to 6 minutes. Pour the *hot* sugar syrup evenly into four heat- and pressure-safe 1-cup ramekins, preferably Pyrex custard cups. Grasp the cups with hot pads or oven mitts and tilt them a little this way and that to coat their sides a bit. Cool at room temperature for 15 minutes.

2. Whisk the eggs, cream, milk, vanilla, salt, and the remaining ⅓ cup sugar in a medium bowl until the sugar dissolves and the mixture is smooth. Divide this mixture evenly among the coated custard cups. Cover each tightly with aluminum foil.

3. Pour the remaining 1½ cups water into a **6- or 8-quart cooker**. Set a heat- and pressure-safe trivet in the pot, then stack the filled custard cups on the trivet, probably three below and one balanced in the center on their rims. Lock the lid onto the pot.

4.

Set the machine for	Set the level for	The valve must be	Set the time for	If necessary, press
PRESSURE COOK	MAX	—	7 minutes with the KEEP WARM setting off	START
PRESSURE COOK or MANUAL	HIGH	Closed	9 minutes with the KEEP WARM setting off	START

5. When the machine has finished cooking, turn it off and let its pressure **return to normal naturally**, about 20 minutes. Unlatch the lid and open the cooker. Transfer the *hot* custard cups to a wire rack, uncover them, and cool for 10 minutes. Then set them in the fridge and cool for 1 hour. Cover and continue cooling for at least 1 more hour or up to 3 days. To serve, turn one upside down on a serving plate, jiggle it a bit, and release the custard and sugar sauce from inside.

Beyond

- Because of the size of the ramekins, this recipe won't work in a **3-quart cooker**.

- Add up to ½ teaspoon orange extract with the vanilla.

- Or sprinkle up to ¼ teaspoon finely minced culinary lavender on top of each custard before sealing and steaming.

Buttery Caramel Pears

4 servings

Strangely enough, this dessert returns to the butter-and-baking-soda technique we used when we poached vegetables to make a creamy (but cream-free) soup. In this recipe, you don't puree the mixture. This isn't soup, after all. Instead, the pears get poached in a sweet butter sauce that is thickened after cooking.

1.

Press the button for	Set it for	Set the time for	If necessary, press
SAUTÉ	MEDIUM, NORMAL, or CUSTOM 300°F	5 minutes	START

2. Put the butter, brown sugar, cinnamon, nutmeg, baking soda, and salt in a **3- or 6-quart cooker** and stir until the butter has melted. Stir in the apple juice until smooth, then add the pears and stir well. Turn off the SAUTÉ function and lock the lid onto the pot.

3.

Set the machine for	Set the level for	The valve must be	Set the time for	If necessary, press
PRESSURE COOK	MAX	—	3 minutes with the KEEP WARM setting off	START
PRESSURE COOK or MANUAL	HIGH	Closed	4 minutes with the KEEP WARM setting off	START

4. When the machine has finished cooking, turn it off and let its pressure **return to normal naturally**, about 15 minutes. Unlatch the lid and open the cooker.

5.

Press the button for	Set it for	Set the time for	If necessary, press
SAUTÉ	MEDIUM, NORMAL, or CUSTOM 300°F	5 minutes	START

6. As the sauce comes to a simmer, whisk the cornstarch and water in a small bowl until smooth. Stir this slurry into the pears and sauce. Stir constantly until thickened a bit, about 1 minute. Turn off the SAUTÉ function and remove the *hot* insert from the machine. Cool for 5 to 10 minutes before serving.

½ cup (1 stick) butter, cut into four or five pieces

⅔ cup packed light brown sugar

1 teaspoon ground cinnamon

¼ teaspoon grated nutmeg

¼ teaspoon baking soda

¼ teaspoon table salt

½ cup unsweetened apple juice or cider

4 large firm ripe pears, peeled, cored, and each cut into 4 to 6 wedges

2 teaspoons cornstarch

2 teaspoons water

Beyond

- For an **8-quart cooker,** you must increase all the ingredients by 50 percent.
- Split a vanilla bean lengthwise and add it to the pot with the pears.
- Spoon the pears and syrup over a small mound of soft goat cheese or fresh ricotta.
- Sprinkle coarse graham cracker crumbs over each serving.

6 ounces wide egg noodles (3 cups)

1½ quarts (6 cups) water

2 large eggs

6 tablespoons granulated white sugar

6 tablespoons regular or low-fat sour
cream

6 tablespoons regular or low-fat
cream cheese

¼ cup regular or low-fat evaporated
milk

2 tablespoons butter, melted and
cooled, plus more butter as needed

½ teaspoon ground cinnamon

½ teaspoon vanilla extract

¼ teaspoon table salt

¼ cup raisins

Noodle Kugel

6 servings

A New York deli favorite, noodle kugel (*KOO-guhl*, which means something like "baked casserole") is often served with brisket. We think kugel's better as a dessert, falling somewhere between a rice pudding and a sweet custard with egg noodles. While you can use low-fat dairy, do not use fat-free, which has stabilizers that can break down under pressure. As with other savory dishes that use wide egg noodles, the best gluten-free alternative for a pressure cooker are noodles made with a mix of grains, preferably corn and rice.

1. Put the noodles into a **6- or 8-quart cooker** and pour in the water. Lock the lid onto the pot.

2.

Set the machine for	Set the level for	The valve must be	Set the time for	If necessary, press
PRESSURE COOK or MANUAL	HIGH	Closed	4 minutes with the KEEP WARM setting off	START

3. Use the **quick-release method** to bring the pot's pressure back to normal. Unlatch the lid and open the cooker. Drain the noodles out of the *hot* insert and into a colander set in the sink. Wipe out the insert and return it to the pot. Cool the noodles for 10 minutes, tossing occasionally to keep them from sticking.

4. Meanwhile, generously butter the inside of a 7-inch round springform pan. Put the eggs, sugar, sour cream, cream cheese, evaporated milk, melted butter, cinnamon, vanilla, and salt in a blender. Cover and blend until smooth, stopping the machine at least once to scrape down the inside.

5. Pour the egg mixture into a large bowl; stir in the noodles and raisins until uniform. Pour and scrape this mixture into the prepared springform pan, packing it down a bit (if not tightly). Cover tightly with aluminum foil.

6. Pour 1½ cups water into the cooker, then set a heat- and pressure-safe trivet inside the pot. Make an aluminum foil sling (see page 20) and set the covered springform pan on it. Using the sling, lower the pan onto the trivet; fold the ends of the sling down into the pot. Lock the lid onto the cooker.

7.

Set the machine for	Set the level for	The valve must be	Set the time for	If necessary, press
PRESSURE COOK	MAX	—	15 minutes with the KEEP WARM setting off	START
PRESSURE COOK or MANUAL	HIGH	Closed	20 minutes with the KEEP WARM setting off	START

8. When the machine has finished cooking, turn it off and let its pressure **return to normal naturally**, about 20 minutes. Unlatch the lid and open the cooker. Use the foil sling to lift the *hot* springform pan out of the cooker. Set on a wire rack and cool for 10 minutes. Unlatch the ring of the springform pan and remove it. Cool another 5 minutes before slicing into wedges and serving warm — or cool to room temperature, then wrap in plastic wrap and store in the fridge for up to 3 days.

Beyond

- For a **3-quart cooker**, you must halve the ingredients and use a 1-quart, high-sided, round soufflé dish (rather than a springform pan). Scoop out big spoonfuls, rather than cutting it into wedges.

- Drizzle servings with heavy cream and maple syrup.

- It's unheard of among traditionalists, but try substituting dried blueberries, cherries, or cranberries for the raisins.

- Or omit the raisins, go old-school, and use ½ cup drained canned fruit cocktail.

1¼ cups graham cracker crumbs

5 tablespoons butter, melted and cooled, plus additional butter for greasing the pan

1 pound regular cream cheese

½ cup granulated white sugar

2 large eggs

¼ cup regular sour cream

2 teaspoons finely grated lemon zest

1 tablespoon fresh lemon juice

½ teaspoon vanilla extract

¼ teaspoon table salt (optional)

1½ tablespoons all-purpose flour

1½ cups water

Classic Cheesecake

6 to 8 servings

If social media is to be believed (does Facebook lie?), a cheesecake is one of the first things people make in their Instant Pots. We've seen a lot of techniques over the years — and written a lot of pressure-cooker cheesecake recipes, too — and we can tell you we heartily don't get why people tend to overcomplicate what can be a fairly simple process for a rich, mousse-like (*not* New York–style) cheesecake.

First, don't cover the cheesecake. True, it can get a drop or two of moisture on top. You can blot these off with a paper towel when you open the lid. A cover on the pan gets in the way as the batter rises. You end up with a top that's partly fused to the foil, often a mess.

Second, never use the quick-release method — which instantly brings any liquid left in the cheesecake to a near boil even after the cake has mostly set, resulting in bumps and cracks. Instead, use a natural release for a better texture, set, and look.

Finally, cook the cheesecake only on HIGH pressure, not MAX, which is too aggressive for a successful cheesecake.

1. Generously butter the inside of a 7-inch round springform pan. Mix the graham cracker crumbs and the melted butter in a medium bowl, then pour this mixture into the prepared pan. Press this mixture evenly across the bottom and about halfway up the sides of the pan to make a crust.

2. Put the cream cheese and sugar in a food processor, cover, and process until smooth, about 1 minute. Add the eggs one at a time, processing each until smooth. Open the machine, scrape down the inside, and add the sour cream. Cover and process until smooth.

3. Add the lemon zest, lemon juice, vanilla, and salt (if using). Process again until smooth — and again, stop the machine and scrape down the inside. Add the flour and process for 1 minute. Pour this mixture into the prepared crust in the pan (it will rise above the crust on the sides). Do not cover the pan.

4. Pour the water into a **6- or 8-quart cooker.** Set a heat- and pressure-safe trivet in the cooker. Make an aluminum foil sling (see page 20), set the filled springform pan on it, and use it to lower the pan into the pot. Fold down the ends of the sling so that they do not touch the batter in the pan. Lock the lid onto the pot.

5.

Set the machine for	Set the level for	The valve must be	Set the time for	If necessary, press
PRESSURE COOK or MANUAL	HIGH	Closed	25 minutes with the KEEP WARM setting off	START

6. When the machine has finished cooking, turn it off and let its pressure **return to normal naturally**, about 20 minutes. Unlatch the lid and open the cooker. Use the sling to transfer the *hot* springform pan to a wire rack. Cool for 15 minutes, then refrigerate for 1 hour. Cover and continue refrigerating for at least 1 more hour or up to 2 days.

7. To serve, uncover and run a thin knife between the pan and the cake. Unlatch the sides of the pan and open it to remove the cake inside. If desired, use a long, thin knife to slice the cake off the pan's base and use a large metal spatula to transfer the cheesecake to a serving platter.

Beyond

- Unfortunately, these ratios and this pan won't work in a **3-quart cooker.**

- Top the slices with strawberry or raspberry jam, warmed for a few seconds on high in the microwave and then whisked until smooth.

- Or top with slightly warmed chocolate sauce.

- Or make a cherry sauce: Mix one 16-ounce bag frozen sweet or sour cherries (do not thaw), ½ cup granulated white sugar, and ½ cup water in a medium saucepan; bring to a boil over medium heat, stirring often. Whisk 1 tablespoon lemon juice and 2 teaspoons cornstarch in a small bowl until smooth, then stir this slurry into the bubbling cherry mixture. Cook, stirring constantly, until thickened, about 1 minute. Immediately remove from the heat and continue stirring until the bubbling stops. Cool for at least 30 minutes at room temperature before serving with the cheesecake.

See photo in insert.

1¼ cups graham cracker crumbs

5 tablespoons butter, melted and cooled, plus additional butter for greasing the pan

1 pound regular cream cheese

¾ cup granulated white sugar

2 large eggs, at room temperature

1 large egg yolk, at room temperature

¼ cup regular sour cream

12 ounces bittersweet chocolate, melted and cooled

2 tablespoons unsweetened cocoa powder

1½ cups water

Chocolate–Sour Cream Cheesecake

6 to 8 servings

This cheesecake is thick and chewy, sort of like a cross between chocolate frosting and cheesecake. Even more than the classic cheesecake, this one needs to ripen in the fridge, if only to develop its sophisticated flavor.

For the best success, start with bittersweet chocolate (around 70% cocoa solids). Chop it and set it in a microwave-wave safe bowl. Microwave on high in 5-second bursts, stirring after each, until about two-thirds melted, then remove the bowl and continue stirring until smooth. Cool to room temperature, 20 to 30 minutes.

1. Generously butter the inside of a 7-inch round springform pan. Mix the graham cracker crumbs and melted butter in a medium bowl, then pour into the prepared pan. Press this mixture evenly across the bottom and about halfway up the sides of the pan to make a crust.

2. Put the cream cheese and sugar in a food processor, cover, and process until smooth, about 1 minute. Add the eggs one at a time, processing each until smooth. Then add the egg yolk and process until smooth. Open the machine, scrape down the inside, and add the sour cream. Cover and again process until smooth.

3. Add the melted and cooled chocolate and the cocoa powder. Process again until smooth — and once again, stop the machine and scrape down the inside. Pour this mixture into the prepared crust in the pan (it will rise above the crust on the sides).

4. Pour the water into a **6- or 8-quart cooker.** Set a heat- and pressure-safe trivet in the cooker. Make an aluminum foil sling (see page 20), set the filled but uncovered springform pan on it, and use the sling to lower the pan into the pot. Fold down the ends of the sling so that they do not touch the cheesecake batter in the pan. Lock the lid onto the pot.

5.

Set the machine for	Set the level for	The valve must be	Set the time for	If necessary, press
PRESSURE COOK or MANUAL	HIGH	Closed	25 minutes with the KEEP WARM setting off	START

6. When the machine has finished cooking, turn it off and let its pressure **return to normal naturally**, about 20 minutes. Unlatch the lid and open the cooker. Use the sling to transfer the *hot* springform pan to a wire rack. Cool for 15 minutes, then refrigerate for 1 hour. Cover and continue refrigerating for at least 1 more hour or up to 2 days.

7. To serve, uncover and run a thin knife between the pan and the cake. Unlatch the sides of the pan and open it to remove the cake inside. If desired, use a long, thin knife to slice the cake off the pan's base and use a large metal spatula to transfer the cheesecake to a serving platter.

Beyond

- Unfortunately, these ratios and this pan won't work in a **3-quart cooker.**

- Top the cheesecake with curls of chocolate, shaved off a bar of bittersweet chocolate with a cheese plane.

- Or top the cheesecake with a sprinkling of crunchy sea salt.

⅔ cup sliced almonds

⅔ cup graham cracker crumbs

½ cup plus 2 tablespoons granulated white sugar

3 tablespoons butter, melted and cooled, plus additional butter for greasing the pan

1 pound regular cream cheese

1 small very ripe banana

⅓ cup packaged, dehydrated, crisp, unsweetened, unsalted banana chips

2 large eggs

1 tablespoon all-purpose flour

½ teaspoon almond extract

1½ cups water

Banana Cheesecake

6 to 8 servings

This cheesecake requires a very ripe banana: one with black spots on its skin, quite soft, beyond what you'd slice onto cereal. A banana with a few brown spots won't cut it. We also add dehydrated banana chips (rather than artificial banana flavoring) to make the cheesecake a banana lover's paradise.

1. Generously butter the inside of a 7-inch round springform pan. Mix the sliced almonds, graham cracker crumbs, 2 tablespoons sugar, and the melted butter in a medium bowl until uniform; then pour into the prepared pan. Press this mixture evenly across the bottom and about halfway up the sides of the pan to make a crust.

2. Put the remaining ½ cup sugar, the cream cheese, banana, and banana chips (if using) in a food processor, cover, and process until smooth, about 1 minute. Add the eggs one at a time, processing each until smooth. Open the machine, scrape down the inside, and add the flour and almond extract. Cover and process until smooth. Pour this mixture into the prepared crust in the pan (it will rise above the crust on the sides). Do not cover the pan with foil.

3. Pour the water into a **6- or 8-quart cooker**. Set a heat- and pressure-safe trivet in the cooker. Make an aluminum foil sling (see page 20), set the filled springform pan on it, and use it to lower the pan into the pot. Fold down the ends of the sling so that they do not touch the cheesecake batter in the pan. Lock the lid onto the pot.

4.

Set the machine for	Set the level for	The valve must be	Set the time for	If necessary, press
PRESSURE COOK or MANUAL	HIGH	Closed	25 minutes with the KEEP WARM setting off	START

5. When the machine has finished cooking, turn it off and let its pressure **return to normal naturally,** about 20 minutes. Unlatch the lid and open the cooker. Use the sling to transfer the *hot* springform pan to a wire rack. Cool for 15 minutes, then refrigerate for 1 hour. Cover and continue refrigerating for at least 1 more hour or up to 2 days.

6. To serve, uncover and run a thin knife between the pan and the cake. Unlatch the sides of the pan and open it to remove the cake inside. If desired, use a long, thin knife to slice the cake off the pan's base and use a large metal spatula to transfer the cheesecake to a serving platter.

Beyond

- Unfortunately, these ratios and this pan won't work in a **3-quart cooker**.

- To make a simple chocolate sauce, stir together 1 cup water and ½ cup granulated white sugar in a small saucepan over medium heat until the sugar dissolves. Whisk in ⅔ cup unsweetened cocoa powder, 2 teaspoons vanilla extract, and ¼ teaspoon table salt. Continue whisking until slightly thickened, about 2 minutes. Remove from the heat and cool for at least 15 minutes, whisking occasionally (the sauce will continue to thicken off the heat).

Eggnog Cheesecake

6 to 8 servings

A cheesecake for the holidays! Eggnog is sometimes made with brandy and sometimes with a mix of brandy and whiskey — so feel free to use 1½ tablespoons brandy and 1½ tablespoons whiskey in this recipe. Or go all out with 1 tablespoon brandy, 1 tablespoon whiskey, and 1 tablespoon gold rum.

1. Generously butter the inside of a 7-inch round springform pan. Mix the cookie crumbs, melted butter, and confectioners' sugar in a medium bowl until uniform; then pour into the prepared pan. Press this mixture evenly across the bottom and about halfway up the sides of the pan to make a crust.

2. Put the cream cheese and sugar in a food processor, cover, and process until smooth, about 1 minute. Add the egg and process until smooth. Then add the egg yolks one at a time, processing each before adding the next.

3. Open the machine, scrape down the inside, and add brandy and cream. Cover and process until smooth. Add the flour, nutmeg, and salt (if using). Process again until smooth. Pour this mixture into the prepared crust in the pan (it will rise above the crust on the sides). Do not cover the pan with foil.

4. Pour the water into a **6- or 8-quart cooker.** Set a heat- and pressure-safe trivet in the cooker. Make an aluminum foil sling (see page 20), set the filled springform pan on it, and use it to lower the pan into the pot. Fold down the ends of the sling so that they do not touch the cheesecake batter in the pan. Lock the lid onto the pot.

5.

Set the machine for	Set the level for	The valve must be	Set the time for	If necessary, press
PRESSURE COOK or MANUAL	HIGH	Closed	25 minutes with the KEEP WARM setting off	START

6. When the machine has finished cooking, turn it off and let its pressure **return to normal naturally**, about 20 minutes. Unlatch the lid and open the cooker. Use the sling to transfer the *hot* springform pan to a wire rack. Cool for 15 minutes, then refrigerate for 1 hour. Cover and continue refrigerating for at least 1 more hour or up to 2 days.

7. To serve, uncover and run a thin knife between the pan and the cake. Unlatch the sides of the pan and open it to remove the cake inside. If desired, use a thin knife to slice the cake off the pan's base and a spatula to transfer the cheesecake to a platter.

1½ cups vanilla wafer cookie crumbs

¼ cup (½ stick) butter, melted and cooled, plus additional butter for greasing the pan

2 tablespoons confectioners' sugar

1 pound regular cream cheese

½ cup granulated white sugar

1 large egg, at room temperature

3 large egg yolks, at room temperature

3 tablespoons brandy

3 tablespoons heavy cream

2 tablespoons all-purpose flour

½ teaspoon grated nutmeg

¼ teaspoon salt (optional)

1½ cups water

Beyond

- Unfortunately, these ratios and this pan won't work in a **3-quart cooker.**

- Sprinkle up to ¼ cup finely chopped candied citron over the crust before you pour the cheesecake batter into the pan.

- Crumble amaretti cookies over each pieces as a garnish.

1½ cups water

Flour-and-fat baking spray

⅔ cup granulated white sugar

1 large egg, at room temperature

1 large egg white, at room temperature

5½ tablespoons butter, melted and cooled to room temperature

¼ cup regular sour cream (do not use low-fat or fat-free)

¼ cup fresh lemon juice

1 teaspoon vanilla extract

½ teaspoon lemon extract

1 cup all-purpose flour

½ teaspoon baking powder

½ teaspoon baking soda

¼ teaspoon table salt

Beyond

- For even more lemon flavor, add up to 2 teaspoons finely grated lemon zest to the processor with the vanilla and lemon extracts.

- Add up to 1 tablespoon poppy seeds or 2 teaspoons stemmed fresh thyme leaves after the batter has been made. Pulse the processor once or twice to combine them.

- For a lemon glaze, put 2 cups confectioners' sugar in a medium bowl. Whisk in lemon juice in 1-teaspoon increments until the mixture forms a thick paste that holds its shape but runs off the whisk, like super thick honey. Drizzle the glaze over the cooled cake and serve at once, or set aside for 20 minutes for the glaze to set firm.

Lemon Sponge Cake

8 servings

Here's a Bundt sponge cake, a springy, light cake that's great with fresh berries (particularly hulled sliced strawberries macerated with a little sugar and a touch of vanilla extract). As with most sponge cakes, this one's better the day it's made since the cake continues to collapse and condense even after it has cooled. If you have leftovers, consider cutting them into wedges and frying the pieces in butter (in a nonstick skillet set over medium heat) until lightly browned on both cut sides.

1. Pour the water into a **3-, 6-, - or 8-quart cooker**. Set a heat- and pressure-safe trivet in the pot. Generously spray the inside of a 7-inch Bundt pan with baking spray, taking care to get the fat and flour into all the crevices. Make an aluminum foil sling (see page 20) and set the pan into the middle of the sling.

2. Put the sugar, egg, egg white, melted butter, sour cream, lemon juice, and vanilla and lemon extracts in a food processor. Cover and process until smooth. Stop the machine and scrape down the inside. Add the flour, baking powder, baking soda, and salt. Cover and process until smooth.

3. Pour and scrape this mixture into the prepared pan. Use the sling to lower the pan onto the trivet in the cooker. Fold the ends of the sling down to fit inside without touching the batter. Lay a large paper towel over the top of the Bundt pan. Lock the lid onto the cooker. (Take care in a **3-quart cooker** that the paper towel doesn't block the seal.)

4.

Set the machine for	Set the level for	The valve must be	Set the time for	If necessary, press
PRESSURE COOK	MAX	—	18 minutes with the KEEP WARM setting off	START
PRESSURE COOK or MANUAL	HIGH	Closed	25 minutes with the KEEP WARM setting off	START

5. When the machine has finished cooking, turn it off and let its pressure **return to normal naturally**, about 20 minutes. Unlatch the lid and open the pot. Remove the paper towel. Use the sling to transfer the *hot* Bundt pan to a wire cooling rack. Cool for 5 minutes, then invert the pan onto a cutting board and release the cake. Slip it from the board to the cooling rack and cool for at least another 15 minutes before cutting into wedges to serve.

Chocolate Lava Cakes

4 servings

There was a point in the early 2000s when just about every celebrity chef claimed to have invented the molten cake, the lava cake, or whatever they called it. Not one of them made the cake in a multi-cooker! Too bad, because the steam creates a super light cake surrounding a liquid chocolate center.

You can unmold these cakes on plates, although they can tear (and immediately run) if you haven't greased the ramekin well enough for the cake to pop loose. Run a flatware knife around the inside perimeter, put a dessert plate over the ramekin, turn the whole operation upside down, and tap gently until the cake comes free. Or simply serve the warm cakes in their ramekins with spoons and plenty of whipped cream.

1. Put the butter and chocolate in a large, microwave-safe bowl. Microwave on high in 10-second bursts, stirring well after each, until a little over half of the butter has melted. Remove from the microwave oven and continue stirring until smooth.

2. Set the chocolate mixture aside and cool to room temperature, stirring occasionally, about 20 minutes. Meanwhile, generously butter the inside of four heat- and pressure-safe 1-cup ramekins.

3. Stir the confectioners' sugar into the chocolate mixture until smooth. Stir in the eggs one at a time, making sure each is well incorporated before adding the next. Stir in the egg yolk until smooth, then the flour and salt, stirring again until smooth. Divide this mixture evenly among the prepared ramekins. Do not cover the ramekins.

4. Pour the water in a **6- or 8-quart cooker**. Set a trivet in the pot, then stack the four ramekins on the trivet, placing three on the bottom layer and one on the top, balanced on the three below. Lock the lid onto the cooker.

5.

Set the machine for	Set the level for	The valve must be	Set the time for	If necessary, press
PRESSURE COOK	MAX	—	8 minutes with the KEEP WARM setting off	START
PRESSURE COOK or MANUAL	HIGH	Closed	10 minutes with the KEEP WARM setting off	START

6. When the machine has finished cooking, turn it off and let its pressure **return to normal naturally**, about 20 minutes. Unlatch the lid and open the cooker. Transfer the *hot* ramekins to a wire rack and cool for 15 minutes. Serve warm or cover and chill in the fridge for up to 1 day, serving them right in their ramekins.

½ cup (1 stick) butter, cut into small chunks, plus more for greasing the ramekins

8 ounces bittersweet chocolate, preferably 70% cocoa solids, chopped

1 cup confectioners' sugar

3 large eggs, at room temperature

1 large egg yolk, at room temperature

6 tablespoons all-purpose flour

¼ teaspoon table salt

1½ cups water

Beyond

- Because of the shape of the ramekins, this recipe will not work (even halved) in a **3-quart cooker**.

- Add up to 2 teaspoons vanilla extract, ½ teaspoon almond extract, or ¼ teaspoon orange extract with the eggs.

⅓ cup orange marmalade

½ cup (1 stick) cool butter, cut into chunks, plus additional for greasing the pan and the foil

¼ cup granulated white sugar

¼ cup packed light brown sugar

2 large eggs, at room temperature

3 tablespoons Triple Sec or Grand Marnier

1 tablespoon vanilla extract

¾ cup finely ground pecans

½ cup all-purpose flour

¼ teaspoon table salt

1½ cups water

Orange Pecan Pudding Cake

6 servings

Here's the first of two recipes for "pudding cake," a cross between a steamed pudding (think of a Dickens Christmas dessert) and a more traditional cake. They both have an exceptionally light texture, which unfortunately tends to turn a tad gummy if they're left too long before serving. We found a way to improve their longevity by increasing the flour, although doing so also made the cakes tough. So you'll need to serve them the day they're made. But since they're both so easy, you'll have no problem whipping them up.

This one's a bit of a marvel: a cake with a marmalade sauce that soaks into the crumb to make a sticky, caramel topping.

1. Generously butter the inside of a 2-quart, high-sided, round soufflé dish. Spread the marmalade over the bottom of this dish.

2. Using an electric mixer at medium speed in a large bowl, beat the butter and the white and brown sugars until creamy and light, about 5 minutes. Beat in the eggs one at a time, making sure the first is well incorporated before adding the second.

3. Scrape down the inside of the bowl. Beat in the Triple Sec or Grand Marnier and vanilla until smooth. At low speed, beat in the ground pecans, flour, and salt just until incorporated. Pour this batter into the prepared pan and smooth the top. Butter one side of a piece of aluminum foil and use to cover the dish, buttered side down. Tightly seal this foil over the baking dish.

4. Pour the water into a **6- or 8-quart cooker**. Set a heat- and pressure-safe trivet in the pot. Make a foil sling (see page 20), set the baking dish on it, and use the sling to lower the dish onto the trivet. Fold down the ends of the sling and lock the lid onto the pot.

5.

Set the machine for	Set the level for	The valve must be	Set the time for	If necessary, press
PRESSURE COOK	MAX	—	25 minutes with the KEEP WARM setting off	START
PRESSURE COOK or MANUAL	HIGH	Closed	35 minutes with the KEEP WARM setting off	START

6. When the machine has finished cooking, turn it off and let its pressure **return to normal naturally**, about 20 minutes. Unlatch the lid and open the cooker. Use the sling to transfer the *hot* baking dish to a wire rack. Uncover and cool for 5 minutes. Run a flatware knife around the inside perimeter of the dish to loosen the cake. Set a large platter or cake stand over the baking dish. Turn the whole operation upside down, then tap and jiggle the baking dish to make the cake come free. Serve warm or cool to room temperature, about 1 hour. The cake can stay uncovered at room temperature for about 3 hours.

Beyond

- For a **3-quart cooker**, use 1 cup water, halve the remaining ingredients, and use a 1-quart, high-sided, round baking dish.

- Skip the whipped cream and go for clotted cream on each serving.

- Or drizzle the pieces with Dulce de Leche (page 455).

½ cup chopped baking dates

½ teaspoon baking soda

⅓ cup boiling water

1 large egg, at room temperature

¼ cup whole or low-fat milk (do not use fat-free)

3 tablespoons butter, melted and cooled, plus more for greasing the ramekins and the foil

2 tablespoons bourbon, whiskey, or rum

⅔ cup all-purpose flour

¼ cup finely chopped walnuts

1 teaspoon baking powder

½ teaspoon ground dried ginger

½ teaspoon ground cinnamon

1¼ cups plus ½ teaspoon granulated white sugar

½ teaspoon table salt

2 cups water

1 cup heavy cream

1 teaspoon vanilla extract

Date Nut Pudding Cakes

4 servings

Dextrose-coated baking dates are found in the baking aisle of almost all large supermarkets. The dates are already sweet, but these individual pudding cakes aren't terribly so. Rather, they're a rather savory date nut bread pudding with a sweet sauce poured on top. The cakes are so light and tender, they may break apart if they're not cooled before serving — which gives you time to make and cool the sauce. If you want to eat them very warm (a comforting dessert indeed!), don't bother turning them out. Keep them in their ramekins and serve with tablespoons, the caramel sauce on the side.

1. Mix the baking dates and baking soda in a small bowl until uniform. Stir in the boiling water and set aside to cool to room temperature, stirring occasionally, about 30 minutes. Meanwhile, generously butter the inside of four heat- and pressure-safe 1-cup ramekins.

2. Whisk the egg, milk, melted butter, and bourbon in a large bowl until smooth and uniform, about 2 minutes. Whisk in the flour, walnuts, baking powder, ginger, cinnamon, the ½ teaspoon sugar, and ¼ teaspoon salt. Add the date mixture and stir well. Divide this batter among the four prepared ramekins.

3. Butter four small pieces of aluminum foil and use these, buttered side down, to seal the ramekins. Pour 1½ cups of the water into a **6- or 8-quart cooker**. Set a heat- and pressure-safe trivet inside the pot. Stack the four filled ramekins on the trivet, using three for the first layer and balancing the remaining in the center on the edges of the three below. Lock the lid onto the pot.

4.

Set the machine for	Set the level for	The valve must be	Set the time for	If necessary, press
PRESSURE COOK	MAX	—	25 minutes with the KEEP WARM setting off	START
PRESSURE COOK or MANUAL	HIGH	Closed	35 minutes with the KEEP WARM setting off	START

5. Meanwhile, make the caramel sauce: Whisk the remaining 1¼ cups sugar, the remaining ½ cup water, and the remaining ¼ teaspoon salt in a medium saucepan set over medium heat until the sugar melts. Continue cooking undisturbed until the mixture turns amber, 5 to 6 minutes. Reduce the heat as low as you can. Taking care because the mixture will roil, whisk in the cream and vanilla. Continue whisking until smooth. Remove the pan from the heat and cool at room temperature in the pan for at least 30 minutes or up to 2 hours, whisking occasionally.

6. When the machine has finished cooking, turn it off and let its pressure **return to normal naturally**, about 20 minutes. Transfer the *hot* ramekins to a wire rack and remove the foil coverings. Cool for 5 minutes, then invert the ramekins onto serving plates; gently tap and shake the ramekins to release the cakes inside. Spoon some of the warm caramel sauce over each.

Beyond

- Because of the size of the ramekins, this recipe cannot be made (or even halved) in a **3-quart cooker.**

- If you don't want the alcohol in the cakes, substitute orange juice.

1 cup all-purpose flour

1 teaspoon baking powder

1 teaspoon ground cinnamon

9 tablespoons (1 stick plus
1 tablespoon) butter, plus more for
greasing the pan

¼ cup maple syrup

2 medium baking apples, preferably
McIntosh apples, peeled, cored,
and thinly sliced

1½ cups water

½ cup granulated white sugar

2 large eggs, at room temperature

2 teaspoons vanilla extract

3 tablespoons whole milk

Apple Maple Upside-Down Cake

6 servings

Why go with the standard pineapple upside-down cake when you can make one with apples and maple syrup, an autumnal treat any time of year? Don't let this cake sit in its baking dish too long or it will begin to stick — not only to the caramel apple sauce on the bottom but also to the sides of the pan as the cake cools. This sweet dessert also makes for a great brunch entrée, particularly with a strong cup of coffee.

1. Whisk the flour, baking powder, and cinnamon in a medium bowl. Set aside. Generously butter the inside of one 2-quart, high-sided, round soufflé dish.

2.

Press the button for	Set it for	Set the time for	If necessary, press
SAUTÉ	MEDIUM, NORMAL, or CUSTOM 300°F	10 minutes	START

3. Melt 2 tablespoons of the butter in a **6- or 8-quart cooker**. Add the maple syrup and stir until warmed. Add the apples and cook, stirring often, until softened, about 5 minutes. Pour every drop of the mixture from the *hot* insert into the prepared baking dish; smooth the apple mixture into an even layer.

4. Clean and dry the insert, then return it to the machine. Pour the water into the cooker. Set a heat- and pressure-safe trivet inside.

5. Using an electric mixer at medium speed, beat the remaining 7 tablespoons butter and the sugar in a large bowl until smooth and creamy, about 4 minutes. Beat in the eggs one at a time, making sure the first is thoroughly incorporated before adding the second. Beat in the vanilla extract, then reduce the mixer's speed to low. Beat in the flour mixture just until incorporated. Add the milk and beat until uniform. Pour this batter over the apples in the prepared pan. Cover tightly with aluminum foil.

6. Make a foil sling (see page 20). Set the baking dish on the sling and lower it onto the trivet. Fold down the ends of the sling so they don't touch the batter, then lock the lid onto the pot.

7.

Set the machine for	Set the level for	The valve must be	Set the time for	If necessary, press
PRESSURE COOK	MAX	—	25 minutes with the KEEP WARM setting off	START
PRESSURE COOK or MANUAL	HIGH	Closed	35 minutes with the KEEP WARM setting off	START

8. When the machine has finished cooking, turn it off and let its pressure **return to normal naturally**, about 20 minutes. Unlatch the lid and open the cooker. Use the sling to transfer the *hot* baking dish to a wire rack. Uncover and cool for 5 minutes. Run a flatware knife around the inner perimeter of the dish to loosen the cake. Set a large platter or cake stand over the baking dish. Turn the whole operation upside down, then tap and jiggle the baking dish to make the cake come free and let the apple "sauce" pour over the cake. Cool for 15 minutes, then serve warm.

Beyond

- For a **3-quart cooker**, use 1 cup water, halve the remaining ingredients, and use a 1-quart, high-sided, round baking dish.

- Drizzle slices with warmed heavy cream.

- Substitute 2 medium Bosc or Bartlett pears, stemmed, cored, and thinly sliced, for the apples.

- Stir in up to ¼ cup raisins after adding the milk.

Butter for greasing the pan and foil

1½ cups water

3 large eggs, separated and at room temperature

¾ cup granulated white sugar

1 cup regular cultured buttermilk

1 tablespoon finely grated lime zest, preferably from key limes

4½ tablespoons bottled or fresh key lime juice (from 3 to 4 key limes)

2 teaspoons vanilla extract

½ teaspoon table salt

6 tablespoons all-purpose flour

Beyond

- For a **3-quart cooker,** use 1 cup water, two-thirds of the remaining ingredients, and a 1-quart, high-sided, round baking dish.

- Skip the whipped cream and serve the pudding soufflé topped with sweetened sour cream: Whisk ¼ cup confectioners' sugar and 1 teaspoon vanilla extract into 1 cup regular or low-fat sour cream until smooth.

- Bottled key lime juice is widely available. If you use it, you won't have a key lime for the zest. Use a standard (Persian) lime for the zest but make sure the zest is finely minced. You can also substitute Persian lime juice for the key lime juice — just use ¼ cup lime juice and ½ tablespoon fresh lemon juice for a more key-lime-like pop.

Key Lime Soufflé Cake

6 servings

This dessert is a hybrid of a pudding, a soufflé, and a cake. It's quite soft and can't be unmolded, so serve it up into bowls. Like so many desserts, it calls out for whipped cream (see the *Beyond* section on page 457).

1. Generously butter the inside of a 2-quart, high-sided, round soufflé dish. Pour the water into a **6- or 8-quart cooker**. Set a heat- and pressure-safe trivet inside the pot.

2. Using an electric mixer at high speed, beat the egg whites in a medium bowl until they make soft peaks off the end of a spatula, about 3 minutes. Beat in ¼ cup of sugar in a slow, steady stream until the mixture is thick and can form silky peaks that hold their shape on a spatula, about 2 minutes.

3. Clean and dry the beaters. In a large bowl, beat the egg yolks and remaining ½ cup sugar until thick and pale yellow, about 4 minutes. Scrape down the inside of the bowl, then beat in the buttermilk, lime zest, lime juice, vanilla, and salt until smooth. Scrape down and remove the beaters.

4. Use a rubber spatula to fold the flour into the egg yolk mixture until thoroughly moistened. Fold in the egg whites gently until incorporated but not completely dissolved. There should be white streaks in the batter.

5. Pour and scrape the batter into the prepared baking dish. Lightly butter a piece of aluminum foil and cover the cake loosely with it, buttered side down. Make a foil sling (see page 20), set the baking dish in the center of the sling, and use the sling to lower the baking dish onto the trivet. Fold down the ends of the sling so they don't touch the batter, then lock the lid onto the pot.

6.

Set the machine for	Set the level for	The valve must be	Set the time for	If necessary, press
PRESSURE COOK	MAX	——	15 minutes with the KEEP WARM setting off	START
PRESSURE COOK or MANUAL	HIGH	Closed	20 minutes with the KEEP WARM setting off	START

7. When the machine has finished cooking, turn it off and let its pressure **return to normal naturally**, about 20 minutes. Unlatch the lid and open the cooker. Use the sling to transfer the *hot* baking dish to a wire rack. Uncover and cool for at least 10 minutes or up to 1 hour. Serve by the big spoonful in bowls or small plates.

Blueberry Bread Pudding

6 servings

There are two bread puddings in the breakfast chapter (starting on page 41) that you could also make for dessert. This version is sweeter than those, with a bright fresh taste, thanks to the blueberries. Use only fresh, not frozen. And check out the headnote to the Peanut Butter Bread Pudding recipe on page 41 for a discussion of the best sort of bread to use in an Instant Pot bread pudding. After that, just make a pot of coffee. Even in the evening, you'll want it with this sweet, berry-filled dessert.

Butter for greasing the baking dish and foil

1½ cups water

4 large eggs, at room temperature

2 cups whole or low-fat milk (do not use fat-free)

½ cup granulated white sugar

1 teaspoon vanilla extract

¼ teaspoon table salt

8 ounces white bread, preferably country-style bread, cut into 1-inch squares (do not remove the crusts)

1 cup fresh blueberries

1. Generously butter the inside of a 2-quart, high-sided, round soufflé dish. Pour the water into a **6- or 8-quart cooker**. Set a heat- and pressure-safe trivet in the cooker. Also, make a foil sling (see page 20) and set the buttered baking dish in the center of this sling.

2. Whisk the eggs in a large bowl until uniform. Whisk in the milk, sugar, vanilla, and salt until the sugar dissolves. Use a rubber spatula to stir the bread cubes into the egg mixture until evenly coated. Add the blueberries and fold very gently until evenly distributed.

3. Pour and pile this mixture into the prepared baking dish. Butter one side of a piece of aluminum foil and cover the baking dish tightly with it, buttered side down. Use the sling to pick up and lower the baking dish onto the trivet. Lock the lid onto the pot.

4.

Set the machine for	Set the level for	The valve must be	Set the time for	If necessary, press
PRESSURE COOK	MAX	——	20 minutes with the KEEP WARM setting off	START
PRESSURE COOK or MANUAL	HIGH	Closed	26 minutes with the KEEP WARM setting off	START

5. When the machine has finished cooking, turn it off and let its pressure **return to normal naturally**, about 20 minutes. Unlatch the lid and open the cooker. Use the sling to transfer the *hot* baking dish to a wire rack. Uncover and cool for 10 minutes. Serve by large spoonfuls in bowls.

Beyond

- For a **3-quart cooker**, use 1 cup water, halve the remaining ingredients, and use a 1-quart, high-sided, round baking dish.

- Substitute raspberries or blackberries for the blueberries.

- For a more exotic flavor, add up to ½ teaspoon ground cardamom to the milk mixture.

Acknowledgments

When we're writing a cookbook, it seems as if the whole thing's no more than two guys in a rural New England home, cooking, writing, arguing (lots), and eating (lots more). Then the manuscript goes to our publisher — and wow, it commands a lot of people!

Many thanks to the editor of our dreams, Mike Szczerban: conscientious, smart, honest about what he needs, and absurdly faithful to our vision, too.

Thanks, too, to his assistant, Nicky Guerriero, for being so eagle-eyed and so quick to reply. Did we even hit send on that email?

Deri Reed, you are the best copyeditor, hands down, no questions, period. (Try to edit that sentence, will you?) Thanks, too, to Jeffrey Gantz for proofreading this book under a crazy deadline and to Amy Novick for indexing it.

We owe a big debt to Laura Palese for turning this beast into a beautiful book, better than we could have imagined. And to Julianna Lee and Kapo Ng for designing the cover, perfect for what we wanted to do.

At Little, Brown, we stand "hats off" to our publisher, Reagan Arthur, and our deputy publisher, Craig Young, for taking on another Bible. Thanks, too, to Lauren Velasquez for marketing our tome; to Jules Horbachevsky and her assistant, Elora Weil, for working on its PR; and to Lisa Ferris, Mike Noon, and Michael Gaudet for working magic to produce a five-hundred-pager in, oh, five weeks or so, right?

We truly couldn't have done this book without Robert Wang at Instant Pot who was so fast to answer our texts and emails, sometimes in the wee hours. And to Anna Di Meglio for working out the details and sending us a dozen (!) cookers.

And much gratitude to Lori Sobelson and Brenda Gibson at Bob's Red Mill for a ginormous box of rice, wheat berries, and other grains. Beyond helpful. Even more delicious!

Closer to home, we couldn't have done the last seven (!!) books without Eric Medsker, a no-drama photographer extraordinaire (and a great friend). Many thanks, too, to Caroline Dorn, a prop stylist with some of the best eyes we've ever seen. Those photo shoots with the four of us! So many bottles of wine, so much food!

Finally, how can we ever thank our agent, Susan Ginsburg, at Writers House, or her assistant, Stacy Testa? Thirty books? In nineteen years? What's next?

Index

Bold type indicates road map recipes.